Imports of Post-Archaic Greek Pottery into Cyrenaica

From the end of the Archaic to the beginning of the Hellenistic period

Faraj Mohmoud Elrashedy

BAR International Series 1022
2002

Published in 2016 by
BAR Publishing, Oxford

BAR International Series 1022

Imports of Post-Archaic Greek Pottery into Cyrenaica

ISBN 978 1 84171 403 5

Typesetting & layout: Darko Jerko

BAR Publishing is the trading name of British Archaeological Reports (Oxford) Ltd. British Archaeological Reports was first incorporated in 1974 to publish the BAR Series, International and British. In 1992 Hadrian Books Ltd became part of the BAR group. This volume was originally published by Archaeopress in conjunction with British Archaeological Reports (Oxford) Ltd / Hadrian Books Ltd, the Series principal publisher, in 2002. This present volume is published by BAR Publishing, 2016.

Printed in England

BAR
PUBLISHING

BAR titles are available from:

BAR Publishing
122 Banbury Rd, Oxford, OX2 7BP, UK
EMAIL info@barpublishing.com
PHONE +44 (0)1865 310431
FAX +44 (0)1865 316916
www.barpublishing.com

TO MY PARENTS, MY WIFE FAIZA AND CHILDREN

NAHLA, MAYSOON AND FATHEL

TABLE OF CONTENTS

ACKNOWLEDGEMENT

In the course of the years during which this study was produced, I have become indebted to many individuals and institutions. The work itself was made possible by a generous scholarship from Libya. Thanks to the administrations in both the Department of Scholarship in Tripoli and the Faculty of Arts in Benghazi.

I would like to thank individuals in the following museums for allowing me to examine objects in their collections and for providing photographs or letting me take my own. In Europe Dr. A. Prag of the University Museum in Manchester, Mr. Michael Vickers of the Ashmolean Museum in Oxford; I am grateful for their encouragement, advice and hospitality. Dr. D. Bailey of the British Museum in London. Professor Francois Villard of the Louvre, Mme Aghion and Mlle Dominique Gerin of the Bibliothèque National in Paris. Professor F. L. Bastet of the Rijksmuseum Van Oudheden in Leiden, Dr Sekallarakis and Alexandra Karestou of the Herakleion Museum, Vanna Niniou of the Chania Museum in Crete.

At home my thanks go to Abdusalam Bazama, Inspector of Tolmeita, Al-Haj Breyik Attiyeh Controller of Antiquities, Ramadan Kwader, Keeper of Collections, Saleh Wanis, Departmental Librarian and Adullatif Al-Jerbi Inspector of Antiquities in Cyrene. I am also indebted to Professor Donald White of the University Museum in Pennsylvania for allowing me to examine and publish material from his excavation of the extramural sanctuary of Demeter at Cyrene.

Here in England, Dr. David Gill has generously shared now for several years his experience of knowledge on black-glazed pottery and also allowed me to use profiles of pottery drawn by him. My thanks go to him and to Dr. Breyik Buckshiem for the computer drawings of the Histograms used in this book. A word of thanks are due to Mr. Lazenby, the Head of the Department of Classics and to Mr. E. M. Caldwell, Senior Administrative Assistant at the Registrar Office of the University for their understanding and help.

A final expression of thanks has been reserved for two individuals to whom I owe most. Professor Brian Shelton, my supervisor, has seen the work through from the beginning. He was an unending source of encouragement, direction and unfailing help right up to the very last minutes. While the final conclusions remain my own responsibility, the result has been materially improved by his care and insight. I have enjoyed working with him enormously and my debt of thanks to him is immense.

And to my wife, who has shared the experience with me, my gratitude and thanks.

Chapter One

INTRODUCTION

Cyrenaica's extensive commercial relationships with the rest of the Greek world during the Archaic, Hellenistic and Roman Periods have been the subject of much modern scholarship[1]. The continuation of these relations from the Archaic into the Classical period has received very little attention. Scholars concerning themselves with historical issues of the Classical period have mentioned in passing Cyrenaican commercial activities, but the full range of evidence of such activities has never before been examined. A comprehensive investigation of the evidence - literary, historical and archaeological - documenting these activities in the Classical period is indeed justifiable.

Cyrenaican trade can be defined as the exchange of goods from foreign commercial centres as identified by commodities and/or artifacts of Cyrenaican origin. This definition immediately raises questions about the nature of the archaeological evidence. For instance is it representative of the range of goods actually exchanged? Is the nature of the exchange direct and reciprocal, or indirect and complex? Is it in the form of regular, organized commercial transactions, or is it more casual, occasional or due to special circumstances? Such questions must be kept in mind as the evidence described here is discussed[2].

I. THE SOURCE OF POTTERY

Attic pottery reached Cyrenaica in quantity, and on some sites we may judge the result of this trade not merely from sherds but from a good number of complete vases. The bulk of these, mainly from necropoleis, are The Leiden, the Louvre, The Bibliothèque Nationale in Paris, and the British Museum. These were brought to Europe in 1837, 1846 and 1864 by the then Dutch consul in Tripoli, the French and British consuls in Benghazi, the ancient Euesperides and western-most city state of the Pentapolis[3].

The vases in Leiden were apparently presented in 1837 by Clifford Kocq van Breugel, the Dutch consul in Tripoli, as a result of the excavation he undertook in Cyrene and the surrounding areas[4].

In 1846, a French consular official, Vattier de Bourville went to Cyrenaica with the support of the French Ministry of Education, to undertake a certain amount of excavation. The main object of this expedition was to find 'objets d'art' worthy of being sent to the French museums. De Bourville wrote a very brief report on his finds from the Cyrenaican Necropoleis. As a result of his work, he sent to France a great number of objects, among which are a number of Panathenaic amphorae and many terracotta figurines[5]. The bulk of the Attic red-figured vases, brought by Vattier in 1946 went to the Cabinet de Medaille of the Bibliothèque Nationale in Paris. The rest, mostly non-Attic seem to have gone to Sèvres: after 1951 he excavated systematically for the Louvre[6].

Mr. G. Dennis was attracted to Cyrenaica as a source of "painted vases". accordingly he succeeded in getting an appointment as Vice-Consul at Benghazi. This being accorded

1 Coster, "The Economic Position of Cyrenaica in Classical Times" in *Late Roman Studies*, Cambridge (Mass.) 1968, 104-44. Boardman and Hayes, *Excavation at Tocra 1963-1965* (1966) 19-20; (1973) 3-5 *id.* 'Reflections on the Greek Pottery Trade with Tocra', in *Libya in History* (1968) 89-91, Schaus, *Archaic Pottery from the Demeter Sanctuary, Cyrene*, 212-257. Chamoux, *Cyrene Sous La Monarchie Des Battiades*, 213-263.

2 The subject is discussed by Hammond in the *Archaeology of Trade in the East Mediterranean*, 33 ff.

3 Dennis, G. in *Transaction of the Royal Society of Literature*, 2nd Series, a, (1850) 135-82; Vattier de Bourville, in *Revue Archeologique* 5(1), (1848), 150 ff; b(1849) 56 ff, in Rapport au *Ministre Archives des Mission Scientifiqe* (1850) 580-86. Introductory remarks may be found in Louvre *CVA* 8 (12) P.34.

4 These are placed in Rijksmuseum van Oudheden in Leiden, Holland. See Holwerda, and *CVA* Leiden III, see Kern, in *Oudheid Kundige Mededelingen* 38, (1957) 35.

5 See note 1.

6 See Louvre *CVA* 5 (8) pls 5, 6, *CVA* 8 (12) 34 pls 48, 49 *CVA* 9 (14) pls. 53, 54 and Sèvres *CVA* 1 (13) pl 25 for the material in Bibliotheque National see De Ridder *Catalogue des vases*, XI.

in 1864, he then started exploring systematically the cemeteries of Cyrenaica. In 1867, he read a paper before the Royal Society of Literature, in which he stated the following:

> "The great majority of the tombs were sunk in the rock, in the form of pits, from 6 to 7 feet long, from: 3.5 to 4.5 feet wide, and from 5 to 6 feet deep. Vases were sometimes placed in all four corners of the sepulchre, but this was rare; they were generally confined to two corners, often to one. The most usual place was the corner to the right of the head, and this was the place of honour; for here a Panathenaic vase in the tomb of a victor, a ribbed amphora of glazed black ware, or more commonly an ordinary wine-*diota*, would be deposited upright, with a number of smaller vases within it, or at its foot, either figured or of black or plain ware, according to the circumstances of the deceased. Occasionally small vases, or sometimes terracotta figures, were placed along the sides of the tomb, between the head and feet of the corpse; but I do not remember ever to have found vases deposited on the breast, or under the arms of the deceased, as was often the case in the Greek tombs of Sicily"[7].

The result of his excavations seemed disappointing, for only a few painted vases, some glass bottles and unguentaria of alabaster were found. This he presented in his lecture, in which he stated, "Before leaving Teuchira (Tocra), I had urged some of the resident Arabs, who had been daily watching my operation, to make excavations on their own account". This they did to such effect that soon he was invited to return to Tocra to purchase the finds. After a long journey from Benghazi to Tocra he found, "The ground in front of my cave was strewed with Greek pottery"[8]. This included several Panathenaic amphorae. Most of the pottery from Cyrenaica in the British Museum was probably acquired from that source[9].

Soon after the Italian occupation of Cyrenaica, Italian archaeologists began to excavate on a larger scale especially after the creation of the *Regia Soprintendanza delle Antichita in Cirenaica*. An enormous wealth of material, including pottery, came to light as a result of systematic excavation conducted with great enthusiasm on the sanctuary of Apollo, the Agora, the forum of Cyrene and other sites of the Pentapolis. Unfortunately, the material was not adequately published and the record of the finds are far from complete.

The Department of Antiquities in Cyrenaica was active after 1951, when Libya became independent. Its reports, together with those of various foreign expeditions, are published in *Libya Antiqua*. Pottery is among the material recovered mainly as a result of rescue excavations and chance surface finds.

Of primary importance for the study of pottery from Cyrenaica, especially of the archaic period, is the report by J. Boardman and J. W. Hayes of their excavations at Tocra. It is an account of stratified pottery mainly from votive deposits of the later 7th century to the late 6th century B.C.. The imported wares, which comprised about 85% of the total pottery in the period, were mainly from Sparta, Corinth and Rhodes, and after *c.* 590 B.C. from Attica[10].

The massive deposit of the Sanctuary of Demeter at Cyrene, excavated by a team from Pennsylvania University, has also produced much stratified pottery of the period. As an example of the wealth of the material, in 1978 the sanctuary yielded a total of 4,014 sherds. These were recovered from behind the wall which separates the lower from the middle sanctuary: of these 21.85% were Attic. By contrast, the excavation of the Agora in Cyrene and other sites directed by Professor Stucchi produced less Attic pottery[11].

II. STRUCTURE OF THE BOOK AND NATURE OF THE MATERIAL

The chronological limits of the thesis, broadly speaking, are the end of the Archaic and the beginning of the Hellenistic eras. Evidence of the late sixth and early fifth century, as well as the late fourth and early third is included here to add depth to the pattern of trade during this period.

After detailed discussion of the commodities exported to the Greek world, the pottery which is studied here is divided into three parts or sections: the Attic red-figured pottery, the Panathenaic amphorae, and the black-glazed pottery. There is a small section on the imported non-Attic pottery. Each piece has a basic description followed by a discussion of the subject represented and the various stylistic features used in the painting in the case of the painted pieces. Among the material discussed here are pieces which have already been attributed to painters and workshops by Sir John Beazley, although some are presented for the first time. Some are known to the author only through photographs and profiles, especially the black-glazed ware.

Only a limited amount of Classical pottery has been adequately published, namely the corpus from the important tomb group from Aslaia near Barca (Modern Al-Merj), and selected pieces from Cyrene and Benghazi[12].

This study does not claim, in any way, to be a statistical survey of the known fifth- and fourth-century pottery from the region. The archaeological record is far too incomplete, and the manner in which the finds have been reported is far too haphazard to allow pieces of pottery to be quantified and compared in terms of absolute number.

Although some of the objects discussed in this work have already appeared in the CVA, namely those of the British Museum, the Louvre in Paris and Sèvres, the author was able

7 Dennis, *op.cit.* 135-82.

8 *Ibid,* 155-7.

9 The inventory numbers for the acquisition of these materials by the British Museum are 1866 4-15, 1967 5-12, 1868 7-5.

10 Boardman and Hayes *op.cit.* 13-30.

11 White *AJA* 85 (1981) 13-30; Stucchi, *Cirene* 158-9.

12 *CVA* Leiden III mainly black-glazed pottery. Vickers and Bazama *Libya Antiqua* 8 (1971) 69-85.
EL-RASHEDY in *Cyrenaica in Antiquity* 205-217. Other publications are quoted in connection with each individual piece in this study.

to collect unpublished material from excavations and museum storerooms. It has to be stressed, however, that availability of material for handling, drawing and taking photographs, especially those in the Museums of Cyrenaica, depended, largely, on the personal cooperation of the officials of these establishments. In most cases the author had the help and cooperation of the individuals concerned, but in a few cases however, cooperation and help were not forthcoming. At Suss (Apollonia), for example, the author was prevented from even handling material which had already been published, namely those items recovered by the University of Michigan (1965-1967)[13]. Enquiries at Benghazi proved fruitless. The pieces attributed by Beazley in *ABV* and *ARV* are all untraceable[14]. They appear to have been lost as a result of the continuous shifting from one location to another. On these few occasions when unpublished pieces were provided for publication many were found to be without exact provenance or even inventory numbers. The picture is different in relation to the material in European museums; the Cyrenaican material in these establishments was available for study. The exception is the Sèvres Museum in France, which claims a large collection of pottery mostly from Euhesperides. The author has also visited Crete to survey sixth- and fifth-century Attic pottery, to see if there is a possible connection between the island and Cyrenaica.

Because of these limitations the number of vases and fragments documenting the exchange between Cyrenaica and Attica, as shown in this work, are in no way representative of the trade in absolute terms, but only in relative terms. Furthermore, in order to have a complete picture of the trade pattern represented by the fifth- and fourth-century pottery, the material should be correlated with other imported goods to provide evidence for the commercial activities of this region. No parallel work has yet been undertaken in this line, but there is an attempt in the final discussion of this work to correlate other contemporary Attic imports with the pottery discussed here.

This study hopes to re-examine and discuss the published and unpublished fifth- and fourth-century pottery imported into Cyrenaica, to see what conclusions might be suggested about the relationship between Cyrenaica and the rest of the Greek world.

[13] J. H. Humphrey (ed.) *Apollonia, The Port of Cyrene*, Excavation by the University of Michigan 1965-7, published as supplement to *Libya Antiqua* IV, in 1976.

[14] See *ARV* 1956, *ABV* 717.

Chapter Two

THE ECONOMIC POTENTIAL OF CYRENAICA AND EXPORT

The Cyrenaica region was destined to be one of the wealthiest of the agricultural districts of the Greek world. This was due to two main elements: climatic advantage combined with a fertile soil. The Theran settlers, apparently, were well aware of this fact. This was indeed implied by the answer of the Pythia of Delphi when the initial settlers of Cyrenaica returned from the island of Plataca and complained about their misfortunes there. Her famous answer was:

> "If you know Libya, the nurse of flocks, better than I do, when you have not gone there, and I have, I admire exceedingly your wisdom"[1].

Moreover, the moving of the original colony from Aziris to the west in its final site of Cyrene is a clear indication to the region's wealth. The Libyans who guided the settlers to the new site, according to Herodotus, described the site as a place where "The sky is pierced" ("ὃ οὖρανός τέτρηται")[2] as a symbol of fertility and implying an adequate supply of rains suitable for agriculture.

I. THE PHYSICAL ENVIRONMENT OF THE REGION

Cyrenaica may generally be described as a large peninsular plateau on the shores of North Africa, projecting northward into the Mediterranean. The region is only 300 km south of Crete and lies between longitudes 19° and 24° east. To the south, the arid Sahara is within a few kilometres of the Mediterranean cost in the Gulf of Sirte and, save for a narrow coastal strip at the northern extremity between Derna and Alexandria, barren desert isolates Cyrenaica from the remainder of the African continent (Maps 1, 2).

1 Parke and Wormell, *The Dephic Oracle* 76.

2 Hdt., IV, 158, 3.

The only part of Cyrenaica suitable for settlement is the coastal strip and the adjoining limestone plateau (known as the Jebel Al-Akhdar or the Greea mountain, about 250 by 80 kilometres in extent), formed by two successive escarpments that rise up to between 200 and 300 metres (Map 3). From this height it falls gently away over 200 km towards the southern steppe and desert region where it is bounded by a series of oases on the edge of the Sahara that offers the possibility of inland communication between the Nile Valley and the Sirtic region[3].

Cyrenaica, being a Mediterranean region, enjoys a concentration of heavy rainfall occurring in a period from November to February. This precipitation is the product of cyclonic storms that are generated in the Atlantic or in the western Mediterranean basin, and then move eastwards, or of local disturbances originating in the Tyrrhenian and Adriatic Seas which then travel directly south to the African coast. Most of the Jebel receives 400 to 650 mm of rain a year and part of it as much as 600 mm (Map 4). Since 200 mm of rain is generally considered the minimum necessary for dry agriculture, the rainfall is only really adequate on the Jebel Al-Akhdar and is barely sufficient for the Benghazi area[4].

The permeable character of the region's soil causes the loss of much water by infiltration to deep strata, in so far as the runoff does not flow to waste in the wadis. On the other hand,

3 Useful accounts of the area's geography and topography are: D.L. Thomson, *Jabal Al-Akhdar, Cyrenaica* 10 f. *Economic Development of Libya*, 29 f. Area handbook for Libya, Washington D.C., U.S. Government Printing Office, 12 f.

4 We have the figures for the annual rainfall in millilitres quoted by C. Kraeling, *Ptolemais*, City of the Libyan Pentapolis 68, from a rainfall map of Cyrenaica prepared by Dr. Lamer E Fort of the Libyan USOM in co-operation with the Metropolitan Office of the Libyan Nazaret of Communications: Agedabia (Corniclanum) 129; Bengahazi (Euhesperides Bernice) 266; Tocra (Tauchira) 311; Tolmeita (Ptolemais) 350; el-Merj (Barca) 485; Suza (Apollonia) 403; Shahat (Cyrene) 596; (Antipyrgos) 146; see also D. Johnson: *Jabal al-Akhdar*, Cyrenaica 11-12 and fig.4.

the Jebel's relatively high rain fall has caused the formation over certain areas of a layer of *terra rossa*, the residues of limestones in dissolution; this is a fertile water-retaining soil which possesses most of the elements required for the successful growing of cereals. These soils are distributed along the plateau between Al-Gubba on the east and the Al-Abbiar on the west. Permanent sources of water were to be found in the flowing streams. These are the series of springs at the foot of the Jebel on the edge of the coastal plain. Wells are common but most of them are dry in the summer months[5].

These conditions, which the indigenous population must have made good use of, prevailed during the second and first millennia B.C. Indeed, it is believed that the resource base was the same in its general characteristics as that found in Cyrenaica today. This is because there was no long-term climatic change recorded in the eastern Mediterranean since the end of the subpluvial, around 2,500 B.C.[6]. Later, when the first Greek settlers arrived in 632, they found, not an unoccupied and virgin land, but rather good arable soil used by a viable and largely self-sufficient population[7].

II. FORESTRY AND EXPORT (Map 5)

Our information about the composition of the flora of Cyrenaica is derived mainly from the classical literature. Pliny divided Cyrenaoca into three latitudinal zones along a north-south axis, beginning with the *arboribus fertilis*. The first zone is a forested and fertile zone along the coast with terraces, springs and short streams where gardens, orchards and vineyard thrived. The second zone is good only for agriculture and incapable of supporting trees, and the third is where siliphium grew[8].

According to Strabo and Pliny, wooded areas were confined to the coastal belt extending more than 24 km inland, and we have Herodotus' remarks that there were few woods from Egypt to Syrtis Minor[9]. A few kilometres west of Appolonia is a district overlooking the Gulf of Phycus called, in Pseudo-Scylax, the Garden of the Hesperides[10]. He describes it as "a place 28 fathoms (32 m) deep, sunk in ground and without access, its length and breadth are not less than 2 stades (350 m). Dense intertwined trees shade it, and include the lotus, apples of every kind, pomegranates, pears, blackberries, vines, myrtles, laurels and ivy".

The Fresco in Thera and the Garden of the Hesperides

It is relevant at this stage to bring in the controversial subject of the miniature fresco from the west house of Akrotiri in Thera that was excavated by Spyridon Marinatos in 1971 and 1972[11]. The miniature fresco was found in Room 5 and is dated between 1550 and 1490 B.C. Marinatos' theory concerning the interpretation of the painting was that it represented an expedition to the North African coast, where flowed the only river west of the Nile. It depicted African flora and animals such as panthers, lions and various North African peoples with crested or tufted hairstyles, and wearing skins dyed with red and madder. The purpose of the expedition, according to Marinatos, was to acquire corn from the rich grain lands there. The whole setting, according to Marinatos, depicted the trip to Libya, the campaign there, and the voyage home again to Thera.

Sandro Stucchi appears to support Marinatos' arguments for a North African setting for the whole scene[12]. Furthermore, he suggests that the river scenes, with their flora and fauna, are, in fact, the Garden of the Hesperides, located in Scylax, near the Gulf of Phycus, west of Apollonia.

On the other hand, Peter Warren convincingly dismisses Marinatos' interpretation of a North African setting for the fresco. Instead, he suggests a Cretan setting, among Cretan people, buildings, flora and fauna[13].

Scylax's suggested site, however, was not the only location for the famous garden. Other names in the district seem to be connected with the same myth, such as the river Luthon (or Leth) and Lake Triton, located in the town of Hesperides (or Euhesperides)[14].

The Lumber Trade

It is Pliny who stated that Cyrenaica was rich in trees for a distance of 15,000 paces from the coast[15]. The Cyrenean Cathartic Law of Apollo, which reaches us in a 4th century version, contains a clause permitting the felling of the trees of the sacred groves by licence from the Temple authorities[16]. This is a clear indication of the importance of lumber to the region's economy. Among the trees cut primarily for lumber is cypress, but the wood that interested the Greeks the most

5 Johnson, *op.cit.*, 8 f. and Barker in Lloyd J.A. (ed.) *Excavations at Sidi Khrebish*, 4 f.

6 It is believed that conditions in classical times were similar to that of today. See W.B. Fisher "Agriculture in Modern Libya" *Geogr. Magaz.* 52 (1952) p 187; R. Goodchild "Farming in Roman Libya" *Geogr. Magaz.* 52 (1952) p 75. Giotto Dainelli "The Italian Colonies" *The Geogr. Review* XIX (1929) pp 410-411.

7 Semple, The Geography of the Mediterranean region, 99 f. Johnson, *ibid*, 93. Goodchild, *Cyrene and Apollonia*, 8.

8 Pliny, *N.H.*, V.5 31-33. In the Pythian Odes, Pindar speaks of the "pleasant garden surrounding Aphrodite's temple in Cyrene where the Cyreneans maintained consecrated groves. Pinder, *Pyth.* 5.24 and 9.53. Theoph., *H.P.* 6.65. See also E.C. Semple, "Ancient Mediterranean Pleasure Gardens". *Geogr. Review* 19 (1929) 433.

9 Strabo, *Geography* 17. 3. 23. Pliny *N.H.*, V.5. Hdt. IV, 175.

10 Pseud-Scylax. *Peripl.* 108.

11 *Thera* V. 17-20 and pl.27b. *Thera* VI 19-31, 38-50. pla. 42a, 91-112, colour plates 7-9 and plans 3-7.

12 Sandro Stucchi, in *Quaderni* 8 (1976) 17-73.

13 P.M. Warren : *JHS* 99 (1979) 128 f.

14 Pliny, *N.H.*, V.5, 31. R.G. Goodchild, *Benghazi, the Story of a City* 5 & 6.

15 Pliny, *N.H.*, V.5. 33.

16 *S.E.G.*, 9. 72. G. Oliverio, *Documenti antichi dell' Africa Italiana*: II Cirenaica ii (1936) no.57.

was citron wood (known as Thuon (hìom) by the Greeks, citrus by the Romans, and to botanists *Calliitris Quadrivalvis*). Pliny mentions it and Theophrastus describes the tree briefly. It is like the cypress in its branches, leaves, trunk and fruit. Pliny states:

> "it grows at its best near the temple of Zeus Ammon, and in the district of Cyrene... Men can still recall that some of the roofs in Ancient times were made of it, for the wood is absolutely proof against decay"[17].

The tree was known to have provided material for merchant shipping, the construction of buildings and various other domestic purposes. As it enjoys decay-proof qualities it was considered most valuable for sculpture and furniture making.

Both cypress and thuoya are believed to have been exported to the Greek world by way of Crete or Egypt, or both. We know that Athens acquired her supply of cypress in the fifth century through Crete, and we can infer from a list of Athenian imports in a comedy of the last third of the fifth century that cypress was more widely used in the Parthenon:

> "Crete sends us cypress for the gods" says Hermippus, referring no doubt to the use of cypress in temples[18].

When Cyrene was brought under Egyptian control in the third century B.C. it was natural that a wood which was so much appreciated in Cyrene should be imported by the Ptolemies. It is not surprising, therefore, that Ptolemy Philopater, in designing his luxurious river-boat should have chosen citrus-wood for the doors[19]. Later in the Roman period we have ample evidence its export all over the Mediterranean world. Today, although the concentration of woodland area in the district is limited to the area between Messa and Mameli, we have evidence that areas such as Taucheira (Tocra), which is today surrounded by a barren rocky terrain, was wooded as late as the 14th century[20].

Many factors are believed to have contributed to the destruction of the forests of Cyrenaica. We know that timber is fabricated by the inhabitants of the post-classical period into agricultural tools and household implements, but fuel requirements, i.e. the charcoal industry, is considered another cause for the degradation of the district's natural vegetation[21]. Russell Meiggs made a recent study on timber in the Ancient Mediterranean world. In the section dealing with the reason for deforestation, he states that forests were lost to flood and fire. More serious was the cutting down of trees to satisfy the demand for wood, which increased as a result of the rising standard of public and private building. Meiggs stresses further that the conversion of the forest to agriculture was an important factor in the deforestation process. This was in response to an increase in population, at the expense of forests, especially in the Roman period, a process which was probably started in the Classical period[22]. Later Tertullian, an African priest of the third century remarked:

> "Wildernesses have been replaced by most attractive estates and woods have yielded to the plough. The cover of wild beasts has become grazing land, sandy areas are sown, stones are broken up and marshes are drained"[23].

Such a remark reflects the condition of the forests of North Africa in the Roman Period. The forests of the Jabel Al-Akhdar must, no doubt, have experienced a very similar fate.

III. AGRICULTURE, PRODUCT AND EXPORT

Agriculture was carried on by the ancient Libyans, especially those living close to the coast, perhaps as a subsidiary to their pastoral activities and taking advantage of the better watered and the more fertile area of the Jebel Al-Akhdar which they occupied.

According to Herodotus, it was possible to use the growing seasons successively so that harvesting was done at successive periods commencing with the crops on the coastal plain and then working upward through the hilly region to the inland plateau[24]. Moreover, Strabo has stated clearly that both the Marmaridae and the Nasamones tribes were very familiar with the art of farming[25].

Cereals

One of the important products of Cyrenaica was wheat, a grain which was very suited to its climate, soil and rainfall. During the great famine in Greece, which lasted from 330 to 325 B.C.[26], and following the treaty of friendship between Cyrene and Alexander in 330, when, on his way to Zeus Amon[27], Cyrene offered no less than 805,000 medimni[28] of wheat to forty-one different communities of the Greek mainland and the islands, as well as to important individuals, to relieve the shortage. This is, no doubt, a clear indication of the economic power enjoyed by the Cyrenaican cities and the quantities of wheat produced. An inscribed stele containing the names of

17 Pliny, *N.H.*, 16, 139-42, 215.14.12. Theoph., *H.P.*, 5.3.7.

18 Hermippus, quoted in Athen., 27 d-e.

19 Athen., 2056.

20 Strabo, IV.6.2.202. Pliny, *N.H.*, XIII, 30 (100). Edrisi, transl. R. Dozy, M.J. de Geoje, *Description de l'Afrique et de l'Espagne* (1856) p 162.

21 Johnson, *Jabal Al-Akhdar; Cyrenaica*, 22-28.

22 Meiggs, *Trees and Timber in Ancient Mediterranean* 373 f.

23 The quotation from Tertullian is taken from Meiggs *op.cit.* 373 (Tertullian, De anima 30.3).

24 Hdt., IV 198, 199.

25 Strabo, *Geography* 2.5.33.

26 Demosthenes, 34. 37. 39. Describes the situation then in Athens. Rostovtzeff, *SEHHW,* 94 ff.

27 Jean Machu, "Cyrene, La cite et la Souverain a L'epoque Hellenistique". *Rev. Hist.* (1950-1) p. 42.

28 The medimnus was a Greek corn-measure equivalent to 52.53 litres or 1.5 bushels. See Seyffert, in *A Dictionary of Classical Antiquities* (London 1891) p. 386. H. Liddle and Scott *Greek English Lexicon* (Oxford 1811-1887), 1089.

the states to which the donation was made, was found in Cyrene and the text was published[29]. This emphatically implies that wheat must have been one of the major exports of Cyrenaica[30].

From the inscribed stele we are informed that communities scattered all over the Greek world as well as two important persons, Alexander's mother, Olympia, and his sister, Cleopatra, were the recipients of the large consignment. The load totalled 805,000 medimni, probably of Aeginetan standard, and was the equivalent of 1,207,500 Attic medimni. It is also equivalent, as Finley has suggested, to a year's rations for some 150,000 men[31].

The consignment was distributed as follows[32]: To Athens went the largest amount - 100,000 medimni - in one consignment; the next largest - 72,600 - to Olympia; the third largest - 50,000 medimni - went to Alexander's sister. A special meaning must have been attached to these last two assignments, perhaps a token of friendship to Alexander after the Alliance which took place in 331 B.C. The consignment also included 50,000 medimni each to Corinth, Argos and Larisa in Thessaly, 30,000 to Rhodes and so on (see the following page).

Some scholars are skeptical of the nature of this consignment and suggested that it was probably a free gift[33]. We are informed that a number of merchants at Athens were invited to supply grain at cheaper prices during food shortages[34]. Although the shipment of grain was made during that famine period we have yet to find sufficient evidence to show that Cyrene acted in the same way, nor do we have any hint that Cyrene was invited to do so. On the face of it, the shipments appears to have been a free gift, clearly implied by the un-prefixed verb in the text (line 2) that has been translated as: "to alleviate the stress"[35]. Waisglass supports this and thinks it would have been a hollow pride that could have inspired a state as wealthy as Cyrene to commemorate its generosity by supplying grain at a rate that was either the market price, or even below it[36]. Moreover, there are authentic cases of gifts of grain in the classical period. One such case was the donation of 45,000 bushels of corn to Athens by Egypt that took place in 445 B.C. Later, by the end of the first century A.D., Cyrenaica, together with the rest of the Roman provinces of Africa, was said to be sending sufficient grain to Rome to maintain a population of nearly a million people for two-thirds of the year. This tremendous increase in production may have been due in part to more skillful management[37].

The wealth of Cyrene from its wheat production was such a great source of pride that it was illustrated on the coins of the period, perhaps in commemoration of such enormous donations[38]. This, no doubt, emphatically implies that wheat must have been one of the major export commodities, not only in Cyrene but also in the other city-states of Cyrenaica. Barka, for example, was favoured with an even better location than Cyrene. It is true that the city received between 450 and 480 mm of rainfall less than Cyrene (600 mm), but fertile plains very suitable for farming surrounded it. They extended in all directions and the inhabitants must have made good use of such favourable positions[39]. Euhesperides is no less important than the rest of Greek cities and there are references to the city's prosperity and its grain surpluses[40].

As cereals comprised the stable element in the normal Libyan diet, it is assumed that the indigenous population knew how to harvest them before the arrival of the Greeks. The first-settlers must have observed carefully the sowing, cultivation and harvesting methods of their neighbours and later, after the Greek population had grown and taken over part of the adjacent grasslands, their grain production must have been in line with the seasonal pasturing and cultivation requirements of the Libyans. The importance of grain production to the Cyreneans may explain the importance of the Demeter cult (as the guardian of agriculture) in the district. This is borne out by the multitude of various motives that habitually turn up in the Demeter Sanctuary of Wdi Bel Gadir, south west of Cyrene[41] and, indeed, in Tocra[42].

Olive Oil

Olive oil was also an important export commodity; the ancients used it as cooking oil, soap, lamp oil, and ointment for the skin. The olive tree (Olea europaea var. Oleaster) is an indigenous species throughout the Mediterranean region. By reason of its elaborate root system, which penetrates down

29 S.E.G., IX 2. M.N. Tod, *A Selection of Greek Historical Inscriptions*, Vol.2, 403-323 B.C. (Oxford 1948), No. 196. G. Oliverio, "Iscrizioni de Cirene" *Riv. Fil.* 66 (1928) pp. 232-235. *Ibid*, *DAAI* II, Cirenaica I (1933) pp. 29-35. More discussion about the text may be found in A.A. Waisglass, *An Historical Study of Cyrene From the Fall of the Battiad Monarchy to the Close of the Fourth Century B.C.*, 82-91.

30 During the Republic it is stated that Pompey gathered stores of grain from Cyrenaica in preparation for his war with Caesar (Caesar, *The Civil War* 3.5.), and later in the Byzantine period we are told by Synesius that his farm produced wheat and other items such as barley, honey, olive oil and figs (Synesius, 148).

31 M.I. Finley, *Ancient Economy*, 170.

32 According to G. de Sanctis, in *Riv. fil* 63 (1935) p. 124, the consignment of grain was valued at over 223 talents. This estimation was reached on the basis of Cyrene's market price of 2 drachmas and 4 obols per medimnis during the 4th century. The maximum price being 2 drachmas, 2.5 obols. See also Waislgass, *op.cit.* 85.

33 Tod, *A Selection of Greek Historical Inscriptions*, Vol. II, 274f. G. Oliverio, *Documenti antichi dell' Africa Italiana*, 85f.

34 W.W. Tarn, *CAH*, VI, 449.

35 *Ibid*, 449.

36 Waisglass, *op.cit.*, p.90.

37 F.E. Adcock, *CAH* p.167. Meiggs, *Trees and Timber in the Ancient Mediterranean*, 373 f.

38 L. Naville, *Les monnaies D'or De la Cyrenaique* (450 a 250 avant J.C.) 27 and pl.11 32-34.

39 The discovery in 1969 of a fifth-century Greek tomb at Aslaia, 18 km west of Barca, in an area considered within the territory of this city, points to this fact. The deceased was presumably a Perioikos farmer of Barca. M. Vickers "A fifth-century B.C. tomb in Cyrenaica", *Lib. Antiq.* VIII, (1971) 81.

40 J. Lloyd, *The historical development of Benghazi*, 60.

41 D. White, *Expedition* 17, 4 (1975) 2 ff.

42 J. Boardman. *Excavations at Tocra 1963-1965*, The Archaic Deposits I, 15.

GREEK SUPPLIES OF CORN TO GREEK CITIES (330-26 B.C.) A marble stele from Cyrene (After Tod, *A Selection of Greek Historical Inscriptions* Vol.II, No.196).

[᾽Ιαρ]εὺς Σωσίας Καλ[λιά]δα. | [Π]όσοις σῖτον ἔδωκε ἁ πόλις, | ὅκα ἁ σιτοδεία ἐγένετο | ἐν τᾶι ῾Ελλάδι· || Ἀθαναίοις δέκα μυριάδας, | ᾽Ολυμπιάδι ἓξ μυριάδας, | Ἀργείοις πέντε μυριάδας, | Λαρισαίοις πέντε μυριάδας, | Κορινθίοις πέντε μυριάδας, || Κλευπάτραι πέντε μυριάδας, | ῾Ροδίοις τρῖς μυριάδας, | Σικυωνίοις τρῖς μυριάδας, | Μελιβοέσσι δύο μυριάδας, | [Μ]εγαρέσσι δύο μυριάδας, || Τ[ηνέσ]σι δύο μυριάδας, | Λεσ[βώιοι]ς μυρίος πεντακιχηλίος, | Θηραίοις μ[υ]ρίος πεντακιχηλίος, | Οἰταιέσσι μυ[ρίο]ς πεντακιχηλίος, | Ἀμβρακιώταις μ[υρί]ος πεντακιχηλίος, || Λευκαδίοις μυρίος [πε]ντακ[ι]χ[ηλίος], | Καρυστίοις μυρίος πεν[τακιχηλίος], | ᾽Ολυμπιάδι μυρίος δισχηλ[ίος] | ἑξακατίος, | Θεσσαλῶν Ἀτραγίοις μυρίος, || Κυθνίοις μυρίος, | ᾽Οπουντίοις μυρίος, | Κυδωνιάταις μυρίος, | Κώιοις μυρίος, | Παρίοις μυρίος, || Δελφοῖς μυρίος, | Κνωσίοις μυρίος, | Βοιωτοῖς Ταναγραίοις μυρίος, | Γορτυνίοις μυρίος, | Ἀλείοις μυρίος, || Ἀκαρνάνων Παλαιραίοις μυρίος, | Μεγαρέσσι μυρίος, | Μελιβοέσσι ὀκτακισχηλίος | πεντακατίος, | Φλειασίοις ὀκτακισχηλίος, || ῾Ερμιονέσσι ὀκτακισχηλίος, | Οἰταιέσσι ἑξακιχηλίος | τετρακατίος, | Τροιζανίοις ἑξακιχηλίος, | Πλαταιέσσιν ἑξακιχηλίος, || Κήιοις Οὐλιάταις πεντακιχηλίος, | Αἰγινάταις πεντακιχηλίος, | Ἀστυπαλαιέσσι πεντακιχηλίος, | Κυθηρίοις πεντακιχηλίος, | ῾Υρτακινίοις πεντακιχηλίος, || Αἰγινάταις πεντακιχηλίος, | Κήιοις Κορθαιέσσι τετρακιχηλίος, | Κυθηρίοις τρισχηλίος ἑκατόν, | Κήιοις τρισχηλίος, | ᾽Ιλυριοῖς τρισχηλίος, || Κήιων Κορησίοις τρισχηλίος, | Ἀμβρακιώταις χηλίος | πεντακατίος, | [᾽Ι]κετυρίοις χηλίος, | [Κ]νωσίοις ἠνακατίος.

Line	City	Amount	Line	City	Amount
46, 50	Aegina	10,000	58	Icetyrii ?	1,000
19, 56	Ambracia	16,500	54	Illyrii ?	3,000
7	Argos	50,000	45	Iulis (Ceos)	5,000
47	Astypalaea	5,000	8	Larisa	50,000
5	Athens	100,000	16	Lesbos ?	15,000
24	Atrax (Thessaly)	10,000	20	Leucas	15,000
51	Carthaea (Ceos)	4,000	14, 36	Megara	30,000
21	Carystus	15,000	13, 37	Meliboea	28,500
53	Ceos	3,000	18, 41	Oetaei	21,400
10	Cleopatra	50,000	6, 22	Olympias	72,600
31, 59	Cnosus	10,900	26	Opus	10,000
55	Coresus (Ceos)	3,000	35	Palaerus (Acarnania)	10,000
9	Corinth	50,000	29	Paros	10,000
28	Cos	10,000	39	Phlius	8,000
27	Cydonia	10,000	44	Plataea	6,000
48, 52	Cythera	8,100	11	Rhodes	30,000
25	Cythnus	10,000	12	Sicyon	30,000
30	Delphi	10,000	32	Tanagra (Boeotia)	10,000
34	Elis	10,000	15	Tenos ?	20,000
33	Gortyn	10,000	17	Thera	15,000
40	Hermione	8,000	43	Troezen	6,000
49	Hyrtacina	5,000		Total	805,000

to the moisture conserved deeper in the layer of soil, the tree is equipped to withstand summer droughts[43].

No work has yet been undertaken on the subject of olive farming and industry in ancient Cyrenaica, yet a region such as Tripoli to the west of Libya, was renowned in the classical literature for the abundance of its olives[44]. Mago of Carthage[45] was said to have prescribed the equivalent of twenty three feet metres each way between the trees, or fourteen metres in cases where the soil was poor and exposed to the winds of Tripoli, illustrating the importance of trees on the one hand, and the state of the climate in Mago's time on the other. Later, the same region was destined to be one of the principal centres of those whose economies were based on the export of olive oil. We know that Leptis Magna was fined 3,000,000 pounds of olive oil by Caesar as punishment for having allowed Cato to winter in the region after his epic march across the Syrtic desert. To Stephane Gsell, a quantity of 3,000,000 pounds suggests the vast extent in terms of trees and territory[46]. We are also told that olive farms densely occupied the whole of the Eastern Gebel, from Tarhuna to the sea, and from the escarpment to the Wadi Tareglat[47].

Oil presses have already been reported in Cyranaica and are said to be even more common than in Tripoli. Our best evidence for the export of oil is Synesius. In a letter[48] to his friend Pylaemenes in Thrace, he informs that he is going to ship some oil to him, as its quality is so excellent. Again we have to rely on Syensius, who actually owned a farm in the country a few kilometres west of Cyrene. In another letter he boasts about the quality of the Cyrenean oil:

> "As to the olive oil of this country, it certainly is the best if one does not listen to people whose taste is depraved, for they persist in judging oil by weight, and the less heavy they hold to be more valuable. With us scales are not forged for oil, but we assert that if this must be done, it would be natural to give preference to the heavier. Moreover, their oil, however famous and costly, when once put into a lamp, is so feeble that it scarcely gives any light at all. But our oil is so good that it gives out a complete flame, and when a lamp is needed it produces artificial daylight"[49].

Wine

The widespread cultivation of vineyards in Cyrenaica stimulated the early manufacture of wine and consequently its trade. We are not sure, however, how extensively it was exported across the Mediterranean. It is to Egypt, however, that Cyrenian wine was normally exported, where it was mostly consumed by the inhabitants of Alexandria[50]. On a number of occasions we are informed of cargoes of wine bound for Greece from Cyrenican ports[51]. Nevertheless, the Cyrenican wine was apparently not very popular outside Africa, and Strabo says that this was due to its mediocre quality[52].

Silphium

Cyrene, as is well known, was the sole, or almost the sole, exporter of the plant silphium[53] which was greatly in demand throughout the classical world. Similar species were said to have grown in Syria, Aremenia and Media, but these were considered to be poor substitutes for the silphium of Cyrene[54].

Silphium grew as a wild plant in a broad strip of territory stretching from the Syrtes on the west to the Gulf of Bumba on the east. To the south, it reaches the southern slopes of the Gebel and the steppes bordering the desert[55]. It is claimed, however, that it was more abundant in the Euhesperides region and around the Syrtic in the mostly Libyan tract of 4000 furlongs[56]. In the Cyrene region, according to Pliny, about 30 miles inland from the coast, an area of about 30 miles wide and 250 miles long grew nothing but silphium.

There is no doubt that the plant was of great antiquity even before the classical time. This is despite Theophrastus' claim that it was discovered only after the Greek settlements in Cyrenaica in 631 B.C. According to him the plant appeared after a heavy shower of rain[57]. Evans thinks the Cyrenaican silphium was possibly exported to Crete. It was also Evans who described a hieroglyphic sign used by the Minoans in Crete as representing silphium[58].

The botanical identification of silphium is not clear. Liddle and Scott define σίλφιον (silphoin) as laserwort *Ferula tingitana*[59]. There is the suggestion that the Libyan term for

43 E. Semple, *The Geography of the Mediterranean Region and its relation to ancient history*, 391.

44 Theoph., *H.P.*, IV.3.1. Pliny, *N.H.*, XVII. 133.

45 Quoted by Pliny, *N.H.*, XVII 93. He was quoted as advising that in Italy the olive should be planted at most 9 m. apart. It is relevant to recall that olive trees have wide-spreading roots. A law in Attica was passed prohibiting a farmer from planting his trees within nine feet of his neighbour's boundary line, lest the roots should encroach. Plutarch, *Solon*, 23.

46 Caesar, *Bellum Africae* 97, 3. Stephane Gsell's original study is his article 'L'huile de Leptis' in *Rivista della Tripolitania* I, (1924), republished in S. Gsell, *Etudes sur L'Afrique Antique'*. Scripta varia (Lille, PUL 1981) 15-156. Review by D.J. Mattingly in *Libyan Studies* 15 (1984) 165f. See also *id.*, *Histoire de l'Afrique du Nord* V, 200-1.

47 D.E.L. Haynes, *Antiquities of Tripolitania*, 51, 142-145. R. Goodchild, "Farming in Roman Libya", *Geograph. Mag.*, 25 (1952) p. 72. F. Begninot, *Encicl. Iitaliana* (Rome, 1929-1939) X, 417 f. S. Applebaum, *Jews and Greeks in Ancient Cyrene* 77. Di Vita-Evard, in *Quaderni* 10 (1979), 67-98.

48 Synesius, 134.

49 Synesius, 148.

50 W.J. Derby, *Food: The Gift of Osiris* (London 1977), 616.

51 Synesius, 134.

52 Strabo, 17. 1. 14.

53 Strabo, XV ii 10. *RE* 3A 103-114. E.S.G. Robinson, "Silphium", in *BMC* (Cyrenaica), British Museum 1927, pp, ccli-cclvii. F. Chamoux, *Cyrene Sous La Monarchie des Battiads* 246-263. *Id.*, in Barker (ed.), *Cyrenaica in Antiquity*, 165-172.

54 Coster, *op.cit.*, 115. Pliny, XIX 13.40.

55 Hdt., IV 169. Strabo, XVII, iii 12. Pliny, *N.H.*. 5.5.33.

56 Theoph. *H.P.*, 6.3.3. (cf. 3.1.8. and 9.1.3 and 4). Pliny, *N.H.*, 5.5.33. Strabo, 2.5.20; XVII 3.20. Pliny puts it in a tract of land some 30 miles wide and 250 miles long.

57 Theoph., *H.P.*, 6.3.3.

58 A.J. Evans, *The Place of Minos*, Vol. I 284-5.

59 H.G. Liddle and R. Scott, *A Greek-English Lexicon* (Oxford 1940), pp. 1031, 1599.

the plant was σιρφι (sirphi) and the Romans may have converted it, hence the Latin term La Sirpe, which is the equivalent to the Greek term[60]. The term was first used in Greek literature by Solon[61]. D'eniau[62], quoted by Gemmill, seems to suggest that there might be a relation between the origin of the word 'silver' and silphium, both being regarded as a valuable medium of exchange. Indeed, we are informed by Pliny that at one stage, when the plant was already difficult to obtain and worth its weight in silver, a stalk was transported to Rome from Cyrenaica. But already before this, 1500 pounds of silphium were kept in the Roman treasury together with gold and silver[63]. That is the time when Pliny complained:

> "... for a long time now no laserwort has been imported to us except what grows in Persia or Media and Armenia in abundant quantity, but of a much inferior quality to that of Cyrenaica[64].

Theophrastus, who was born about 370 B.C. and therefore lived during the peak of the silphium popularity, described the plant as having:

> "... a great deal of thick root; its stalk is like ferula in size and is nearly as thick; the leaf, which they call maspeton, is like celery. It has a broad fruit, which is leaf-like, and is called the *phyllon*"[65].

Silphium seems to have been widely used as a condiment vegetable, and believed to have been good for domestic animals. It was also used as a growth stimulant for plants and helpful for food preservation[66]. But its most important use was medicinal[67]. Pliny gives a full list of the different uses of the plant[68]. According to him it was useful for quartan fever, removal of hair, skin diseases, removing the contents of the uterus, soreness of the trachea, removal of extravasated blood and warts, promoting menstruation, removal of corns, as a diuretic and as an antidote for the poison of weapons, snakes and scorpions. It was also useful for massage, coughs, tetanus, quinsy, epilepsy, sciatica, and lumbago, etc.

The plant, therefore, must have met a variety of the needs of the ancient world, making it, no doubt, among the most valuable of Cyrenaican products. It is natural that it was well advertised by the people of Cyrenaica; we have Athenaeus, quoting Antiphanes, speaking of Cyrene:

> "I want to say goodbye to all horses, silphium, chariots, silphium stalks, steeple-chasers, silphium leaves, and silphium juice."[69]

He also writes of Lynceus of Samos, the intimate friend of Theophrastus, as being very familiar with a punch flavoured with silphium extract, and quotes him as saying:

> "A punch was served round, made with vinegar and silphium juice."[70]

Silphium was also mentioned frequently in the classical plays, for example in the works of Aristophanes[71]. In *Plutus*, one of the characters remarks: "Then you won't change, not if you give me all Battus' silphium". And there is a remarkable statement in *The Knights*: "Don't you remember when a stalk of silphium sold so cheaply?"[72]

Silphium seems to have become a royal monopoly soon after the establishment of the Greek settlements in Cyrenaica. The scene on the famous Laconian cup by the Arkesilas painter shows the king, Arkesilas II (569-568), supervising the loading of what is thought to be silphium for export (Plate 1,1). The spelling of the inscription (Silphomachos) was taken to mean Σ(ι)λφομαχος (S)(i)lphomachos) in order to connect the scene with the export of the silphium. However, other interpretations have been given. Lane suggests that the material in the basket is not silphium but wool[73]. But we should keep in mind Theophrastus' remark that silphium was packed in jars and not in open wicker baskets. However, the open basket may contain the leaves of the plants, which we know were in great demand and also exported.

The maximum peak production of the plant seemed to have been between the establishment of the Greek settlements in 631 and about 200 B.C. Besides the literary sources already mentioned, we have reliable coin evidence. The earliest coins of Cyrene, minted between 570 and 525 B.C., show the silphium fruit, its leaf, or the plant[74]. The last date for coins with silphium engraved on them was for the period between 246 and 221 B.C., during the reign of Ptolemy III.

Hence, the peak of its export was during the archaic and classical periods. Athens is certainly among the Greek states that imported Cyrenaic silphium[75]. Egypt too, especially in the Ptolemaic period, made use of the plant[76]. In the west we

60 Charles L. Gemmill, "Silphion", *Bull. of Hist. of Medicine*, Vol. XL, 1966, pp. 295-313. R.E. 113-114 (Silphion).

61 Solon was quoted by Pollux, *Onomasticon* (Ed. I. Bekker, Berolini, librarian F. Nicolai, 1846), p 427.

62 P.C.F. D'eniau, *Le Silphium* (Paris 1868) 1-160. Gemmili, *op.cit.*, 299.

63 Pliny, *N.H.,* XIX, 38-40.

64 Pliny, *N.H.,* XIX, 13.40.

65 Theoph., *H.P.*, VI 3.I. A plant of nearly similar description on a late 5th-century amphoriskos is thought to be that of silphium. See Sparkes and Talcott, *Ath.Agor.*, XII, No.1153 (pl.48).

66 Waisglass, *Historical Study of Cyrene*, 10-11.

67 For a general survey of the plant's medicinal uses until the middle ages, Gemmill, *op. cit.*, 305-313.

68 Pliny, *N.H.,* XVII, 259 XVIII, 308 XIX 38-44, XX 56, 105 XXII, 100-106.

69 Athen., *The Deipnosophist*, pp. 433-435.

70 *Ibid.*, p.433.

71 Aristophanes, *The Comedies*, trans. by B.B. Rogers (London, Pitman 1924), Birds, Vol.2, 181, 275.

72 *Ibid., Plutus,* 925, Vol. 3, p.445. *Knights*, Vol. 1, p. 213.

73 *CVA,* Bibl. Nat. I 17-18. E.A. Lane in *BSA*, 34, (1933-34) 161 ff. B.B. Shefton in *BSA* 49. 1954. p 399 no.14; 308 ff. The cup is discussed by Hooker, *The Ancient Spartans,* 88 f.

74 Robinson, BMC, ccli, pl.1.

75 Athen., 1, 27e. Theoph., *H.P.,* 6.3.2.

76 P.M. Frazer, *Ptolemaic Alexandria,* 149-150.

have evidence that the plant was smuggled to Carthage in exchange for wine[77].

By the time of Pliny, in the first century B.C., we are told that silphium had become scarce. Later, by the time of Synesius, silphium seems to have become extinct in the wild and only found in private gardens[78].

The disappearance of the plant in later antiquity is still a mystery. Many explanations have been given: climatic change, the methods used in harvesting, lack of government control, over-grazing and cultivation, etc.[79]. One reasonable explanation is given by Pliny, who stated that those who rented the pastures stripped it clean by grazing their sheep on it. This is supported by Arrian's comment that sheep had a habit of digging up the roots of silphium and that they needed supervision[80].

Excessive land use must have contributed to the plant's extinction, and also disregard for the traditional methods of cultivation could have killed the plant[81]. It is likely that a combination of all these explanations was the reason.

Other Products

Dates from Augila and Siwa[82], soda[83], honey, vegetables[84], perfumes[85], and salt were all exported. Salt, Cyrenaica's only mineral, was produced chiefly along her north-western shore in the salt lagoon near Benghazi[86]. Herodotus states that Libyan salt was of two colours, white and purple[87], and we are almost sure that it was exported to Egypt, especially that which was quarried in the south and around the oasis of Amon. It is Arrian who claimed that the priests of Ammon took salt with them for religious rites whenever they went to Egypt[88]. The fruit pine nut (pinus pinea) was also exported to Egypt and it was frequently found represented on Egyptian tombs, despite its limited cultivation there[89].

77 Strabo, 17. 13. 39.

78 Pliny, *NH* 22, 100. Seynesius, letter 134.

79 R. Goodchild, "Farming in Roman Libya", *Geogrph. Mag.* (1952) 25 pp. 70-78. *Idem.*, "The decline of Libyan agriculture", *Geogrph. Mag.* (1952) 25, pp. 147-155. W.B. Fisher, "Agriculture in Modern Libya", *Geogrph. Mag.* (1952), 25, pp. 184-194.

80 Pliny, *N.H.*, 18.13.39. Arrian, *Anab.*, 3.28. 6-7.

81 Theoph., *H.P.*, 9.1.7. Robinson, *BMC, op.cit.*, ccli.

82 Strabo, 17.3.23. Hdt., IV. 172. Pliny. *N.H.*, 13.4.9.

83 Diodorus, 3. 50.

84 Applebaum, *Jews and greeks in Ancient Cyrene*, 129.

85 Pliny, *N.H.* 6. Theoph., *H.P.*, IV, 3.1. An inscription of the 4th century A.D. refers to the perfume dealers' quarter of the city (αργοσ μυροπωλας). Reported in *Annuario* I (1914), 184.

86 R.G. Goodchild, *Benghazi, the Story of a City* (Dept. of Antiquities Cyrene, Shahat 1962) p 3.

87 Hdt., III 168; IV 18 2. Synesius. 148.

88 Arrian, *Anab.* 3.4.3. W.J. Derby, *Food, the Gift of Osiris* 44-50.

89 Derby, *op.cit.* 294, 753.

IV. THE FAUNA OF CYRENICA AND EXPORT

Stock rearing was certainly a source of wealth in ancient Cyrenaica and since Neolithic times, herds and flocks appear to have formed the inhabitants' principal wealth[90]. The Egyptian pharaoh Merneptah (1236-1223 B.C.), in his wars with the Libyans, boasted to have taken hundreds of thousands of cattle from the invading Libyans[91]. Similar claims were repeated after the campaigns of Ramses III (1198-1166 B.C.) against the Libyans and their allies, "The People of the Sea"[92]. There are also references to sheep[93], asses[94], and dogs[95], which were among the domesticated animals of the Libyans. We have already seen the emphasis with which Apollo spoke of the pastures of Libya. No doubt this was due to the relief of the Jabel Al-Akhdar, which is high enough to condense winter rains in this otherwise semi-arid steppe and to support such good pastures. It is believed that stock rearing was practised mainly by those who were living further south of the littoral. These were the more mobile tribes, who moved freely over greater distances looking for pasture[96].

It is relevant to stress the importance of the rhythmic seasonal movement of flock-owners from the southern steppe to the plateau. It illustrates the way of life of the nomadic pastoral and settled farmers and cattle owners who were concentrated on the plateau. The flocks usually spent winters on the steppe, by late April they needed to move to the plateau in search of water as the steppe-land wells gradually dried up[97]. It would be logical to suppose that this annual transhuman, which was until recently a regular phenomenon in Cyrenaica, was also undertaken by the Libyans in the Greek period. The Theran settlers, who occupied the plateau, moved only enough to secure fresh pasture for their herds and flocks, an arrangement that worked smoothly as long as the Gebel was not densely settled and space was left to provide enough pasturage. As the Greek settlement network grew into these traditionally free spaces, the pastoral tribes were excluded from access to the plateau and the coastal plain. This forced them to seek an alliance with Egypt, but eventually they were defeated by the Cyreneans at Irasa about 570 B.C.[98].

Sheep must have been important to the economy of the region. But while cattle are mostly found in the Jabel, sheep on the other hand were at home in the steppe, due to the fact that sheep drink little, and in the winter hardly at all[99].

90 McBurney, *Hawa Fteah* 313-319.

91 Breasted, *Ancient Records* III. 589. p.250.

92 *Ibid.* IV 111. p.66. 6. 224. p.125. Gsell, *op.cit.* v. p.173.

93 Homer, *Odys.*, IV. 65. Strabo, XVII.

94 Breasted, *op.cit.* III. 584. p.240.

95 Raymond Mauny, "Pre-Arab Trans-Saharan Trade-Routes between Libya and the Nigero-Chachic Savannes". *Trans-Saharan Trade-Route Conference*. 3.

96 Johnson, *Jabal Al-Adhdar* 97.

97 S. Applebaum, *op.cit.* p. 20.

98 Herodotus, IV, 159. Diodorus, *Library of History* 1, 68. 1-5.

99 S. Applebaum, *op.cit.* p.20.

In the classical period, our first evidence is the Homeric passage, which testifies to the fitness of the country for sheep breeding, where the ewes wean three times a year[100]. Cyrenaica's name was often associated with the term "flock-feeding" (μηλτρόφος) and "of many sheep" (πολύμηλος)[101]. Sheep meat, we are told, acquired an exceptionally fine flavour if they pastured on silphium[102].

A recent study of the animal bones recovered from Bernine (Benghazi) shows that in the Hellenistic and Roman periods there was a dominance of sheep and goats in the stock economy of the city. The obvious reason was that both animals were far better adapted to local grazing conditions than other animals[103].

Textile manufacturing from the home supply of wool must have existed. These no doubt ranged from fine woolen cloths to blankets and carpets. The question of colour is an important one and it is believed perhaps that the wools were used in their original shades, which were very fine. We have yet to find evidence for manufactured wool being exported outside Cyrenaica, but if the material being weighed on the Arcesilas kylix (Plate 1,1), is, as some suggested, wool instead of silphium, then this indicates that the king, besides his monopoly of silphium, had a decisive share in the production and marketing of wool[104].

Cattle were raised in large quantities in Cyrenaica. Indeed, it is believed that they formed the principal wealth of the region since the Neolithic period[105], and we have more evidence from the Pharaonic period: hundreds of thousands of cattle were seized by Merneptah (1236-1223) after his fight with invading Libyans[106]. In the classical period, Arrian speaks of the abundance of cattle in Cyrenaica. We have also the testimony of Herodotus, who stated that the inhabitants of the interior had a breed of bulls which, on account of their long curved horns, had to graze backwards[107]. Barca seemed to have been prominent in this field. Its mixed population was initially attracted by its fertile red soil and cattle rearing potential[108]. The coins of the city stand witness to this and bulls were shown on the obverse[109]. We are not sure, however, of the level of beef consumption by the ancient population. The investigation of the animal bones from Bernice showed that beef, in contrast to lamb, was rare as an element in the diet of ordinary people. It was also shown that many of the cattle killed were immature, suggesting that the young animals were being raised for meat; but at the same time there are several mandibles and maxillae from very old animals. Barker suggests that these were probably plough-cattle killed when there working lives were finished. It is also expected that hides were among the principal exports of Cyrenaica[110].

Most important for the economy of the region was the horse. The horse was first introduced to Libya in the last quarter of the 2nd millennium B.C.[111]. It was adopted first by the Egyptians around 1600 B.C. through their contact with the Hyksos. Through the Egyptian contact with Libyan Berbers it reached Cyrenaica. It is assumed that shortly after that date the Libyans were equipped with the chariot and that perhaps, about 1100 B.C., it became familiar to the Libyans of the interior[112].

The earliest notice of the horse in Libya occurs in the reign of Merneptah. The Pharaoh boasted to have captured "horses which bore the fallen Chief of Libya and the children of the Chief of Libya, carried off alive, pairs, twelve". At the time of Rameses III, 183 horses and asses were taken by the Egyptians[113].

More information about the Libyan horse is provided by the classical authors. We have Herodotus' statement that the Garamantes of Fezzan chased the Ethioplaios Troglydites on chariots drawn by four horses[114]. In recent years this statement has been confirmed and supplemented by the evidence provided by the rock-carvings and paintings of the Sahara. It was possible to classify the paintings and carvings into various groups and styles that can then be arranged in chronological order. What concerns us here, however, is the style, marked by the presence of men riding on horse-drawn chariots. Over three hundred representations of chariots have been found in the Sahara, confirming Herodotus' claim[115].

Horsemanship, we are told, was begun in Libya. The Berbers appear to have had a reputation for horse rearing. "Horse breeding", says Strabo, "is followed with such exceptional interest by the kings that the number of colts every year amounts to one hundred thousand"[116]. These horses were often so well schooled as to be easily guided when not ridden, "they would follow their masters even without being led, like dogs."[117]

With horses, the use of chariots was also mastered in Libya. Among the booty taken by Rameses III from the Libyans were one hundred chariots[118]. We have already mentioned the Garamentes who chased the Troglydites in chariots drawn by four horses.

100 Homer, *Ody.* 4, 86 ff.

101 Hdt., IV *Pyth.*, 6.

102 Homer, *Ody.* 4, 85-9. Cf. Pind. IX *Pyth.*, 6. Arrian, *Anab.* 3. 28. 6-7.

103 Barker, in Lloyd (ed.) *Excavation at sidi Khrebish*, 18.

104 Lane, *BSA* 34 (1933-4) 161-2.

105 McBurney, *Hawa Fteah* 313-319.

106 Breasted, *Ancient Record* III 589, p 250.

107 Hdt., IV. 185.

108 Polyb., v. 65-8.

109 Robinson, *B.M.C.* clxvi no.1A, clxviii.

110 Barker, *op. cit.* 19 f. For the export of hides see *Hermippus*, quoted in Athenaeus 1. 27 G. See also Hdt. IV 188 and Synesius *Ep* 130 & 147.

111 F. Chamoux, *Cyrene* 234-237.

112 R. Mauny, "Pre-Arab-Saharian Trade-Routes between Libya and the Nigero-Chadic Savana". A paper presented to the conference on *The history of the Trans-Saharan Trade-Routes* (Tripoli 1979) p 3.

113 Breasted, *Ancient Records* III 589, p.250 (4).

114 Herodotus, IV, 185.

115 L'hote, *Tassili Frescoes*, 124-132.

116 Strabo, 17. 3. 19.

117 Strabo, 17. 3. 7.

118 See notes 112, 113.

It is not surprising, therefore, to know that it was the Libyans who taught the Greek settlers how to handle the quadriga and provide them with their best breeding stock; hence the fame Cyrenaica gained for its horses. Pausanias recalled a Cyrenian named Theodorestus, who bred horses according to the Libyan custom. He, and his parental grandfather before him of the same name, gained victories at Olympia with four-horse chariots. His father gained a victory at the Isthmius[119].

Libyan charioteers were greatly praised and held in distinction in the Greek world. We hear of fine horses of racing stock brought as early as 494 B.C. to compete in the Greek sacred games at Corinth, Delphi and Olympia. With the Persian campaign in Greece, we know that a Libyan contingent took part with Xerxes; all of them were mounted on chariots[120]. By the end of the Battiad Monarchy, we hear of the Arkesilas chariot victory at the Pythian games of 462[121].

In 331, when Alexander the Great penetrated the Libyan desert on his way to the Oracle of Amon at Siwa[122], he was met on his way by Cyrenians who offered their friendship and presented him with three hundred horses and five chariots[123]. Later, when Cyrenaica was a dependency of Egypt during the Ptolemaic period, it was suggested that horses were exported in large quantities to Egypt. Synesius we are told, sent a horse abroad as a present to a friend[124].

One important factor to be considered when discussing the economy of Cyrenaica is related to hunting. The presence of wild animals in Libya was commented on by Herodotus. He stated that, with the exception of the coastal zone, which was occupied by Libyans, Greeks and Phoenicians and the upper zone, which was occupied by the Libyans, the country was infested with wild beats[125]. On the old site of Cyrene today, the nymph Cyrene is represented in the Apollo Sanctuary strangling a lion with her bare hands, a useful accomplishment in a country where lions roamed[126]. Further information is supplied by both rock drawings of big game and Roman mosaics of such animals as lions, leopards, wild asses, etc.

Hunting, therefore, took place further inland, in an area from the southern slopes of the Jebel and those parts of Marmaraica to the east, and the coast of Syrtes to the west, where pastures become scarcer. Wild animals were known to be fairly plentiful in these areas. Pursuit and capture of such animals had, as believed, an origin much earlier than that of animal domestication. One may assume therefore that the skin of these beasts and other domestic animals would be used for clothing and other purposes. We are told about a tribute paid by the Tehenu tribe to Queen Hatshepsut (1503-1482). This included: "many panther skins of five cubits long and four cubits wide"[127]. On the so-called "Chieftain Vase" from the Minoan palace at Haghia Triada, there is a scene representing five figures, three of them carrying objects explained by Evans as elephant skins, the spoils of hunters returned from Libya[128].

Cyrenaica must have supplied the Mediterranean world with these beasts to be used for games, and the inhabitants of the interior were no doubt the main beneficiaries of such trade. E. Price in her investigation into the origin of the bears that took part in the grand procession of Ptolemy Philadelphus (285-246 B.C.), considers them to be Cyrenaican and that they may have been traded to Alexandria[129]. The bustard (otis retrac and related species) was also traded with Alexandria in very large quantities[130]. Our best evidence does not, however, come from Cyrenaica itself, i.e. the eastern part of Libya, but rather from the west, where the prosperous inhabitants of Ghirza decorated their tombs with sculptured hunting scenes (now in the Tripoli Museum). These show lions, hares, ostriches and antelopes[131].

In later periods, it is believed that the passion of metropolitan Rome for the slaughter of thousands of large Libyan animals in the circuses was a major factor in the extermination of big game near the coast of Cyrenaica and Tripolitancia, and, to a lesser degree, in the hinterland. After the fall of Carthage, the export of these animals was said to be second in importance only to the export of olive oil for the lamps of Rome[132].

Also a good source of wealth for Cyrenaica were the riches of the sea. Marine life along the coast must have attracted fishermen in search of sponges and the Cyrenaican coast enjoyed a large variety of fish and shellfish. We remember that it was the purple fisherman of Itanos, from a Phoenician settlement on eastern Cretan, who piloted the first Theran settlers to the African coast[133].

Among the edible marine molluscs, murex was particularly valued in the ancient world as a source of purple dye. This

[119] Pausanias, VI 12.7.

[120] Sophocles, *Electra* 702. Pindar, *Pyth* IV, V. Hdt., VII 86 and 184.

[121] Pindar, *Pyth* I. II. III, IV. *Olymp*. I, III-IV *Nem* IX.

[122] J. Machu, *Rev. Hist*. 204-205 (1950-1) p 42.

[123] Diodorus, 17. 49.

[124] M. Rostovtzeff, *SEHH*. 1. p 293, 385, 396. Synesius, Letters, 40.

[125] We can have an idea of the familiarity of the foreign artists with the fauna of Cyrenaic (e.g. monkeys, cheetahs and cranes) in the famous Arcesilaos Laconian cup, (Paris Bibliotheque, Nationale). See Herodotus II, 32 and Mela I, 8, Strabo XVIII.

[126] Cyrene and the lion are represented on a Laconian cup in Taranto (about 520 B.C. or a little later, contemporary with the last work of the Amasis Painter). B.B. Shefton, BSA 49 (1954), 310, and C.M. Stibbe, *Lakonische Vasenmaler* 192. See also the Roman representation in sculpture, the Roman examples published in Paribeni *Catalogo Delle Sculpture Di Cirene* nos 176-178 pl. 102.

[127] Bates, *The Eastern Libyans*, 93.

[128] Evans, *The Palace of Minos* 2, 742.

[129] The detailed account of the Procession is to be found in the fifth book of the *Deiprosophistai* of Athenaeus of Nancratis (203 B= FGrH 627 F2) and the account is quoted from a larger work by Kallixeinos of Rhodes about Alexandria. The comment of E.E. Price is from his publication *The Grand Procession of Ptolemy Philadelphus* (Oxford University Press, 1983) 96.

[130] Athen., 390 d.

[131] Haynes, *The Antiquities of Tripolitania,* 154-155.

[132] E. Hufnal, *Libyan Mammals,* 14. On one occasion Caesar was said to have put in the arena 400 lions to battle with the gladiators. Titus celebrated the inauguration of the Colosseum with 9,000 animals; Trajan had 2,246 large animals killed in a single day. It is believed that large numbers of these came from Africa. See: J. Carropino, *Daily life in ancient Rome* 239. E.W. Bovil, *The Golden trade of the Moor* 6.

[133] Hdt., IV, 151-3.

dye, which is secreted from a gland in the mantle cavity of the molluscs, was found widely distributed on the Mediterranean littoral; heaps of shells have been found in many parts of the Mediterranean region. To the west, the Phoenician cities on the African coast enjoyed similar raw material[134]. The shallow coast of Syrtis Minor offered thriving murex fisheries that supported Punic dye-factories at Carthage and Attica.

We know very little of the dye production in Punic Tripolitania. However a tomb belonging to a Garamantian lady in Fezzan, dated to about 300 A.D., revealed purple dyed textiles, believed to be imported from one of the coastal centres[135], perhaps Leptis Magna, which was one of the important trade centres in the Mediterranean.

In Cyrenaica no serious investigation into the exploitation of the murex shell in the Greek period has taken place despite the presence of many signs that may be taken to indicate the existence of such an industry.

A large deposit of murex shells dated from the second century B.C. to the third century A.D. was found and reported in Bernice. These shells, however, were thought to be food debris and may have also been used for lime production. Since the late stage in the history of Cyrenaica is considered to be a decline in the social, cultural and physical structure of the district, a state of affairs which was made worse by earthquakes, D.S. Rees, in his investigations of the murex shells from Bernice, thought that such a state of affairs would not be conducive to supporting a labour-intensive industry, either for local use or for export[136]. It is therefore justifiable to conclude that a murex-dye industry must have existed in Cyrenaica, but at an earlier period, perhaps before the 2nd century A.D.

To sum up, Cyrenaica managed to produce a notable wealth for the citizens resulting from production of food and livestock enough to sustain the population. The products were typical of forest, field, grazing land and pasture and were known to be fundamental commodities of ancient trade.

V. THE SAHARA CONNECTION

How far these commodities were supplemented by luxury goods arriving from central Africa along the Sahara caravan routes, depends on the solution of the general problem presented by these routes. Sandro Stucchi has asserted recently that there was a trade route between Egypt and Greece, via Cyrene, dating back to the four decades which preceded the historical date of the foundation of Cyrene in 631 B.C.[137]. Stucchi and Milne before him, contended that the Assyrian invasion of Egypt in 672 B.C. created a disruption in the flow of trade down the Nile, and consequently trade traffic was diverted through the western desert, via Siwa Oasis into the Giarbub Oasis, and then north to the sea by the Gulf of Bomba on the eastern outskirts of the Cyrenaica plateau[138]. Are we now to consider Stucchi's[139] further claim that the foundation of the Cyrene itself was a direct consequence of the existence of two caravan routes linking the region to central Africa when goods from the Sahara are scarcely represented among the Cyrenaica finds? Yet many may rightly argue[140] that the district could not have attained the level of wealth attributed to her by classical authors unless she had possessed a share of the export trade in such goods from central Africa.

We are certain that the ostrich was exported. The bird is well known to the Graeco-Roman world in West Africa, Syria and Mesopotamia; Pliny gives a detailed account of it. Diodiorus Siculus remarks that it is the bird's weight that makes the ostrich unable to fly and that it sometimes threw up stones behind it violently enough to avoid its predators. Xenephon had already noted the creature's extraordinary speed and the way it used its wings like sails when running[141]. The earliest illustration of the ostrich is on a black-figure skyphos in Boston, where the bird is shown ridden by members of a comic chorus[142]. Such a representation suggests that the bird was used as a mount. Oppian say that the Ostrich was large enough to carry a youth on its back, and Firmus, the rich pretender in Egypt, is described as riding on the back of a huge ostrich[143]. No less than eight pairs of ostriches walked in harness in Ptolemy Philadelphus' grand procession[144]. Lucian lists ostriches among the quarry of the Garamenties of Fezzan and states that they prized the birds' eggs both as food and for their use as cups when halved[145].

The evidence for the role of the bird is plentiful. The bird was used in amphitheatre shows and for food. Its shell was greatly in demand and its plumes was prized decorations on the crests of ancient helmets[146]. Its illustrations on Roman

134 Among the centres of production in that part of North Africa was the 4th - 2nd century B.C. Kerkouane (Dar Essafij on Cap Bon) and the famous centre on the island at Djerba (ancient Mennix), as described by Strabo (Geography XVII, 3.18) in the late first century B.C. and Pliny (Natural History 1 X: 127) in the first century A.D. Pliny described Mennix as producing the best African purple, along with that from the Gaetulian cost. The dye from the latter area was also noted in the first century B.C. by Horace (Ep.11.2, 181).

135 D.S. Rees in *Libyan Studies* 11 (1979-80) 79 f.

136 *Ibid* 87 f.

137 Sandro Stucchi, "Cyrenaica as head point of two possible caravan routes". *Trans-Saharan Trade-Route Conference*. 1.

138 J.G. Milne, *JEA* 25. (1939). 177-183. S. Stucchi, *op.cit.* 3. The Gulf of Bomba contains the small island of Platea where the Therans founded their first settlement before they moved to the African shore proper in 639 B.C. See R. Goodchild, *Cyrene and Apollonia*, 7.

139 Stucchi, *op.cit.*, 3 f.

140 Applebaum, *Jews and Greeks in Ancient Cyrenaica*, 129.

141 Pliny, *N.H.*, X, 1, (1, 2), Diodorus Siculus 11, 50 3-6. Xenophon, *Anabasis* I 5, 3.

142 Sifakis G.M., *Parabasis and Animals Choruses* (London 1971), pls. III-IV.

143 Oppian, *Cynegeticus* III, 482-563, especially 490, 491, and *Scriptores Hisoriae Augustae* Firmus, VI, 2.

144 E.E. Price, *The Grand Procession of Ptolemy Philadelphus*, 1a, 90; from Athenaeus V, 200 f.

145 Lucian, *De Dipsadibus* 2, 6, 7.

146 Synesius, 129, 134; *cf.* Haywood in, *An Economic survey of Ancient Rome*, IV, (1938) 55. Gsell, *Histoire de l'Afrique du Nord* I 128-9.

mosaics are indications of its importance[147]. The lines in which Claudian compares Eutropius to an ostrich, indicate clearly that the bird is associated with regions of the interior of Cyrenaica and the west.

> "Even so the great Libyan bird, hard pressed by the cries of the hunters, speeds across the burning sands and rushes through the dust with wings carried like sails before the breeze; but when it hears the clear sound of feet behind it, it forgets to flee and stands with eyes closed, hiding its head and imagining, poor soul, that it cannot be seen by those whom itself it cannot see."[148]

Fifty-four fragments of ostrich shell were recovered from Bernice. These were found in contexts ranging from Hellenistic to Islamic in date[149]. Later, Synesius of Cyrene (c. 370-413 A.D.) states that ostriches were still being shipped abroad from there in the early fifth century for the amphitheatre shows. He explains to his friend Phlaemeues, one of his correspondents, that he has acquired some ostriches, taken in the hunt, but cannot send them at once by sea owing to enemy activities. He promises, however, to send them later by another boat[150]. African ivory and ostrich shells were found in Etruscan tombs, though it is more likely that most of these were shipped through western ports, following the ancient inland trade route to Tripoli[151].

[147] For the ostrich in Roman life and a discussion of the mosaics. See Toynbee *Animals*, 237 ff.

[148] Quoted by Toynbee, *ibid* 237 f. from *In Eutropium* II, 310-16.

[149] Barker in Lloyd (ed.) *Excavation at Sidi Khrebish*, 24.

[150] Synesius Epistolac, 133.

[151] Evans, *The Palace of Minos*, I 285, 170. Bates, *The Eastern Libyans,* 101.

Chapter Three

THE RED-FIGURED POTTERY

I. FIFTH CENTURY

1. *Alabastra* [two fragments] (Cyrene Museum) (Plate 11, 2)

The first fragment [la] is from the base section of an alabastron, with a tondo containing a palmette painted in silhouette. From the very small part of the remaining figure zone, this fragment appears to be from a white-ground alabastron, as it seems to show traces of white colouring. The Paidikos Group[1], in the early red-figure period, was familiar with such a technique, i.e. ornaments in black silhouette, a figure zone in the centre of the alabastron body with a tondo at the bottom filled with a palmette, either in RF or silhouette technique[2]. On an alabastron in Paris by the same group (Louvre CA1920), both the vase's lower and body sections have circumscribed palmettes drawn in silhouette[3].

The second fragment [1b], too, is probably from a white-ground alabastron. Only a small part of the figure zone remains. It is painted with white slip; a chevron band in black glaze separates this zone from the wide lower section, which is painted in black glaze.

This piece very probably belongs to the so-called 'Negro Alabastra' group. Sixty-two of them are known[4]. Their exceptional feature is the representation of figures with African appearance on the main figure zone[5]. The reverse displays a tall palm tree. This type of alabastron is mostly dated to the first two decades of the fifth century[6].

The ethnic origin of the warrior is uncertain. The racial type is that of the inhabitants of the upper Nile and the Sudan. One may ask the question whether this is an illustration of the so-called Ethiopians, frequently mentioned by classical authors. The reference in Herodotus to Ethiopiaus in Xerxes' army, and the representatives of blacks on Athenian vases of the fifth century B.C.[7], have led to the conjecture that it was at this period that blacks were seen for the first time in Greece in large numbers. Frazer calls them eastern Ethiopians since he takes them to be mercenaries in the Persian army from India or Baluchistan[8]. Consequently he dates the group after the Persian War.

The familiarity of Greek artists with the indigenous population of Africa is nothing new. From the seventh century onwards the Greeks lived in Egypt and no doubt had daily contact with its diverse ethnic inhabitants[9]. The palm tree may in fact allude to the environment to which these indigenous blacks belonged. All this may reflect the influence of the region of North Africa on Greek artists who, no doubt, paid an occasional visit to the area, especially Egypt.

It is also reasonable to suggest that a number of blacks lived in Athens, for they were often shown as warriors, particularly in vase-paintings from the third quarter of the sixth century, in association with Memnon[10]. They are seen on the neck-amphora in London and on amphora type A in Philadelphia; both vases painted by Exekias. They also appear on another neck-amphora in New York, associated with Exekiasl. One is also represented as an archer on a neck-amphora in Brussels by the Swing painter[11].

1 *ARV* 98-101, see especially 99, 3-6.

2 Wehgartner, *Attisch Weissgrundige Keramik*, 115.

3 Mertens, *Attic white-ground,* 129, no.3, pl. XVIII, 4. See Wehgartner, ibid 115 f. for more examples.

4 *ARV* 267-9, *par*. 352. Mertens, *op. cit.* 132ff. Neils, *Antike Kunst* 23 (1980) 13-18.

5 Thimne, in *Jahrbuch der Staatlichen Kunstsammlungen in Baden-Württemberg*, 7 (1970), 7 ff.

6 Mertens, *op. cit.* 134.

7 Hdt. VII, 70.

8 D. Frazer, *AJA* 39 (1935) 35-45.

9 Boardman, *The Greek Overseas,* 152-3. Snowdon, *Blacks in Antiquity,* 121f., 184. Cf. also Rack, *Zum Barbarenbild Derin Kunst Athen*, 164-213.

10 Pinnev, in Moon W.G. (ed.), *Ancient Greek Art and Iconography,* 131-132.

11 London, BM B 209, *ABV* 144,8. Philadelphia Ms. 3442, *ABV* 145,14. New York, 98.8.13, *ABV* 149. Brussels, A 130, *ABV* 308, no.82. Snowdon, *Blacks in Antiquity,* fig.15.

In sculpture, stone statues from Ayia Irini in Cyprus (about 560 B.C.) were identified by E. Gjerstad as representing blacks, perhaps in the civil and military service during the Egyptian occupation of the island under Amazis (568-525 B.C.). Terracotta masks portraying blacks are known from Sicily in the late sixth and early fifth centuries B.C.[12].

It has been suggested that the presence of Ethiopians on these flasks may serve as labels, or advertisements of exotic Egyptian products, possibly perfumes or unguents[13].

Alabastra were usually suspended by leather thongs attached to the vessel's neck[14]. They were not designed to stand on their round bases, which, therefore, were suitable areas for decoration. The date of the two Cyrenaican alabastra is about 500 B.C., and they were probably painted in the workshop of the Syriskos group, where similar Alabastra were painted. This workshop may have had an influence on the Negro Alabastra group[15].

2. *Head Vase* - fragment from a Kantharos (Cyrene Museum) (Plate 12,1)

Only part of the head, forehead, left eye, eyebrow-ridge and ear survive.

This type of vase was usually formed of a wheel made lip attached to a mould-formed lower portion in the shape of a head of a black female, which had a snail-curl hair applied with pellets of clay. The surface appears to have been covered with a shiny black glaze of good quality. Incision was used to indicate the pupil of the eye. This type of physiognomy, and the pellet treatment, of the hair characterizes the development of Attic black faces throughout the archaic and classical period.

Beazley has classified attic head-vases of the sixth and fifth centuries by their moulded portions[15]. There is no exact parallel to our piece in this classification, and because only small fragments of the head remain it is difficult to determine precisely the shape, but I think our piece is likely to be from a Kantharos, and it is certainly close to class B (the Epilykos Class). Representative of the group are the Janiform "black heads" from Boston[16].

The name Epilykos was found inscribed on a Janiform (white females) aryballos in the Louvre [17]. The name has been found on vases of early red-figure painters of the last quarter of the sixth century (Skythes, *c.* 520-505)[18]. The boy Epilykos was apparently the artist's favourite athlete and he is represented on a vase by Phintias[19].

A second Janiform (black and white) aryballos from the same class, also in the Louvre (CA987) is known[20]. The treatment of the hair and forehead of the black woman is close to ours. The top of the white woman's head is decorated with a cock and a hen, framed by florals. The composition is closely comparable with an unattributed Oxford lekythos from Agrigento[21], whose shoulder bears a large cock and a small hen between a pair of linked, circumscribed palmettes with ribbed petals. This lekythos is dated around 500 B.C.

Head-vases were common and at the time they were no doubt novelty and luxury items[22]. Biers has rightly observed that of the thirteen complete vases in Beazley's first four groups and subgroups, twelve are fully, or in the case of Janiform vases, half modelled in the head of a black[23]. The use of the head of a black for the body of many of these plastic vases has no more significance than that of a topical reference, as souvenir-mugs in the form of human faces have today. There is no doubt, however, that the subject held great appeal for Attic potters and as Beazley has pointed out, the nature of Attic black glaze was particularly suited to the rendering of this subject. Date, late sixth to early fifth century B.C.

3. *Cup, Type Concave Lip* (Cyrene Museum) (Plate 12,2)

The body forms a continuous curve with stem; filled at the junction of stem and foot with a scraped groove above and below it. Practically intact. Brilliant black glaze applied throughout except for the interior of the handles and outer of face and underside of foot.

This is an exceptionally well preserved type C Cup[24], the interior medallion of which shows a naked man balancing himself on a wine skin, seated to left with knees bent and both legs drawn in three-quarter view. Shoulders are frontal and the bearded head is in left profile. The right arm is raised and the hand is extended with the two fingers visible. The tip of the beard is preserved and the sketch line of the figure clearly visible.

This piece is very close to the style of Epiktetos, the master cup painter of the early archaic red-figure style, who flourished during the last two decades of the fifth century B.C.[25]. Good

---

12 Gjerstad, *The Swedish Cypus Expedition* IV. Pt 2, 103-104, 466-467. Snowdon, *Blacks in Antiquity*, 122-123, fig.1. Biers, in Moon M.G. (ed.), *Ancient Greek Art and Iconography*, 120.

13 Winnefeld, *AM* 14 (1889) 49 f.

14 Haspels, *ABL*, 101, no.2.

15 *ARV* 264, 267.

16 A general classification of the type was first made by J. Beazley, *JHS* 49 (1929) 38-78, pl.1-6. Cf. also *ARV*², 1519-52, 1697-98 and 1704, and par. 501-505 and 552. Boston 98.888. Beazley, *op. cit.* 42, pl.1,3, E.A.A. *i* 973, *ARV* 1530/3.

17 Louvre, CA 986, *ARV* 1530,1, 1578. The vase was commented on by Pottier in *Mon Piot* 9 (1902) 135-140 *ARV* 1578.

18 Ibid 82 and Boardman, *ARFV* 59-60.

19 Boardman *op. cit.* 59 f. Beazley, *JHS* 49 (1929) 26, 43.

20 Louvre, CA 987, *ARV* 1530,2, par. 501, Addenda 194. Hoffmann, *RA* 1974, 203, fig.8.

21 Oxford, Ashmolean Museum, 1932-33, *ARV* 1644. Kurtz *Athenian white lekythoi*, 123, pl.65.1. Haspel *ABL*, 75.

22 Croissant, *BCH* (1973) 205-25.

23 Biers op. cit. 120 (n.12).

24 Sparkes and Talcott, *Ath. Agora* 91, figs. 389-413.

25 *HGVP*, 319-320. Kraiker, *JdI* 44 (1929) 151.

illustrations of his work, which are similar in style to our cup, are the Greek examples in Copenhagen[26]. For the most part, Epiktetos cups have no pattern-work: the rim is plain black, and the black tondo - only slightly larger than the picture generally in a cup - has only a figure or two as decoration. The black background itself becomes a positive element in the decoration, thus setting the fashion for much that is best in subsequent red-figure work. The man on the Cyrenaica cup, like most of the Epiktetos figures, is neatly drawn and with only a few anatomical markings. Our artist, who must have been contemporary with Epiktetos, was clearly interested in outline, which he had a sure grasp of. The figure shown on the inside of our cup is nicely adapted to the round space provided.

Date of the cup, late sixth or the beginning of the fifth century B.C.

4. *Cup* (Cyrene Museum) (Plate 13,1)

A fragment. Only part of the reserved circle bordering the tondo is preserved. In it is a wreathed head of a boy. A relief contour for the forehead-nose line. Outline of hair reserved, purple colour for the wreath.

This piece [4] is assigned to an archaic cup painter similar to that of the Chelis Group. The work of the group is represented by the cup in the Louvre from Vulci[27]; alternatively, the workshop of Epictetos is a possible source of inspiration. Date late sixth or the beginning of the fifth century B.C.

5. *Cup: Fragment, part of the cup Tondo* (Cyrene Museum) (Plate 13,2)

Surface abraded. Glaze is flaking. Relief contour throughout. A dilute is used.

On the fragment, a youth appears to be leaning forward "stooping", supporting himself with a staff held by the left hand. His right hand is apparently extended downward over his knee, which appears to be lifted up.

This could well be an educational scene where the youth is supervising another or he could be in dancing pose. Alternatively he could be holding an object or an animal, pet, etc.

The style of painting is that of the late Archaic Period, which is, in fact, a continuation and expansion of the early red-figure technique, but coarse in style.

A similar scene, in style and subject, perhaps, is to be found on the unsigned kyathos attributed to Onesimos (the Panaitios Painter)[28], one of the important cup-painters active in the closing years of the sixth and early fifth centuries. The scene shows a youth reading aloud from a book to two listeners. The pose of one of the listeners is close to that of the youth on our fragment[29].

We can also compare the hand on our piece to those drawn by Makron[30], another influential Cup-painter, especially the outline of the hair, which is usually reserved and not incised. The eye is long and narrow, the lower lip droops, the chin is protruding. A good example of these features in the work of Makron, is the cup in Bryn Mawr[31].

The painter of our piece belongs to a workshop no doubt influenced by one or all of these famous cup-painters. But he is more likely to have been active in the early years of the period, during the second decade of the fifth century.

6. *Epinetron* (Onos) (Cyrene Museum)[32] (Plate 13,3)

This Onos fragment is the only example to be found in the region so far. The upper part is ornamented with an incised scale-pattern, and on what is left of its long side there is a meander, or snake-like line, painted in white on a black ground. This is separated from the scale section by a black line.

An epinetron was usually placed by women on the thigh as a protection during the task of carding wool. The plain type of epinetron found in the Athenian Agora is the practical version for daily use[33]. The decorated type was probably a special gift. An elaborate example is the one from Berezan (South Russia) painted in the BF tradition. The figures were carefully drawn and the scales were meticulously incised[34]. On a complete BF epinetron in Leiden the long sides are decorated with a panel of men, women, klismoi, a stool and a dog[35]. An epinetron from Copenhagen, like the Cyrenaican piece, is decorated on the long side with only a panel of meanders and painted in black on red clay[36]. The meanders of the Cyrenaican piece, however, are somewhat different, drawn in a snake-like manner in white on a black background. We have yet to find a similar example, but the Louvre loutrophoros, by the Kleophrades painter, has similar white wavy lines on its lip and outer surfaces of the handles[37]. The date of the Cyrenaican fragment is early fifth century.

---

26 *ARV* 75, 59.

27 Paris, Louvre G15, in Hoppin, *Attic Red-figured vases*, Vol.I, 190.

28 *ARV* 313-330. Caskey and Beazley, *Boston* II, 23ff.

29 Berlin, Staatliche Museum, 2322, from Vulci, *ARV* 329, 134. J. Boardman, *ARFH*, fig. 234.

30 *ARV* 458-481. *HGVP* 132-3.

31 CVA, *USA* (13) pl.19.

32 Elrashedy, in Baker (ed.), *Cyrenaica in Antiquity*, 212 f. pl.17 III, 3.

33 Robinson, *AJA*, 49, (1945) 488-490. Sparkes and Talcott, *Pots and Pans of Classical Athens*, fig.57. The most celebrated example is the vase by the Etetria Painter in Athens, *ARV* 1250, 34.

34 Gorbunova, in *Archaeologia Polona*, 14 (1973), (Festschrift Casimro Majewski), 79-85.

35 *CVA*, Leiden, 2, pl.68 1-2.

36 Copenhagen, National Museum inv. 1636. *CVA*, 3(3) 89, 1 pl.120 (122) 1.

37 *CVA*, Louvre 8, (III,1c), pl.56-7.

7. *Column-Krater, fragment* (F11, Tr.2, St.3, Cyrene Museum) (Plate 14,1)

A fragment from the shoulder of the vase. Only parts of the heads of the painted two figures remain. On the right the head of a male figure, probably Dionysus, likely to be walking to the right, but turning around as he goes to look at a female figure, whose hair is in a Sakkos. The wreathed Dionysus is holding a vine branch (part of which remains), probably in his right hand as the left usually holds a kantharos.

Dionysus and a Maenad are shown on this piece. The style is close to that of Myson, who marks the beginning of the mannerist movement. His works date from the turn of the sixth century and continue into the first two decades of the fifth[38]. Characteristic rendering on our piece include his narrow eyes, the ear formed by interlocking areas, and the row of dots edging the hair at forehead and temple. We may compare our Dionysus with a similar Dionysus by Myson on a krater in the Metropolitan Museum, and probably of about the same date, between 500 and 490 B.C.[39].

The bulk of vases attributed to Myson were found in Etruria, outside this region only Athens, and now Cyrene, had pottery attributed to him.

8. *Krater* (A fragment, Cyrene Museum) (Plate 14,2)

A shiny black glaze evenly applied. Black relief line applied to the outline of the phiale, the inside of the oinochoe's handle, outline of woman and man's fingers of both hands, part of the spear shaft and arms of the man. Dark red glaze applied to the woman's bracelet.

A woman and a man in the act of pouring a libation. Only the arm of the woman remains. She is facing left and holds an oinochoe[40] in her right hand. Facing her, a man, likely to be a warrior, holds a stick, or spear, in his left hand. With the right hand he extends a broad phiale, behind which part of the oinochoe is hidden.

The nearest parallel is the Attic Nolan amphora in the Kelsey Museum in Michigan, where a similar scene is represented[41]. This is attributed to the Berlin painter, who is responsible for the innovative placement of one or two figures as an important theme in the composition of the subject[42]. This innovative composition of free field, or spotlight technique as it is often referred to, emphasizes the orange-red figures against the shiny black ground, and was highly effective. These features are illustrated by the Michigan amphora, dated to the mid seventies.

Our fragment from Cyrenaica is very close to the Michigan amphora and could well be by the same artist or one of this circle.

There is another similar scene, by the same painter, on a kalpis in the Kunsthistorisches Museum in Vienna[43]. This represents Artemis pouring a libation for Apollo, who holds out a phiale as shown on our fragment and on the amphora of the Kelsey Museum. The scene on the Cyrenaica fragment is most likely to be a sacrificial one before a young warrior's departure for, or on his return from, battle. The military subject, if it is a military scene, may reflect the Athenian political events at the end of the first quarter of the fifth century, after the Persians had been defeated by the Greeks. Alternatively[44], the figures may represent a Triptolemos and Kore scene, like those illustrated on a Kalpis by the same painter, now in the museum of the University of Graz[45].

9. - 11. (Cyrene Museum) (Plate 15, 1-3)

These three pieces are from large vessels. They are close in style and could well be by the same hand.

On No.9, figure moving left, dressed in a himation. The archaic drawing of the folds of the himation, ending in arcs, is reminiscent of the Pan painter[46].

Fragment No.10 preserves part of the head, chest and right arm, and shoulder of a bearded figure, likely to be Dionysus. He is probably moving to left, but looking around to the right. He wears a plain chiton and has a kantharos raised in his right hand. The painting is by the hand of one of the mannerists, likely to be the Pan painter.

Fragment No.11 preserves the mouth, beard, right shoulder and arm of a male figure moving to the right, with a vine-branch. He is Dionysus. The nearest parallel for this composition is the bellcrater in Palermo by the Pan painter[47].

12. *Fragment* (Oxford from Euhesperides) (Plate 16,1)

Part of a head of an attendant of Buisiris, facing left, with a bundle of sacrificial sticks over his shoulder.

---

38 *HGVP*, 130.

39 Richter and Hall, pls.23.2, 170.20.

40 Clearly intended to represent a metal vessel. The oinochoe in the scene is Shape 1, which appears commonly in designs involving the use of phiale on oinochoai in general. Cf. Green, *BISC* 19 (1972) 1-17 and *JHS* 81 (1961) 70, on the identification of metal oinochoai, and especially the elaborate oinochoe on a fragmentary stamonos of the early 5th c. in Oxford. Oxford, 1911, 627.

41 Moon, *Greek Vase-Painting*, fig.91. Kelsey Museum of Archaeology (An Arbor Museum purchase, 77.7.1, ex-collection of Lord Belper, Kingston Hall, Nottingham, England).

42 Beazley, *ARV* 31f. Robertson, *JHS* 72 (1950) 55f.

43 *CVA*, Vienna 3, pl.140, nos. 1-3.

44 Other common scenes involve the presentation of wine to a god, whether by another god or mortal, e.g. Zeus/Ganymede, Zeus/Athena, Apollo/Artemis, and (with Kantharos) Heracles/Athena, Dionysos/Satyr, Dionysos/Maenad. Cf. Simon, *Opfernde Götter*, passim.

45 Schwarz, *ÖJh* 50 (1972-75), 125-6, 128-9, 132-3, fig. 1-4. *ARV* 1634, 183, Addenda 97.

46 Beazley, *ARV* 550-61, examples of his work in *The Pan Painter*, passim. Richter, *A Survey*, 94.

47 Palermo, Museo Nazionale, V 778. Beazley, *ARV* 550, 2.

This is another fragment by the Pan Painter from Cyrenaica, now in Oxford[48]. The attribution to the artist, passed on by M. Vickers, was made by Beazley. The small ear and heavy jaw are characteristic of that artist.

The scene, probably, depicts Heracles and Buisiris, King of Egypt (the confrontation took place in North Africa). During a prolonged drought, according to mythology, Busiris took the advice of a Cypriot sect and, to make the crops grow, sacrificed to Zeus all foreigners who entered Egypt. Heracles, unwilling to become a victim himself, managed to kill the King and all his followers.

The best representation of this event can be seen on a pelike by the Pan Painter[49]. The reverse of the vase shows three Egyptians rushing off in horror, holding the implements of the cults as Heracles slaughters their King and the rest of the followers (shown on the obverse). The man in the middle bears a table on his left shoulder and drags a bundle of sticks from his right hand. He is perhaps the same man on our piece, but here the bundle is carried on the shoulder.

This man is depicted with a shaved head adorned with a wreath. As always with Greek vases, the Egyptian are shown with their hair, and occasionally their beards, closely cropped and shaved (and sometimes rendered by simple dots of diluted black pigment[50]). The custom is reflected in classical literature by a statement from Herodotus, who indicates that Greek priests wear their hair long whereas in Egypt they shave it off[51]. We may also see this characteristic in the Egyptian Arts; the bronze figure of Khonsirdais, dating from the reign of Psammetichus I (664-610 B.C.), is a closely shaved priest[52].

Returning to Heracles and Buisiris, M. Vickers has stated that this is the only example of the story found, so far, at a North African site[53]. The same is true for the Attic ware. There is a fragment (from the shoulder of a late sixth century amphora in Oxford - of the Fikellura type from Naucratis) that bears a human head and this is identified as the head of Busiris, wearing a serpent helmet[54]. Our fragment is dated to about 470 B.C.[55].

13. *Pelike* (Cyrene Museum) (Plate 16, 2-3)

Convex mouth[56], segmented handles in section and spreading foot with torus edge; the underneath of the foot reserved. Relief lines are used extensively on both sides for the garment edges, faces and the stick. A dilution is used as well for the chiton sleeves, basket, and parts of the cockerel.

(A) A man is standing to the right in a himation; he holds a bird by the wings as if to offer it to the woman who is standing to the left. The woman wears a sakkos and chiton, with a himation over everything. She carries a box in her right hand; between them is a basket of wool.

(B) A youth stands to the right with a thick, knotted stick in his right hand; his chest and shoulders are well wrapped with a himation. He chats to a woman dressed in a chiton and himation. She receives (or offers) perfume from a *Plemochoe* (πλημοχόη) - a vase frequently drawn on fifth century vessels. It was mostly used by women, in conjunction with the alabastron, at their toilet, in religious and funeral ceremonies[57].

The vase is attributed by Beazley to the Perseus Painter[58], one of the earlier mannerists named after a hydria in Berlin[59]. There is another pelike by the same painter in Berlin. This is identical to the Cyrene example and shows a herm, a bird and an altar[60]. Berkeley has a further pelike by the same painter: it is closer to our example in its composition and subject matter (preparation for a bride's toilette)[61]. Our vase is the only pelike by the Artist to be found overseas in the Mediterranean area. Date 470 B.C.

14. *Column-Krater Fragment* (Cyrene Museum) (Plate 17, 1-2)

The fragment is from the rim and neck of a column-krater. Lustrous black-glaze.

On the upper surface an animal frieze (not incised and in silhouette) of goats to the right. The exterior has ivy leaves above and below a line.

Column-kraters with rims decorated in this manner usually have palmettes and scrolls over the handles. It is difficult to determine whether this fragment was part of a black- or red-figure krater, as features such as animal friezes in silhouette were often used in both techniques[62].

At the turn of the fifth century, and in the two subsequent decades, a number of painters appear to have turned out red-figure column-kraters, several of which show similarities to

48 Vickers and Gill, *Libyan Studies* 17, (1986), 104, no.60.

49 Brommer, *vasen listen* 35. Beazley, *The Pan Painter*, 3 pelike. Athens 9683, *ARV* 554, 82.

50 For a comment on such customs in the Greek arts see D. Williams, in Brijder (ed.), *Ancient Greek and related pottery,* 275 ff.

51 Hdt. II, 36.

52 London, *Egyptian Antiquities,* 142166. T. James, *Ancient Egypt* 27.

53 See note 48.

54 Oxford, G.121-5. Price, *JHS* 44, 1924, 185, fig.5. *CVA* ii, II D pl.6 (397) 8. Cook, *BSA* 34, 1933/4 19, no.7, pl.10d.

55 Vickers and Gill, *op. cit.* 106.

56 Richter and Milne, *Shapes and Names,* 5. Sparkes and Talcott, *Ath. Agora,* XII, 49-50.

57 Richter and Milne, *op. cit.* 21 f., figs. 146-148.

58 *ARV* 581/3.

59 Berlin 2377. *ARV* 582/16.

60 Berlin, Staatliche Museum 2172. *ARV* 5814 and Boardman, *ARFH* fig. 330.

61 Berkley 8.4582. *CVA,* Berkley I, pl.XLIII,I.

62 Such elements of decoration can be found on a number of column-kraters painted in the black-figured technique. Cf. R. Lullies, *Griechische Kunstwerke,* 58-61 fig. 25. J.N. Coldstream, *BSA* LXVIII (1973), 57, pl. 22-23. *CVA,* Boston 2, pl.108 (11). Cf. also Peters, *Studien zu den Panath,* pl.6. ARV^2 11, (5, 6).

black-figure Leagros group vessels[63]. There are obvious connections between these and the red-figure column-krater works of Myson, his followers, and the so-called mannerists. Hence the difficulty in determining the technique applied on the krater from which our fragment comes. But since the figure painting in our example appears rather degenerate, it is likely that our piece was part of a red-figured krater. The main scenes on both sides are usually framed with tongue borders above and ivy borders at the sides.

Two column-kraters may serve for comparisons. The first is in the Gallatin Collection[64], and the second in the Lecce provincial museum[65]; the latter is attributed to the Leningrad painter (470-460 B.C.).

15. *Column-krater*[66] (London BM 1914.5-20.1) (Plate 17, 3-4)

There are the remains of leaves, mostly restored by plaster, on the rim's external surface. The neck of side B is undecorated and was painted black. Side A is decorated with inverted lotus buds and dots. Each scene is framed with a tongue pattern above and ivy-wreaths on either side. Below the scene there is a reserved thin band. There are ray patterns around the body base.

(A) Two groups each consisting of a youth and woman conversing. The youths wear mantles and hold sticks in the right hand. The women wear chiton mantles and fillets round their heads; the left figure is well wrapped whereas the one on the right is uncovered.

(B) A woman stands facing the right. She wears a chiton and mantle, and holds a thyrsus. She is facing a man who stands to the left, wrapped in a himation, supporting himself with a stick. What remains of a third man, behind the woman, appears to be standing to the right; he is also wrapped in a himation and holds a staff.

This vase, though it appears to have been hastily done, has typical loop handles and the subsidiary decoration of an early classical period column-krater.

The vase's shape, and treatment of the subsidiary decoration, point to the mannerist workshop. The rim and handle-plates of mannerist column-kraters are usually quite flat. The lotus decoration - particularly that on the neck, a trade mark of the mannerist workshop - is characterized by bean-shaped lower tendrils that do not cross each other. The features of the subsidiary decoration are so consistent that it is probable that one potter, or a set of potters, were producing vases which various painters then decorated. It is also possible that one painter might have been doing the subsidiary decoration for others, or for himself and others[67].

Beazley attributes our vase to the Orchard painter[68] (460 B.C.). The style of the mantled figures, with their sticks, is typical of this artist and is usually a helpful clue in identifying his work.

Interior scenes of young men and women appear to be popular with artists. This is to be found on the named piece of the artist, a column-krater in New York[69]. The composition of the scene on side B on this vase is repeated on side A of our krater, where four figures are divided in to two groups, each consisting of one man and one woman facing each other. The men on both vases hold knotted sticks wrapped in a similar way; their poses are identical.

16. *Pelike, fragment* (Cyrene Museum) (Plate 18,1)

This is a large fragment of a pelike, with part of a scene that probably tells the story of Kephalos and Eos. A youth (Kephalos) is striding rapidly to the right. His head is turned and he is apparently pursued by another figure (Eos), the dawn goddess, who is being attacked by the youth's hound. Kephalos wears his regular hunting apparel - a short, belted chiton with folds, a black bordered chlamys (fastened with a large brooch on the chest) and a sun hat, or petasus, hanging around his head by a string. He holds a lagobolon in his left hand. Only the feet of Eos and part of her chiton remain.

The amorous Eos was given to carrying off beautiful young men. Some say this was the result of her jealousy for Aphrodite, as Eos had been the mistress of Ares. Stories about her always involve the rape of a succession of young boys, usually flying off with them in her arms prior to assaulting them. One of her lovers was the hunter Kephalos, married to Procris. Eos allowed him to return to his wife after she became, by him, the mother of Phaethon[70].

Vase scenes showing Eos pursuing a young hunter start in the early classical period. A number of these have inscriptions naming the hunter as Kephalos[71]. On our pelike, Kephalos appears to be fleeing the goddess, and if the vase were intact

63 *ARV* 235 (below).

64 *CVA*, USA I, pl.9 (5,7,8).

65 Bernardini, *I vasi attici del Museo Provinciale di Lecce*, figs. pp. 84, 85.

66 On the column-krater and its name, A. Rumpf, *Chalkidische Vasen* (Berlin and Leipzig (1927), 43, 123. Beazley, *AJA* (1927) 351. *AJA* 45 (1941) 597. Amy 20, *Hesperia* 27 (1958), 198 n. 79. Richter and Milne, *Shapes and Names*, 6.

67 There are column-kraters of Mannerist shape and subsidiary decoration that are not pained by the Mannerists, i.e. one in Bologna by the Alkimachos Painter, Bologna p. 236. Berard, *Anodoi*, pl.17m, fig.59. *ARV*² 532, 44, Addenda 132.

68 Beazley, *ARV* 523-11.

69 New York 07.286.47. Richter and Hall, *Red-figure vases*, 117 f., pls. 90, 91, 170.

70 This is a common scene on Archaic and Classic Attic vases. For Eos in general cf. Rosche, *ML*, 1.1 1252 ff. Vermeule, *Aspects of Death*, 162-165. Eos is reported to have carried off four youths in her time, Tithonos (Apollod. III, XII, 4, *Odyssey* V), Kleitos (*Odyssey* XV, 250), Orion (*Odyssey* 5, 121-4), and, most relevant to the subject on our vessel, the lover Kephalos. Cf. Apollod. III, XIV, 3. 0vid.*Met.* 711f. Caskey and Beazley, *Boston* II (1954) 37 and III (1963) 57. Also Kaempf-Dimitriadou, *Die Liebe der Götter*, 16-21.

71 *ARV*² 603, 43.

we might perhaps see the hunter wearing the usual startled expression.

In his attributed 121 works, the Artist appears to favour larger vessels (including 41 kraters). He nevertheless did paint small vases, of which our pelike is a good example. These depict the familiar thems of gods and human activities[72].

The painting on our pelike is typical of both the artist's style and composition. A favourite detail of his was Kephalos' hound, seen trying to protect his master from the goddess. This is not the first time hounds were represented on vases. The animal appears frequently on the vessels of the Pan Painter[73]. More relevant to our vase, however, is the Konigsberg pelike by the Niobid painter[74]. The subject is identical, showing Kephalos, holding a rabbit and his lagobolon, about to be caught by Eos.

It is worth noting that the presence of a pelike by the Niobid painter in the Cyrenaica region is indeed a significant find, as we know that the number of the artist's painted pelikai is very low (about 8) compared to the other shapes he favoured[75].

17. *Hydria Type II [Kalpis]* Louvre MN712 - H. 33.5 cms. (Plate 18, 2-3)

Neck, body and shoulder forming a continuous curve with a gradual narrowing of the body; overhanging rim and a base in two stages, the lower a flat and narrow disc, the upper curving outwards. The inside of the mouth is painted black. The glaze, unevenly laid, appears also to be unevenly fired. The lip's upper surface, and a narrow band at the bottom of the base, are both reserved.

The exterior rim has a band of egg pattern; the upper border of the figure zone, and below, have groups of meanders alternating with cross-square ribbed side-frames; the figure covers the whole side from shoulder to the meander's lower band.

Two men and a woman.

Two bearded men stand one to the right, the other to the left. They are represented in a similar pose, both wrapped in a himation and leaning forward, supported by knotted staffs. The one on the left is wrapped completely in his himation, both arms inside. The right figure holds his staff, at the top and middle, with both hands. In the centre a woman, dressed in a long Ionic chiton, himation, and with a fillet on her head, extends her right arms, holding honeysuckle between her fingers; she appears to be offering the flower to the man on the right.

This is a street scene probably representing a hetaera and two customers. She appears to be persuading a clearly reluctant man, offering him a flower and, more than likely, herself as well. Such scenes seemed to have been in vogue among artists working during the middle of the fifth century. Two cups in Oxford carry a very similar scene. The first has external painting by the Curtius painter and internal work by the London Painter E777[76]. Both sides represent scenes of men and women in conversation. The second cup is the work of the Euaichme Painter 470 B.C.[77]. The inside shows a bearded man in a similar pose to that of the man on our example. He leans on a knotted stick, offering a cockerel to a boy. Men and women are represented on the cup's exterior surface. On side A, a woman stands between two bearded men. Both are partially draped and lean on knotted sticks as they talk to the woman, who is probably a hetaera. On a stamnos by the Chicago painter (450 B.C. or a little later) a woman similarly dressed holds a honeysuckle between her fingers. She is gazing, appearing to admire the flower rather than offer it for her body[78]. The artist of these vases must have depicted real scenes from the streets of classical Athens[79].

Beazley has already attributed this hydria to the Syracuse painter[80]. Nine hydriae by the artist were known to Beazley[81], and we may now add another from the Kranert Art Museum (University of Illinois), which depicts the story of Heracles in the garden of the Hesperides[82]. His hydriae were mostly of the normal workshop type, distinguished by size, shape of lip and foot, subsidiary decoration, and the placing of the subject high on the body. Such features are represented on our hydria, and another one in Oxford[83].

The painting style of our hydria is typical of the Syracuse painter, having few, but large figures, and less interest in the human form. Close in style is the artist's pelike at Galaxidi (Locris). On Side A of the vase there is a bearded man and a youth conferring. The pose of that man, his hairstyle, beard and folds of himation, resemble those of the old men on our vase[84]. Our vase is reasonably dated 460-450 B.C.

---

72 *HGVP,* 345. *ARV* 589-608.

73 Beazley, *The Pan Painter,* pls.24 (1,3) 27 (2), 31.

74 Once in Koenigsberg, F 162 (or 66). *ARV* 603, 44. Webster *op. cit.* 12 pl.11, b, *op. cit.* Cf. the neck-amphora from Vulci by the Niobid Painter. The scene on it also illustrates the story of Eos and Kephalos. *CVA,* Leiden 3 pl.130, 1-4, 132, 4-7, figs. 16-17.

75 The only evidence of large vases by the artist reaching Libya is a fragment of a bell-krater from Benghazi, showing the right hind leg of a horse (*ARV* 603, 33).

76 Oxford 1925, 74. *CVA,* i 7 pls. 3 (1), 10 (1-2). *ARV* 934 63, 940, 16.

77 Oxford 517. *CVA,* i, 7 pls. 3 (1), 8 (1-2). *ARV* 785, 8. Boardman, *ARFH,* 195 fig. 373.

78 St. Louis, Missouri, 2015, 1951. Philippaki, *The Attic Stamnos,* 112, pl.43. B.Grossman in Moon, *Greek vase painting,* 202, no.113. *ARV* 629, 9, Addenda 132.

79 Boardman and Eugenio La Rocca, 48 f.

80 *ARV* 520, 38.

81 Ibid 520, 35-42. *Paralip.* 383, 35.

82 Kranert Art Museum, University of Illinois, gift of E. Moor (70-8-4). The vase was attributed by Cahn to the Syracase Painter in *Antike Kunst* 5 (1972), advertising page vi, Lekythos. Ann Perkins, in Moon, *Greek vase* painting, 177, entry 100. The attribution is confirmed by Robertson, *History of Greek Art,* 375 (top), and n.35, p.685.

83 Oxford 531. *JRS* 25, 68. *CVA,* 1 pl.32, 9. *ARV* 520, 36.

84 L. Ghali – Kahil. *BCH,* 74 (1950), 52f., pl.5. *ARV* 520, 34.

18. *Pelike* Tolmeita Museum, from Asleaia (near El-Merj) (Plate 19,1-2)

Mouth convex, handles segmented in section, disc foot, lipped at top, intact. Entire vase black except for the pictures. The scene in A and B is framed by bands of dotted-egg with relief line borders above picture, thick reserved band with black pattern at the side (not applied on side B). The scenes are framed with bands of egg patterns above, reserved lines below and thick reserved band with black dot pattern at the sides.

Michael Vickers, who has published the content of the Aslaia Grave speaks of orange added to the vase. I do not know what this means. This is perhaps the diluted colour, which often fires orange[85], used for the muscles of the Satyr's stomach and some of the details of the woman's dress on side B.

(A) Satyr chasing a maenad fleeing to the right looking back and making some kind of gesture.

(B) A woman addressing a youth to the left leaning on a staff. Both figures wrapped in a himation.

Drawing careless and sketchy.

This is a mid-fifth century pelike. The decoration, however, appears to be post rather than pre 450 B.C.

The pelike, according to Vickers, is attributed by Brian Shefton to the Munich Painter 2333[86]. Vickers further pointed out that the plump hands of the figures, with their stumpy fingers, and the rough-hewn faces of the women, are among his characteristics[87].

19. *Hydria Type II (Kalpis)* Louvre MN 710 - H. 29.5 cm. (Plate 19, 3-4)

Overhanging rim, foot in two stages, lower section flat with narrow disc, the upper section curves outward. Black all over except for a reserved band below the figure scene. No frame for the scene.

Subject: Two women fleeing from a youth.

The youth, presented in the middle to the right, is dressed in hunting gear with a black-bordered cloak fastened over his right shoulder. He wears a petasos and holds two spears in his right hand. He is striding to the right, trying to reach a fleeing woman. The women wear transparent chitons with over garments. The chitons are embroidered with crosses, and the necks and edges of the sleeves with a dot pattern. The hems have dark crosses. The fleeing woman escapes to the right while looking back at the youth, raising her right hand in a startled gesture. To the left, another woman is dressed in a chiton under a himation. This woman is completely wrapped. She wears a sakkos and is also running away to the left, but looks back.

The theme showing a youth attacking a woman with a weapon – usually a sword, but occasionally a spear - is commonly interpreted as Theseus and his mother Aithra, or stepmother Medea[88]. Most of the scene follows the same iconographical pattern. The youth advances on the woman with his sword in his right hand. The woman flees to the right of the spectator, and turns towards the youth making a gesture of supplication. The youth usually wears chiton and cloak, or cloak alone. He also has a petasos over the head, or hanging at the back of the neck. Such themes, almost certainly, represent a serious attack with murderous intent; the youth drawing his sword from a scabbard and advancing fiercely towards the woman.

Sourvinou-Inwood, in her interpretation of the scenes, made an exhaustive list showing the distribution of the imagery and its variants[89]. The list included two hydriae - one in Taranto by the Niobid Painter, and the other in the Louvre by Geneva Painter[90].

The scene on both hydriae, as on our vase, shows a youth with spear pursuing a woman. This is certainly not a hostile scene. It is, rather, an erotic one, with a youth chasing a woman, who, significantly, is wearing a transparent garment. The youth draws the two spears towards himself with his right hand, while trying to reach the fleeing nymph with the left, but he has not succeeded. In a similar scene on a hydria in Mississipi[91], the youth succeeds in reaching the woman: he touches her shoulder with his hand.

The youth is identified as Theseus. His name has been found inscribed on three vases: a bell-krater by the Kemaris Painter in the Louvre, a hydria from Sorrento by a follower of the Polygnotan Group in Worcester, Massachusetts, and a lekanis fragment in Leningrad[92].

Our hydria is attributed by Beazley to the Brussels Group A3069, whose artist was probably a follower of Polygnotos[93]. Indeed Polygnotos is known to have painted similar types of hydria with a very similar subject. We may refer to the hydria in the Robinson Collection, where an identical subject to ours is represented[94]. The two fleeing women here wear peploi, but with similar poses and gestures. This is the nearest example

85 Vickers, *Lib.Antiqua* 8 (1971) 75.

86 Brian Shefton has communicated to me that he does not recall expressing an opinion on this vase.

87 Vickers, *op. cit.* 75. *ARV* 1161-70.

88 The subject is studied by Sourvinou, in Wood, *Theseus as a son and stepson, passim.* Suppl. no.40 to *BICS*.

89 Sourvinou, in Wood, *op. cit.* 72, n.157.

90 i. Taranto, *ARV* 606, 74. Sourvinou, in Wood, *op. cit.* 72, n.157 (15).
ii. Louvre 427, *ARV* 615, 2. Sourvinou, in Wood, *op. cit.* 71, n.157 (16).

91 Mississippi, *CVA,* Robinson ii, 32 pl. 44. *ARV* 1032, 64.

92 i. Bell-krater, Louvre G.423. *CVA,* d pl.23, 1 and 3. *ARV* 1064, 6. *JHS* 47 (1927) 147.
ii. Hydria in Worcester, Massachusetts. Beazley and Caskey, ii 81.
iii. Lekanis fragment. *CR*, 51m 1877 pl.5,6. Beazley and Caskey, ii 81.

93 Louvre MN 710. *CVA*, 9, pl.15, 2. *ARV*^{2}, 1033, 2.

94 Beazley, *V. Pol.* 53, no.3, p.54. *CVA,* The Robinson Collection ii and 32 pl. 44.

we can find to our vase. We may compare the woman on the right of our hy dria to the one on the left of the Polygnotan example.

The subject is also found on an Oxford volute-krater, also attributed to the Polygnotos Group[95] (about 440 B.C.). We may especially compare the pose of the woman on the left of our hydria to that on the right of the Oxford vase. Both women are similarly dressed, with arms wrapped inside their himations. We may also use a hydria in Brussels by Polygontos[96] for comparison, since the figures on that vase, especially the woman on the left, recalls the same idea.

The artist of our hydria was simply repeating a subject very popular at the time of Polygnotos and before. Third quarter of the fifth century.

20. *Hydria (Kalpis)* Louvre N 3478 (MN 708) (Plate 20, 1-2)

H. 0.34

Surface of the vase slightly worn. The inside of the neck is glazed. The overhanging rim is decorated with a band of egg pattern, as is the band on the neck above the picture, which is placed between reserved lines. Below the picture a band of meander in three groups alternating with squares. The side handles are twisted slightly upwards, and both are reserved on the inside.

Subject: Seated woman (bride?) with attendants.

In the centre, a woman seated to the right, on a klismos. She wears a chiton, mantle, sakkos, and ear-ring. She holds a diadem in both hands, ready to be placed on her head. Above her is a wall-mirror. On the left, a woman stands in three-quarter view looking to the right. She wears a chiton and mantle, and has her hair tied up with sphendone. With her right hand she adjusts her mantle.

This vase belongs to the Polygnotos Group, to which the Klephon Painter belongs[97]. The subject of women at home, mistresses and maids, or bride with friends, is one of the popular subjects of this period[98].

Beazley attributes our vase to the style of the Klephon Painter[99] 440-430 B.C. Four kalpides in the same tradition are useful for comparison; two from Delos, one in Laon, and the fourth in Leidon[100].

21. *Pelike* Louvre inv. N.3344 (Plate 20, 3-5)

H. 0.29 D. 0.13

This type of pelike has a torus mouth. The handles are segmented in sections with a small disc foot. Above and below the scene, bands meander in groups of three, four and fives, interrupted by chequered squares. A palmette is placed under each handle.

(A) An indoor farewell scene in which a bearded man and a woman are waving to a departing youth, who is probably their son. The man is draped in a himation and leans on a stick. The woman is seated in a three-quarter view on a chair (klismos). In the background is a Doric column. The youth is dressed as a hunter, with cloak and two spears held erect in the left hand. He appears to be walking away while looking and waving to the man and woman. The heads of the three figures are crowned with wreaths.

(B) Two youths, draped in himations, are conferring.

The shape of the pelike is of the mid-classical type, popular during the middle quarter of the fifth century. Our vase, however, probably represents the end of the style. Early on in the first half of the century, the pelike has a triangular look, narrow neck and splayed foot. The low centre of gravity is characteristic of the shape. Such features were borrowed, no doubt, from the black-figured pelike[101]. The mannerists used the shape frequently. Important among their work is the famous pelike by the Pan Painter, the subject of which is Heracles and Busiris[102].

Pelikai of the later years of the fifth century are only slightly different to ours. The best representations of pelikai in this period are the examples in Boston by the Lykaon Painter, and the example in Munich by the Kadmos Painter[103]. Each has a bulging broad body with relatively narrow neck and high disc foot. The elegant Munich Pelike appears to be slightly advanced. The profile of the mouth is nearly perpendicular and the handles do not reach the lip as is the case with our vessel.

The style of the painter is typical of the third quarter of the fifth century, or slightly later, with a few figures always drawn on the same line and without regard for depth and perspective. Two pelikai appear to be close in style and composition to ours. The first one, in San Francisco, is by an artist named by Smith as the Spreckles Painter, a follower of the Niobid Painter[104]. On side A of this pelike, Apollo sits on a klismos

95 Oxford G275 (525). *CVA*, i 18f. pl.21, 1-2. *ARV* 1562 (under the Kalos-name Alkimachos ii no.4). Paralip. 506.

96 Brussels R 226. *CVA* 2, pl.9,1. *ARV* 1032, 65.

97 *ARV* 1149/18. *CVA*, Louvre 9 (14)m, pl.54, 6-7.

98 See E. Gotte, *Frauengenmachbilder in der Vasenmalerei des 5.Jh*. Diss. (Munich 1957) 36ff.

99 *ARV* 1149, 18.

100 Dugas, *Delos* XXI, pl.XXXI 74, 75. *ARV* 1149/21, 22. For the kalpis in Leiden, *CVA* 3 pl.143, 1-6. For the Kalpis in Laon 37. 1065 *ARV*², 1149, 25. The four vases are in the manner of the Klephon Painter.

101 A good example of a black-figure pelike of this type by the Eucharides Painter (490 B.C.) is in Chicago (David and Alfred Smart Gellery). Johnson, *AJA*, 47 (1943) 313f., no.9 and fig.9 on p.394. Bothmer, *JHS* 71 (1951) 42, no.7, 45, 46. *ABV*, 396, 23. Louis Berge, in Moon *Greek vase painting*, 149 f., entry 29.

102 Athens National Museum 9683, *ARV* 554, 82. Boardman, *ARFH*, fig. 336.

103 Boston 34.79, *ARV* 1045,2, Paralip, 444. Munich 3260, *CVA*, pl.81 (277), 1-2, *ARV* 1186, 30.

104 San Francisco (Palace of the Legion of Honour, 1814), Smith, *CVA LVA* i, 40f., pl. XVIII I, a-b *ARV* 617, 1.

between two women and there is a Doric column is in the background. This is obviously an earlier work with a different style of painting despite the similarity in the composition. Indeed the hairstyle, the treatment of the garment, and the poses of the figures are different. The second pelike, in Athens, is by the Peleus Painter and has a similar composition and not dissimilar style[105]. On side A the subject is the arming of Achilles. Three figures are represented. Achilles is in the center, seated on a klismos, in three-quarter view. His right arm rests on the top of the klismos in a pose similar to that of the woman in our pelike. The woman on the right also stands in a pose similar to that of the youth. The work on the Athens pelike, however, is more carefully executed and the overall scene appears more elaborate. The painter may have also been influenced by the style of the Washington Painter, who was active during the middles years of the second half of the fifth century. Although most of the output of this workshop are loutrophoroi, pelikai constitute the second largest shape produced. The lebes gamikos in New York may be compared to our vessel, as regards style of painting and drawing[106].

22. *Calyx-krater (fragment)* Oxford P513 [E/AR3/2] Euhesperides (Plate 21,1)

This fragment[107] is from a double-registered calyx-krater. Only part of the painting remains. Above is a reserved line. The shank and foot are that of a figure, probably involved in a violent act. Below, the banded head of a figure facing right.

Although calyx-kraters were made in Athens in the Archaic period, those with double registers do not appear until the second quarter of the fifth century; their use continued only for a very short period. The earliest example dates to *c.* 460 B.C., the latest to shortly before the end of the fifth century, with the majority being produced during the forties and thirties.

Jacobsthal, in his 1936 study of this type of krater, listed some forty-one examples; Trendall added another ten in 1951[108]. Oakley, who also discusses the style of decoration in respect of the different painters and workshops that used this shape[109], has recently published a complete list, including newly discovered pieces.

Jacobsthal further observed that in double-register kraters, the artists gave greater attention to the upper register that has the advantage of not being interrupted by handles. It appears from Oakley's examination that most of the attributed examples are connected with two workshops of Attic painters: The Niobid Painter and his followers, and the Phiale Painter and other painters connected with him[110].

The painting on our small fragment is not attributed. On the upper section the position of the figure's shank and foot is indicative of a person involved in a violent act. The pose of the figure must be similar to that of the Satyr facing Prometheus, the bringer of fire, on a double-register calyx krater in Oxford by the Dinos Painter[111], except that the Satyr is facing right. The weight of the Satyr, in the Oxford krater, is on his right foot, the left advances towards Prometheus; he leans backwards to left. On our example, the figure appears to be facing left. The weight of the body is on the left foot, while he advances the right leg towards the left side. We cannot determine the style of painting from such a small fragment, but like the Oxford example, the painting must have been executed during the third quarter of the fifth century.

23. *Cup with offset lip; a fragment* (E11/12, Tr.I, St.2) Cyrene (Plate 21,2)

Relief lines used for the horsemen, arm, hand, spear, folds of chlamys, and horse. A youthful horseman in chlamys riding towards the right. His spear is in his right hand, held at rest.

There is a series of stemless cups in which incised or stamped patterns are found, sometimes combined on the same pot with red-figure paintings. A.D. Ure [112] discussed a group of these. Each stands on a thick spreading ring foot, the bowl is broad and shallow with an average diameter of roughly 20 cms. The rim reaches a depth of about 3 cms. There are two horizontal handles attached just below the lip, rising to the level of the rim. The series was arranged in groups according to the character of the incised decoration. In one of these groups, a cup (Bowdoin College) was decorated with a star-rosette pattern incised in the medallion. The outside of the cup is decorated in red-figure technique[113]. On one side a horseman, in chlamys and petasus, rides to the left, and as with our fragment, the tail of the horse extends backwards in a straight line indicating the speed of the galloping horse. His spear is in his right hand, poised to throw. The other side has a similar representation but the spear is held at rest in his hand. Cups with a similar representation and painting style come from Etruria, Nola and Camarina[114]. These are catalogued in the tradition of the Sotades Painter, about the third quarter of the fifth century, of which the Hippacontist Painter is a prominent follower. This dating agrees with development of the shape, also found in black-glazed pottery. The Cyrene piece resembles the group and could well be in the same tradition, probably from a stemless Cup[115].

---

105 Athens 12 229, *BCH* 71-72 (1947-8) 389 fig.4 *ARV* 1040, 14.

106 New York 16.73, Richter and Hall, No.144, Pl.147, *ARV* 1126, 6.

107 Mentioned in D. Gill, *Euthesperides* 1968-69, a suppl. to Libya Antiqua. G.D.B. Jones and J.A. Lloyd (eds.). Oakley, in *Ancient Greek & Related Pottery,* 127 No.70 (originally identified by Brian Shefton).

108 Jacobsthal, *M.M.S.* 5 (1934-1936). See Appendix III, 136-140. Trendall, *JHS* 71 (1957) 191 f.

109 Oakley *op. cit.* 119 f.

110 Jacobsthal *op. cit.* 119 f.

111 Oxford 1937 983(T), Dinos Painter, *ARV* 1153, 13 *para.* 457, Addenda 165. Schefold, *Die Göttersage in Der Klassischen*, 88 fig. 112, *para.* Oakley, *op. cit.* 125 No.25 fig.2.

112 Ure *JHS* 55, (1936) 205-215.

113 Ibid, 206 No.10 fig.10.

114 Naples 2525 Ure *op. cit.* 207 fig.7. *ARV* 519, 1 Nola, London C 125. Ure *op. cit.* 209 fig.9, pl.II, 3-4, *ARV* 770 (below). Camarin, Syracuse 25512, *ARV* 770, 3.

115 For the Sotades Painter see Peredoilski *AM* 53 (1928) 9 ff., *ARV* 763 f. for the Hippacontist Painter *ARV* 770, 1-4.

24. *Stemless Cup, a fragment* Manchester M 1308 (N.81 - AN) from Cyrene (Plate 21,3)

Fine dark orange clay, lustrous black glaze. Relief line used for the elbow, couch, cushion and table. Foot in two stages, separated by a groove and carefully moulded. Fine concentric rings of varying width were alternately drawn in black and reserved[116].

The shape of the vase is akin to mid-fifth century cups, having a shallow bowl curving up to a plain rim on the outside, but with an offset on the inside[117].

The painting on what is left of the tondo appears to represent a symposium within a concentric circle in reserve. We see the elbow of a man reclining to the right on a couch with cushions decorated with black stripes. Beneath the couch is a stool and below this there is an exergue in reserve.

The style of the piece is that of the Marlay painter, whose name appears on a calyx-krater. This was formerly in the Marlay collection and is now in Cambridge[118]. Two similar stemless cups, one in New York and the other in Los Angeles, are useful for comparison[119]. The Cyrenaican example was painted around 430 B.C.

25. *Stemless Cup, a fragment* Cyrene (Plate 21,4)

A bearded figure standing to right in a himation, holding a staff in his right hand. Subject and style of painting similar to that on a stemless cup in Naples by the Marlay Painter. The interior shows a woman playing the flute and a youth moves to the right with stick and cloak[120].

26. *Hydria Type II [Kalpis]* Louvre MN 714 (Plate 22, 1-2)

H. 17 cm

Neck, shoulder and body form a continuous curve; mouth in two stages. The horizontal handles curve inwards and are round in cross section; the foot has an ogee profile.

Glazed throughout except for the groove on the lip and the edge of the foot, a dilute for kalpis neck, chiton folds, and the dots on the dragon. Egg and dots decorate lower part of neck and band below the scene around the vase.

Subject: Kadmos and the Dragon.

Kadmos was the legendery founder of the city of Thebes, whose ancient acropolis was called The Cadmeia. He was the son of Agenor, King of Tyre or Sidon. When his sister Europa, was kidnapped by Zeus, Kadmus and his brothers were ordered by Agenor to find her or never return. In Greece he consulted the oracle at Delphi and was told to find a city where a cow was laying down; this led him to the site of Thebes beside a spring, where he killed its dragon guardian with a stone and sowed the dragon's teeth. Kadmos married Harmonia, daughter of Ares and Aphrodite, and had several children, including Semele[121].

On our hydria, Kadmos, armed with large stone held in the right hand and a hydria in the left, is stepping forward in the direction of the supposed fountain of Ares to fetch water. A dragon in the shape of a large serpent stands erect, ready for the attack. A woman sits in three-quarter view, clad in a chiton, gesticulating to Kadmos and perhaps warning him of the danger. He is represented nude, holding his cloak over his left arm. Kadmos has not yet engaged in the fight with the dragon, but he clenches the stone in his extended hand, ready to fling it at the monster.

There are examples showing the fight in full swing. A comic scene on a Beotian skyphos in Berlin, by the Painter of Cabir (440-420 B.C.)[122], shows Kadmos helplessly retreating and falling on his back while the huge dragon advances towards him. On two southern Italian red-figured bell-kraters - one by Asteas (360-350 B.C.), the other by Python (about 325 B.C.) - Kadmos is shown gaining the upper hand, raising the stone in his right hand while the dragon is coiled and ready to strike[123].

The woman standing between Kadmos and the dragon has been wrongly called Harmonia by Plaoutine, Richter and Trendall[124]. She is, in fact, Thebe[125], her name is inscribed on a hydria by the Kadmos Painter in Berlin, and on the Naples Bell-krater[126]. She is represented here in her capacity as the local deity[127].

The fountain is not depicted on our hydria, but the artist has suggested its presence by the vessel Kadmos is holding.

---

116 Sparkes and Talcott, T*he Agora* XII, 102 No.481 and p.269 pl.22 fig.5.

117 A.D. Ure's list of RF stemless cups, *JHS* 55 (1936) 2-6.

118 *CVA*, Cambridge pl.37, 2; *ARV* 1276,3.

119 *CVA*, Gallattin Collection N.Y., pl.24. Los Angeles, *CVA*, 39, 1-6.

120 Vatican. Once Naples, Astarita, see Bothmer, *Am.* p.180. Beazley *ARV* 1281, 74.

121 Kadmos was known to all Greek writers and his stories were often referred to. The fullest narrative is that of Apollodorus [3.4.1-2, 3.5.2, 3.5.4]. Kadmus appears prominently in Euripides *Bacchae*, the story of Pantheus, is frequently alluded to in his *Phoenician Women*. Details are added by Herodotus [2.49, 4.147], Diodorus Siculus [5.58.2], and Pausanias [3.24.3, 9.5. 1-3, 9.12 1-3]. See also Beckel, *Götterbeistand*, 74-76. Vian, *Les Origines De Thebes* Passim, but see especially 35-50.

122 Berlin inv 3284. Neugebauer, *Führer durch das Antiquarium Vasen*, 138. Vian, *Les Origines De Thebes* 37 No.9 pl.IV. Trendall, *Paestum Pottery*, 23 n.14. Brommer, *Vasenlisten* 480, D1.

123 i) Naples 3226 (82.258). Trendall, *Paestum Pottery*, 20, 24, pl.5a. Vian, *op. cit.* 40, no.19, pl.VIII.

ii) Louvre N 3157, Trendall, *Paestum Pottery*, 64, 121 no.152, pl.16c. Vian, *op. cit.* 40, no.20 pl.18.

124 Plaoutin, *CVA*, Louvre 9, p. 42 f. Richter and Hall, 160. Trendall, *Paestum Pottery*, 23.

125 Also identified as Thebe by Enrico Stefani, in *Mem. Linc* 1935, 172, and Vian *op. cit* 48.

126 Berlin 2634, *ARV* 1187, 33. Brommer, *Vasenlisten*, 480 87. Vian *op. cit* 38, no. 11 pl. V (for the bell-krater in Naples).

127 Froning, *Dithyrambos und Vasenmalerei*, 49 f.

The subject is found on a bell-krater in New York, painted by the Cassel Painter[128] (440 B.C.). The composition of the subject is identical to that on our hydria, with Kadmos approaching in a similar pose. The dragon stands erect with its upper part curving forward in a threatening gesture. Thebe sits between the two. The similarity in the composition may suggest a common source, either in wall painting or sculpture, as an inspiration for the artist of both vases.

Two vases, a pelike in London[129] and a hydria in New York[130], have different subject matter but are quite similar in style. They are, probably, contemporary and can be compared stylistically to our hydria. The pose of Thebe, sitting in three-quarter view, and the treatment of her chiton, especially the line of the folds, are similar to that of both Ariadne on the pelike and Amymone on the hydria. The physical details of Kadmos are also repeated on the male figures of the other two vases, as are the hairstyles of both Thebe and Eros.

The New York hydria is attributed to the Meleager painter (400-380 B.C.), but such features are not limited to that artist. We may find them on the Jena painters work too, and his work on the pelike in Exeter (380 B.C.)[131] is characteristic.

Our hydria was probably painted in the later years of the fifth or early fourth centuries.

27. *Pelike* Louvre MN. 735 (Plate 22,3)

H. 0.32 D. 0.165

Torus mouth, handles segmented in section and with high disc foot. On the neck a band of laurel or olive leaves. Below the figure scenes a reserved band of hooks or wave pattern placed between two thin reserved lines.

This pelike with a triangular style and subsidiary leaf decoration on neck and a band of wave pattern below the scenes, recall the early phase of Italian vases in the second half of the fifth century[132]. Early Italian painting of this period was found to be closely modelled on contemporary Attic work, especially that of the school of Polygnotus and his followers[133].

The artist must have had in mind a similar subject to that of the Al Mina Pelike - dated by Beazley to the later years of the fifth century - with its two figures. A woman and an athlete are standing together, leaning on a staff[134]. Our pelike is certainly not Apulian but rather an Attic work of the second half of the fifth century. Beazley classifies this vessel with the Al Mina example, and considers them to be the work of one artist. Indeed the two Pelikai are identical with similar profile and almost the same height (the Al Mina Pelike is 34 cm high). They have similar torus lips and bulkier, high disc feet. However, the subsidiary decorations on the Al Mina Pelike are somewhat different. Here on the neck and below the figure scenes the decorated band consists of meanders and tongue patterns. On side A the pattern below the fight scene, like that on our pelike, is a reserved wave pattern between two reserved thin lines. The composition of the scenes, on both sides, is also similar, with two figures standing beside an altar. Moreover, the pose of the nude athlete, standing to the right on side B of our pelike, is identical to the athlete's on the Al Mina Pelike.

The style of painting on both vases is nearer to that of the Prouomos Painter. His best work can be seen on the Volute-krater in Naples. There are similarities in the poses of the male figures and the details of their physiques[135].

28. *Skyphos (fragments a-f)* (Cyrene) (Plate 23,1)

The shape was huge in size[136].

Fragment of part of the body and lip. The lip is decorated with laurel between two reserved lines.

The scene on fragment *a* shows a woman, Aphrodite or a bride, represented in a skillfully drawn chiton, painted with great elaboration and with billowing folds. She is busy adjusting the diadem on her head. Other fragments (*b-f*) possibly from the same pot, show palmettes, lotus and laurel decorations. These elements contribute to the beauty of the scene. In fragment *e* a woman's arms hold a musical Lyre.

This is the style of the Meidian School[137] and should be by the master's hand. The drawing of the figures, with these elaborate garments and the gesticulating hand, are typical of his style. There is a fragment of a skyphos in Oxford[138], of a later date (early fourth century B.C.), with laurel decoration on the lip. Nearest to the Cyrene piece in style, however, is the famous hydria in Florence, which illustrates the scene of Phoane in a bower, with Dimonassa surrounded by nymphs and gods[139]. Date about 410 B.C.

29. *Loutrophoros* Louvre MN 558 (Plate 23, 2-3)

Exceptionally well preserved.

This is the hydria type with two horizontal, and one vertical, handles. It has a slim body and tall spreading neck, with flat

128 New York 22.139.11. Richter and Hall, pl.131, pl.171, 132. *ARV* 1083, 5.

129 See entry (No.44) (London E435 435).

130 New York 56.171.50 (ex Hearst). *AJA* 1962, pl.825. Richter and Hall, pl.167, 168. *ARV* 1412, 46.

131 See Entry No.42.

132 See Entry No. 21 for a discussion of the shape.

133 The principal work on Apulia red-figured vases is in Trendall and Cambitoglou, *The Red-Figured Vases of Apulia*, 3 ff.

134 Antioch 6711. *ARV* 1342, 1. *JHS* 59, (1939), 23 No.57.

135 Naples, 3240. *HGVP*, Pls.218, 219. *ARV* 1336, 1.

136 For very large versions of normally small vessels, cf. the red-figured mug by the Meleager Painter, in Lazaridis, *Neapolis* and Romiopolou, *A. Delt.*

137 *ARV* 1312-1332. Hahland, *Vasen um Meidias*, passim. *HGVP*, 375-376.

138 *CVA*, Oxford, I pl.XLIX, 16.

139 Florence, Museo Archeologico, inv. 81947. *HGVP*, pl.213-217.

and wide mouth. The foot is echinus-shaped with a reserved channel. Top of rim unglazed; vertical handle glazed from outside, reserved from inside. Horizontal handle glazed entirely. Wide fillet decorated with line of palmette patterns between neck and shoulder. On shoulder enclosed tongues. A thick reserved band separates the palmettes and the tongues. Band of egg and dot pattern circles the body above and below the scene. Rays and tongue pattern decorates the lower part of the body.

The technique of both relief lines and outlining was used for figures. Barbotine for necklaces and bracelets of the central women, bride and attendants, earring of right attendant, and rays of her diadem. Bosses on the bride's hair, fillet and face of Eros. White is used extensively (black for the drapery borders).

In the loutrophoros[140] (from λουτρόν [bath] and φέρω [bring]), maidens brought water, in which the bride was bathed (in Athens from the Kallirhoe fountain). The water was also placed on tombs of unmarried persons – for marriages that might occur later in the Underworld.

The Cyrenaica loutrophoros is the only known example from North Africa. The scheme of decoration is the one usually found on loutrophoroi. On the neck, each side features a woman draped in chiton and himation. On the body an Epaulia scene[141] continues around the vase. The main scene is composed of a seated bride on a klismos to left, in a three-quarter view, while a little Eros is flying towards her; as if he has just finished placing the diadem over her head. She is wearing an elaborate belted chiton, the end of which she raises with her right shoulder; her left arm rests on the klismos. Her knees are wrapped with a himation that also covers the rear of the klismo. Two maidens attend her. The one in front is walking away but looking back, carrying ribbed bowl, or lekanis, decorated with vertical lines and covered with a knobbed lid. The bowl has no handle, but the maiden holds it by the stem; a scarf drapes from it. Below the scarf, there is a cushioned stool on the floor. The maiden is dressed in chiton under a himation. The other maiden, in a peplos, stands behind the bride, approaching to left carrying a chest, no doubt filled with wedding finery. A scarf is suspended from it. There is another cushioned stool below on the floor. Behind this maiden, Nike stands in a peplos, trying to place more gifts on the chest before it is presented to the bride. Below the vertical handle a woman in a chiton and himation also approaches, more than likely the bride's mother. The three women in the centre wear diadems, necklaces, earrings and bracelets. All the himatia and peploi have broad black borders.

This vase is distinguished by its fine overall design, the rich drawing of garments, and the grace of the figures adorned with diadems, necklaces, earrings and bracelets.

Beazley places this loutrophoros in the Meidian school[142], and used its Louvre inventory number as a name to distinguish it from the rest of the workshop[143]. There is a lebes gamikos in California[144] very close to our vase in style. The artist of both vases must have been greatly influenced by the work of the master of the School in its latest period, around 420 B.C. or a little later.

30. *Pelike, a fragment*[145] (Cyrene) (Plate 24,1)

A small body fragment, probably of a pelike, and of the section near the vertical handle. Part of the scroll, which usually accompanies the double palmettes, remains. Our pelikae no.40 (pl.29, 1-4) has similar decoration.

A woman is dressed in an oriental costume. She wears a tiara, and a chiton under a long sleeved jacket, richly decorated with various patterns. In her left hand she carries a metal vase (phiale) also decorated, with laurel leaves, while in the right hand she carries an oinochoe. Close to the woman appears to be another figure, whose double spear remains. A third female figure is seated, probably cross-legged, at the bottom of the fragment, her leg and foot are the only parts of her body showing.

We know from mythological sources that the sorceress Medea attempted to poison the hero Theseus upon his arrival in Athens, before he was recognised by his father Aigeus. The representation of such a story was echoed on fifth century vases. The paintings were apparently inspired by Euripides' *Aigeus*[146].

A group of such vases was assembled by Brian Shefton[147]. On these, Medea usually identified by her tiara and oriental costumes, an illusion to Medea's non-Greek origin[148], carries a phiale and oinochoe. Other figures on the vases include Theseus, the bull, and an old man holding a staff. It is therefore possible that what is represented here on the Cyrenaican fragment, though not complete, is a representation of that same story.

This is an iconographic tradition started in the early classical period and continuing through most of the rest of the fifth and fourth centuries. The double spear is, perhaps, held by Theseus. On a bell-krater in Madrid (by the Munich Painter 2335[149] and dating to between 430 and 420 B.C.) Theseus is shown attacking the bull with a stone in his right hand while

[140] For shape see Richter and Milne, 5 ff. fig.41-42. J.V. Noble, *The Techniques,* 27 ff. and figs.166-167. For the literature on Loutrophoroi, cf. Wolters, *AM*, 16 (1891) 372 f. Collignon on Loutrophoroe, Daremberg, *Dictionnaire des Antiquities,* I,318.

[141] This is the festival which took place in the court of the bridegroom's house on the day after the wedding, when relatives and friends of the bride would come and with gifts. On the Epaulia & wedding scenes, see Deubner, *Jdi,* 15 (1900) 144-154. H. Metzger, *Les Representations* 15.

[142] *ARV* 1312-1332. Hahland, *Vasen um Meidias, passim*. Richter, *Survey,* 146 ff.

[143] *ARV* 1320/3 (The Louvre Painter MN558).

[144] *CVA,* Berkeley, I (5) pl.LI, 1a-c.

[145] Stucchi, *Cirene 1957-1966*, 159, fig.174 (The section on pottery was written by Luciana Pandolfi).

[146] Webster, *Tragedies of Euripedes*, 77.

[147] B.B. Shefton, *AJA,* 60 (1956) 159ff.

[148] Trendall and Webster, *Illustration of Greek Dama,* 71 (Aigeus III 3, 1-3).

[149] *ARV* 1163, 45.

holding a double spear in the left. The story on the Cyrenaica fragment could well be a "variant" version of the legend, with Medea taking the place of the nymph as a witness to Theseus' struggle with the bull[150].

The style of painting seems to be very much influenced by the Medean school, but it is likely to be from the closing years of the fifth, early fourth, century.

A Volute-krater, by the Talos painter, found in the necropolis of Ruvo and now in the Jatta Collection[151], has a different subject (the Death of Talos), but otherwise is in a similar painted style. The phiale, or rather the basket carried by Medea, is also like that on our piece. The krater, as with our fragment, has a similarly rich design.

The phiale on our section, as well as the pattern on what is left of the tiara and the shoulder, are all similar elements to that of Medea on the krater. The patterns on the garments, too, are identical to those on the Cyrenaican piece. The Talos Painter was a follower of the Meidias Painter. The painter of our piece is also very probably a follower of the Meidias Painter, working in the late decades of the fifth century.

31. *Oinochoe [Shape III]* Choes. London PM 1868.7-5.131 (Plate 24,2)

Trefoil lip, squat bulging body resting on a ring foot. Surface glazed in full except for the underside of the foot. Relief lines employed.

The reserved figure on the front is a child, or rather a fat boy crawling to the right to reach a cart, or getting on his feet and about to walk for the first time with the aid of the cart. An ivy-wreathed chous is placed in front of the cart. A band of egg and dots under the scene. The only relief lines are on the right arm and left knee of the boy.

This vessel, like much of the pottery from Cyrenaica now in the British museum, was probably found in a grave.

The chous, the standard item in a child's grave, is the jug used primarily in the celebration of the Anthesteria, a three-day Athenian festival, held late in February every year, to honour the wine god, Dionysus, who was thought to have brought the gift of wine[152].

On the second day of the festival, newlyweds, and all citizens, celebrated the choes, or the feast of jugs in which they drank the new wine. Miniature replicas were then given along with toys and other gifts. Carts, frequently represented on choes, appear to be one of the most popular of children's toys. Each cart seems to be simply made with two wheels joined by a cross piece, and with a pole for pulling or pushing. Some of these choes, however, may also have been used for funeral purposes, and were placed in the graves of infants who died too young to take part in the festival (just as nuptial vases were often placed in the graves of unmarried young women). At this time, three year-olds were initiated into this religious ceremony and received their first taste of wine. The iconography of many choes provides evidence of the festival[153].

The popularity of the chous seems to have started during the Peloponnesian War, and the years immediately following, continuing until the early years of the fourth century when the vessels seem to have gone out of fashion. Van Hoorn[154] made an exhaustive and reliable catalogue of the style, but it was J. R. Green who made an extensive study of the shape[155]. The choes were manufactured in two sizes. The larger is a general-purpose jug, it may, but need not, bear scenes related to the celebration of the Anthesteria, where the vessel had a particular role. To judge by the scenes depicted on them, such miniature jugs were made for children (these have a wider range of height, the greater number between 7 and 8 cm). In general these largely come from Attica. Very few come from outside. It was observed that by the late fifth century, the neck and body of the chous exhibited important changes. The easy flow of the neck, which the jug exhibits at the beginning of its history, gradually changed, the body becoming plumper and wider. The diameter of the ring foot became a little narrower than the maximum diameter of the body.

Green divided the chous into two main workshops according to the variations in the mouth and foot, as well as the decoration: these are the "chevron workshop", which takes its name from the chevron pattern on the sides of the figure scene, and of high quality, with thin clay and fine feet. The other, the "crawling body" workshop is of lower quality by comparison. The interest of these vessels lies more in the childhood scenes painted on them; the clay is thicker, the body globular, the foot large.

The Cyrenaica chous, not mentioned by either Van Hoorn or Green, belongs to this workshop which is divided into three classes (Sydney, Copenhagen and London E535)[156]. The shape probably lasted until around 415-410 B.C. at the latest.

32. *Oinochoe [Shape III]* Chous: Manchester M 1300 (Cyrene) (Plate 24,3) Miniature

H. 6.8 D. 5.2

The picture is framed with two reserved lines on the side and a band of egg pattern above and below. The reserved figure

[150] For more discussion on this theme see Shefton, *op. cit.* 162-163.

[151] Ruvo, Jatta, 1501. *ARV* 1338,1. Nicole, *Meid.* pl.6,2. Cook, *Zeus,* i pl.41.

[152] Parke, H.W., *Festivals of the Athenians,* pp.107-120. Hoorn, G., *Choes and Anthesteria,* 15 ff.

[153] On choes and their signifiance see in particular Deubner, *Attische Feste,* 9B-123. The evidence concerning the history and function of the choes and links to the Anthesteria was first marshalled by him. See especially 96-98 and also 238-247. Karouzou, *AJA,* 50 (1946) 245-60.

[154] Hoorn, *Choes and Anthesteria,* no.255-60.

[155] Green, *BSA* 66 (1971) 189. 224 f. Green and Sinclair, *Historia,* 19, (1970), 523. See also Sparkes and Talcott, *Ath.Agor.*, 60-63.

[156] *A)* Sydney Nicholson, *Museum Handbook* (1948), 307 fig.76b. Van Hoorn, *op. cit.* 916, fig.328. B) Copenhagen 10120. Van Hoorn, no.486, fig.538., *CVA* viii, p.1353,2. C) London E535, Van Hoorn, no.639. Green, *BSA,* 66 (1971) pl.33.e.

is a child, or rather a fat boy, crawling to the right to inspect an oinochoe or chous. An amulet hangs around his neck. A bunch of grapes is suspended from above. Relief lines are visible.

Described wrongly by Rowe as an aryballos, this vessel was found in the courtyard of tomb N.81-AB, in the North Necropolis of Cyrene with a black-glazed skyphos, type A, dated to the late fifth or early fourth century B.C.[157].

33. *Oinochoe [Shape III]* Chous[158] Louvre N 3408 (Plate 25, 1-3)

Four centaurs pull a chariot driven by Nike, in which Heracles stands. A wreathed man goes ahead holding two torches.

The scene appears to be a comic one; the figures wear comic costumes and masks.

The caricatured Heracles is very evident. He resembles the New York Heracles in a set of actor-terracottas there, having staring eyes and wide-mouthed comic mask[159]. We can distinguish him by his club and headdress. He wears a long sleeveless chiton and himation. Nike holds the reins, with wings and himation; her snub-nose and black-hair mask, recall the women of a comic female chorus frequently represented on vases[160]. The four centaurs have hairy faces and chests, with well-marked brows and equine ears[161]. The dancing man carries two torches and wears tights, shown by the wrinkles on his legs and the lines around the right wrist and ankle. He is also provided with a scarf. His bearded face is represented with one eyebrow up, one down[162], and resembles the masks on a late-middle comic relief[163]. His pose is very similar to that of Perseus shown on an Attic chous in Athens[164]. Nike, Heracles, and the torch-carrier are presumably actors, and the centaurs may be members of the chorus. There is mention in Plato[165] of a drama with centaurs, and these may have been the centaurs of Nicochares or Apollophanes[166].

157 Rowe, *Cyren. Exped.*, 21, Pl.37. For an Attic black-glazed Skyphos (type a) see Entry No.9 in Chapter 5 (Black-glaze).

158 See Beazlev, *ARV* 1335/34. Metzger, *Representations*, 212/35. Rumf, *AJA*, 55 (1951), 10, fig.5-7.

159 New York, 13.225.27. Trendall and Webster, *Illustrations of Greek Drama* (1971) IV, 9(27). A. Picard-Cambridge, *The dramatic festivals of Athens,* p.211 and fig.91.

160 Comic chorus women on an early 4th c. bell-krater, Heidelberg B 134. Webster, *Greek Theatre Production,* pl.15.

161 Compare the children's comedy masks on a chous in Leningrad. Leningrad oA 1869.47. From Phanagoria, South Russia. The Meidias work-shop, see Picard-Cambridge, *op. cit.* fig.78. Trendall and Webster, *op. cit.* IV,3. For children's comedy, E.J. Jory, *BICS,* 14 (1967) 84ff.

162 For such phenomena see Rumpf, *AJA,* 55 (1951), 10.

163 Athens, Epigraphical Museum 1338, marble relief, 340 B.A. Trendall and Webster, *op. cit.* IV, 8a.

164 A chous from Anavysos, 420 B.C. Athens, Vlastos Collection in Trendall and Webster, *ibid* 117, fig.IV,I.

165 Plato, *Politicus* 303d, cf. 291a.

166 Webster, *Art and Literature in Fourth Century Athens,* 34.

This is not the first representation of centaurs with chariots on Greek arts. They were found on reliefs as well as vases[167]. This appears to be an archaic tradition, though they may not be connected with comedy. On a late sixth century black-figure lebis gamikos, from the Agora, Heracles is shown driving a chariot pulled by centaurs[168]. Here, Nike drives the chariot and the torch-carrier runs ahead.

The scene on the Cyrenaican chous was probably inspired by a satyr play parodied by a comedy writer. Here Heracles is driven not to Olympus[169] but to marriage. The dancer with two torches here is similar to the old man in Euripides' *Helen* (723), who bears the torches and escorts Helen of Troy to her wedding with Paris[170].

Marriage scenes on vases are plentiful. They usually show the wedding procession with bride and groom in a chariot or on foot. In the sixth century, Peleus and Thetis were often represented in a chariot surrounded by gods and led by Hermes. On a black-figure amphora in Naples[171], the bride and groom ride in a chariot, and behind the horses come the gods Apollo, with his kithara, and Artemis, with a young fawn, while the herald Hermes leads the procession. On a pyxis by the Marlay Painter (430 B.C.) in London[172], the groom mounts his chariot beside his bride, while behind follow a youth with a torch, a girl with a basket on her head, and finally a woman carrying a lebes gamikos. Behind the chariot stands a woman with a torch in her hand. A youth, holding a caduceus, leads the procession in place of Hermes.

A wedding procession on a fourth century pyxis in Athens[173] follows the same tradition, but here two Erotes were added as well as the usual characters.

Heracles, Hebe's wedding is rarely represented on vase paintings. On a Pyxis in Philadelphia and another one in a private collection, the bride and groom were portrayed in a procession on foot[174].

It may well be, therefore, that the scene on our choes is supposed to represent a stage in a wedding where Heracles is being driven to Hebe's home. The presence of Nike next to him is only natural since it is an essential element in a wedding scene, especially in the bridal quarter. The replacement of horses by Centaurs may indicate their defeat by Heracles, and symbolise the subordinate role they are

167 Matz, in *Festschrift für Carl Weickert,* 41-58.

168 Agora Pl.2571. E. Vanderpool, *Hesperia,* 7 (1938), 393, no.31.

169 On a pelike by the Kadmos Painter, Heracles is driven to Olympus by Athena while satyrs steal the arms from his pyre. Kadmos Painter, *ARV* 1186; 30. Trendall and Webster *op. cit.* p.117.

170 Illustrated on an Apulian bell-krater, 370-360 B.C. Matera 9579, *PhV*², 48, no.44 pl.3c. Trendall and Webster, *ibid*., fig.IV, 28.

171 *CVA,* Naples i (20) HE Pl.3, 3-4.

172 London, *BM* 1920.12-21. *ARV* 1277, 23. *JHS* 41 (1921) 144 pl.6 1-2 and 4-5.

173 Athens 1630. Bruckner, *AM* 32 (1907) pl.5,1. Schefold, *UKV,* 59.

174 University Museum MS 5462. The two pyxides are discussed in Roberts, *The Attic Pyxis,* 181.

now leading. They are in a subservient position to the now immortal Heracles[175].

Our choes has already been attributed by Beazley to the Nikias Painter (last decade of fifth century), an artist probably influenced by the style of the great painter Parrahsios, one of the celebrated painters in antiquity[176].

34. *Oinochoe [Shape II]* Paris Cab. Med. 471 (Plate 26,1)

On the lower part of the neck a reserved band decorated with egg and dot patterns between two black lines. On the main body of the jug a maid with sakkos, earrings, and chiton, standing in three-quarter view and to left on a short thin reserved line. She carries a wicker basket under which falls a broad sash.

Solid black for the maid's hair and for part of the basket, white for the sash. Relief lines only used for the basket.

This oinochoe was attributed by Beazley to the Ferrara Painter (T.28)[177].

There are many examples of this style of oinochoe by The Ferrara Painter (T.28) from Spina. Closest amongst these is the oinochoe recovered from Tomb 494 in Ferrara. The maid represented on the vase is very similar to that on our piece, with an identical pose but different gesture. The Ferrara maid faces left with both arms extending symmetrically, but while the left hand holds the chest and the sash, the right is extended freely. This oinochoe is also by the Ferrara Painter (T.28)[178].

It is significant to note that among the Painter's 29 oinochoi listed by Beazley, the Cyrenaica vessel is the only one to have been found outside Italy. The rest come from Spina and date late fifth century.

35. *Askos*, London BM F.32 1866.4-15.44 (Plate 26,2)

A disc foot, dome-shaped top, small flaring spout, an arched handle from mouth to the other side of the body. Glazed all over except for the underside. Two animals are represented: a goat and (perhaps) a wolf or hound. Both face across the spout. No relief line was used.

Askoi are known as perfume holders during the fifth and fourth centuries, but the name given them by ancients has not survived. Its conventional name was (possibly) given to it for its resemblance to the wine skin. It is probably meant to represent an animal. They were occasionally found in tombs as purifying offerings and could also be used for pouring wine libations to the dead on the occasion of burials. The basket handle, which comfortably accommodates four fingers of the hand, makes it well suited for carrying a small amount of liquid from home to the tomb.

Like the Cyrenaica askos, most of Athenian askoi are decorated with two pictures and these frequently form an opposing pair (pursuer and pursued)[179]. Usually a rapacious animal - hound, wolf, eagle, lion - pursues a hare, fox, fawn, or ram. The animals are either presented head to tail, or the pair aligned face to face indicating that pursuer has brought quarry to bay. Our askos is of the latter scheme, where the goat and wolf face each other at the spouted area of the vessel.

The style of drawing is close to the two askoi in Castle Ashby[180], dated late fifth century.

35. *Askos with strainer top* London BM F.33 1866.4-15/101 (Plate 27,1)

Ridged, strainer top. Low flat base, slightly projecting at lower part of body. A small, ridged ring-handle set at right angle to the spout (on the circumference opposite spout). A palmette occupies the space between the handle and spout.

The main scene is a hound and lion confronting each other.

This askos is a slightly different version to the previous one, where the over-arching handle was removed and substituted by a ring handle; the centre drops down slightly, and was subsequently provided with a strainer edged with a lip. This development occurred in the late fifth century[181].

A further Spina example resembles the Cyrenaica askos[182], although the subject matter differs (a fox is pursuing a rabbit). Date end of fifth or early fourth century.

37. *Miniature Hydria* [Kalpis] London BM 239 (Plate 27,2)

H. 13.6 cm

Black except for the figure scenes, bands of decoration on edge of foot. Overhanging rim a two stage foot. The design covers the whole side and shoulder. Picture framed on three sides, top, and bottom with a band of egg and dot pattern and spiral designs from the scene on the right.

---

175 See the discussion in Matze, *op. cit.* 41 f. (note 167).

176 Rumpf A., *AJA*, 55 (1951) 10 f.

177 *ARV* 1355, 16.

178 Massei, L., *Gli Askoi*, 103, pl.XXVI (the two oinochoai in the central row, nos.1,2). Alfieri, *Spina*, 105 fig.260. *ARV* 14355, 15. See also *Enciclopedia dell'Arte Antica* III, 626.

179 For the shape with similar subject see Beazley, *AJA* (1921) 325-326. *ARV* 1504 f. For South Italy and Etruria, see Beazley, *EVP*, 272 f. Cf. Waldhauer, *AA* (1929), 235 f. and Rudiger, *Askoi* (unpublished dissertation, University of Freiburg, *Br.* (1960). Cf. *idem*, *RM* 73-74 (1966-67)i f. The composition corresponds to H. Hoffman (Type A) when classifying askoi with such representations. H. Hoffmann, *Sexual and Asexual Pursuit* (1977), II, pl.I.

180 *CVA*, Britain 15, Castle Ashby pl.53, 1-2.

181 *Olynthus* XIII, pls. 73-177. Sparkes and Talcott, *Ath. Agor.* 159f.

182 Massei, L., *Gli Askoi, A figure Rosse*, 101 ff no.67 pl.XXV.2 T.494 (Askos inv.22796). The composition corresponds to Hoffmann (Type B). Hoffmann, *op. cit.* pl.11, fig.5,6.

The subject is the grown figure of Eros, with large wings, moving to the right and holding an object (a strigil?).

38. *Miniature Hydria* [Kalpis] Leiden KVB 52 (Plate 27,3)

H. 13.5 cm, Dia. 9.5 cm

Black, including neck and top of the mouth overhanging rim, foot in two stages. A band of egg and dot pattern frame the picture from top and below. A spiral design provides a natural border to the right of the picture.

A woman dressed in a chiton and long sleeved tunic. Her hair is kept in place by a fillet. She carries a chest and moves to the right.

Both hydrias appear to belong to one group of the same size. They only have a single painted figure and share similar decoration, namely the spiral plant design. The second example has already been examined[183] and compared to the work of the L.M. Painter, an artist who specialised in lekythoi, each with a single female figure[184]. Indeed, the type of chiton, with fine lines, folds and a richly embroidered tunic, was in vogue during the last quarter of the fifth century. A pelike in New York by the Meidias Painter has a woman wearing a richly embroidered tunic over a long chiton, but her tunic, unlike the woman on our hydria, has short sleeves[185]. On a bell-krater, also in New York, a woman wears a long tunic with long sleeves, the embroidered pattern on that tunic is not dissimilar to that on our Pelike[186].

II. THE FOURTH CENTURY

39. *Pelike* Paris Louvre N 3403 (MN 734) (Euhesperides) (Plate 28, 1-2)

H. 26 cm

Large pelike with flaring neck, overhanging rim, handles with central ribs, disc foot in two stages. The underneath is reserved. The outer edge is also reserved. On the overhanging rim there is a continuous band of egg and dot pattern, framed by a relief line. Above the scene, on both sides, is a band of egg and dot pattern, with a relief line above and behind. Encircling the vase below the scene is a band of similar pattern, boarded by relief lines. Below each handle is a double palmette.

(A) In the centre Heracles sits naked, his garment tucked underneath. He is presented front on in the upper half and shortened in the lower, drinking from a kantharos. He sits in the presence of two women, the Hesperides, probably after having arrived from his long journey. He leans on his club while looking towards a man on the right, who leans on a staff. This is probably Atlas. On the left are two women. The one near Heracles is holding an oinochoe, having emptied its contents into the kantharos. The second extends her arm towards the hero, perhaps to receive the empty pot from him.

(B) Three draped youths, the one in the centre offers a strigil to the youth on the right, while leaning on a stick.

Relief lines were used for limbs, club, oinochoe, and necks of figures.

Metzger has interpreted the subject of our pelike as the apotheosis of Heracles[187]. That is the stage when the hero achieved immortality after the Twelve Labours and ascended to Olympus. Metzger groups six vases that carry scenes representing the final stage in the Hero's life. The group includes our pelike. The representation is almost indistinguishable on these vases: Heracles sitting, often with a kantharos in his hand, among his well-wishers, Athena, Nike, Hermes, Iolaos, Satyrs, and Maenads. Hebe, the daughter of Demeter and the hero's new wife, also appears occasionally (she is represented on three of Metzger's group, Nike on four). None of Heracles' company can accurately identified on our pelike.

The subject on these vases may complement one another, representing various stages in the story of the theft of the golden apples of the Hesperides, the last Labour of Heracles. On the New York pelike, Heracles has just arrived at the garden of Hesperides. He now has the task of persuading the Hesperides to give him the apples[187 bis].

This stage of the story has been reconstructed mainly from fifth century B.C. vase painting by the German scholars of the 19th century[188]. This view has been discussed and accepted by Homer Thompson, who states that Heracles does not wrest the apples himself from the dragon, but charms the Hesperides with love and lets them drug the dragon and bring the apples to him[189]. This is certainly the mood and interpretation of the late fifth and fourth centuries artists[190]. Archaic painting presents a different version of the story, where the hero appears to secure the apples himself without the assistance of the Hesperides. This contrasts greatly with earlier representations of the story: lively and often violent action scenes showing the battle of the hero with the snake, or the taking of the apples. On three Attic black lekythoi[191], Heracles is represented either

[183] *CVA*, Leiden iii (5) 39 pl.142, 6-7.

[184] *ARV* 1364 - 1365.

[185] Richter and Hall, 199, entry 159, pl.159.

[186] *Idem*, 195, entry 155, pl.155.

[187] Metzger, *Represent*, 212 f and no.41. p.216 f.

[187 bis] See note 195.

[188] Roscher, *Lexikon*, "Herakles", 2228 (Furtwangler), 2594.

[189] Thompson, *Hesperia*, 18 (1949) 250 f., 254.

[190] Brommer, *Jdi*, 57 (1942) 112, 116-117. Metzger, *Representation*, 205 ff.

[191] i) Attic black figured lekythos, Berlin inv. 3261. Haspel, *ABL* and 51.62.110.198 pl.18,1. Brommer, *Jdi*, 57 (1942), 108 fig 2. Cactus Painter, *ABV*, 472.

ii) Attic black-figured lekythos, Athens 1132 (CC 957). *JHS* 13 (1892/3), 9 ff. pt.3. Haspel, *ABL*, 150, 155, 256. Brommer, *op. cit.* 108 no.4 fig.3. Athena Painter, *ABV*, 522, 50.

iii) Attic black-figured lekythos (private collection, Marburg). Brommer, *op. cit.* 110-111, figs.4-5. The Athens Class 581. *ABV*, 499, 33.

about to snatch the apples from the tree or departing in haste after securing the golden apples. On these vases the tree is shown, while the vicious dragon is about to attack the Hero. The Hesperides are nowhere to be seen.

A silver coin, significantly also from Cyrene, depicts Heracles and one of the Hesperides standing on either side of the tree. The hero is shown about to pluck the golden fruit[192]. Another version of the story is shown on the temple of Zeus at Olympia (457 B.C.). Heracles, according to this version, sends Atlas, who is standing at the outer edges of the Earth, holding the sky on his shoulders, to the garden of the Hesperides in his place; the Hero holds the sky up while Atlas goes for the apples[193].

The last stage in the story is shown on a hydria in Illinois. Heracles is shown holding three apples. He moves rapidly away while one of the Hesperides follows him with open arms, a gesture of protest perhaps[194].

Although the scene on our pelike appears to show the first stage of the story, we are not certain of the identity of the figures in Heracles' company: who is the bearded man and who are the two women? The man could be either Atlas or Oceanus. Atlas is normally represented, especially in sculpture, as supporting the sky on his shoulder, while Oceanus can be given horns, as shown on a pelike in New York[195]. The presence of either of the two may indicate the locality of the scene. The two charming hostesses can be identified as the daughters of Atlas. They are depicted as well-mannered girls, eager to serve and please. One of them offers the Hero a drink from an oinochoe, and the other extends her arm to receive the empty kantharos. The two girls may also be identified as the Hesperides. Beazley recognizes them as such, and to him the bearded man is Atlas[196]. If so, the dragon and the apple tree are not shown here. The picking of the golden fruit is perhaps undertaken by the other absent sisters, and Eros, but since all the known representations of Heracles in the Garden of Hesperides show the apple tree and the dragon, our identification of the figure as Atlas, and his daughters, is the more likely one.

The kantharos that Heracles holds is probably a metal one, as a similar example was made in silver at Trebenischte, and there is a bronze one in the museum of Thebes[197]. Beazley calls the shape the 'Sotadean Type', after a Goluchow vase of this style was found signed by the Attic potter Sotades[198]. Beazley compares its beautiful simplicity to the late Chalcidian eye-cup: very few examples of the shape survive and all date from the fifth century. Important among these are Goluchow vessel and the one in Munich by the Penthesilea Painter (450 B.C.)[199]. The kantharos is also represented on other shapes; it appears, for example, on a stemless cup (beginning of the fourth century) in Tarquinia, and on a calyx-krater in Athens, where a Satyr is shown bringing a kantharos to Heracles[200].

The Pelike is attributed by Beazley to the Pasithea Painter[201]. Resembling our piece in subject and composition is the pelike by the same artist in New York, which is dated to the first quarter of the fourth century[202].

Only three pelikai are known to have been painted by the Pasithea Painter[203]. He is an artist who flourished in the first quarter of the fourth century but appears to have been influenced by earlier artists in the later years of the fifth century. The idea of presenting intimate groups in physical contact, as shown on our vases, is an interesting feature. The two Hesperides in front of Heracles are represented in close proximity, with the one at the back leaning forward, touching the back of the other, with her arms extended forward. The scene is repeated on the Metropolitan Museum pelike by the same hand. The Hesperides and Oceanus, as with the Hesperides figures on our pelike, are intimately placed in front of Pasithea and Heracles[204]. Such intimacies are to be found on the vases of the last quarter of the fifth century. The best example is to be found in the work of the Meidias Painter. In the lower zone of his hydria in London, close to the apple tree on the left, Asterope leans with her left elbow against the back of her sister, Chrysothomis. Only these two are physically close, while the rest are distributed evenly around the vase[205].

40. *Pelike* Louvre MNB 1036 (Plate 29, 1-4)

H. 25.5 cm

Shape as Louvre MN 734.

(A) Dionysos in a chariot drawn by a griffin, panther, and bull.

The wreathed Dionysos leans forward with the reins and thryson held in both hands. He is represented nearly naked (his cloak is tucked underneath him, extending to his back and around his right arms).

(B) Three draped youths, the two on the side hold strigils.

[192] Muller, *Numismatique* i p.11, No.23. Head, *Historia Numorum*, 866. Brommer. *Jdi*, 57 (1942) 121 fig.13.

[193] Robertson, *A History of Greek Art*, 274. Ashmole and Yalouris, *Olympia* pl.188.

[194] Ann Perkins, in Moon, *Greek Vase Painting*, 177 entry 100.

[195] Richter and Hall, 211 f., no. 166, pl. 163.

[196] *ARV* 1472, 2. See also Brommer, in Brijder (ed.), *Ancient Greek and Related Pottery*, 178 and no.3 id *Heracles* 50.

[197] Both are reported by Beazley in *EVP*, 72.

[198] Beazley, *V. Pol.* 27 f., pl.15-6.

[199] Munich 2565. *CVA*, Munich 2 P.25 f., no.3-4, Pl.95.

[200] For the stemless cup, *ML* 36 487 left, p.210, n.1 for the Athens calyx-kraters 14902. *AM*, 62 (1937), pl.25.

[201] *ARV* 1472, 2.

[202] Richter and Hall, pl.162, 188, pl.163, 166. Metzger, *Represent*, pl.27,2. Thompson, *Hesperia* 18 (1949), pl.52,2. *ARV* 1472,1.

[203] *ARV* 1472, 1-3.

[204] Richter and Hall, 211 f.1, no.166, pls.162-163.

[205] London, *BM*, E 224. Arias, Hirmer and Shefton, in *HGVP*, 375, entry 214, 215.

The subject on side A is not easy to interpret. In Greek art, Dionysos is usually seen in company with these three creatures, not as a single group but separately; he appears more frequently with the panther and griffin.

Dionysos and the Panther: On a bell-krater by the Filtrano Painter from Cumae[206] Dionysos is riding a chariot drawn by a panther and pantheress. On a pebble-mosaic floor in Peila, dated to the late fourth century, the god is shown sitting sideways on a panther. On an ivory relief in Milan, the young Dionysos is shown riding a chariot drawn by two panthers[207].

Dionysos and the Griffin: Inside a cup by the painter of Vienna, 202, in Enserune, the god rides a griffin. This scene is repeated on a hydria in Barcelona (second quarter of the fourth century)[208].

Dionysos and the Bull: A rare and important representation of the god on a bull is the unattributed black-figured vase in Wurzburg, which shows him pouring wine from a kantharos[209]. In sculpture, we find the effeminate god in a bull-hide, as represented by a statue in Berlin. The god is draped in hide, while the animal head hangs down his back. Occasionally the god's physical powers, and links with the bull, are symbolized by the two horns occasionally shown on his forehead[210].

The god is represented on a chariot in a similar way to that of Heracles on the Choes from Cyrenaica[211]. Chariots are usually shown drawn by two or four horses[212]. Heracles is drawn by four Satyrs, but Dionysos' chariot is drawn by three incompatible animals, the bull on one side, griffin and panther on the other.

There must be a reason for combining these three animals together. A simple, yet not entirely complete explanation is that, like Heracles with the Satyr, it may indicate the power and mastery of Dionysos over these creatures: they are tamed and now live in harmony. Another explanation might be that the scene could represent a Gigantomachia. If so, then Dionysos is on his way to fight the Giants, creatures of great size and strength. These, according to legend, rebelled against the Olympian gods and attempted to reach Heaven. Eventually they were defeated by Zeus with the help of Heracles. Dionysos like the rest of the gods took an active part in the fight.

There are a number of representations showing the god, and/or his companions, either on their way to fight, or in the middle of the fight[213]. On a fragment from a crater in Athens by the Pan Painter[214], Dionysos is shown striking a fallen Giant with his thyrsos while holding a vine branch in the left hand. Two animals, one of them a panther, take part in the attack. Two stamnoi, one in Orvieto[215], by the Painter of the Yale Lekythos, and the other in Boston[216] by the Blenheim Painter, show similar representations. On side A of both vases, similar to that seen on the Athens krater, Dionysos charges at the falling Giant with the butt of his thrysos in his right hand, while holding a vine branch in the left. On the Boston stamnos he is assisted by two Maenads. One is hurling a huge rock at the enemy, the other beats him with a thrysos. The Maenads are not present on the Orvieto stamnos, instead the god has the help of the Satyr and his favourite animal, the panther.

Side B, of both stamnoi, proves the most relevant to the analysis of the scene on our pelike, where one satyr ride in a chariot drawn by two others. This is probably, as Beazley suggested, a continuation of the scene represented on the other side[217]. The pose of the satyr on the Boston stamnos is similar to that of Dionysos on our pelike. The satyr leans forward, holding a goad in his right hand. The other hand rests on the shoulder of one of the satyrs, who looks around. On the Orvieto stamnos, the two satyrs drawing the chariot stretch their arms and legs in a way similar to that seen in the short-distance runners on the Panatheneni Amphorae. Two other satyrs, a charioteer and follower, are added to the scene. Both are armed with shields and spears and provided with Attic helmets. The charioteer holds the goad and reins with the spear.

A similar Gigantomachia is to be seen on an Archaic Greek gem, formerly in the Bartholdy Collection[218]. The gem shows a satyr in a chariot, but this time the chariot is not drawn by two satyrs, but by two lions. It is suggested that this satyr has probably stolen the chariot from Dionysos, or he might be the god's charioteer in the battle against the Giants[219].

Dionysos on our pelike is, most likely, on his way to the battle after harnessing these wild animals, including the bull, a fact that both Metzger and Vian miss. Metzger has failed to see the subject as a Gigantomachia. This is probably the reason behind its exclusion from Vian's list of Gigantomachia themes.

[206] Paris Market (Mikas, ex Borelli), *ARV* 1453, 12.

[207] Robertson, *A History of Greek Art* 457, fig.153b. Cook, *Zeus* II, 245².

[208] *CVA*, Enserune, 18, pl.11, 1-3. Schefold, *UKV*, no.589. Barcelona (Muzeo Arqueolgica). Schefold, *UKV*, no.141. Metzger, *Represent.*, 140 no.61. Trias De Arribas, *Ceramicas Griegas*, 186 f pl. CV1.

[209] Farnell, *Cults of the Greek State*, Pl.XXXIX. Reinach, *Repirtoir* II, 35 (1-33).

[210] These examples are mentioned and discussed by Farnell, in *ibid* vol.5, 252, pls.XXXIX,a,b, and XL.

[211] See entry No.33.

[212] In early paintings, it has been occasionally noticed that there is an outline of a third horse running beside the two-wheeled chariot drawn by a pair of horses. Anderson, *Ancient Greek horsemanship*, 31. This can be seen on a hydria in Berlin, by Psiax, where three horses are represented (two chariot horses and a third trace-horse), Berlin 1897. Beazley *Develop*, 78, pl.36, 2. (I am grateful to Susan Wood for this observation.)

[213] Vian, *Repertoir Des Gigantomachies*, 83 ff.

[214] Athen. Acrop. 760 (Acrop. G.160). *ARV* 552, 20. Vian, *op. cit*. no.375, pl.XLI.

[215] Orvieto 1044. *CVA*, pl.9-10. *ARV* 6471. Vian, *op. cit*. pl.XL, 376. Caskey and Beazley II, 71-72. Philippaki, *The Attic Stamnos*, 37 f.

[216] Boston, oo.342. *ARV* 598,4. Vian, *op. cit*. XLI, No.382. Caskey and Beazley II, pls.55-56. Philippaki, *op. cit*. 73 f. pl.47,1.

[217] Caskey and Beazley II, 71.

[218] Caskey and Beazley II, 72. Furtwangler, *Die Antiken Gemmen*, pl.8, 42. Boardman *Greek Gems*, 147 pl.347.

[219] Boardman, *Greek Gems*, 147.

It is evident that the representation of Dionysos in connection with the Gigantomachia either, shows the god and his companion in a chariot on the way to the battle, or in the middle of the struggle, with a chariot represented. Our pelike, most definitely, represents the first stage.

A combination of the two stages is to be found on an unattributed Attic lekythos in Berlin, belonging to the first quarter of the fourth century[220]. On it Dionysos is seen in a chariot drawn by two griffins painted white, while the two griffins charge fiercely at the two Giants. Dionysos holds his thrysos poised for attack. One of the two Giants has snake legs.

This Pelike, like No.39, is attributed by Beazley to the Pasithea Painter[221].

41. *Pelike* Leningrad B.4528[222] (Euhesperides) (Schefold UKV No.483) (Plate 30, 1-3)

(A) The Calydonian Boar Hunt.

Artemis, according to mythology, was the cause of this incident – an act of revenge. Oeneus, King of Calydon in Aetolia, and the father of Tydeus, Meleager and Deianeira, offended the goddess by failing to include her with other gods and goddesses in his harvest sacrifice. Angry at such neglect, she took revenge by sending a mighty boar to devastate the local crops.

The Hunt for this monster was celebrated on account of the heroes who took part in it - Theseus, Jason, Peleus (father of Achilles), and others - and for the story of Meleager and Atlanta, who were also associated with it. Many of these heroes lost their lives, and in the end the mighty boar was killed. Meleager, in love with Atlanta, gave her the head and hide of the animal as a reward as she was the first to hit the monster. This act led to quarrels with Meleager's uncles on his mother's side, and eventually to his death. That happened when his mother angrily extinguished the torch the Fates had given to Meleager on his birth, and to which his life was tied[223].

Seven hunters are present on our vase, six males and one female; the scene is watched by the goddess Artermis. The boar is in the centre running to the left, the object of the attack by the hunters and their hounds. The figure above the animal is presumably Theseus or Ankaios, placed at a point half way along the length of the animal's back (slightly higher than the boar). Theseus advances forward, swinging an axe in both hands, over or behind his head and about to strike the animal. Next to the Hero, close to the boar's head, is a hunter, probably Peirithoos (Ovid. Meta. 435). The hero, whom Ovid tells us rushed to the boar after Ankaeus, falls and was protected from a similar fate by his friend Theseus. He leans away from the boar, left leg advanced towards the animal. He raises his right arm over his head, holding and swinging a club in his hand, while the left arm is extended towards the boar, with his chlamys draped over it. Meleagros stands in front of the boar. In both hands he holds two spears, pointing them towards the animal. He is nearly on the same level as the beast. On a level just below the boar is a dead hound lying on its back with head bent downwards. To the left, on higher level than Peirithoos, is a clothed female archer wearing a phrygian cap. She is presumably Atlanta, who was fond of such headgear (or a hunting cap) and chiton. On coins she is represented in similar caps and chitons, confronting the boar[224]. The legend tells us that she was the first to shoot and hit the animal. On our vase she is seen holding a bow in her left hand, drawing back the string with her right. A quiver is slung on her shoulder. A hound is seen on a higher level looking back with raised tail. On a level higher than Theseus and Atlanta, behind Theseus, there is a spear thrower seen from the rear. He leans back to hurl a spear from his right hand while holding another in an outstretched left arm, wrapped in his chlamys.

We are not sure of the identity of this last figure, nor do we know the next hunter, who advances directly behind the boar in a position symmetrical to that of Meleagros. This hunter, accompanied by a hound, is nude with only his chlamys fluttering over his shoulder. He leans forward, with both hands thrusting two spears towards the back of the boar. A hound is shown in profile to left, and slightly in front of the hunter. On the far right there is a figure who does not seem to be taking part in the action. He looks as though he is running away, but looking back to survey the scene with horror. He wears a piloi and chlamys, holding a bow in his left hand. In the background, on a higher level, is the goddess Artemis, face on but turning to the left towards the figure there. She holds two spears vertically in her right hand, and, like Atlanta, wears a phrygian cap.

All the hunters, except Atlanta and the figure on the far right, wear taenia, symbols of victory.

More important is the position of Thesus. He is now the focus of the entire composition, shown about to strike the boar with an axe[225]. He is clearly made to upstage Meleagros, who in all versions of the myth was the one who killed the animal.

It has been observed that the classical representations of the Calydonian Boar Hunt all seem to repeat certain selected motifs. These are uniformly inter-related and thus reflect a common source, perhaps a lost monumental painting by

[220] Berlin inv. 3375. Neugebauer, 133. Jacobsthal, *Ornam. Gr.*, pl.126, a-b. Vian, *op. cit.* pl.XLVIII, No.400 Metzger, *Represent*, 334, no.64.

[221] *ARV* 1472, 3.

[222] Reinach, *Repertoir* I, 322 fig.2. Schefold, *UKV*, no.483. Metzger, *Represent.*, 313, no.26, pl.XLI,4.

[223] For an account of the story see *Iliad*, IX, 529-99. Ovid, *Metamorphoses*, viii, 270-546. Pausanias, viii 45. Fragment of Euripides, *Meleager*, Nauck^2, 515-39.

[224] Severan Coin of Tegea (200 A.D.), Paris, Bib.Nat. Mionnet, *Medailler Antique* ii (1807), 256, No.75. Illustrated in Stewart, *Skopas of Paros*, pl.29.a, and referred to in F. Imhoof-Blummer, P. Gardner, "Numismatic commentary on Pausanias" (*JHS* 7 (1886), 112.

[225] Similar poses of "hammer swingers" representing the wedding of Peirithoos, probably inspired by the painting of a lost monumental painting, are reported by Brian Shefton in *Hesperia* 31, (1950), 350 ff.

Polygnotos, or his circle (460-450 B.C.)[226]. The Athens dinos, datable to about 450 B.C., is perhaps the earliest surviving reflection of this 'Polygnotan' composition[227]. But the Calydonian Boar Hunt, was a favourite subject with artists long before this, presumed lost, mural. We know that, as early as the sixth century, vase painters used the subject but in an extended composition with many figures. So, on an Athenian dinos in Boston, by the London Painter B 76 (575-550 B.C.), no less than fourteen hunters, including five horsemen, are involved. More important among sixth century representations of the story is the famous François Vase (volute-krater) by Kleitias (570-565 B.C)[228].

Looking at these two examples one would observe that among the sixth century painters the boar always runs to the left, in its path a wounded man and a dead hound. A group of hunters, varying in number, were drawn more or less symmetrically and arranged either side of the animal, sometimes accompanied by archers and horsemen. As a rule, every figure is placed on the same plane, in a typically sixth century scheme. Attempts to render perspective were minimal.

We know now from the Benghazi example that this scheme was abandoned. But this is not the first or, indeed, the last example to represent this break from the old method. An Attic red-figured dinos in Athens, by the Agrigento Painter (450 B.C.)[229], seems to be the first known example that introduced the new scheme. The composition of motifs and figures could not be clearer than shown on the Benghazi Pelike, presenting an extraordinary break with the archaic scheme. The figures no longer stand on a common plane - they are placed on different levels in a setting of hills. The boar here is in the centre of the foreground.

A closer and more relevant comparison to the Benghazi example is the relief shown on a bronze mirror in Boston (350 B.C.)[230]. Only two figures are represented. In the centre, presumably, is Theseus, in a position and stance very similar to that of the Benghazi Pelike. The Boar is also identical. There is no doubt that both represent the true spirit of the fourth century.

(B) Maenad in full frontal view to the right, but looking back over her shoulder.

Her left arm is extended and holds a thrysus. Her right arm is adjusting her sleeveless chiton, which is fastened over the shoulders. The garment is banded with a thick line at the hem, waist and lower apoptygma. She is followed by a nude, bald, and bearded satyr. Another nude satyr, clad in a lion skin, advances in front of the maenad, but he is looking back while raising his right arm above his head, perhaps in an attempt to stop the fleeing maenad.

The Benghazi Pelike is very important. It is the only fourth century Attic vase to represent the story of the Calydonian Boar Hunt, yet it is unattributed[231]. The Attic Pelike from Derna (Cyrennica) (Entry No.48) has a very similar size and profile to the Hermitage example. This is the early fourth century style of pelike. Side B on the Yale Pelike is indeed very close to side B of the Hermitage vase. The composition is almost the same, with a group of three and the fleeing maenad as the central figure. The pose, gesticulation, and painting itself are not dissimilar to the Yale Pelike, which has already been attributed to the Hippolytas Painter *c.*375 B.C.

Side A, on the other hand, is indistinct, with inner details obliterated, and with an absence of close comparable work it is difficult to decide who the artist was. There are, however, some elements in the style of painting, as well as the composition of the whole subject, that indicate that the painting was executed during the first quarter of the fourth century. The idea of arranging figures on different levels was tried by different artists as early as the second half of the fifth century. More relevant to us, however, is the fact that the Jena Painter, during the first decade of the fourth century, used the same method on his pelike (Entry No.42), in Exeter. Indeed, if we compare the style on the Hermitage Pelike to that of the Exeter vessel (by the Jena Painter), we find that both vases share certain characteristics in style. Compare, for instance, the poses of Pylades on the Exeter pelike to that of Artemes on the Hermitage vase. Compare, too, the pose and gesticulation of Hermes to that of the unidentified figure with Pilo, to the very right of the Hermitage vessel. The hairstyle is also similar, and Hermes' hairstyle resembles that of the hunter. From such similar characteristics on both vases we may conclude that the Hermitage Pelike artist was a contemporary, or follower, of the Jena Painter, a fact that may date the pelike to the first two decades of the fourth century.

42. *Pelike, Exeter University*[232] (Plate 31, 1)

Part of the lip and lower part of the body are restored. This is the pelike style with flared neck. Oval patterns on the lip and base of neck.

The figures are arranged on an uneven ground. They represent the mythological scene illustrating the meeting of Orestos and

[226] For a discussion on the subject and attempts to reconstruct this supposed lost work from the circle of Polygnotos, see Kleinder, *Antike Kunst*, 15 (1972). 9 ff. A list of representations of the subject has been compiled by Brommer, *Vasenlisten*, 310-315. See also R. Blatter, *Antike Kunst* 5, (1962), 45 ff. D. von Bothmr, *Bull. Metropolitan Mus. of Art* 27, (1969), 425 ff. P. de la Coste-Messelière, *Au Musée de Delphes* (1936), 120 ff. K. Schauenburg, *AA* (1962), 765 ff. For representations of the story in all media, Roscher, in *Lexikon* "Meleagro", 2591 ff. *EAA*, I, P.753. *Atalanta*, II P.983 f., "Meleagro".

[227] Athens National Museum 1489 (cc 1597). The Agrigento Painter, *ARV* 577, 52. Brommer, *Vasenlisten*, 314, B1. Kleiner, *Antike Kunst*, 15 (1972), pl.2, 1-3.

[228] Boston 34.212. *ABV*, 87,18, Addenda, 9 87 (18). *CVA*, 2, pl.5. 64, 65.1. Florence 4209, *ABV*, 76,1, *para.* 29 and Addenda 7-8. Beazley, *Develop*, 26-37 pl.II,1. Boardman, fig.46.3. Simon and Hirmer, fig.53. Shefton, *HGVP*, fig.42. See also the representation of the story in Jacobsthal, *Die Melischen Reliefs*, No.103 (P.78), Pl.60.

[229] Athens National Museum 1489 (cc 1579). *ARV* 577, 52, Addenda, 128. Kleiner, *Antike Kunst*, 9, pl.2, 1-3.

[230] Boston, Museum of Fine Arts, 05.59. Zuchner, *Griechische Klappspiegel*, 60 f. KS 82, fig. 29. *Greek Gods and Heroes* (Museum of Fine Arts, Boston 1962 57).

[231] An Apulian 4th c. amphora in Trieste depicts the story. Trieste, *CVA*, IV d Pls.14-15 (C. 330).

[232] Exeter University. *ARV* 1516, 80. The picture is in Cook, *GPP*, pl.50. It is also reproduced by N. Bozana (Kourou), *AAA*, 4 (1971), 260.

Electra at the tomb of Agamemnon. In the middle is Agamemnon's tomb in the shape of a stele with a two-stepped base. This is inscribed Ism[ene], and decorated with white fillets tied around the column; they appear to have been provided with offerings. Of these, a small perfume vase falls onto the tomb steps.

The meeting of Orestes and Electra at Agamemnon's tomb was a very popular subject in the second half of the fifth and the fourth centuries, especially in southern Italian vase painting. The number of figures represented varies considerably, but the central group is fairly constant. This generally shows Orestes, often with Pylades, Electra, and a companion around the tomb monument of Agamemnon, which takes the form of a stele or column on a stepped base[233].

The painting was probably inspired by the *Choephoroi* the second play of the *Oresteia,* which Aeschylus produced in 458 B.C. The play opens with Orestes, in the company of Pylades, praying to Hermes as he offers two locks of his hair on the tomb of Agamemnon. Before withdrawing they leave their footprints (205-210). Electra follows, with the chorus, bringing libations. She recognises her brother by the lock of hair he offers and by his footprints. This leads to the meeting scene (Electra and Orestes), where they pray to the shade of Agamemnon and vow to kill his murderer (211)[234].

On the Cyrenaica Pelike, the woman (in peplos) to the right of the stele is Electra. She carries a large hydria. From this she makes her libation, before the emergence of Orestes and Pylades.

Electra is balanced on the other side of the vase, left of the stele, by a male figure whose identity is not certain. He is very probably Hermes, to whom Orestes addresses himself in the opening lines of the play, and whose presence would have been indicated, at least symbolically, on the vases. He is nude, sitting in a relaxed pose, and gesturing to Electra with his left hand.

The identity of Pylades is almost certain; he was Orestes' constant companion and usually represented with a staff and/or spear. He is sitting naked on the step of the grave monument, part of his cloak (chlamys) rolled about his thigh. He holds two spears and looks over his shoulder towards his friend. On a calyx-krater in Syracuse - by the Sicilian Dirce Painter (380-370 B.C.)[235] - a figure, who must be Pylades, holds both a staff and a spear. He is always represented at the edge of the vessel, in a subordinate position. On our vase he is placed at the lower right hand corner.

We can also be certain of the identity of the figure standing to the left of the stele. It is Orestes, wearing a large hat (petasos) fixed around his neck. A chlamys cloak (fastened in front by a brooch) hangs over his shoulder and down his back. His stands close to the stele and his proximity to Electra seems further to confirm his identity. Orestes raises a sword with one hand and holds his hair with the other to cut the offering of his two locks.

An earlier representation of these three principal figures in a very similar composition can be seen on a terracotta relief from Melos (450-440 B.C.)[236]. Here Orestes and Electra are placed on the steps of the tombs, on either side of the stele, while Pylades sits apart from them on the lowest steps.

We are not sure, however, of the identity of the female figure behind Orestes. The identification is made even more complicated by the presence of the inscription ISMENE next to her. Why should the painter want to make a point of identifying her and none of the other figures? Brian Shefton suggests that the artist was probably confusing the identity of this woman with a character from another play by Sophocles, in which Ismen, the daughter of Oedipus and Jocasta, has a principal role[237]. These plays also include Oedipus and Antigone. Our female figure, on the other hand, must rather be a servant, or companion, of Electra, as she appears on many contemporary vessels.

Our vase is attributed by Brian Shefton to the Jena Painter, a painter of cups of the early years of the fourth century B.C.[238]. His workshop was in Athens, where most of his attributed work, now in Jena, was found in fragments. Our vase is the only pelike so far attributed to the artist, and possibly dated to the first decade of the fourth century. Prag, in his recent work on the Oresteia, considers a skyphos by the Penelope Painter in Copenhagen (440 B.C.) as the only existing vase to illustrate the Cheophoroi, before the large south Italian pots of the fourth century[239]. He could not have been aware of the existence of our pelike. Indeed, this is the only Attic vase that illustrates the Cheophori in the early years of the fourth century.

43. *Pelike* Cyrene Museum (Plate 31, 2)

(A) A youth (hunter?) bends forward to the right, over his left foot, which rests upon a rock. He is nude, leaving his cloak draped over his raised thigh. He covers his head with pilos, a head covering usually worn by hunters. He confers with a woman (maenad?) seated on the left. She wears sleeveless chiton, decorated in front with a sea-horse version pattern (reserved) against a black background. Her hair is covered by a sakkos, but some strands escape in front and around her ear. She looks as though she is wearing earrings. Her right hand is held out high in a singing gesture. The left hand rests on a

[233] For treatment of the subject see Jacobsthal, *ibid*, 16 ff. Sechan, *Studies sur la tragedes Grecque*, 56 f. *EAA*, v. 741-3. Trendali J. Webster, *Illustration,* 41-44. Prag, *Oriesteia* 51-57. Kossatz-Deissman, *Dramen des Aischylos,* 92-102.

[234] Translated by Tucker in *The Choepohroi of Aeschylus*.

[235] Syracuse 36334. Trendall and Webster, *Illustration* 42, III 1, 3. Prag, *Oresteia*, 56.

[236] Berlin, Staatliche Museum, Terr. Inv.6803. Trendall and Webster, *op. cit.* 41, III, 1, 1. Jacobsthal, *MR*, nos.104-105.

[237] Shefton in a Jackson Knight Memorial lecture, May 1983, Exeter University, (unpublished) and *idem*, *The Eye of Greece,* 177 f.

[238] *ARV* 1516, 80. Cook, *GPP,* 184-5 pl.40. Shefton, *op. cit.* 177 f.

[239] Copenhagen, National Museum, Inv.597. Prag, *Oresteia*, 56.

tympanum (tamborine). Behind the youth another woman approaches from the right. She also wears a chiton and faccus and holds a tamborine by the left hand, while beating it with the right. A sash falls below the tamborine.

(B) Two youths draped in hymatia face each other and converse. The one on the right holds a staff in his right hand.

The pelike shape is that of the early fourth century B.C. type. The composition and style are not easy to determine. On an unattributed hydria in the Hermitage, telling the story of Poseidon and Amymone[240], we find the same composition, but the style of painting seems rather different. (Although the treatment of the lower half of the chiton on the seated woman is somewhat similar.) The woman behind Poseidon on the hydria holds her right arm out in a manner similar to that of the seated woman on the pelike. On the other hand, the patterns used differ on both Amymone and the seated woman on the pelike. On the hydria, a wave pattern was applied in black on a reserved background, whereas on our pelike we find a degenerate sea-horse pattern.

A number of pieces attributed to the Jena painter show the sea-horse pattern. It was, apparently, a popular motif on contemporary vases, and on earlier and later examples. It appears on the sleeved chiton of tragic actors, most appropriately that of Andromeda, as she prepares to step down after being saved by Perseus[241]. The scene is portrayed on a calyx-krater in Berlin, dated to the late fifth or early fourth century[242]. Later the sea-horse pattern degenerates when used by the painters of the fourth century. The Meleager Painter, on his hydria in New York[243], depicting the story of Poseidon and Amymone, has the garments of the figures, both men and women, richly decorated, and the most prominent decoration used is the sea-horse pattern. It decorates the lower sections of the men's attire, and both the bodice and lower sections of the women's garments. The poses of the figures, and the gesticulations, on the New York hydria are similar to those shown on our pelike. For example, note the pose of the seated woman talking to the satyr, and how it also resembles that of the maenad on the pelike.

Our pelike was probably made a generation later than the Jena Painter, and is, perhaps, contemporaneous with Meleager Painter, who was working during the middle years of the first quarter of the fourth century.

240 Leningrad B 4125. Schefold, *UKV* pl.9, 2. Metzger, *represent,* P XL, 3.

241 Johnson, *AJA,* 42 (1938) 348, 360 no.36. Hahland, *Vasen um Meidias,* pl.22.9.

242 Berlin Staatlich Museum 3237. Neungebauer, 126 pl.68. Phillips, *AJA,* 72 (1968) 7, pl.7 fig.16). Beazley did not attribute this vase to the Pronomos Painter, as Phillips, *op. cit.* and others (in *Rendiconti della Pont Acad. Rom. d'Arch* 38,61), assumed. He quoted the vase because it depicts tiaras like those on the Pronomos Volute-krater in Naples (inv.3240) *ARV* 1336,1 and 1690. Beazley corrected them in *Paralip,* 480.

243 New York. Acc.no.56.171.56 (ex Hearst). *ARV*[2] 1412,46. Caskey and Beazley, *Boston* II 9. *AJA,* 66 (1962), pl.82,5.

44. *Pelike* London B.M. E 435[244] (Plate 31, 3)

H. 29 cm

(A) In the centre, the young Dionysos, wreathed with ivy, sits naked on his cloak, in three-quarter view to left. He leans on his left elbow and carries a thrysos in his right hand, turning his head towards Ariadne, who is similarly seated next to him, partly wrapped in a himation that covers her only to the waist. She wears a saccos over her head. She, too, leans on her left arm and outstretches her right towards Dionysos. On her arm, stands the young boy Eros, kneeling and extending both arms towards Ariadne. A panther, shown in right profile, approaches Ariadne, perhaps sniffing at her garment. To the left of this main scene, a satyr advances with his right hand on his hip. To the right, Pan sits on a rock raising a lagobolon in his right hand.

(B) Three draped youths. Two stand to the right confronting a third to the left. Between them is a stele, or an altar.

His wreath of ivy leaves and thrysos identifies the god Dionysos. The identification of Ariadne is equally certain, since, on vase painting, Dionysos never appears with any other identifiable female figure. Next to her is Dionysos' favourite animal - the panther -, which is frequently represented on vases next to him[245].

Dionysos is by far the most often represented divinity on Greek vases. He was a very popular god and appears to have played a great role in the everyday religious life of the average Greek; more so than any other divinity[246]. His importance is born out by his appearance on painted pottery, probably far out numbering any other mythological figures. More often than not, Dionysos is alone, or with one or more members of his retinue. Chief among these is Ariadne, the Cretan princess, whose help was needed by Theseus, when the Athenian hero came to Crete to free the Athenians from their tribute of seven youths and seven maidens, sacrificed to the Minotaur[247]. After killing this creature, he carried Ariadne off as his bride, but deserted her on the island of Nuxos. There, Dionysos saw her, fell in love and married her. This last phase of Ariadne's story is the one represented on the London Pelike.

244 London E 435. Smith, *Catalogue of the Greek Etruscan vases* III 265 f. Schefold, *UKV,* no.514, pl.7, 2 Metger, *Represent,* 119, no.26, pl.XIII, 3.

245 On an Attic black-figured neck amphora in Butnam Museum (Davenports Iowa) [AR47.58]. R.D. De Puma, in Moon, *Greek Vase Painting,* 124, no.71, and on another neck amphora in London: B258, *CVA* 4 pl.63,41, and on a hydria in Harvard: 60.347 (Bequest of D.M. Robinson 1960-347). Robinson *CVA,* 3 pl.13. *ARV* 1341, 2. The last example is in the manner of the Meidias Painter (400 BC). On it a panther stands to the right while Ariadne walks to the left with arms outstretched to touch the animal.

246 An historical sketch of the conception and cult of Dionysos has been drawn by Burkert, *Greek Religion* 161-167. Guthrie's chapter on Dionysos in *The Greeks and their Gods.* M. Robertson, *A History of Greek Art,* 1237 and 388-389. Otto, *Dionysos, Myth and Cult,* passim.

247 For a list of vases representing Thesus and the Minotaur see Brommer, *Vasenlisten* (3, 226-243).

The composition of our vase is similar to that of the Yale Pelike (to be discussed) (Entry No.48). The figures cover the whole scene. The Satyr to the left, and the Pan with his lagobolon to the right, effectively frame the composition and echo the shape of the vase. The attention is focussed on Dionysos, who is represented larger in scale than the other figures. Eros and the panther are more dominant elements of the total composition.

We may compare our hydria to the example in the Metropolitan Museum, attributed to the Meleager Painter[248]. The composition of the scene is similar. Poseidon, seated with his trident, recalls Dionysos on the London Pelike. The Amymone figure seems identical to Ariadne. Both have saccos and sitt in three-quarter view, nearly naked. The treatment of the himation is similar. On the Metropolitan Hydria, Eros is grown and effeminate, and the water bird replaces the panther. The painters of both vases must have been closely associated.

45. *Hydria, "Exeter"*[249] (Plate 32, 1-4)

This is a Type II hydria, with neck, shoulder and body forming a continuous curve. Egg and dot pattern decorates the lips, and below the scene around the vase.

On the reverse there are three large palmettes; one below the upright handle and two on a higher level at the shoulder, close to the horizontal handles. Scroll pattern also used.

Subject: Dionysiac Thiasos.

The scene's main figure is a woman (maenad) in a special posture indicating dancing movements. This is shown by the position of her feet and the flow of the lower part of her sleeveless chiton in a ballooning curve. She is, in fact, in the act of pirouetting. Her right arm is bent towards her chest, the left holding a tambourine. To her left, a satyr moves rapidly to the left, but looks back towards the dancing maenad. He leans away from her. His weight is placed on his right foot, which advances towards the maenad on the left. His left arm bends towards him while the right extends downwards. The scene is framed by two figures. To the left there is a standing maenad, her right arm bent, holding a tambourine in her left hand. To the right of the scene, a youthful Eros sits to the left on his cloak. He extends both arms towards the dancing maenad. In contrast to the central figures, Eros and the standing maenad seem quieter.

This scene probably represents the revelries of Dionysos' companions: the god himself is not present here. Occasionally Pan figures replace the satyrs, Eros too appears more frequently than before[250]. Dancing maenads and satyrs are usually shown moving wildly, drawing inspiration for their ecstatic mood, no doubt, from Dionysos, the god both of ecstasy and the suspension of all things rational[251]. The tambourine held by the dancing maenad, like the thrysus, is very much a symbol of Dionysiac revelries. The instrument in these scenes was an innovation of the second half of the fifth century (about 440 B.C.), transferred from the ecstatic cult of the Asiatic goddess, Cybele[252].

This tradition probably originated in Thrace, before spreading rapidly across the Greek islands as early as the Mycenean period. The female figures known as Maenads are often depicted as heavily cloaked, or wearing fawn or panther skins. They frequently carry, and occasionally tear to pieces, snakes or small forest animals. Such a representation mirrored real cult association thiasoi, especially in the emphasis on music and violent dance. This dance had a marked effect upon bystanders, especially women, who succumbed to the mass hysteria in large numbers. As time went on, the god became Hellenized, acquiring new influences, notably over the vine, as wine god, and as patron of the theatre, when old rituals became gradually more sober, and were eventually replaced by formal festival ceremoniess[253].

The scene on the Exeter vase does not necessarily represent a performance or special occasion. Satyrs and Maenads are Dionysos' constant companions and this is how they are considered, especially the capering Thyiads. A representation of their image goes hand in hand with the gradual "civilizing"of Bacchic ceremonies. These scenes were popular subjects on Attic vases from the mid-sixth century B.C. until the fourth century B.C.[254].

We have yet to find an exact parallel to the Exeter hydria. In terms of shape we can perhaps compare our vase with the unattributed hydria in the Metropolitan Museum[255]. As for the subject, it is relevant, perhaps, to cite the calyx-krater in Athens, the named piece of the Athens Painter 12255[256]. On it, three maenads and one satyr are engaged in a violent, frantic dance. The three maenads are shown floating above the ground, with heads pointing up. The line of their garments, and the position of their feet, indicate the frenzied dance they are performing. For composition and style we are less fortunate. The only example that might provide a parallel for

[248] See note 243.

[249] The information and photographs were kindly provided by B.B. Shefton.

[250] For a discussion on the subject see Pauly Wissowa, *RE* s.v. "Dionysos". Farnell, *The Cults of the Greek State* V, chapters 4-5. Daremberg-Saglio, *Dictionnaire des antiquities Greques et Romains*, s.v. Dionysia, "Maenades", "Thyiades". Metzger, *Represent.*, 142 f.

[251] Lawler, in *Mem. Acad Rome* VI (1927), 69-112.

[252] *HGVP*, 373.

[253] See Note 250.

[254] See Euripides, *Bacchae*, 488, 482. Sophocles, *Antigone*, 1128, 1153. Aristophanes, *Clouds*, 603. *HGVP*, 323. For fifth century representations:
i) Cup 1 painted by Macron in Brussels (A 247). Lawler, *op. cit.* pl.20, 1. *ARV* 462, 41.
ii) Stamnos by the Dinos Painter in Naples (2419). Lawler, *op. cit.* pl.15 1-2. *ARV* 1151/2.
iii) Bell-krater in Providence (23.324) by the Pothos Painter. Lawler, *op. cit*, 20,2. *ARV* 1188, 1.
iv) Squat lekythos in the Louvre (MNB 2110), by the Meidias Painter. Lawler, *op. cit. ARV* 1314, 14.
For fourth century representations see the list in Metzger, *Represent.*, 140 ff.

[255] Richter and Milne, *Shapes and Names*, fig.86.

[256] Athens 12255 (N.1113). *ARV* 1435. Metzger, *Recherches*, 94, No.3, Pl.XLIV, 1 and 2.

the treatment of the dancing maenads' garments is the unattributed bell-krater in the Louvre. Maenads play the tambourine and satyrs engage in a frenzied dance in the presence of the god Dionysos on both vases[257]. The lower sections of the chitons flowing with the movement, but the garments on the krater are transparent whereas the chiton on the Exeter hydria is not. The Exeter hydria is an example of the early phase of the Kerch style, and the style of painting style looks as if an artist, who was probably a follower of the Jena workshop, painted it during the second quarter of the fourth century. The profile of the shapely Eros is typical of that period.

46. *Hydria, London* BM E 226[258] (Plate 33, 1-3)

H. 42 cm.

Restored; nearly half the scene and one handle is missing. The design is arranged in two bands. To increase the area for an ambitious subject, the neck ornamentation is set high. The border of the base grouping is a uniform pattern of three keys of stopped meanders between chequered-squares. Egg pattern around the handle-stems and rim, its intersections dotted. The upper-most flange of the mouth is glazed, as is the bell of the foot, including the bell of the grooved roll below.

Subject: The toilet of Helen.

In the centre Helen is seated in a chair (inscription ελένη). She sits in three-quarter view, wearing a thin chiton and a richly decorated cloak around her lower body. Next to her, on a level with her head, is a small Eros (inscription πύθος). He crouches to adjust a fillet on Helen's forehead. There are four female figures on the right four women. The first stands to the left before a thymiaterion, or incense burner; the second sits to the right on a lower level, but she turns her head towards Helen: above her the inscription καλή. The third figure is Klio "κλε(ι)ώ". The fourth woman is also sitting; she holds a tambourine. On the left, behind Helen, there are three other standing women, all three looking towards Helen. The first holds a palmette fan ("flabellum"). The second leans on the first. She is inscribed καλή. The third figure seems to balance the figures on the right of Helen, on the same level. She, too, has a tambourine. In general, the scene is distinguished by the grace of the figures and the rich drawing and wealth of linear draftmanship. All the women have elaborately long chitons, bracelets and necklaces, except for Klio, who has no necklace.

There are nine figures on the higher plane, including Eros. Helen is clearly the focal point of the whole scene; she has the rapt attention of her seven companions and maids. The two women on the outside balance the composition of the scene. Each sits with one hand resting on a tambourine, and the other adjusts her shawl. The figure on the right leans forward on a rock, in a pose that recalls a very many figures on vase painting of the time. She is balanced by the second figure on the left, but leans forward to rest her arm on the figure behind Helen. Such a pose is found in the later fifth and early fourth centuries. White paint was used for Helen's flesh. She is only partly covered. Her richly embroidered chiton is draped over her right shoulder and from the waist downwards. Her companions are dressed in chitons, with borders or panels of two narrow stripes (see especially the women under the side handles). The belts are also rendered by two pairs of lines. All the figures wear wreaths of myrtle, earrings, necklaces and bracelets.

The shape of the hydria, in general, represents a type favoured in the late fifth and early fourth centuries, with a squat, steep body, almost rounded below. Although the foot is similar to those of the Meidian Hydria, the body is much slimmer and taller. The style of painting, the poses of figures, and the decorative elements, are all elements to be found in the painting of the period.

Close to our hydria in composition and style of drawing, is the hydria in the Pelizaeus Museum, Hildesheim[259], which is dated to the beginning of the fourth century. The subject on this vase is Helen and Paris.

Our hydria has already been attributed to the Painter of the Athens Wedding[260], and consequently dated by Schefold to 390-380 B.C., representing the early period of the Kerch style. But as the main elements in this style of painting seem to be taken from the painting of the late fifth century, I am inclined to date the vase to the later years of the fifth and beginning of the fourth century B.C.

47. *Cup-Skyphos (Heavy Wall)* London BM 67.5-12.33[261] Euhesperides (Plate 34, 1-3)

This is a deep bowl with strong concave lip above, slightly thickened at the rim[262]. The two handles, one partly missing, are attached below the lip and curl up just above the level of the rim. It has a moulded ring foot in two sections – an upper, and a wider, lower part – in effect divided in two by a horizontal groove placed a little above the middle, forming a large lower section and a narrow, sharper, upper one. The underneath is reserved and painted with two black circles: a thick one away from the centre, and a narrow, smaller one close to it. There is also a groove above the junction of the wall and foot. No relief line is used. Diluted black paint has been used for the sakkos of the maenad, and the upper part of the dress, as well as the hair and beard of the right satyr.

Inside, there are four linked palmettes enclosing a small circle. These are placed within a circle of incomplete, impressed ring of ovules.

[257] Louvre G.507, *CVA*, Louvre V, pl.(365) 5.

[258] E226, Smith, *Catalogue* III 178. *CVA*, British Museum, 6 pl.95,1. Schefold, *UKV*, 138. *ARV* 1318, 3. Ghali-Kahil, *Les Enlevements*, 165 no.124, pl.XXVIII,3.

[259] G. Röder and A. Ippel, *Die Denkmaler des Pelizaus Museum zu Hildesheim* (1921), 177, no.1252. Schefold, *UKV*, 143, figs.68-69. Ghali-Kahil, *op. cit.* 169, no.129, pl.XX.

[260] Ghali-Kahil *op. cit.* 165 no.124 pl.XXVIII, 3. Metzger, *Represent.*, 279, no.30. Schefold, *UKV*, 138 f. *ARV* 1318, 3.

[261] *ARV* 1519, 21. Sparkes and Talcott, *Ath. Agora*, 30.

[262] For this type in black-glaze, see Sparkes and Talcott, *Ath.Agora*, XII, 111 f. For the red-figure type, see Ure, *JHS* 64 (1944), 67-77.

The painting on both sides of the wall shows a maenad between two satyrs. On each handle there are three reserved palmettes.

Of the many skyphos cups, with interior stamps resembling ours, the most useful for comparison is the one in Leningrad[263]. The style of painting is very close.

The Cyrenaica cup has already been assigned by Beazley to the Q Painter[264], whose work is dated to the first and second quarters of the fourth century. Our cup was probably painted during the later years of the first, or early years of the second quarter of the fourth century.

48. *Pelike Yale University Arta Gallery 1913, 138 [Stoddart Collection]*[265] from Derna (Plate 35, 1-2)

H. 39.1 cm.

Handles broken and repaired. Neck and mouth restored incorrectly; the lip should overhang. Uneven glaze; surface worn and unevenly preserved. Some preliminary drawing in inner markings of anatomy and drapery. Added white flesh of Erotes and snake (now largely missing); also perhaps for added clay of apples and jewellery (also missing). Above the figures on side A, is a broad band of egg-and-dot pattern. Below a narrow band of the same patterns. On side B, another broad band of the same pattern runs above the figures. Circling the vase below the figures is an egg-and-dot band. Below and at the base of each handle are palmettes.

(A) Heracles in the garden of Hesperides. This is a scene from one of the twelve labours of Heracles: the theft of the golden apples of the Hesperides. In the centre of the scene is the miraculous tree of the golden apples, the wedding gift of Ge to Zeus and Hera, and the symbol of eternal life and youth. A snake, sent to guard it, coils around the tree. Here the snake is represented in a passive attitude, suggesting, as the story goes, that it has already been drugged and immobilized. The apples, the goal of Heracles' last mission, are being gathered by a Hesperid to the far left of the scene. She is dressed in a long garment. To the right of the apple tree, there is a second Hesperid [resembling Aphrodite?], only partly covered by her richly decorated himation. She sits on a rock and looks towards Heracles, offering herself, perhaps, as bride to the Hero. Heracles sits in three-quarter pose on his lion skin, in a relaxed posture, appropriately responding to the Hesperid next to him. Eros, perched on the Hero's knee, makes Heracles the centre of attention.

A third, and fully draped Hesperid, is placed to the right to balance the scene. Next to her, a seated Pan effectively frames the composition. Both figures are watching and looking with great interest in the direction of Heracles.

This is, no doubt, a good example of the representation of remote locations (The Garden of the Hesperides). The Garden was supposed to have been found in Benghazi Libya (ancient Euhesperides). So the presence of this vase in Cyrenaica may not be a coincidence: it was very probably imported deliberately because of its subject matter[266].

Heracles' venture in the Garden of the Hesperides appears to have beeen depicted more frequently in the fourth century than ever before. Yet in most versions of the story, Heracles does not wrest the apples by force from the snake[267]. On our pelike, as, indeed, on a number of late fifth and early fourth century vases[268], Heracles amorously charms the Hesperides and then succeeds in persuading them to bring the apples to him after drugging the snake.

We may witness the earlier phase of the Hero's last labour on a pelike in the Metropolitan Museum[269]. Heracles has just arrived and the hostile, aggressive looking snake has not as yet inclined to part with the fruit. The second sister also looks agitated, as does her father, Oceanus, who lends support from behind. On a slightly earlier representation, a London hydria by the Medias Painter[270] shows Heracles accompanied by Iolaos, who looks at the Hesperide, Lipora, who already holds an apple in her hand. Meanwhile her two sisters, Asterope and Chresothemis, on the other side of the tree, proceed to gather more apples. This is a later phase of the story.

On a hydria by the Syracuse Painter (470-460 B.C.)[271], the artist depicted the moment after the theft. Heracles rapidly departs, holding three apples close to his body. One of the Hesperides pursues him, the second looks towards the fleeing hero, while the third faces the apple tree over which the snake is entwined, its mouth open as if in conversation with the maiden.

The Yale pelike, like the London hydria, both represents the time Heracles rests in the Garden, while the apples of eternal life and youth are gathered and brought to him, and the moment when the Hesperides offer themselves to him as brides.

(B) A maenad running to the right, looking back over her shoulder. She is presented in frontal view but her head is in profile. She holds a thyrsus in her left hand, while raising her right over her head. She wears a chiton, and

263 See the examples in The Hermitage, 22 63. *ARV* 1520, 25. Ure, *JHS* lXIV (1944) 74 and pl.IV, 32. See also *CVA*, Britain 12 (Reading) pl.27, 2a-d, *CVA*, Poland 6 (3) pl.41, 43, 6-7. *CVA*, Poland 2, pl.10,4. Beazley, *V.Pol.* p.71. *CVA*, Germany, 30, Pl.67 5-6 and pl.68, 1-2. *CVA*, Germany, 18, pl.72 (3,5,8,9), (6,9).

264 *ARV* 1519, 21.

265 Brommer, *Vasenlisten*, 72, 16. Schefold, *UKV*, 57, 66, 90, 145, No.543. Brommer, *JdI* 57 (1942), 118,6. Metzger, *Representa.*, 203, no.20, Burke and Pollit, 81 f.

266 See discussion by Bronnner, in Brijder (ed.), *Ancient Greek and Related Pottery,* 178 f.

267 See the discussion on Entry No.39 for more discussion on different versions of the story.

268 See Entry No.39.

269 Pelike in the Metropolitan Museum. Richter and Hall, pl.163.

270 BM E224. *HGVP,* 376, 214-215.

271 Krannert Art Museum, University of Illinois (70-8-4). Ann Perkin, in Moon, *Greek Vase Painting,* 117, no.100.

the lower section and hem of the apoptygma are banded with thick lines. She is pursued by a bearded and apparently slightly built satyr, who raises his right arm and tries to grab the maenad with his left. To the right of the scene, an Eros, holding a tympanum in his left hand, flys away in front of the maenad, but looks back.

The composition and style of painting is identical to side B of the Hermitage Pelike[272], which makes them both contemporary, perhaps belonging to the same workshop.

The Yale Pelike has already been attributed to the workshop of the Hippolytus Painter C.A. 375[273], whose work represents the earlier phase of the Kerch style.

49. *Hydria, Type II (Kalpis)* London BM E 231[274] (Plate 35, 3-4; Plate 36, 1-3)

H. 41 cm.

This is a Type II hydria with neck, shoulder and body forming a continuous curve. The mouth in two stages. Ogee foot. White paint, with details in yellow, is used for the bull and the flesh of the two Erotes. Diluted colour is used for the hair. Egg-and-dot pattern decorates the lips and the band below the scene around the vase. The lower part of the neck is also decorated with egg-and-dot pattern. Above this is a reserved band decorated with black dots between two black lines. The reverse of the vase has three large palmettes: one below the upright handle and two placed on a higher level. The design of these curves up over the shoulder, close to the horizontal handles, under each of these the artist has placed a small palmette.

Subject: Europa and the bull crossing the sea.

Europa is the daughter of the legendary King of Tyre and sister of Cadmus. She was carried away by Zeus in the form of a bull to Crete, where she bore him Minos, Rhadamanthys and Sarpedon.

The bull, luring Europa on to his back and then abducting her across the sea to Crete, is sometimes said to have been sent by Zeus[275]. On a hydria, by the Painter of the Munich Amphora, Europa is shown approaching Crete where she is met by a Zeus-like King, presumably Zeus Asterius as the Sun-God[276]. On a fish-plate in Leningrad from Taman (Elreghen), Zeus is shown waiting on his throne as Europa arrives on Crete with the bull[277]. Nevertheless, the bull is usually considered as the God himself in animal form.

On our vase, Europa is not actually mounting the bull, instead she is presented floating alongside the animal holding it by the neck with one hand, holding up her robe with the other. She is dressed in a chiton and sphendone. As she is meant to have just made a sea crossing, wave patterns are used, and dolphins and large fish swim by. Two Erotes escort Europa. One in front leads the bull, the other follows behind. The two Erotes carry taenia in one hand and beckon to the bull with the other. Three young male figures are also present. One steps forward while looking back, gesturing to the bull to follow. He is almost naked, his arm and left shoulder only are covered by his himation. The other two, in contrast to the other figures, are sitting quietly. Both are placed on the vase's shoulder to frame the scene, one to the right, the other to the left. Both are beckoning to the bull.

The subject of Europa and the bull was popular in Attic arts since the Archaic period. In sculpture, Europa appears seated on her bull in a metope of the mid-sixth century from the Siphnian treasure at Delphi[278], and she was a popular subject for later painters.

Nearest to our vessel, in both style and composition, is the hydria in the Hermitage[279]. But in that example, unlike the representation on our vase, Europa is actually mounting the bull. There are two Erotes present, and here they fly alongside the animal. The three male figures, however, are identical in pose to those on our vase.

Although the two vases may not be by the same hand, it is very likely that both vases are contemporary and could well have been painted in the same workshop.

The fish-plate, too[280], seems to be contemporary with the two hydriae. Europa here, as on our vase, is presented floating alongside the bull. She is wearing a long chiton, the lower end of which is blown by the wind, indicating the speed with which the bull is cruising; large fish are also shown, indicating the trip across the sea. Our vase is an early example of the Kerch style, painted, perhaps, about 370 B.C.

50. *Hydria, Type II (Kalpis)*[281] BM E 227 (Plates 37, 1-2; 38, 1-2; 39, 1; 40,1)

H. 40 cm.

White with yellow flesh tones. Gilding for jewellery, fruit and wreath around the neck of the vase. Below, a continuous band of egg-pattern. Beneath each side handle, a palmette; and on the reverse, an elaborate pattern of four palmettes. The design curves up over the shoulder.

Subject: Heracles in the Garden of the Hesperides.

---

[272] See Entry No.41.

[273] Burke and Pollit, *Greek vases at Yale*, 81 f.

[274] London E231. *CVA*, 6 Pl.96,2. Schefold, *KV*, pl.1. *UKV*, H.174. Metzger, *Represent.*, 306, no.l5.

[275] Ovid, *Metamorphosis* 2, 836-875. Homer *Iliad*, 14.321-322. Apollodorus, 3.1.1-2. Overbeck, *KM* 1, p.420 f. Metzgers, *Represent.*, 307 f. Cook, *Zeus* I, 544.

[276] Leningrad (St. 1637). *ARV* 245. Cook, *Zeus* i, 531, fig.405.

[277] Kertch Museum Fo (or Leningrad). Schefold, *UKV*, 12 No.51, fig.2. Cook, *Zeus* I 546, fig.414.

[278] Pierre De la Coste-Messelière, *Delphes*, 319, pl.40. See also the Metope from Temple Y at Selinus, Palermo, Maseo Civiro.

[279] See Note 276.

[280] See Note 277.

[281] FR Pl.79,2. *CVA*, London 6, pl.93 (368) a-c. Schefold. *KV* pl.7 a. *UKV*, no.170, Thompson, *Hesperia* 18 (1949), 254 pl.641. Metzger, *Represent.*, 202, no.19, pl.XXVII,1.

Heracles sits in the garden of the Hesperides, leaning on his club; behind him the tree bearing the golden apples. Here the apples are being picked and offered to the Hero by Eros, the representation of Love. He is assisted by Aphrodite, who sits on a plane, nude to the waist. To the right, on ground level, a youth, Iolaos, moves away and looks behind him. On the left, another nude youth sits facing the right, but looking back. With his left arm he draws forward the edge of his cloak over his shoulder. There are three maidens (The Hesperides) on different levels. The first, in the foreground, stands and looks at Heracles, while the others are shown at a higher level (on the shoulder of the vessel), looking in the direction of Heracles. They all wear elaborately drawn chitons.

This is typical of fourth century representations of the Hero's adventure in the Garden of The Hesperides[282]. We may recognise the scene thanks to the tree, which is placed in the centre. It is meant to symbolize the locality of the scene - usually there is a dragon coiled around the tree (not represented on the vase). Here there are no violent scenes spoiling the peace of the Garden.

The position of the maiden in the foreground is significant in relation to Heracles. We know that one of the Hesperides has fallen in love with the Hero, who will leave once his task his achieved. The moment has come when the Hesperide has to give up the apples and part with her beloved [283]. This is the maiden who pursues him - in an attempt to restrain the hero as he moves rapidly away with the golden apple - on a hydria by the Syracuse Painter (470-480 B.C.)[284]. There is a painting - on a late fifth-century relief - in a house at Pompeii that seems to show one of the maidens grieving[285]. (The work is a Roman copy, part of a set of four architectural reliefs, tentatively identified as those once flanking the two entrances in a low wall surrounding the Altar of Pity in the Athenian Agora[286].) Heracles is sitting between two standing Hesperides, who have just plucked the golden apples for him. Now, in his triumph in achieving his task, there is the painful thought of parting. The one in front of the Hero has her hand to her chin, and seems to look sadly at Heracles. On our hydria, the intimacy and pose of the maiden in the foreground (in relation to Heracles) can, therefore, be explained in this light.

Our hydria has yet to be attributed to a particular painter, or group of painters[287]. It can, however, be compared to another hydria in Istanbul depicting the birth of Plutos[288]. The profile of both vases is similar, with a short neck and squat, bulging body. But though the number of figures on both vases is not the same (ten on the Istanbul hydria, eight on the London vase), the drawn composition is similar (Plate 40,2). While on the London hydria Heracles is the central figure in the scene, it is the boy Plutos who take centre stage on the Istanbul vessel. Of the three figures to the left of the scene on the Istanbul example, Aphrodite at the top emulates the women at the similar place on the London hydria. Of those figures on the right side of both vases, there are difficulties in comparing them, especially the two appearing to be leaving in haste. The hairstyles, drapery, use of jewellery, are all features common to both vases.

The supposition that the two vases are contemporary is confirmed by the sophisticated decoration on the reverse of the two hydrae[289]. The design on both vases does, indeed, similar; note the two palmettes below the vertical handle, the two on the shoulder, and the single example under each horizontal handle. The spaces left are filled with spirals, leaves, lotus flowers, and other ornaments.

Our hydria appears to have been painted during the early period of the Kerch style, and dated by Schefold to 360 B.C.[290]. I suggest placing this between 370 and 360 B.C. This is among the generation of hydria that succeeded ours, executed by the painter of the Athens Wedding, with a squat shape, bulging sides, and reverse decoration recalling late fifth century vases.

51. *Hydria [Kalpis]* London BM E 228[291] (Pl. 41,1)

H. 31 cm.

The general shape represents a type favoured in the early years of the fourth century. A squat, oblong body, with neck and shoulder forming a continuous curve. Good examples are to be found in early Kerch ware. Part of the centre of the design, including the heads of the two central figures, is broken away. White, with yellow details on a red ground, is used for the flesh of the maenad on the right, and for Eros. There is gilding on raised ground for the jewellery, the details of the thyrsos, ivy wreaths, and harp strings. Diluted colour for the hair. Below the figure scene, and circling the whole vase, there is a painted band of sets of four meanders between chequered-squares. The pairs of lines enclosing it show some relief. Around the neck there is a necklace of pendants, raised in relief that has probably been treated with gilding. In keeping with the shape, the ornament on the reverse is drawn rather broadly and densely patterned. There is a fine pattern composed of six palmettes, and another with spirals and smaller palmettes used as filling. There is a single palmette below each horizontal handle. The designs curve over the shoulder. There is a reserved band around the stems of the horizontal handles and the edge of the base.

[282] See discussion on Entry No.39.

[283] For the love of Hesperid see Gotze, in *JdI,* 63/4 (1948/9) 91-92. Thompson, *Hesperia* 21, (1952) 59.

[284] The Krannert Art Museum, University of Illinois, gift of Harlan E. Mour (70-8-4). Ann Perkins, in Moon, *Greek Vase-Painting,* 177 No.100. Robertson, *A History of Greek Art,* 375 (top) and n.35, p.685.

[285] For Pompeian painting (House 1.7.7.). Maiuri, *Mon.d.Pitt* 3,ii, 2 pl.A.

[286] Rome, Villa Albani inv. - Nr.100. For this relief of Pit see Gotze, *RM* 53 (1938), 220 ff., pl.37,1. *Idem, Jdl,* 63-4 (1948-9) 95 ff. fig.5. Thompson, *Hesperia* 21 (1952), 69, pl.17,C.

[287] See Note 281.

[288] Reinach *R.A.* 1900, Part I, 87 f., illustrated in P.93. FR II 59, fig.29, Jacobsthal, *Ornament* 128, 192, pl.131.

[289] Jacobsthal, *ibid,* pl.131, a.

[290] Schefold, *KV,* 22, pl.7, a.

[291] Walters H.B. *CVA,* London 6, P.6. Smith, *Catalogue* III, 180 E 228. Metzger *Represent.*, 120.

Subject: Dionysos, Ariadne and Thiasos.

In the centre, Dionysos sits, or rather leans back, in three-quarter view. A female figure with a wreath, probably Ariadne, stands, or leans against him, with her left arm passing under his left, in front of his body. He appears to be touching, or drawing, her head towards him with his right hand. Dionysos wears a richly embroidered costume; a mid calf-length chiton (misinterpreted by Walters, Smith and Metzger as trousers, *anaxyrides*[292]), and jerkin: a sleaved tunic under a panther skin cloak. He wear ornamented, long boots fastened in front. He sits on his himation. A thyrsos rests against his right arm, its upper section is reserved and the lower black with reserved borders. Ariadne has flowing hair and wears a long-belted chiton underneath a himation. To the right, behind Ariadne, a female figure moves to the left, playing on a tympanum held in the left hand. The tympanum is decorated with stars and a wave pattern.

This woman is only partly covered in a himation, leaving the upper part of her body bare. Her hair is drawn back and held by a fillet. She wears earrings, a beaded necklace armlet (bracelet), and shoes. Her flesh is painted white. The artist has mistakenly placed her feet in front of Pan - she is supposed to be behind the seated god, who plays the "trigonon", a triangular harp[293]. A similarly shaped instrument can be found on a volute-krater by the "Sisyhos Painter" in Munich, and two lebetes gamikoi by the Washington Painter in New York[294]. The frame of the trigonon, like the tympanum, is decorated with a wave pattern. Pan is bearded, with shaggy hair falling in ringlets. The lower part of his body is wrapped in a himation.

To the right, above the right horizontal handle, there is a winged female figure, on a smaller scale, completely wrapped in the himation that envelopes her body and both arms. It also covers her head and mouth; only eyes and fringe are shown. She appears to be dancing to the sound of the music, while looking in the direction of the central figures.

To the left, immediately next to Dionysos and Ariadne, is the seated figure of Aphrodite, in three-quarter view. Her hair is bound in a chequered *sphendone*. Some of her hair escapes in curls and ringlets around her ears. She wears a belted chiton and sits on a himation, wrapped around the lower half of her body. Part of this himation extends up over her left side and drapes over the left shoulder. She holds a tympanum, in her left hand, vertically placed on her thigh. This instrument is decorated with a star and dotted lozenges; a young Eros stands on its edge. He is shown with short hair, held up in a fillet. Eros looks down at Dionysos, apparently fanning the god with the palmette-like fan ("flabellum") he holds in his left hand. Behind the seated female, a youthful Pan, with goat horns, ears and tail, plays on a syrinx pipe (σύριγξ). He is partly nude, with his cloak hanging from his left shoulder, falling to the left thigh and knee. Behind the standing Pan, at a higher level, above the left horizontal handle, there is another Pan figure. He is short, bearded, with shaggy hair. He has goat legs and ears, and has a hide over his back. Like the veiled, winged female to the right, he is dancing to the music. In his left hand he holds an oinochoe, that is probably full of wine from the calyx-krater beneath him. Smith and Mitzger classify this vessel as a pithos[295].

One important side of Dionysos' character has its expression in Greek Art, epitomized as Dionysos-Melpomenos, God of Music, who loves the wild, pathos-filled voices of wind instrument[296]. Our fragment appears to illustrate Dionysos' cult association with musical and dramatic arts. Two types of instrument are represented on the vase. The first is a wind instrument, the syrinx pipe, the other the stringed harp. Another instrument favoured by the god is the lyre. On the London cup, by the Meleager Painter[297], the god is seen carrying a tortoise-shell lyre.

Although most of the thiasos representation shows the participants moving in a violent dance, our vase was meant to show a peaceful group in meditative pose. Dionysos here is dressed as a Thracian, in a sleeved jerkin, perhaps suggesting the god's, non-Greek, origin[298].

The winged female figure seen above the horizontal handle to the right is not without interest; there is a mystery concerning her appearance. Erika Simon has interpreted her as Parthenos, occasionally found in association with Pan[299]. Webster has challenged Smith's suggestion (supported by Metzger[300]), that this winged and veiled figure may represent Echo. He prefers her as Night (μελανόπτερος) [301]. Although this interpretation is the more favoured, an interpretation as Echo might not be out of the question. Echo seems to suit the whole atmosphere of music and sound as represented on our hydria. However, the example cited by Webster for comparison is not applicable here. The Taranto lekythos represents the male figure "Sleep", in the form of a small, winged boy[302]. Our fragment, however, shows the winged female "Night"[303].

Karouzou has confirmed the interpretation in relation to the representation of Night on a lekythos from Odos Pandrosou,

[292] See previous Note 291.

[293] For this type of instrument see Wegner, *Das Musikleben der Griechen,* 47 fl.

[294] New York 07.286.35 and New York 16. 73. Richter and Hall, 182 f. pl.146. *ARV* 1126, 1 and 6. Wegner, *op. cit.* pl.23. See also the volute-krater in Munich, 32 68. Wegner, *op. cit.* 232, pl.22 (lebes gamikos).

[295] See Note 291.

[296] Farnell, *The Cult of the Greek States,* 143 f.

[297] Stemless cup, London British Museum E 129. *ARV* 1414, 82. *HGVP,* 382 f.

[298] Harrison, *Prolegomena,* 373.

[299] Simon, *JdI* 76 (1961), 165 f.

[300] Smith, *op. cit.* 180 f. 228. Metzger, *op. cit.* 120.

[301] Stated in his review of Metzger H., *Les representation.* In *JHS* 73, (1953), 186.

[302] *ÖJh* 38, 1-2. *ÖJh* 41, 78-81. *ARV* 560,5. Illustrated in Belli, *Il Tresoro Di Taras,* 160-161 (near the Pan Painter).

[303] For a general discussion on such representations see Karouzou, in *LIMC* II, 904 ff., but especially 906 no.6. *Idem, JHS* 65 (1945) 43 ff.,Yalouris, *AJA* 84 (1980), 316 f.

coming from the workshop of the Icarus Painter[304]. Night is portrayed walking quietly to the left. From her face down she seems to be completely wrapped in a himation over a chiton. This is repeated on another lekythos by the Tymbos Painter in Athens[305]. Here as well, Night is wrapped in a himation over a chiton. On both lekythoi the figures' arms are concealed within the himation. Our vase is the only one to show Night completely covered and veiled. The tradition continued into Roman and later times[306]. Indeed, our closest parallel is in the terracotta figurines of the Hellenistic period, where representations of completely veiled and covered dancing girls is very common[307].

Like the other hydria in London (BM E 229; No. 42, pl. 42, 1)[308], our vase can be placed stylistically near the Helena Painter. There are distinct similarities between the two hydriae. The scenes on both vessels are tranquil ones. Eros is in an identical pose on both examples, looking down at the central figure. Compare also the position of the head of the female figure (with the tympanum) on our hydria with Helen's head on the London vase (BM E 229). Compare also our vessel's treatment of the drapery folds on the female figure seated next to Dionysos with those of the figure sitting on the far right of London BM 229, and also with Helen's on the Munich krater[309] (located near the Helena Painter's work). Of what remains of the palmette decoration, I think that the arrangement on the reverse of both vases in London may have been similar: note the spiral below the standing figure on the right of London E 229 to the spiral on our hydria.

Another work attributed to the Helena Painter is the painting on a hydria in the Hermitage, portraying the story of Paris and Helen[310]: nine figures are arranged in a very similar way as those on our hydria. The two women behind Paris recall, in style, Aphrodite, who sits next to Dionysos. The cloaked woman above the handle is a copy of the winged female figure on our vase. The profile of the face and the way the hair is seen escaping underneath the head covering, are identical features on the two figures of both vases.

The same hand did not necessarily paint London E 228 and E 229: hydria E 228 appears to be finer, with more careful execution. Such fine detail and elaboration are to be found in works as late as the middle of the century represented by the work of the Marsyas Painter, and other artists connected with him. This is the period when the Kerch style reached its peak, and many of its masterpieces may be assigned to this period[311].

[304] Karouzou, *JHS* 65 (1945) 43, pl.VII,a (Athens, National Museum).

[305] Athens, National Museum 17761. *ARV* 756,61. Karouzou, *op. cit.* pl.VII, b.

[306] Karouzou, *op. cit.* 44. Roscher, *ML* s.v. NYX 574-575 fig.1-2.

[307] After Weege, *Der Tanz in der Antike,* 63f., fig.82 (S. Sabourff II, Taf 139).

[308] See discussion on next Entry No.52.

[309] Calyx-krater, Munich, Museum Antiker Kleinkunst, 2388. Ghali-Kahil, *Enlevement,* pl.22. *HGVA,* 385, no.223.

[310] Hermitage St. 1924 FR II, 72, pl.79,2, Schefold, *KV*, pl.2,b. *UKV* 20, no.159, fig 22. Metzger *Represent.,* 280 no.35. Ghali-Khahil, *op. cit.* 171 f. pl. XVIII, 1.

[311] For the painting of the period see Richter, *Attic Red-Figured Vases,* 159 ff. Robertson, *A History of Greek Art,* 435.

The Eleusinian Painter, whose style is not very dissimilar to that of our piece, favoured crowded compositions showing assemblies of gods and heroes, seated or active, sometimes with a central drama, but the overall effect is static. On one of the artist's two pelikai in Leningrad[312], below the central scene and in a style similar to that of our piece, there is a band of sets of four meanders, separated by chequered squares. But the composition on our fragment is less crowded by comparison. The Helena Painter (The Pompe Painter), who is probably earlier than the Eleusinian Painter, used a similar style with nicely composed subjects with fewer figures. As with our fragment, the painting is extremely delicate, carefully drawn with very fine lines. The artist's work is represented by an Oinochoe and skyphos in New York[313]. There are several features on these that make the style of painting comparable to that on our fragment. The garment of the standing women on the skyphos has similar ornamentation to that worn by Dionysos.

The hairstyle of the women, as well as the treatment of the satyr's beard is close. The thrysos has heart-shaped leaves. Our piece, while looking back at the style and modes of late fifth and early fourth centuries, is definitely a mature Kerch work in its style and execution, painted by an artist probably active during the last years of the second quarter of the fourth century. It is contemporary, perhaps, with the Helena Painter.

52. Hydria, Type II [Kalpis] London BM E 229 (Plate 42, 1)

H. 30 cm.

The neck, shoulder and entire reverse of the vase are missing.

White, with details in brown, is used for the flesh of Eros. A dilute is used for hair, details of the decoration on cushions and drapery folds. Gilding on raised ground for jewellery. Egg-and-dot pattern on reserved band below the scene encircling the whole vase.

Subject: The Toilet of Helen.

In the centre of the scene, Helen sits on a four-legged couch that is covered with embroidered cloth. Two decorated cushions are placed on the two ends of the couch. Helen, apparently wearing a wreath, is dressed in a long chiton, with a himation wrapped around her legs and up to her shoulder from the back. She sits in three-quarter view with her head turned to the left, as if in deep thought. Above her, to the left, a winged Eros hovers with his feet touching the left cushion. He looks down at Helen. Behind Helen is a pair of folding doors, shown partly open. To the right of the picture, again

[312] i) Leningrad (St.1792), *ARV* 1476, 1. Metzger, *Represent.,* pl.34,2, pl.8.3. *Idem, Recherches,* pl.24. Simon, *Antike Kunst,* 72 ff.
ii) Leningrad (St.1793), *ARV* 1476, 2. Metzger, *Represent.,* pls.36,1, 15,1. Simon, *op. cit.* 73-74, pl.19,3.

[313] i) Oinochoe, New York 25.190. Richter and Hall, *Vases in the Metropolitan Museum,* No.169, pl.164 Richter, *Survey* 161. Schefold, *KV* pl.10. Arias, Hirmer, Shefton, *HGVP,* no.224.
ii) Skyphos, New York 06.1021.181. Richter and Hall, *op. cit.* No.170, pl.165. Schefold, *op. cit.* pl.9.

behind Helen, stands Aphrodite clad only in a himation with her torso and right arm bare. She, too, looks in the direction of Helen. Next to her is the lower part of a male sitting to the left. This part figure is also wrapped in a himation, and, probably like the latter woman, the upper part of the body is bare. To the far right are the feet of a standing male figure, Paris perhaps. A standing woman, dressed in a long chiton and himation, balances him to the far right. He also looks at Athena. Helen and her companion wear earrings, necklaces and armlets (these are gilded on raised ground).

The scene does not seem to be a cheerful one. On the contrary, Helen appears pensive and distressed. This is reflected in the posture and expression of the faces of Eros and Helen's companions.

Beazley places this vase, and the London example (E 230), in one group (Group of London, E 230)[314]. There is a lot in common between this hydria and the Munich calyx-krater from the Munich Group, 2388[315] (370 B.C.), especially on side A, where similar treatments were applied to the drapery, shoes, and the figure poses. Schefold, however, attributes our vase to the follower of his Hippolytus Painter[316]. This hydria has to be dated to 370-360 B.C.

53. *Hydria, Type II [Kalpis]* London BM E 241[317] (Plate 43, 1-3)

H. 29 cm

White was used, with yellowish details, for the flesh. Gilded details. Red for wreaths, pink and blue for drapery. Hair drawn in a fine brown line in brown wash. Egg-patterns below the design and around the lip. A palmette below each side handle. On the reverse an elaborate pattern composed of six palmettes.

Subject: The Adonia.

A ladder rests in the foreground of the central scene; a woman pauses on the third rung as she descends. She scatters something (grain) into the vessel that is being held up to her by a woman with plaits around her head. A tall plant with berries grows to the right of the ladder, beside which a woman, muffled in a mantle, dances to the music of the flute, or autos, played by a woman behind and Eros, who flutters between the two women on the right. Two mantled dancers respond to the music. Beyond, another woman dances and clicks her castanets. A small Pan figure is seen dancing on the upper left.

The subject of this vase is repeated on the two lekythoi. The first, from Apollonia in Thrace, is now in Berlin, and the second can be found in the Hermitage Museum[318]. The scene on the Berlin lekythos shows Aphrodite, and the woman with the vessel, in poses identical to those on our hydria in the British Museum. Eros floats above the small vessel, and a large themlaterion, on the Hermitage lekythos). But we notice that, instead of Aphrodite, it is Eros descending the ladder. And, again, it is Eros, not Aphrodite, who is seen throwing the grain into the small vessel held by the woman standing to the left of the ladder. Here Aphrodite sits behind her, while other women play various musical instruments.

Principal vase scenes showing women climbing ladders were long considered to be depicting incense gathering, as part of an Epaulia scene. These vases include an epinetron by the Ereteria Painter, and a lebes gamikos by the Athens Painter 1455 (both in Athens), and a fragment of a lebes gamikos in the Louvre, also by the Athens Painter 1455[319].

Such opinions were held from the middle of the 19th century, beginning with Otto-Jahn and Jean de Witte, who discussed the matter in an exchange of letters in the Annali (1845)[320]. Smith also described the scene on our hydria in such terms. Furtwangler, Nickle and Schefold held similar opinions also. All take the view that the scene on these vases represents women gathering incense. Cook commented: "Not improbably, the gatherer mounted the ladder as a symbol of the celestial nature of such harvesting"[321].

F. Hauser, in 1909, was the first to interpret and recognise the scene as a celebration of the Adonia[322]. He went on to assemble a series of vases, from the late fifth through to the mid-fourth centuries, all showing women assembled around a ladder, which to him signified the activities of the cult of Adonis. He interpreted the ladder as a reference to the act of transporting pots and flowers to the roof. N. Weill has also collected a series of Adonis scenes from the mid-fifth to the mid-fourth century B.C. Hauser accepted that the prominent woman on the ladder, or seated close to it, was, in fact, assuming the role of Aphrodite in a rite associated with Adonis. That it is the goddess herself on the vases is confirmed by the presence of Eros. That she has associated with Adonis is, indeed, indicated, by an inscription found at Piraeus, dated

[314] *ARV* 1481 1,2. Munich 2388. Schefold, *UKV*, 23, No.172. Ghali-Kahil, *op. cit.* 167, no.227, pl.XVIII. Arias, Hirmer, Shefton, *HGVP*. Metzger, *Represent*.

[315] Munich 2388, *ARV* 1448,1. Metzger, *Represent.*, 48, 28V *HGVP*.

[316] Schefold, *UKV*, 23, No.172 a. Ghali-Kahil, *Les Enlevement*, 167, no.127.

[317] Nicole, *Meidias*, 150. Cook, *Zeus* II 124. *CVA*, London, VI pl.95,4, Schefold, *KV*, pl.519, *idem*, *UKV* No.181, pl.19,2. Metzger, *Represent.*, 94, no.43, pl.VII,5. *ARV* 1482,1.

[318] Both vases are reported respectively in Metzger, *Represent.*, 93, no.44 and 45 pl.VII/3,4. Nicole, *Meidias* (Supplement) pl.VIII 5,6. Cooker, *Zeus* 11, 124 pl.VII 1. Schefold, *UKV*, no.290, 292, figs.32, 34. pls.19,1/18, 1,2.

[319] Epinetron, Athens 1629. *ARV* 1250, 34. *LIMC* 1, pl.399. Simon and Hirmer, pl.218. Lebes gamikos, Athens 1454. *ARV* 1178, 1. Weil, *BCH* 90 (1966), 669. Nicole, *Meidias*, 145. Brueckner, *AM* 32 (1907) pl.5,2. Fragment of lebes gamikos, Louvre, CA 1679. *ARV*. 1179, 3 Addenda 167. Nicole, *Meidias* pl.9; pl.8,2. Deubner, pl.25. Weil, *op. cit.* 668 f. fig.4; B. Servais-Soyez in *LIMC* I 227, no.46 pl.169, Adonis.

[320] O. Jahn, "Sur les representations d'Adonis. Lettre a M.S.DE Witte", *Ann Inst.* 1845, 347-358. J de Witte "Sur les representation d'Adonis. Lettre a M.O. Jahn, *Ann Inst.* 1845, 387-418. (The reference is taken from Metzger, *Represent.*, 95, n.1).

[321] Smith, *Vases in the British Museum,* 186 no.241 and 355 no.721. F.R. II 98 f. Nicole, *Meidias,* 149-150. Schefold, *UKV*, 154. Cook, *Zeus*, II 124 n.1.

[322] Hauser, *ÖJh* 12 (1909) 90 ff. Weill, *BCH*, 90 (1960) 564 f. Metzger seems to reject the possibility of any depiction of the cult on vases of the fifth century.

302-301 B.C., in which mention is made of a thiasos of the Syrian Aphrodite, rewarding one Stephanos for enacting "the procession of the Adonia" according to the old usage[323]. Such an explanation appears to have been accepted by Beazley, and to also have been acknowledged by Cook and Metzger[324]

The festival of Adonia is confined to women lamenting the dying god Adonis. It included women mourning, followed by rejoicing at the god's rebirth. The cult is Semitic, and its origin can be traced back to Byblos and Cyprus. It also resembles the Syro-Mesopotamian, Dumuzi-Tammuz cult[325].

In that the god's death corresponds to the dying of nature in summer, the Adonia were celebrated at the time of Tammuz (June/July). This coincides with Theopharastus' remark that the Gardens of the Adonia were sown in the summer, and cultivated when the sun was at its most powerful (Theophrastus, *HP*, 7, 3).

The Alexandria festival is described by Theocritus (Idyll. 15), where the rite consisted of a magnificent celebration of the wedding of Adonis and Aphrodite. Women carried his image the following day to the seashore amid much lamentation.

It was, however, from Cyprus that the cult was brought during the fifth century to Athens, where Adonis was identified with Eros. The cult existed in conjunction with rites to Aphrodite, where Athenian women placed pots of flowers and herbs (the Gardens of Adonia or 'κήποι') on their flat rooftops, in celebration of the god[326]. The Adonia, therefore, is a women's cult. The activities included music, dancing, and the burning of incense. Metzger's suggestion that the rituals represented the celebrations following Adonis' mourning, appears to have been accepted[327].

The second half of the fifth century witnessed the interest of painters in the representation of Adonia. Some of these have already been mentiond[328], and two more examples may be included here. The first is a fragment from Argos by the Melthyse Painter, and the second a hydria by the Meidias Painter. Both vases are in Athens[329].

From the scenes on these vases, two separate phases of the festival can be recognised. In the first phase the women climb the ladder to the roof and arrange their pot plants in such a way that they are fully exposed to the burning sun. This can be seen on a squat lekythos in New York[330]. A woman, partly uncovered, climbs a ladder. As she does so, she turns around to receive from Eros a pot filled, perhaps, with earth. This pot was unidentified by Richter, who described it as a funnel-shaped vase[331]. On the floor, and also higher up, there are two larger pots with ring handles. These are the perfume burners usually found on fourth-century vases on similar scenes. The funnel-shaped pot is, in fact, the mouth, neck and shoulder, inverted, of a wine-amphora of the painted kind used for storage, but used here as a flower pot, or 'garden' for Adonis, taken to the rooftop. The other two pots are perfume burners.

This interpretation is confirmed by a similar representation on a second squat lekythos in Carlsruhe, painted by a follower of the Meidias Painter (390 B.C.)[332]. It is clear here that the pot handed by Eros to the woman on the ladder, is actually the upper part of a broken amphora. The other half may still be seen on the floor, waiting to be lifted up[333]. Both vases were used for incense planting, seen sprouting from the tops of each of them. The perfume-burner, or thymiaterion, may be seen behind Eros. Women can be seen on either side of the central scene, their hands raised in surprise.

In the second phase of the festival the women climb down the ladder, bringing the myrrh and frankincense to fuel the incense burners in honour of Aphrodite and her lover, and to provide the devotees of Adonis with perfumes and seducing ointments[334].

Representations of this phase of the festival are found on a number of fourth century Greek vases; our hydria is perhaps the most important among them. In all these scenes, the ladder appears to be central to the theme, constituting the main link in these paintings. Three principal figures can be recognized: one brings the incense down from above, the second receives the items, and the third fuels the incense-burner (situated near the foot of the ladder). In one example, Eros is shown holding out the perfume-burner (or thymiaterion).

Mrs. Brouskari understood the scenes to be representations of mourning and lamentation[335]. Metzger adds that the scents used were either grains of frankincense or leaves of myrrh. He rightly interprets the paintings as joyful scenes: "Les 'jardins' transportés sur le toit, la jeune femme qui s'est chargeé de cette mission, redescend à l'interieur de la maison et son retour est le signal de fêtes chorégraphiques et musicales: il lui reste à déposes les grains d'encens du sacrifice dans une coupe qui a été prepareé d'avance et c'est le moment précis qui les imeglers attiques ont choisi de representer"[336].

[323] I.G., II-III², 1261, 9. Quoted by Deubner, *Attische Fest*, 222 n.6 and Richter and Hall, 220 n.10.

[324] Beazley, *JHS* 47 (1927) 230. Cook, *Zeus* III, Addenda 1118. Metzger, *Represent.*, 94f.

[325] Burkert, *Greek Religion* 177. In classical literature the father of Adonis is mentioned as Phoinix (Hes. Fr. 139) and also as Kinyras, of Paphos in Cyprus (Appollod.3.182). On the origin see Burkert, *op. cit.*177.

[326] Deubner, *Attische Feste,* 220 ff.

[327] Metzger, *Represent.*, 95-99. Attallah, *Adonis,* 191. Brouskari, *The Acropolis,* 119.

[328] See note 322.

[329] i) Athens 19522. Weil, *BCH* 90 (1966), 665. *Paralip,* 400.

ii) Athens 1179. Nicole, *Medias* pl.4.Wein, *op. cit.* 673, fig.5. *ARV* 1313,2.

[330] New York 22.139.26. Richter and Hall, 219, no.173, pl.168.

[331] Richter and Hall, *op. cit.* 219 f.

[332] Karlsruhe. B 39 (278). *CVA,* Karlsruhe 2 pl.27 (325). Hauser, *ÖJh* 12 (1909), 91-92. Metzger, *Represent.*, 91 no.41 B. Servais-Soyez in *LIMC* I, 227 no.47. Adonia, pl.169 (Berard), *La cité des images*, 93 fig.131.

[333] See Beazley's identification of the pot in *JHS* 47, (1927), 230.

[334] Detienne, *The Gardens of Adonis,* 991 ff.

[335] Brouskari, *The Acropolis Museum,* 119.

[336] Metzger, *op. cit.* 97 f.

The descending figure, Eros, or the woman, places the grain, or incense, in a small bowl usually offered out by another woman. This is a deep dish with a base and removable ring handles that fold down when not in use. Among the treasures of ancient Macedonia, there is a similar small bronze bowl, or phiale, dated to the fifth century[337]. This has two removable handles with a palmette attachment. The vessel, a multi-purpose shape, 9.7cm high and with a diameter of 23cm, is a very appropriate size for the festival of the Adonia.

Of the group of vases Schefold calls the "Apollonia Group", three, including our hydria, show Adonia themes[338]. These are closely associated, but appear to have been painted by different hands. Nearest of these to our hydria is the name piece of the group in Berlin, where a semi-nude Aphrodite descends the ladder. All the other features appear on the vase, including the covered dancing women.

Our hydria, like the London BM E 228[339], is probably related to those of either the Hellena or Eleusinian Painters. It shares with those the excellent fine line drawing, and, as with BM E 228, it is less crowded and depicts fewer figures in a perfect composition. The semi-nude figure of Aphrodite, shown descending the ladder, and the woman presenting the vessel, constitute the central element of the scene. These are balanced by a few figures, two on each side of the ladder. Each of these is either dancing or playing a musical instrument, and the joyful atmosphere is shared by the small figures of Eros and Pan. Both appear to be convenient 'extras' in the composition of the total scene, in which all the figures are beautifully arranged and carefully balanced.

Our hydria must be contemporary with the hydria in London, E 228. Both vases have similar profiles and identical bases. The hair treatment is similar. The dancing Pan on E 228 is repeated here on E 241 at the same location, over the left horizontal handle. Moreover, the arrangement of the palmette decoration on the reverse is not dissimilar on both hydriae. The inspiration must have been taken from a single reportoir. The design consists of two large palmettes under the vertical handle. The space between these and the horizontal handles is occupied by two large palmettes on each side. There is also a single, large palmette under each horizontal handle. The remaining space is taken up with either small palmettes, or delicate spirals and other filling ornamentation[340].

London E 241 is likely to be contemporary with E 228, executed perhaps during the latter part of the second quarter of the fourth century[341].

54. *Hydria, Type II [Kalpis]*, London BM E 230[342] (Plate 44, 1-2)

H. 31 cm.

Egg-pattern around the overhanging rim.

Above and below the scene there are bands of egg-and-dot pattern. White is used for Eros' flesh, diluted for other details of hair and garments.

On the reverse, there are two large palmettes at the shoulder. Below the vertical handle two similar ones, one pointing up, the other pointing down; these are surrounded by petals and spirals. Below each horizontal handle there is another palmette.

Main Scene

The Toilet of Aphrodite: In the centre, a stool (diphros), its legs shown in perspective. To the right of it the goddess Aphrodite appears to be removing her chiton over her head. There is a broad band (στρόφιον) around her breast. She also wears shoes and earrings. Her hair is plaited. Facing her is a woman in a long chiton with short hair. She holds out her hands to receive the garment. Between them, above the stool, Eros flies forward to assist Aphrodite with the task. On the right stands another woman, a servant, in long chiton with overfull saccos and earrings. She holds up a square box and a long sash. To balance her on the left, a satyr stands in an attitude of astonishment at the beautiful scene.

An alternative interpretation of the scene might be that this is a nuptial scene, where a bride is preparing herself for the wedding. There are a number of elements that might support this. A woman approaching with a box, from which a sash hangs, Eros and the stool, are all elements usually found in connection with a nuptial scene[343].

The presence of the satyr is hard to determine; he has nothing to do with the subject, which is supposed to be a private affair, taking place in the women's quarters. He is probably used here as a frame to the scene, and to balance the woman holding the box.

A similar representation with a satyr present is to be found on a lekythos in Baltimore of a slightly later date (360-350 B.C.). Aphrodite is shown sitting on a stool surrounded by attendants and companions. Two satyrs are placed between

---

337 *Treasurers of Ancient Macedonia* (Archaelogical Museum of Thessaloniki 1979), 82, no.337, pl.44.

338 i) Squat lekythos in Berlin from Apollonia. Berlin inv 3248. Schefold, *UKV*, pl.19,1 and fig.32. Cook, *Zeus* II Pl.7b. *ARV* 1482, 5. Addenda 192. *LIMC* 1, pl.170, Adonis 48. Metzger, *op. cit*. Pl.VII,3.

ii) Squat lekythos in Leningrad from Apollonia. Leningrad 928 (inv.20.24). Schefold, *UKV*, pl.18. Cook, *Zeus* II, pl.7a. *ARV* 1482,6 (Berard), *La cité des images*, 94, fig.134.

339 See entry no.51.

340 Jacobsthal, *Ornamente*, 128, 163, 194, pl.131,b.

341 I also believe this is probably the date for the red-figured skyphos published by Brouskari M. in *The Acropolis Museum* description catalogue (Athens 1974) 119, fig.230-231 (1960-Nak 222). The vase illustrates the festival of Adenia. Here the poses of the figures and the style of the palmettes and other ornaments is not dissimilar to that of London E 241; it is even more close to the two squat lekythoi in Berlin and Leningrad that were placed together with the London E 241 in one group (The Apollonia Group). See note 22. On the skyphos the scene is framed on the top by a chain of laurel leaves as on the Berlin lekythos. The bottom is described with alternate clockwise meander with chequer boards. This skyphos can be included with the Apollonia Group and is dated the second quarter of the fourth century B.C.

342 London, BM E 230. Smith, *Catalague of Greek & Etruscan Vases in the British Museum*, 181. *CVA*, London, 6, pl.97,2, 1481,2.

343 Roberts, *The Attic Pyxis*, 184.

the figures, sitting on a rock. They are passive and appear only to be scene-fillers[344].

The vase, together with London E 229, also from Cyrenaica, were grouped by Beazley as the London Group E 230[345], and attributed by Schefold to the Hippolytos Painter. But while we can date London E 229 to the last ten years of the second quarter of the fourth century, I feel that London E 230 appears to be much earlier in date: it is much smaller in shape and with a slightly different profile. While E 230 is triangular, what remains of E 229 appears rather to be oval. But most significant for any comparison, is the palmette and floral pattern that decorates the reverse of hydria E 230. The palmette arrangement is excellent. Two palmettes occupy the space below the vertical handle. One points upward towards the handle's lower section and another down towards the band of egg-and-dot pattern that circles the lower section of the body. Spirals, lotus flowers, and other filling ornaments, are symmetrically placed to the right and left of the design. Such an arrangement was the favourite of the Shuvalov Painter during the third quarter of the fifth century. An oinochoe in Ferrara (from Spina), by the artist bears a very similar design[346]. The same design is copied on an oinochoe in Berlin that belongs to the later years of the fifth (and early years of the fourth) century[347]. An oinochoe in New Orleans, in the manner of the Nikias Painter (400 B.C.), also features the same design[348]. The painting on our hydria is similar to that later Oinochoe, but with minor differences. The artist added two large palmettes to the shoulder. His source of inspiration must have been an earlier work of the first quarter of the fourth century, for such a design was never encountered on the vases of the second quarter of the fourth century. This is the accepted date for the London E 229. There seems, therefore, little justification for Beazley's placing of the two vases (E 229 and E 230) in one group. The painting on our hydria (E 230) was carried out, perhaps, during the first decade of the second quarter of the fourth century.

55. *Hydria "Kalpis"* Louvre N 3371 = (MN 718) (Plata 45, 1-2)

H. 0.185 cm.

A small hydria[349] with an elongated neck (exactly one third of the height of the hydria) that flares downwards and upwards reaching a wide, spreading mouth. The mouth has a raised upper section, with sloping, overhanging lips. The two side-handles twist sharply towards the shoulder, perhaps indicating that their function is ornamental rather than functional (for lifting). The vase sits on a wide, flat, ogee base that emulates the mouth in shape and size. Two grooves mark the sides. The side of the base, and the section where it joins the body, are reserved. The rest of the body is glazed black.

Above and below the figure scene there is a band of tongues. Relief lines were used for the woman's hands, the border of her face, arms, and feet of the Erotes. Dilute colour for the figure's hair and outline of the woman's chiton.

Subject: Aphrodite and Erotes.

The goddess, who is presented with face in three-quarter view, wears a chiton and adorns herself with bracelets, necklace, and earrings. Her hair is held up by an elaborate, chequer-patterned fillet and a triangular scarf in a palmette design. The goddess pulls up, or adjusts the edge of her garment, with her left hand. Two diminutive Erotes, placed symmetrically, hover around the edges. The one on the right is landing on the index finger of her left hand. As face of the goddess is not in profile, the presentation of her scarf appears rather awkward to the viewer. The painter wanted to have the face in three-quarter view and showed the side section of the scarf. The goddess is painted large-scale, her bust filling the available space on the hydria.

Up until now there has been no attempt to examine this hydria, interpret the subject, consider its style, and consequently date it. Although N. Plautine classes the painting as an Attic work, Beazley does not include it in his *ARV* catalogue[350]. Metzger must have known about its existence, but chose to ignore it.

At first glance, one might be justified in interpreting the subject on our hydria as the birth of Aphrodite: she appears to be emerging from below. While her bust is fully presented, the elbow of her right arm, and part of the left arm, are not shown, giving the impression that the goddess is in the process of rising up.

A hydria in Brussels by the Herakles Painter[351], has the large head of Aphrodite in front of two hovering Erotes, flanked by two satyrs. The subject of this hydria, and indeed other vases with similar representations, appears to be different from that of our hydria. While Eros (or the Erotes) is frequently shown hovering around the head of the goddess, other figures are always fully presented standing on the ground. These may be maidens waiting to receive and dress the goddess, or satyrs, standing armed with great mallets, or hammers, ready to strike at the rising head[352].

The goddess on our pelike (given her pose, and flanked by small Erotes) does not seem to be emerging from below. She

344 Baltimore, Walters Art Gallery 48-54. *LIMC* II, 30, No.191.

345 *ARV* 1481,1 & 2. Schefold, *UKV*, 23, 88-90 and 159 nos.172, 174 Pls.12, 1-2 (Gahli Kahil, *Les Enlevements*, 67 pl.18), 13, 3-4. For London cf. *BM*, 229. See Entry No.52.

346 Ferrara T 264. Alfieri *Spina*, 102, fig.252. Tezzi Hafter, *Der Schuvalow-Maler*, 111,58, pl.162 (012,013).

347 Berlin, F.2651, illustrated in Jacobsthal, *Ornament* pl.83. Dated by Metzger to early fourth century, (*Represent.*, 338 no.69) but placed by Lezzi-Hafter earlier, in the time of the Ereteria Painter (*Der Schuwalow-Maler*, 38 n.157).

348 An oinochoe from the Collection of the New Museum of Arts, Gifts of Alvin. P. Howard (16.11). Published in *Greek Vases from Southern Collection*, (New Orleans Museum of Art and Tulane University 1981).

349 Louvre N 3/371 - MN 718. *CVA*, IX, 44, pl.55, 15-16.

350 Plautine in Louvre. *CVA*, IX, 44 f., pl.54, nos.15,16.

351 Brusselles, R 286. *ARV* 1472,4. Schefold, *UKV* pl.1. Metzger, *Represent.*, pl.4,2. Berard, *Anodoi* 44, pl.7,25.

352 For such a representation on vases see the list of *LIMC* II (s.v.Aphorodite) 114 f. no.1170-1182, pls.117-118.

is not looking upwards, as she usually does when she is represented as rising from the underworld. With her head shown in three-quarter view, what we have is more of a portrait, or rather an abbreviation of a fully represented Aphrodite. Similar depictions in other forms of Greek art are readily available.

The series of Caryatid mirrors that was produced in the second half of the fifth century provides a comparable representation. On a mirror in Paris[353], the area between the cradle that supports the mirror's disc and the Caryatid is filled by two winged Erotes suspended from the cradle. They are hovering, ready to touch the Caryatid's head. The representation on our pelike is not very dissimilar to these Caryatid figures, which are, incidentally, intended to represent Aphrodite[354]. Indeed, the goddess on our hydria may well be an abbreviation of this Caryatid mirror. If so the Providence representation on a gold medallion, dated to the second quarter of the fourth century, may also be interpreted as such[355]. The bust of the goddess projects forward, with her face in three-quarter view. She is flanked by the figure of Eros and another figure.

Dating this hydria is not an easy task. While the shape of the vase, with its squat body, elongated neck, and concave sides, is very common during the second quarter of the fourth century, the composition of subject and style of painting indicate an earlier date. We can trace the style in the first quarter of the fourth century, or even in the later years of the fifth. While some of the physical details of the Erotes' bodies were similarly used on male figures during the first quarter of the fourth century, the pose of the goddess, with its three-quarter view, as well as the hairstyle and scarf, are all reminiscent of the style of the Meidias Painter and his follower[356].

Our hydria appears to be a fourth-century work with a style of painting influenced by the work of the later years of the fifth century. It is safer, therefore, to give the vase the broad daring of the first half of the fourth century.

56. *Pelike* 746 Paris, Louvre N 3470 (MN 746) (Plate 46, 1)

Pelike with flaring neck, overhanging rim, moulded base. Added white colour for Aphrodite's face. Bands of egg-and-dot pattern on lip and around the body below the figure scene, and on the base of the neck.

Side A: Aphrodite's head in left profile. The face is partly painted white with no facial details. She is partially veiled and wears an embroidered sakkos on her head. To the left of the scene, the figure of Eros hovers over her head. To the right a female figure stands to the left, gesticulating towards the head and Eros. She is clad in a sleeveless chiton with simple fold.

Side B: Two youths facing one another.

There are two other vases very similar to the Cyrenaica pelike in composition. The first is in Lausanne[357]. It portrays the large head of Aphrodite, emerging from below, and facing the figure of Hermes, who presents a large alabastron to the goddess. The second hydria is in the Louvre[358]. On it we see the head and part of the shoulder of Aphrodite to the left. She holds a mirror in her right hand while Eros hovers in front of her head. This example is the nearest in composition to ours, and the goddess also appears to be emerging from below, whether from the waves of the sea, or underground, we do not know.

This pelike has already been attributed to Group G[359], and is dated, according to its shape, to the third quarter of the fourth century.

57. *Pelike* Paris Cab. Med. 411 (Plate 46, 2)

H. 18.5 cm

Pelike with flaring neck, overhanging rim, two-stage base. Added white colouration for Eros.

There is egg-and-dot patterning on the bands around the body, below the figure scene, and at the base of the neck.

Side A: A woman's head, with embroidered sakkos, in left profile. There is a rosette on her ear. She wears earrings and a necklace. Eros flies towards her with a mirror in his right hand. In the space between them are tendril designs and a tympanum.

Side B: Two cloaked youths face one another. The left-hand figure holds up a tympanum. The other extends his right arm to grasp a rounded object (a ball or disc).

The pelike has been attributed to Group G. Date: third quarter of the fourth century.

58. *Pelike* London BM F 11

H. 18 cm.

Size, profile and subject identical to that of previous entry (No.57).

---

[353] See for instance the Caryatid mirror in Paris, Louvre, inv. BC 1692. Congdon, *Caryatid Mirrors of the Ancient World,* 195 no,87 a, pl.82.

[354] Congdon, *ibid*, 18.

[355] Providence, Rhode Island School of Design 29.256. Amandry, *AJA*, 59, (1955), 219-222, pl.64. *LIMC* II, 112, No.1137, pl.113 (1137).

[356] The three-quarter view of the head is rare in the later years of the 5th and early 4th centuries. On the white ground lekythos in Athens (inv.1816, Group R, the Reed Painter, end of 5th century) a warrior is represented with body and head in three-quarter view (Louvre, 534 no.1.67. *CVA*, Athens (Papaspyridi) pl.18, 1-3; pl.17,2. *HGVP,* 396 pl.XLV). There is also the volute-krater in Ruvo (inv.1502, 68, The Talos Painter 400-390 B.C.). Medea's face is drawn in three-quarter view (*ARV* 1338, *para.* 481. Simon, *Die Griechische Vasen,* 154 f. fig.230. For the fourth century see Entry Nos.56, 57.

[357] Berard, *Anodoi*, 68 pl.7, fig.29.

[358] Louvre MN 719. Metzger, *Represent.*, 78. *Idem*.19 and Berard, *op. cit.* pl.7, fig.26.

[359] *ARV* 1468, 129.

The practice of painting a head in profile as the main decoration of a vase (as seen on Nos. 57-60) goes back at least to the seventh century B.C. It continued in Greece over the next two centuries[360]. By the fourth century the practice had become very common, and large numbers of small vases decorated in this manner have been found at Al Mina, Olynthus and elsewhere[361].

Von Vacano states that in the sixth century it was always the full figure of the gods that appeared to emerge from below, and that from the end of the sixth century onwards the head only seemed to emerge: signifying the rise from the Underworld[362]. Many of these heads appear to represent a benign and majestic maiden, or young woman. She is usually shown either in profile, three-quarter, or almost frontal view.

Representations of the female head or bust, whether in traditional or naturalistic form, appear in other fields of Greek arts, namely terracotta figurines and sculpture. The heads of many of these are represented with veiled faces, as on No.56. These are usually found as grave goods or above ground, used, no doubt, as votive or funerary offerings. Such representations were in demand from Cyprus to Italiote Kyme, and from Cyrene to the Crimea. Beyond the limits of the Greek world, Sardis, Carthage and Sardinia have yielded them up[363].

From Neapolis (Thrace) we have a small and richly painted terracotta figurine bust, representing a veiled maiden shown with both hands held close to her breast, probably holding a dove[364] From the sanctuary of Demeter and Kore at Serra Orlando (Area IV, Morgantina, Sicily), a bust of a maiden was found among material belonging to the third quarter of the fourth century. It is a less than life-size figure of a woman in a high-waisted chiton.

Morgantina has also produced considerable numbers of fully modelled protomes. Some of these are larger than life-size, others approximately so. The subjects are fully clothed and always face frontally, the arms cut off above the elbow[365].

The identity of the female head, or bust, is uncertain. H.R. Smith suggests that this sort of protome was meant to represent a consort of Zeus – Hera, Aphrodite, or Athena[366]. The representations have also been identified as Persephone, the daughter of Demeter, and this seems to have been confirmed by certain coins from Syracuse (end of the fifth century onwards). The head of Persephone became the most important of all Syracuse coin types, as she was worshipped as a bringer of fruitfulness and life, as much as for being the great deity of Death[367].

[360] Vacano, 14 ff. Schauenburg, *AA*, 1974, 149 ff.

[361] Woolley, *JHS* 58, (1938), 23 fig.8. Beazley, *JHS* 59 (1939) 26-7. *ARV* 1366-7. *Olynthus* XIII, pl.58 (43,44). For vases such as askoi and pelikai cf. Massei, *Gli askoi* 55 (3), 58 (1), 79 (1), 71 (2).

[362] Vacano, 122 f.

[363] For a discussion on the description see H.R.W. Smith in *Hesperia* (suppl.VIII, 1949), 355, Note 78.

[364] E 450,839, 449. Lazarides, *Neapolis*, 132 f.

[365] Zuntz, *Persephone*, 156.

[366] Smith, *op. cit.* 355.

[367] Hill, *Coins from Sicily*, 102, 157 pl.XI,4. Zuntz, *Persephone*, 157.

Female half-length figures and busts are frequently found standing in the graves of the Cyrene necropolis[368]. Most of these feature the upper mantle worn as a veil over the back of the head, some depict a veil drawn over part of the face, and a great number show only the smooth, curved, plane of the face (pl. 46, 3). It has been suggested that they represent a local goddess or even Persephone. Elizabeth Rosenbaum, who worked on Cyrenaican portrait sculpture, wrote of them as figures of mourning women[369]. They are dated to the fourth century and the custom for them appears to have extended into the Roman period[370].

For the identification of this emerging deity on the vase painting, we may choose between Pandora, Persephone and Aphrodite. As a model for the first, there are the certain representations on both black and red-figured vases. On a black-figured lekythos in Paris[371], the colossal head of a female is portrayed rising from the ground. Two men armed with great mallets or hammers are present: one of them strikes the rising head. An explanation for this scene may be found on an amphora in Oxford[372]. The design on this vase shows Pandora rising from the ground. Inscriptions near the figure reveal the identity of the goddess. She is shown rising with outstretched arms and, again, we have male figures with hammers standing next to Hermes.

On this representation, and other examples, Pandora is always depicted in the company of the deities clearly involved in her creation[373].

There is a tendency to interpret many of these female heads accompanied by Eros or the Erotes as the birth of Aphrodite, rather than the emergence of Persephone from the Underword. In fact many of these heads show a beauty that would associate them with Dione's daughter, and such a theory is augmented by the frequent presence of Eros or Erotes close to the Aphrodite representation. The significance of the goddess being regarded in this way has been demonstrated by H.R. Smith in his funerary Symbolism[374]; her head depicted in company with Eros would be highly appropriate[375].

[368] Discussed in connection with the Garamantian gravestones, by Elrashedy, *Garamantian Burial Customs,* 124 f.

[369] Rosenbaum, *A Catalogue of Cyrenaican Portrait Sculpture,* 14 f.

[370] Chamoux, *Cyrene sous la monarchie des Battiades,* 360.

[371] De Ridder, *Cab.Med* (Bibliotheque Nationale) and discussed by Fürtwangler, *JdI* (1891), 13. Harrison, *JHS* 19 (1899), 232. Gardiner, *JHS* (1951), 5.

[372] Gardiner, *JHS* 21 (190a) pl.1. Berard, *Anodoi,* 114 and pl.19,71.

[373] See the vases mentioned by Beazley in his list of mythological subjects in *ARV* under Pandora and Anesidora. There is an agreement between A.H. Smith [*JHS* 11 (1890), 278 f pl.XI-XII], C.H. Smith [*Catalogue,* 285 (E 467)], Beazley (*ARV* 601, 23, *para* 395, Addenda 130), Beck [Album pl.61.316 (BC)], Metzger (*Represent.,* (73), and Fulvio Canciani (*LIMC* I, 790 f. no.2 pl.643) that the rising woman on a valute-krater in London (E 467) by the Niobid Painter is Pandora. While Brommer (*Satyroi,* 14) and Rumpf [*JdI* 65-66 (1950-1) 171], because of the presence of Eros, interpret her as Aphrodite.

[374] H.R.W. Smith, *Funerary Symbolism in Apulian Vase - Painting* (see index s.v. Aphrodite).

[375] On Greek mirrors Erotes create an important feature of the Caryatid, where they are usually suspended from the support and hover near the head of the goddess. Congdon, *Caryatid Mirrors of Ancient Greece, passim..*

Buschor appears to believe that the goddess is emerging from the sea, however no evidence for that is present on any of our vases having Aphrodite as the principal figure on side A. Rather than waves, what seems to be represented on our vase (No. 57 in the Louvre, No. 3470 = MN 746) below the chin of the goddess is likely to be her hands wrapped. Other scholars accept the idea that the goddess was earth borne and she is seen rising from the ground[376].

Berard argues that the large head, rather than representing the birth of Aphrodite, is in fact the personification of the chthonic power of the goddess, who adopts the shape of a human head[377]. Indeed, examining these heads they appear to have been deliberately painted in larger scale than the other figures represented in the scene. The huge head appears to be emerging from below and small figures of satyrs and other characters are placed on the ground.

It is not difficult to differentiate such scenes from those representations of the actual birth of the goddess. The latter always present the goddess wholly or partially in the same proportion as the other figures in the scene, emerging from below, while the immortals (and/or mortals) wait to receive and cloth her. The classic representation of this is the so-called 'Ludovisi throne', where Aphrodite rises from the sea (indicated by a pebbly beach), assisted by two women[378]. The representation of such scenes on vase paintings are numerous[379].

The head of Aphrodite is a very common feature on Apulian vases of the fifth and fourth centuries. The goddess is sometimes used only for subsidiary ornamentation, not on the main body of the vase but on the neck of volute-kraters, and shoulders of amphorae and loutrophoroi. The heads are usually painted in added white colour and surrounded by elaborate floral settings. The goddess may also appear as the sole or principal decoration on the reverse of Apulian vases, occasionally with some adjunct like a fan or a mirror. Eros is occasionally present on the obverse[380].

Fifth century representations on Attic vases are also numerous, for example the small hydria in Genoa and the skyphos in Boston, both by the Penthesilea workshop[381].) On the hydria, the emerging Aphrodite is helped dress by an Eros and a maid. The skyphos shows the goddess rising, nearly a third of her figure appears between two women. There is also the cup in the Villa Giulia Museum by the Sabouroff Painter[382]. Here a dancing Pan fills the medallion. Below him, the head of Aphrodite rises from the ground. Aphrodite emerges in the presence of Eros, Pan, a man and two women, on the shoulder of a hydria in Syracuse by the Polygnotos Group[383]. Most important, however, is the pelike in Rhodes by the Erichthonios Painter[384]. The inscribed figure of Aphrodite emerges in the presence of Hermes and an ithyphallic Pan.

In the fourth century, the large representations of the goddess appear most popular. The earliest known is on the squat lekythos in Copenhagen from Fikellura (380 B.C.)[385]. This is a large head of Aphrodite represented flanked by two Erotes. On a hydria in Paris (Louvre MN 719, mid-fourth century)[386], the goddess is seen holding a mirror while Eros hovers near her. On a pelike in Polygyros (Thessaloniki, mid-fourth century)[387], the bare-breasted goddess of Love emerges between two Pans. On a hydria in Brussels[388] by the Heracles Painter (350 B.C.), the large head of Aphrodite rises in the presence of two Erotes and two Pans holding hammers. Also important is the cup in Paris (Cab. Med. 821)[389]. It has a composition similar to that of the fifth-century example in the Villa Giulia. The figure of a hovering Eros fills the medallion. He is approaching the emerging Aphrodite. It would be highly appropriate on our two vases (Nos. 57 and 58) for the head shown in company with Eros to be interpreted as that of Aphrodite.

59. *Oinochoe, Shape 2* Paris (Cap. Med. 472) (Plate 47, 1-3)

H. 14.7 cm.

Low disc base, flat below short, offset neck. Low handle projecting in to the trefoil mouth[390].

Apart from the figure drawing, shoulder pattern, and underside of vase, the whole pot is glazed black, including the inside of the mouth.

---

[376] Buschor, *Feldmause* 31. Metzger, *Represent.*, 72 f. Cambitoglou, *JHS* 76 (1955) 7. Berard, *Anodoi*, 61 f. *ARV* (see index, s.v. birth of Aphrodite).

[377] Berard, *op. cit.* 43 f.

[378] Rome, Terme Museum 8570. Lullies R, *Griechische Bildwerk in Rome* (1954), fig.9-12, fig.15.

[379] For the representation of the birth of Aphrodite on vases see the list in *LIMC* II (s.v. Aphrodite), 114 f., nos.1170-1182, pls.117-118. E. Simon, *Die Götter der Griechen,* 246 f.

[380] Jucker, *Das Bildnis im Blatter Kelch,* 200 f, figs.125-128. Trendall and Cambitoglou I, 189-90, nos. 8-5 and 11. The volute-krater in Boston, 1970, 235, pls.61, 3-4, 124,5.

[381] Hydria Genoa 1155 (71). *CVA,* pl.6 1-3. *ARV* 917, 206, *para.* 43. Addenda 140. Berard, *Anodoi,* pl.14, fig.47. Skyphos Boston 01.8032. *ARV* 888,155, *para.* 428, Addenda 148. Schefold, *Die Gottesage,* 9, fig.1. Berard, *Anodoi,* pl.12, fig.12.

[382] Villa Guilia 50329. *ARV* 840, 60. Addenda 145. Berard, *Anodoi,* pl.12. 43.

[383] Syracuse 23912. *CVA,* pl.24. *ARV* 1041,11, *para.* 443, Addenda 156. Berard, *Anodoi,* pl.18, 62.

[384] Rhodes 12.4.54. *Cl.Rh.IV*, 103 f. *BCH* 48-49 (1944-45), 305 fig.6. *ARV* 1218, 2, Addenda 173. Berard, *Anodoi*, pl.18, fig.63. The inscription is reported by Metzger, *Represent.*, 72, no.3.

[385] Copenhagen inv. 5183. *CVA* 4, pl.168 (170), 11 a-c.

[386] Louvre MN 710. Metzger, *Represent.*, 81 no.24. Berard, *Anodoi,* 66-68, 122, pl.7, 26.

[387] Thessaloniki, The Archaeological Museum of Polygyros. *Arch-Delt.* 24 1969. Chron. 2, 312, pl.32. Berard, *Anodoi,* 32, pl.13.46.

[388] Brussels R 286. Schefold, *UKV,* pl.1,1. Metzger, *Represent.*, pl.4,2. *ARV* 1472,4. Berard, *Anodoi,* 67, pl.7, 25.

[389] Cab. Med 821 De Ridder 485 no.821 Metzger, *Represent.*, 81, no.23, pl.6,1. Berard, *Anodoi,* 172, list 3c, No.c and Note 393.

[390] For the shape cf. *ARV* Xlix-1. Richter and Milne, fig.126. Caskey, *Geometry,* 138, no.90.

Tongue pattern on shoulder.

Relief contours were used for the hand of Athena where she holds a spear. Diluted paint is used for the snake and the hair of the figures. Athena's head shown in profile between two youths. She wears a Corinthian helmet decorated with a snake. The helmet is pushed up to show the goddess's face. She holds a spear.

The vase has been attributed to the F.B. Group[391]. This type of oinochoe appears to be the favourite shape employed by the artists of this group, but the form had long been in use. Early in the closing years of the fifth century the oinochoe was already experiencing a rapid development in form. By the early fourth century the Oinochoe type I (disc base and high handle), disappeared, and type II (wide flat base and low handle) develops from it, to be used by the F.B. Group[392].

The composition on most of these vases is the same: a central main figure (an athlete, Arimasp or Eros) standing between two other figures. Numerous examples show the head of the central figure in profile. The Cyrenaica piece is the only example I know that represents, as the central figure, the head of Athena in profile between two youths.

Representation on Athenian vases of profile heads is not a new development. Numerous examples are readily available from the fourth century. Later, the Kerch vases are our main source. Such a tradition, however, may go back as early as the fifth century B.C. The Achilles Painter was among fifth-century artists who painted profile heads on a number of his vases. One of these is a squat lekythos showing the bust of Artemis in three-quarter view armed with her quiver and a bow[393].

The Cyrenaica oinochoe is an important vase. It is the only example by the F.B. Group, or other contemporary artist, that represents the head of the goddess Athena in profile. From early in the fifth century, a white-ground lekythos in London shows the head of Athena in right profile. The style seems to have been a popular one of the time[394]. Myron made a marble statue of the goddess of which the head remains. She wears a Corinthian helmet in a similar fashion to that illustrated on the vases[395]. The painting on our oinochoe appears to have been inspired by a contemporary work, for we find the style copied on the coins of the period[396]. Both the coins and the painting on the Oinochoe are probably copies of the cult statue. On the oinochoe, Athena was probably meant to represent the divine scale, larger in size than the two human figures flanking her head.

[391] *ARV* 1489, 156.

[392] *ARV* 1484-1494.

[393] De Ridder, *Catalogue*, pl.20. Cab.Med. 479. ARV 499, 107.

[394] Illustrated in Cook, *Zeus*, III, 620 (*BMC* III, 396, no. D 22). See also the example in Beazley, *Attic Red-Figured Vases in the American Museum* (Cambridge Mass. 1918), 71, no.22.

[395] See the head in Dresden, *Staatliche-Kunst Antikenabteilung im Albertinum* (Dresden 1978). The cover.

[396] G.K. Jenkins, *Ancient Greek Coins* (1972), No.404, p.1.

A similar composition was represented on an oinochoe in Oxford: an athlete between two youths[397].

A good number of these oinochoae have been found in Spina[398], but very few in Greece itself. This example from Cyrene, and others, show that there was an overseas market for such vases. Dated to the first half of the fourth century B.C.

60. *Pelike*[399] (Plate 48, 1-2)

Large pelike with flaring neck, overhanging rim and disc-base. On lip egg-and-dart pattern. On neck above the scene on side A, stripes of double slanting palmettes and egg-and-dot pattern. On side B a band of wave pattern. Below scene double interlocking meander in groups of fives and sixes, alternating with dotted chequered squares. Under handles designs of large palmettes and scrolls.

Side A: In the centre a Doric structure with three columns, the one to the rear intended to suggest depth. In front of the structure Heracles sits naked, in three-quarter view to right. His garment is tucked underneath him and he leans on his club, placed under his armpit. Across his chest he wears a baldric, and the handle of the sword it supports appears close to the left arm. (The scabbard in which the sword is kept is hidden by Heracles body.) A high handled kantharos[400] is held in his left hand as he looks around to watch a dignified bearded man half wrapped in a richly decorated garment. A nude Hermes is behind him, whose garment (chlamys) is draped over his left arm, while he holds his *kerykeion*, rendered in black, in his right hand. He is leaning against the bearded man, touching him with the left arm[401]. All these three figures are crowned with laurel-wreaths. Facing Heracles to left, is a Nike dressed in a richly decorated chiton. She holds an oinochoe in her left hand, from which she is about to pour a libation into the kantharos held by Heracles. To the right, Ioloas sits in three-quarter view on his garment (chlamys), holding two spears. He turns around to watch the scene.

Side B: Three youths (ephebi) conferring, wrapped in himation. Between them is an altar. The central figure holds an astrigil. In the space above the altar, or stele there is a round object (disc or ball).

The subject represented on this vase is not entirely clear, as there is no exact parallel for comparison. The architectural structure must be a building relating to the cult of Heracles,

[397] *CVA*, Oxford, pl.42,5.

[398] *ARV* 1484-1494. Massei, *Gli Askoi,* 144, pl.XXXIV 1-87; p.153, pl.XXXV 2-94; pl.182, pls.LVII 3-113; p.225, pl.LII 2-140; p.236, pl.LVI 1-146; p.250, pl.LVIII 2-152; p.298, pl.LXXI 2-177.

[399] Until 1975 in Topsham, Devon. Ms Radford now in USA with other branch of the family (information communicated through B.B. Shefton).

[400] Beazley's kantharos Type D. Richter and Milne, *Shapes and Names*, 25 f., fig.167.

[401] Figures leaning forward against other figures are frequent in the late 5th and early 4th centuries, e.g. the late 5th c. example on the work of the Meidias Paint on the hydria in London (BM E 224). For the 4th century see Entry No.39.

who appears to have been widely worshipped throughout Attica. By the fifth century, it was stated that Heracles even overtook Theseus, Athens' national hero, in the number of sanctuaries dedicated to him[402]. These were found represented on vases[403], and relief[404] and architectural remains[405].

These structures were two or three meters high, square in plan, and built on a foundation of two or three steps, with columns (either Doric or Ionic) at the four corners supporting an epistyle[406]. When there was no temple available, banquets were originally offered to Heracles in the open air, under the shade of a tree. Later, wooden or stone edifices (the four-column Heracleions) were constructed for the purpose of ritual meals prepared in honour of the hero. De Visscher has further suggested that in the cult of Heracles the hero was also thought to receive the homage of the gods in his Heracleion[407]. A good number of vases represent the hero as being greeted by Athena, or conversing or receiving libations from her. This role is often taken over by Nike[408] and what we see on the Cyrenaica pelike is an example of this[409].

The presence of two figures on the far left and right is commons on vases of this period. Hermes is on the left, waiting to guide the far-wandering Heracles to one of his adventures. The youth on the right, perhaps, is Iolaos, Heracles' young nephew and frequent companion in his labours.

Who we cannot identify is the dignified man with the sceptre who is approaching our hero. Perhaps he represents a king, or the priest of Heracles?

On side B, the stele-like structure between the two ephebes is perhaps an altar relating to the Heraclion, represented on side A, since celebrations with sacrifices, and distribution of meat and wine as part of the rituals in these buildings, seem to have been frequent occasions in Athens. We learn from Hesychius that the ephebes poured libations to Heracles before they cut their hair[410]. This libation was called "oinisteria". The Boston relief, showing Heracles and Hermes approaching a four-column Heracleion, was, as Frickenhaus suggests, dedicated to Heracles by an Athenian youth who participated in such a ceremony[411].

Our pelike is unattributed. Among the nearest in theme is a krater in London showing Apollo surrounded by the followers of Dionysos at Delphi[412]. From the shape of our pelike, and its painting style, it appears to belong to the second quarter of the fourth century B.C., and perhaps related to the workshop of the Erbach painter. The composition and style closely resemble the painting to be seen on his bell-krater in London.

61. *Pelike* Manchester M680 (N 83 BH)[413] (Plate 49, 1)

H. 24.8 cm

Rim, neck, handles, and part of the shoulder and body preserved. Reddish buff clay. Black glaze.

Around the rim there is a band of egg and dot pattern. Similar hand is on the neck above the scene.

The scene is the obverse of the vase showing the upper part of a maenad wearing a chiton, with belted waist. Her breast is in three-quarter view. Her hair is covered in a sakkos, but some of it escapes in front and at the side. She wears earrings. She is beating a tambourine from which a sash hangs. The maenad is moving quickly to the right towards a sketchily drawn satyr, who is also moving to the right in a three-quarter view and looking back. He is probably holding a thyrsos. The maenad is also looking back and apparently running away from another satyr, who is trying to reach her by extending his left arm towards her.

The style of this sketchy painting is similar to that seen on another pelike from Olynthus[414], in the manner of the Hippolytus painter (360 B.C.). Another pelike, found in southeast Yugoslavia (Demir Kapija)[415], shows an identical subject and composition, but unlike the Manchester pelike, the scene moves to left. A maenad holds a thrysus in her right hand and a tambourine in the left. She is running away from

[402] For the cult of Heracles see Pauly-Wissowa, *RE* Suppl.3 (1918), 923-931 and Woodford, *Studies presented to George M.A. Haufmann,* 211 ff.

[403] Eight kraters:

i) Ferrara, T.IBVP, from Spina. *ARV* 1337,3 (Pronomus Painter).
ii) Athens 12682. *ARV* 1418,4. Metzger, *Represent.,* pl.XXXI, 2, no.58.
iii) Athens 14902. Metzger, pl.XXXI,3, no.56.
iv) Villa Guilia 3619, from Faleri. *ARV* 1420,7. Mingazzini, *Mem Linc,* pl.8, 2, no.257.
v) Paris, Musée Rodin, 1. *CVA,* pl.23,1-2 and pl.25. 3-5.
vi) Louvre G.508. *ARV* 14361. Metzger, *Represent.,* pl.29,2.
vii) Louvre G.509. *CVA,* Louvre 5, pl.7-8 (3781). Mingazzini, *Mem Linc,* no.263.
viii) Würzburg 645. *ARV* 1427, 39.

[404] Athens, National Museum 1404, from Ithome, Frickenhaus, *AM* 36 (1911), 122, no.3, Venice, Dodge's Palace, Frickenhaus 122, no.4 and pl.II/2. Rome, Masco Baracco (from Athens), Frickenhaus 123 no.7. Athens National Museum 2723 (from Marusi), Frickenhaus 122, no.2 and pl.III/1. A lost example, once in Kaki, Thelessa, Frickenhaus 123, no.6. Athens, Acropolis Museum 2586, Frickenhaus 123, no.9. Boston Museum of Fine Arts 96.696 (from Attica), Frickenhaus 122, no.1 and pl.II Naples, National Museum (from Attica), Frickenhaus, 123 no.8.

[405] Frickenhaus, *op. cit.* 113 ff., especially 117-8, 132-3. J.H.Young, *Hesperia* 10 (1941), 169 ff.

[406] Woodford, *op. cit.* 213. Walter, *AM* 62 (1937), 41 ff.

[407] De Visscher, *Ant.Cl.* 30 (1961), 67 ff. See also Metzger, *Represent.,* 225-230.

[408] Walter, *op. cit.* pl.28. Beazley, *EVA* 72. Metzger, *op. cit.* 212, pl.XXXI.

[409] Nike was found, on some examples, replacing Athena on the chariot taking Heracles to Olympus. Discussed, *supra*, Entry No.33 (Louvre N 3408).

[410] Hesychius s.v. "Oinisteria". See also Photius s.v., "Oinisteria" and Athen 11.494 f.

[411] Boston Museum of Fine Arts 96.697. Frickenhaus, *op. cit.* pl.II.

[412] London BM F 77. *ARV*[2], 1418,5. Metzger, *Represent.,* 177, no.33, pl.XXV,1.

[413] Rowe, *Cyren.Exped.,* 12, 26 (frontispiece).

[414] *Olynthus* XIII ,pl.64, 50. See also the example in V pl.126.

[415] Vuckovic-Todorovic, *RA* (1973), 44, fig.5.

one satyr to the right, only to be confronted by another to the left. Both pelikai have similar painting styles, and are likely to be from the same workshop. Date 360 B.C.[416].

62. *Bell-krater*[417] *(fragments)* Cyrene Museum (Plate 49, 2)

This piece belongs to the fourth century type of bell-krater, with handles and widely flaring rim and. Fragment of side A only, with part of rim, one handle. A part of the other handle has survived. Relief and diluted colour are used for the garments.

Laurel leafs are painted around the outside of the rim. At the bottom of the scene there is a meander and chequer-board pattern.

The scene represents a symposium[418]. Two youths, wreathed and nude to the waist, are seated on couches. Each is leaning on pillows. Below each couch is a three-legged table. The figure on the right rests his left arm on the white pillow while holding an object in his right hand (a mirror or rhyton). He faces left. The second youth looks to the right, resting his left arm on a pillow and holding "a phiale". Between the two youths is a woman painted entirely in white[419] except for her hair. She wears a long chiton with her hair bound in a fillet. She advances to the right extending her arm towards the figure on the right in a dancing gesture[420]. Black bunches of grapes are shown in the background.

The painting is in the manner of the Black-Thrysus Painter[421] (350-340 B.C.). Most useful for comparison are kraters in Paris, Copenhagen and Torino, which are attributed to that artist[422]. Our piece is almost certainly from his workshop, or by a member of his circle. Date 350-340 B.C.

63. *Pelike* London BM E 434 (Plate 50, 1-3)

Large Pelike with flaring neck, overhanging rim, handles with central rib, disc-base in two stages. The underside and outer edge are reserved. On the overhanging rim there is a continuous band of egg-and-dot pattern, framed by a relief line. Above the scene, on each side, is a band of egg-and-dot pattern with relief lines above and behind. Encircling the vase below the scene is a band of similar pattern, boarded with relief lines. Below each handle is a double palmette. White with yellow details on the red ground is used for the griffins, except for their wings, which are in the usual red figure technique.

The subject on this Pelike is a 'grypomachy', the right side involves Arimasps and Griffins. According to Herodotus, the Arimasps were people from the Scythian Steppes (Hdt: 3.116, 4.13, 4.27). Aeschylus (Prometheus Bound, 804-807) said that their country had a gold-bearing river, but most accounts have it that the gold was in the keeping of Griffins living beyond the Arimaspians, near the Hyperboreans. They may at one time have lived in the gold-bearing Altai Mountains of Central Asia[423]. The Arimaspians were perpetually at war with the Griffins, stealing their gold at every opportunity.

There are three beardless Arimasps on our vessel, colourfully and elaborately dressed in a typical oriental fashion. They are fighting three Griffins. The Arimasps wear shoes, jerkins and anaxirides decorated with rows of various patterns, and a short chiton, also elaborately decorated. They wear tiaras.

The Arimasp in the centre of the picture appears to be the main target of the attack by these creatures. He is shown desperately defending himself with his crescent shaped shield (pelta) and axe (sagaris). The other two Arimasps are coming to the rescue. One behind the wings of the Griffin on the left, is in the act of thrusting a spear in the back of the monster, while the other, above the central figure, holds a huge rock and is ready to hurl it down on one of the Griffins.

There are a good number of vases similar in drawing style and composition to the Cyrenaica pelike. One may compare especially the pelike in Castle Ashby, and the one in Baltimore, for both subject and style[424]. In the last example on side (B) there are marks on the hem area of the youth's garments that are identical to side (B) of the Cyrenaica pelike. Yet this does not necessarily mean that they are by the same hand. The drawing on our Pelike is better executed.

Beazley lists the Cyrenaica vase under the Helbig Reverse-Group, dated between 360-350 B.C.[425]. Two other Pelikae from the same group were found in Cyrenaica. Both are in the Louvre[426].

---

[416] For a discussion on the dating of the contents of the sarcophagus N.83-BTT, see entry No.35 in Chapter Four (black glaze) in this study.

[417] For 4th century B.C. bell-kraters, *Ath.Agor* XII, 55. Richter and Milne, 8. Schefold, *UKV*, pls.26-27. *Olynthos* XIII, 81-92 Pls.36-55. *Hesperia XXVII* (1958), 199.

[418] For Symposia, see Tomlinson, in *Ancient Macedonia*, 308-315. G.M. Richter, *The furniture of Greeks, Entruscans & Romans*. Vickers, *Greek Symposia, passim*.

[419] Similar examples in *Olynthus XIII*, pls.38 & 41. Schefold, *UKV* pl.15,4. *CVA*, Louvre V III, 1, pl.5 (4 & 9).

[420] Similar examples in *Olynthus XIII* pl.38, V, nos.133, 137. *CVA*, Robinson Collection III, pl.XVII, 2. Schefold, *MKV* 14-16, 182, 138, nos.82, 117, 118, 127, pl.15 no.239.

[421] *ARV* 1431 - 1434, 1893.

[422] *CVA*, Louvre 5 III 1, e pl.5, 9-10. CVA, Copenhagen 8. CVA, Torino II, Italy XL, pl.11 5,6.

[423] For arimasps and griffons see Fürtwagler in Roscher, *Lexikon* 1.2 P.1742, s.v. Gryps. Durrbach in *Dict Ant*, 11, 2, P 1668 s.v. Gryps. Prinz-Ziegler, in Pauly-Wissowa *R.E.* VII (2) P.1902 f. s.v. Arimasp. Schefold, *UKV*, 174. For representations of The Grypomachy on vases see W. Wrede, *AM* il (1924), 212-215. Schefold, *UKV* 153, vases listed under "Arimaspen und Greifen". Metzger, *Represent.*, 329 f. For a recent but general study see Flagge, *Untersuchungen zur Bedeutung des Greifen*, 75, 52 ff. Delplace, *Le Griffon*, 124 ff.

[424] Castle Ashby. *CVA* pl.44. Robinson Collection, *CVA*, 3, pl.15-16.

[425] *ARV* 1474. Smith, *Catalogue of Vases*, 265, pl.XIV. Metzger, *Represent.*, 328, no.51.

[426] i) Louvre MN 738. *ARV* 1474, 6.
ii) Louvre MN 747. *ARV* 1474, 8.

64. *Pelike* Paris Cap. Med. 406 (Plate 51, 1)

H. 25.5 cm

Pelike with flaring neck, overhanging rim. Base in two stages. On lip, base of the neck (on both sides) and around the body below the figure scene there are bands of patterns. Diluted colour is used for the garment of the Arimasp.

Side A: Subject is a 'grypomachy'. An Arimasp on horseback confronting a griffin.

Side B: Two youths clad in himation, facing one another. The one on the left holds a tympanum. In the middle between them a round object (ball) is suspended.

The style of painting on this pelike is typical of the middle Kertch style attributed by Beazley to Group G[427]. Our vase is especially close to a pelike in Spina and another in New York. There are also examples in Olynthus and in Munster (Germany)[428]. All of these are dated to the second quarter of the fourth century B.C., however, the pelike from Spina is the nearest example to ours. It is attributed to Group G and dated to 380-360 B.C.

65. *Pelike* Paris Cab. Med. 408[429] (Plate 52, 1-2)

H. 30.5 cm.

Pelike with flaring neck, overhanging rim. Base in two stages. The lip, base of the neck, and bands below the figure scenes are decorated with egg-and-dot patterns. Added white for the two Griffins and dilute colour for Arimasp's costume.

The subject is a 'grypomach', but it does not appear to represent the normal grypomachy scenes of griffins fighting griffins that are frequent in Greek art of the fourth century. On these scenes Griffins are usually represented either attacking other animals, such as stags and horses, or attacking figures such as Arimasps or Amazons. These scenes are to be found on vases as well as on gems[430]. The Arimasps are usually distinguished by their exotic costumes - oriental cap, jerkins and trousers[431].

The subject on our vase is not very clear. The two griffins are facing each other, mounted by two Arimasps. This probably symbolises their victory over the Griffins, the legendary guardians of the central Asiatic gold fields. Here the two Griffins are not only defeated, but also subjugated and tamed for the Arimasps' own use. The scene, therefore, does not appear to represent a fighting scene. The Arimasps are holding a javelin, but not in a threatening manner, aiming it downwards as if in exercise. Clumsily drawn in the background, in two-dimensional form, is a bi-corporate, horned lion-griffin who crouches. The beast is joined at the chest to make one head. The whole scene, excluding the mounted Arimasps, is probably meant to be a backdrop, a motif seemingly unparalleled on any red-figured picture.

A plate in Copenhagen is decorated with a similar subject[432]. Two Griffins facing each, mounted by two Arimasps in a very similar pose to that on our Pelike, but here the bi-corporate beast in the background is absent. Instead, over the heads of the two Griffins is an Eros, who appears to be playing with a large bird - duck?

The meaning of the bi-corporate beast is not easy to explain. It clearly has an artistic value when used as ornamentation. Its use may also signify the intensification of power, or accumulation of facilities. A beast with two bodies is stronger and more formidable than a single-bodied one.

The bi-corporate monster in Greek Arts was borrowed from the Near East. They were well known in the Orientalizing period in the seventh century[433]. From the transitional period to the early Corinthian, we have an alabastron in London decorated with two Sphyinxes, whose bodies face one another. Their two necks are joined to end as one head[434]. In the early Corinthian Orientalizing style, bi-corporate creatures were not uncommon. A painted alabastron in Syracuse shows a bird with a Gorgon's head and a lion's claws on two bodies[435].

The motif seems to have disappeared mysteriously from the vase painting of the sixth and the fifth centuries, but it continued on other types of art. Outside Greece the monster is found on Tarentine capitals and clay arulae[436]. On mainland Greece, the creature was used for the decoration of mosaics from Olynthus[437], on a strip of thin gold of Greek workmanship form Olbia[438], on gems (chalcedony scaraboids)[439], and on Attic tomb slabs decorating the base of a loutrophorus[440].

---

[427] Cab.Med., 406. De Ridder, *Cab.Med.*, pl.16. *ARV* 1462, 7.

[428] For the Pelike from Spina see Massei, *Gli.Askoi*, 269, no.I, fig.7. Cf. also the bell-krater from Olynthus, Olynthus XIII, 90, no.37, pl.46, and the pelike from Munster (Germany) [inv. 723 in the University Museum of Archaeology. Boreas, *Münsterische Beiträge*, 190, no.16, pl.33 (1-2)].

[429] Cab. Med. No.408. De Ridder, *Ca.*, 298 No.408. Metzger, *Represent.*, 328. No.50, pl.42,2. Jacobsthal, *Early Celtic Art*, pl.231, c. Schefold, *UKV* 57, No.550. Delplace, *Le Griffon*, 133.

[430] See discussions on Entry Nos.63, 66. See note 423. For the griffon on gems see Boardman, *Greek Gems and Finger Rings*, 305 f.

[431] For Arimasp costumes see Marie-Theres Picard, in *Studi Antiqua*, 1955, 152 f.

[432] Copenhagen inv.9411, *CVA* Denmark VIII, pl.358 15. Delplace, *op. cit.* 133, fig.142.

[433] For the origin see Kraus, in *AM* 68-70 (1953-55) 123 f. Cook R.M., *Greek Painted Pottery*, 41 f. Jacobsthal, *op. cit.* 48.

[434] London, *BM* 99.2 28.68. Payne, *NC* 51, n.8, pl.15, 14.

[435] Syracuse, from Megara Hyplaea tomb 501. Payne, *op. cit.* 52, fig.12.

[436] For Tarentine capitals, Ronezewski, *AA* 42 (1927), 271, 3a, p.274, 4. Jacobsthal, *op. cit.* K 48. For Tarentine clay *aurulae*, Van Buren, *MAAR* 2 (1918), 25, pl.17.

[437] *Olynthus* V, 10 ff. pl.6. Lorentz, *RM* 52 (1937), 168, No.XX, pl.44.

[438] Minns, *Scythians and Greeks*, 392, pl.288.

[439] Boardman, *Greek Gems and Finger Rings*, 305 f., fig.836.

[440] See the list of Attic Stelae, ornamented with the double sphinx, in Woysch-Meautis, *La representation des aimaux* 83 f, 135 f, Nos.375-381, Pls.62-63. See also Luschey, in *Festschrift, B. Schweitzer*, 243 ff., and pl.53,2.

The fifth and fourth centuries witnessed the development of the animal style on Iranian soil. The gold armlet from the Oxus Treasure, with foreparts of horned griffins at the open ends is, indeed, a manifestation of this creation[441]. Dalton's comments on the monster representation are still valid[442]. He stated that Persians had employed the combined monster, that is a winged lion with long, pointed ears and a crested eagle's head, legs and tail, used by the Babylonians and Asyrians, but adding horns as a new feature. A lion-griffin, with unusually large horns, was used to decorate the frieze of coloured tiles from the Palace of Darius[443].

The lion-griffin with Persian style horns is to be found on a late fifth century Greek gem in Oxford. On Greek vases the beast is featured on two fourth-century vases in Leningrad. The first is a pelike by the painter of the Griffin-Lions, and the second is a squat lekythos by the Xenophantos painter[444].

The Greek painter of our vase appears to have been copying an imported fabric. The delicate textiles of tapestry, decorated with intricate and elegant designs in many colours (from the Acheminid style) as witnessed by these imported fabrics, were found in the Altai Barrows. A third-century painting from Dion in Macedonia, was rightly described by Boardman as inspired by Persian art[445]. The painted frieze of a lion on a woven textile, and the frieze of stylized lion heads, was executed in felt on cloth. Both finds, recovered from the frozen tombs of Pazyrik in the Altae region (Barrow, 5 and 1), were very probably the product of the Acheminid Culture in Persia, and could be identified by the subject depicted. The motif can also be found on friezes (of animals in heraldic fashion) on Susa glazed-bricks and on gold plaques from Hamadon.

Foremost among these textiles recovered from Pazyrik are the saddle-covers with animal designs[446]. The large motif used on the cover is the attack of a carnivore on an ungulate, or a struggle between beasts represented by whole animals, or their heads. The technique employed is appliqué, or pasted-on silhouette, or figures made up of polychrome pieces of felt sewn on to the cover.

Barrow No. 1 in Pazyrik yielded a number of these saddle-covers. Two examples were sufficient to show the artistic composition of this production. There is a lion decoration on the first cover. The details are indicated on the body of the animals (the ram and lion) by cuts, through which the light colour of the saddle is visible.

On these woven textiles, the indication of the animals' musculature on the shoulders and thighs is done by specific decorative motifs - circles, commas, and figures-of-eight with polychrome inlays. These are all obvious imitations of the style of the Chaemerian gold and silver smiths. If we examine the gold armlet from the Oxus Treasure we can see on the legs and the main body of the monster large areas that have been deeply chased with hollows and that follow the lines of the monster and emphasize them in a bold, conventional style. These hollows create an abstract shape, meant to be inlayed with coloured stones. The colour of these armlets, with their relatively large inlays, must have been very striking.

These large coloured inlays on Acheminid gold, are indeed, the abstract ornaments, or slashes, on the bodies of the animals portrayed on Acheminid carpets, as seen on the examples surviving in the frozen barrows of the Altai, at Pazyrik[447]. These same abstract ornaments are imitated on Attic vase painting of the fourth century. On the pelike in Leningrad, a horned lion-griffin is shown with a similar body and abstract ornament[448]. On our vase the bi-corporate lion-griffin has circles, or comma-shaped forms, on the shoulders, fore legs, and hind legs that can be already seen on the armlet from the Oxus Treasure.

Although this is a 'Kerch' pelike, it is not easy to date by its style of painting. Jacobsthal dates it between 330 and 320 B.C.[449], but the shape of the vase may suggest an earlier date, probably the second quarter of the fourth century. The body is still globular and the neck has not shrunk yet to form concave side. Such features are to be found on those pelikce produced in the third quarter of the fourth century onwards[450]. One device that is frequently employed during the second quarter of the fourth century is to paint one or more figures on the vase in white, as is shown here in the case of the two griffins that have been mounted by the Arimasps.

66. *Pelike, Exeter 40 1922-14*[451] (Plate 53, 1-2)

Moulded base and ring, the handles triangular in cross-section. Egg-and-dot pattern on the overhanging rim, also above and below the painted scene. Below handles there are double palmettes and scroll.

White colour used for the face of the woman and the Griffin's protome. Relief and silute colour for inner details of the cap and wings of the Griffin.

441 Dalton, *The Treasure of the Oxus* 32 f., No.116, pl.1 fig.64. Porada, *Ancient Iran,* 170 f., pl.51. Jettmar, *op. cit.* 223 f., pl.49.

442 Dalton, *ibid.*, 3.

443 From Susa, the Lion Griffon in the Louvre. Ghirshman, *Persia*, 142 fig.191. Rudenko, *op. cit.* 80, fig.96.

444 Gem. Oxford, 1885, 491, from Nymphaeum, blue chalcedony scaraboid. Boardman, *Greek Gems and Finger Rings,* 306 pl.838. Pelike, Leningrad inv. st.1873. KAB 51a K. Schefold, *UKV* 44, no.381, pl.5,1. *ARV* 1473,1. Wienser, *JdI* 78 (1963), 209 fig. Delplace, *Le Griffon,* 129, fig.138. Picard, *Studi Antiqua*, 1955, 152 f., pl.VII,3. Squat lekythos, Leningrad inv.st.1790. Schefold, *UKV*, fig.67. Blavatski, *History of Ancient Painted Pottery*, 269 E.A.A. ii, 935. *ARV* 1407,1.

445 Boardman, *Antiquity* 44, 143 f.

446 Discussed in Rudenko, *Frozen Tombs of Siberia,* 220 f., figs. 112, 114. Wiesner, *JdI* 78 (1963), 210 f., fig.4.

447 i) Saddle cover in the Hermitage (1684/326) from Pazrik, Kurgan. Illustration in *From the Lands of Scythiaps* (The Metropolitan Museum of Art), pl.23, Cat. No.113.
ii) Leather ornament from saddle pillow, first Pazrik Barrow. Rudenko, *op. cit.* 100, fig.87,6 (tiger attacking mountain ram).

448 See Wiesner, in *JdI* 78 (1963), 209, fig.3. Delplace, *op. cit.* 129, fig.138.

449 Jacobsthal, *op. cit.* 48.

450 See commentry on Entry Nos. 44, 63.

451 *ARV* 1467, 110.

Side A: Large scale head of an Amazon in profile to right. She is placed between a horse head and a protome of a griffin both to right. The woman wears a phrygian cap.

Side B: Two cloaked figures facing each other. The one on the left is holding a tambourine while the figure on the right extending his arm towards a round object (ball).

There are a number of interpretations of the scene on side A. One of these interprets the female heads as those of Amazons walking beside their horses. The use of white colour suggests that it is the head of a woman, and the absence of Eros rules out the figure as being Aphrodite. The scenes were probably intended as abbreviated representations of combat between griffins and barbarians, since there are many pelikai that carry scenes of Amazons on horseback in combat with griffins[452].

This Pelike, which is attributed to Group G, can be compared to two others in the Louvre. The first is from Cyrenaica (MN 751) and the second from Kerch [S 1378 (S 1668)][453]. Identical subjects (Amazon between a griffin and a horse), composition, and style can be recognised on the three pelikai (including our pelike No. 67).

The three pelikai, therefore, can be dated to the third quarter of the fourth century.

67. *Pelike* Paris, Louvre MN 752 (Plate 53, 3-4)

Egg-and-dot pattern on lip above and below the scene. Palmette under the handles.

Side A: The head of an Amazon, in an Amazon cap, in right profile. In front of her is the head of a horse, also in right profile. White colour is used for the face of the woman, diluted paint for the inner sakkos and horse's mane[454].

Side B: Two cloaked youths facing one another. No added colour, diluted paint, or relief lines.

Of the many red-figure horse pelikai resembling ours, those most useful for comparison are those from Olynthus, the Athenian Agora, and an example in Leningrad[455]. The style of drawing, however, on these examples is slightly different. The horses were drawn with thinner faces, and sometimes with open mouths. The female head is also different. In general, the drawing and painting is hasty and sketchy. Remains of added white, especially on the Agora examples, are visible on the horse's bridle, the veil and the woman's neck.

The closest (indeed identical) pelike to ours is an example in Stuttgart, where a female head is confronted by a griffon[456].

[452] Discussion in Thompson, *Hesperia* 3 (1934), 427.

[453] *ARV* 1467, 109 and 111.

[454] For subject see Entry No.66.

[455] *Olynthus* XIII pl.60, 46A. *Hesperia* 3 (1934), 333-335, 427, fig,13,14. Schefold, *UKV*, no.496, pl.25 (Leningrad st., 1789).

[456] Stuttgart, in Schefold, *UKV*, no.596, pl.25. Münster inv.737, University Museum of Archaeology. Boreas, *op. cit.* 195, no.17, pl.33, 13 and 4.

The style of drawing, especially the face of the woman and the inner decoration of her sakkos, is the same as our vessel. Both vases appear to be by the same hand, painted during the third quarter of the fourth century B.C.

68. *Pelike, Paris Louvre MN 753 - N 3459* (Plate 54, 1-2)

Egg-and-dot pattern on lip, above and below the scenes.

Side A: A female head (Amazon), wearing an Amazon cap, in right profile. Next to her, also in right profile is a griffin's protome. White colour was used for the woman's face, "repainted after restoration". Relief line for the woman's face and upper part of cap. Dilute colour for inner marking.

Side B: Two cloaked youths facing one another. The one on the right holds an object (discus or tambourine)[457].

Beazley attributes the pelike to the Amazon Painter. The shape of the Cyrenaica pelike is very close to two Pelikai from the Athenian Agora that are dated to the last quarter of the fourth century B.C.[458]. The three vases have a pear-like shape, with a wider neck that flares upwards. The subject and composition of the vases are also similar, but the Amazon on the Agora pelike is placed between the horse and the griffin, and the horse is not represented on the Cyrenaican vessel. The style of painting on these vases is identical. If we examine the protome of the monster and the Amazon on our example, we will notice that they are inadequately drawn, while the mantled figures on side B, by contrast, are very sketchily represented and drawn with no facial details. Such characteristics are indeed shared by the two Agora pelikai. Dated the last quarter of the fourth century B.C.

69. *Pelike*, Leiden KVB 57 (Plate 55, 1-2)

Side A: The head of an Amazon wearing an Amazon cap and holding a spear in left profile. The head of a griffin in right profile faces her. This pelike is dated to the third quarter of the fourth century B.C.[459].

70. *Pelike, London BM F 12* Euhesperides

H. 18 cm

Shape, ornamentation and subject as entry No. 69.

Dated to the third quarter of the fourth century B.C.

71. *Pelike, Londan F* (11) (Plate 55, 3)

H. 18 cm

Shape and ornamentation as entry No. 69.

[457] For subject see Entry No.66.

[458] For the attribution see *ARV* 1479, 23. For the Pelikai from Athens see Thompson, *op. cit.* (3, 1934), 332-3, 427, figs.13, 14 and 114.

[459] For subject see Entry No.66. For dating see discussion on Entry No.68.

Side A: An Amazon wearing an Amazon's cap in right profile. Facing her a crane painted white and between them a tambourine. Behind the crane is a pelta, ornamented with a star.

Side B: Two cloaked youths facing each other, with a round object between them.

Same style as entry No. 67 and probably by the same workshop.

Dated to the third quarter of the fourth century B.C..

72. *Pelike* Paris Cab. Med. 407 (De Ridder 297-298) (Plate 56, 1-2)

Pelike with a flaring neck and overhanging rim. Base in two stages. Oval patterns on the lip, around the body below the figure scene, and on the base of the neck (on side A). There is an egg-and-dot pattern on side B.

Added white for shields. Diluted colour for inner details and Amazon's costume.

Side A: Battle between Amazon and Greeks: The figures are set at different levels on a rocky ground. The Amazon is, as usual, distinguished by her special headgear, jerkin and trousers (distinguished by small circular pattern in diluted colour). She is mounted on a rearing horse, and attacking the Greeks with a javelin in her right hand. The three Greeks are nude except for their headgear - one with a Corinthian helmet of a later type, and the other two with piloi[460]. The Greeks are retreating and appear to be losing the fight to the mounted Amazon, while protecting themselves with their large shields. The one on the left is already fleeing. He leans away with his right foot shown in profile. The left foot, which is foreshortened, advances forward. His companion in the background is holding a short slashing sword, which he swings over his head, ready, perhaps, to strike at another Amazon (not shown). The third Greek is crouching in the foreground. He supports himself on his right foot and knee, his right hand touching the ground and holding something; a sword perhaps, to use against his mounted attacker. There are shield devices of which A alone is visible.

Side B: Three cloaked youths, two of them facing one another. Between them a stele or altar. A round object is suspended in space.

Of the many pelikai representing battles between Amazon and Greeks the most useful for comparison is the pelike from Crete[461]. The neckband decoration is similar and the subject on side A is the same, but each of the two vases differ in the use of the white colour. On our pelike, the shields are painted white, not the horse. Moreover, the number of figures on each of the two vases is four, but on our example we have one Amazon and three Greeks, instead of two Amazons and two Greeks.

The shape of the pot may suggest a date later in the fourth century. It is, however, useful to cite examples of other pelikai in the period so as to understand the development of the so-called Kerch style form. Most relevant to the discussion are two pelikai, with roundly bulging bodies, from Olynthus. Similar shapes are dated by Schefold to the middle of the fourth century B.C.[462]. Examples such as the one in Yale and the one from Alexandria show reduced bulging, a more drawn in neck, and more angular handles. The shape of these last two is comparable to examples in Leningrad and London, dated respectively by Schefold to 345 and 333 B.C.[463].

Our vase, although not attributed, is of the same class as the last example (represented in Alexandria, Leningrad and London) to be dated to the third quarter of the fourth century B.C.

73. *Squat Lekythos* Cyrene Museum (Plate 57, 1)

Flat handle and long neck. The body rests on a low ring-base. Shoulder slopes to the narrow base of the neck. The line of the neck continues from the shoulder to the slightly flaring mouth. The clay glaze covers the entire vessel, except for the underneath, and the reserved design is of poor quality.

The decoration consists of a single, very conventionalised palmette of angular outlines, bordered by lotus-like petals. The palmette is bordered by a reserved line, and this is pierced by the central leaf of the palmette.

The lekythos is generally known to be the most common container of oil and one of the vases most generally associated with burial customs throughout Greece. Among these, the squat and palmette decorated lekythos was most abundant throughout the fourth century B.C.[464].

Robinson has divided the fourth century squat lekythi into two distinct groups according to the variations appearing in the palmettes. The earlier group has rounded petals bordered by narrow reserved lines. The execution of this group is very good by comparison[465]. Vases of this group are few and thought to belong to the first quarter of the fourth century. On the later group[466], we find plain reserved lines as borders, but on many of these the border is pierced by the central leaf of

[460] The type is discussed by Snodgrass, *Arms and Armour of the Greeks*, 93 f., 97.

[461] Athens 1445 (cc 1860). Schefold, *UKV*, no.343, pl.24,4. *ARV* 1464, 56.

[462] *Olynthus*, V, nos.267, 268, pl.120, 121. Schefold, *KV*, pl.24,b.

[463] Baur, *Stodart Collection* 109, no.136, fig.37. Thompson, *Hesperia* 3 (1934), 427 no.4. Breccia, *Sciatbi*, 49 no.91, pl.XLVII (71,72), Leningrad st. 1789. Schefold, *KV* pl.16,a. London, BM E 424. Schefold, *ibid*, pl.16,b.

[464] Richter and Milne, 14-15. Sparkes and Talcott, *Ath.Agor.*, XII, 150-155.

[465] Robinson, *Olynthus* XIII, 146 f., pl.103 (109) and pl.105 (108), V pl.141 (408), pl.142 (429).

[466] Robinson, *Olynthus* XIII, 147 v pls.,142-143 (434-43), pl.105 (110, 111, 114, 115, 116). See also, Ontario Museum, fig.479. Ure, *Black Glaze Pottery from Rhitsona*, 50, pl.XV,1.

the palmette. This is the second type of palmette according to Robinson's classifications.

One can therefore observe the deterioration in the quality of the glazing by contrast to the overall attention to detail apparent in the earlier pieces. This last group makes up the majority of the fourth century squat lekythi and was dated to the second quarter of the fourth century B.C. The Cyrene piece belongs to this group.

74. *Squat Lekythos* London BM E 711[467] (Plate 57, 2-3)

H. 18 cm

Ovoid body with broad base ring and long off-set neck with flat handle at back; bell shaped mouth[468].

Red and white with black background and accessories in white. Myrtle wreath, tongues on lower part of the neck. Below this there is a floral ornament between two reserved lines flanking the lower end of the handle. There is a complex palmette ornament beneath the handle, tongues at the base of the neck, a wreath or myrtle leaves on the shoulder and below there is a continuous band of egg pattern. Flesh white with brown details. Drapery has been rendered in colours, but now faded. Gilding is used for gold and the side of Eros' wings, jewellery, and the berries of the wreath around the shoulder.

"The myth of Danae receiving the shower of gold". Learning from the Oracle that his grandson by Danae would kill him, Acrisius had her imprisoned (either in a tower or in an underground chamber). However she bore a son, Perseus, by Zeus, who appeared as a shower of gold in her room[469].

On our lekythos, Danae is seated to the right on the ledges of a landscape, partly clad in a himation. Her body is bare in front to the waist. She also wears a sphendone, necklace and bracelets. She holds out her left arm to accept the shower of gold that falls upon her in a continuous stream of large circular drops. On the right, Eros moves away, looking back with a gesture of encouragement. On the left, an attendant woman, in a long chiton, with saccos, earring, bracelets and necklace, is backing off in surprise. The presence of Eros is natural in such scenes, since intimate relations are about to take place between Zeus and Danae.

On vase painting, two episodes of the story appear to be the most popular among artists of the classical peried[470]. The first shows Danae immediately after her imprisonment, always looking upwards at the ceiling. She is frequently represented with her torso uncovered while holding the edges of her garment as if to expose herself to Zeus. The scene is also represented on a mirror in London[471]. The sudden trickle of a gold shower, as a manifestation of Zeus, is depicted to the astonishment of her attendants.

The second episode of the story relates to events after Akrisius has discovered the birth of Perseus. Danae and her child are always shown near, or about to enter, or actually inside the chest that was destined to carry them across the sea.

One important kalyx-krater, by the Triptolemos Painter[472] in Leningrad, shows both episodes of the myth. On side B Danae is already with Perseus in the chest that is to be their floating prison. Akrisius stands to supervise the operation. He is gesticulating to the carpenter, who is concentrating on his tools as he work. The name of Arkrisius is inscribed next to him. Side A is most relevant, however, which, as with our lekythos, carries the first episode of the story. On this side, Danae, her name inscribed next to her, is shown seated on a grand couch looking at Zeus as he descends into her lap in the form of a shower of gold. The scene is also represented on coins and on gems[473].

The Cyrenaica lekythos is unusual in terms of the presence of Eros with Danae; and the nurse in this episode of the story is not common, a fact noticed by Cook and Metzger[474]. Danae's nurse, the woman behind Danae on our vase, is not presented on any other example showing the first episode of the myth. Eros here appears to be leaving in haste, after his successful mediation, while Danae is opening up to the trickle of gold. A squat lekythos in San Francisco, dated to the middle of the century - showing Eros standing between two seated women - may well represent the first episode of the story, but so far the representation is only interpreted as a woman and Eros[475]. Along the top edge of the scene, over the head of Eros, there are six pellets, with four more on the ribbon between Eros and the woman on the right. These pellets do indeed look similar to those falling on Danae's lap on our lekythos. I also like to believe that the two lekythoi are nearly contemporary: they share a number of features. Both lekythoi, with their contracted bodies, slender necks, and wide flaring mouth pieces, should be grouped among the later type of squat lekythoi[476]. They have reserved areas on the neck and where the body joins the base. The San Francisco lekythos has a similar composition. The compactness of the pose of the sitting women is identical, and Eros, on both vases, is provided with flattering drapery that is considered an innovation at the close

[467] Smith, *Catalogue of Vases* 351 (E 711). Cook, *Zeus* III, fig.297. Schefold, *Die Gottersage,* 241, fig.338.

[468] For shape see Richter and Milne, 14-15. Rudolph, *Die Bauchlekythos, passim*, but especially 72, pl.34.1, in connection with our vase.

[469] In classical literature the story is told by: Hyginus, *Fabulae* 63; Apollodorus, 22-4; Ovid, *Met.* 4, v.611. See also Roscher, *Lex. Myth.*, 946 f.. Rose, *A Handbook,* 272, 284, n 51.

[470] Cook, *Zeus* III, 455 f. Metzger, *Represent.,* 51m, 335 f. Karouzou, *BCH* (1946), 439 f.

[471] Schefold, *Die Gottersage*, 241. See the illustration compiled by Karouzou, *Ant.Kunst* 13 (1970), 34 ff., figs.1 & 2, pl.24, 1-4 & 6. The London Mirror is illustrated in Schefold, *op. cit.* 241, fig.339.

[472] Leningrad 637 (st 1723) 1, *para.,* 365, Addenda 110. Cook, *Zeus* III, 457. *LIMC* I, pl.343. Atkinson, 3. Simon and Hirmer, pls.154-65. Boardman, *ARFH,* fig.306.

[473] Boardman, *Greek Gems,* 210, pl.637, 216, pl.667 (inscribed Danae). A bronze coin of Argos, struck by Hadrian, was found to represent Danae seated on a thrown. British Museum Cat., *Pelopon.,* 148, pl.28,11.

[474] Cook, *op. cit.* 467. Metzger, *Represent.,* 337.

[475] *CVA,* San Francisco 1, p 50 f., pl.XXVIII (488).

[476] Schefold, *UKV*, 140.

of the first Kerch period, before 360 B.C. Distinctive too, is the symmetrical palmettes and filling ornament at the back of the vase[477]. The main element of decoration consists of large palmettes, triangular in shape at the bottom of the body, below the handle. Above is a smaller one. To the right and left of the handle, palmettes, spirals and other filling ornaments are placed symmetrically. This type of ornamentation is not at all dissimilar to that on our hydria in London (E 241)[478].

At any rate, our vase, like the San Francisco lekythos and the London BM E 241, was probably painted in the later years of the second quarter of the fourth century (365-350 B.C.).

75. *Oinochoe, Shape III* London BM E 554[479] (Plate 58, 1-2)

A maenad (or Komos Girl) running to the right but looking back. She wears a long sleeved, blue and white-bordered jacket. She carries a jug and torch. She appears to be pursued by a naked youth who is balancing a tympanum in his left hand and snapping the fingers of the right hand. His garment hangs on his arm. Below the scene there is an egg-and-dot pattern. This is an early Kerch style. The pose of the maiden and the type of garment she wears are to be found on a squat lekythos from Olynthus, and on a lebes gamikos (from Boetia) in Berlin[480]. A nude male figure (his garment hanging on his left arm), in an identical pose to that on our piece, with a tympanum in his left hand, is to be found on another chous from Histria, dated by Alexandrescu to the second quarter of the fourth century B.C.[481]. Both vases are probably from the same workshop. Ours is attributed by Beazley to the painter of the Ferrara chous, and dated to the second quarter of the fourth century B.C

76. *Lebes Gamikos* Cyrene Museum (no number) (Plate 59, 1-2)

This is a miniature vase, Type II.

It has high vertical handles. The lid is lost and there is no stand.

On the shoulder of the vase there is a tongue pattern.

The painting represents part of an Epaulia scene continuing round the vase. In the centre is a draped female figure dressed in a long elaborate chiton, and wearing a fillet in her hair. She advances to the right but looks back. In her right hand she holds a fan. Above it there is a sash hanging. On her left arm she supports a box, under which fall the ends of a broad scarf. Approaching her from the right and left are two flying Nikai. Both have unusually long, extended wings decorated with black dots. The lower bodies stretch far back under the wings. The one on the right of the main scene has a scarf in her left hand. The one on the left supports a chest. Both wear chitons with thick black borders.

The lebetes gamiko[482], with similar scenes, were probably used (suggests Brueckner) for food or drink by the bridal couple[483]. Another theory is that they held water for the bridal bath[484]. The water may have been mixed with perfume for sprinkling and purification. (This could be true in relation to the small size of our vase from Cyrenaica.) The suggestion that the vase was even used for funerary purposes is not entirely supported[485], for lebetes gamikoi, unlike the loutrophoroi and the louteria, have nothing to do with the cult of the dead, or with the funeral bath, and there is no lebes gamikos found within a funeral scene[486].

Our earliest evidence for the production of lebetes gamikoi, with such features as ours, seems to emerge around 430 B.C. The Marlay Painter is known to have decorated lebetes gamikoi[487]. After him, many were attributed to the Washing Painter[488], and the manner of the Meidias Painter[489].

In the fourth century, the Marsyas painter is known to be responsible for the production of a number of such pots[490].

The iconography of lebetes gamikoi deals, overwhelmingly, with the manifold aspects of a wedding. On many of these the artist depicts a file of women bringing gifts to the bride in Epaulia scenes. Two winged figures appear frequently among the women with their gifts[491]. On a pyxis in Athens (by the Athens Painter 1585), a winged figure is shown with a wreath leading the procession to the seated bride[492].

On lebetes gamikoi, these winged figure are occasionally shown hovering symmetrically beneath the handles, carrying

[477] See H.R.W. Smith, in San Francisco, *CVA* i 50 f., pl.25.

[478] See Entry No.53.

[479] Smith, *Catalogue of Vases* III, 320 (E 554). Hoorn, *Choes & Anthesteria*, No.168. *ARV* 1504, 2.

[480] i) Squat lekythos, Olynthus, inv.34-43. *Olynthus* XIII, 141, No.85, pl.84 (84).

ii) Libes gamikos, Berlin Antiquarium F.2937. Schefold, *UKV* 29, No.276, fig.66.

[481] *Histria* IV, 79, No.459, pl.55.

[482] Richter and Milne, *Shapes and Names*, 11. Brueckner, *AM* 32 (1907), 98. Metzger, *BCH* 66-67 (1942-43) 22-247. Cook, *GPP*, 232. Ginouves, *Balaneutike*, 276-282. See Robinson, *AJA* 40 (1936), 507 ff., and 518 for a list known as lebeles gamikos.

[483] Brueckner, *op. cit.* 98.

[484] Neugebauer, *Führer durch das Antiquarium*, 98. Fürtwangler, *La Collection Sabouroff.*

[485] Kurtz and Boardman, *Greek Burial Customs*, 151, 241.

[486] Kenner, *OJh* 29 (1935), 152.

[487] *ARV* 1277, 14-15, 17-18, 22-25.

[488] *ARV* ,1126-1128 and 1133, 196, *par* 454, 4 *bis* and 3 *ter*.

[489] *ARV* ,1322, 11-18, 1322-23, 19-32 *ter*, 1326-27, 77-90; 1328, 92-99. *Paralip.* 479, 14 *bis*, 20 *bis*, 91 *bis*, and 96 *bis*. See also Athens 1659. Richter and Milne, *Shapes and Names*, fig.74. Collignon and Couve, pl.XLVIII, 1575. *ARV* 1322, 11.

[490] *ARV* 1475, 1-2, 7.

[491] Athens National Museum 1681. Brueckner, *op. cit.* pl.VIII. *ARV* 1322, 16.

[492] Athens 1367a, from Athens. *ARV* 1360, 3. Roberts, *The Attic Pyxis*, 110 f., pl.101,2.

baskets and a taeniae, a kalathos or wedding torches[493]. While Beazley always referred to those creatures as Nikai, a personification of female beauty, Kenner considers them to be winged spirits or beings connected with demonic winged creatures (Sirena, Sphinxes, Gorgons, Harpies, Eos)[494].

Since the seventh century, creatures such as Sirens and Gorgons appear regularly on vases. If these winged figures were connected to these early representations, then the explanation would be that they were in the processions to ward off evil, bring blessings, and share in the pleasant occasion.

Lebetes gamikoi are often found in pairs, and occasionally threes, as part of matched sets including red-figured lekanides, and pyxides. The paintings on these sets were often proved to have been carried out within one single workshop. One example of these sets is the group found in the offering areas of the Kerameikos of Athens. No less than three lebetes gamikoi Type I pyxides, red-figured lekanides, and other black and plain pots were found. The pattern on the bodies of the lekanides and pyxides is similar. It consists of palmettes, presented alternately vertical and reserved within a triangular frame.

A pair of lebetes gamiko, by the Washing Painter (430-420 B.C.)[495], was found with a black glazed lekanis and two red-figured Pyxides. The subjects on the two lebetes gamikoi proved to be complementary. The bride is portrayed on each of the two vases in a different stage of her life. On one of these she sits in preparation for her marriage. On the other the bride becomes a mother and holds up her child. The presence of the basket on the woman's lap in the two scenes identifies her as the same person[496].

The subject on another set of lebetes gamikoi is a nuptial scene where a bride stands holding a fan. Eros hovers at her side and a woman approach with gifts. Published by Schlorb-Vierneisel, the vessels were considered to belong to a single workshop[497]. This workshop was first recognised by Roberts as the Otchet Group (370-360 B.C.)[498].

Spina also provided sets of finds. Many of these included nuptial lekanides, but instead of pairs of lebes gamikoi we have pairs of oinochoi, many with nuptial scenes[499].

[493] *AM* 32 (1907), pl.5, 7-8. Kenner, *ÖJh* 29 (1935), 109 ff., 53 (once owned by Sammlung Lan and Koronski and now in the Greek Museum, Newcastle upon Tyne).

[494] Kenner, *OJh* 31 (1939), 81-95, figs. 33, 34.

[495] Vierneisel, *AA* (1964), 431-434, fig.24. *Paralip.* 454, 3 *bis* and 3 *ter*. A *Deltion*, 18 ii, pl.23.

[496] The idea was first summarized by Buschor in *AM* 71 (1956), 205-207. Beil, 115, 117, 118.

[497] Schlorb-Vierneisel, *AM* 81 (1966), 77-75. Beilagen, 48-50.

[498] Roberts, *AJA* 77 (1973), 435 ff.

[499] Massei, *Gli. Askoi.*, 46, pl.XI 2-30; p.60, pl.XV 1-38; p.175-177, pl.XLII 3-110; p.257-258, pl.LX 2-157; p.260-261, pl.LXI 2-158; p.271-273, pl.LXV 2-163; p.298-299, pl.LXXI 2-3, 177.

We have yet to find any other lebes gamikos to match our piece, or any other relevant item as part of a set. There are fragments of lekanides, but these are from Euhesperides[500].

However, there is a lekanis from Olynthus that is very close to the Cyrenaica piece[501]. The zealous maid wears a peplos with an overall. The upper part of the dress is decorated in a similar fashion and the marking of the chest is identical.

What makes the Cyrenaica lebes gamikos exceptional, however, is the nature of the presentation of the scene. This is clearly an abbreviated nuptial scene, but certain elements such as Eros and the seated bride were left out. The artist was clearly only interested in the zealous maid, who rushes to deliver the gift to the bride, surrounded by the two Nikai.

Stylistic traits characteristic of the Otchet Group workshop are present on our vase. These are the delineation of the peplos of the female figure, the embroidared taeniae, and the marking on the chest carried by the maid[502]. The patterns on the large fan and the scarf are also characteristic. These stylistic features may be seen on a lekanis belonging to the Otchet Group in Toronto and Adria[503].

77. *Lebes Gamikos* Cyrene Museum (no number) (Plate 60, 1-2)

Neck and handles lost. Shoulder decorated with black tongues on a reserved background.

On one side there is the head of a woman drawn in right profile. She wears embroidered Phrygian headgear, her hair escaping from the side. In front of her is a water bird[504].

On the other side of the pot there are the heads of two women, also wearing Phrygian headgear. Between them there is a roughly drawn scroll pattern.

A closer representation of the treatment of the head cap, the drawing of the birds, as well as the style of painting in general from Olynthus, is found on more than one example[505]. Athens, too, provides a number of lekanis lid fragments painted in similar style[506]. These are attributed to the Group of the Vienna Lekanis[507].

[500] See Entry Nos.78, 79.

[501] *Olynthus* V, pl.III, 215.

[502] Cf. for example: Athens pnyx 166-67, FR. Talcott and Philippaki, pl.14. *ARV*², 1497, 11-2. Salonica, *inv* 38.216. *ARV*² 1497,18. Robinson, *Olynthus* XIII, pl.87; Salonica fragment, *ARV*², 1497,23. *Olynthus* XIII, pl.114, 1962.

[503] Toronto, 450. Robinson, *Ontario* Vol.11, pl.LXXXIII. *ARV* 1497, 14. Adria, *Mostra*, pl.CXXV.

[504] Cf. entry No.71, a woman and a bird on a pelike.

[505] *Olynthus* V, pl.114/234 and pl.122/270. *Olynthus* XIII, pl.84/58, pl.86/63.

[506] *Hesperia*, Suppl. X, nos.178, 179, 183, pl.16 and p.43.

[507] *ARV*², 1501, 2 1691. Beazley, *JHS* 59 (1939), 34; *Olynthus* XIII, 119 f.. Eichier, *CVA*, Vienna, text to pl.50, 6-7 and *CVA*, Cambridge, pl.27,10.

Our hydria was painted around the second quarter of the fourth century B.C., which is the date of the Group of the Vienna Lekanis.

78. *Lekanis (fragment from the lid)* Oxford GP 509 (E-AQ5-1) (Plate 61, 1)

Part of the cover of a lekanis. The knob is missing, painted in black glaze, egg-and-dot pattern around the vertical edge of the lid. On top near the centre is a black dot, originally part of the row of dots surrounding the knob.

To the right the lower part of a woman wearing a chiton. The folds of the drapery are indicated by thin black lines. She sits to the left and appears to be holding a rectangular box. Towards her, on the left, is the left arm of our well-known running maid. She hastens to the right, holding a rectangular box, under which fall the ends of a broad scarf decorated with black dots. The maid is clad in a sleeveless chiton, pinned to her shoulder by a black brooch. Her hair is dressed simply in a knot at the back.

This is a nuptial scene usually taken to represent the day after the marriage, when relatives and friends of the bride would come in a procession to present their gifts. Such scenes, which are very common on Athenaian vases, have been interpreted as Epaulia.

Lakanides painted with such scenes are considered as bridal utensils used during the Epaulia. They carried the gifts to the bride, probably food (cakes) to the newly married couple[508]. There is no shortage of such illustrations showing the vessels' importance on such occasions. On a pyxides (dated to 360-350 B.C.) of the Kerch style, a woman, among the file of women carrying different bridal gifts, is shown carrying a lekanis[509].

Like the lebes gamikos, the lekanis is usually found as part of a set including lebetes gamikoi and pyxides. As with the lebes gamikos, the iconography on the lekanis always depicts the bridal quarters during the Epaulia, the day after of the wedding day[510].

A fourth-century lekanis, from the offering area of the Kerameikos, was found with a group of vases and considered to form a set. The painting on it belongs to one workshop of the Otchet Group[511]. Three or four elements were recognized to identify this group[512]. Eros approaches a seated woman as a maiden runs to the right, looking around. This last element, described by Beazley as the "zealous maid", is very noticeable and prominent in the composition. Characteristic, too, is the heavy, bold, curved line creating the hemline of the dress of the seated woman.

The composition on a lekanis in Toronto[513], by the same group, consists of the repetition of one element: a seated woman and a maid, with the "zealous maid" separating the two. Sometimes the painting is handled in plain style. Alternatively, another figure, usually Eros, is presented in white, as shown on a lekanis from the Kerameikos[514].

The body of the lekanis is usually decorated with a pattern of alternating palmettes, vertical and reversed within a triangular frame. These are to be found on examples from The Keramikos, as well as from Leningrad, Adria and Ancona[515].

The compositional scene and figurative style of our Oxford vase link it to the Otchet Group (370-360 B.C.). It features two of the four main Group elements noted by Beazley. The "zealous maid" approaches the seated woman and hands to the bride the box of wedding gifts. The seated bride is clad in a chiton, the base of which is marked by a heavy, bold, curved line. The box's shape and the embroidery on the taenia, are characteristic of the Group.

79. *Lekanis (fragments from the body of a lekanis)* Oxford (Plate 61, 2)

These are painted black and the paint was also applied to the ledge supporting the lid. The end of one ribbon-like handle remains.

The body design emulates the Otchet Group technique, where alternating palmettes within triangular frames usually feature. Here the frame appears to be circular. Such decorative methods can be observed on examples from Leningrad, Adria, Ancona, Este and Numana in Italy, Athens, and Agighiol in Romania[516]. These are dated to the second quarter of the fourth century B.C.

Lakanides from the Otchet Group workshop are numerous, with the overwhelming majority of them found on mainland Greece. There are at least twenty from Athens and six from Olynthus. In the north, one has been found on Thassos, two from Kerch, and one from Agighiol in Romania. From the Aegean islands there is one from Delos and one from Rhodes.

---

[508] Richter and Milne, *Shapes and Names*, 23 (with illustration) and Deubner *JdI* 15 (1900), 151.

[509] Berlin 3373. Schefold, *UKV*, pl.16,17,2. Roberts, *The Attic Pyxis* 124. Richter and Milne, *op. cit.* 23.

[510] See discussion on Entry No.76.

[511] Discussed in connection with Entry no.76. Cf. also Schlorb-Vierneisel, *AM* 81 (1966), 77-75. Beilagen, 48-50. Roberts, *AJA* 77 (1973), 435 ff.

[512] *ARV* 1496-1498.

[513] *Toronto* 451. Robinson, *Toronto*, 22.3, pl.LXXXIII. *ARV* 1497, 14.

[514] Schlorb-Vierneisel, *op. cit.* Beilagen, 48, 2.4,4.4.

[515] See discussion on following Entry No.81.

[516] i) Two in Leningrad from Kerch. *Otchet* (1913-1915), 85, 95, figs.135,154. *ARV* 1496,1,2. *Para.* 499.
ii) Adria, *Mostra*, pl.123 and pl.124,1. *ARV* 1496, 3 *bis*.
iii) Ancona from Monte Fortino, *ML* 9 (1899), pl.12,7. *ARV* 1497, 19.
iv) Este. *Studi Entruschi* 44 (1876), 54, nos.36,37, pl.XXII (36,37) [Favaretto].
v) *Numana*, inv.279. Fabrini, *Numana*, no.109, pl.LXVI, c.
vi) Athens. Schlorb-Vierneisel, *A.M.* 81 (1966), pl.48,4.
vii)Agighiol (Romania). *Bericht der Römisch-Germanischen*, 50 (1969) pl.130, A-C. Two lekanides also bear similar patterns are in *ARV*², 1498,9. *CVA*, Stuttgart I (26), pl.33.

They are known as far west as Capua, Montefortino, Numana, Adria, Esti, Spina and Numana[517].

80. *Lekanis (fragment from a lid)* Louvre CA 963 CA 964 (Plate 61, 3)

A remnant of a scene showing a griffin in profile and the front detail of a swan separated by a tree branch. The style of painting is similar to one found on a bell-krater from Olynthus by the Griffin Painter[518]. The subject is not clear. Dated to the second quarter of the fourth century B.C.

81. *Lidded Lekanis with ribbon handle* Cyrene Museum (Plate 62, 1-2)

Low ring base with a broad surface area [519]. Horizontal ribbon handle.

The exterior of the bowl is painted black. The lid rim is decorated with black dots on a reserved background and the knob features an egg pattern in a faded, black-glazed circle. The lid itself is decorated with two crouching panthers separated by a scroll.

A somewhat similar composition is found on an askos and lekanis from Olynthus (both fourth century B.C.[520]). Our vase can be dated to the second quarter of the fourth century B.C.

82. *Fish Plate* Leiden KVB 148 (Plate 62, 3)

The 'fish plate' takes it name from the marine creatures decorating its surface. Typically, the plate has an overhanging rim, a concave centre forming a depression "for the sauce or drainage", and is a ring-based.

Our example is a small fragment of the central depression area with part of the ring base.

The remaining decoration shows one large and one small fish. Only parts of the large fish (back and fins) remain, but most of the smaller fish can be recognized. It is not possible to detect the species the artist had in mind for the smaller fish, but the larger one is probably meant to represent a kind of sea perch. This species, together with the sargus, mullet, labrus (rock fish), cephalopod, and especially the torpedo, are among the most common fish, and all great favourites with the Attic Artist[521]. Shellfish and molluscs of every sort, not to mention squid and octopus, were very abundant off the shores of Euboea. They provided the fishermen of Ereteria with so important a livelihood that the town even had a squid as its numismatic device[522].

Although fishing was a full-time occupation in the ancient world, the Greeks regarded it as a far less noble pursuit than hunting. Plato was advised specifically in the *Laws* against acquiring a taste for sea-fishing or angling[523]. Plutarch held the view that fishing was an inglorious pursuit unworthy of a free man, because it required more cunning than strength, and did not, like hunting, provide one with healthy exercise[524]. In fishing centres, such as Olynthus, many fishhooks, netting needles and weights were found throughout the residences of the north hill. (The same finds occur extensively in southern Italy, where many citizens were fishermen[525].)

Fish plates have been found in both residential areas and cemeteries. This would imply that they were used for daily meals of fish. Fish was a staple of the Greeks and was in great demand, and highly favoured, since Homeric times. Most Athenians were obliged to rely on fish rather than meat[526]. The fish market was one of the most crowded and picturesque in the whole of the Agora.

Schefold argues that fish plates might also have been used at funeral feasts. He suggests that the fish decoration is a reference to Europa crossing the sea, and also symbolizes, perhaps, the flight of the dead to the other world[527]. Indeed, there are a number of fragments of fish plates that illustrate the abduction of Europa amidst shoals of real and fantastic sea creatures[528]. Fish plates painted this way, and with other mythological scenes, were probably intended primarily for ritual use.

Schefold's suggestion, however, that the fish plates were broken after the funeral feast and then buried in the tomb has yet to be proved as common practice; the series of fish plates found in the Leptis Magna cemetery were found intact[529]. Both H.B. Walter and D. Robinson suggest that fish plates might also have been hung up as votive offerings in marine deity temples, such as Poseidon's sanctuary at Paestum[530].

---

517 i) Athens. *ARV* 1496-98, 4-13, 15, 17, 21, 27-33. Talcott and Philippok, pl.14-15.
ii) Olynthus. Toronto 451. This is associated, by Robinson, to Salonica inv.38-216. *Olynthus* XIII, pl.87. Salonica inv.124. (R.213). Robinson, *Olynthus* 5, pl.110,213 (*ARV* 1297, 20). Salonica, fragments in Robinson, *Olynthus* XIII, pl.114, 195c, pl.115, 197, b,d (*ARV* 1497, 23-25).
iii) Thasos. Limenas, fragment (*ARV* 1497,22).
iv) Delos. Dugas, *Delus,* pl.56,24 (*ARV*², 1497,26).
v) Spina Ferrara inv. 2003. Alfieri, *Spina,* fig.291. For those from Agighiol, Capua, Adria, Numana, Este.
See Note 516 above.

518 See for comparison *Olynthus* XIII pl.45 and Schefold, *UKV* 159.

519 For the shape see discussion on Entry No.36, Chapter 4 (black glaze).

520 *Olynthus* V, 114, nos.233-235.

521 Trendall, *JHS* 57 (1937), 268.

522 Flaceliere, *R.E.A.* 50 (1948), 211-217.

523 Plato, *Laws,* 823 e.

524 Plutarch, *De Sollertia animalium,* 9.

525 Robinson, *Olynthus* XIII, 127. Aristotle, *Politics,* 1291,b.

526 Davidson, *Mediterranean Sea Food*, 109 f. See also the section on food in Flacière, *Daily Life in Greece*, 170.

527 Schefold, *UKV*, 147 f. See the representation of the story on our hydria in Entry No.49.

528 See the collection from the northern cities of the Black Sea reported by Zimmermann, *infra*. See Note 531.

529 De Miro – Fiorentini, *Quaderni* 8, fig.94.

530 Walters, *History of Ancient Pottery* I, 487. Robinson, *Ontario,* 229.

Excavation has produced many red-figured fish plates from southern Italy[531], but surprisingly very few Attic examples. Attic types were comparatively late introductions to the repertoire of the Athenian potter. Although an earlier type, without a rim and with a higher base, may belong to the fifth century[532], fish plates in their developed forms seem not to occur in Athens before the late fifth or early fourth centuries, from when they quickly became popular and were copied in the west. Our only examples of the early Attic painted type are the two plates from Leningrad and the fragments from Istanbul, dated respectively by Schefold as 430 B.C. and 450 to 430 B.C.[533]. However these dates are not entirely accepted, as the plates were not dated within their find contexts. A more likely date for these early examples is 400 B.C.[534].

Although the earliest examples of black-glazed fish plates from the Athenian Agora can be dated to the later years of the fifth century B.C.[535], the earliest evidence for the standard red-figured fish plate seems to come from Motya (destroyed in 397 B.C.). Excavations carried out around the quays of the inner harbour *(Cothon)*, near the City gate, revealed Greek material from the late fifth and early fourth centuries B.C. The finds included two painted fish plates, with dates that cannot be later than 397 B.C. (when Motya fell)[536]. A date of around 400 B.C. is accepted as a *terminus post quem* for the production of red-figured Attic fish plates.

Spina (Tomb 136, Valle Pega) has revealed a set of four Attic fish plates, all black, but the contents of the tomb take us well into the first quarter of the fourth century B.C.[537]. Tombs T.369BVP, T.1064BVB, T.909VT, T.863VT produced four Attic red-figured fish plates, all dating to the first half of the fourth century B.C.[538]. Of probably the same date is the fragment from Histria[539], and another piece from Euhesperides (not seen by the author). The biggest collections, however, come from excavations of ancient cities of the northern Black Sea coast. Fragments of some seventy-five Attic fish plates have been published by K. Zimmermann[540].

Attic fish plates were not produced over a long period and lasted approximately from the end of the fifth, or early fourth, to around the middle, or just after the middle, of the fourth centuries B.C. Their final date of occurrence is generally held to be contemporaneous with the destruction of Olynthus (349/348 B.C.). Indeed, examples of painted Attic fish plates are not known after the middle of the fourth century B.C. On the other hand, black-glazed fish plates continued to be produced during the second half of the fourth century and after[541].

We may now discuss the criterion by which one can differentiate Attic and south Italian styles. Although both manufacturing areas seem to show common marine species, the actual arrangements of the fish by individual artists can be indicative of the place of production.

On Attic plates, Trendall and McPhee have proposed[542] that the backs of the fish (with fins) seem to be always shown on the inside, close to the central depression, while the bellies are towards the outside, near the rim. With south Italian production the opposite is the case. The backs of the fish are always on the outside of the plate, near the overhanging rim, while the bellies are shown inside, near the central depression.

Accordingly, the finds from Motya may not be Attic; they are probably south Italian productions of a later date. The collection (reported by Zimmermann) from the northern Black Sea coast conforms to such patterns of fish arrangement. Our fragment would thus appear to be of Attic production, dated, perhaps, to the first half of the fourth century B.C. The fish plate from Spina (Tomb T.909VT) seems to be the nearest parallel to our fragment, showing, coincidentally, the same species, a sea perch[543].

---

531 For south Italian fish plates see K. Zimmermann, in *Wissenschaftliche Zeitschrift Rostock* 16 (1967), 561-70. La Croix, *La faune marine dans la décoration des plats à poisons,* 19-20. Trendall, *JHS* 57 (1937), 268, and *The Art of South Italy,* vases from Magna Graecia, Entry nos. 82, 83, 102, 110, 111.

532 For possible antecedents of fish plates, see the section on stemmed plates in Sparkes and Talcott, *Ath.Agora* XII, 142-143. Shefton, *JHS* 85 (1965), 259.

533 Leningrad. Schefold, *UKV,* figs.1-2. *Larisa* III, 177, pl.59,10.

534 Corbett, *BSA* 50 (1955), 265. Shefton, *op. cit.* 259.

535 Sparkes and Talcott, *Ath.Agor*. XII, 147B.

536 Motya inv. 157. Isserlin B50, *I.L.N.* Sept 21, (1963), 426, fig.6. Leeds Annual, IV, (1962-3), pl.13, 7. Sparks and Talcott, *ibid*, 147, no.20. I am not sure, however, that the fragment also from Motya is Attic, see Isserlin, in *Archaeology* 27, 3 (1974), 191 (I am grateful to D. Gill for the reference). D. Gill informed me of a fragment from Selinus in the Antiquarium in Sicily. He says that the fragment seemed to him to be Attic, but he was not able to handle it.

537 *RIASA* 1955, 140, fig.66 and p.159, fig.196. Shefton, *op. cit.* 259.

538 T.369B VP (inv. 14 834), T.1064B VP (inv. 38011), T.909 VT (inv. 2433), T.863 VT (inv. 2436). See Alfieri, *Spina,* 118 f, nos.306-7, 308, 309, 310. Alexandrescu, *Histria* IV (1978), pl.59, *bis* for the piece from Euhesperides, see D. Gill's report in (eds.) G.D.B. Jones and J.A. Lloyd, *Euhesperides* 1968-69.

539 Alexandrescu, *Histria* IV, pl.59, 509 *bis.*

540 K. Zimmermann, in *Iz istorii Severnogo Prichernomoria v antichnuiu epokhu*. Sbornik Statei, 59-92. The next examples were kindly indicated by David Gill: Frel J. in *Listy Filologicke*, 92 (1969), 291-293, and the examples in The Louvre CA 2265, from Kertch; Brauron 478, from Brauron; Larnaka (Pilrides), from Cyprus (probably Marion).

541 See the section on black-glazed fish plates and Sparks and Talcotte, *Ath.Agor*., 147 ff., for the third century type. See Jehasse, in *Salamine De Chypre* VIII, 33 f.

542 Personal communication (Brian Shefton).

543 See *supra* 538.

Chapter Four

COMMENTARY ON THE IMPORTED ATTIC RED-FIGURED POTTERY

I. STYLES, ARTISTS AND GROUPS

The Late Sixth- and Fifth-Century Attic Pottery

The Attic Red-figured vases in this study fall within the limited period of nearly two hundred years: from the last quarter of the sixth century into the last quarter of the fourth. None of the production of the pioneer groups appears to have reached Cyrenaica, but we have examples that seem to represent the early red-figure painting. The Type C cup No.3 is probably by the cup painter Epictetus (520-490 B.C.), one of the important artists who, after the pioneers of the newly discovered red-figured style, perfected the red-figure techniques. In the last years of the sixth century we have the two alabastra No.1 a-b. 1(a) is by the Paidikos Group 1(b), while the other is to be placed with the so-called Negro Alabastra. We also have the head-vase No.2 that is close to Beazley's Epilykos class (Class B).

Myson, whose work marks the beginning of the mannerist movement, is probably responsible for the painting of column-krater No.7, while the style on krater No.8 is close to that of the Berlin Painter. The painter must be a follower of that artist. There are also the two lost cups by the painter of the Yale Cup and the Brygos Painter from Cyrene[1].

Of the early Classical period, hydria No.17 is by the Syracuse painter, showing a street scene. This is one example from eleven Hydriai, attributed to the artist[2]. Nearly contemporary with the Syracuse painter are two other artists. The first is the Orchard Painter who painted column-krater No.15. The style of mantled figure with a stick is typical of the painter and taken as a useful clue for identifying his work. The Sotades Painter is probably responsible for the work on cup No.23[3]; only five cups are attributed to this artist. A.D. Ure discusses cups with representations such as horsemen in chlamys, petasus, and holding spears[4].

Pieces Nos.9-12 appear to have been painted by the hand of one of the mannerists. The drawing of himation folds that end in arcs are characteristic of the Pan Painter. Among the early mannerists, and probably contemporary with the Pan Painter, is the Perseus Painter, whose pelike No.13 is one of five pelikai grouped together and identified by Beazley[5]. On the surface of the small rim fragment of column-krater No.14, there is an un-incised animal frieze in silhouette of goats and on the outside there are ivy leaves above and below lines. There must be a connection between these and the work of the red-figured column-krater of the other early mannerists. The Leningrad Painter used such types of decoration on his bell-krater. His column-krater in Lecce serves as representative of his style[6]. The Niobid Painter's style is identified by Beazley on pelike No.16 and the lost bell-krater from Euhesperides[7].

Of the production of the classical period we have the work of a number of artists who were either contemporary to, or a follower of, Polygnotos.

On hydria No.20 there is a seated woman (bride?) with attendants. The style of painting is close to that of the Klephon Painter who seems to have been working in the years c.a. 435-420 B.C. He is fond of portraying bridal quarters, or

1 *Africa Italiana*, 4 (1931) 211(5), 212(2). *ARV*, 497, 45, 397, 44.

2 *ARV*, 520, 32-42.

3 *ARV*, 763-4, *Para* 415, *Addenda* 140.

4 A.D. Ure, *JHS* 55 (1936) 205-215.

5 *ARV*, 581.

6 Bernardini, *Ill Vasi attici* 84, 85.

7 *ARV*, 603, 33.

women preparing for Dionysiac festivals. Hydria No.19, with women fleeing from a youth, is attributed by Beazley to the Group of Brussels (A 3069)[8]. Polygnotos is known to have painted hydria with similar subjects[9].

The accidental discovery of the tomb at Asleaia near Al-Merj (Barka) produced a pelike attributed to the Munich Painter (2335). This is not the only work by the artist known to have reached Cyrenaica: two lost bell-kraters reported by Beazley are known to have been painted by the same Artist[10]. The Marlay Painter (active around 430 B.C.) is responsible for the painting of the two fragments Nos.24 and 25 from two stemless cups. In the tondo of No.24 a symposium was painted within concentric circles in reserve. Four skyphoi from Al Mina, and one from Naucratis, were attributed to the Marlay Painter (ARV 1278, 28-31, 32). These are among the earliest Attic productions to have reached the eastern Mediterranean. We may add to these the lost fragments from a bell-krater by the Cassel Painter, and calyx-krater by the Kadmos Painter[11].

The production of the Meidias Painter in the late fifth century is most important as he had a great influence on the following periods. He continued the style of the Eretria Painter and developed it into a softer and more luxurious form. The painting on the skyphos fragment No.28 is representative of his exquisite style. The loutrophorus No.29, too, was executed in the Meidian workshop or by an artist who followed the master's tradition. The Nikias Painter, who is responsible for the painting on chous No.33 (with Heracles and Nike in a chariot pulled by centaurs), is one of the better followers of the Meidias Painter. The work of the Talos Painter on No.30, and that of the painter of the Ferrara vessel T.28 as No.34, can be placed in the 'ornate' tradition of the late fifth century. To these we include the work of the Painter of the Louvre Maid (L.M.) on the two miniature hydriai Nos.37 and 38, and the two squat Lekythoi[12]. The Stragly Painter is also contemporary; the painting on two squat lekythoi are attributed to him[13].

Fourth Century Pottery

Of the vases that reached Cyrenaica during the fourth century very few can be attributed with certainty. Beazley has attributed the two pelikai Nos.39 and 40 to the Pasithea Painter[14], who was active during the early years of the century. The activities of the Jena Painter may be placed in the first decades of the fourth century. Brian Shefton has identified the painting on pelike No.45, which illustrates the meeting between Electra and Orestes, as the work of this artist[15]. I also believe that pelike No.41, which carries the story of the Calydonian boar hunt, is probably the work of a follower of the Jena Painter, as is the painting on pelike No.43. Probably contemporary with the Jena Painter, or slightly later, is the work of the Meleager Painter. Our pelike No.44 with Dionysos and Ariadne, was probably executed by a follower of the artist. His work is best represented by the painting on a hydria in the Metropolitan Museum[16]. In the same tradition as that of the Jena Painter is the Erbach Painter. His work is quiet and refined. The painting on our pelike No.60, showing Herakles in front of a Doric structure (Herakleion?), was, probably executed by a follower of this artist. Our hydria No.46 is among the excellent production of the first quarter of the fourth century (390-380 B.C.). The exquisite painting, showing the toilet of Helen, is by the hand of the Painter of the Athens Wedding. To the middle years of the first half of the fourth century (380-370 B.C.) belong the works of the next two artists. The skyphos cup No.47, with maenads and satyrs, is attributed to the Q Painter. Pelike No.48, carrying the story of Herakles in the Garden of the Hesperides, is the work of the Hyppolytus Painter. One particular artist whose earlier work may be associated with the years 380-370 B.C., and whose activities continued well into the second quarter of the following century, is the Retorted Painter who appears to have preferred to work on bell-kraters. Only small fragments from a bell-krater (Side B) found in Euhesperides (now lost) have been attributed to this artist[17]. Good representations of his work are the pair of bell-kraters in the Louvre (G 514 and 514 *bis*). The painting on these kraters is similar in style to that of contemporary bell-krater artists, such as the painter of the Oxford Grypomachy and the Telos Painter. Talcott and Philippaki are followed by Robertson in recognizing that the work of these artists is closely related[18], and that they usually decorate the reverse of their bell-kraters not with the customary draped youths, but with a figure of Nike standing between two youths and crowning one of them[19]. The Black Thrysus Painter, too, can be associated with these bell-krater specialists. His painting on our fragment No.62 is probably later and to be dated nearer to the middle of the century or after. Probably contemporary is the Filotrano Painter. Nearly half of his 35 attributed bell-kraters were found in Spina; significantly four were found in Al-Mina. The lost fragment from Euhesperides[20] is the only example by the artist which reached Cyreanica.

To the two middle quarters of the fourth century belongs the style known as 'Kerch', from the south Russian location of many of these pieces. The inhabitants of this region - Greek colonies and Scythian tribes - must have had close commercial contacts with the Athenians at that time. The Kerch style must have been the direct development from the preceding periods. In a way, it resembles that of the Jena Painter and appears to

8 *ARV*,1033.

9 Robinson Collection, *CVA* 11, 32, pl.44.

10 *ARV*, 1163, 38, 39.

11 *ARV*, 1278, 28 - 31 (Marley Painter) 1084, 8, 1186, 26, Leiden KVB 157 (XVIII C14), *ARV* 1223.

12 *ARV*, 1364, 8, 1365, 14 (Louvre MN 763, MN 764).

13 *ARV*, 1367, 13 (MN 770), 1368, 20 (MN 768).

14 *ARV*, 1472, 2, 3.

15 B.B. Shefton in the *Jackson Knight Memorial Lecture*, May 1983, Exeter University (unpublished), also in *The Eye of Greece,* 177 f.

16 New York, 56.171.56. *ARV*, 1412, 46.

17 *ARV*, 1453, 5.

18 Talcott and Philippaki, *Hesperia* suppl X, 9. Robertson in *Excavation at Kition* 68.

19 *ARV*, 1428, 1, 4, etc. For examples of the painter of the Oxford Grypomachy, and *ARV*, 1429, 4, 1430, 19-20, 25 for the Retorted Painter. *ARV*, 1428, 13, 21, 22, 25, 30, 33 for the Telos painter.

20 *ARV*, 1453, 5.

be derived from that of the Meidias Painter in terms of its polychrome effect, but it avoids the latter's clean, sharp outlines and multitudinous drapery lines. Our hydriae Nos.49 (Europa and the bull), 52 and 54 (the Toilet of Helen and the Toilet of Aphrodite and both from the London Group E 230) and 50 (Herakles in the Garden of the Hesperides) are fine examples of the style in the second quarter of the fourth century. The Kerch style appears to have reached its acme nearer to the middle of the fourth century, and although the compositions appear to have become crowded many of its masterpieces may be assigned to this period. In this study the best representations of it are the kalpis No.51, with Ariadne and Thiasos (close to the style of the Helena Painter and the Eleusinian Painter), kalpis No.53, with the Adonia festival, and the two pelikai Nos.63 (Helberg-Reverse Group) and 64, both with Grypomachy scenes. Of the Helberg-Reverse Group, we have two more pelikai from Cyrenaica in the Louvre (MN 738, MN 747 = ARV 1474, 6, and 8).

Lekanides with figured lids showing scenes interpreted as Epaulia were popular in the second quarter of the fourth century. Schefold[21] considers these a coarse reflection of the early Kerch style in this period. The painting shows a woman (bride?) seated and attended by Erotes. Other women bring toilet boxes, alabastra and gifts. Examples of these are reported by Talcott and Philippaki from the Pnyx Hill of Athens. Fragment No.79 from Cyrenaica, from the wall of a lekanis, is decorated with a pattern of palmettes alternatively vertical and reversed with a triangular frame. Such a compositional scheme may be attributed to the Otchet Group (370-360 B.C.). The painting of the lebes gambos No.76, also with an abbreviated Epaulia scene, is probably related to the Otchet Group.

To the second quarter of the century belong the vases attributed to the workshop of the F.B. Group that appears to have favoured the shoulder oinochoe (Shape II). The bulk of the production of this workshop is found in Spina. Four oinochoi from this workshop found their way to Cyrenaica[22] and No.59 is typical of this production.

Of the nine chous attributed to the painter of the Ferrara Chous, one vase was found in Kerch and a second (No. 75) was found in Cyrenaica, the rest are from Spina.

The largest single group to have reached Cyrenaica during the fourth century is Group G, produced during the middle two quarters of the century - the period of the Kerch style. These are pelikai that feature overhanging rims, flaring necks and bulging bodies in the second quarter of the century, and pear-like shapes in the second half of the century. Their bodies are usually occupied by a female head wearing an amazon cap in profile to right or left. Behind the head was painted the protome of a horse and/or griffin. Some of these, such as No.68, are attributed to the work of the Amazon Painter. Nearly half of the 136 pelikai attributed to this workshop were found in Russia, 25 were found in Cyrenaica, and 12 in Spina[23].

[21] Schefold, *UKV* 138.

[22] *ARV*, 1484, 17; 1488, 85; 1487, 153, 158.

[23] *ARV*, 1463-8.

II. THE IMPORTED SHAPES

Among the imported shapes (fig 2) there is a noticeable absence of the stamnos and the amphora and its varieties. The pelike was probably meant to replace the amphora. This shape is known to have become very popular after 500 B.C. Those from Cyrenaica started arriving during the second quarter of the fifth century. The earliest is vessel No.13 by the Perseus Painter (470 B.C.). To the late fifth century belongs fragment No.30, which carries the story of Medea and Theseus. From now on the pelike continues to be imported until the second half of the fourth century without interruption, forming nearly one-third of the imported vessels into Cyrenaica (fig 2). These can be divided into four groups. The first (Nos.13, 16, 18, 21, 27, 30) is the one that reached Cyrenaica in the fifth century. These usually have a triangular shape, narrow neck and splayed foot. The low centre of gravity is characteristic of the shape. Such features were no doubt derived from the black-figured pelike of the later years of the sixth century. These have a bulging broad body with relatively narrow neck and with a high disc foot, as in example No.27. Of the second group, pelikai Nos.39-44, with bulging body, drawn in neck, overhanging lip, and low foot, are typical of the pelikai produced and imported to Cyrenaica in the first quarter of the fourth century. Those produced in the second quarter of the century (Nos.48, 56, 60, 61, 63) constitute our third group. These have less of a bulge and are the type found in Olynthus. In date, therefore, they cannot be much later than mid-fourth century. Pelikai of the fourth group (Nos. 67-752) are roughly pear-shaped, with a wider neck that flares upward. The Amazon head, usually flanked by a horse and griffin, is the usual decoration on these.

Like the pelike, the water jar, or hydria, was a very popular vessel. This is the one-piece hydria, also known as the kaplis. This was introduced to the Athenian workshops by about 520 B.C., but their import into North Africa started nearly a century after that date. Hydriae Nos.17, 19, 20 are typical of those imported in the third quarter of the fifth century. On these early examples the neck, shoulder and body form continuous curves with a gradual narrowing of the body, overhanging rim, and a foot in two degrees. The lower flat and with a narrow disc, the upper curving outwards. The type continues into the fourth century. These usually carry mythological scenes.

Of the various types of oinochoai produced by the various Attic workshops, only the plump type with trefoil mouth, Shape III, the so-called chous, and Shape II (Shoulder Type) were imported to Cyrenaica. Three of these, Nos.31-33, are the standard type which were used primarily in the celebration of the Anthesteria. Their popularity was at its height in the later years of the fifth century. Five examples of the shoulder type were found in Cyrenaica. The first, No.34, is by the Ferrara Painter T.28. The painting on another four oinochoai, all imported to Cyrenaica, is attributed to the F.B. Group[24], and No.59 in this catalogue is a typical example. All of these were produced in the second quarter of the fourth century.

[24] See note 22.

Of the wine-mixer and cooler vessel, the krater, very few were found in Cyrenaica. We have three column-kraters. The painting on No.7 is probably by the column-krater specialist Myson, whose work marks the beginning of the Mannerist movement. The painting on No.15 has already been attributed by Beazley to the Orchard Painter (460 B.C.). This is the last column-krater known to have reached North Africa. Only one calyx-krater was found (Cyrenaica No.22) and it is of the double-register type, dated to the second quarter of the fifth century. Bell-kraters appear to be most in demand from now on. Surprisingly enough no early bell-krater is thought to have been found. The earliest is one by the Niobid Painter[25]. From the fifth century there are examples by the Cassel Painter, two by the Munich Painter (2335), and one by the Kadmos Painter[26]. Of the second quarter of the fourth century, two attributed kraters are lost, one by the Retorted Painter and the other by the Filottrano Painter[27]. No.62 in this study is representative of those imported during this period. There are also a number of fragments from Euhesperides, now in Oxford, and they are probably contemporary with those already mentioned[28].

The small number of Attic cups suggests that they were not common in Cyrenaica. The earliest example by far is the fine Type C Cup (No.3), very probably by the painter Epiktetus (520-500 B.C.). Our Cup is the elegant Type C with concave lip, shallow, wide bowl, curving into a slender short stem standind on a flat foot. No.4 is probably painted by one of the late Archaic cup painters, Onesimos, Makron or even the Chelis Group.

The last cup known to have reached Cyrenaica is the skyphos cup No.47. The type has a deep bowl, heavy wall, a concave lip, slightly thickened at the rim, and a moulded ring-foot. The cup is dated to the first quarter of the fourth century.

Of the deep vessels with horizontal handles, the single example No.28, with straight-lipped skyphos, is very important. The Meidias Painter must be responsible for the excellent and elaborate drawing of the women.

The lekanis, the heavy dish with lateral handles, is among the type of small bowls imported to Cyrenaica. More of these have been found in black glaze than in red-figure. The four examples in this study, Nos.78-81, belong to the second quarter of the fourth century. Two examples, Nos.78 and 79 from the Otchet Group, carry an Epaulia scene.

Oil flasks were also brought to Cyranaica, but these are very small in number. The two fragmentary white ground alabastra are of the type usually suspended by leather thongs and attached to the neck of the flask. No.1(a) is of the Paidikos Group (520-500 B.C.), while the second fragment, No.1(b), belongs to the so-called Negro Alabastra Group, a type which seems to have rarely travelled outside Greece. Among the 34 known examples of this Group, only three or so have been found overseas.

Nos.35 and 36 are the only red-figured Askoi known to have reached Cyrenaica. No.35 is the type with a dome-shape top, flaring spout, and an arched handle from the mouth to the other side of wall, resembling a wine skin. The second Askos (No.36) is of the type with a strainer top and a ring handle set up at right angles to the spout.

Among oil flasks, lekythoi appear to have reached Cyrenaica in the second quarter of the fourth century. These are of the ovoid body style, with a broad base ring and a long offset neck with a flat handle and a bell shaped mouth. No.73 is to be classed as a palmette lekythos, the type investigated by Robinson[29], who divided this type into two distinct groups - earlier and later, according to the variation of the palmette. Nos.74 and 74 *bis* belong to the later group dating to the second quarter of the fourth century. Lekythos No.74 is contemporary with No.73. It is a very important piece as it carries a subject representing the myth of Danae and the shower of gold. Another squat lekythos, painted with Aphrodite and Erotes, comes from Cyrenaica[30]. The type was also found in Taranto and Ruvo[31]. The style of painting on these is close to our lekythoi Nos.74 and 74 *bis*. These seem to form one group, probably produced and painted in one workshop. The almost total absence of the regular, 5th-century lekythos is remarkable, particularly as so many of them reached Sicily.

Of the vessels used for special occasions, we have the well-preserved loutrophorus. This is a hydria type with two horizontal and one vertical handles. In the loutrophorus maidens brought water in which the bride was bathed. The pot was also placed on tombs of unmarried persons. Loutrophorus No.29 is unique, as this is the only known example in the tradition of the Meidian School. Our two lebetes gamikoi Nos.76-77, like the loutrophoros, are connected with the bride and wedding. They usually show scenes in the bridal quarters.

Only one fragment (No.82) of a red-figured fish plate was found[32]. This is clearly a very important fragment, for it is evident that while black-glazed fish plates appear to have enjoyed a wide distribution in the Mediterranean region and beyond (Map 7), red-figured examples are rarely found.

Only one example of the epinetron was found in Cyrenaica (No.6). The epinetron is the knee-piece used by women over which wool was worked. The presence of fragment No.6 is significant. From the published account, it is known-that the epinetron rarely travelled outside Attica. The epinetron found

25 *ARV*, 603, 33.

26 *ARV*, 1084, 3; 1163, 39; 1186, 6.

27 *ARV*, 1430, 28; 1453, 5.

28 Seen by the author, now in the Ashmolean Museum.

29 *Olynthus*, XIII, 146 f.

30 *BM*, E712. W.W. Rudolph, *Die Bauchlekythos*, pl. XXXIV, 2, No.74 *bis* (London BM E712), not discussed in this study, is of the same shape and class.

31 For the example from Taranto, see De Julliis, *Gli Ori Di Taranto*, 375 No.11 (inv 4.555) and 12 (inv 4.557). The examples from Ruvo (Jatta) were seen by B.B. Shefton who confirms their similarity to our example.

32 See the discussion on No.82.

on Rhodes are known to be of local ware. Apart from the single example in Berezan (south Russia), our piece is the only example of the red-figured type to have been found in the eastern Mediterranean[33].

Fragment No.2 is to be classed as a figure-vase taking the form of a human head. This is the type classified by Beazley on the basis of their moulded portions. Our fragment was probably part of a kantharos (Class B), according to Beazley's classification (The Epilykos class). The rhyta, the figure-vase in the shape of an animal form, the equivalent of a human form, has never been found in Cyrenaica.

Cyrenaica, then, appears to have enjoyed a wide variety of shapes, such as are to be found only in Greek settlements. The Greek nature of these North African settlements may thus be clearly identified.

III. THE SUBJECT-MATTER

Mythological Scenes

Of the 84 pieces presented in our study, the subjects on the majority of them appear to deal with mythology, providing us with a rich corpus of mythological scenes. Among these the characters of Dionysos, Aphrodite, Heracles, and related subjects are the most popular.

Dionysos

Dionysos, the wine god, is usually shown with his retinue of satyrs and maenads. His representation on column-krater No.7, painted probably by Myson, is typical of the representations of the Archaic period. On pelike No.44, the wreathed god, with kantharos in his hand, is seen sitting nude next to his consort, Ariadne, and a panther, his favourite animal, in the fourth century manner. By contrast, on the large fragment No.51, he is seen in a richly embroidered costume, consisting of chiton and jerkin, in a Thiasos scene. On this fragment, and indeed with most fourth-century representations of the god, he sits quietly while his followers, satyrs and maenads, dance and play about him. On the fourth-century pelike No.45, Dionysos is not present, only his followers, who are shown engaged in frenzied movement. Occasionally, as on Nos.44 and 61, the maenads are seen being chased or flanked by satyrs, who are about to grab them. Fragment No.40 is very important, as it is the only representation in the fourth century of the young Dionysos in a chariot on his way to fight the giants. Dionysos, in his chariot, is pulled by the unlikely team of panther, bull and griffin. The composition was the creation of the Pasithea Painter during the first quarter of the fourth century.

Aphrodite

There are two types of representation of the goddess of love, Aphrodite. In the first type the goddess is presented as the main figure in the scene and in the second she is not the main figure but nevertheless she is in a prominent position. On hydria No.54 the goddess is engaged in her toilet. She is the central figure in the presence of Eros and a satyr. On hydria No.53 the scene shows the ritual festival of Adonis. Aphrodite, as the main figure in the scene, is seen climbing down the ladder. On hydria No.5l, illustrating the meeting between Dionysos and Ariadne, the goddess is placed behind Ariadne. There is also the representation of the head of goddess on many Attic vases, mostly pelikai, in Cyrenaica. Important among these is kalpis No.55, dated to the first half of the fourth century, where the head of the goddess is symmetrically flanked by two small, flying Erotes. On pelikai Nos.56-58, the goddess is shown in profile next to Eros, and holding a mirror.

Other Gods

Other immortals are represented on vases imported to Cyrenaica. Such vases are not important in terms of their number but rather for their subject. Two vases, a hydria (No.49) and the squat lekythos (No.74) illustrate the Zeus romance. On the hydria he takes the form of a gentle bull, carrying off Europa, the Phoenician princess, to Crete. On the squat lekythos, Zeus visits the imprisoned Danae in the form of a shower of gold and consequently impregnates her.

Athena appears on only one vase, painted by the F.B. Group during the first half of the fourth century. Oinochoe No.59 shows the bust of Athena between two youths. She is presented in profile to left with a spear, wearing a Corinthian helmet pushed up to show her face.

None of the other immortals are represented on Attic red-figured vases in Cyrenaica. Not even Apollo, next to whose temple the nucleus of Archaic Cyrene was built, or Demeter, to whom two sanctuaries, one in Tocra and one Cyrene, were dedicated.

Heroes

(A) Herakles

Fragment No.12 by the Pan Painter is very important, being the earliest Attic work from North Africa to show Heracles as part of the scene that represents the fight of Heracles with the attendants of Buisiris. The presence of such a piece in Cyrenaica is of some significance, as the confrontation between Heracles and the King of Egypt was supposed to have taken place in North Africa. Chous No.33 belongs to the later years of the fifth century B.C. The painting, by the Nikias Painter, shows a parody of the Apotheosis of Heracles. He is taken in a chariot, driven by Nike and pulled by four centaurs. Here the centaurs are subjugated to replace the horses, and so made to pull the Hero's chariot.

The other representations of Heracles are dated to the fourth century. Three of these represent the hero in the last of his twelve labours, the fetching of the Golden Apples of the Hesperides. On his way to Libya, Heracles, we are told, met

[33] See the discussion on No.6.

the Libyan native, the giant Antaius, who forced strangers to wrestle with him and then slew them - until he met Heracles. Scenes representing the Hero and the giant wrestling appear to have come late into pictorial tradition. No representation of such a confrontation was found in Libya. We may cite, however, the fine calyx-krater by Euphranios from Cervetri[34], for the illustration of such a fight.

Vases showing Herakles in the Garden of the Hesperides appear to represent the later version of the myth. This is the late fifth- and fourth-century representation after other versions of the story had faded from the vase painters' stock scenes. They now show quiet scenes, with figures sitting or standing about the tree of the Golden Apples. On pelike No.48 we recognize the scene because a serpent is coiled about the tree. The Hesperid on hydria No.50, helped by an Eros, is represented plucking the Golden Apples from the tree to offer them to Heracles. Here there is no struggle to spoil the tranquility of the garden. The whole picture shows the Hersperides as a garden party in paradise.

These vases appear to have been especially intended for trade with the Greek settlements of Cyrenaica, where that myth had special relevance. It should be stressed that Cyrenaica, Euhesperides in particular, is the only Greek settlement that claims such a number of vases showing Heracles, and, more importantly, the vases that represent the myth of the Hesperides in the fourth century B.C.[35].

(B) Other Heroes

Kadmos is represented on Hydria No.26. The subject is related to the myth of Kadmos and the dragon. Theseus is found on two vases. If fragment No.30 represents the story of Theseus and the sorceress Medea, then this must be an important piece. Also important is pelike No.41, with the story of the Chalydonian boar hunt in which Theseus take part. Our pelike is the only fourth-century Attic pot that carries the illustration of this myth. Meleager brought together a mighty band of Heroes: Jason, Peleus, Ankaios and others, to hunt the great wild boar that was sent by Artemis to savage Kalydon, by way of revenge, and to punish Oineus who forgot the goddess when making a sacrifice.

Grypomachy and Amazonmachy Scenes

In the Gryphomachy scenes, the Arimasps, colourfully dressed in oriental fashion, fight the legendary griffons that guarded the gold beyond the Arimasps' plains, next to the Hyperboreans of central Asia. Two of the representations show the fight in equal terms and there is no hint in the painting as to which side is winning.

On pelike No.64, a griffon confronts a mounting Arimasp. The scene on No.65 seems to represent the subjugation of the griffon by the Arimasps. Two griffons face one another, mounted by Arimasps.

Amazonmachy scenes became really prolific on red-figured vases after the Persian War. These are not uncommon among imported vases. Amazons, like the Arimasps, are usually dressed in oriental gear. While only one example shows the usual battle between Amazons and the Greeks (No.72), the rest of the representations are abbreviated scenes where only the head of an Amazon is shown in profile, either next to a horse and/or a griffon, as on Nos.66-71.

Scenes from the Trojan Cycle

The subject on the two hydriae Nos. 46 and 52, and pelike No.42, relate to the Trojan cycle. On both hydriae, the subject is the Toilet of Helen. She is represented sitting, flanked by a maiden in the presence of Eros. The story on the pelike deals with the meeting between Electra and Orestes at the tomb of Agamenon, a subject which is common on the painting of the later years of the fifth and fourth centuries, especially on south Italian production.

Scenes from Everyday Life

Myth is by no means the only source of inspiration for the subjects on the imported Attic vases to Cyrenaica. Nearly half of these vases show scenes from everyday life, whether religious, sport or other scenes.

The scene on hydria No.53 is related to the religious festival of Adonia, a theme found on a number of fourth-century Greek vases. The scene is usually recognized by the presence of a ladder in the centre of the representation. Three principal figures are shown in the scene. The first climbs down a ladder bringing incense from above. The second figure receives the incense and the third hands it to the incense burner.

The scene on fragment No.8, whereby a woman pours a libation into a phiale held by a man before departure, or after arrival, can be classified as a religious scene. The choes (Nos.31-33), mostly produced in the later years of the fifth century, are standard items from children's graves, used primarily in the celebration of the Anthesperia in honour of the wine god Dionysos. Children shown crawling on these vases is very much a trademark of these choes.

There are also vases that depict Epaulia scenes. From the Median School we have the well-preserved loutrophoros No.29. On it there is a scene of the women's quarters that continues around the vase. The bride, surrounded by maidens, sits on a klismos while Eros flies towards her. The scenes on Nos.20 and 28 are also related to the Epaulia, or at least to depictions of women's quarters. The subject is also repeated on fragment No.79, which is related to the Otchet Group and dated to the second quarter of the fourth century. The lebes gamikos No.76 also appears to be related to the Otchet Group. The subject is similar but the scene here is abbreviated: the bride is not represented, instead two Nikai flank the maiden who is carrying gifts.

The painting on pelike No.21 shows a farewell scene, taking place indoors. A youth is departing, possibly for adventure

---

[34] Louvre G. 103 from Cervetri *ARV*, 14, 2 *Para.* 322, *Addenda* 73. Boardman. *ARFV*, fig.23 *Lime* 1, pl.651, Antaius I 24.

[35] See the discussion on Nos.39 and 48.

rather than war. Holding a long spear, he is dressed as a hunter with a black-bordered chlamys fastened by a brooch on his shoulder.

Sporting scenes are represented on two pieces. Fragment No.23 depicts a youthful horseman with a long spear held at rest. On pelike No.27, two naked youths in palaesta are shown probably after exercise; one of them holds a strigil (scraper).

Symposia, drinking parties, are represented on two fragments (Nos.24 and 62). The scenes show dining rooms with couches set along the wall below three-legged tables for food. On the couches, men are shown in the middle of a drinking party. They are partly naked as they recline on the couches, leaning on striped cushions while occasionally women play the double pipes.

A number of scenes show interaction between men and women. Hydria No.19 depicts two women fleeing from a youth. The scene on pelike No.43 shows a youthful hunter(?) chatting with a woman in a relaxed manner. Two men and two women on both sides of column-krater No.15 are also engaged in conversation. We are not sure, however, of the interpretation of the scene on pelike No.13. A man is holding a cock towards a woman who is holding a closed chest. Are these gifts being offered to the women, or is she a maidservant accepting gifts on behalf of her mistress, the bride? There is no doubt, however, about the interpretation of the subject on Hydria No.17 by the Syracuse Painter. In a street scene, a woman, probably a hetaera, is flanked by two bearded men, possibly customers; she offers a honeysuckle to the man on her right (and more than likely herself as well).

Chapter Five

THE BLACK-GLAZED POTTERY

Attic black glaze is among the important ware representing the plain version of black- and red-figure vessels, employing essentially the same technique[1]. The typical fabric of its product is a fine orange-brown, apparently the result of mixing red and yellow clays in suitable proportions, and reveals a sprinkling of very fine mica particles. Its distinctive feature is a fine lustrous or metallic black slip surface that contrasts with the underlying clay, which, owing to an oxidizing firing, is red, brown or yellowish - never intentionally grey or black. This surface can then be enlivened in different ways[2]. The paint, for practical or aesthetic reasons, may not cover the whole of the surface. Thus areas such as the resting surfaces of the pot, elements of the foot (i.e. the top of the stem, the outer edge, the resting surface, the section above the foot), and various parts of the lip and knob are reserved. In some cases a red wash may be applied to these reserved areas, while the underside is often decorated with a series of black circles around a central dot on the reserved surface. Added clay with gilding was frequently used in the 4th century, especially on the neck of closed pots[3]. Ribbing[4] was also popular in both fifth and fourth centuries, again especially on closed pots, and occasionally on other vessels such as kantharoi and stemless cups. Such features, together with other characteristics on many of these vases, such as the metallic surface, the thin body wall, and indeed their very shapes, are most probably to be attributed to the influence of contemporary metal work[5].

Just before the middle of the fifth century the technique of incised pattern and stamping was introduced[6]. A variety of decorative elements may thus appear on the vessels, all covered by the black slip. The shapes which carry incised or stamped decoration are mainly the different styles of drinking cups, bowls, flasks and amphoriskoi for scented oil.

The main centre of production of this class of pottery was Athens[7], from roughly the sixth century to the end of the fourth century B.C. Its distribution was widespread, for it was, no doubt, appreciated throughout the sphere of Greek influence and had a wide export market, equaling and even exceeding that of the figured wares in extent. It has thus been found in Italy[8], in most Near Eastern countries[9], and it ranges from the towns of the Black Sea[10], through Bulgaria, to Germany in

---

1 Farnsworth, *AJA* 48 (1964), 223 pl. 68, 13. Noble, J.V., *The Techniques*, 31-33. Skomorowska and Swiecki, Z., *Archeologia* (Warsaw) 28 (1977), 37-47. For the most recent discussions, with full bibliographies, see Maggetti et al., *Archeologia* 23, 2 (1981), 199-207. Tite, Bimson and Freestone, *Archeometry* 24, 2 (1982), 117-126.

2 Hayes, *Ontario 1*. Sparkes, *Ath. Agora* XII, 17-31.

3 Kopcke, *AM.* 79 (1964), 22-84. Beil, 8-47. Wolters, *A.M.* 38 (1913), 198-199. Thompson, *Hesperia 11* (1934), 339.

4 See Kopcke *op.cit.* 22-84. Beil, 8-47. Noble *op.cit.* 31-33. Shefton, in *Annals Archeologiques*, 109-110. Gill, in Vickers (ed.) *Pots and Plans*, 19 f.

5 D.K. Hill, *AJA* 51 (1947), 248-56, pls. LVIII-LXI. Robertson M., in Kurtz (ed.) *Beazley and Oxford*. See also Shefton *op.cit.* 109-110, and the discussion of the technique in an unpublished paper delivered to the International Vase Symposium at Amsterdam (12-15 April 1984) in *Ancient Greek and Related Pottery*. (Brijder ed.) M. Vickers, J. Allan & O. Impey, *From Silver to Ceramic* (Oxford 1986). Gill *op.cit.* (n 4).

6 Ure in *JHS* 55 (1935), 209-210. Corbett in *Hesperia* 24, (1955), 172 ff. Gill *op.cit.* (n 5). These authors discuss the technique of 'stamping'. See also Hill *AJA* 51 (1947), 248-58, pls. LVIII-LXI. For the influence of Achaemenid gold and silver shapes see Shefton *op.cit.* 109 ff. and Strong *GRGSP* 78, 84-88, 93-101. Sparkes and Talcott, *Ath. Agora* XII, 15.

7 Important discussions on Athenian black-glaze of the fifth and fourth centuries are: Talcott in *Hesperia* 4 (1935), 476-523 and Corbett in *Hesperia*, 18 (1949), 298-345. C. Dugas in *Delos* XXI on the black vases from the Rheneia Purification Pit, is a valuable contribution providing *terminus ante quem* of 425 B.C. For mid fifth century cf. Boulter, in Hesperia 10 (1953), 59-115. For the fourth century see Robinson *Olynthos* V, text to pls.148-195 and XIII, text to pls.142-245. Gill, in Kenrick (ed.) *Sabratha*. Jehasse, in *Kition* iv. Alexandrescu in *Histria* IV, 82 ff., pls.60-67.

8 Cf. Aurigemma, *Spina* I, text to pls.17, 19, 117, 134, 139, 212, 214, 218, 219 par. II, see Pls.104 and 145 for examples on material from Spina on the Adriatic. Also Alfieri, *Spina*, 122 f., figures 324-344, and for finds from Lipari (an island near the North-Eastern Coast of Sicily), see Bernabo-Brea and Cavalier, *Meligunis-Lipara*, text to pls. 18, 56-70, 77, 127-135.

9 Clairmont, *Berytus* (1956-57), 1-34. For fourth century export and *idem* Cyprus, L, see Jehasse, *Salamine de Chypre* VIII, passim.

10 Boardman, *A.R.* for 1963-63, pp.34-51 and *Greek Overseas*, 238-245. Gaidukevich, *Nekropl. Bosporskich*, 43 f. Onaiko, *Madozhda Anisimouna* 1966, notes to pls.VIII-IX. *Idem*, 1970, notes to pls.VII-X. Petrenko, *Provoberezhe Sednego*, notes to pls. 11-13. Vickers, *Scythian Treasures*, 40, Pl.9a,b. Alexandrescus *op.cit.* 82 ff.

Central Europe, France and Spain[11], and North Africa[12]. This is particularly true of the region of Cyrenaica[13], where the range of fifth and fourth century material is remarkably wide in quantity and quality, indicating that black-glaze vessels constituted a large percentage of the imports to the Greek Cities in the region of Cyrenaica, as to most other Greek cities of the same period.

I. THE FIFTH-CENTURY TYPES

SKYPHOS (1-13, pls.63-66)

Skyphos of Corinthian Shape

Skyphoi of a traditional Corinthia type were apparently among the earliest imports to Cyrenaica. It is easy to recognize by the reserved band with fine black rays above its foot. The top of the foot is usually black; the underside is reserved with concentric black rings around a central dot[14]. Not all these characteristics are applicable to our two skyphoi. Skyphos No.1 is a miniature shape with ring foot, dated to the middle of the fifth century. Of this small type, a series of skyphoi are reported from the Athenian Agora and elsewhere, dated to the same period[15].

Skyphos No.2, on the other hand has a thin, well-rounded wall curving into a small splayed foot, the upper-side of which is spreading, the lower is convex, forming a continuous curve down to its meeting with the outer surface. Horseshoe handles are attached to the wall, but unlike the typical Corinthian type it has no reserved zone above the foot; the vase is glazed inside and out. Such types of skyphoi are reported from the Athenian Agora. These are datable to the third quarter of the fifth century[16].

Skyphos of Attic Shape

I. Type A: (3-11, pls.64-65)

The skyphos is one of the most popular Attic drinking cups used during the Archaic and Classical period. It was produced in varieties that developed and changed with the time.

Although Attic production of this shape started in the early years of the fifth century[17], the importing of the type to Cyrenaica does not seem to have occurred before the third quarter of the century. This was the period when this Attic shape was evolving into its standard form[18].

The earliest among our group (No.3) has a ring foot with an outer profile, recognizable with a more or less torus outline. The walls swell upwards slightly, in an outline continuous from the foot, to reach its widest diameter at the rim. Attached to the latter we find triangular handles. The shape is fully glazed apart from the underside, which is reserved and decorated with glazed circles. Examples in dated contexts come from Leptis Magna, Delos, and the Athenian Agora[19]; our vessels 4-11, belong to the last quarter of the fifth or early fourth centuries B.C. Two of these, in particular, are from dated contexts. No.9 was found in a sealed tomb in the North Necropolis of Cyrene. This tomb (N-81-A.C.) contained red-figure fragments. We are almost certain that the red-figured chous found in the same tomb belonged to the later years of the fifth century[20]. No.11, too, came from a tomb in Apollonia. The black-glazed materials here belong to the late fifth and early fourth centuries[21].

II. Type B (so-called Glaux): (12-13, pl.66)

Nos.12 and 13 represent the type of skyphos with one horizontal and one vertical handle, similar to a mug shape. The idea was, perhaps, for the item to serve as a dipper, or small jug, as well as for drinking purposes. The shape is similar to Skyphos Type A, the only difference being that in Type B the body narrows slightly at the bottom of the wall to rest on a smaller ring foot with torus profile. Beazley suggests that the vessel's shape is intended to represent the back and tail of an owl[22]. The owl itself is found painted in red-figure style on the closely related skyphos type known as Glaux[23]. This

---

11 For Bulgarian finds see the grave at Dalboki, near Stara Zagora, *Ashmolean Museum* report for 1948, 20-21, pl.3. *Apollonia 1946-1949, passim*. Filow, *Duvanlij*, p.65, 78, 93-94. For Germany, see the finds at Klein Aspergle (near Ludwigsburg), Ebert, Reallexikon, S.V. (Klein Aspergle and p.103). For France, Villard, *Marseille*. Mouret Collection, Fouilles d'Enserune (CV France 6). *Ruscino*, 163-188. For Spain, Kern, Lamboglia and Mezquiriz in *Archivo Levant*, V, (1954) and Diehl on the Los Nietos material in Madrid, *Madrid Mitt*., III (1962), 55-61. M. Picazo, *La Cearmica Atica de Ulastrat*, 99-118. Trias, *Ceramicas Griegas, passim*. Jully, *La Ceramique attique* (black-glazed pieces are discussed in Part 2, p.93 ff.).

12 For material from North Africa see Morel, *Antiqutie Africaine* 15 (1980), 29-75. Villard, in *Libyca* 7 (1959), 7-25. Cf. *Quaderni* (1971), *passim*. Gill, in Kenrick (ed.) *Excavation at Sabratha, passim*.

13 For 6th c. black-glaze pottery from Cyrenaica, see *Tocra* I, pp.105-109, pls.84-88. For later materials see A. Row and J. Healy, *Cyrenaica Expedition*. See also *CVA*, Sevres, pl.25 and M. Vickers, *Libya Antiqua*. 18 (1971), 69-85.

14 For the various stages of development see Vanderpool, *Hesperia* 15 (1946), nos.243-245, pl.63. Talcott, *Hesperia* 5 (1936), 340, fig.8, P2732. Boulter, *Hesperia* 22 (1953), nos.23-26, pl.29. Sparkes and Talcott, *Ath.Agor*. 81 f.

15 Sparkes and Talcott, *Ath. Agora* XII, no.1379, pl.45. *Eph.Arch*. 1958, pl.22Y, on the left, grave XXI.

16 Sparkes and Talcott, *op.cit*. nos.220-322, fig.4, pl.15, A text p.81-83. Talcott, *Hesperia* 4 (1935), 505 No.21.

17 For the development of the shape see Talcott, *Hesperia* 4, (1935), 505, no.21. Corbett, *Hesperia*, 18 (1949), 317, no.20. For distribution in North Africa and the West see Gill, in Kenrick (ed.) *Sabratha*, 275 ff.

18 See especially Boulter, *Hesperia* 22 (1953), 74, no.28, pl.28, fig.2. Sparkes and Talcott, *Ath. Agor.* XII, no.346, pl.16.

19 For the skyphos from Leptis Magna see Ernesto De Miro-Graziella Fiorentini in *Quaderni* 8 (1977), skyphos 5 from Tomb 2, p.7 f., fig.1, a, pl.III, 5. For Delos, Dugas, *Delos* XXI, 61, Skyphos 181, pl.XLIX (181). For the Athenian Agora see Sparkes and Talcott, fig.4, no.342.

20 Rowe, *Cyrenaican Expedition* 8, Tomb N.81-43, pl.35c and pl.37a,c. Our red-figured Catalogue No.9.

21 Ghislanzoni, *Notizie Archeologiche* 1905, 90 Fig.49 *bis* and 49 *ter*.

22 Beazley and Magi, 87, no.110, pl.31.

23 *ARV* 982-984, for bibliography. Beazley, *EVP*, 200. Johnson, in *Studies Robinson* II, 96-104 and *AJA*, 59 (1955), 119-124. *JHS*, 71 (1951), 192 under No.136 (Trendall). *Hesperia*, suppl. X, 1956, p.22 under No.54.

shape has a thicker wall than the Corinthian type, with no reserved zone above the foot. The handles too are stronger[24]. The two examples from Cyrenaica are similar except that the vertical handle in No.12 is thicker. This piece was found in the sealed tomb (N.81-RR) in the North Necropolis of Cyrene. Skyphos No.13 was discovered in the vicinity of El-Merj. Among the grave goods of the Cyrene tomb was a fifth-century type lamp[25]. Similar examples to our vases, from Kerameikos, the Athenian Agora, and other sites[26], put the dating of the Cyrenaica pot to the second quarter of the fifth century.

FEEDER (14, pls.1,1 67, 1-2)

The deep bowl No.14, partly closed from the top with a rather high foot, is known as a 'feeder', and is among objects usually found as grave furniture[27]. Feeders are thought by some as to have been used a lamp fillers, and by others as cups for feeding babies or invalids[28]; they could just as well have been used for other purposes of daily life. However, its similarity in shape to some types of askoi would also suggest that it was used for oil.

There are many varieties of feeder, forming a consistent group that shows development over nearly a century. Feeder No.14 belongs to an early type that had a prototype in the late Corinthian[29].

Similar to our vase is the feeder once exhibited in Geneva[30]. This has nine linked palmettes and tongues bordering the central opening, but unlike the Cyrenaica example the palmettes here are encircled by another chain of impressed tongues on the shoulder. Similar to the feeder from Cyrenaica are ones in Newcastle and Edinburgh[31]. The nearest examples to No.14 are a pair of feeders found in 1936 in a grave in Lenormant Street, near the Athenian Agora. They, too, have nine palmettes and are bordered by impressed tongues, but here each tongue is impressed with a double line. Both vases are contemporary, and may be dated to the third quarter of the fifth century[32].

CUP (15-25, pls.1-2, 68-71)

i. Cups with Stems: Vienna Cup ("Vicup") (15-16, pl.68,1-3)

The stemmed cup is one of the commonest drinking cups that the Attic workshop produced, with great variety, during the late Archaic period[33]. After 480 B.C., only the Vicup and the Acrocup appear to have been produced in any number in black. The reason, it seems, was that after this period there was less market demand for the stemmed cup in its many variations. No acrocup, however, has yet been reported among the finds of Cyrenaica during this period[34]. Our two examples (Nos.15 and 16) are vicups[35]. Both represent the typical form, with wide shallow bowls, straight inset lips, and horizontal handles rising to the level of the rim. The bowl stands on a short stem that runs into the bowl with no interruption. The handle zones, the outer face of the foot, the resting surface, and the centre of the curve underneath, are all reserved.

To my knowledge there are no other examples of these cups anywhere in Cyrenaica, but similar examples from elsewhere are readily available. In Dublin there is a cup of the same shape and class but this contains three pellets in the foot, as revealed by an X-ray examination, which makes a rattling sound[36]. We do not know if the Cyrenaica cup held pellets, because its foot and stem were broken and restored.

The Vienna cups seem to have enjoyed only the briefest existence and, according to Bloesch, the majority of them is

24 A somewhat heavier version of this shape was used by the Brygos Painter. *ARV* 2, 253-4).

25 For the Cyrene skyphos, Rowe. *Cyrenaican Expedition* 8, pls.33b, 34b.

26 *Kerameikos* IX (1978), 153, Grave 295, No.7, pl.79 (Mid. 5th century B.C.) *Corinth* XIII, 237, pl.48,3 and North Cemetery Grave 325 (486-50 B.C.). Deposit 11, D11-d, pl.53, *Ath. Agor.* XII, 260, P 25699, no.362, pl.17. *CVA* Oxford 2, pl.65.2. *CVA* Bologne i, pl.46, 11, 12. *CVA* Vienna 1 pl.44 (one from Corinth Grave 324,3. *Corinth* XIII 237, pl.48,3). For distribution: R.A. Tomlinson and D.W.J. Gill "Two Type B Skyphoi in Birmingham". *BSA* 80 (1985), 115 f. See also other examples of Skyphoi 'Type B', most of them without provenance. *CVA* Norway 1, pl.52, 4. *CVA* Providence 1, pl.26,5. Ashmead and Philipps, *CVA* Poland 2, pl.3:12. *CVA* Goluchow, pl.46:12. *CVA* Oxford 2, pl.652. *CVA* Cambridge 1, pl.41:35. *CVA* Tours and Bourges, pl.13,8. *CVA* Limoges and Vannes, pl.14:5. *CVA* Rennes pl.27,3. *CVA* Brussels 3, pl.2 (137):12, 14, 15. Ostschweiz Ticino inv. K.18 (*CVA* Switzerland 5, 204, pl.2:8).

27 For the shape and usage, G.A.S. Snijder, "Guttus und Verwandtes", *Mnemosyne*, 3rd series, 1 (1934), 34 sqq. H. Kern, *Mnemosyne*, 4th series 10 (1957), 16-21. H. Klebe, *Schadwaldt, Gefässe zur Kindernahrung im Wandel der Zeit* (1955). K. Schauenburg, *JbRGZM* 4 (1957), 71 no.42. N. Kunisch, *Antiken der Sammlung Funcke,* no.114. Sparkes and Talcott, *Ath.Agora* XII, 161 f.

28 Walters, *Catalogue of Lamps in the British Museum,* 219. Ure, *Black glaze pottery from Rhitzona in Boeotia*, 54.

29 Payne, *Necrocorinthia,* 335, fig.185, no.1527.

30 *Art Antique,* "Collections privées de Suisse Romands" Jose Borig (ed.) No.250. See also *Kerameikos* IX, pl.41,3,42,1. For the types, see Sparkes, *Agora* XII 161, with reference cited and list of other stamped examples, no.7.

31 On Newcastle 165, 10 linked palmettes were placed around the central hole. David Gill, in Brijder (ed.), *Ancient Greek and Related Pottery,* 106, has shown that these feeders were made in the same workshop as amphoriskoi.

32 Sparkes, *Ath. Agora* XII, 320 nos.1197 pl.39 and *idem, Pots and Pans,* fig.52. C.G. Boulter *Hesperia* XXXII (1963) 121, D.8, pl.39. See also *Kerameikos* IX, Grave 295, no.8 pl.42. Cf. similar examples of feeder vases in the Fitzwilliam Museum, Cambridge, inv. G.218 (*CVA* 6, pl.XLI:14) and one in Musée Majewski, Warsaw inv. 7267 (*CVA* Poland 3, pl.100 4,8).

33 On kylikes in general see F.Brummer, in *Arch.Anz* 1967, 546. See also Richter and Milne, *Shapes and Names,* 24-25. Caskey, *Geometry,* 167-207. Sparkes and Talcott, *Ath. Agora* XII, 88-97.

34 For acrocup see Beazley, *Potter and Painter in Ancient Athens* (London 1948), 22-23. For acrocup and vicup. *ARV,* li. Sparkes and Talcott, *Ath.Agora* XII, 93 f. I have recently been informed that there is an acrocup from Euhesperides, London 1974, 9-2.32.

35 On vicups, Bloesch *F.A.S.*, 139-141, with list pls.38-9. Talcott *Hesperia* (1936), 336-338.

36 Vickers, *JHS* 90 (1970), 199-201 pl.IV-5. *Idem, AJA*, 77 (1973), 196-7 pl.40. *Idem, AJA* 78, (1974), 429-30, pl.88. Another vicup with rattling pellets but earlier in date is the one in Leningrad (Hermitage 5721), in *idem*, *JHS* 90 (1970), pl.VI. See also Boulter, *Hesperia*, 12 (1953), 76, no.32. Sparkes and Talcott, *Ath. Agor.* XII, 93 and 265, nos.435-438.

confined to the second quarter of the fifth century B.C. This is confirmed by examples attributed to the painter of the Yale Cup[37]. Moreover, the examples come from graves in the North Cemetery of Corinth and were found among material belonging to the second quarter of the century. The Fikellura cemetery examples, too, are all dated to the same period[38].

A group of Vienna cups reported from the Athenian Agora have similar characteristics, with very few variations, and are also contemporary. The example P-5117 from the same group is particularly close to ours[39]. It has a similar thin, neat stem, as well as similar reserved areas. Both cups (Nos.15 and 16) from Cyrenaica appear to belong to the second quarter of the fifth century B.C.

ii. Stemless Cup:

1. Cup with inset lip (Castulo cup) (17-19, pl.1)

We begin with three fragments which I believe belong to a series of stoutly made cups, whose main characteristics are the elaborate ring foot, which is thick and spreading, and a lip which also is slightly thick but inset. Its exceptionally thick wall is fitted with handles of solid girth[40]. The small fragment No.17 is from a cup of this class. It has an inset concave lip on the outside with a wide flat offset rim band inside.

Fragment Nos.18 and 19, on the other hand, preserve part of the body wall, interior and foot of the cups; the interior piece appears to be shallow and the foot is low and heavy with a convex interior.

Brian Shefton was the first to name this style the 'Castulo Cup'[41], after a site in the Iberian Peninsula known through Professor J.M. Blazquez's work[42]. Excavations there revealed a number of them in a late context. The cup seems to have had a remarkably wide distribution pattern. It occurs in Black Sea regions (one has been found as far as Askyutintsy, 170 km east of Kiev) and in the North East (as far as Durrnburg/ Hallein, just south of Salzburg, north of the Alps). To the west it has been found in Campania and Sicily (e.g. Populonia, Orvieto), Sardinia, Ibiza, and even the Levant coast. To the south there are a number of examples from the North African coast, including Leptis Magna (Map 6)[43]. The shape appears to have been created before the middle of the fifth century, continuing into the second half of the fourth century.

2. Cup with Plain Rim (20, pl.69,1)

No.20 can be described as a shallow bowl with no internal floor decoration. Two horizontal handles are set halfway down the wall, projecting in a straight line and then turning up. The wall curves to end in a plain rim. The foot resembles that of the Castulo cup, since it projects slightly from the bowl with its lip on the torus face meeting the lower part of the body in a concave curve. The cup was found in the Aslaia tomb, its material ranging in date between the first and last quarters of the fifth century[44]. The Athenian Agora provides a series of plain rim cups, as does the site of Stryme near Komotini (Thrace). Here, although the underside of the cup from this site is slightly different to ours, the item is painted completely black (except for the reserved underside)[45]. Our find is close to the developed version dated to 425 B.C.

3. Delicate Class (21-25, pls.2, 69-71)

Among other varieties of the stemless cup, the large type of delicate class[46] is well represented in imported black-glaze material to Cyrenaica. Characteristic of this class is the shape's high elaborate foot and plain rim, which has an offset on the inside[47]. Moreover, its large flat interior is ingeniously decorated with incised and stamped patterns. Apart from these features, the delicate class cup is basically similar to the plain rim cup. No.21 (pls.2,1, 69,2-3) in our collection has a shallow bowl that curves up to a plain rim with two horizontal handles set halfway down the wall and rising to the rim. Before the moulded foot there is a 'jog', or step, which separates it from the wall. The foot itself is divided into two parts: on the top there is a 'neck' (upper part) acting as a joint between the bowl and the lower member. Below this there is a lower section, wider than the neck. This, too, is divided in two by a groove on the outer face. The inner face is shaped into a convex curve. The cup's underneath is more distinctive, with its mouldings, raised rings, scraped groove, and raised areas.

37 Bloesch, *F.A.S.*, 139-140, pl.38. *ARV*, 395-397.

38 For Corinth north cemetery, *Corinth* XIII, 160, Grave 282-3, pl.37. Grave 300-5, pl.44. Grave 306-3, pl.45. Grave 308-3. (F.43), 64.10-7 1517 (F.53), 1952.2-4.31 (F.56), 64.10-7 2114 (F.128), 1949.2-20.24 (F.149); 64.10-7 1518 (F.251). (References taken from Sparkes, *Ath. Agora*.)

39 *Ath. Agor*. XII, 265, No.437, pl.20, Fig.5. Other examples of vicups are to be found in Cambridge (*CVA* I, pl.41;32) from Marion (Cyprus) in Verona (*CVA* 1 pl.2,3), in Poland (*CVA* Goluchow, pl.46,2 in Warsaw inv. 1980-77), and an example in the Fogg and Gallatin Museum, *CVA* pl.XXIV, 15, probably from Gela.

40 For discussion of the type, Sparkes, *Ath. Agora* XII, 101-2 (under "stemless cup with inset lip").

41 *Madrid Beitrage* 8 (1982), 403-405.

42 J.M. Blazquez, Castulo 1 (*Acta Arqueologica Hispana* 8 (1975), 192 ff.).

43 De Miro and Fiorentini, *Quaderni* 9 (1977), 27, fig.31, pl.XV, tomb 4, No.11, from Leptis Magna. Gill, in Kenrick (ed.), *Sabratha*, 27 f. *Ath. Agora* XII No.471, fig.5. M. Vickers, *Scythian Treasures in Oxford* 40, with fig.7, pl.IX a-b, and *CVA* Oxford 1, pl.48.2. Parallels are also in *CVA* Goluchow, pl.46.6. For other versions of the shape, *CVA* Geneva I, pl.26,6-7. *CVA* Tours and Bourges, pl.9.6-9. *Olynthus* XIII, pl.210, No.648 (400 B.C.). Lamboglia, *La Ceramica Precampana dell Bastida*, pp.127-128. See also examples in *CVA* Brussels 3, 137:17. *CVA* Altenburg ii pl.80; 8. *CVA* Stuttgart, pl.36:7,8,9. *CVA* Mainz pl.14:9. *CVA* Oxford, pl.48. *CVA* Verona, i pl.2:2 a-b. *CVA* Goluchow, pl.46:6,a. *CVA* Poland 3 pl.4 (100), 30. *CVA* Bucarest 2, pl.32:2. *CVA* Zurich, pl.29. *CVA* Ostschweiz Ticino pl.2:11. *CVA* Fogg and Gallatin, pl.62:5. *CVA* Warsaw 6, pl.8:2,3,4,5,6,7. See distribution of the vessel on map 6 compiled by B.B. Shefton.

44 Vickers, *Lib. Antiqu*. 8 (1971), 76, pl.XXX,b.

45 Sparkes *Ath. Agora* XII, 102, No.481. Bakalakis, 99 Fig.36, pl.54,2. For similar examples see *CVA* Galatine, pl.62, 4. Delos (Dugas, *Delos* XXI pl.48, 148) and in *CVA* Gotha ii, pl.76:7.

46 Ure, *JHS* 56 (1936), 205-215. Corbett, *Hesperia* 18 (1949), 322 f. Sparkes and Talcott, *Ath. Agora* XII, 102-103.

47 The shape is found in bronze (Salonica from Derveni). *Arch. Delt* XVIII, 1963, (Xpovika), pl.224y. Wurzburg inv. H767, *JdI*. LXV-VI i 1950-1, pp.175-177, fig.1-3. *Olympische Forschungen*, V, 186, fig.59, and see 185, no.49 - incised decoration of rosettes, tongues and linked palmettes and the example in Newcastle University Museum (Newcastle 577).

The floor of the cup is decorated with tongues, arranged in two zones, with a smaller, central zone left undecorated. This pot represents the early version of the shape, of which numerous examples come from dated contexts in Smyrna, Delos and elsewhere, dated to the third quarter of the fifth century B.C.[48]. However, the closed double lines (used in the internal decoration instead of the single line), outlining the tongues and rosettes, is a feature that appears on slightly later examples. Two other finds exhibit such features. The fragment (P4846, 430 B.C.) from the Athenia Agora is from filling excavated behind the retaining wall of the Stoa of Zeus. The other fragment (P9448), a cup excavated in the area below the Areopagos, is dated to the later years of the fifth century, and this context may date our cup to the last quarter of the fifth century B.C.[49].

Fragment No.22 has an elaborate treatment of the underside consisting of concave moulding and raised rings. The floor of the cup is decorated with an incised central rosette, two circles, a zone of linked palmettes, and two circles and tongues. There are two parallels to this piece. The first is a cup from the Athenian Agora, which has a similar treatment of the underside, and similar interior floor decoration[50]. The second is a red-figured cup, found in a tumulus at Klein-Aspergle in Wurtemberg, with a similar treatment of the underside. Both the Athenia Agora and Klein-Aspergle cups belong to the same workshop of the Amphitrite Painter[51]. To these two we can add the Cyrenaica example, which was very probably influenced by the same workshop.

Fragment No.23 is also an early piece, the underside of which is lightly moulded, but the floor decoration, which appears to have been made with a ruler and a compass, seems the most distinctive feature of it. In the centre there is a star with a large number of closely set rays, surrounded by two zones of ovules and separated by concentric circles. The scheme of decoration on a group of red-figured cups of the same class, studied by A.D. Ure, is very similar to that on this fragment (No.23), and her valuable remark on the star-rosette pattern is applicable to our cup[52]. But here it is both the second and third zones that were ornamented with arcs near the upper and lower circles of each zone. This was, apparently done to create the design, which is analogous to the simple tongue pattern. The star rosette pattern disappeared about 440 B.C. and was replaced by the tongue pattern.

Among the red-figured cups, two are relevant, one in Bowdin College and the other in Boston. Both are attributed to the manner of the Sotades Painter[53]. The floors of both cups are decorated with the usual star pattern, together with little arcs around the central inner, and outer, zones. Another fragment from the Kerameikos, also attributed to the same workshop, has an identical floor design[54]. The pattern on the Cyrenaica piece is very neat and sophisticated, proving it to be slightly earlier, or at least contemporary, with the workshop of the Sotades Painter.

The floor decoration of piece No.24, on the other hand, represents the development and growing sophistication of stemless cup decoration in the last quarter of the fifth century. The inner zone of the floor is occupied by an eight-rayed star. The outer zone is decorated with the tongue pattern. The narrow space between the inner and outer zones is left undecorated. All the lines making up the overall pattern (stars, circles, tongues) are doubled.

Among the same group of red-figured cups discussed by Ure are two further examples: one in London by the Carlsruh painter, and the other in Syracuse (Camarina) by the Amphitrite painter. Each has an inside decoration consisting of an eight-rayed star, placed in the centre. The rays here pass beyond their own zone reaching the outer circle. The Athenian Agora also provided a parallel[55], a cup with a central star and twelve rays, but like the Cyrenaica piece, the rays do not pass their own zone and are surrounded by two zones of tongues separated by concentric circles. The Cyrenaica piece is definitely later than the first two examples, for it appears that cups with large stars, whose rays pass their own zone, to intersect the outer circles, are the earlier ones. So the Agora piece seems to be contemporary with the Cyrenaica example. This is dated by Sparkes to 420 B.C. on the strength of the red-figures pottery found in a late fifth century well.

Cup No.25 has a concave lip and ribbed wall. In general, cups with such features occur in a relatively small number[56]. In terms of its style, the body forming a foot moulding and the underside treatment, i.e. the presence of raised rings, makes our cup very similar to the item from the Athenia Agora[57]. The floor decoration is also similar: a tongue pattern forming a rosette in the centre, then an empty zone followed by another outer zone filled with tongue pattern. In cup No.25 the arc designs completing the rosette pattern were not applied. Moreover, the projecting handles on our cup, unlike the Athenian Agora find, do not finish in upward turns. Such a cup feature is shared with another example in Oxford that

48 From Symrna, Boardman *BSA* 53-54 (1958-9), 176 f., nos.178-84, pl.43,44, fig.11, and from Olympia, Eilmann, *Olympia Bericht* III (1941), 38 ff. See also Schiering, in *Olympische Forschungen* V, 155 ff. and Delos, Dugas *Delos* XXI, 51 f. No.149, Pls.48 and 50, No.156, Pl.47.

49 See Corbett, *Hesperia* 18 (1949), 342, under no.142 (P-4846). Sparkes and Talcott, *Ath. Agor* XII, 259, no.490 (P-9448), pl.50, p.270, no.493, pl.22.

50 *Athenian Agora*. XII (P-5332), 269, No.484, pls.23,50, fig.5.

51 Stuttgart, KAS 113. *LVA* 1 (26), pl.28 (1240), 1-3. *ARV* 831, 25. Lindenschmit, III, part 12, pl.6,l. Ebert, S.V., Klein Aspergle, pl.1. Jacobsthal and Langsdorff, pl.33. Schaal, Vom Tauschhandel, pl.11,1. Die Antike, X, (1934) 19, fig.1. Jacobsthal, ECA, pl.26a 168-169. Hinkel, *Arch. Anz.* (1968), 652 ff. N. Kunisch, *Antiken der Sammlung*. Similar example also came from Stryme near Komotini (Thrace). Bakalakis, 9,7, fig.33, with general discussion.

52 Ure, *JHS* 55 (1935), 205-215.

53 Boston Museum of Fine Arts 13.203. Ure *op.cit.* fig.10,8. Caskey, *Geometry of Greek Vases*, 208. Beazley, *ARV* 2, 831, 5. See also Peredolski, *AM*, 53 (1928), pl.5,2 and VI,1.

54 *Kerameikos* X (1976), 204 K 43, and other examples in *Ath. Agor*. XII, 269, no.492 (P-23612), pl.51. *CVA* Wurzburge ii, pl.29,2 (2,5,6), pl.30 1-3. *CVA* Adolphseck ii, pl.88,1,3. *CVA* Geneva, pl.1 10-11.

55 See Note 52. Cf. *Ath. Agor*. XII 270, no.500 (P-9201), pl.23, 51. Carbett, *Hesperia* 18 (1949), 342, no.144.

56 See list in *Beazley's Gifts* III, No.415 (1966.417), Pl.LVIII. Most of it quoted in Sparkes and Talcott, *Ath. Agor*. XII, 104, no.27.

57 *Ath. Agor*. XII, 270, no.483 (P-9448).

has a different incised and stamped decoration. This is dated to the later years of the fifth, or early fourth, century B.C.[58]. Closer still to No.25 is another cup recovered from a fifth century well, south of the Stoa of Attalos in Athens, in the area below the Areopagos[59]. The cup was found among a number of red-figured pots dated to the later years of the fifth century B.C., but here the middle zone of the cup's floor is stamped with linked palmettes. This cup is dated by Talcott to the later years of the fifth century. It appears that this was the time when artists crowded and over elaborated their designs. Indeed, this is the period that witnessed the downturn in the fine stamped ornamentation.

Our cup, therefore, appears to be earlier than this stage in ornamentation and perhaps contemporary with the cup from the Athenian Agora[60] dated to about 430 B.C.

MUG

[Oinochoe Shape VIII B] Pheidias Shape (26, pl.72)

The well-preserved mug No.26 is a variety of oinochoai classed as Shape VIII B[61], the so-called Pheidias shape (after a find from Olympia bearing the graffiti of Pheidias)[62]. This round-mouthed mug continued as one of the most popular of all small closed shapes in black-glaze during the second quarter of the fifth century B.C. Its uses were, perhaps, as Beazley has suggested, a soldier's or traveller's mug serving a number of purposes: drinking, libation, measuring, ladling[63]. Schiering has provided a survey of the shape's development, use and metal counterparts in his discussion of the Pheidias mug at Olympia[64]. We are also reminded of the silver mug found in Bulgaria in the Bashova Mogila (Mogilanska) mound near Vrasta[65]. A black-glaze mug was found next to the mug in the Bashova Mogila mound[66]. The shape was also produced in bronze. On a mug in Boston, the double-handle is decorated with raised palmettes and ends in a satyr's head[67]. Such examples indicate that the Shape VIII B has a metal prototype.

Our mug is the standard type with squat body, ribbed wall, concave lip and double-rolled handles with shouldering. Such features are to be considered a change from those of the early types, such as the style classed as Shape VIII A, dating to the first quarter of the fifth century, which has a broad and flat base, round wall, wide offset neck, and a banded handle. Examples of such types are products of the Berlin Painter 2268 workshop[68], and the Brygos Painter.

Among the metal prototypes, the silver mug from the Bashova Mogila mound is a close parallel to our vase in that it has the double-handle, but not the rope pattern on the junction of neck and body. Moreover, the vertical ribs on the silver mug do not reach the top of the body. But the general features are the same, suggesting that such a shape was common throughout the third quarter of the fifth century: among the other finds with this silver mug was a hydria by the Kadmos Painter[69]. The 'Grave of the Corcyraeans', in the Kerameikos, is very important for dating purposes, as an example of a black-glazed mug was found among its contents and dated about 433/2 B.C.[70]. A series of similar mugs from the Kerameikos and Athenian Agora are dated to the third quarter of the fifth century[71]. The ribs on many of these mugs vary in their technique. The earlier types seem to have narrow-set ribs. Later types have heavy moulded ribs with arcs elaborated with reeding technique and applied in a distinctive manner to produce a special shine on the black glaze. This is the so-called 'Thericleian technique'[72]. The vertical ribs on our mug, on the other hand, appear to have been made as a result of raised moulding, but from wide-set regular grooves pressed probably with a spatula onto the surface of the mug. Similar application of such types of ribbing can be seen on a mug, a broad, squat variant with no provenance, in the Toronto Museum (ROM) and dated to the third quarter of the fifth century B.C.[73].

BOWL (27-35, pls.3, 73-75)

i. Echinus Wall (27-33)

There is a good series of bowls types from Cyrenaica. In general, their shape conforms to the modern idea of the bowl - a serving dish of varying degrees of depth. The echinus bowl, its wall profile representing the outline of the echinus of the Doric capital, is the most numerous of the Cyrenaica finds of black-glaze vessels. They represent the shape in its advanced stages in the second half of the fifth and fourth centuries. Their use is exactly the same as the earlier types, for salt and other condiments, and they could also have been

58 Oxford 1966, 417. *Beazley's Gifts*, 111, no.415, pl.LVIII.

59 Talcott, *Hesperia* 4 (1985), 520, no.108. Finds include several vases of late 5th century as "P-5482", a fragmentary large open pot (stamnos?) attributed by Beazley to the Pathos Painter, *Hesperia* 18 (1949), pl.78,5, and pl.79, Beazley *ARV* 1190, 32.

60 P-9448, in *Ath.Agor*. XII, No.483, fig.5, Pl.22.

61 Beazley *ARV*, xlix-1.

62 General survey of the shape: Sparkes and Talcott, *Ath.Agor*. XII, 72-74. *Neue Deutsche Ausgrabungen* 309, fig.44. *AJA* 63 (1959), pl.75, figs.9-10. *BCH* 83, 1959, pl.33. *Archaeology*, 12, (1959), 137. Olympia-bericht 7, (1961), 16-17, figs.8-9. Schiering, in *Olympische Forschungen*, V (1964) Pl.64 and Fig.45,1. *Arch. Delt*. 16 (1960) B, pl.113.

63 Beazley, *V.Pol*., 59-60.

64 Shiering, *Olymp. Forsch* V (1964), 169-182. See Gill, in Vickers (ed.) *Pots and Pans*, 16.

65 Strong, *GRGSP*, 84, pl.17. B. Nikolov, *Musée Archeologique De Vratza* No.50. *Archeologia* (Sofia) a, (1967) Part 1, 14, fig.4.

66 Filow, *Duvanlij*, 78, fig.100, *JdI* 45 (1930), 301, fig.24. (Filow) Plovdiv (inv. no.1530) Danov H. and Ivanov, 36, no.18, pl.18.

67 *CB* P.21, fig.20 of Comstock and Vermeule 317, No.443. See also the example from Dodona, Carapanos: *Dodona*, pl.24, 4 and 5.

68 London, BM E565 from Camairos, *ARV* 157/71.

69 Boston, 00.339 from Locri, *CB1* pl.VIII, 20. *ARV* 385/386. *V.Pol*.15.

70 Filow, *Duvanlij*, 75 f., Figs.95-99, pl.XIV. Cf. *JdI* 45 (1930), 297-299, Fig.18-23. *ARV* 1187/36.

71 *AA* 1972, 604-605, fig.23,1 No.5, fig.24,1 No.5. *Kerameikos* IX, pl.112, 1 No.5, pl.113,1, No.5.

72 For the nature of the technique see B.B. Shefton: Annales Archeologique (1971), 110 pl.XXI, fig.8a and b.

73 Hayes, *Ontario* 33, No.52.

used for drinking and perhaps, as suggested, as doorknobs and as targets in the game of Kotabos[74].

The earliest example of the echinus bowl among the Cyrenaican black-glaze finds is No.27, the wall of which curves up gently to the rim in the same thickness. It also sits on a disc-foot that is flat underneath. I have yet to find an exact parallel to this piece among the finds of the classical sites. There is, however, among the small bowls classed by Sparkes[75] as salt-cellars, an example that appears to be a small version of the Cyrenaica bowl; the date of the Agora salt-cellar is 500-480 B.C.[76]. Our bowl, however, could extend to the second quarter, if not to the middle, of the century.

To the early echinus bowl we may add No.28, a contemporary salt-cellar of the same shape. This example is of the heavy type, with a thick wall, of which there are parallels from both the Kerameikos and the Athenian Agora. Each of these vessels has a disc-foot, which is flat underneath and outward projecting; a rare type found to belong roughly to the second quarter of the fifth century. Both bowls are closely dated. The Agora bowl is dated by a succession of ostraka from the 480s, while the Kerameikos example was found in a grave whose contents are dated from 460 to 450 B.C.[77].

Bowl No.29 (pl.73, 1-2) in the group also represents the heavy type. It has a thick rim sloping down inwards, and a wall incurving towards the solid foot, which is reserved underneath. The floor is elaborately decorated, consisting of a zone of linked palmettes surrounding ovules within two circles. This type of decoration is typical of the middle years of the second half of the fifth century[78].

This heavy bowl appears to have been replaced by a lighter version consisting of a plain rim, rounded above to the same thickness as the rest of the wall, as in vessel No.30 (pl.74,1-2). The foot is usually concaved from the inside.

Another version of this shape can be seen in Nos.31-32 (pl.3), where the wall curves up to the rim in the same thickness, and this, too, has an incurve. The bowl sits on a ring foot, concave inside and convex outside. Similar examples from the Kerameikos and the Agora[79] belong to the last quarter of the fifth century. The salt-cellar 32 (pl.3) is clearly related to this type of bowl. Here the wall curves up to the rim, but unlike the bowl version, the rim does not have the sharp incurve. The treatment of the foot, however, is identical - concave inside, convex outside - and so is likely to belong to the same date of production, i.e. the last quarter of the fifth century[80].

ii. Convex Wall (34)

We may also include in this group the salt-cellar 34 (pl.74,3) that represents the standard form with a convex wall and flat underside[81]. The wall is drawn in at the top and descends to the resting surface, which is reserved. The earlier version of the shape has a recessed underside, a criterion that helps in dating both versions[82]. The flat underside salt-cellar, however, did not go beyond the end of the fifth century.

iii. Out-turned Rim[83] (35, pls.3,6; 75,1-2)

The shape represented by vessel No.35 is not very common among the finds of Cyrenaica: it was the only example found there. This is a shallow pot resting on a high ring-foot, a broad, gently rising lower wall, and a steep upper wall. The rim turns out, projecting outwards and making a pronounced double curve. The underside is reserved, save for a glazed band that borders the reserved area. As usual, the floor of the bowl is decorated handsomely with impressed patterns[84] consisting of central linked palmettes surrounded by another row of palmettes also linked. These are separated by a chain of ovals.

Our bowl was found in the intact sarcophagus (N.83-BH No.3) at Cyrene's North Necropolis[85]. The finds from this rich grave consisted of local as well as imported materials. The material included silver coins. The grave was dated to the early years of the third century, according to the numismatic evidence. This was done without considering the fact that all the other imported material points to an earlier date around the first half of the fourth century. This creates a big hiatus between the dating of the grave, based mainly on the numismatic evidence, and its contents.

It is desirable, therefore, to examine the datable material and the evidence for their dating, and to have a fresh look at the coins as evidence, in an attempt to narrow this gap

The material from sarcophagus N.83-BH, now in Manchester, includes:

---

74 *Archaeology* 13 (1960), 207, Fig.9.

75 Sparkes, *Ath. Agora*. XII, 135-138.

76 *Hesperia* 15 (1946), pl.66, 288. See especially: *Ath. Agora*. XII, No.939, fig.9.

77 *Ath. Agora*. XII, No.939, pl.34, fig.9. *Kerameikos* IX, 125, No.151 (2), 141, No.228 (3) fig.20.0.

78 See the example from *Tocra* II, 94, fig.42, inv. 2361 (unstamped). *Ath. Agora*. XII, No.839, pl.33.

79 *Kerameikos* X, p.203, K.30, fig.219. *Ath. Agora*. XII, no.870, fig.9. See also J. Hayes: Ontario No.66, fig.11. The Punic Cemetery of Leptis Magna produced similar examples but this is perhaps a development from the same series, as the foot is slightly higher. *Quaderni* 9 (1977), 10-11, Fig.4(c), pl.V(15).

80 Also *Ath. Agora*. XII, no.870, fig.9. *Kerameikos* X, p.203, K.30, Fig.219.

81 For a discussion about this version see Sparkes, *Ath. Agora* XII, 135 (salt- cellar, convex wall).

82 *Ath. Agora*. XII, no.897, pl.34, fig.9. This is, however, not an exact parallel as it is wider and lower (shorter) than our example, but the profile is close enough.

83 The best survey so far of the bowl is Sparkes and Talcott, *Ath. Agora*. 128-138. Olynthus provides many of the fourth-century bowls, but the presentation is not adequate: *Olynthus* V, 230-232, pls.175-6. *Olynthus* XIII, 346-354. *Kerameikos* IX pl.82. *Kerameikos* X, 204,5, K 212, figs.218, 219, 236, 237.

84 For decoration of fourth-century bowls see Corbett, in *Hesperia*, 24 (1955), 172-186, and see especially *Ath. Agora*. XII, P-22576, pl.67,8., P-22578, pl.66,14, P-22579, pl.69,22, P-22627, pl.180, fig.2,10 and pl.67,10, P-22634, pl.67,11, P-22639, pl.67,12. D.W.J. Gill informs me that this shape is particularly common in the eastern Mediterranean.

85 Rowe, *Cyren. Exp.* 12.

i) A red-figured pelike[86], dated to the second quarter of the fourth century.

ii) A lamp (M 698). This is of the same class as another lamp, now in the British Museum, studied by D.M. Bailey, who suggested a date around the middle of the fourth century B.C. The late date for this class of lamp was made after consideration of the numismatic evidence[87].

If we ignore the coins, we would, then, be free to date the lamp to an earlier date, since we have another example from a grave in Cyrene's Necropolis, from which the material can be dated between the end of the fifth and the middle of the fourth centuries[88]. Indeed, this type of lamp may be classified as Howland Type 21 C., which is usually dated from the end of the fifth century to the early years of the fourth[89]

iii) The amphora (M 677)[90]. This has a sloping shoulder, relatively short neck, and a large foot. These characteristics, together with the slight bulge on the upper part of the neck, indicate a Hellenistic date[91].

One can see from the imported material in grave N.83-BH that their dates range from the late fifth century through to the first half of the fourth, a fact that makes examination of the dating of the coins imperative.

In dating the silver coins from the grave, J. Healy[92] simply compared these to a group of silver obols with "no provenance", from the region of Cyrene[93]. These are obols of uncertain standard and their dating may, therefore, have to be reconsidered[94].

It is, then, far more difficult at this stage to accept an early third-century date for grave N.83-BH, as the dating of the coins is not certain. But, according to the rest of its contents (i.e. the imported material), it could well be earlier in date than has been supposed.

86 Rowe, *op.cit.* front piece discussed *supra*.

87 Bailey, *Catalogue of The Lamps*, 287 under Q.622.

88 *Annuario*, XVII-XVII (1969-70), 161, fig.198.

89 Howland, *Ath. Agor.* IV, 48, pl.34.

90 Rowe, *Cyren.Exp.* Pl.

91 Cf. Riley, Type 2. See Lloyd (ed.), *Excavation At Sidi Khrebish*, 22 Fig.68 (I am grateful to David Gill for the observation).

92 In Rowe, *op.cit.* 32, no.XV, XVI.

93 G.S.G. Robinson, *Catalogue of Greek Coins,* Cyrenaica CVII, no.271 a-c, CXIX, 57 pl.XXV-5.

94 I have corresponded with Professor J.F. Healy who was responsible for the report on the coins (see Rowe, *op.cit.* 32) and raised these issues with him. I am grateful for his reply, from which I quote the following: "The bronze coins (*sic*) were in a very poor state of preservation and I based the dating on comparison with similar coins in the British Museum collection. At the time I felt that it was possible that the coins might have been earlier (i.e. 4th century B.C., but not before). My view is that the bronze coins can only give a very approximate indication of date and that the weight of evidence of other finds should not lightly be set aside. I am sorry that the numismatic evidence, on this occasion, is not more conclusive".
Professor Healy must be referring to the silver coins from the grave.

The Athenian Agora provides us with a series of out-turned rim bowls that have the same characteristics as No.25. Of these, close among to our bowl is a vessel[95] with an identical profile but with different underside treatment and floor patterns. The sophisticated stamp pattern does place the Cyrenaica bowl slightly earlier than the Agora example. Such characteristics may link the Cyrenaic bowl to the earlier series from the Athenian Agora[96] of similar interior floor decoration. Our bowl, therefore, was probably made during the first quarter of the fourth century B.C.

LEKANIS (36-38) (pls.4, 76)

Lekanides[97] are particularly common finds among Cyrenaican sites, and show considerable variation in form and decoration. These are the broad, lidded bowls having two horizontal handles. Their primary use would be as serving dishes, toilet articles, and bridal gifts.

Three types of lekanis are found in Cyrenaica[98]:

The lidded lekanis, with ribbon handle.

The lykinic.

The covered bowl, Pyre type[99].

i. Lidded with ribbon handles (36-37)

Find No.36 represents the first type. One of the main features of the pot is the heavy foot, which is slightly flaring with a broad resting surface, usually reserved, illustrating a development that occurred after the middle of the fifth century. These features were retained until the fourth century. It has a shallow, round bowl with a slightly in-curving rim, ledged on the outside to receive the lid. Attached to the wall of the bowl is a horizontal handle. The handle zone is reserved and decorated with slanting zigzag lines. So, too, is the area above the foot that shows rays radiating towards the body. The same pattern is repeated under the stem of the lid. This treatment with such a decorative scheme has lead some to consider the shape as Chalcidian[100]. However, from a number of examples quoted by Boardman, the shape, its profile and decoration, is Attic. One particular fragment from Eretria, reported by him, is

95 Sparkes and Talcott, *Ath. Agor.* XII, 293, no.803, pl.32, fig.8.

96 *Ibid*, no.783, pl.57, fig.8.

97 On the identification of the name, see Deubner *Jdi* 15 (1900), 152. Richter and Milne, *Shapes and Names*, 23. Amyx, *Hesperia* 27 (1958), 202-205.

98 Rowe, *Cyrene. Exp.* 15, N.83-BG, pl.8.1, 18, N.81, pl.24,c pl.35,b. White *AJA* 70 (1966), pl.68, fig.17,18. *CVA* Sevres 1 (13), pl.25.

99 To be discussed in connection with Entry No.152.

100 Professor Friis-Johansen was largely responsible for some of the lekanis being identified as Chalcidian (*CVA* Copenhagen 3, 77-78 pl.98.2, lekanis no.521). In fact the same design of zigzag on the oblique can be found under a lotus frieze on a black-figure psykter in the same collection (*CVA* Denmark 3, pl.98.1, Copenhagen no.326), which is believed to be Chalcidian. See Beazley *JHS* 49 (1929), 109.

certainly later in date than he has assumed[101], for although the pattern on the vase, namely the zigzag is early in date, the shape is certainly later.

A similar Lekanis to No.36, from Nola, was found in a grave whose contents are dated to the second and third quarter of the fifth century. A red-figured amphora of the Owl-Pillar group was among its important finds. This is considered an imitation of the Attic red-figures and is dated to the second and third quarter of the fifth century[102].

Our vase appears to have been produced in the third quarter of the fifth century and it has the main features of that period. Its ring foot, instead of finishing in a sharp flaring edge, is round, forming a torus outer face. We can easily compare it to examples in Bern[103], London (from the Fikellura Cemeteries)[104], and the Athenian Agora[105], which are possibly from workshops active at the same period (or even by a single workshop active around 425[106]).

This is also the date of the other lekanis No.37[107], which, by contrast, is completely glazed with the exception of the top edge and centre of the lid, the resting surface of the foot, and the point inside the foot where it joins the body: these are all reserved. From the development of the shape, it can be said that the height of the stem of the knob, the shape of the body, and the broad resting surface, all suggest a date around 425 B.C.[108].

This lekanis was found together with a red-figured pelike, from the workshop of the Painter of Munich 2335, and a Panathenaic amphora by the hand of the Kleophrades Painter[109].

ii. Lykinic

The lykinic lekanis[110], represented by No.38, is a shallow bowl with its rim slightly tilted inwards and ledged on the outside to receive the lid. Attached to the bowl are two horizontal cup handles that rise and twist towards the top. The lid is very slightly convex with vertical sides, fitting over the bowl, and with an elaborate knob, thought to be an imitation[111] of woodwork. The foot of the bowl resembles that of some of the stemless cups, especially those with a plain rim; it projects slightly from the bowl and the torus foot is lipped - a feature that places our vase in the early third quarter of the fifth century[112]. A similar lekanis from Gela was found in a tomb with Attic vases attributed to the Syracuse Painter (460-440)[113], and the manner the Achelis Painter.

PELIKE (39, pls.5,1, 77,1)

Lidded Pelike

Of the two pelike presented in the collection, the lidded pelike No.39 is more interesting[114]. Beazley listed nine of this type and Sparkes added twelve to the list[115]. This is the 'squat type' that is classed as a variation of the type C amphora. Here the greatest diameter is set not high up on the vase, but, as in the standard Attic form, at the midpoint or well below, giving the pot a pear-shaped appearance and greater stability. Our vase was found in the intact sarcophagus (N.83-BH No.3) at the Cyrene Northern Necropolis. The date of the finds range from the late fifth to the middle of the fourth century[116]. Similar lidded pelike in Copenhagen originally came from Athens, the Athenian

[101] The identification is accepted by Rumpf, in *Chalkidische Vasen*, IX and *Sakonides*, pl.6. Boardman classes this shape among a group of black-figured vases from Ereteria as Attic, *BSA* 47 (1952), 42 no.16, fig.24 b, pl.13. But see especially Sparkes and Talcott, *Ath. Agor.* 164 ff., with list of varieties and shapes.

[102] M.B. Jovino and R. Donceel, *La Necropoli di Nola Pre-Romana* 19, 84 pl.XX, No.1, 6. A. Trendall, *The Red-figured Vases of Lucania Campania and Sicily* (Oxford, 1967), 668, Wo.23.

[103] Lezzi-Hafter, *Antike Welt* (1980), lekanis No.36.

[104] London 64.10-7.1569 from the Fikellura cemetery, Grave 73, *JHS* 60 (1940), 36-73.

[105] *Ath. Agora.* XII, no.1220-1. The Athenian example is particularly close as the underside is decorated with glazed circles. But we are not sure whether our example, like the Agora example, has the central date.

[106] See this list compiled by Sparkes in *Ath. Agora.* XII 166:

1) Athens, Kerameikos HS 89. *Arch. Anz.* 1964, cols.435-436, fig.24, upper left, XVIII, 1963, (Xpovika), pl.23.
2) Capua, old inv.243. *CVA* 2 (23), pl.20 (1095), 3, noted above, no.14,
3) Copenhagen, inv.Chr.521. *CVA* 3 (3), pl.98, (100) 2.
4) Geneva 8898, *CVA* 1 (1), pl.23 (23) 7 and pl.A, 16.
5) London 64.10-7.1567 (F 129).
6) London 64.10-7.1569 (F 73). Mentioned in *J.H.S.* LX, 1940, pp.36-37.
7) Wurzburg 163: Langlotz, Wurzburg, pl.120.

[107] Vickers, *Lib. Antiqu.* 8 (1971), 75, pl.XXX 6.

[108] *Ath. Agora.* XII no.1220, pl.40, fig.11. Similar examples are also found in *CVA* Altenburge ii, pl.80:14. *CVA* Oxford I, pl.48:17. *CVA* Oxford ii, pl.65:11,14. *CVA* Verona I, pl.1:3. *CVA* Warsaw vi, pl.8:10. *CVA* Bucarest ii, pl.34:5. *CVA* Ostschweiz, pl.14:18. *CVA* Norway i, pl.52:1-2.

[109] See section on red-figured pottery. Chapter Three, entry 18 and Chapter Six, Panathenaic amphora no.3.

[110] On this class of lekanis in general see Kern, in *Mededeelingen* (Leiden) 38 (1957), 53 ff. Sparkes and Talcott, *Ath. Agor.* XII, 169.

[111] *A.A.* 55 (1940), 616 f.

[112] For an identical find to the Cyrenaica piece from the Athenian Agora, *Ath. Agor.* XII, no.1242, pl.42, fig.11. See also the example in *CVA* Altenburg ii, pl.87:13. *CVA* Oxford, pl.45:13. *Beazley's Gifts* no.406, 108 with reference to other examples.

[113] *Mon.Ant.* 17 (1906), 344. Grave 30, 342 f., figs.252-256, *ARV* 519/18-20. Syracuse Painter and *ARV* 1003, 19 *bis*, also P.1677.

[114] Second pelike to be discussed. For pelike in general see Richter and Milne, *Shapes and Names*, 4-5. Cook, *GPP*, 224. For discussion of the function see *Jdi* 8 (1893), 180-184. (Pernice) de Waele *R.A.* Ser.5, XXIII, 1926, 282-295. Sparkes and Talcott, *Ath. Agor.* XII, 49 f.

[115] Beazley, *EVP* 178, Sparkes and Talcott, *op.cit.* 50.

[116] Rowe, *Cyrene Exped.* 12, 16, pl.11,a. The lid of the pelike was not found in the same sarcophagus (N.83-BH) No.3 as the body, but in No.4 (N-.83-Bj). Rowe, *ibid.* pls.11(a) body, 12(a) lid. Both tombs were found occupying courtyard BK with another two sealed sarcophagi, indicating that they were contemporary. Based on numismatic evidence, the dating of tomb 3 was put to the early fourth century and tomb 4 to the early third. Since the dating of the coins from tomb 3 is not convincing, while the majority of the imported materials are dated to the first half of the fourth century, the dating of both tombs should be shifted to the first half of the fourth century.

Agora and the necropolis of Pontamo at Rhodes, all belonging to the later years of the fifth century.

Two lidded pelikai (one in Copenhagen, the other in Leiden), originally came from Athens and are very similar in profile to ours[117]. So is another example from the Athenian Agora[118]. This was discovered in a well fill, and the finds are dated to the last quarter of the fifth century. One particular fragment of bell-krater (P 1264) is attributed to the workshop of the Semele Painter and the Suessula Painter. Also among the finds of the same fill was a louterion (P 12641) dated to the late forties or the early thirties of the fifth century[119]. To the same period belongs another example from the necropolis of Pontamo in Rhodes. Among the finds from this necropolis (Tomb No.8) was a red-figured squat lekythos of the Meidian Style[120].

BOLSAL (40-55, pls.6-8; 77-82)

Bolsal[121] appear to have been popular articles imported into Cyrenaica[122] during the second half of the fifth and fourth centuries. Earliest among these is No.40, found at Aslaia near Al-Marj[123], and described by Vickers as Proto-Bolsal.

This bolsal has a ring foot similar to that on the Type A skyphos. Its wall is potted in one curve. Among the contents of the tomb where it was found was a red-figured Pelike attributed to the Munich Painter 2335, and a prize Panathenaic amphora by the Kleophrades Painter. A bolsal from Camairos similarly shared the same context as a work (a red-figured cup) of the Kleophrades painter[124].

A bolsal in the Greek Museum in the University of Newcastle (Newcastle 572)[125] is contemporary with the Aslaia one, but the lower wall of the Newcastle example has a moulded ridge and the foot is rilled. Similar, too, are two proto-bolsals, one from Elaious[126] and the other from Camairos[127]. The latter is the closer of the two to the Aslaia bolsal. But whereas the Aslaia bolsal has no floor decoration, the Camairos example has eight palmettes and two circles stamped on its floor.

Also early are Nos.41 and 42 in our collection, where the feet, like the Corinthian-Type skyphos, have a continuous curve for the inner and the resting surface[128]. These early examples from Cyrenaica have interior floor decoration.

Slightly later examples from elsewhere, many of which are intact, acquired the main elements that comprise the shape, and whose main characteristics are that of a bowl with a wall that rises vertically to the rim. The floors of these bowls are frequently decorated with stamped patterns. Two horizontal handles are attached just below the rim[129].

These differ from the early examples in the way the lower part of the pot was shaped. A raised ridge and/or a groove were applied to the lower part of the wall. Below this we witness the introduction of the concave lower wall, a feature apparently was used on metal shapes as well[130]. On clay pots, such an exercise seems to have been known before 433/2 B.C, since a bolsal with such features was found among the contents of the grave of the Corcyraeani in the Kerameikos[131].

By 426 B.C. we have examples from Delos (Rheneia Pit)[132] that combine both the concave curve with the stamped pattern consisting of closed ovules and linked palmettes. A number of bolsals from Cyrenaica were found to represent this stage (Nos.43 to 49)[133].

Each has a single curve with a maximum diameter at the rim. At the lower part of this wall there is a groove acting as the joint between the concave lower part of the wall and the vertical upper part. The underside has a glazed centre surrounded by a reserved area; the rest is black. The floor of the bowl shows a stamped pattern of linked palmettes around a circle. This is the intermediate stage in floor decoration, after the elaborate design of two zones of linked palmettes

[117] *CVA* Copenhagen IV, pl.178:1,2. *CVA* Leidon 3, pl.152,1.

[118] *Ath.Agor*. XII, 51, 238 no.25-31. *ARV* 1344, 2. Corbett, *Hesperia* 18 (1949), 343, no.151 (Corbett).

[119] Shefton, *Hesperia* 33 (1952), 330 ff., pl.105-110.

[120] *Clara Rhodes* II, 141, Fig.19. See especially p.140, no.13889, fig.20.

[121] For a recent study on the shape see Gill, in Brijder (ed.), *Ancient Greek and Related Pottery*, 102 f.

[122] Rowe, *Cyrenaica Expedition* (1959), N.83-BG, pl.8, fig.a, N.83-BJ, pl.12, fig.a, N.81-AG, pl.24, fig.b-c, Tomb A. See T. Brown, *JHS* 68 (1948), 149-150, fig.1, nos.42/47 and 43/47. *CVA* Sevres 1 (13), pl.25, fig.44. *Tocra*, Cist Grave 2. See G. Wright "Excavation at Tocra", *PEQ* (1963), 59-60, pl.14, fig.9.

[123] M. Vickers, *Libya Antiqua* 8 (1971), 75-76.

[124] Bolsal, London 1949 2-20, F8, red-figured cup, London E 73. *ARV#2*, 192, 106, para.341, Addenda 94.

[125] Newcastle 572 (The Greek Museum), ex. Nostell Priory, No.34. Gill, *Attic black-glazed pottery,* no.30 (not published), p.103, fig.1 (stamped decoration). Sparkes and Talcott, *Ath.Agor*. 273, No.534.

[126] Louvre 1915-45, *BCH* 39 (1915), 194 (S-X).

[127] London 64.10-8 1635 (F.163), in D. Gill *op.cit.* 102 f.

[128] This feature is discussed in *idem* 102 f. Other examples include bolsals from Eleusis (*Eleusis* iii, pl.344,b, no.680), the Dema house, along the Dema wall in Attica (J.E. Jones, L.H. Sackett, A.J. Graham, in *BSA* 57 (1962) 90, fig.5,21), the Rheneia pit (*Delos* XXI, pl.LXIX, 171), Camiros (London 1952.2-4.39, F181), Tamassos Nymphaion (Oxford 1885.497. *CVA* 1,3, pl.48 [140] 3. Vickers, *Scythian Treasures*, 39 fig.6 and pl.VIII,b).

[129] Sparkes and Talcott, *Ath. Agora*. XII, pl.107.

[130] See Vickers, *op.cit* 42, fig.9 and pl.XIII. A Strong, *GRGSP* pl.17, A. *Silver for the Gods,* 31, no.6.

[131] *AA* 1972, 604, fig.23,3, no.9, 605, fig.24,3 no.9, 606, fig.25,3. *Kerameikos* IX, pls.112,3, no.9, 113,3 no.9.

[132] The majority of finds from the Rheneia pit belong to the years before 426 B.C., providing a useful *terminis ante quem* for the type of foot and the stage of development in the impressed pattern. For bolsals from the Rheneia pit see *Delos* XXI, 167-168, pls.49-52 and *JHS* 75 (1955), 182. On the context see D.W.J. Gill, "The date of the Porticello shipwreck: some observations on the Attic bolsals", *IJNA* (1987).

[133] Bolsal 47 was found in a sarcophagus (N.81-AC0 in the North Cemetery of Cyrene. The majority of the material from this sarcophagus is dated to the early years of the fourth century, but one small lekanis is dated to the late fifth century. Rowe, *Cyren. Exp.* pl.35,b. Bolsal 48 in Manchester (III.L.173, M 752) was found in sarcophagus N.83-Bd of the same cemetery. Rowe, *Cyren. Exp.* 12 and 32, pl.12,a.

on the early examples was abandoned and replaced by various, less complicated, designs. Two bolsals demonstrating such characteristics were found among groups of two dated tombs (404-3 B.C.). The interior floors of both of these have simple arrangements of four palmettes in a circle. The first group was found in the tomb of the Lakedaimonians (404-3 B.C.). The second is the tomb group from Rhodes city, now in Exeter. Two small bowls (Exeter 87.10.77a 78) were found with the bolsal (Exeter 87.10.79), one of which is stamped with ovals and four palmettes, as well an askos with a strainer top (Exeter 87.10.76)[134].

OINOCHOE (56-67, pls.8/83-86)

i. Shape 5 (Nos. 56-60)

Of the oinochoe imported to Cyrenaica, Beazley's shape 5[135] appears to have been more in demand. The shape is divided into three types: a, b and c. Of these, only shape 5c (Nos. 56-60) has so far been encountered.

The variety 5a has a tall, slender body with a rounded mouth and low handle, usually figured[136]. 5b is similar, but with high handle[137]. On 5c, unlike the other two variants, the neck is wide and the juncture of the neck and body is much less sharply defined, but like 5b it has high handle. This variety therefore appears to be a hybrid of the other two types[138].

Our vase 5b was found in a sealed grave (N.81-AC)[139], among material of a datable range from the end of the fifth to the first half of the fourth century. It is not, however, easy to give our vase a precise dating at this stage, but similar examples are usually dated to the later years of the fifth and early fourth centuries (mainly those from the Kerameikos and the Athenian Agora[140]).

ii. Shape 2: Shoulder Oinochoe (No.61)

The characteristics of shape[141] include its low foot, flat underneath, and a fairly slim body rising to a flat shoulder. Its short neck forms a continuous curve ending up in the trefoil mouth. It has a low handle projecting from the shoulder joining the mouth. Its cut-off base makes it easier to fit into a krater, although its narrow neck and elaborate lip make its use as a ladle unlikely. One illustration of it on a red-figured Oinochoe of the same shape shows it in the hand of a youth, presumably attending a sacrifice.

Spina has so far revealed the largest number of black-glazed oinochoi, of the same class, from dated contexts. The majority of these are dated around the middle of the fifth century and after. They were produced by several workshops, in particular the workshop of the Achilles Painter and the Shuvalov Painter[142]. It has been observed that oinochoi of this shape were placed in tombs in pairs, a reminder of the red-figured lebes gamikoi that were treated in a similar fashion[143]. Examples of such a class of black-glazed oinochoi were reported from the Athenian Agora[144]. In the large red-figure vessels, the shape was very popular, especially in the first half of the fourth century. A number of these were imported to Cyrenaica[145]. They have also been found in the Greek sites of the Black Sea[146], but, again, Spina appears to have had by far the lion's share of the market[147]. Our black-glazed oinochoe (No.61), while very similar to both those of the middle of the fifth century reaching into the second half of the sixth century, and those red-figured examples of the first half of the fourth century, is exceptional in the sense that it appears to be the only known black-glazed Oinochoe Shape 2 decorated with impressed ornaments on the shoulder angle (but very common on other shapes). These usually consist of a row of small palmettes, points downwards on top, a row of ovules below. We encounter it on the feeder from Cyrenaica[148] and also on an Oinochoe Shape 5b in Toronto[149]. Both examples are dated

---

[134] Discussed by Gill *op.cit.* 104.

[135] See Beazley's classification in *ABV* XI and *ARV* ILI. For a discussion on the development see Sparkes and Talcott, *Ath. Agor*. XII, 68. Green, *BICS* 19 (1972), 7. For a local version of the shape see *Olympische Forschungen* V, 208-211 and especially 208, no.97.

[136] See the example in London British Museum E559, *ARV* 539, 45, Boreas Painter, and the London E 555, *ARV* 1065, 1, Mannheim Painter.

[137] Oinochoe Type 5b also carry occasionally decoration below the angle that forms the junction between the body and neck, the decoration sometimes takes the form of a red-figure pattern and sometimes the red-figure pattern is replaced by stamped palmettes and ovules, a feature which is not present on one from Cyrenaica. For Oinochoe 5b with such features see Newcastle 162 (Greek Museum), and Toronto (Ontario Museum) 925-28.2. Hayes, *Greek and Italian Black-Glazed Wares,* 26 f., no.41.

[138] See *Kerameikos* IX, 154, Grave 299, no.1, fig.41. *Ath. Agora*. XII, p.248, no.176, pl.10. A. Hundt and K. Peters, no.369, pl.43. See also Altenburg 32 (*CVA* pl.80, 15). Carlsruhe 216 (B 936, *CVA* pl.35,6). Tubingen G.36 (Watzinger pl.50). Oxford 394A (*CVA* I pl.48, 13). The same shape with impressed decoration as in Copenhagen inv. 1687 and 1686 (*CVA* 7, pl.286 (289) 12-13). Vienna: (*Laborde* ii pl.48, 5). Naples from Cumae, *Mon Ant*, XXII, 1913, pl.105,4b. *Beazley Gifts,* no.390. Jovino, *Necropoli di Nola* 46, pl.4, A,2.

[139] Manchester M 1247, M 1248, in Rowe, *Cyrene Exped.* 8 pls.24,c and 38,b. Oinochoe 41 (M 658) was found in the sarcophagus N.83-BG. The material found in the tomb is of an early fourth century date. Rowe, *Cyrene Exped.* 12, 15 pl.9,a.

[140] See note 138.

[141] Richier and Milne, fig.126. Caskey, *Geometry* 138, no.98. Green, *BICS.* 19 (1972) 6. Beazley, *EVP*, 258- 257. Kern. in *Mededeelingen* 34 (1953), 1-12.

[142] Massei, *Gli Askoi,* 4 no.5, pl.1,2 (Tomb 1), 25 no.5, pl.V,2 (Tomb 16), 30 no.5, pl.VI,1 (Tomb 18), 62 no.5, pl.XVII,1, 150 no.2, pl.XXXVII (Tomb 99), 146 no.1, pl.XLI,1 (Tomb 80); 199 no.2, pl.XLV 2 (Tomb 123). Achilles Painter, London E 523,*ARV* 992, 76 and Louvre G 438, *ARV* 992, 77. For the Shuvalov Painter see Lezzi-Hafter, *Der Schuwalow Maler* 9-11, and London E 522, *ARV* 1207, 32.

[143] Roberts, *AJA* 77 (1973), 435-7.

[144] Sparkes and Talcott, *Ath.Agor*. XII 60, 243, no.103, pl.5, fig.2.

[145] Entry No.59 in Chapter 3 (red-figure).

[146] See Venedikove (ed.), *Apollonia* pl.78.

[147] Massei *op.cit.* 144, pl.XXXI V, 1 (Tomb 87), 153 pl.XXX, 2 (Tomb 49), 182, 2 pl.XL VII, 3 (Tomb 113), 226, 4 pl.LII, 2 (Tomb 140), 236, 3 pl.LVI, 1 (Tomb 146), 250 no.3, pl.L LVIII, 2 (Tomb 152), 298, 2 pl.LXX 1, 2 (Tomb 177).

[148] Entry No.14.

[149] Hayes *op.cit.* 28 f, no.41.

to the third quarter of the fifth century. This is the most likely date of our oinochoe.

iii. Shape 3: Chous (No.65)

Of all the shapes of Oinochoe in the fifth century, the chous is the easiest to follow in terms of its development of shape, and consequently to date. Thanks to the sequence provided by the Kerameikos and Agora deposits that have helped in their study[150].

The earliest black-glazed chous from Cyrenaica (No.65) belongs to the later years of the fifth century. This is the time when the body becomes squat and golbular. However, the shape is now comparatively slimmer than those made a quarter of a century earlier. The trefoil mouth now curves gently, but the rim becomes blunt, forming a flat edge, slightly thicker than the neck. The foot, however, becomes low and wide. Such features can be noted on a black-glazed chous from the Athenian Agora (P 2086), which is dated by Sparks to 420-400 B.C. The filling of the well from where it was recovered is dated to 410-390. Among the finds of the filling are two red-figured chous, also dated to the same period[151].

Green's 'crawling boy' workshop production appears to be the red-figured equivalent to the black-glazed vases of the later years of the fifth century[152]. This is the type with children painted on, as they had a connection with the festival of the Anthesteria. These small red-figured chous were found to be standard items in children's graves of the period. Two of these red-figured chous came from the North Cemetery of Cyrene[153].

OLPE (Nos.68-88) (pls.9/86-88)

Footed (Nos.68-74)

There is a good series of the small-footed olpai from Cyrenaica. These can be divided into two groups: earlier and later. Olpai of the early group[154] have ovoid bodies resting on a small disc-foot. The shape has a rounded mouth and a strap-like handle that curves up gently from the shoulder to join the slightly projecting lip. One criterion that can be used for dating olpai is the nature of this strap-handle, which now rises above the level of the rim, a change that begins during the third quarter of the fifth century. Later, by the end of the fifth century, and through to the fourth, the handle appears to be angular. This is in contrast to the sixth and early fifth century olpai, where the handle rises in a graceful curve.

[150] Sparkes and Talcott, *Ath. Agor*. XII, 60 f.

[151] Sparkes and Talcott, *ibid.* 244, no.118 and 392 (H12:11). pl.6, fig.5. *Hesperia* 8 (1979), 275 no.4. Van Hoorn, *Choes and Anthesteria*, no.167, fig.68 and no.168, fig.177.

[152] Green, *BSA*, 66 (1971), 213 ff.

[153] Rowe, *Cyrene Exped*. pl.37,a.

[154] For more discussion on the shape see *Olynthus* XIII, 228-229. Sparkes and Talcott, *Ath. Agora* XII, 78 ff.

There are a number of olpai of the early group from Cyrenaica (Nos.68-74), however only the two that were excavated from the Artemision of Cyrene, are from a dated context. Olpai Nos.68 and 69 were found among a wealth of material, published in some detail in 1931, and as such comprise one of the very few instances of the publication of small finds in conjunction with their contexts. This was undertaken by the Italians before 1939[155].

Outside Cyrenaica there are two similar examples coming from dated contexts. The first was a find from the Eridanos Necropolis, and the second from the Kerameikos, both in Athens[156]. The handle on each is slightly higher than those of the very early types, where the handle is low and curvy. The disc-foot is still low, with little protrusion and reserved underneath. The tombs where they were found with their contents are dated from 451 to 440 B.C. Our two vases were probably made during the later years of the third-quarter of the fifth century.

II. THE FOURTH-CENTURY TYPES

BOLSAL (Nos.52-55) (pl.8/80-82)

In the early part of the fourth century no significant development seems to have been applied to the shape of the pot, although the cavity appears to be more pronounced. One may notice, however, a slight change in the style of the inside decoration as seen on No.51[157], where the palmette cross pattern now substitutes the earlier sophisticated design. Slightly later, perhaps during the second quarter of the century, as No.52 indicates, the palmette design is now circled with rouletting, a pattern common to other contemporary and later shapes[158]. Moreover, the most frequent treatment now for the underside is a black band and a circle, with the rest of the area reserved[159]. Bolsals Nos.54 and 55, on the other hand, illustrate the development that occurred about the middle of the century, namely the canonical black underside with rising central cone and groove resting surface. The handles now tilt upwards and

[155] Pernier, *Africa Italian* IV (1931), 213, fig.35 from a pit in the treasury foundation in the Artemesion (intramural).

[156] *AM* 81 (1966), pl.27, 3, Grave 58, 3. B. Schlorb-Vierneisel, in Knigge, *Kerameikos* IX, 151, Grave 287, 1 pl.78. Cf. *Ath. Agore* XII, pl.13, nos.278-281.

[157] Bolsal 51 was found in the same sarcophagus as Bolsal 47, see note 133.

[158] The floor of a cup-skyphos from a cistern, south east of the Kolonos Agoraios in the Athenaian Agora, has a palmette-cross decoration designed in a similar way. The pottery from this cistern, including the cup-skyphos, is dated to the second and third quarters of the fourth century. *JHS* 18 (1949), 343 no.149, pls.86, 89 and 90 (Corbett).

[159] For a similar version see Ure, *Black Glazed Pottery,* 52, pl.XVI, no.24. *CVA* Cambridge 1, pl.XLI.24. *CVA* Fogg Museum, pl.XXIII.II. *CVA* Geneva 1, pl.27.3-9. *CVA* Gotha 2, pl.77.4-6. *CVA* The Hague 2, III L.pl.3.13-14, 17-18. *CVA* Reading 1, pl.34.12-34. *CVA* University of Michigan 1, pl.XXXIII. *Histria* IV 87, no.554, pl.65. For similar stamps cf. *CVA* Geneva 1, pl.27.17-18. For the palmette pattern with rouletting, see Sparkes, *Ath. Agora*. XII, 107 f., 275, no.559, pl.53.

have a triangular look about them[160]. No.54 has a lot indication of 28 in the normal Attic acrophontic numerals[160bis].

OINOCHOE (Nos.62-64, pls.84-85)

Shape 2: Shoulder Type

The Kern Class (Nos.62-64)

There were three fourth-century oinochoi found in Cyrenaica: Nos.62-64 are typical examples. The body appears triangular in shape with a very broad shoulder, and a low foot, which is flat beneath. The shape of the handle is low and projects from the shoulder to join the trefoil spreading mouth. The inside of the curvy neck, and all the outside, except the underneath, are glazed. Vertical broad ribbing was applied to the wall, ending a little above the foot, and was joined at the top by incised arcs. B.B. Shefton terms this rib-moulding technique 'Thericleian', and he suggests that it is an imitation of Persian objects[161]. The shape appears to be very popular and was widely exported during the first half of the fourth century. Kern had made a list of the known examples at the time[162]. Of the three finds from Cyrenaica, only No.62 is included. Of these the pair in Manchester (Nos.63 and 64) are from a dated context (from the sealed tomb N.82-BJ). All the black-glazed objects found in it are dated to the first half of the fourth century, a date that was supported by numismatic evidence[163]. Both vases have exactly the same profile and dimension. The two are a pair and probably belonged together. There is one similar example from Olynthus and two from Alexandria[164]. The three make perfect parallels to the Cyrenaican oinochoe, all belonging to the mid-fourth century, a time when Shape 2 was very popular both in the Athenian local market and for export[165].

160 See for comparison, *Ath. Agor*. XII, fig.6, no.558. Hayes, *Ontario*, no.61 and Clairmont, *Berytus* 12 (1956-57), 19, no.450, pl.v,3. *Histria* IV, 87, no.555 Fig.13. Ure, *Black Glaze Pottery*, 52 f., Grave 33 no.4, pl.XVI, 4.

160 bis For such indication see Johnston, *Trademarks*, 27 f.

161 Shefton, in *Annales Archeologique*, 109 f.

162 *Archivo Levant* V (1954) 141-3. An example from the Agora is fairly slim in body, with slightly wide shoulder. This appears to represent the early fourth- century type, see Sparkes and Talcott, *Ath.Agor*. XII, 244, no.104, pl.5.

163 Rowe, *Cyren.Exped*. 16 pl.12, N.83-Bj, p.32, coins no.XVIII.

164 *Olynthus* XIII, 217 (295), pl.154 (295). Alexandria Breccia, *Sciatbi*, pl.49, nos.77, 83. There is also the example in Newcastle 389 in the Greek Museum. For Spain, Trias de Arribas, *Ceramicas Griegas*, pl.126,2 and also the example from Apollonia, in Vendikov (ed.), pl.81, 291.

165 A list with more parallels is given by Kern, in *Archivo De Prehistoria Levantina* 5 (1954), p.142-3. Other examples are Masner, pl.8, no.563, National Museum Warsaw 6 (*CVA* Poland 9, 389, pl.13:6), Schloss-museum Gotha (no number) (*CVA* Germany 29, 1409 pl.78:1), Archaeological Museum, Sofia inv.7186, Cracow, inv.1460 (*CVA* Poland 2, 68, pl.14:3), National Museum of Antiquities, Bucarest inv.03385 (*CVA* Romania 1, pl.43:4). Beazley, *EVP*, p.256-7. N.Kunisch, no.116.

Shape 3

Chous (Nos.66-67; pl.86)

Chous Nos.66-67 represent the development of the shape in the third quarter of the fourth century. The vase now has a tall slender body with small foot. Its trefoil mouth spreads outwards and droops over the rim. Both vases have the shape, dimension and same colour of clay. These two (as with Nos.62 and 63) appear to be a pair and probably belonged together. The series from the Athenian Agora provides the best sequence for comparison. Three similar chous are relevant (P5384, P12989, P7772), all coming from fills and dumps of certain material, dated to the second half of the fourth century[166].

OLPAI

i. Footed (Nos.75-86, pls.9/83/87)

The style of the second group (Nos.75-84) has similar features, but here the body is gently rounded. The strap-handle is nearly vertical as it rises high and curves well above the level of the rim, then recurving to join it. It also has a high foot that protrudes from the wall. Such features appear to show the development of the shape in the first half of the fourth century.

The majority of olpai from Cyrenaica are of this stage of development. A number of these are from dated contexts, namely those in Manchester and the one excavated in Apollonia. The Manchester olpai, from the North Cemetery in Cyrene (Nos.77-80), were found in a sealed tomb that contained mostly black-glazed material, dated to the first half of the fourth century[167]. The Apollonia example (No.75) was found in a grave, though disturbed, the contents of which had not been removed. The material, which is mostly black-glazed, is dated to the second and third quarters of the fourth century[168]. That is the likely date for our olpai.

Two similar examples come from the Athenian Agora. The first was recovered from the accumulated dumped fill of a well, dated to 375 B.C. The second is from the third quarter of the fourth century[169].

The two olpai (Nos.85 and 86), although different in shape, are also to be dated to the middle of the century. These are of the tall vase shape, cylindrical in form, broad in the shoulders, the walls of which narrow downwards. The strap- handle springs from the shoulder and curves to join the lip on the same level. The foot, too, is different to that of ordinary olpai. It is high and splayed. This type is not frequent among the finds of the period and none have been reported from the

166 (P 6384) *Athenian Agora*, 245 no.127, pl.7. (P 12989), *Athenian Agora*, 245 no.128, pl.7 Fig.2. (P 7772), *Athenian Agora*, 245 no.129, pl.7.

167 Rowe, *Cyrene Exped*. The two pelikai (M685 and M683), 16 and 32 Pl.11,a. Pelike (M761), pl.12,a.

168 Apollonia, inv. 66461. K.M. Phillips, in White *Apollonia*, 122, Tomb e, Pl.XXIC. *Idem*, *AJA* 70 (1966), fig.18.

169 Sparkes and Talcott, *Ath. Agora* XII, 255, Nos.282-3, Pl.13.

Agora or the Kerameikos. Outside mainland Greece and Cyrenaica, Rhodes is the only place where examples of such types of olpai are found. They are dated to the middle of the century[170].

ii. Footless (Nos.87 and 88, pl.88)

The footless type, as represented by Nos.87 and 88, is a tall, slender vase, cylindrical in form. The wall bulges at the shoulder, but narrows down towards the lower section, then flares slightly before it reaches the bottom. The handle, like the late, footed version, is nearly vertical. It rises high and curves sharply, well above the level of the rim before curving again to join it. Our two vases from Cyrenaica can be compared with an example from the Athenian Agora, found in house fill, dated to the second quarter of the fourth century[171]. This is likely to be the date for our footless olpai (No.87), since the majority of the material from the tomb where the vase was found belonged to the early years of the fourth century. This dating is supported by coins from the same tomb[172].

AMPHORA (Nos.89-92, pls.89-91)

Large vessels are not uncommon among the black-glaze imports to Cyrenaica, but all the finds are those of the closed types. Nos.89-93 are amphorae of the fourth century. This is a type easily compared to contemporary Panathanaic amphorae, whose main characteristics were flared mouths, vertical handles, and convex feet[173]. It appears that the majority of the surviving examples of this class of amphorae are of high quality, with their bodies covered with vertical ribs.

None of these appear to have been made before the third quarter of the fourth century. Generally, the shape is similar to those made in the first half of the fourth century, but some features make it later in date. We know that the amphora after the middle of the century acquired larger lips, sloping shoulders and elongated slender ankles. We can apply such characteristics to No.89, which is preserved with its lid. A Panathenaic amphora, also from Cyrenaica, made at the time of the archon Theophrastos (340/339)[174] is similar to No.89 in that it has a short, wide neck, ornamented with an olive-wreath. Such an ornament at this time is common on Panathenaic Amphorae[175].

Amphorae (Nos.90-92) have short, slender and pronounced concavity of neck. The handles emulate this feature in the neck by being slightly concave from the outside. The mouth has experienced a change with low wall and spreading, flat lip. The ankle, too, is now short and slender. The body appears more bulged with broad shoulders. The result is that we have an amphora with a disproportionate shape. Such features seem to indicate a later production; they are found on contemporary Panathenaic amphorae. Kopcke has placed vessel No.92 among the group, which was produced between 330 and 310 B.C. Indeed these features, on vases produced at such a late date, are found on those Panathenaic amphorae from Cyrenaica, and during the archonship of Archippos (320/10 B.C.)[176].

PELEKAI (Nos.93-94, pl.91,2)

Pelikai Nos.93 and 94 are some of the excellent examples of closed vessels imported to Cyrenaica. Both are of the large type with flaring neck and overhanging rim. Among the style's main features are the central rib of the handles and the disc-foot. The ribbing is skillfully applied from shoulder to foot in the so-called Thericleian technique. There are two other pelikai sharing the same characteristics as those frfom Cyrenaica: one in Munich and the other in Leningrad[177]. The necks of these vases are decorated with gilded wreaths. Our pelike, however, are closer to the Munich vessel in that the handles on both vases, where they join the neck, touch the overhanging rim and so are likely to be of the same date, about 360 B.C.

Regarding red-figured technique, we may use two pelikai (one in Paris, the other in Leningrad) for comparison. Both are considered to be of the Kerch style and dated by Schefold to 360-350 B.C. They are typical of those pelikai produced during the second quarter of the fourth century with a bulging body, broad neck with a concave side overhanging the rim, and a disc-foot in three degrees[178].

SKYPHOS (Nos.95-96, pl.92)

The skyphos is one of the shapes that experienced transformation during the fourth century. As can be seen on Nos.95-98, the rim is now sharply outturned, with the consequent contraction of the part of the wall immediately below it. Furthermore, the lower part of the wall tapers sharply with concave sides[179]. This is the distinctive element of the shape that characterizes its walling in the second quarter of the fourth century; shaped into a stem to make it suitable to hold as a drinking cup. The handle is set high

[170] *Clara Rhodes* 11, 160, fig.45 left, and 165, fig.46 above left. *Clara Rhodes* 11, 144, fig.22, 145, fig.24, 147, fig.27, 148, fig.28, 154, fig.36.

[171] Sparkes and Talcott, *Ath.Agor*. XII 255, No.274, Pl.13.

[172] Olpe (M759). Rowe, *op.cit.* 16f, 32, Pl.12,a and Pl.32, XVIII for the coins.

[173] See Kopcke, *AM*, 79, (1964), 40 ff., pls.26-27.

[174] Louvre MN 706. *CVA* V, pl.5,8-14 and pl.6,1. *ABV* 415, 3.

[175] See Berlin inv.3981. Also *AJA* (1943), 460. Beazley, *Develop*. 99.

[176] Louvre MN 705. *CVA*, pl.6 (4-7, 11).

[177] Munich, Staatliche Antikensammlungen 8436, see G. Kopcke, *AM* 79 (1964), 41, (134) pl.28,1. Leningrad, the Hermitage, see Kopcke, *AM*, 41 (135), pl.29,3. See also Mainz, Römisch-Germanisches Zentralmuseum, *CVA* Germany 42, pl.40, also E. Zervondaki, *AM* 83 (1968), 1 ff.

[178] Paris, Schefold, *UKV* No.558, pl.22,1. Leningrad B 2232. *UKV* No.474, pl.8. For the dates of these pelikai, Schefold, *ibid*, 141.

[179] A similar example from Corinth is separated from earlier series and given the name "laphaes skyphos" on the basis of the graffito of a Corinthian owner (Grave 476-1, P.193, fig.22). *Corinth* XIII, 125 and 287-288.

above the wall just below the lip. It flares slightly from the root, placed with a slight upward tilt. The pot sits on a ring-foot, with an outer profile, torus in shape. The resting surface and the underside are reserved with concentric circles in the centre.

The popularity and wide distribution of this shape make it possible to find parallels to our vases. These come from the Sciatbi Necropolis in Alexandria[180], and other parts of the Greek world. Of these the example from the Athenian Agora[181] is indeed close. In the red-figured pottery a skyphos showing the preparation for a Dionysiac festival is most relevant for comparison. It belongs to the Kerch style and is dated to 350 B.C. It has a similar profile, but the lower part of the wall is slightly wider[182].

HYDRIAE (Nos.99-111, pls.93-99)

The hydria[183] appears to be one of the commonest vessels in plain ware imported to Cyrenaica[184]. None, however, appear to have reached Cyrenaica before the fourth century. The reason being that it was not produced in Attica in any number before the end of the fifth century. It was then made in various sizes[185] and developed into one of the most majestic shapes in the Attic black-figure workshops, with elaborate foot and mouth, often ribbed, and with gilded decoration on the neck[186].

The clear-cut line of fourth-century, black-glaze hydria, particularly its general shape, lip and foot, might have derived from bronze prototypes[187]. The wreath around the neck, added in thin clay and probably gilded, also points to metal work[188].

[180] Inv.15578. Breccia, *Sciatbi*, P.162, and pl.56, 120.

[181] Sparkes and Talcott, *Ath. Agor*. XII, 260, no.352, pl.17, fig.4. Similar examples were found in Salamis (Cyprus) in Jehasse, *Salamine De Chypre*. 74 f., nos.709-720. *Olynthus* XIII, pl.200, 500-582.

[182] Schefold, pl.9a,b. Richter and Milne, *Shapes and Names*, fig.177. Richter and Hall, *Red-figured Athenian Vases*, pl.165 (170) and pl.178.

[183] Amyx, *Hesperia* 27 (1958), 200 f. Diehl, *Die Hydria, passim*, and the addition by Bothmer, in Gnomon, 37, (1965), 599-608. Fulzer, *Die Hydria, passim*. Sparkes and Talcott, *Ath.Agor*. XII, 53, Kopck, *AM* 79 (1964), 22 ff., especially 34 ff. for a list of such hydriae, and 69 f. (on their dating).

[184] Rowe, *Cyrenaican Expedition of the University of Manchester* 1955, 1956, 1957. Manchester (1959) N.810A6, pl.24, fig.c, N.83-BG, pl.8, fig.c. Brown, *JHS* 68 (1948), 149-150, no.40/47, fig.1. From Benghazi, *CVA* Sevres 1 (13), pl.24 (553), 7. In his review of the Sevres fiscule, Beazley dates the Benghazi hydria to the fourth century B.C. (*JHS* 56 (1936), 253). The shape in red-figure from Cyrenaica is represented by a hydria in Plymouth Museum and another one in the British Museum (*CVA* British Museum 6, pl.93, 2 E227).

[185] As the examples from the Rheneia Pit: *Delos* XXI, pl.51, 128-134; those in New Haven, Yale 378-380; Baur, p.234, fig.104; in Oxford 408, *CVA* 1(3), pl.32 (124) 11.

[186] As Winterthur Art Museum inv.308: Bloesch, *Antike Kunst*, pl.47,25; Lane, *GRK Pottery* (1948), pl.96; Schefold, *Mgk* 237, no.328; Bloesch *Antike Kleinkunst*, pl.9, 32, and Kopcke, *AM* 79 (1964), 34-39 and 69-70, and see Sparkes, *Ath.Agor*. 53.

[187] E. Diehl, *Die Hydria*, pls.10-12.

[188] G. Kopcke, *AM* 79 (1964), 22-84, pls.8-47, and p.25 for a discussion of the influence of metalwork.

Many of these, especially the late fourth century examples, had their bodies covered with vertical ribs from shoulder to foot[189].

Earliest among the collection are the fine pieces Nos.99-101. They represent well the type, with ovoid bodies and wide shoulders. The overhanging rim is divided into two rounded mouldings by a groove and prominent ridge at the top. The lower moulding covers part of the vertical handle. Another characteristic is the moulded ring-foot, concave, with double torus at the edge.

A fine and well-preserved Attic hydria in the Louvre is very close to the Cyrenaica piece[190]. It has a similar profile and decoration, especially the painting on the overhanging rim and the garland on the neck. This is indeed a masterpiece. The quality of the vase is shown by its elegant shape and metallic glaze. The potter must have had a metal counterpart in mind. Both vases belong, no doubt, to the class of hydria that has slightly curved side handles, a bulging body and a short neck placed on a broad shoulder.

It is not difficult to find parallels to this vase in red-figure production. Indeed, the hydria E 227 in London, also from Cyrenaica, is its twin[191]. As well as the already described typical features shared by both vases, the necks of the vases are ornamented with olive leaves. Accordingly, our black-glazed hydria can be dated around 370-360 B.C.

Nos.102-104 appear to represent the next development during the end of the second quarter of the fourth century. The hydria shows a triangular appearance with broad, almost flat shoulders. In red-figured vases such features can best be observed on a hydria by the Apollonic group, also from Cyrenaica[192], dated to 360-350 B.C.

On many of these hydriae the overhanging rim is left plain. The neck, however, may be decorated either with the usual garland and ivy leaves or with added clay in the shape of plastic dots circling the neck, as seen on No.102. Close to this class of hydria is a neck fragment from a vase from the Athenian Agora[193]. This is also decorated with added clay in the form of an ivy wreath.

No.103 is a complete, but smaller version of this type of hydria, with similar neck decoration. No.104, which is probably later in date (350 B.C.), has a slightly thicker neck and is without the usual decoration.

[189] Close to our examples in red-figure: British Museum, *CVA* 6, pl.99,13 E242, E243. In black glaze: London, British Museum 64, 10-7, 1512; Kopcke, *AM* 79 (1964), N88, pl.24,1; Leningrad, the Hermitage, *AA*. 28 (1913), 188 Abb.20. Examples with ribs: *Clara Rhodes* VI-VII, p.772 (2L4); Robinson *Catalogue of Greek Vases* 11, pl.LXXXVII (543), and from Alexandria, Breccia, *Sciatbi* XXXVI (44).

[190] Louvre CA 2272, G. Kopcke, *AM*. 79 (1964), No.71, p.34, pl.23(1).

[191] See Entry No.50, Chapter 3 (red-figure).

[192] See Entry No.53, Chapter 3, see also the example in Munich, *CVA* V (26), 20 and pl.235.

[193] *Ath. Agora* XII, P-8280, 239, No.51, pl.3. See also *CVA*, the example in Oxford *CVA* (3), 123, pl.48 (140) Fig.35.

Olynthos has revealed a number of this type[194], which was produced during the third quarter of the fourth century B.C.

Later types of hydriae, like the amphorae, have their bodies covered with vertical ribs. Fragments Nos.105-107 are indeed representative. These are of the same class as the published hydria (No.108), also from Cyrenaica, and now in London. This has a triangular, slightly slim body. On the side, the horizontal handles re-curve very sharply and tightly to the body. The tall, slim neck is decorated with a gilded wreath and the neck flares upwards - to be crowned with a spreading overhanging rim. Ribbing was skillfully applied from the shoulder right down to the foot. The abundance of hydriae with similar features indicates both the popularity of such types and the activity of the Athenian market at this later period[195]. We are almost certain that its production went on until the latter years of the century. Indeed the three hydriae (Nos.109-111) in Leiden[196] appear to have been produced during the last decade of the century. A hydria in Munich (dated 320-10 B.C.) is the counterpart of the shape in the red-figure technique[197].

CUP-KANTHAROS (Nos.112-115, pls.9/99-100)

i. Moulded rim (No.112, pl.98, 1-2)

Among the finest of all the Cyrenaica finds are the cups-kanthoroi[198]. No.112 is of the moulded rim type that evolved with other related shapes between 390 and 380 B.C.[199], and continued into the Hellenistic period to 275 B.C.[200]. The inspiration for this elegant shape appears to have come from the heavy-walled cup skyphos[201] that stopped appearing after the cup-kantharos became very popular. It is not difficult to see the similarity between both shapes.

Like the heavy-walled skyphos, our cup has a narrow neck and thick, moulded rim and deep bowl. The lip has two divisions. The upper has a slight protuberance, and the lower is thick and widely projecting and curved in profile. The handles are horizontally set, wide-slung. In the complete examples the loops are slightly higher than the lip and fixed with an upward tilt. The foot is wide spreading and low. The upper narrow section is separated from the lower by a slightly depressed reserved line. There is no stem to separate the bowl and the foot.

One criterion for dating cup-kanthoroi is to note the proportion of bowl to its neck, which appears to change with the time. In the earlier types (second quarter of the fourth century) the ratio of height to diameter of mouth was 1:2, here the bowl is shallow and the neck is low with concave sides[202]. Our cup (No.112) has a high neck and deep bowl. Such a development seems to have occurred during the third quarter of the fourth century. Dated examples with similar features come from Olynthos, the Athenian Agora and the Sciatbi Necropolis in Alexandria[203].

ii. Squat rim (No.113, pls.9,5/99,1-2)

Among the features of this shape[204], as represented by No.113, is the vertical upper wall with concave sides that turn out at the rim. The floor of the bowl, as usual, is filled with palmette patterns within rouletting.

This type of cup-kantharos has a profile similar to that of the stemless cup ("delicate class") with concave rim[205]. Both cups have a similar shape of bowl (deeper in the cup-cantharos). The handles project from the bowl to a level higher than the rim and then turn inwards slightly. The only difference between the two cups is the shape of the foot. The stemless cup has a broad moulded ring-foot. In the cup-kantharos the foot is also moulded but it is narrower than that on the stemless cup. Moreover, it is concave beneath and made in several degrees with a reserved groove. There are, however, two examples from Olynthus, one of them with a rising foot similar to that on stemless cups. These were found in a grave dated to the first quarter or the second quarter of the fourth century[206]. Other examples from Rhodes, the Athenian Agora

194 *Olynthus* V pl.118, 262; *idem*, XIII pl.144, 219.

195 See Kopcke's list, in *AM*, 79, (1964) 36, 70f., Nos.88-94.

196 Leiden. *CVA* iii, 52-53, pl.154, 1, 2, 3.

197 Munich 2439 inv. 6011. *CVA* V (20), 20, pl.235 (1-2), pl.236 (1-6), pl.237 (7-9). Beazley *JHS* 59 (1939), 39. Metzger, *Represent.*, 271, No.15.

198 For a discussion on this type see Corbett, *Hesperia* 24 (1955), 177. *Idem, Gnomon* 23 (1951), 61-64. *Olynthus* XIII, 274-294, pls.183-192. *Olynthus* V, pls.148-150. Talcott, *AJA* 55 (1951). Kopcke, *AM*. 79 (1964), 47-55, 77-81. Sparkes and Talcott for a detailed study, *Ath. Agora* XII, 117-121.

199 This is the date for the earliest examples of this type from the Athenian Agora. *Ath. Agora* XII, 117 f., and nos.648, 649, fig.6.

200 The Agora provides examples of Hellenistic date. Cf. P-5719 *Hesperia*, (1936), 38, fig.38 (1961), pl.93d (early third century).

201 *Ath. Agora* XII, 280, no.621, pls. 27, 55, fig.6.

202 Cf. example in *Athenian Agora* XII, 282, No.652, pl.28, Fig.7. See also the example in Newcastle (Greek Museum), 163. Shefton, *AR* (1969-70), 61. This example in Newcastle has four pellets in the hollow of the lip and these were inserted through a hole pierced into the lip.

203 *Olynthus* XIII, 286, No.504, pl.187. For the Athenian Agora, *Hesperia*, 20, (1951), 114, 2, 4 Pl.50,b. Corbett, *Hesperia* 25 (1955), 185, fig.3, P-51, pl.70. Sparkes and Talcott, *Ath. Agor*. XII, 283, No.661, pl.28, fig.7. Breccia, *La Necropoli di Sciatbi* I, 65, No.1707 and II, Pl.LIII. See also the examples in Staatliches Museum, Schwerin, inv. 734 (*CVA*, Germany, 1 582, pl.48:2). Schlossmuseum at Gotha, inv. Ahv, 116 (*CVA*, Germany 29, 1408, pl.77:1-3). Fitzwilliam Museum, Cambridge, inv. CE.F1890 (*CVA*, Great Britain 6, 279, pl.41:40) from Poli, Cyprus. Musée d'Art de d'Histoire, Geneva, inv. 10775 (*CVA*, Switzerland 1, 28, pl.28:7). Fogg Museum inv. 23.1908 (*CVA*, USA, 8, 362 pl.XXIV:44). See also *Hesperia* 23 (1954), pl.24f. *Mon. Linc* 22, 1913 pl.106,21. Museo Campano at Capua (*CVA*, Italy 29, pl.IV,7). See also Baur, 216, fig.99, no.391/392, Musees Royaux d'Art et d'Histoire at Brussels inv.A1714, A1715 (*CVA* Belgium 3, 138, pl.3:15,18); (Museo Nazionale), Naples, inv. 85838 (*CVA* Italy 24, pl.4, 7); Musée National des Antiquities, Bucarest, inv. 03226 (*CVA*, Romania 1, pl.42:6). For the palmettes see Corbette, *Hesperia* 24 (1955), pl.66,71.

204 See Sparkes and Talcott, *Ath. Agora* XII, 120 for a discussion on the shape, and *CVA*, Reading 1(12), text to plate 34 (561):7.

205 See discussion on entry No.25. Sparkes and Talcott, *Ath. Agor*. XII, fig.5, Nos.493-494.

206 *Olynthus* XIII, 280, Nos.498, 499, pls.187, 183.

and the Sciatbi Nicropolis in Alexandria are in the same class as our cup[207]. These are from contexts dated to the third quarter of the fourth century. The Sciatbi example, however, could be slightly later as it has a narrow foot and a more sharply twisted handle. The example from Rhodes is the closest to ours. Both cups have stems separating the foot from the bowl. Our cup was probably produced during the two middle quarters of the fourth century and other material found with it in the sealed sacrophagus (N.83 BG) from the North Cemetery of Cyrene is dated to the first half of the fourth century[208].

iii. Bowl shape (Nos.114-115, pl.100)

This type is similar in shape to the cup-skyphos and very probably developed from it[209]. Indeed, chronologically this type appears to follow the cup-skyphos, starting probably during the second decade of the fifth century.

No.114[210] is an open bowl with no concave wall above it. Instead, the wall of the lip continues with the line of the body, curving inwards slightly at the top, setting, therefore, the maximum diameter a little below it. The handles, like all cup-kantharoi, project nearly half way from the wall, curl up over the rim, and turn inward. The foot too is typical of the cup-kantharos.

After the publication of the Agora Series it is now possible to follow the line of development of the type. The earliest of the series (380 B.C.) is a low bowl, wide at the top with maximum diameter at the rim[211]. The last in the series (325-310 B.C.) is very close to our bowl (No.114). It has a similar profile of bowl angle, handles, and size of foot (separated from the bowl by a stem)[212].

In later examples, the walls flare upwards, forming the widest diameter at the top; the lips no longer turn inwards. Such a development occurred during the last quarter of the century and carried on even further into the Hellenistic period.

No.115 has a deeper bowl and high stem with a two-step foot. The first part is splayed and concave beneath. The most important development, however, is the fact that the lip, instead of turning inwards, as seen in earlier examples, is now outward spreading and the handles incurve strongly. There are a number of examples with similar features, such as those in Wurzburg and London[213]. Among these the one in Wurburg is the nearest to ours. The decoration on the wall of both vases is indeed identical. It is a vine-branch arranged with alternating leaves and grapes clusters with tendrils in white. The dating of such a development is probably the late fourth or first quarter of the third century.

KANTHAROS (Nos.116-121, pls.100-101)

i. Moulded rim (No.116 and 117, pl.100)

The shape of this type of kantharos, as represented by Nos.116 and 117, is close to the cup-kantharos[214]. I find that these two examples share the same profile of rim, neck and body with cup-kantharos No.112, and with cup-kantharos No.113 the same neck and body, and, most importantly, the high stem that separates the body and foot.

Like most cup-kantharoi, the moulded rim has two divisions; the upper with a slight protuberance and the lower thick and widely projecting. The handle projects from the body to join the rim and make spurs, also projecting slightly, and set on a level with the rim. In case of No.116, the body is covered with vertical ribs. The foot similar to that of the cup-kantharos, made in several degrees with a reserved groove.

For ribbed kantharoi, we may compare ours to those from Olynthus and the two examples in Alexandria. These are dated to the second quarter of the fourth century. The two ribbed examples from Alexandria are from the last quarter of the fourth century B.C.[215].

Similar examples to No.117 were found in the Athenian Agora, at Olynthus, and Rhodes from a context dating to the third quarter of the fourth century B.C.[216].

ii. Plain rim (Nos.118-121, pl.101)

Like kantharoi with moulded rims, the handles on Nos.118-120 project from the body to join the rim. The horizontal spurs project slightly and are level with the rim. Our examples, however, have taller necks and a deeper body. These appear to be later developments to the plain-rimmed kantharos, and

[207] *Clara Rhodes* II, 122, fig.4, middle left (Tomb 2, La Necropoli di Pontamo). *Hesperia* Suppl.IV, p.133(a), fig.98. *Hesperia* 2u (1951), 115 (2,3) pl.40b. *Ath. Agora* XII, No.684, pl.28. *Olynthus* V. pl.148, 511. Breccia, *La necropol. di Sciatbi,* pl.LIII, 102. See also University of Reading inv.37.vii3 (*CVA,* Great Britain 12, 561, pl.34,35:7). Collection de l'Université Cracow, inv. 281, anc. 1234 (*CVA,* Poland 2, 84, pl.11:31). Romisch-Germanisches Zentralmuseum, Mainz, inv. 0.4169 (*CVA,* Germany 42, 2055. pl.42:8).

[208] M656 Rowe, *Cyren. Exp.* 14, pl.8,c R.1.

[209] For the shape see Kopck, *AA*, 79 (1964), 55-56, 81-82. Sparkes and Talcott, *Ath. Agor*. XII, 121. Ure, *Black Glaze Pottery*, 31. Beazley, *EVP*, 239. Thompson, *Hesperia* 23 (1954), 74 (under 9).

[210] Sevres, inv. 4166, 11. *CVA*, pl.25, 22.

[211] *Athenian Agora* XII, 285, No.686, pl.28, fig.7. Also the example in Rhodes, dated to the second quarter of the century. *Clara Rhodes* 11 (1932), 155, Fig.38 (top left and right).

[212] *Ibid*, 285, No.690, pl.28, fig.7.

[213] i) Wurzburg, L.728. Kopcke, *AM* 79 (1964), pl.46,8.

ii) London, BM, 86.3-10.13. Kopcke, *op.cit.* pl.46,7.

iii) London, BM. Kopcke, *op.cit.* 46a.

See also Brussels, inv. A-1668. *CVA* 3 (3), pl.7 (138), 12.

[214] For the shape see Sparkes and Talcott, *Ath. Agor*. XII, 122. Thompson, *Hesperia* 23 (1954), 73. See also *CVA*, Reading 1 (12), text to Plate 33 (560).

[215] *Olynthus* V, pl.150, 525 and XIII, pls.190 and 192, 522 A and B. Alexandria (no provenience), see Clairmont, *Berytus* 12 (1956-58), 21, Nos.565 and 566. Breccia, *Necropoli di Sciatbi,* pl.53, no.103, has a higher neck. This is probably a later date, as one would expect from the location of the find.

[216] *Ath. Agor.* XII, 285, Nos.696-700, pl.29, fig.7. *Olynthus* XIII, pl.185, Nos.512, 513. *Clara Rhodes* 11, 147, fig.25, P.145, Tomb 11 (No.13916).

the cup-kantharos for this type is not represented at Olynthus[217].

The neck on No.121 is decorated with olive (or laurel?) wreaths (pairs of leaves flanking a straight stalk) added in white. Kantharoi with similar neck decoration are found on Samos, Alexandria and the Athenia Agora[218]. There are also kantharoi with ribbed bodies. A number of these have a combined wreathed neck and ribbed body[219], but examples of the plain type are innumerable. Many of these are from contexts dated after the middle of the fourth century, probably to the last quarter of the century[220].

CALYX CUP (No.122, pl.101)

The calyx cup was probably used in drinking rituals. The shape[221] is represented by only one example, No.122. In this cup the combination of a convex lower wall, approaching hemispherical, and a concave upper wall flaring outwards above, is characteristic of cups without handles, or foot: like the phiale, it has a central boss inside. This probably makes the two shapes related in view of the elaborate ribbing and the presence of the central boss.

Examples of such shapes were found in the Achaemenid pottery and silver work[222]. This appears to be a possible source of influence. If so, the influence may have come in the middle of the fourth century from the Achaemenid deep bowl[223]. This is a small toasting-cup already represented on the Greco-Persian Gems[224], of which actual examples in silver and bronze have survived from later fifth and early fourth century contexts[225].

This Achaemenid influence must have been felt well before the conquest of Alexander paved the way to direct contact between Greece and the East.

The Greek silver examples are, usually respousse decorated: the body with elongated petals radiating from the bottom, the shoulder with a band of guilloche pattern. A bowl from Nikisiani, Macedonia, dated to the third quarter of the fourth century, is decorated with such patterns[226]. Around and throughout Macedonia the type was found also in Vergina, Derveni, Sedes, and Stavroupoli. In Thrace it was found in Arzos and Mesemvria[227].

In clay, the earliest example in Attica is dated to the second quarter of the fourth century. There is also and example from Olynthus that was evidently in use at the time of the destruction of the city in 348 B.C.[228]. On our calyx cup from Cyrenaica, the upper body wall is taller and narrower than in the early types. The wall of the bowl is decorated with only ten vertical ribs, spaced equally around the bowl. Such features would place it after the middle of the fourth century[229].

ONE-HANDLED CUPS (Nos.123-125, pl.102)

Conical

Of the one-handled cup (κάναστρον/κάνασθον)[230], the conical shape appears to be the type favoured type by Cyrenaicans. We have three complete examples, Nos.123-125, and a number of fragments from Euhesperides[231].

The vase was probably used for solid and liquid food and was a very practical vessel for travellers and soldiers.

The three examples are of the conical type, each consisting of a deep bowl with flaring wall, broad rim and a horizontal handle attached to it. The bowl rests on a low ring-foot. There is an identical example from Alexandria. Although all classes of the one-handled cup are represented in the Athenian Agora in quantity, surprisingly, the collection contains only a single

[217] See the examples from *Ath. Agor.* XII, Nos.707 and 708, fig.7. Rotroff, *Hesperia* 52 (1983), 283 No.2, pl.51. *Hesperia*, 53 (1984), 348f., pl.67. *Hesperia* 3 (1934), 320, A28. *Hesperia* 6 (1937), 165, Fig.98,c. *Clara Rhodes* II (1932), 121, fig. 3, lower row, left. Breccia, *La Necropoli di Sciatbi* II, pl.LIV, 109.

[218] Samos (fragment) see Kopcke, *AM*, 51, No.282, pl.42,3. Agora (P-13526, fragment), Kopcke, *op.cit.* 51, No.281, pl.42,1. For the example from Alexandria, Clairmont, *Berytus* XII (1956-58), 20, No.561, pl.VI, 10. See also the example in *Clara Rhodes* 11 (1932), 160, Fig.45.

[219] Koroni Peninsula (east coast of Attica), Vanderpool, McCredie, Steinberg *Hesperia* 31 (1962), 37, No.37 (PR17) and P.59. *Clara Rhodes* 11 (1932), 161 (Tomb 22) fig.47.

[220] See the examples in the Agora. Thompson, *Hesperia*, 3, (1934), 320, A28; 6 (1937) 165, fig.98,c. Rotroff, *Hesperia* 53 (1984), 353, No.11, pl.67. *Clara Rhodes* 11 (1932), 121, Fig.3. Alexandria, Breccia, *La Necropoli di Sciatbi* II, pl.LIV, 109.

[221] For the shape: *Bull. Vereen*, 28 (1953), 1-21 and 32 (1957), 62-65; Von Bothmer, *Ancient Art from New York* (private collection, New York 1961), 70 text to 276; Kopcke, *op.cit.* 53-55 and 81. See also Sparkes and Talcott, *Ath. Agor.* XII, 121f. Oliver, *Silver for the Gods,* 40, no.10.

[222] Strong, *GRGSP,* 99f. Dalton, *Treasure of the Oxus*, 45, fig.72, 182. *AJA* LXVII (1962), pl.41, fig.1a,b.

[223] Strong, *op.cit., ibid*, 90f. Shefton, in *Annales Archeologiques* 1971, 109-111.

[224] Richter, *Engraved Gems,* fig.506 (in Berlin from Megalopolis).

[225] See the examples in A. Fol, *The New Thracian Treasure*, 16 f., nos.i-45, Filow, *Duvanlij*, 88, no.8, Fig.110.

[226] No. A869, Kavalla Museum (Nikisiani, Macedonia). *BCH*, 84, (1960), 799, fig.12, and *The Search for Alexander,* 160, No.120.

[227] See Rhomipolou (ed.), *Treasurer of Ancient Macedonia,* No.103 (Vergina), No.194, 261 (Derveni), No.280, 283, both Pl.41 (Stavroupoli), No.317, pl.45 (Sedes), No.433 (Mesemvria), Nos.464 (pl.61), 465 (Arzos).

[228] Shefton, *Annales Archeologiques* 111. Sparkes and Talcott, *Ath. Agor.*, 122. *Olynthus* V, pl.150, 530, XIII, pls.190-191, No.521A, pl.215, 520A.

[229] See later example from the Athenian Agora. Sparkes and Talcott, *Ath. Agor.* XII, 285, No.692 (350-325 B.C.). Hesperia XX (1951), 124, 8, 2, pl.52b. See also Breccia, *La Necropolis di Sciatbi,* pl.LVI, 118, 124. Also the example Romisch-Germanisches Zentralmuseum in Mainz, inv. 04178 (*CVA,* Germany 42, 2056, pl.43:7), Oxford 1937.303, in Shefton, *op.cit.* fig.14. H. Palmer, C. Vermeule, *Archaeology* 12 (1959), 4. V, figs.14-16.

[230] See Noble, *Techniques*, 102-113 and 210, figs.260-261. Also R.M. Cook, in *CR* 65 (1951), 9. On a fragment of a one-handled example from Naukratis, (the Fitzwilliam Museum, Cambridge).

[231] See David Gill, in Jones and Lloyd (eds.), *Euhesperides 1968-69*. There are numerous examples from Euhesperides. See also the example from Alexandria, in Clairmont, *Berytus* XII (1956-58), No.412, pl.2,2.

find of the conical, one-handled cup[232]. Both examples from Alexandria and the Athenian Agora are of the same class as those from Cyrenaica, and if they are not from the same workshop, they must at any rate be contemporary (second quarter of the fourth century B.C.).

SMALL BOWL AND SALT-CELLAR (126-133, pls.10/102-104)

i. Echinus wall (Nos.126-130, pls.10/102-104)

Of the fourth century version of the echinus bowl, No.126 is the earliest. This, like the previously discussed bowls[233], is heavily made, with a thick incurving rim and curving wall standing on a solid ring-foot, only partly reserved underneath. The underside has a broad, glazed band surrounding a reserved area decorated with two thin rings, the smallest of which is at the centre. The floor of the bowl is occupied with a palmette-cross. The design of the palmette-cross is similar to that on a cup-skyphos from the Athenian Agora dated to the second quarter of the fourth century[234]. The palmette-cross design was introduced in the early fourth century. A bolsal with similar design and date was found in the same sealed sarcophagus together with bowl No.126. The date of the bowl must be early fourth century, confirmed by the context and other finds, including coins, of the tomb[235].

A later series of the echinus salt-cellar was introduced around the second quarter of the fourth century to replace earlier types that had a flat underside. This is also the period when the salt-cellar with concave wall and recessed underside was popular. No.127, from Tocra, represents the development of the shape in this period. The foot here is less broad and the resting surface is grooved while the wall is now high and the rim, by comparison, is slightly thinner with a pronounced incurve. These new features place our piece in the middle two quarters of the fourth century[236]. Similar examples from the Athenian Agora were found in a well, the contents of which belong to the second and third quarters of the fourth century.

Cup No.128, also from Tocra, is of the same type. This is a shallow vessel with a short, upright rim and sloping sides resting on a high foot that is grooved on the resting surface. The junction of the wall and foot is scraped. This is a development, no doubt, from earlier examples, but unlike those, ours appears to be less solid and less compact by comparison[237]. The piece has a particular interest through the local graffiti, which is discussed by its editor.

Find No.129, on the other hand, has a round wall forming a shallower bowl sitting on a very broad resting surface surrounding a small, glazed area of underside with a central nipple, indicating that it belongs to the middle of the fourth century[238].

To this period, too, belongs the echinus bowl No.130 with its projecting rim. Only one example has been reported. There is a close parallel to this pot among the finds of both the Athenian Agora and Salamis (Cyprus)[239]. The Cyrenaica bowl has a foot with a very broad base, and, like other contemporary shapes, the underside is painted black. This is matches the Agora example and must be dated to the middle of the fourth century B.C.

ii. Concave wall (Nos.131-133, pls.10/104)

Among the salt-cellar group, Nos.131-133 represent the type with concave wall, a shape which is also known in silver: a pair were found in the burial mound at Dherveni (Macedonia)[240]. The shape belongs in the main to the fourth century, as it appears to have replaced an earlier series, also concave, but with a flat underside, which was popular during the fifth century. The Cyrenaica pieces, however, are the fourth-century type, each consisting of a low, strongly concave wall, topped by a rounded rim and sloping down to the resting surface, which is clearly marked off from the wall and the inner face of the foot. The underside is totally glazed[241].

PLATES (Nos.134-137, pls.10/105)

i. Rolled rim (Nos.134-135, pl.10)

There are many varieties of plates produced in the Attic Workshop. These range from the very elaborate to the very

---

232 P-8288, *Ath. Agora* XII, 127, No.776, pl.31, fig.8.

233 See the discussion on Entries Nos.27-33.

234 Corbett, *JHS*, 18 (1949), 343, No.149, pls.86, 89, 90.

235 J. Healy, in Rowe, *Cyren.Exped*., Nos.XVII, XVIII. For other examples from Cyrenaica: Holwerda, No.78, 8-81; Sevres, *CVA* pl.25,27, and the No.80. A good number of these were found in the Sidi Abeid Cemetery (Euchesperides) [unpublished].

236 See especially, *Ath. Agora* XII, nos.948-9, fig.9. Lamboglia, *Studi Liguri,* 173. *Idem*, *Arc. Levantina* V (1954), 122f. Robinson, *Olynthus* XIII, pl.224. *BCH* 90, (1966), 589, fig.2,d. Technau, *AM* 54 (1929), 43, fig.31, No.4,5. Coldstream, *Knossos*, 23, fig.14, No.H48. Cuadrado, *Archivo Levantina* X (1963), 16, fig.11, Nos.48-59. From Cyprus, Jehasse, *Salamine De Chypre* 42, fig.28. J.J. Maffre, *BCH*, 95 (1971), 681, No.39. *Beazley's Gifts,* pl.LIX, 431.

237 This piece from Deposit III, level five, from a site excavated at Tocra. *Tocra* 11, 92, 94 No.2360, fig.42. Compare these with examples from the Athenian Agora, *Ath. Agora* XII, nos.833-5, fig.8, pl.33. *Quaderni* (1977) 20, Fig.19"b", pl.XI (22), pp.22-28, fig.32,a, pl.XV (10).

238 *Athen. Agor*. XII, 299, No.887, fig.9. Corbett, *Hesperia* 18 (1949), 329, Fig.5, 155.

239 *Ath. Agor*. XII, No.881, pl.33. Jehasse, *Salamine De Chypre,* 45-46, No.196.

240 Archaeological report for 1961-62, 1963-64, 19; *AJA* 66 (1962), 389-390. Strong, *GRGSP,* 217 and *Delton* 18 (1963), 193f, pls.223-234.

241 See *Agora* xii, 136-137, fig.9, Nos.921-937 and pl.34. *Kerameikos* ix, 43, fig.20 (9, 3-203, 7-216,2). To the north, they are found at Olynthus (*Olynthus* xiii, pls.238 and 239) and the Black Sea. For examples from Panticapaeum: Cracow, Museum of Archaeology 3591 (*CVA* 2, pl.4 (93) 19); Zurich 2536 and 2537 (*CVA* 1 (2), pl.28 (70) 20-21 and 22-23, fig.9, 6-7). They are also found at Old Smyrna (*BSA* lx (1965), 151 fig.9,1), Kalymnos (Brussels A1723, *CVA* 3(3), pl.2 (137) 2), Rhodes (Copenhagen 6448 (two) and 7623 (*CVA* 4(4), pl.177 (180) 11-13), Tamassos on Cyprus (Reading 47.ii.10, T.75.I, and 47.ii.11, T.146.II), and A1 Mina (Reading 83.9.1). An example from Egypt (Brussels A1749 (*CVA* 3(3) pl.2 (137) 6)). For other examples from Cyrenaica, Holwerda No.93-95, Sevres *CVA,* pl.25,24. A number of these were found in the Sidi Abeid Cemetery (Euhesperides unpublished).

plain types. Starting from the later years of the Archaic down to the Hellenistic periods[242].

The two examples from Euhesperides (Nos.134 and 135), according to Sparkes' classification, must fit into the type with rolled rim. These are the slightly plain type, totally glazed with plain rim and a thick wall, usually marked off on the outside by a simple groove. The ring-foot is convex on the outside and concave on the inside with a flat resting surface. Our two plates appear to mark the end of the series as I find them very comparable to those produced during the last quarter of the fourth century, especially the Agora P 6964. This was recovered from a dumped fill with an accumulation mostly of the last quarter of the fourth century[243].

ii. Fish plate (Nos.136-137, pls.10,105)

For the black-glazed fish plate we have the complete example in Leiden, No.136. In order to classify and date our plate, we have to refer to the red-figured type, since the fish plate in both techniques shares the same characteristics and follows the same line of development. Its broad floor slopes down to a central depression and has an overhanging rim. The floor stands on a high ring-foot. Indeed, the only difference is the red-figured characters that adorn the upper surface of the figured type, consisting of fish and marine creatures and a wave pattern decorating the overhanging rim[244].

To date the number of fish plates found in Cyrenaica is surprisingly small in comparison to the other type of material; there was a good series of such plates found in Sabratha and Leptis Magna further west of Cyrenaica on the North African Coast. They were even found in the Tipasa (Algeria) and in the land of the Garamantes further south in the heart of the Sahara. An excavation carried out in 1968-69, in the Cemetery of Sidi Abid of Euhesperides, produced one decorated fish plate, No.137, and numerous fragments[245].

The best published examples are from the series of plates from Salamis (Cyprus) and those from the Athenian Agora[246]. Both sites produced a series of fish plates that started from the end of the fifth century and continued well into the third century, in the case of the Salamis finds, and into the end of the fourth century in the case of the Agora Series. Our example is close to those plates produced during the third quarter of the fourth century from Salamis and the Athenian Agora, which I believe have similar features to ours, namely unmoulded ring-feet with broad resting surfaces.

Fish plates travelled far and were widely exported. On the North African coast they are found in Kerkuan, Carthage (Tunisia), and Tipasa (Algeria). They have also been uncovered in Italy, Spina and Motya (Sicily). To the west of the Mediterranean, there are finds from Tharros, shipwreck discoveries from near Majorca, and a number from Spanish sites. The eastern Mediterranean has examples from Salamis (Cyprus) and as far distant as Histria on the Black Sea[247]. On the mainland they are known Olynthus and the Athenian Agora. In the Aegean they have been found on Thassos, Samos and elsewhere (Map 7).

LEKYTHOS (Nos.138, pl.106)

Black lekythoi[248], the most common oil container among the vases, and also associated with burial customs, were not, in general, imported to Cyrenaica. Example No.138 is the only exception[249]. This has a fourth-century elongated egg-shaped body covered with vertical ribs and fitted with a conical mouth and moulded foot. It was recovered from an adult cist burial and dated by K.M. Phillips to 375 B.C.[250].

ASKOI[251] (Nos.139-146, pls.107-110)

i. Shallow (Nos.139-140, pl.107)

Nos.139-140 represents the shallow type which has a broad body and a wall sloping in to a broad flat base; it was fitted

---

[242] Sparkes and Talcott, *Ath.Agor.* XII, 14ff., fig.10, Nos.1022-1045, and pl.36. Corbett, *Hesperia* 18 (1949), 325, fig.3, No.153, fig.4. Robinson, *Olynthus* XIII, pl.227, Nos.854, 858, 861, 862, pl.228, No.859, pl.229, No.869.

[243] Sparkes and Talcott, *op.cit.* 310, No.1060 (325-310 B.C.). Corbett, *Hesperia*, 24 (1955), 178 (under No.2).

[244] See the discussion on red-figured fish plates in the study (Entry No.82, Chapter 3).

[245] See D. Gill, in Kenrick (ed.), *Excavation at Sabratha,* 291 (Nos.i35-165). De Miro-Graziella Fiorentini, *Quaderni* 9 (1977), fig.94 (XVa and XVb), from Leptis Magna. For a fragment of a fish plate from a site in Wadi Al Ajal (The Land of the Garamantes) in Fezzan (information provided by Brian Shefton and Charles Daniels of the Department of Archaeology, Newcastle University). For the fish plate from Tipasa see J.P. Morel, in *Antiquities Africaines* 15-16 (1980), 85, fig.41.

[246] Jehasse, *Salamine de Chypre,* 34f., fig.22 (36-47). Sparkes and Talcott, *Ath. Agor.* XII, 147f., 310f., pl.37, fig.10 (Nos.1061-1073).

[247] Note in the section dealing with red-figured pottery in this study.

i) The Kerkuan information was provided by B.B. Shefton for Carthage, A. 74.III.31 and A.78.XI.228 (Archaeometry 25.1, 1983, 77-86). For Tharros, see B.A. Sparkes, in Barnett (ed.), *Tharros* (Nos.17/2, 29/5) pls.18, 106, 129.
ii) Tipasa, Morel, *Antiquities Africaines*, 58 f. and fig.41.
iii) For the plate from the shipwreck (Majorca), see Guerrero Ayuso, *Los Nucleus Arqueologicos De Cavalia*, fig.96, 2, 3, 4, and Salvador *Rst. Lig.* 38 (1972), 307, fig.25.
iv) For Spain, see E. Cuadrado, *Madrider Mitteilun,* 181, fig.32, 7.
v) Salamine (Cyprus). Jehasse, *Salamin de Chypre*, 34.
vi) Olynthus. Robinson, *Olynthus* V, pl.190, No.1044 and XIII, pl.221, No.903.
vii) Thasos. Gali Kahil, *La Ceramique grecque,* pl.56, Nos.41-42.
viii) Samos. Technau, *AM* 54 (1929), 46, Fig.35.
ix) Histria. Alexandrescu, *Histria* IV, 92, No.609, fig.15.

[248] For the name and ancient usages, cf. Richter and Milne, pp.14-14. The early history of the shape and its decoration throughout the Bf. period has been presented by Miss C.H.E. Haspels, *ABL, passim*.

[249] See D. White, in Humphrey J.H. (ed.), *Apollonia, The Port of Cyrene,* 118-119.

[250] See Phillips, in Humphrey J.H. (ed.), *op.cit.* 118-119. No exact parallels have been encountered, but R. Edwards (quoted by Phillips) compares this to the oinochoe from Tomb 814 at Spina with similar body and foot. S. Aurigemma, *Scavi di Spina*, pl.104,a. Ignoring the neck and mouth of an oinochoe in the Gallatin Collection, the body, handle and foot, as well as the ribs, in both vessels are similar (*CVA* USA 1, 52 pl.31:7).

[251] For the varieties of askoi, see *AJA*, XXV, (1921), pp.325-326 (Beazley), and *Mnemosyne*, third series, I, (1933-34), 34-60 (Snijder). The name is obviously conventional. See Richter and Milne, 17-18. Sparkes and Talcott, *Ath. Agor.* XII, 157f., 210.

with a large spout with rounded lip and a long and high arched strap-handle linking the spout to the body on the opposite side. All this indicates that it was made for liquids and especially the pouring of small quantities at a time. These liquids were likely to have been perfumes or even honey. The peak in popularity of this vessel was seen to be around the last thirty years of the fifth century, when it was produced in both figured and black[252]. Our askoi, however, has features that place the shape in the first half of the fourth century[253]. The top of the vessel rises slightly, forming a high breast. This feature, on askoi later than ours, rises more markedly to the centre and in certain cases was elaborated into a nipple, perhaps in imitation of a lid. Moreover, the broad handle rises above the body and the trumpet-shaped spout has a more pronounced flare.

ii. Relief top[254] (Nos.141and 142, pls.108-109)

Two askoi (Nos.141 and 142) are classed under this heading. The body appears to take the shape of a duck[255], with the neck flaring upward in a trumpet-like spout. The overarching strap-handle projects from the tail end and joins the rim. Most characteristic of the shape, however, is the fact that the convex top takes the shape of a medallion. This is usually decorated with high relief.

From the little that remains of No.142, Rowe failed to recognize the shape as an askos. He described it as a model pot or a lid[256]. He also suggested that the relief on the top was that of a Medusa-head. But although the Medusa-head, during the fourth century, can be portrayed with no protruding tongue and without the snakes, the face on our vase, with buffed cheeks, appears to be a mask rather than a Medusa-head[257]: that, on our askos, the face fills the medallion and there is an absence of hair, may well confirm this fact.

There is a series of askoi with relief tops in the Athenian Agora. Unfortunately none of these were found complete. These are dated by Sparkes to the end of the fifth and the early years of the fourth century B.C. Two of these (P 24197 and P 10918) are from a datable context, both at the end of the fifth century[258].

[252] *CVA* Oxford 1 (13), pl.45 (137), 1, 2, 4.6, 8. *CVA* Munich 2(6), pl.100 (296), 4-11 and pls. 101-102 (297-8). Massei, *Gli Askoi*, *passim*.

[253] See the example from the Athenian Agora (probably contemporary to ours), *Ath. Agora* No.1177, pl.39. In red-figure, see Massei, *ibid*, T.207c (inv. 12278), pp.224-7, no.139-140, pl.LII, 2; LXXX, 3. Similar examples can be found in Staatliches Lindenau, Museum Altenburg, inv.81 (*CVA* Germany 18, 865, pl.80:22). Ashmolean Museum, Oxford, inv.371 (*CVA* Great Britain 3, 140, pl.46:31). Offentliche Sammalungen, Zurich inv. 2522 (*CVA* Switzerland, 2, 70, pl.28:16). Rhode Island School of Design, Providence, inv. 16543, C-2362 (*CVA* USA, 2, 80, pl.26:6).

[254] For this type of askos see Sparkes and Talcott, *Ath. Agor.* XII, 159.

[255] There are two askoi from Corinth in schematized duck form with tail and neck. See R. Edwards in *Corinth* VII, Part III, (1975), 148, pl.64 (776).

[256] Rowe, *Cyren. Exp.* 22 (N.83.BJ, M770), pl.40a,b. There is a fragment of a relief top from Euhesperides in Oxford (D.W.J. Gill).

[257] For a discussion of the relief-decorated askos, see Pagenstecher, *Die Caleuische Reliefkeramik* No.666, Fig.48. See also Hayes, *Greek and Italian Black-Glass Wares,* 53f, Nos.86 and 87. Jentel, *Les gutti et les askoi à reliefs* 365-68, *AP* XI, 1a, pl.LIX, figs.193-194.

[258] Sparkes and Talcott, *op.cit.* 159, 319 (Nos.1181, 1187).

Of our two examples, askos No.142 was recovered from the sealed arcophagus in the North Cemetery of Cyrene. The material found with it belonged to the first half of the fourth century[259]. Although the relief on the top of askos No.142 is not visible, it appears, however, to feature in the medallion in a similar way to that of No.141. Moreover, the shape of the vessel as a whole has a very similar profile with a high ring-foot. Both askoi were probably made during the first half of the fourth century.

iii. Strainer top (No.143, pl.110)

The second type of askos imported to Cyrenaica (No.143) is the style topped with a moulded. The form appears to have been introduced into Greek households by the late fifth century[260]. Here, a ridged ring-handle substituted the arched strap-handle on the shallow shape askos. The strainer on the top sinks down and is surrounded by a moulded ledge. Askoi of this type are not frequently found in the Athenian Agora, but sites such as Olynthus and Spina have parallels to our example. Many of the Spina askoi are contemporary to red-figure types of the first half of the fourth century[261].

iv. Guttus type (Nos.144-146, pl.110)

Askoi Nos.144-146 represent the Guttus type. This is a squat wine decanter with a body that curves onto a broad base, usually reserved underneath. Its ring-handle and mouth enable the contents to be poured with exceptional care. As with the previous shape it has a ring-handle, which is also ridged. The mouth is set on top of the vertical neck, marked off from the body by a ridge.

We are not sure whether all the examples of gutti from Cyrenaica are Attic. No.144, in particular, has buffed clay and a dull glaze. There is the possibility that these were made locally in an imitation of imported Attic examples. Chronologically they are probably contemporary with the series from the Athenian Agora, which is dated to the middle quarters of the fourth century. In later examples, the body becomes higher and narrower and the foot higher, but smaller. Examples of these vessels come from Alexandria[262], Lindos[263], and Olynthus[264], but closest to No.144 is a group of gutti from the Athenian Agora[265].

[259] Rowe, *op.cit.* 12 (N.83-BJ), 32. Coin pieces XVII-XVIII, pl.6, P-15.8,b; 12a; 40 a-b.

[260] Sparkes and Talcott, *Ath. Agora,* pp.159-160. *Olynthus* XIII, 257-258.

[261] *Olynthus* XIII, Pls.176, 177 (Nos.469-72). Massei, *op.cit.* 141-143, no.86, 165, pls.XXXIII, 1-2, LXV, 4; 279-283, no:167, pls.LXVI, 2-3; LXXV, 3; LXXVI, 2; LXXVII, 1.

[262] Breccia, *La Necropoli di Sciatbi,* 59, no.147, and pl.L, no.89.

[263] *Lindos* I, pl.149, 3147. *Clara Rhodes* VI-VII (1932), 447, fig.1 and 457, fig.12.

[264] *Olynthus* V, pl.172 and XIII, pl.168, 414-421.

[265] *Ath. Agor.* XII, P-6952, 319, no.1194, pl.39, fig.11. See examples in Schlossmuseum Gotha, inv.H.A.502, *CVA* Germany 29, 149 pl.78:7. Collection de l'Université Cracow, inv. 638, 88 pl.14:25. Musée National des Antiquities, Bucarest, inv. 03245, *CVA* Romania 1, 43 pl.43:2.

LEKANIS, Lykynic Shape[266] (Nos.147-152, pls.4/8/111-112)

Nos.147-151 are of the same class as the fifth century lekanis with mushroom-knobbed lid, shallow bowl, and the typical horizontal cup handles that rise and twist inwards at the top. They differ, however, in the form of the foot. Here the style is given a heavier, flared, foot with basal moulding, a feature that dates these later examples to the fourth century B.C.

Kern discusses lekanis No.147 and dates it to 400 B.C.[267]. His dating is based on comparisons made with similar vessels recovered from Ialysos (Rhodes)[268]. They were found in a grave with an Attic red-figured lebes gamikos, attributed by Beazley to the manner of the Meidias Painter[269]. Accordingly, Kern dates the lekanis to the end of the fifth century. There are two more similar lekanides from dated contexts. Both are cited by Kern as good parallels to our piece and dated to the late fifth century[270].

I feel, nevertheless, that our piece is likely to be of an early fourth-century date. The foot, our best criterion for dating, consists of two sections, nicked off by a marked groove from the body. The upper section of the foot broadens downwards so that the lower part attains a greater width, but has less height than the upper one. The lower section shows a pronounced tapering profile again. These feet characteristics are found among fourth-century examples such as the examples from Toronto and the Athenian Agora. Both have very similar feet and are dated to the first quarter of the fourth century[271]. This is also the date of the series of similar lekanides from Olynthus[272].

The other style of lekanis (No.152) found in Cyrenaica is the pyre-type bowl, probably intended for use with sacrificial pyres. This is a small bowl, similar to the lekanis in shape, but with no handles. There is a series of this type from Kerameikos and the Athenian Agora[273]. These were poorly made and of a thin fabric. However, The Cyrenaica bowl appears to be of a stronger fabric and elegantly made and ornamented. The lid's shoulder and the wall have horizontal grooves. The flaring disc-foot is heavy with a broad surface. The underside is black and rises to a nipple, a feature that dates our bowl to the second quarter of the fourth century.

FEEDER (Nos.153-155, pls.112-113)

The top of pot No.153 slants upwards to the filling hole. The loop handle is broader and the disc-foot is heavier and edged on the outside, but of most interest is the decorated pattern on the top. This is a concentric arch formed by alternate reserved and glazed bands. This pattern is more likely to represent a core of palmettes rather than a mere abstract type of decoration.

There is a series of fourth century feeder vases from Olynthus[274] on which the top decoration is a wave pattern. The Cyrenaica vase is a rare example, on which the pattern is a palmette core. The only other example of a feeder with an identical shape and decoration comes from southern Russia[275]. We are familiar with artists who used such patterns around the middle of the fourth century on other shapes. Our best example is by the Vienna Painter (No.155), who decorated the cups with large palmettes, the cores of which are identical to the designs on the Cyrenaica feeder vases[276].

Nos.154 and 155, however, have deep round bodies with flattened incurving rims, broad stemmed feet, rather high and bulky, and with heavy bases. They were fitted with vertical broad looped handles and tubular spouts. The tops are reserved and decorated with spiral patterns instead of the palmette cores[277]. This feeder vase appears to represent the latest version in the development of the so-classed Type 2 shape in Robinson's classification[278]. It was widely distributed in the second and third quarter of the fourth century. Our feeders are particularly close to a vessel from Toronto and further example from Naucratis in the British Museum[279].

III. COMMENTARY ON THE IMPORTED ATTIC BLACK-GLAZED POTTERY

The group of Attic black-glazed pottery from Cyrenaica is impressive in its variety. The geographical location of the region meant that it was well placed to receive the Athenian production that was circulating overseas. It is however

[266] For the class, see Beazley, *CVA* Oxford 2, pl.65-13, with accompanying text. Kern, *Mededeelingen* 38 (1957), 53-57, with list. Sparkes and Talcott, *Ath. Agor*. XII, 168-7, with list.

[267] Kern, *op.cit.* 53ff.

[268] Jacopi, in *Clara Rhodes* III (1929), 155, no.2 (6641) and fig.148, on p.155, centre.

[269] Rhodes, acc. No.6640. *Clara Rhodes* III (1929), 154-155, no.1, with fig.149 on p.156. *ARV* 1322, 14.

[270] *Clara Rhodes* VI-7 (1932-33), 465, Sub XXII, 3, and fig.18, 11 (6th vase from the right on p.466). *Clara Rhodes* VIII (1936), 157, fig.144, 11 (right on p.158).

[271] Hayes, *Ontario* 36, Nos.58-59 (figs.15 and 6). Sparkes and Talcott, *Ath. Agor*. XII, 321, No.1246, (P-6198) pl.42.

[272] *Olynthus* XIII, 316 ff., pl.206 (Nos.632, 633).

[273] *Kerameikos* IX, Nos.301(2), 202(5). *Athenian Agora* XII, No.1276-79.

[274] For the type, see especially J.H.C. Kern, "An Attic 'feeding bottle' of the fourth century B.C., Leyden". *Mnemosyne*, 4th ser. 10 (1957), 16-21. Robinson, Olynthus XIII, p.265, Nos. 479, 480 for the wave pattern.

[275] Gaidukevich *Nekropoli Bosporskich Gorodow*, 35, Fig.12.

[276] Vienna 155. *CVA*, pl.32, 1-2 pl.31, 4-5. *ARV* 1522, 1. Vienna 95, *CVA* pl.32, 3-4 pl.33, 4-5. *ARV* 1522, 2.

[277] For the type see J.H.C. Kern, *Mnemosyne* 4th ser. 10 (1957), 20, who lists 25 published examples from various sites.

[278] *Olynthus* XIII, 265, especially no.1480.

[279] Hayes, *Ontario*, 165f., No.267, fig.5 (909.70.1). Walters, *BMC*, Lamps 219, Nos.1438-42, fig.346. See also other examples in *CVA* Cracovie (Pologne 2), pls.93.18, 96.23 (both from Kerch), and variant pl.96.5. C.W. Clairmont, *Berytus* 12 (1956-57), 12, nos.434-440, pl.111.6, with variant no.441, pl.111.7 (all Benachi Collection, from Egypt). *CVA* Zurich 1 pl.25.15,17. A.W. Johnston, *Proceedings of the Royal Irish Academy* 73 (1973), section C, no.9, 401, no.582 (Dublin, National Museum 1903:382). See also *Clara* Rhodes 11, 155, fig.37. J.J. Maffre, *BCH* 85 (1971), 697, no.44, fig.52.

impressive only in qualitative rather than quantitative terms, as the finds are not great. The answer lies in the nature of the material. This is a collection of pottery acquired partly from museum stores and partly as the result of successive excavation at ancient sites such as that of Euhesperides, originally from tombs.

Of the 155 pieces presented here the series of black-glaze falls within the limited period of nearly one hundred and fifty years, ranging approximately from the second quarter of the fifth until the third quarter of the fourth century (Figure 3), the earliest being the skyphos of the Corinthian type (No.1), the Attic Type B (the so-called glaux, No.13) and the Vienna cup (Nos.15 and 16). Assuming that this material is a fair representative of the type of black-glazed pottery that reached Cyrenaica during late Archaic and Classical periods, one must observe that, during the first half of the fifth and even part of the third-quarter of the fifth century, imports appear to have been sporadic. Only by the third-quarter onwards do we notice what appears to be a greater flow of imports. There was a further slackening of activities for a short period during the first quarter of the fourth century to be followed by a very large group produced mainly in the second quarter of the century. Such an observation can be correlated with the rhythm of the imported red-figured vases, and indeed with the Panathenaic Prize Amphorae. David Gill has recently studied and published the black-glazed pottery from Sabratha. He also investigated the batch of black-glaze fragments from Euhesperides[280]. These are the results of the unpublished excavation of Johns and Wilson in 1952-4 (on behalf of the Cyrenaican Department of Antiquities and the Ashmolean Museum, Oxford)[281], and of the rescue excavations of 1968 and 1969 conducted by the British School at Rome under the direction of G.D.B. Jones[282]. For comparison with materials from other sites in Libya there is the publication of the black-glazed pottery found in the Punic cemetery of Leptis Magna, by De Miro and Fiorentini[283]. Gill's investigation on the pottery from the two sites revealed that the Attic forms of skyphos and the bolsal were the most popular shapes among the imported black-glazed pottery. Such an observation can also be said of our material in this study. In fact, most of the shapes present in our collection are to be found in the Sabratha and, indeed, in the Lepcis Magna material (Figure 4).

There are, however, shapes included in this study (mainly from Cyrene and Tocra), which are not present in the sites of either Sabrath or Leptis Magna. The fifth and fourth century feeders (Nos.14 and 153), the shallow askoi (Nos.139 and 140), and the kalyx cup (No.122) are not represented on these western sites.

280 D. Gill, in *Excavation at Sabratha,* 275-296, and *idem* in *Euhesperides* 1958-69.

281 H. Sichtermann, *AA* 74 (1959), 239-348. Boardman, *BSA* 61 (1966), 155-156.

282 Jones and Little, *JRS* 61 (1971), 64-79. Jones, in *Cyrenaica in Antiquity,* 31-32. Vickers, *AR* (1971-2, 4). Selective material from the Archaic period is published by Vickers and Gill in *Libyan Studies* 17 (1986), 97.

283 This is material from the Phoenisian cemetery at Leptis Magna, published by De Miro-Fiorentini in *Quaderni* 9 (1977), 7-75.

The feeder (No.14) is dated to the third-quarter of the fifth century. This is of the type found in the Kerameikos and Athenian Agora[284]. No.153, on the other hand, is of the mid-fourth century. It is of the type found frequently in Olynthus[285].

The shallow askoi (Nos.139 and 141) are of late fifth or early fourth century production. Both Spina and the Athenian Agora provide a number of examples of the same type[286]. Examples of the single calyx cup (No.122) are to be found in the Achaemenid pottery and silver work. This appears to be a possible source of influence. The earliest example in Attic pottery is dated to the second quarter of the fourth century. The example from Olynthus, which is evidently nearer to our example, is dated to near the middle of the fourth century[287]. The most important shapes, which are found only in Cyrenaica, are closed shape pots, e.g. the lidded pelike (No.39) of the fifth century, and the examples with ribbed walls (Nos.1, 93 and 94) with a fourth-century date. There are few amphorai (Nos.89 and 92) of the Panathenaic Shape with wide spreading lip, and raised fillet between neck and body, naturally meant to carry olive oil or wines. All date to the third-quarter of the fourth century. There are no less than 12 olpai (Nos.8-20) of the type found in the Kerameikos and the Athenian Agora[288], imported in the fifth and fourth centuries, and 13 hydriai (Nos.99-111), most of them ribdbed, dated to the second quarter of the fourth century. The series of 'cup vi' vessels (Nos.15 and 16) and stemless cups (Nos.16 and 25), including the 'delicate class', is significant. These can be closely compared with examples from the Athenian Agora, the Kerameikos, and Stryme (near Komotini, Thrace)[289].

In the discussion on black-glazed pottery from Sabratha, Gill compared those of the second half of the fifth century to what is known of imports at Al Mina, and to some extent Spina, and since Jully's studies of Athenian pottery in Languedoc, Rousillon and Catalonia show different levels of trade[290], he suggested that Sabratha was not using the same traders[291]. Such a suggestion may apply to Leptis Magna when dealing with the series of black-glazed pottery recovered from its Phoenician cemeteries. Perhaps we should consider the presence of such Attic material in these two Phoenician sites, and indeed other North African sites further to the west, as part of the commercial activities of the Phoenician traders. Such activities are indicated by Phoenician graffiti on the foot of an Attic bell-krater of the third-quarter of the fifth century B.C. from Galero in Spain. This graffito, as shown by A.W.

284 *Hesperia* 32 (1963), 121, D.B, pl.39. *Ath.Agora* XII, wo.1197, pl.39. Knigge, in *Kerameikos* IX (1976), pl.42.

285 *Olynthus* XIII, Nos.479, 480. Hays, *Ontario,* No.267.

286 Massei, *Gli Askoi.* Askos No.88 (inv.6567), 145-6, pl.LXXX,I. *Ath. Agora,* Nos.1176-77, pl.39.

287 Shefton, *Annales Archeologiques Arab Syriennes* (1971), 110, pl.XXI, Fig. 8, a and b. *Olynthus* V, pl.150, 350, XIII, pl.190-191, No.521A, pl.215, 520A. Later examples are to be found in Alexandria. Breccia, *La Necropoli di Sciatbi,* pl.LVI, 118, 124.

288 Knigge, in *Kerameikos* IX (1976), pl.78. Sparkes and Talcott, *Ath. Agor.* XII, pl.13.

289 Sparkes and Talcott, *ibid*, 102 f., fig.5. Hoepfner, *Kerameikos* X, fig.218. Bakalaki, 917, fig.32.

290 Jully, *Cyramique grecques,* 295-326.

291 Gill, *op.cit.* 276 f.

Johnston, can be interpreted as a merchant's mark quantifying a set of kraters in a formula closely similar to Attic usage[292]. In Pseudo-Scylax 112, there is a passage referring to the Phoenicians as trading, among other goods, Attic pottery on the Atlantic Coast of North Africa. Brian Shefton's findings concerning the routes followed by the Castula Cup is in agreement with the Pseudo-Scylax passage[293]. The cup type, which is found on all the sites of the north African coast, is extremely frequent on south Italian and Sicilian sites. Westward it was found in Sardinia, Ibiza, the Levant Coast, and inland sites (Map 6).

Brian Shefton believes that, during much of the fifth century, the bulk of Greek imports to the Andalusian plain and North Africa came via the Levant coast, along the route indicated by the finds of these Attic cups. The Phoenician sites of Sabratha and Leptis Magna were probably part of this trading pattern. I do not think the Cyrenaican sites used the same merchants who traded with Sabratha and Leptis Magna. Judging from the red-figured pottery, and indeed the Panathenaic Prize Amphorae, we have to think of Cyrenaica as part of eastern Mediterranean, rather than the west, in terms of its commercial activities.

[292] Johnston, *BICS* 25 (1978), 82 f. Shefton, *Madrider Beitrage* 8 (1982), 366, n. 87.

[293] B.B. Shefton, *ibid*, 366, 404.

Chapter Six

PANATHENAIC PRIZE AMPHORAE

One of the most famous of the Athenian festivals was the Panathenaea, the festival dedicated to the goddess Athena on the occasion of her birthday. Although the origin of the festival is not known, historical tradition dates the reforms of the festivals to 566 B.C., during the tyranny of Peisistratos. This was really an adaptation of the old yearly festival, the Athenea, which continued to be celebrated every year as the lesser Panathenaea. But every fourth year from, 566 B.C., there was a celebration of special magnificence and the procession carrying the peplos to the temple of Athena on The Acropolis was the most important event of the festival. A further element that greatly enhanced the popular interest of the festival was added in the sixth century. The year 566/5 B.C. saw the institution of organized competitions, especially horse racing and music; but most important was the introduction of athletic games. These consisted of foot races, the pentathlon (foot race, long jump, discus, spear throwing, and wrestling), wrestling, boxing, and the pankration, a form of free-style fighting. There was also a race in armour for men[1].

In the course of his reforms, Peisistratos seems to have introduced the awarding of 'Panathenaic amphorae' as prizes to the victors in these competitions. These were a special kind of Attic vase, filled with oil (or holding olive trees from the sacred grove of Attica).

The Panathenaic amphora[2] was an egg-shaped vessel with a short, narrow foot and neck. In height, the early vase (sixth and fifth century) was between 62 and 67cm but later models (fourth century) were between 68 and 82cm. The decoration on these vessels soon assumed a fixed style that remained unchanged for centuries, although its character was gradually transformed to suit changing taste.

The subject of the picture and other ornamentation remained the same: on the neck a double lotus flower and palmette chain. Below this is a broad band of tongues. On the body, in reserved panels, Athena stands to one side, with her shield and raised spear in war-like attitude, between two columns, each supporting a cockerel, with the inscription: ΤΟΝΑΘΕΝΕΘΕΝΑΘΛΟΝΟ "I am (or 'this is') one of the prizes from the games at Athens"[3]. On the other side there was a representation of the event for which the prize was given.

Participation in these games was not restricted to Athenians, a fact that explains the diffusion and distribution of prize amphorae all over the classical world, and they have been found in remote, non-Hellenic places. According to the testimony of two inscriptions (of a second century B.C. date), most of prize amphorae were won by non-Athenians[4]. From a total of nearly 50 extant names stated on inscriptions, only 10 are clearly identified as Athenians. Since these prize amphorae were filled with olive oil, it is stated that the winner had the right to sell his oil tax-free. The oil was then exported probably in these amphorae[5].

We know, that the inhabitants of Greek colonies, and Athenians overseas, were expected to participate in the festival by sending a heifer and a suit of armour on each occasion as an offering[6].

For Cyrenaica, we are not clear of the circumstances concerning the export of these vessels to the region. It is

1 The early years of the sixth century saw considerable development in many Greek festivals on the model of the four-yearly festivals at the great inter-state sanctuaries like Olympia and Delphi. It is evident that the Athenians were not far behind in the organization of other festivals, like the Pythian, Isthmian and Nemean events, in feeling that their great festival should be brought into line with the new ideas. For a discussion of these ideas and the origin of the festival and the new reforms, see Davidson, *JHS* 78 (1958), 24-29. Corbett, *JHS* 80 (1960), 57-58. Parke, *Festivals of the Athenians,* 34 f.

2 Peters, *Studien zu den Panath. Idem*, *JDI*, 57 (1942), 143-157. Beazley, *AJA* 47 (1943), 441-465. *Idem*, *Develop.* ch.8. Smet, *Ant. Class.* 5 (1936) 87-104. Brauchitsch, *Die Panath. Passim.* Davidson *JHS* 78 (1958), 52. Frel, *Panath.* Edwards, *Hesperia* 26 (1957), 320-349.

3 Shefton, in *HGVP*, 314.

4 *I.G.*, II^2, 2313-2314.

5 Cf. Peters, *op.cit.* 11f. Amyx, in *AJA* 27 (1958), 182f.

6 Meiggs-Lewis, No. 40, 1.3 ff. (Erythrai), No. 46, 1.42 ff. (decree of Cleinias), No. 49, II, II ff. (Brea), No. 69, 11.56 (Tribute reassessments 425-424 B.C.). F. Chamoux, *Cyrene Sous la Monarchie des Battiades.*

evident that the Cyrenaicans took great interest in sport inside, and outside, of the city-states of Cyrenaica. Moreover, we know, for certain, that classical authors frequently mentioned the Cyrenaicans as taking part in the various Greek festivals and winning chariot races in the Pan Hellenic games. Our best evidence comes from Pindar, who dedicated three poems in honour of two Cyrenean citizens. The first two poems (Pythian IV, V) were to be performed in celebration of the victory won by King Arkesilaos IV in the four-horse chariot race at Delphi, about 462 B.C. The third (Pythian IX) was composed to celebrate a victory in the hoplite race - the race run in full armour - by Telesikrates at the Pythian Games of 474[7]. But although there are a number of Panathenaics representing chariot race events, surprisingly the majority of these found in Cyrenaica are connected with athletic events. Alternatively, these Panathenaic vessels might have been exported as regular vessels serving as ordinary containers for oil it: it is known that the average vessel contained between thirty-eight and thirty-nine litres of oil. We also know that this oil was exempt from taxes, and duty-free for export. As the Athenian Potters produced more Panathenaics than were ordered by the state, they evidently sold the surplus without difficulty (as empty vessels, each fetched between 2.4 and 3.7 obols). But because many of these were actually inscribed, they were more likely to have been associated with an event, and would have belonged to regional victors in the Panathenaia[8].

With the exception of a very few and insignificant fragments, all known Panathenaic amphorae from Cyrenaica were found in tombs[9]. Outside of Cyrenaica, the site yielding Panathenaic vessels most abundantly is Athens, especially the Pompeion, in the Kerameikos[10]. This funerary use of Panathenaics, however, was not limited to Cyrenaica and Attica, but extended over all of the Mediterranean Greek settlements and the Black Sea area[11].

I. THE SIXTH-CENTURY TYPES

The earliest imported Panathenaic vessel to Cyrenaica is represented by the small piece (No.1, pl.114, 1) found on the third terrace of the Demeter Sanctuary of Cyrene[12]. Three fragments of the same amphora were collected and when joined they appeared to be from the reverse of an early Panathenaic amphora. There were two male nude figures painted on its lower section, heavily built athletes, standing foot to foot, possibly in the middle of a boxing match.

This amphora was probably painted during the first few years of the last quarter of the sixth century. The style of painting is typical of that period: in particular it is very similar to that of the Euphiletus Painter. The painting on a Panathenaic vessel in Munich is typical of his style[13].

The scene on fragment (No.2, pl.114, 2) is a four-horse chariot race. The style and detail of what remains of the wheel and hind legs are comparable to that on side B of Panathenaic vase No.6. It is fair to assume that the vase was painted in the last quarter of the sixth, or early fifth century B.C.

II. THE FIFTH-CENTURY TYPES

The earliest, and indeed the finest, Panathenaic amphora from Cyrenaica (of the fifth century) was the vase found in the spring of 1969 at Aslaia, some eighteen kilometres southeast of El-Merj (Barca)[14]. The vase (No.33, pl.115, 1-2), which is typical of early fifth-century Panathenaics, has a well-proportioned, compact shape, with echinus mouth and a rather short neck separated from the shoulder by a raised fillet. Its cylindrical handles are set close to the neck, from which they spring upwards and then turn down to join the round shoulder. The vase is triangular in shape with a swinging, round wall that tapers sharply, from the base's greatest diameter, towards a very small, torus foot. This intact vase was attributed by Vickers to one of the great red-figured artists active in the first two decades of the fifth century, the Kleophrades Painter[15].

This vase represents the second stage in the evolution of Panathenaics amphorae, which started in the third quarter of the sixth century B.C., displaying certain features that were to remain canonical until the end of the fifth century. Its shape by now has a well-proportioned form, gradually larger and more compact, with a round shoulder and curved base. Handles are close to the neck and with a torus foot replacing the echinus one. The profile of the goddess here, as on coins, is majestically represented in an archaic manner. The Kleophrades Painter gave her a distinctive facial type: massive chin, full sensual lips, and a straight nose. She appears less stout and more energetic, with one heel raised from the ground.

7 Schol.Pin. *Pyth*. 4 (Drachmann, 11 P.92), *Pyth* IX (Drachmann 11, P.220).

8 Amyx, *Hesperia* 27 (1958), 178. See also M.A. Tiberios, *A Delt*. 29 (1974), 142ff.

9 G. Dennis, Transaction of the Royal Society of Literature 9 (1870), 22-25. Smith C., *BSA* 3 (1896-7), 192. Dennis believes that they came from a special quarter of the city reserved for heroes in this connection. See Luni, in *Quaderni* 8 (1976), 281 n.259. Vattier de Bourville, *RA* 5(1) (1848), 150ff. *Idem*, *RA* 6 (1949), 65ff. *Idem*, *Archivis des mission Scietifique* (1850), 580ff. Chamoux, *Cyrene Sous la Monarchie des Battiades*, 28.

10 Frel, *Panathenaic* 6-7 and *Kerameikos* 10 (1976), 238f.

11 See the examples from a Taranto Grave, reported by Lo Porto, in *Atti e Memorie della Societa Magna Grecia,* 69 ff., pl.XXXIII-XXXVII. The example from Vulci in Riccioni, see G, *Panatenaica di Vulci*, 33f. See also the other example in the Villa Guilia Museum reported in *Il Musea Nazionale Etrusco di Villa Guilia* (1980) Nos.55, 287-288, and the example in *Il Museo Civico Archeologico di Bologne* (1982) 267, 274.

12 White, *Lib. Antiq*. 8 (1971), 92, pl. XXXIV, b.

13 See the reverse of this vase in Munich, Antikensammlungen 1453, from Vulc. *ABV* 322. Boardman, *ABFH* No. 298. For a representation of this style of boxing and wrestling see the black-figure neck amphora in the British Museum B. 295 (The BMN Painter). Beazley, *ABV* 226 1, Para 106, Addenda 27. Gardiner, *Greek Athletic*, 420, fig. 143. Harris, *Sport*, figs. 6-7.

14 M. Vickers, J. Reynolds, *AR*. 1971-2, 38, figs. 14a to 15b. M. Vickers, *Lib. Antiq*. 8 (1971), 74-75, XXVII 1-b, XXVIII a.

15 For the name of the artist see Boardman, *AA* 1981, 329.

She begins now to wear a chiton instead of the peplos, in keeping with the changing fashion.

On every Panathenaic vase by the Kleophrades Painter, the goddess has the same shield device, the winged horse Pegasus, which must have served as a form of official trademark, not only of the painter, but also of the potter, who turned all of his Panathenaics.

The reverse of the amphora (pl.115, 2) shows a boy holding up a discus, in preparation for a throw, in the presence of a flute player and a judge[16]. The flute player is represented, as usual, in long, white robe. The judge is clothed in a himation and carries the palm-branch that is to be presented to the victor in this competition. The boy has exaggerated long limbs, with rather unsuccessfully drawn anatomical details. There is, therefore, the suggestion that this side of the Panathenaic vessel was not executed by the Kleophrades Painter himself but by someone from his workshop[17]. On another Panathenaic by the artist, the anatomical details (the stomach muscles) were drawn more successfully[18]. There are seven intact Panathenaic amphorae by this artist (as well as some fragments[19]), and we can now add this fine piece from Cyrenaica. A particularly close parallel to ours is his amphora in the Metropolitan Museum. The garments worn by Athena are similarly designed, the upper parts with no folds and the surface decorated with stars (the lower part does show folds). A similarly close example is the vase in Taranto, by the same painter[20].

Among the imported non-Panathenaic shapes, the Attic kalpis (pl.115, 1), painted in the black-figure technique, is not without interest[21]. On the preserved side, Athena is painted, black-faced, and looking left. As represented on Panathenaic amphorae, she wears a high-crested helmet. In front of her there is a floral design (half-palmette) and behind her there is a small owl with tendril. Although only the bust of the goddess is presented, the painter must have had the figure of Athena, as portrayed on Panathenaics vessels, in mind. He presented her in similar fashion, with the usual Attic helmet, aegis and spear. This kalpis is attributed by Haspel to the Painter of the Half-Palmette, whose basic motifs, in drawing, are owls and females, either full figure or bust[22]. It is no surprise, therefore, that the painting of this piece (500-480 B.C.), and its import to Cyrenaica, happened at a time when we are witnessing the start of the flow of Panathenaic prizes to the region.

After the retirement of the Kleophrades Painter (as a producer of Panathenaic vessels), the Berlin Painter[23] seems to have become the main producer of the form. There is a restored vase in the Cyrene Museum that, if not by the artist's hand, must at any rate have come from his workshop. Luni mistakenly places the vase in the fourth century[24]. Only the reverse (No.4, pl.116, 2) survives, representing a short-distance foot race undertaken by four, tall, elegant figures. This is clear from the way they run, all of them raising their front leg high, while the arms are moving too. On a Panathenaic amphora by the same artist in London (Market Christie, once Castle Ashby[25]), a long-distance race is represented. On this vase a post is shown, not the finish, only the turning point in the race.

The composition and arrangement of figures on another vessel from Cyrenaica by the Berlin Painter is slightly different (No.5, pl.116, 3); here, too, a short- distance race is represented, but the spacing of the competing figures is somewhat different. They are identical to those on another Panathenaic (from Nola) by the Berlin Painter[26]. The two middle athletes partly overlap, while the front one forges ahead; the last figure is desperately trying to catch up with the rest. The arm and leg movements are diagonal; the left leg and right arm move forward together, so does the right leg and left arm. The figures appear to be executed in three-quarter view: front, chest and back.

The Panathenaic No.6 (pl.117, 1-2) has not been attributed. Neugebauer broadly places it in the first half of the fifth century[27], while Schmidt and Smets narrow the date to the second quarter of the same century[28]. It is not unreasonable, however, to place the date of the painting of this amphora earlier than that. Although the shape of the amphora was very common during the first half of the fifth century, the date of the painting can be pushed back to the early years of the century. Side B on the vase represents a quadriga, a racing chariot, in which a bearded charioteer is bent forward, pressing his four horses to the finish. Such a representation is very close, if not identical, to Side B of a Panathenaic vase, painted by the Kleophrades Painter (in Malibu)[29]. Closer examination

16 There are a number of sports that were accompanied by double-flute players in the Athenian festivals. These included the high jump, wrestling, boxing and discus-throwing, a fact which is augmented by the classical authors. Pusanias (VI, 14, 10) states that the flute player Pythokritos, who had been successful in the flute competition at the Pythian games, had been given the task of accompanying the pentathlon events at Olympia.

17 M. Vickers, *Lib. Antiq.* 8 (1971), 74, n.22. Although this amphora is dated to the first quarter of the fifth century other material in the tomb appears to have been produced more than fifty years later, implying a wide range of dates for the tomb. See Chapter 5 (Black-glaze) in connection with entries Nos.20-37.

18 Munich, Antikensammlungen, inv. 1456. *ABV* 44.

19 *ABV* 404. Beazley, *AJA* 47 (1943), 445. *Develop*, 94.

20 The vase is part of a group of Panathenaics by the Kleophrades Painter and his Workshop, published by Lo Porto, in *Atti e Memorie della Societa Magna Grecia* 8 (1967), 75ff., pl. XXXIV, C.

21 BM 359 from Tocra. *CVA* BM, 6, pl. 97, 11 (356). *LIMC* II (1984), 982 no. 277.

22 Haspels, *ABL* 248, 205. Kurtz, *Athenian white lekythoi,* 104, 109, pl. 621. The vase is also discussed by Schauenburg, in *AA* 1974, 149-157, fig.6, but he attributes it to the Bowdoin painter. For another hydria with a similar motive see *Clara Rhodes* IV (1931), 181, fig. 187.

23 *ARV* 197-198 and *AJA* 47 1943, 449, under 212. *ABV* 408/11. His Panathenic are all late. Frel, *Panathenaic Prize Amphoras*, 13f.

24 Luni, *Quaderni*, 202.

25 *CVA*, Castle Ashby, pls. 17, 18 (1,2), 61.

26 Berlin, Staatlich Museum 1832 from Nola. *ABV* 408/4. Boardman, *ABFH,* 169, no. 302.

27 Neugebauer, *Führer durch das Antiquarium*, 83.

28 Schmidt, *Archaistische Kunst*, 73, Cl., pls. 2,1 and 3,1. Smets, *L'Antiquite Classique* 5 (1936), 94.

29 Frel, *JPG* 4 (1977), 7u f., fig. 19.

of both amphorae suggests that the same hand may have painted both vases. However, the A Sides on both vases are in no way similar: the clothing of Athena in a chiton, under an *ependytes* decorated with stars, was an idea also used by the Kleophrades Painter. On another Panathenaic in New York[30], Athena, like on our amphora, has a longer and more slender figure than that drawn by the Kleophrades Painter. Among other artists worth considering for a comparison of style, is the Eucharides Painter, who was active in the early fifth century. A similar looking Athena appears on another vessel in Toronto by the Eucharides Painter. Her garment has the same style; the upper part decorated with crosses within squares[31].

Considering both sides of vase (No.6), we can assume that the artist, whoever he was, must have been active in a period no later than the first quarter of the fifth century B.C.

No major changes seem to have taken place in relation to the shape of Panathenaic amphorae during the fifth century. In the later years of this same century, however, we notice that the walls of these vases no longer taper sharply downwards towards the foot, as was the case with early types. Instead, it now curves until it reaches the torus foot, giving the Panathenaic an egg-like shape. Such features remained canonical, with minor changes, throughout the later years of the fifth and fourth centuries. This is typically the time we start to see the Panathenaics in terms of groups, rather than as being identified with known red-figure artists. Among these is Beazley's 'Kuban Group', whose name-piece came to light in the south Russian Kuban region. Cyrenaica offers three vases from this group (Nos.7-9, pls.116-120)[32].

Although the shield devices are different on each vessel, the style and composition are the same, especially on Nos.6 and 9 (pls.119-120). Elements such as the shape of the aegis, form of the garments, the stars on Athena's skirts, the big stars on her sleeves, and the use of ornaments in white, are characteristics of the group.

On No.7 (pl.118), the smallest vase in the group, the device of the shield is a Nike with a long sash held in both hands[33]. The reverse illustrates a newly introduced event, the quintain (javelin throwing from horse back). The target is a shield fastened to a post. The game may have not been regarded as a very serious athletic performance, for we know that only five amphorae appear to have been awarded for first prizes[34]. On our vase, the front rider has already lodged his javelin in the target, and is still maintaining his arm in the throwing position while the back rider is about to make his throw. There are some peculiarities about the painting of this vase. The riders appear too large compared to the size of the horses, whose hind legs are longer than their front ones. The tail of the front horse is painted behind the target post while the hind legs of the same horse are in front of it. The tail of the back horse is allowed to cross the border of the picture. The vase has other characteristics that may place it earlier than the accepted date for the rest of the group bearing the 'tyrannicide device' (403 B.C., the date of the overthrow of the tyranny in Athens and the restoration of democracy)[35]. Such characteristics can be noticed on groups of Panathenaics from earlier workshops, namely the Robinson Group[36]. Vase No.7, although small, has clearly a shape and profile closely akin to that group. Moreover, we notice that the slim figure of Athena used for this group has been copied onto our amphora with a garment similar in terms of its folds and filling ornaments. One important difference, however, is the absence of white colour on the Robinson Group: it has not been selected for either Athena's skin or ornament and decoration. This is a feature that characterizes our vase. The Robinson Group appears to be among the earliest on which the Ionic alphabet was employed instead of the Attic. The innovation, however, was only official by 403, but its use must have started earlier nevertheless. The group was thus dated by Robinson to between 422-414 B.C. Our vase must have been produced and painted within the ten years prior to 403, the traditional date for the expulsion of the Tyrants from Athens[37].

On vase No.8 (pl.119), from Tocra[38], Athena is represented looking lean with long legs, long feet and a small head. Her garment has no folds but rich, florid ornamentation. The lower edge of the chiton is decorated with a frieze of dancing girls. The device on the goddess' shield is a star with a small 'gorgoneion' in the middle. A similar device is found on a Panathenaic from the same group in Leningrad[39]. The cockerels appear slightly distorted on the column. The reverse features a quadriga, a chariot with four horses, charging at full speed. They rear in the air, all at once, with forelegs thrashing, represented at the point when they are turning round the white post. This is an extremely successful attempt to capture the impression of the speed of the race. Such mood is, of course, paralleled in sculpture and our best example is the marble relief from Phaleron, now in the National Museum of Athens. The relief portrays the hero Echelos abducting Basile. The whole scene is presented in three-quarter view, with the outside horse in profile and the other horses front on. The garments of Basile billow out from the speed of the race[40].

30 The Metropolitan Museum of Art, Acc. No. 07.286.79 (Ruger's Fund, 1907). *CVA* 3 (12), 35. pl. 43.

31 Robinson D.M. and Harcum C.G., *Catalogue of Greek vases,* No.350, pl.LIV. *ABV*, 395, 2 (Eucharides Painter).

32 Schmidt, *Archaistische Kunst,* 89-91. *ABV* 411. *AJA* 47 (1943), 453-454.

33 London BM 1903.2-17.1. *CVA* London 1, pl. 1 (31) 1, a-b. Beazley, *Develop.* 96. Cf. Boardman, *ABFH,* pl.304.1, for side A of BM 605, and not side A of our vase as shown.

34 Gardiner, *Greek Athletics and Sports*, 167.

35 Bury and Meiggs, *A History of Greece,* 318f.

36 *ABV* 410, 2.4. *CVA* Robinson Collection, pl. 31-32 and text. 46.

37 For the dating of the Robinson Group see D.M. Robinson, in Robinson Collection, *CVA*, p.47, and Sparks, in *A. Kunst* 20 (1977), 11, who places our vases broadly between 415 and 405 B.C.

38 London B 606. *CVA* London 1, pl. 1, (31), 2, a-b. Beazley, *AJA* 47 (1943), 453, 3. *ABV* 411, 3. Beazley, *Develop.*, 69. Shefton, in *HGVP,* 315, no. 81.

39 Leningrad inv. 17553. *AA* 1914, 287 figs. 108-109. Beazley, *Develop.*, 96, pl. 46, 1-2.

40 Athens National Museum, 1783. Boardman, *Greek Art*, 129, fig. 131.

The Panathenaic amphora No.9 (pl.120) is a melon-like form, very probably by the same artist[41] as vase No.8. The device on the shield is interesting, for it recreates a very important Athenian monument dedicated to Harmodios and Aristogeiton, known as the Tyrannicides (The Tyrant Slayers). The original bronze statues, preserved in a Roman marble copy, were created by Kritios and Nesiotes for the Athenian Agora in 477 B.C., to replace an earlier monument to the same political heroes, by the archaic sculptor Antenor, which had been carried away by the Persians in 480 B.C.

The recreation of the Tyrannicides by Kritios and Nesiotes, and their use in the later years of the fifth century as a shield emblem, may, in fact, commemorate the restoration of political freedom to the Athenian Polis. The Panathenaic festival is known to have been held at the end of the first month of the Attic year, which began after the summer and so corresponding roughly to July. The summer event of 403/2 B.C. followed closely on from the expulsion of the thirty tyrants, the brutal oligarchy installed under Spartan patronage after the capitulation of Athens in April 403, and after democracy was restored. These amphorae, therefore, are thought to have been offered in the Panathenaea of 403/2 B.C.[42].

Panathenaic vase No.9, showing the Tyrannicides as a shield device, and Panathenaics Nos.10 and 11 (pls.121-123) with similar devices, are more than likely contemporary, very probably made in the same actual year. Different workshops must have been commissioned by the state to make the prize amphorae for the games of a particular year, and one may assume that it was a condition that Athena should have as her shield device the historical group of the Tyrannicides as a memorial celebration. Examining closely the three-shield device on our Panathenaics [Nos.9-11, pls.120-123), the group is represented looking left, with Aristogeiton in front and Harmodios following, partly overlapping. Aristogeiton is shown in three-quarter view (back view). The sword hilt, grasped in the right hand, is seen clearly on vase 10, but not on Nos.9 and 11, where the hand and the hilt are hidden behind the hips. The left hand extends forward, carrying his cloak, with the scabbard upwards. The folds of the cloak are indicated on vase 10, but not on 9 and 11. Behind, Harmodios is generally shown in the position familiar from the famous copy in the National Museum of Naples, with his right leg and shoulder extending forward. His sword is poised in his right hand, behind his head and back, ready to strike Harmodios. On vase 9 the sword is shown over his head. The sword's scabbard hangs from a baldric over the right shoulder. On amphora 11 the scabbard hangs behind his back, but no baldric is indicated. On No.10 there is a line across the torso, indicating the existence of a baldric, but there is no scabbard. On No.11 neither the baldric nor sword are indicated.

On vase 9 the two figures are painted on a low, rectangular base. It is not clear from the painting whether these statues were conceived of as standing chest-to-chest, or angled and converging on the victim. The latter supposition is probably right. This is also the view taken by B.B. Shefton when discussing the iconography of the group[43].

There are two Attic oinochoi with a similar arrangement of figures. Both are dated stylistically to 400 B.C.[44]. The first, the Dexelios grave in Athens, shows the group seen from Harmodios' side, but unlike those on the shield devices he is here represented facing left. The two figures are separated and do not overlap. Harmodios' pose is similar to that on Panathenaic No.9. On the second oinochoi, in the Villa Giulia Museum, the arrangement of the two figures is similar to that on the shield devices. Aristogeiton here is in front and Harmodios follows. The position of his left hand, holding the scabbard, is high and the right arm is in a similar position[45]. The style of the painting on Side B of No.9 is typical of the later years of the high classical style. The painter seems to have had the statue of the Doryphorus by Polycleitos (440 B.C.) in mind[46]. Each of the three figures is represented supporting his weight on one leg, while the other leg is placed sideways and back a little: like the Doryphorus sculpture, the central figure is broad shouldered. In his left hand he holds two spears, while the right hand is free, extended forwards. The same pose is found on an oinochoe in the British Museum showing athletes in the Palestra[47]. The himation of the judge is also drawn in the fashion of the period, with part of the upper body left uncovered. Looking at the figures of deities on the frieze of the Parthenon (442-438 B.C.)[48], and the relief on the Erechtheion[49] (410-409 B.C.) in the Louvre, both give an impression of the treatment of the drapery in that period. Athena on example No. 10 here is still the slim figure with long legs, but the curve of her buttock is more emphasized and the heel of her back foot is only slightly raised.

The reverse (pl.122) represents a quadriga. The bearded charioteer is stooped forward, pressing his horses on at the point where they are just reaching the final stage of the race, represented by the white post. A similar design can be seen on a chous in Boston[50]. Here, too, the charioteer bends at the knee and rises up pulling back the reins. The style of this chous is described as 'Pheidias' and 'Meidian'[51]. The painting on the Panathenaic is said, by Peters, to be by the workshop of Aristephanes[52]. It should be stated, however, that this style horse drawing was fashionable in the last quarter of the fifth

41 London B 605, *CVA* London, 1 pl. 2 (32), 3, 6. *ABV* 411, 4.

42 For a general discussion on the representation of the tyrant slayers see Brunnsaker, *passim*; Shefton, *AJA* 64, 1960, 178; Susserott, 69-72, 205f.; Beazley, *Develop.*, 69; Vermule, *JDI* 85 (1970), 103-0.7.

43 Shefton, *AJA* 64 1960, 197f., pls. 49-52.

44 Boston Museum of Fine Arts 98.936. Hahland, *Vasen um Meidias,* 6f., pl. 69. Brunnsaker, *The Tyrant Slayers*, 105, pl. 24. Vermeule, *Jdl* 85 (1970), 103f., fig.7.

45 Museo Villa Guilia Rome inv. 44.205. Brunnsaker, *The Tyrant Slayers*, pl. 24.

46 D. Arnolds, *Die Polykletnachfolge*, 217f., pl.1,a.

47 BM E 524 8 (photograph in D. Arnold, *ibid*, pl. 4.B).

48 Robertson, *The Parthenon Frieze*. See especially the North Frieze, Slab X. Brommer, *Der Parthenonfris*, pl.68.

49 Susserott, *op.cit.* pl. 1.1.

50 Museum of Fine Arts 98.935. Van Hoorn, *Choes and Anthesteria*, 32.111 no. 372, 6, pl. 24. Hahland, *Vasen um Meidias Vermeule*, 98f., figs 4-6.

51 Vermeule *op.cit.* 102.

52 Peters, *Jdl* 57 (1942), 143.

century, taking its inspiration, no doubt, from the Parthenon frieze[53].

The reverse of No.11 (pl.123), on the other hand, shows a short-distance foot race. This is indicated by the position of the arms and legs. But the arm and leg movement is not particularly natural. The rather old-fashioned manner of presenting the runner is used, with left leg and left arm advanced.

This Panathenaic amphora, too, is attributed to the Aristophanes workshop. On an oinochoe attributed to the workshop in the Louvre, showing a torch-race, the competitors are depicted running flat out to reach the winning post: they are represented in an identical scheme to that on our Panathenaic[54].

Considering Panathenaics Nos.10 and 11 (from the Hildesheim) stylistically, both appear to have been painted in one workshop. Moreover, on both vases "The Tyrannicides" was used as a shield device. Panathenaic No.9 (from London) also employs the same shield device, but this, though contemporary, was certainly painted by a different workshop. One has only to look at the treatment of Athena's garment to see the difference. Her garments on the two Hildesheim Panathenaics are indeed identical in their use of white colour, inner ornamentation, dress length, and the treatment of their hems. Moreover, Athena's head appears too small on the Hildesheim Panathenaics.

Working only from photographs, the author was unable to examine the inscriptions next to the left columns of the two Panathenaics to determine their similarity. It appears that the painter mixed old Attic with the Ionic way of writing. Friedrich Behn reports that the painter used the Θ on No.10 (with an interior vertical interior 'hasta'), and a dot on No.11 instead of the 'hasta'[55]. But more significant is the same spelling mistake made on both vases: The suffix 'θεν' is written 'θην'. These observations corroborate the assumption that the two vases in Hildesheim were not only painted in the same workshop, but by the same hand as well. The painter must be a follower of the Meidias Painter, for there is a cup in Boston by Aristophanis[56] showing a fight between Greeks and Centaurs where some of the details on the Centaurs (i.e. the treatment of the forelegs and manes) are not dissimilar to those on the horses on Side B on No.11. This indicates that our painter was active in the later years of the fifth century, after the Meidias Painter and near the style of Aristophanis.

Panathenaic vase No.12 (pl.124), which is not included in Beazley's list, appears to have been made in the late fifth century, though mistakenly dated by Luni to the fourth century[57]. The folds on Athena's garments are arranged in a similar way to those of the Robinson Group. We do not know whether it had a similar shield device as it has faded (if, indeed, it was ever there). Features such as the fanciful cockerel on the Ionic column, and the tongues still adorning the foot, are characteristic of that period[58]. Moreover, the scheme of the running youth on the reverse is similar to those on the Hildesheim vase, showing a short-distance race. Our vase is probably contemporary, or slightly later, than the Robinson Group and earlier than the Kuban Group.

III. THE FOURTH-CENTURY TYPES

During the fourth century the body wall of the Panathenaic amphora is still squat and bulging, but the echinus mouth now has a concave look with the lip slightly projecting where it joins the lid. The tongue pattern that used to adorn the lower part of the body has now disappeared. Moreover, the torus foot has now acquired a new feature. It is marked by a deep, reserved groove which.

Among the features of the late fifth, and early years of the fourth, centuries is the introduction of the miniature Panathenaic amphora, with the shape imitating that of the conventional Panathenaic vessel, but miniature in size. The suggestion is that they were toys for children[59]. There are a large number of these in existence, all very similar, but they differ in respect of the representation of the athletes on Side B[60]. Amphora No.13 is an example, although rather an unusual one. The neck of No.13, unlike the others, has no floral ornamentation. Moreover, the painting of the figure on Side A extends upwards to occupy the shoulder, replacing the tongue pattern. In general the decoration of the amphora is unpretentious, with the figures in black silhouette. This vase is probably contemporary with the Kuban group or a little later: its shape lends itself to such a proposition. Additionally, this amphora, and another in the Louvre, are the only examples with columns topped with cockerels. We know that the cockerel still appears on the Kuban group and that it is contemporary with the Hildesheim group. On Panathenaic vase No.14 (in Berlin), which was made during the archonship of Philokles (392-391 B.C.), the cockerel was replaced by a symbol[61].

Earlier still than the Berlin Panathenaic is one from Olynthus in Polygyros. This also has a symbol instead of the cockerel, but there is no archon's inscription[62]. My only reservation in dating this miniature Panathenaic vase to the later years of the fifth century is the way in which Athena's shield is presented: it is painted obliquely. This must be the earliest example in which the shield is shown in this way, for we know that on the standard Panathenaic amphora the first appearance of the oblique shield, with the goddess still looking to the

53 Robertson, *op.cit.*

54 Peters, *op.cit.* 155, figs. 7-8.

55 Behn, *AA* 34 (1919), 84.

56 Boston 00.345. *ARV* 1319, 3. *Hesperia* 31, pl. 108, 84-7. *JdI* 57 (1942), 151, fig. 6.

57 Luni, *Quaderni* 8, 260. The vase illustrated by Luni is shown in a more complete state than that in my photograph, taken in the summer of 1981. Luni's photograph is pre-war.

58 Robinson Group. *CVA* 1, p.46, pl.31.

59 Walters, *JHS* 18 (1898), 300.

60 Beazley, *BSA* 41 (1940-45), 10 f.

61 Berlin 3980, see discussion for Entry No.14.

62 Robinson, *Olynthus* V (1933), 88-9, pl.61. Eschbach, Kat. 5.

left, was during the archonship of Charicleides (363-362 B.C.)[63]. The athletes may be compared with those on early fourth-century red-figured cups, especially those painted by the Jena Painter and the Q Painter[64]. It is, therefore, fair to assume that our miniature was made and painted during the later years of the fifth, and early years of the fourth, centuries B.C.

The first quarter of the fourth century witnessed the introduction of the names of the archons in office onto Panathenaic amphorae[65]. However, none of these archons were found to correspond to the years in which the Great Panathenaea was held. It is therefore assumed that the archon's signature had nothing to do with the festival, but only with the collection of oil[66]. We are informed that festival management was in the hands of the "Athlothetai", elected by lot and holding office for four years, from one great Panathenaea to the next[67]. Aristotle tells us "these Athlothetai arrange the Panathenaean procession, the musical contest, the gymnastic contest, the horse race. They provide, together with the council, the robe for Athena and the prize vases; they also give the oil to the contestants. This oil is collected from the sacred olives. The Archon levies it from the owners of the farms on which the olive trees grow, three quarters of a pint from each plant"[68].

The role of the archon in the festival appears to have been limited to the need for their signature only, and therefore they were connected solely with the collection of oil. The archon, as a rule, could not take his seat in the Areopagus until he had handed over this quota of oil[69]. Gardiner argues that the placing of the Archon's signature on the Panathenaic Amphorae might have been merely to register the fact that he had paid his quota of oil[70]. This innovation constituted a major addition to the inscriptions on Panathenaic amphorae. The practice must have been prescribed by a law passed early in the fourth century. This enables us to date the vase to the early years of the first quarter of the fourth century. As far as we know, from the beginning of the fourth century the name of the archon appears on the obverse, generally running along one side of the right column, but it may instead replace the prize inscription near the left column. Of the ten officials who made up the college of Archons, the names of the so-called eponymous archon designated the year in which he held office[71]. As the year started late summer, the modern transcription covers the last half of one year and the first half of the next.

The small fragment of a Panathenaic amphora found in Lindos, but now in Istanbul, is considered among the early pieces of the fourth century as it bears the name of the archon Hippodamas (375-374 B.C.[72]). After this we have the name of the archon Asteios (in office from 373-372 B.C.) on a reasonably complete amphora in Oxford[73].

Our vase No.14 (pl.126/127) is certainly the earliest known Panathenaic vessel to bear an archon's name. Unfortunately, from a name supposedly consisting of eight letters only the 'sigma' is left ....]s. Beazley agreed with Susserott that the drawing on the vase is stylistically earlier than the Panathenaic in Oxford that named Asteos as archon[74]. Thus we have to look for an archon's name consisting of eight letters, ending in 'sigma', and also prior to the year of Asteos (373-372 B.C.). The name of the archon Kalleas (377-376 B.C.), though only seven letters, is a possibility, but the most likely name is that of the archon [Philokle]s (392-391 B.C.).

The reverse (pl.129) of the vase, as with No.7 (pl.118), represents a quintain scene. Each of the two horsemen wears an Attic helmet, short chiton, and long boots. The front rider has missed the target and his javelin is lodged in the ground while the back rider is approaching and preparing himself for the throw. With his right shoulder twisted, he holds his javelin fairly high in his right hand poised in a downward sharp angle aiming at the target and about to hurl it. In his left hand he grasps the reins pulling them towards him in an attempt to control the horse that rears up, with both forefeet and the left hind foot in the air. The motif of horsemen, hurling down javelins while mounted on running horses with forelegs thrashing, is one that appears during the fourth decade of the fifth century, but it is most common in the later years of that century and on into the fourth. The earliest representation is the Bellerophon on the Melian relief in Nantes, and examples in the later period are numerous[75].

For the placing of vase No.14 early in the fourth century, the stele of Dexelios is our best example of a similar representation: the stele is dated around 394 B.C. An inscription states that the tombstone was erected for Dexelios of Thorikos, who fell at Corinth in 394 B.C. at the age of twenty[76]. He is shown

---

63 See Entry No.23 in this catalogue and Kerameikos 147. Frel, *Panathenaic,* cover picture, fig. 1.

64 See Ure, *JHS* 64 (1944), 67-77 and *ARV* 1219, 21.

65 Peters, *Studien zu den Panath.*, 7 ff. Beazley, *AJA* 47 (1943), 461.

66 Mommsen, *Fest der Stadt Athen*, 82.

67 Parke, H.W. *Festivals of the Athenians*, 42.

68 Aristotle, *Ath.Pol.*, 60, 1-2.

69 *Ibid* 60.3.

70 Gardiner, *JHS* 32 (1912), 191-2.

71 For a list of Athenian eponymous Archons from 403 to 323 B.C. see M.N. Tod, *A Selection of Greek Historical Inscriptions*, Vol. II (Oxford 1948), 316.

72 *AJA* 47 (1943), 456-457 and Beazley, *Develop.*, 97.

73 Oxford 572. *ABV* 412. *AJA*, 14 (1910), 422-425. *AJA* 15 (1911), 505-506, figs. 1-2.

74 Susserott 72. Beazley, *Develop.*, 97. *BSA* 41 (1940-5), 11. See also J. Frel, *Quelques noms d'archontes sur les amphores panathanaiques*. *RA* 972, 285 and *Panathenaic Prize Amphoras* (1973), 18f. Also Sparkes, in *Antike Kunst* 20 (1977), 11, pl. 5 (3-4).

75 The Nantes relief is discussed by B.B. Shefton, in *BCH* 82 (1958), 34 ff. He also lists the late 5th century with similar motifs. *Ibid* 42.
i) Two gigantomachies: A Louvre amphora with the dioskouroi by the Sussula Painter (*ARV*, 852/2), and the Athens pelike in the manner of the Pronomos Painter (*ARV*, 850/6).
ii) Calyx-krater formerly in a private collection in Tubingen. *AM* 35 (1910), 332-3.
iii) Volute-krater in Taranto by the Painter of the Birth of Dionysos. Trendall, *Früh italiotische Vasen*, 42, No. 91. *CVA* Taranto, fasc. 2, 23-26.

76 Brueckner, *JdI* 10 (1895), 204f., No. 16. *Idem*, *AM* 14 (1889). 398, p.9. Lullies and Hirmer, *Greek Sculpture,* 87f., pl.192.

on the stele in a moment of victory thrusting a spear into a fallen enemy, in accordance with a convention already established in the later years of the fifth and early fourth centuries. The composition of the stele is copied on our Panathenaic amphora. The horses appear almost flying, rearing and touching the ground with only their right hind legs. The upper half of the rider is shown in a three-quarter view with his right hand holding a javelin poised to throw.

The earliest vase from Cyrenaica to bear an archon's name (that can plausibly be recognized with confidence) comes from other vessels belonging to the Asteios group. The name piece of the group is a Panathenaic, in Oxford, inscribed with the archon's name Asteios 373/372[77]. Vase No.15 (pl.128), in Alexandria[78], was painted by a different hand at a later date than the Oxford Panathenaic. The date is supported by the archon's inscription, inscribed beside the right-hand column with the name of the archon Phrasikleides in the year 371 B.C. The second example, also from the same group, is the well-preserved vase in Detroit[79]. Panathenaic No.16 (pl.129) is unusual in that it does not bear an archon's inscription, meaning that this vase may have been intended as a competition sample, or souvenir of the Panathenaic games, rather than as an actual prizes.

Another innovation was made at about the same time as the introduction of the Archon's name on these vases. This related to the figures shown on top of the painted columns. The cockerel, which formerly perched on the top (a symbol of Athena's fighting spirit), disappears, his place taken by a different symbol each year, thus providing clues to the dating of the amphora. These symbols are mythological or human figures, often reproducing a statue or a statue group. The symbol may or may not be identical on both columns.

The first known symbol on a Panathenaic is that shown on amphora No.14 in Berlin. Unfortunately, only the symbols surmounting the left capital are reasonably preserved and can therefore be described. The figure (pl.126, 2) represents a man wrapped from the waist down only in a himation. He carries in his left hand a large cornucopia. The subject is repeated on the Detroit amphora (No.16) with two figures. Each carries a large cornucopia in his left hand and a thrysus in the right (pl.129)[80].

There is no indication that these figures are mortals or immortals and it has been suggested that they may well rather be magistrates[81]. An alternative explanation is that they represent Athenian heroes, bearing the attributes of divinities, the thrysus of Dionysos and the cornucopia. This calls to mind the statues that once stood on the pedestal of the Monument of the Eponymous Heroes, personifications of the Athenian tribes. The statues were presented as dignified, draped men, loosely and separately arranged on a long pedestal in the Athenian Agora. The monument was successfully reconstructed with the individual statues arranged on an inscribed base. The reconstruction of the statues, though imaginative, provides examples of the stance and pose and some of the signs are useful for comparison with our symbols[82].

The figures on the Detroit Amphora stand in the familiar stance of the Polykleitan Doryphoros and Diadomenos, i.e. with most of the weight carried on the right foot, while the left foot is drawn behind slightly, with only the toes and ball of the foot attached to the base. The figure on the left column stands on the left foot while relaxing the right. An important work in sculpture is worth mentioning in this context. This is the fine relief of Athena and Erechtheus in the Louvre, dated to 410-449 B.C.[83]. Although earlier than our Panathenaic, the style, pose and stance of Erechtheus is not dissimilar to the two dignified men on the amphora.

The symbols on vase No.16 are similar to those on amphora No.14 in pose and style of painting, a fact which may place it early in the Asteis group. (Perhaps even earlier than the name piece of the group (Oxford 572)[84] and earlier than amphora No.15 (in Alexandria), since the Detroit amphora (No.16 does not carry on archon's inscription.

From the second quarter to the end of the century, two families, possibly related, seem to have influenced the Athenian pottery market[85]. Two fragments, one from the Pompeion in the Kerameikos and the dated Istanbul piece from Lindos (Rhodes), are important in this context[86]. The Pompeion fragment has the signature. ΒΑΚΙΟΣ ΕΓΟΙΣΕΝ (Bakchios made me)[87].

This piece is not dated. The Istanbul fragment, on the other hand, was found to be showing the first four letters of the

77 *ABV* 412.1. *CVA* Oxford 3, pls. 28, 47.

78 Schefold, *UKV*, figs. 46-47. *ABV* 412, 2.

79 Detroit Institute 50.193. E. Bell, in Moon, *Greek Vase Painting*, No. 125. *ABV* 412.3.

80 See Eschbach for the earlier dating of this vase (cat.10). He puts it in one group with our No.14 (his cat.12) of Philocles 492-491 B.C.

81 E. Bell in, Moon, *Greek Vase Painting*, 223. Eschbach, cat.10.

82 The monument was erected just after 430 B.C., beside the corner of the Heliaia and partially obstructing the southwestern entrance to the Agora. It stood there during the middle of the fourth century. The bronze statue of the heroes was erected between 430 and 425 and remained in place until the middle of the fourth century. See the study by T. Leslie Shear, in *Hesperia* 39 (1970), 160f., 212f., pl. 42.

83 Susserott, *op.cit.* 27ff., pl. 1.

84 *ABV*, 412, 1.

85 An inscription dated to before 321 B.C. found at Ephesus (and published by Keil, *Ojh* 16 (1913), 232 and 234, and Preuner, *JdI* 35 (1920), 70-1 and also mentioned by Beazley, *AJA* 47 (1943), 456) records the following as from the Senate and People of Ephesus: "Since Kittos and Bakchios, Athenians, provided the black pottery for the city and the hydriae for the goddess (Artemis), at the price established by Law, they shall be citizens of Ephesos for as long as they remain residents there, and their descendents also". For the potter Bakchios, son of Amphistrator (or the like), we have another inscription dated to 330 B.C. on a tombstone found near Athens. Cf. A Wilheim, *Beitrage* 1909, p. 40, No. 26, fig. 18. This was meant to be Bakchios, the father of Bakchios in the Ephesus inscription. Preuner *JdI* 35 (1920), 69-72.

86 Beazley, *AJA* 47 (1943), 456. *ABV* 413/1. Frel, *Kerameikos* X (1976), 238-245.

87 C. Blinkenberg, *Lindos* (Berlin 1931), No. 3149, pl. 149. Beazley *ABV*, 413/2.

name (Bakchios) of the potter and the first letters of the name of the archon of the year, Hippo, which can only mean Hippodamos.

There is also another potter, Kittos, perhaps related to Bakchios, whose signature is found on vase No.17 from Cyrenaica (London B604). Next to the right column is the inscription ΚΙΤΤΟΣ ΕΓΟΙΗΣΕΝ (Kittos made me)[88].

The style of vase drawing may be compared to that of the Panathenaic of the year 367-366 B.C. (Archon Polyzelos), from which several examples have been preserved[89], all from Cyrenaica (Nos.17-21). The name piece (No.17, pl.130), surprisingly, does not bear the familiar archon's name. The columns are surmounted by the figure of Triptolemos (pl.30, 2). He sits in a chariot, drawn by two winged dragons, on his mission to spread the knowledge of agriculture among men. In his hand we can see the ears of corn given to him by Demeter. A good representation of such a scene in sculpture is the votive relief in the Eleusis Museum. Although it is dated after the middle of the fourth century, Triptolemos is represented in a similar way, sitting on a chariot, drawn by a winged dragon in the presence of Persephone, Demeter and other worshippers[90].

Panathenaic vase No.22 is the only exception in the Kittos group where rams surmount the Doric columns instead of the figure of Triptolemos. Kittos' Athena, with much added white, is shown as a well-proportioned figure. The device on her shield on this vase, and indeed on the rest of the Polyzelos Group, is a star. On all of these vases white was used extensively for the garments of the goddess[91].

Side B on No.17 (pl.130) represents the *pankration*, a combination of boxing and wrestling bout. Two athletes fight in the presence of a judge to the left of scene and a third athlete is on the right. Again, the judge is shown in the manner of Polycleitos and the third athlete is waiting his turn to fight the winner. Side B on Nos.18 and 19 depicts the *dolichos,* the long-distance race. Both vases appear to be similar in style of painting. Indeed the pose of the athletes on both vases is similar. They are well proportioned, shown leaning forward while striding, with their heads tilted forward slightly. Only the treatment of the hem of Athena's garment would prevent their attribution to one hand. No.20 (pl.133) shows a wrestling match. The two competitors grasp each other, leaning, with their heads touching. A judge stands to the left, ready with a palm branch to offer to the winner. His stance and pose are very similar to vase No.17. To the right stands a third athlete, also holding a palm branch, an indication that he was the winner of a previous competition. He is walking away, but the intensity of the fight in the centre appears to capture his attention. Vase No.21 (pl.134) depicts a boxing match. The young athletes face one another with their feet wide apart, the left advanced. They both wear an early type of boxing glove (*meilichai*), formed by a leather throng wound several times around the fingers and knuckles and passing diagonally across the palm before being wound around the wrist. The left hand of both athletes are free, extended guard, but the right is clenched and drawn back, ready for the punch[92].

Looking at the reverse sides of the Kittos group, and due to the similarity in the layout of the scenes on No.17 ("Pankration") and No.20 ("Wrestling") Beazley suggests that the two scenes might originate from a rough sketch by a single artist. He rightly admits, however, that the style of painting is different[93]. The athletes on No.20 are presented as short and stocky, with an emphasis on the torso musculature. I would further suggest that the style of No.20 is very close to that of No.21, and therefore that the two amphorae are likely to have been painted in the same workshop.

Before the middle of the fourth century several further changes appear. Athena now wears a cloak draped over her upper arms that ends in flaring swallowtails. A similar characteristic (the edges of worn material) can also be noticed on the hems of her over-garment and chiton. The edges of these garments are emphasized by thick white borders. This latter detail was perhaps meant to stress the old-fashioned, archaistic character of Athena's ornate drapery. Also at this time Athena's shield is shown at an oblique angle.

These features are found on intact Panathenaic vessels of the second half of the fourth century, but the new style must have started at least fifteen years earlier, before the middle of the century. 363-362 B.C., the year of the archonship of Charicleides, is the year when we have evidence of the new mood. From Eleusis we have the fragments of three Panathenaics. One of these carries the inscribed name of the archon Charicleides (363-362 B.C.[94]), and from the Pompeion of the Kerameikos, Frel has reported fragment finds of more than ten Panathenaics of the same year: but the name of the archon Charicleides does not survive intact on any of them[95]. In Eretria there are three, only partly published, complete vases that reveal the full name of the archon Charikleides[96].

From Cyrenaica we have a further fragmentary and badly restored Panathenaic vessel; nevertheless it is a very important example. Indeed, No.22 (pl.135) has all the elements that identify the Panathenaics of the year 363-362 B.C. On the obverse we can recognize part of the oblique shield and Athena's swallowtail shawl. The symbol crowning the column is a flying Nike holding a lighted torch in her left hand and the end of her swallowtail cloak in the right. She is portrayed as though she has just touched the ground, with her whole body resting on the right foot. Her bare left foot shows from

88 London B 604. Preuner *JdI* 35 (1920), 71.

89 The Polyzelos Group. *AJA* 47 (1943), 455-456.

90 Charbonneaux M. and Villard, *Classical Greek Art*, fig. 246.

91 London B 603. *CVA* 1 (32), pl. 2, (2 and 5). *AJA* 47 (1943), 456, no. 4.

92 Gardiner, *Greek Athl.*, Sp. 402f.

93 Beazley, *Develop.*, 97.

94 Schmidt, *Archaistische Kunst,* pl. 7 (1-3). AJA (1943), 457. *ABV* 414/ 1-3.

95 Frel, *Panathenaic*, 23, and in *Kerameikos* X (1986), 238-245.

96 Themelis, in *AAA* 2 (1969), 409-16. Robertson, *A History of Greek Art*, pl. 137, a, c-e. *Praktika* (1976), 80f. *Stele* (1980), 265 ff., Eschback, cat. 27-29, with plates.

her open peplos. This seems to be the fashionable representation of the goddess of victory in the classical period. A close parallel in sculpture is the group of statues that are supposed to have been erected on the acroteria of the west pediment of the temple of Athena Alea, in Tegea (350-340 B.C.)[97]. The inspiration for both examples must have come from early in the fourth century. The Panathenaic amphorae of this year are unique in one respect; the shaft of the columns flanking Athena are ornamented with pairs of acanthus leaves, a feature which does not occur at any other time[98]. Only a small part of such a column survives on our vase. But most important is the presence of the complete archon's name: Χαρικλείδης[99], but while the Eretria and Eleusis inscriptions are written in Stoicuedon, he inscription on the Cyrenaica vase is written in Kionedon.

Nothing much remains on the reverse of the vase apart from a section of a male figure representing, perhaps, an official judge or a trainer, supervising a wrestling or boxing competition. Such officials are usually shown to the left or right of the scene behind the athletes. The figure on our vase appears to be gesticulating towards the figure in the centre with his right hand. In his left hand he probably holds a palm branch.

The drawing of the fight on this side is typical of the Kerch style, which prevailed during the two middle quarters of the fourth century. The details of the drawing are exceptionally neat and beautiful[100].

On the Panathenaic vase No.22 Athena is shown maintaining her traditional stance and orientation, facing left. This was a feature that did not last much later, for on all amphorae of the second half of the fourth century, the goddess is portrayed facing right. The change therefore must have taken place before the middle of the century. Beazley stated that the change in the position of the goddess must have happened between 359-358 and 348-347 B.C.[101]. There is now more evidence available and the change certainly took place during the archonship of Kallimedes (360-359 B.C.). Six Panathenaic vases inscribed with this archon's name have survived: one in the Athenian Agora[102], and five in Eretria[103]. On two of these (one from the Agora and one from the Eretria group), Athena retains her traditional stance on the left, but on the other four from Eretria, this orientation is no longer maintained. She now faces right and this is how she will be shown throughout the rest of the fourth century, until the end of the Hellenistic period. The six Panathenaics were found to have been painted by different hands and it is not known which of the artists introduced this radical change, nor do we know the reason behind it.

From the period between the archonships of Charicleides (363-362 B.C.) and Nichomachus (341-340 B.C.), that is about twenty years; there are very few Panathenaic amphorae. Only the Agora and the Kerameikos of Athens appear to provide examples of them. However, vases from the later period, until the archonship of Archippos (321-320 B.C.), are very well represented. This is the period that witnessed the start of a new series, the so-called Nichomachus series after one vase (No.23) in Alexandria that is inscribed with the name of the archon Nichomachus 341/340 B.C.

Vase No.23 (pl.136) is the earliest of a series of dated prize vases. All of them appear to have come from one workshop, during the second half of the fourth century. Athena here is facing right according to the new scheme. The inside of her shield is now shown, instead of the exterior, and therefore there are no shield devices to consider. The reverse of the vase represents a short-distance foot race, rather than a sprint, to tell from the easy stride of the runners. The three athletes are shown with a natural combination of right arm and left leg movement, a change from the earlier scheme of left arm, left leg movement, as clearly represented on the Detroit Panathenaic vase of thirty years earlier.

A better example of the new mood is represented by the restored Panathenaic No.24 (pl.137) in the Louvre, which bears the name of the archon Theophrastos (340-390 B.C.)[104]. The garment of the goddess on Side A is now longer than before. The aegis is reduced to a mere cross-cord with a small gorgoneion in the middle, and the garment now clings to her breast and torso. A smaller tailed garment (wrap) is worn over her shoulder, which is echoed in the lower edges of the lower garment above the knee and at the ankle. On the left column the figure of Athena stands to the right, clad in a long chiton. On her head she wears an Attic helmet and holds a short white scepter in her outstretched hand. On the right column there is a bearded male figure, wrapped in a himation. His right arm and shoulder are uncovered, while his left arm is hidden in the garment behind his back. In fact, his pose and the way he is clothed, are the same as the figure of the judge on Side B. His right arm is raised while the figure of a small white Nike hovers close to his left shoulder. It has been suggested that this figure is intended to represent Lykoargos, the Attic orator[105], because of his connection with the Panathenaean stadium. However, the painting contains elements that indicate that this figure must be Zeus. As we have Athena on the left column it is logical to assume that the artist thought it appropriate to balance her with the figure of Zeus on the right column. This same arrangement is to be

97 Andrew Stewart, *Skopas in Malibu* (The J. Paul Getty Museum Malibu, California 1982), fold out.

98 See Frel, *Panathenaic* for illustration of the Nike and the columns with acanthus leaves. However, it was Schmidt (*Archaistische Kunst* 12) who first pointed out the first use of acanthus leaves.

99 Themelis, *op.cit.* 409.

100 Compare the style of painting on side B of our vase to that on the Panathenaic from Eretria. Themelis, in *Stele* (1980), pl.110.

101 Beazley, *AJA* 47 (1943), 457.

102 Agora 355, p 31. Beazley, *ibid*, 457 and *BCH* 55 (1931), 465. K. Peters, *JdI* 57 (1942), 146.

103 Themelis, in *AAA* 2 (1969), 409-16. Frel, *Panathenaic Amphoras*, pl.24. Frel, *RA* 1972, p 288. See note 96.

104 (1) Louvre, *CVA* MN, 706 g, pl. 4, 8-14, pl. 6,1. *AJA* 1943, 462-5 and 415/3. A fragment of a second amphora with the same archon's name was apparently recovered from a tomb at Cyrene in 1911 but never published. See K. Peters, in *JdI* 57 (1942), 147. *CVA* Hoppin and Gallatin Collection, text p.6 (ours No.24, *bis*).

105 Torr, *RA* 26 (1895), 160. Richter, *The Portraits of the Greeks* II, 212.

found on a contemporary Panathenaic vase in Harvard, where the figure of Zeus is identified by the sceptre he holds in the right hand[106].

The Zeus on our amphora (No.24) raises his right arm in a manner identical to that of the god on the Harvard vessel. The arm was probably raised to hold a sceptre, as Zeus does on the Harvard amphora. It cannot be that the white paint has faded, since every other white-painted element on Side B is perfectly preserved. The painter, then, must have deliberately neglected or forgotten to indicate the sceptre in white paint.

On Side B (pl.137) there are four tall figures: two nude victors, a judge and perhaps an official. The two victors can be recognized by their palm branches, the symbols of victory[107]. The first athlete on the left is running away, having received the palm branch for his victory, perhaps, in the foot race. The second athlete, perhaps already the victor of another contest, appears to have just received the symbol of victory and is therefore conferring with the judge, who is wreath-crowned and wrapped in a himation. The identification of the fourth figure on the right is not certain, as there is no similar representation on any other Panathenaic vase in a sporting context. Also crowned with a wreath, he is dressed in a chiton under a cloak that fastened over the shoulder. He wears high boots and carries a torch. If he is not an official rushing away, perhaps to announce the victor or call for another competitor, then he must be a competitor perhaps, in the torch race[108].

As for the style of painting, although the athletes' pose, especially the semi-frontal one, seems to be derived from the later work of the Polykleitan school, other features may have had their inspiration from elsewhere. In sculpture, the nearest in pose and proportion seems to be the statue of the Lansdowne Heracles, which is believed to be the work of Scopas (about 360-350 B.C.)[109]. Features such as the oval face with massive jaw, the slight turn of the head, the slim waist, the placing of the body weight on one foot while relaxing the other, can all seen in the semi-frontal athlete on our amphora. On a contemporary painting, a nude Heracles, identical in pose to our athlete, is copied on a Kerch pelike in the Hermitage[110].

The judge's posture and the way he is dressed in the himation recall the contemporary portrait statue of the tragedian, Sophocles. He is preserved in a good Roman copy in the Vatican, made from the original and sculpted in Athens around 340-330 B.C.[111]. The himation on our figure is similar to that of Sophocles and like him the left arm is hidden, placed on his left buttock. The right arm is left uncovered and extends downwards.

Although both No.24 and the Harvard vase were made in one workshop, each was clearly painted by a different artist. On Side A of our piece No.24, unlike the Harvard amphora, Athena's white face does not extend beyond the line of the picture frame. Her shield appears larger and extends beyond the shoulder of the vase downwards to the body. There are more incised lines working the upper part of her garment, as well as the shawl's ends that hang over her arms at a point nearly at the middle of the shield. In addition, the figures of Athena and Zeus on the columns are well proportioned and neatly drawn. On Side B, each of the judges on both vases is clothed differently, and although the athletes are strong and well muscled, those on no.24 have better physiques, with narrower waists, muscled torsos, and broad shoulders.

Beazley has placed the Harvard vase and our vase No.23 (in Alexandria) in one group. Examining the details of these two vases, one sees certain similarities in the style of painting, including the shape of the shield and its position, diagonally over the shoulder of the vase. Also similar is the treatment of the ends of the goddess' shawl, which is tucked behind her short sleeve and to the left of her breast, and the absence of incised lines on her garments over the torso area. I am inclined to attribute our vase No.23, in Alexandria, and the Harvard amphora to one single hand. The neat, excellent drawing on vase No.24 must have been executed by a different artist.

Regarding the shape of the Panathenaic amphora at this period, as represented by example No.24, one may observe the exaggeration in the overall proportion of the vase with its tall but narrow neck, compared with a noticeable increase in the projection of the lip and long, narrow base.

On Panathenaic vases Nos. 26-28 (pls.138-140)[112], Athena's style and pose on Side A remain the same, but a comment may be made in terms of Side B. On Nos.26 (333-332 B.C.) and 27 (332-331 B.C.), the subject is the long-distance foot race (*dolichos*). Here the athletes' arms are represented at the side, close to the body; their chests project forward slightly and the heads are erect. They move with long easy strides on the balls of their feet. The athletes on No.28 (328-327 B.C.) are competing in a short-distance race (the stade race). They pump their arms vigorously, but in the dated fashion of left leg and left arm advanced. They also run on the balls of their

[106] Harvard 1925.30.124. *CVA* Hoppin and Gallatin, 6 pl. 6, 1-2 .*ABV* 414, 2, para. 178, Addendum, 52. For the figure of Zeus and Athena on the column see *AJA* 10 (1906), 386, fig. 1, a-b.

[107] For the palm branch as a symbol of victory and origin see F.B. Tarbell, "The Palm of Victory", *Classical Philosophy* 3 (1908), 204 ff.

[108] N. Gardiner, *Greek Athletic Sports and Festivals* (1910), 292. The hairstyle is similar to that on the famous bronze statue from Anti Kythera, a Wreck of Perseus (?), which is thought to be a late work of the Polykleitan school, about 350 B.C. See J.N. Svoronos, *Das Athener National Museum* fr. w. Barth (1903), 1, 18ff., figs. 2-14, pls. 1-2. Johnson, *Lysippos,* 44f., pl. 5. M. Bieber, *The Sculpture of the Hellenistic Age*, rev. ed., New York, 1961, 12. P. C. Bol, *Die Skulpturen des Schiffsfundes von Antikythera,* 18f. D. Arnold, *Die Polykletnachfolge*, 207f., 241, pl.2,c.

[109] For the statue of Lansdowne Heracles cf. Andrew F. Stewart, *Scopas of Paros,* Noyes Press (1976), 98f., 142, 147 pls. 42, 52. Howards, *The Lansdowne Heracles* (Los Angeles 1978), *passim*.

[110] Schefold (*UKV* 67) dates the pelike to 346-320 B.C. on numismatic evidence from Pantikapaion (Kerch).

[111] See Helbig W, No.1066. Schefold, *Die Bildnisse der Antiken*, 102. Richter, *The Portraits of the Greeks,* 129, no.2, fig. 680.

[112] London B 609, Archonship of Nikokrates, 333-332 B.C. Sevres 723, Archonship of Nikites 332-331 B.C. London B 611, Archonship of Euthykrites 328-327 B.C. Berlin inv. 3981, Archonship of Euthykrites 328-327 B.C. The symbol on No.25 is the figure of Athena wearing a himation and Attic helmet. She holds an *alpustre* of the goddess Athena holding Nike.

feet and their heads usually appear higher than in the long race[113].

Only one year separates Nos.26 and 27. The compositions are similar although there are only three competitors on the first and four on the second. The style of painting is somewhat different. The three figures on No.26 appear to have something in common with vase No.24 in the Louvre. The central athlete here is very similar to the departing victor on that amphora, suggesting that the painting on both vases was probably influenced by the same sculptural sources. The athlete on No.27, on the other hand, appears tall and excessively thin.

The sprinter on amphora 29 (pl.141), although painted in the same year as No.28, is clearly the work of a different artist, and, whereas the athletes on the first vessel appear natural, with normal physical proportions, those on the second vase look clumsy, with exaggerated body proportions.

The lost Panathenaic amphora No.31 (pl.143, 1)[114] was produced and painted during the archonship of Hegesias (324-323 B.C.), and like vase 30, Nike symbols are shown surmounting the columns on Side A. Athena is in her familiar pose, but the modern drawing made by the French explorer Paul Lucas in 1710 is not accurate[115]. Parts of Athena's head and helmet should extend upwards to the neck of the vase, as is always the case with Panathenaic prize amphorae of the fifth and fourth centuries.

The wrestling scene on Side B is supervised by an old man and witnessed by a young athlete, who is probably waiting for his turn.

The importance of this vase lies in the fact that it is the earliest Panathenaic to find its way into print. On his travels to Africa in the early years of the eightieth century (1710), Lucas saw the vase in the possession of Lemaire, the then French Consul at Tripoli, who appeared to have undertaken the task of excavating some sites in the region. Although Lucas states that the vase was from the Tripolitanea area, it is very likely that it was brought from the region of Cyrenaica, as Lucas also states that Lemaire acquired some artifacts from Cyrenaica. It is relevant to remember that Clifford Kocq van Brengel, the Dutch Consul to Tripoli in 1937, shipped to Leiden material with a report stating that these contents were the result of his excavations in the region of Cyrenaica[116].

Three different sporting events are depicted on the reverse sides of vessels Nos.30, 32, and 33:

On No.30 (pl.142), painted during the archonship of Hegesias (324-323 B.C.), two boxers are shown in action in the presence of a judge. The two combatants are painted with thick limbs, gross bodies, but slim waists. They wear heavy gloves, identical to those worn by the boxers on the Panathenaic bearing the name of the archon Pythodelos (336-335 B.C.) and painted twelve years earlier[117]. This heavy glove, replacing an earlier type, consists of bands of ox-hide covering the whole hand and extending up the forearm. They were secured by crossed and re-crossed thongs[118].

Vase 32 (pl.144), painted during the archonship of Kephisodoros (323-322 B.C.), depicts the h*oplitodromi* (runners in armour). Three men wearing Attic helmets and carrying round shields run to the right. The style is the same as that of the long-distance race, with the arms close to the side and with the athletes striding out easily. An earlier, but unsuccessful, representation of this particular race can be seen on the other Panathenaic vase bearing the name of the archon Pythodelos (336-335 B.C.)[119]. The scene on the vase is rather comic and the painting is poor and clumsy. The athletes on our vase have well-proportioned, muscular limbs.

The reverse of No.33 (pl.145), painted during the archonship of Archippos (321-320 B.C.), shows the victor of a discus throwing competition handing his discus to a friend while he prepares to receive the palm branch, the symbol of victory, from the judge. The style of painting has come a long way since Myron's first representation of the famous discus thrower (460-450 B.C.). More relevant, however, is the early Classical bronze statue in New York, which represents a discus thrower preparing for his throw[120]. The athletes here are shown (like the boxer on vase 30) with small heads, thick limbs, bulky and heavy bodies. This shows well the trends in representation of physical types of athletes at this time.

On stylistic grounds, Beazley places the last three Panathenaic vessels in one group within the Nichomachus series. After careful examination of all the scenes it is possible to trace the hand of one painter on two of these vases. Nos.30 and 32 appear very close. Details such as the frieze decorating the neck, the incision in the central strap of the shield, the line of the goddess' left breast, as well as her left shoulder and hem of her long chiton at the bottom of the picture panel, are indeed similar on both vases. All these features indicate that these two vases are likely to have been painted by one hand. Similarities can also be traced on the reverse of the vases. If we compare the judge on vase 30 with any of the running athletes on No.32, he is shown, like them, in three-quarter view, with a small head, nearly triangular eyes, and a muscled torso, the lines of which are carefully incised (but in an exaggerated manner).

The last archon whose name appears on a Panathenaic amphora is Polemon (312-311 B.C.)[121]. A number of vessels inscribed with his name exist but none of these seems to have

[113] Gardiner, *Athletics*, 137. *Idem*, *Grke Ath*., 278f. J. Pouilloux, *Salamin de Chypre* IV (1973), 108 (for sprinting), pl. 23/a, 24/a, 26/a (for long-distance), pl. 25/a-b.

[114] *ABV* 415, 10. Smets, *L'Antiqu. Class*., 5 (1936), 101, 132.

[115] P. Lucas, *Voyage*, 108-109, pl.2.

[116] Kern, in *Oudheidkundige Mededeelingen* 39 (1957), 53.

[117] London B 607. Beazley, *ABV* 415/4. *CVA* f. pl. 3,1. Beazley, *Develop.*, 99 pl. 47,2.

[118] Gardiner, *Grk Ath.*, 407.

[119] London B 608. Beazley, *ABV* 417/1. *CVA* f. pl. 3,2. J. Frel, *Panathenaic*, fig. 28.

[120] Gardiner, *Greek Athl. Sport*, 328-329, fig. 83. Richter, *Greek, Etruscan and Roman Bronzes*, No.78.

[121] *AJA* 1896, p. 332. K. Peters and *Develop*, p. 100.

reached Cyrenaica. The latest inscribed example from there is the vase 33 (pl.145), now in the Louvre, which was painted during the archonship of Archippos (321-320 B.C.)[122].

Soon after the archonship of Polemon, the long established tradition of inscribing amphorae with the names of presiding archons was discontinued. However, Panathenaics vessels continued to be made in the third and second centuries, naming their officials - treasurers (tamias) or stewards of the games (agonothetes)[123]. But drawing gradually degenerated and pot making similarly declined as an art form; the clay was poorly prepared and the firing often unsuccessful. The amphora became a caricature of earlier shapes[124].

IV. COMMENTARY

The earliest known Panathenaic is probably the so-called Burgon amphora in the British Museum[125], awarded about 560 B.C. Contemporary with it, or a little perhaps, is the amphora in Halle[126]. The latter, whose style is close to that of Lydos is usually taken to be the earliest Panathenaic to show athletic scenes. The appearance of these earliest prize vases no doubt signalled the start of the growth of an industry whose output was destined to reach lands much farther away than was originally anticipated.

The volume of production in the sixth century was modest by comparison with later periods and although the majority of the published examples are of unknown provenance, those with known provenance are mostly from the west, namely Etruria. None has so far been found in the Black Sea regions, nor was there a flow of these prize vases in the direction of North Africa despite the abundance of imported Athenian black-figured pottery. It is true that we have that single fragment from Cyrene, but that is an exception. The presence of the piece in Cyrenaica is certainly not the result of a Cyrenean participation in the Great Panathenaea, but rather the result of a casual import, whether as a gift or an heirloom or a more valued personal belonging.

It is not until the fifth century that we witness regular provision of the Panathenaics (Figures 5/6). Right from the start, in the first quarter of the century, the Cyrenaican athletes appear to have been actively involved in the Great Panathenaics as during the century eleven prize amphorae reached the region.

Surveying all production of Panathenaic amphorae of known provenance within a period of about one hundred years (from the last quarter of the fifth century to the last quarter of the fourth B.C.), it is evident that the majority comes from Attica. Athens and Eleusis between them account for more than half the production. Cyrenaica is the only region in North Africa that appears to have acquired Panathenaic amphorae. More than a quarter of the known output comes from this part of the world. The region's share of Panathenaic vases is second only to that of Attica (Figure 8).

By examining Cyrenaica's share of the Panathenaics of certain groups, it is interesting to note that in this period almost all the vases from the Kuban and Hildesheim group are from Cyrenaica. Regarding the Asteos Group, apart from one example in Oxford from Athens, the rest are from Cyrenaica. Moreover, the Kittos Group, whose vases are inscribed with the name of the archon Polyzelos, are again exclusively Cyrenaican. The Panathenaics produced during the year 362-361, the period of the archon Charicleides, were only found in Eretria and Attica. The large fragment from Cyrene is the only example to be found outside Greece. Lastly, from the Nichomachus series of eighteen known examples, no less than ten are from Cyrenaica.

It is important to examine the types of sporting events represented on the Panathenaics. Of at least thirty-three vases that reached Cyrenaica (Figure 7), the following may be indicated: Two of the three vases depicting the quintain are from Cyrenaica; chariot races appear only on fourth- and fifth-century vases. Two precede the Olympic victory of Arkesilaos IV in 460 B.C., as described by Pindar, while the other two belong to the end of the century. Of some significance are the vases depicting foot race competitions. Nearly half of the vases (thirteen) show this race: only three represent long-distance foot races (one armour race and the others short-distance foot races).

This would seem to indicate the importance of sport in the life of the Cyrenaicans, as well as their contribution to the Greek Panathenaea. The fame of their victor in the Pan Hellenic games is best known from Pindar's fourth and fifth Pythian Odes to Arkesilaos IV[127], but other victors are mentioned by Pausanias. Of the eight Olympic victors he records, probably over half relate to the Republican period, which may indicate that the participation of the inhabitants of Cyrenaica in these contests was greater in this period. This is supported by the number of surviving Panathenaic amphorae (25) that reached Cyrenaica in this period [128] (Figure 5).

---

[122] Louvre MN 705. *CVA*, g, pl. 6, 4-7 and 11. *ABV* 416/13.

[123] R. Edwards, *Hesperia* 26 (1957) 230-349; Frel, *Panathenaic Amphora,* 29.

[124] Frel, *op.cit.* 29f.

[125] London BM B 130. *ABV* 89,1.

[126] Halle University inv. 560. *ABV* 120.

[127] An inscription recording the dedication of a statue, considered the work of a Cyrenaean artist, in the temple of Apollo Hyperteleates at Sparta may perhaps be connected with the victory. *SEG* II #, 170. This was the suggestion of Hilier von Gaetringen, in *Phil. Woch.* 43 (1923), 1002. He also believes the stone may have been the base of a statue of Arcesilaus IV (475-450 B.C.), set up by his queen in honour of the victory in 462 B.C. J. Hondius hand points out the difficulties in precise dating, however, especially because the archaic lettering may have remained in use at the Spartan sanctuary of Apollo much later than elsewhere in Greece. J. Hondius, *BSA* 24 (1919-1920, 1920-1921), 137f.

[128] Pausanias 683. Eubotas was a victor in the foot-race in 408 B.C., and in the chariot-race in 403 B.C. (see Diodor, 13.68 and Xen., *HG* 1.2.1); 6.12.2: Idaios won the foot-race in 276 B.C.; 6.13.7: Mnaseas, nicknamed the Libyan, won the hoplite-race (5th century); 6.18.1: the son of Mnaseas, Kratisthenes won the chariot-race (5th century); 10. 2.2: Poros was the victor in the foot-race in 375 (Diodor 16, 23 f); 10.3.1: Polycles was victor in the foot-race in 348; 6.12.7: Theochrestos who was a horse breeder in the local tradition of Libya, was the victor in the four-horse chariot-race, as was his grandfather before him. Theochrestos's father was victorious at the Isthmian games.

Chapter Seven

NON-ATTIC POTTERY

1. Etruscan plate

Cyrene Museum, H. 4 cm, D. 13 cm (Pl.146, 1)

Broken and restored. Part of the rim missing, yellowish-buff clay with a slip of the same colour, dilute, used for details of features, hair and the lines of the head cover.

Footed plate stands on a ring base. The rim is broad and rolls under at the edge. Its inner and outer edges are set off, both above and below, by incised grooves and ornamented with a bold wave pattern (six in number) in black glaze. The plate has a central depression (medallion).

In the centre a head of a woman, presented to the left, in the same clay colour. She wears her hair in a half-sakkos *(sphendone)*, a "net" simulated by a crosshatched pattern. On her forehead is a *diadem* with two "spikes". Her hair is loose in front but arranged in ringlets falling along the side of the face. In her ear is an earring with a single pendant. Around her neck is a beaded choker.

This plate is characteristic of the Caeretan Genucilia Group, a name derived from an example in Providence, bearing the Latin inscription *P. Genucilia* under its foot[1]. Caere and Falerii Veleres *(Civita Castellana)* were the main centres for production. The Cyrene plate is clearly related very closely to the Caeretan branch of which two plates, one in the Louvre and the other in Portland Oregon, are representatives. The first is attributed by Del Chiaro to the Louvre Genucilia Painter, and the second is by an artist related to his workshop[2]. The artist, according to Del Chiaro's study, painted a number of plates with features common to Caeretan Genucilia plates and decorated with female heads, with net sakkos, spiked diadem, reserved leaf-shaped area and jewellery. Characteristic details included the presence of a dot before the eye, and an earring with a single long pendant terminating in three triangularly placed dots. The spikes, always two in number, are short, thick and placed upright.

The production of the Genucilia Group lasted for more than a century, starting from 400 B.C. and ending some time during the first half of the third century B.C. The Caeretan branch, of which our plate is an example, was probably active during the second half of the fourth century[3]. The distribution of this class of pottery was not confined to the sites of Etruria and Latium but found to reach distant areas as far as Carthage.

One notices from the distribution of these plates that they were restricted to the western Mediterranean[4]. It is, therefore, significant to find the example of the Genucilia Group in the eastern Mediterranean at Cyrene.

2. Campanian hydria (Calpis)

Cyrene Museum (Pl.146, 2)

Parts of the lip, and the vertical and horizontal handles are broken. Yellowish-buff clay, covered with lustrous black glaze. On part of the shoulder and neck (nearly one-third of the space on shoulder) there is a long tongue pattern painted on the yellowish background.

White used for the face, tongues and ornaments, traces of it remain. Relief line used for the head cover. The main scene

1 *CVA* USA Providence, pl.29, 2. Beazley: *E.V.P.* (1947) 10, 175-177. M.A. Del Chiaro, *The Genucilia Group*, 64f., no.91, pl.91, a-c.

2 Paris, Louvre, CA 3187. Portland Oregon, Portland Museum, no.26.249, Collection of Classical Art. Del Chiaro, *Genucilia Group,* 257f., pl.19, c,b.

3 For the chronology of the group see Del Chiaro, *Genucilia Group,* 206-313. *Idem, Etruscan Red-figure vase painting,* 138-140. Ashmead and Phillips, *Classical vases,* 64f., no.91, pl.91, a-c.

4 See the distribution of this class of vases in Del Chiaro, "Distribution of the Caeretan Red-figured pottery", *Acheol. Classl.*18 (1966), figs. 1, 2.

is framed with small palmettes pointing downwards and other decorative elements.

On the main side of the vase a female-like head facing left. The surface of the face has been nearly abraded. Details of mouth and edge are not clear. Only faint traces of the white remain, consequently the loss of facial details that were originally painted in black over the white flesh. Over the head a cap *(kekryphalos)* with traces of open work embroidery consisting of two bands bordered by a series of dots and dashes. The *kekryphalos* contains the hair except for a broad strand at the temple and a dense lock that escapes through an opening at the top or back of the head.

Identification of the head

It is likely that the head, rather than being a representation of Aphrodite or Nike, is in fact an abbreviated representation of an Erotes of the Hermaphrodite type, so frequent in this period. Eros' head always appears in the same fashion. On an Apulian volute-krater in London, the head of Eros appears in profile between two wings, and on an Apulian plate, in Stoke-on-Trent, the head of Eros is represented in profile to the left. Behind the head is a mirror, usually held by Eros, and in front can be seen a section of the decorated wings[5].

The shape of the vase, as well as the style of decoration, can be found on the red-figured production of both Caere and south Italy. From Caere there are examples of vases, including hydriae, which have the same decoration and composition, i.e. the tongue pattern on the shoulder and female heads in profile on the body. With a very few exceptions, all of the heads face to the left[6].

Caere was recognized as the centre of this production. Substantial evidence for the attribution to a Caere School was provided by the style of the profile and more emphatically by the type of the head cover worn by the female figures[7], but after more examination of the head cover it became apparent that there were, in fact, production centres. Del Chiaro put forward two hydriae to represent the two centers, one in Marseilles and the other in Rome[8], both having the tongue pattern on the shoulder and a female head facing left on the front. The two centres of production are the Caeretan Centre, represented by the Torocup Group (Marseille hydria) and the Faliscan Centre, represented by the Barbarano Group (Rome hydria).

In the Caeretan workshop[9] the *kekryphalos* is generally decorated with two bands bordered by a series of dots, dashes, dotted circles and triangles. One band runs from the ear to the back of the sakkos and the other curves upwards from above the ear to the top of the head. A regular feature with the uppermost part of the *kekryphalos* is the presence of a diadem painted in white and usually visible on the Torocup Group (not now showing on the Marseille hydria)[10].

The Faliscan *kekryphalos* is divided into three or four parts but in a different manner. The divided sections are arranged in parallel curves and roughly follow the contour or crown of the head.

Both the Caeretan and Faliscan *kekryphaloi* have a small opening at the top which permits a lock of hair to escape freely. The diadem of the Caeretan *kekryphalos* is never found on Faliscan examples.

Female heads on vases were also found on a group of Apulian vases[11], but the *kekryphaloi* here were richly decorated and the heads were ornamented with earrings and necklaces in white. The faces were painted in the colour of the vase. There is a similarity in the arrangement of the *kekryphaloi* with the Faliscan Centre. The only differences are that in Apulian production the inner details are in white and more relief lines are used.

The Faliscan and the Apulian vases are not very dissimilar to the Cyrene example but the closest to it are vases from Campania. This is clear from the similarity in the rather careless drawing, the arrangement and decoration of the *kekryphaloi,* and, above all, the composition[12].

A group of vases, mostly bell-kraters, are contemporary and seem influenced by the Nicholson Group "Cumae B"[13], whose activities are placed in the last quarter of the fourth century. The decoration and design on the vases of this group tend to be monotonous and there is a considerable decline in the use of added colour and less use of white on the faces.

The head on the bell-krater in Warsaw (Warsaw 147274) may be taken as representative. It has a *kekryphalos* tied around the chignon with a white ribbon. There is a mass of hair over the brow, across which runs a white *stephane*. The *kekryphalos* is decorated with lines and/or dots[14]. Such a description applies perfectly to the head on a lebes-gamikos in Bern[15].

The last example is indeed very close to the Cyrene hydria and is, very probably, by the same hand. The Cyrene head had less use of white and no necklace.

Date: last quarter of the fourth century.

[5] London F 285 Walters, *Catalogue of Greek and Etruscan Vases,* 143. Stoke-on-Trent, Hanley Museum and Art Gallery, 241 p.35, in Cambitoglou *JHS* 74 (1954), 114, pl.III, d.

[6] Del Chiaro, *Etruscan Red-figured vase painting at Caere*, F 974, 63ff.

[7] Beazley, *EVP* (1947), p.168f. Del Chiaro, *ibid*, p.73.

[8] Marseilles, Musée Archéologique (Borely) 7538. Rome, Musée di Ville Juilia, no.7879. *AJA* 65 (1961), pl.31, figs. 1 and 2.

[9] Del Chiaro, *Studi Etruschi* XXVIII, 137-164.

[10] Del Chiaro, *AJA* 65 (1961), 56-57.

[11] Cambitoglou, *JHS* 74 (1954), 111-121.

[12] Trendall, *LCS*, pl.210, 67.

[13] The term is after the Nicholson Painter who takes his name from the University of Sydney Museum. Trendall, *LCS,* 522-537.

[14] Trendall, *LCS,* pl.210, 1.

[15] The Historic Museum in Bern, inv. 12388. Lezzi Hafter, *Antike Welt* (1980), 64, no.149, fig.61.

3. Pelike

London, British Museum (E 430), H. 28 cm (Pl.147, 1-2)

The clay is non-Attic.

Torus mouth, a high disc-foot, the handles are segmented in section. On the neck a band of laurel or olive leaves, below the scene a band of meanders in groups, interrupted by chequered squares.

Side A: A satyr and maenad face each other. The bearded satyr on the right stands leaning forward and places his left foot on a low rock. He rests his left elbow on his left knee and bends his arm towards his head on the right. He stares at a maenad who stands in three-quarter view to the right. She also holds an upright thyrsus in her right hand while extending the left downwards with one finger pointed towards the ground. She is dressed in a *peplos* with overfall, overgirt. Her hair is combed and gathered behind in a knot. Behind the satyr's head hangs a sash.

Side B: Two draped youths facing one another and conversing. The one on the left has his right arm and shoulder bare. He extends his hand forwards with an upright staff. His companion, except for his head, is completely wrapped in his garment.

Although the shape of our vase is not uncommon during the third quarter of the fifth century in Attic work, our vase is very probably the production of a south Italian workshop. The neck decoration (laurel leaves) is typical of that of south Italian painters, but most important is the nature of the glaze and the clay itself, which is grey. Concerning the subject matter, we know that the artists of both Lucania and Campania during the second half of the fifth century did paint figures in a pose similar to these on our pelike, in imitation of contemporary Attic production[16].

4. Footed Apulian alabastron

London, British Museum F 31[17] (Pl.148, 1-2)

Tongue pattern on neck, egg-and-dot on shoulder, hooks below the scene, white colour for box, rocks, ornament and wings of Eros. Relief line for Eros' neck, arm, and other details.

Eros, seated on some rocks, holding a chest or box. Here the god's body and features have assumed characteristic fleshy, feminine forms. He wears boots, and his hair is gathered into a *kekryphalos* or *sphendone,* with an opening at the top for locks of hair to appear. Eros is richly bejewelled; strings of beads encircle his neck, chest and arms. He also wears earrings, bracelets and anklets. Eros, in various attitudes, is one of the most common representations on south Italian vases. The god's role is characterized as both a Dionysian and Sepulchral divinity[18]. The box that he carries here is the sacred mortuary paraphernalia he is supposed to deliver to the tomb. Other objects that are usually carried by him are a situla, phiale, alabastron, a mirror, a long-handled, plumed flabellum, a flaming torch, a sash and strings of rosettes. Other symbols held or carried by the god are more specifically Dionysian: the tympanum, bunches of grapes, an ivy leaf, etc.[19].

Although there is no exact parallel to our vase, its style of painting appears to be late Apulian. The pose of the effeminate Eros, sitting on the white-painted rocks, is a common theme in the work of the followers of the snub-nose vase painters and can also be traced later in the work of the Ganymede Painter[20]. These workshops were active in the second half of the fourth century. Considering the use of white colour for the rocks and the open box, the painter of our vase is probably a contemporary of the second workshop.

Trendall attributes the vase to the Menzies Group.

Date: third quarter of the fourth century B.C.

GNATHIAN POTTERY

5. Bottle

London, British Museum 582, *CVA* (1) pl.4, (40), 5, H. 14 cm (pl.149, 1)

Light brown clay painting, white, yellow or red on black background. Round-bellied form, tapering up to a narrow neck, slightly concave; heavy overhanging rim, comprising a small lip-moulding and a flaring flange below foot with slight stem and heavy near-vertical base-moulding bearing a groove. The black glaze appears to have been applied by dipping, ending on the inside of neck and just over the foot. On the body, a swan to the right stands, with wings spread, on a pedestal. On either side the floral pattern spreads over the body of the vase. The swan is painted in white and red on the

---

16 For Lucania, see Trendall, *LCS* I, 3ff. and 11, but see especially *LCS* (Third Supplement), pls. 11 (3-4), 111 (1-2) and *LCS* II. For comparison see *LCS* 11, pl.88, 4.

17 Walters, *Catalogue* 33 (F 31). Trendall and Cambitoglou, *The Red-Figured Vases of Apulia* 843, no.281. For the shape we can compare our alabastron to two footed examples in Oxford (inv. 1945-55). Ashmolean Museum, *Report of the Visitors* 1945, pl. c and Ashmolean Museum, Department of Antiquities Guide XXXIII. Schauenburg, *JDI* 87 (1972), 270 figs. 16-17. Trendall and Cambitoglou, *Attic Red-Figured Vases of Apulia,* 429, no. 74.

18 For this see Wuilleumier, Tarente, Bieber, *Hesperia,* Supp.8 (1949), 31f., pl.4-5. On the Italian Eros as an Orphic divinity see Brendel, *RM* 51 (1936), 88. Also K. Schauenburg, *RM* 64 (1957), 210ff.

19 See these representations on Tarentine rhyta in H. Hoffmann, *Tarentine Rhyta*, nos. 78, 139 (situla); nos. 62, 68, 76, 188 (phiale); no. 188 (mirror); nos. 78, 113, 145, etc. (flabellum); nos. 14, 66, 81, 261 etc. (ball); nos. 189, 282, 324, no. 22, 162, 490, etc. (rosettes); nos. 282, 323 (tympanum); nos. 9, 86, 70, 2, etc. (grapes); nos. 145, 209 (ivy leaves).

20 These workshops are discussed by Trendall and Cambitoglou, *op.cit.* I, 317, 359 pl.98, 1-2 (bell-krater Milan, Soprintendenz), pl.100, 1-2 (bell-krater in Louvre K 129), 5-6 (bell-krater Lecce 660), pl.116, 3-4 (pelike, Taranto 110035). *Op.cit.* II, 819, pl.307, 5 (cup, Frankfurt B 139), pl. 309, 3-4 (kantharoid skyphos, Oxford 1971, 1025), pl. 312,3 (oinochoe, Shape 8, mug, in Canberra, ANU 65.25).

black background. The floral is in white. On the neck there is a row of white stripes above a circle of white dots.

Middle Gnathian (Stockport Group), 330 B.C.

6. Pelike

London, British Museum, old catalogue C 69, *CVA* (1), pl.5 (41), 22, H. 22.5 cm (Pl.149, 2)

Bulbous body merging with narrow neck, flaring out at top, wide splayed flat-topped rim with overhanging quarter-round moulding on outside and small horizontal below. Foot of flattened low, bell-shaped form. Two round sectional handles from top of neck to shoulder. Belly covered with fine vertical ribs.

Side A: On shoulder and lower part of the neck, a female head to the left. The hair is drawn back from the face and fastened in a knot behind. The head is flanked by elaborate floral pattern. Above: a pair of horizontal lines, egg-and-dot band, two plain bands, and a row of dots.

Side B: Leaves and tendrils as part of a wreath. The painting is in white, red and yellow. Round the foot two bands, painted red.

Date: 300 B.C.

7. Oinochoe

Cyrene Museum (Pl.150, 1-2)

Upper part of neck and lip missing, otherwise well preserved. Light orange clay. Black lustrous glaze over the whole body with the exception of foot and lower part of belly, proving the vase was dip painted. Round-bellied form, tapering up to a concave neck, low rounded foot. Handle projects from shoulder ending in a lion's head, facing across the mouth. Body covered with vertical ribs (except for a small plain panel around base of handle). The ribs are marked with white colour, forming a circle around the shoulder. On neck the remains of florals, probably vertical ivy-sprays and grape clusters with vine leaves, as found on late fourth and early third century vases.

Date: 300 B.C.

8. Oinochoe

Sevres 4166, 2 Benghazi, H. 0.08, D. 0.25 cm (Pl.150, 3)

Slender round-bellied form tapering up to a concave neck crowned by a wide echinus mouth. Low foot concave in shape. Body covered with vertical ribbing, bordered below by a groove just above knot at top. Handle projects from shoulder to join the echinus mouth. Black paint applied to exterior, probably by dipping, ending on inside of neck and just above foot.

Late Gnathian: 300 B.C.

Biblio.: Sevres, *CVA* (Pl.48, 25).

Gnathian pottery is named after the first location where significant finds were made, and Egnezia (ancient Gnathia) on the eastern coast of Apulia. It is now known that pottery was produced at centres other than Egnezia (Taranto in Apulia, and a centre to the north in the Canosa, or Ruvo, area).

The production started from about 360 B.C. to about 270, with the middle group starting about 340 and the ribbed group about 325[21]. Principally three colours are regularly used for decoration: white, yellow and red applied over black glaze. Incised lines often accompany the painting, especially as borders (or as a stem) to leaf bands. The common pottery designs can be seen: arrangements of vine branches and ivy, or female heads, set between florals (used mainly for small size vases).

The examples from Cyrenaica appear to belong to the middle Gnathian period. Characteristic of the painting on the vases of this stage is the colourful and elaborate scheme of vine decoration. The earliest figure-style in the early Gnathia is mostly, though not entirely, abandoned and one finds the substitution of female heads and the introduction of masks as the main features of decoration. From not very too late in the second half of the fourth century we have the tomb in Rocavecchia[22], which contained a footed krater, stylistically placed near the Louvre Bottle Painter[23]. Webster categorizes our bottle, No.5, is, in the Stockport Group, which was named after a squat lekythos in Stockport[24]. The use of floral decorations on the group as a flanking ornament is considered to be a continuation of the tradition of the Konnakis Group[25]. Among the group, a bottle in Oxford (1934.13) is very similar to ours with elaborate floral design with pressed sectionalized flowers. Dr. Green has shown that the Oxford bottle links across to the Dunedin Painter Group[26]. I suggest that our bottle is like the Oxford example and very probably related to the Dunedin group. On vases of this group the side florals are simple tight coils.

Ribbing was introduced (about 320 B.C.) to decorate the surfaces of certain Gnathia vases, such as oinochoi and pelikai, which have a large area of black below a neck or shoulder picture. This area is now ribbed. Ribbing may or may not be broken by a belly-band with subsidiary decoration. On wide-mouthed vases, such as kraters, the ribbing restricts the main decoration to a frieze in the handle zone. The painter responded to that with new pictures and new patterns,

[21] For a general classification of the pottery see Mario Bernardini, *Vasi dello Stile di Gnathia* and Forti, *La ceramica di Gnathia*. A short survey of the ware is provided by J.R. Green, *Gnathia pottery in the Akademisches Kunstmuseum,* Bonn 1-13.

[22] *NSC* 1957, 414ff.

[23] Green, *BICS* 15 (1968), 34f.

[24] London, BM F582. *CVA,* pl.4.5. Webster, *BICS* 15 (1968), 22f., no.11. *JHS* 71 (1951), 227, fig.4.

[25] For the Konnakis Group, see *idem*, *BICS* 15 (1968), 8f.

[26] *Idem*, *BICS* 15 (1968), 23 Green, *BICS* 15 (1968), 44, no.4.

including a new tendency to frame the heads, animals and birds with naturalistic vines or ivies. Early examples of ribbed vases come from a tomb at Carovingo, dated to about 330-320 B.C.[27]. The finds from the Chatby Cemetery in Alexandria belong to the last quarter of the fourth century and the very beginning of the third (including a number of ribbed fragments of Gnathian vases[28].

The technique of ribbing probably came from Athens, where the first examples were produced in the latter part of the fifth century, presumably in an imitation of metal vases. Throughout the fourth century the popularity of ribbing increased and the technique was applied to a wider range of shapes[29].

One fine Gnathia work is the pelike in Lecce (Lecce, 5032), with its excellent ribbing. This is attributed to the Painter of the Louvre Bottle[30]. The shape is indeed similar to our pelike, but the quality of the ribbing is lower in standard. Dr. Green has rightly placed our pelike around 300 B.C. One indication of its late production is the hairstyle of the female on the vase's neck. In chronology, Dr. Green has used Mrs. Thompson's definition of the hairstyle, and its variation, in which she dates more closely a series of Attic terracottas securely by context[31]. She classifies the hairstyle into three phases. The style of hair of the female in the first phase (established in the third quarter of the fourth century) is characterized by eight twists of hair running back towards a carefully painted coil of plates on the back of the head. This phase lasted for approximately twenty to twenty-five years. In the second phase a bun replaces the neat coil. The third phase sees the bun replaced by a knot in the relatively early part of the third century, by a knot[32]. On our vase the female head has her hair drawn back from the face and fastened in a knot behind. On this basis one can, rightly, place the pelike to around 300 B.C.

The partly broken oinochoe (No.7) from Cyrenaica appears to be an important vase. The upper part of the neck joining the vertical handles is missing. The handle projecting from the shoulder ends above a lion's head. The glaze throughout is a good lustrous black. The potter's work is of a high standard with carefully rounded ribbing. Above the rib ends white colour has been rubbed in and around them to set them off. Remains of the floral decoration on the neck are still visible.

There are three Gnathia oinochoe with a similar profile an all dated to approximately 300 B.C.[33]. The closest of these to the Cyrenaica oinochoe, however, is the one in Ontario, with a round-bellied form tapering to a concave neck. Most significantly, as with the Cyrenaica vase, the handle of the Ontario vase terminates in a small mould-made lion's head facing across the mouth. The body of oinochoe No.8 is exactly the same as No.7 with a slender, rounder body tapering to a tall, narrow, concave neck. However, the neck here is crowned with a wide echinus mouth, recalling those on the Panathenaics of the fourth century[34]. Double-stranded handles project from the shoulder to join the rim, tied with a Heracles-knot on top, a characteristic usually found on late kantharoi[35] but very rarely on oinochoi. There is no figure or floral decoration on the neck. The group of kanthoroi with Heracles-knots in Toronto are dated to about 300 B.C. In the absence of similar oinochoe with definite clothing contexts we have to accept such a dating for our example here.

Dr. Green has stressed the importance of the group of Gnathian pottery from Alexandria, and other Egyptian sites including Naucratis and Memphis (130 vases, mostly ring-handled kanthoroi with some oinochoe and few pelikai[36]). Those from Alexandria appear to be from one particular workshop that managed to capture a good share of the market, mainly in the first quarter of the third century. The south Italian vases from Cyrenaica, including the Gnathian production, belong to the later years of the fourth century.

Dr. Green has further suggested, together with Frazer, that the popularity of Gnathian vases on Rhodes, and their remarkable absence on Delos, indicates the important, active role played by Rhodian merchants in the trade with Alexandria in the first quarter of the third century. We should now include Cyrenaica as trading link with Alexandria. More finds may prove that trade connections along the North African coast could have existed [37].

Gnathian pottery was produced in Apulia for approximately one hundred years during the fourth and early part of the third century B.C. It travelled far and has been found in a wide area, including Spain, Corsica, the upper Adriatic, mainland Greece, the Aegean islands, Cyprus and the eastern Mediterranean[38].

The quantity of the none-Attic material from Cyrenaica, although not complete in this study, is impressive nevertheless. Doubtless, more finds are waiting to be identified in Museum collections.

---

27 Forti, *Ceramica di Gnathia* 49, n.43, pl.14a. Webster, *BICS* 15 (1968), 3.

28 Breccia, *La Necropoli di Sciatbi,* pls.81-2.

29 See the section on black-glaze here, also Sparks-Talcott, *Ath. Agor*. XII, 21-22 and Kopck, *AM* 79 (1964), 22-84.

30 London. Green, *BICS* 15 (1968), 47, pls.IX, a.

31 *Hesperia* 21 (1952), 38-9. It is assumed that the Apulian hairstyle must be following that of Athens.

32 Green, *ibid*, 48.

33 i) Ontario 923 13.119. Robinson, *A Catalogue of Greek Vases,* no.521, pl.LXXXXIX (521-C.759). Hayes, *Ontario,* 144 f., no.239.
ii) Bonn, Akademisches Kunst, museum inv. 1950, Green, *Gnathian Pottery*, 12, pl.23, 23.
iii) Lecce, Museo Castromediano. Forti, *Ceramica Di Gnathia,* pl. IIc.

34 See the section on Panathenaics in this study.

35 Kanthoroi 923-13.116, 923.13.123, 923.13.114. See Hayes, *Ontario,* 153-156, nos.254-256.

36 For the distribution of the ware in general see Green, *Gnathia Pottery* 1f. For the eastern Mediterranean, *idem* in *Studies in Honour of Arthur Dale Trendall,* 81 ff.

37 Green, *op.cit.* 84. Frazer, *Ptolemaic Alexandria,* 162, fig.171.

38 See Note 36 above for the distribution.

There is only one piece of Etruscan work (Genucilia plate, Entry No.1). The rest are south Italian work, the majority Gnathian. The bottle and pelike in the British Museum, and the early third-century, ring-handled kantharos from Tocra (published by Boardman and Hayes) are identified by Green and Bailey as local production[39]. If so, this is then a clear indication of the familiarity of the Cyrenaicans with the original production of Gnathian pottery and their attempts to imitate the production were certainly successful. The market must have attracted a whole range of different shapes and sizes. Unique among these is the excellent oinochoe (No.8) in Sevres (with echinus lip), which is unquestionably Gnathian[40].

[39] Boardman and Hayes, *Tocra* ii, pl.42, 2379 and p.93, fig.42. Green, *op.cit.* 84.

[40] Sevres *CVA*, Pl.48, 25.

Chapter Eight

GENERAL DISCUSSION

I. INTRODUCTION

Attic pottery in the fifth and fourth centuries B.C. was fairly widely distributed in overseas markets, reaching the eastern and western Mediterranean, the Black Sea and central Europe. Within this range, in general terms, the same types of Attic pots turn up in various sites, habitations and cemeteries, but the forms and relative proportion of Attic pottery seem to differ from site to site. The difference between the pottery found in Cyrenaica and that from the rest of the Greek world is a classic case.

One question with which the study of fifth and fourth century Cyrenaica will be concerned is the importance of pottery as an indicator of commercial activities between cities. Many scholars have advised caution in the use of pottery distribution for formulating historical conclusions, particularly in regard to commerce. Duncan Jones despite the notion that pottery can be important for its own sake considers that "The staples of long distance trade were luxury goods and government supplies rather than low priced goods intended for sale to a mass market"[1]. Both Hopper and Cook believe that the pottery trade was only a minor one and that not every Greek city was a producer. Aegina, for example, has often been cited as manufacturing practically nothing exportable, and certainly no fine ware of its own, yet the island was a leader in Greek maritime enterprise.

In the fifth and fourth centuries B.C., the city-states of mainland Greece, Athens among them, fed their populations chiefly on grain imported from south Russia and north Africa - Cyrenaica, Libya and Egypt - and to a lesser extent on salt fish from Spain, the Black Sea and elsewhere. They needed timber for their houses and fleets of commercial warships (from Macedon, Asia Minor and the Levant), and incense, hides, textiles and other luxuries from all over the Mediterranean. These imported goods had to be paid for, in part perhaps, by the export of silver and natural commodities, such as olive products, and manufactured goods, such as vases. But these vases, Hopper believes, constituted only a small part of such mixed cargoes[2], and some even think that pottery was merely a space-filler, or ballast, for these merchant ships[3].

The well-published Archaic finds from Tocra, Cyrene, and Euhesperides[4] present a very different picture. From their Tocra excavations, Boardman and Hayes reported no less than 2,400 pieces from the later seventh to the late sixth centuries B.C. The imported ware comprised about 85% of the total pottery of the period. The massive deposits from the Sanctuary of Demeter at Cyrene yielded a total of 4,014 sherds, mainly imported. They were recovered during a controlled test from a single cubic metre of the backfill that was dumped behind the wall separating the lower from the middle sanctuary. The sources of vases from these sites may be identified with some accuracy – Corinth, Sparta, Athens, Rhodes, Chios, Crete, and various other island centres, including Melos and Samos. These shipments cannot all have been mere space-fillers.

It is the quantity of these non-Attic wares discovered on the sites of Tocra and Cyrene that is the significant point, as well as their numbers relative to the amount of pottery found. Boardman notes that there is a remarkable repetition of vases with the same shape and decoration, proving that there was a deliberate traffic in certain shapes[5]. There are grounds, however, for claiming that Attic pottery finds do not necessarily indicate direct commercial contact between cities.

1 Duncan-Jones, *The Economy of the Roman Empire*, 1.

2 Hopper, *Trade and Industry in Classical Greece*, 44. R.M. Cook, *Jdi* 74 (1959), 114-123.

3 M.G. Fulford, a review article in *Libyan Studies* 15 (1984), 162. Gill, in *IJNA*. (1987, 16.1). *Idem*, *Oxford Journal of Archaeology* (1987).

4 Boardman I. and F. Hayes, *Excavation at Tocra* (1963-65). The Archaic Deposit I, 19f. White, *AJA* 85 (1981), 26. Vickers and Gill, *Libyan Studies* 17, (1986) 97 f.

5 Boardman, in *Libya in History* (1968), 89-90.

It was a valued commodity all over the Classical world and its trade was not necessarily in the hands of the Athenian themselves, nor always transported on Athenian ships. Commercial graffiti marks scratched on Attic pottery were often written in non-Attic alphabets[6], but for non-Attic Archaic pottery, such as that found at both Tocra and Cyrene, the quantity certainly indicates regular trade with these centres.

A major contribution to our knowledge of Cyrenaican commercial relations with the outside world was made by the study of the pottery finds from the cemetery of Sidi Krebish (the former Bernice). Dr. Riley has quantified the coarse pottery of the Hellenistic and Roman period. Of the 40,000 sherds classified, local and imports, more than 257 were imported, coming mostly from the Aegean areas but also from the western Mediterranean and the Levant. These vases included amphorae, cooking ware, jugs and plain ware (a class comprising bowls, dishes, mortaria, etc. Dr. Riley concludes: "fine pottery was widely traded throughout the Mediterranean in large quantities, as were coarse functional wares such as cooking pots, frying pans, mortaria, etc.". Cyrenaica no doubt had its share of such trade[7].

This imported pottery was not necessarily the only commodity, but one of the important items among a mixed cargo on ships. Shipwrecks are an important source of information on ancient maritime cargoes in general. Unfortunately, wrecks are far too often looted, only partly excavated and partly published, or only consist of dispersed cargos, and do not reveal the precise details needed to determine the contents of these loads.

Pottery was found among the dispersed cargoes of five shipwrecks of which we know a great deal. These are the Porticello wreck off Reggio Calabria (415 to 385 B.C.), the Madonnine wreck off the coast south of Taranto (dated probably to late in the second quarter of the fourth century), the El Sec wreck off Mallorca (the second half of the fourth century), and the Kyrenia wreck close to the coast of Cyprus (north-east of Kyrenia and dated to the late fourth century)[8]. Of these the Porticello and Kyrenia wrecks are the best known. The Porticello ship[9] was found to be carrying a mixed cargo. There was wine from Byzantion, Mende, salt fish from Motya, lead ingots from Laureion, ink and bronze sculpture from an unidentified source, and consignments of coarse and fine Attic ware, including black-glaze. In the Kyrenia wreck, together with 400 amphorae, Attic ware was evident and plentiful[10].

The pottery that reached Cyrenaica (Archaic and Classic) was very probably part of a similar cargo. Two other significant trade commodities may be added here to that of the pottery finds: marble and silver. The precise origin of the marble, used for both architecture and sculpture in classical Libya, is covered by Kane (for Cyrene), and Ward-Perkins, Walda and Walker (for Leptis Magna)[11]. Using the isotopic method, of the 30 samples of Hellenistic and Roman marble from the Demeter sanctuary of Cyrene, half would appear to have been imported from Greece and the islands, with the remainder equally divided between Turkey and Italy. A corresponding study of samples of marble from Leptis Magna showed that a similar pattern of trade took place with Greece and the islands.

The one product that Cyrenaica could not get from any closer source than Greece, and which Greece could supply in practically unlimited quantities, was silver. It was, of course, imported as bullion to be melted down by silversmiths for manufactured articles and/or struck as coins. Egypt was one North African country that imported silver before the arrival of the Greeks. The Cretans of the Minoan Kingdom appear to have exchanged silver for items from Egypt. There are paintings in Theban tombs of Cretan traders bringing metal vases, which seem to contain silver bullion, to the Royal Court[12]. Through the Archaic and Classical periods, Athenian silver purchased Egyptian wheat in Naucratis[13]. Later, during the Ptolemaic period, we have a clear literary reference to the amount of silver enjoyed by the Ptolemaic Kings. In the fifth book of *The Diephosophistai*, Athenaeus of Naucratis gives a detailed account of the grand procession of Ptolemy Philadelphus (197C-203B). The list of silver items carried and displayed in the procession was impressive: silver kraters (199C), a silver table 18 feet long, a three-legged table covered in silver, eight Delphic silver tripods, 26 hydriae, 6 Panathenaic amphorae, and 160 psyker, all silver (199 C, D, E)[14]. Such was the standard of luxury in which the Ptolemaic Dynasty lived. Knowing the close relations between Alexandria and Cyrenaica in the Hellenistic period, one would expect that the Cyrenaicans would have been living in similar standards.

The same Athenaeus, when listing the possessions of the old temple of Hera at Olympia, states that among the gold and silver items in the temple were a golden mixing bowl and a silver saucer dedicated by the Cyrenaicans. He also mentions that at the annual festival of Artemisia the guests of the priest of Apollo at Cyrene were offered phialai of solid silver[15]. Further evidence of Cyrenaican wealth is demonstrated by a story of Diodorus. He records that in 322 B.C. Thibron, the Lacadaemian adventurer, sailed from Cydonia in Crete to North Africa with 6,000 mercenaries in a fleet of thirty ships. After defeating the Cyreneans he gained control of the harbour at Apollonia. He laid siege to the City of Cyrene and

6 Roebuck, *Ionian Trade and Colonization* 79-82. Johnston, *BICS* 25 (1978), 82-83.

7 Riley, in *Excavation at Sidi Khrebish,* 402.

8 C.J. Eiseman, *The Porticello Shipwreck, passim*. For the Kyrenia shipwreck see Blackman, D.J. (ed.), *Marine Archaeology* 349f. Steffy, *AJA* 89 (1985), 83-84, 89-99. For the El Sec shipwreck, see Pallares Salvador, in *Rivista di Studi Liguri* 38 (1972), 287-326.

9 Eiseman, *op.cit.* 263 f.

10 Gill, *IJNA* (1987), 16.1.

11 S. Kane, *Cyrenaica in Antiquity*, 237 ff. Ward-Perkins, *JRS* 41 (1951), 89-104. H. Walda and S. Walker, in *Libyan Studies* 15 (1984), 81-92.

12 Breasted, *Ancient Records* II, 760, 773, and A. Evans, in *The Palace of Minos* II, 739ff. T.G. Milne, "Trade between Greece and Egypt before Alexander the Great", *JEA* 25 (1939), 178. Boardman, in Jones, *Greek and Cypriot Pottery,* 698 (the section on ancient Naucratis).

13 C.H.V. Sutherland, in *AJP* 64 (1943), 140f. C. Roebuck, *Ionian Trade and Colonization,* 128.

14 Athenaeus, *The Deipnosophistai* V (197-203 = FGrH, 627 f 2). See also E.E. Price, *The Grand Procession of Ptolemy Philadelphus,* 15, 75.

15 Athenaeus, *The Deipnosophistai*, 550 a-b.

compelled the Cyreneans to give him 500 talents of silver and half their war chariots to support his campaigns[16]. Their readiness to pay this amount of silver is further proof of their wealth and the availability of silver at their disposal.

The earliest issue of Cyrenaican silver coins, as far as we know, is dated to about 560 B.C.

It is not unreasonable, therefore, to suppose that these imported items and cargoes, including silver, must have been sufficient to balance the export of the silphium, Cyrenaica's most celebrated export, as well as corn. An inscription found in Cyrene, (between 330 and 326 B.C.) lists 41 cities on the Greek mainland and islands to which it distributed 805,000 Aiginetian medimnoi (1,207,500 Attic medimnoi) of grain[17]. Of all the Greek cities, only Athens received more than 100,000 Aiginetian medimnoi, although other sources are not specific on this point. Laws were enacted in Athens in the fourth century to ensure a sufficient supply of grain to feed the population. The laws prohibited residents to ship grain to any port except Piraeus, or lend money on grain shipments to any city but Athens. Such laws indicate that competition for grain existed among the Greek cities, and that Athens, whose grain imports are well documented, was not the only large Greek *polis* to seek supplementary sources of grain[18]. C.E. Coster has rightly suggested that the fertile region of Cyrenaica must have exported grain on a regular basis[19].

II. COINS AND EXPORT TRADE

The advantages of coinage for commercial use made it an important component in both local and international mercantile transactions. The appearance of a city's coinage in a foreign land, sometimes as part of a hoard, may indicate commercial exchange between merchants of the two areas in question.

Although the overstriking of one state's coins by another with some regularity might imply that trade was largely responsible for the influx of coins, there are factors other than trade that might account for it, for example political, military or casual exchange. The remarkable number of 4th century B.C. overstrikes by Cretan cities of coins from Cyrene is worth noting. This was the result (as mentioned above) of Thibron's expedition[20]. Although he was captured and eventually put to death in 322 B.C., the return of his soldiers to Crete, with the captured treasure of 4,000 silver talents, was responsible for the presence in Crete of so many Cyrenean coins (many were restruck by cities such as Gortyn and Phaestos)[21]. The overstrikes may also testify to close trading links between the two regions of Cyrene and Crete.

It was in Arkesilaos' reign that the introduction of coinage into Cyrenaica began [22]. This would suggest that her external trade had begun to develop more intensively, concomitantly with the royal interest in the export of silphium, wool, corn and agricultural intensification. There is a famous cup in Paris (the Laconian Cup[23]) showing, probably, the fourth Battiad, Arkesilaos II (560 B.C.) overseeing the loading of goods for overseas export. The earliest coin issues are in silver of the Euboic Attic standard, dated to about 560 B.C. Some of these were restruck on Athenian tetradrachous (with Athena's head and owl). This is perhaps an indication of Cyrene's early relationship with Athens[24]. Cyrene was, no doubt, able to strengthen her commercial ties with other Greek commercial centres, but the Athenian influence on coins appears to have continued.

Surveying hoard distribution, the Mit Rahineh hoard, probably the earliest known Archaic hoard of silver coin (buried perhaps about 525), was found to contain two of the earliest Cyrenaic coin types, showing silphium details[25].

Both Heichelheim and Applebaum[26] estimate that from the tallies of coin hoards in other countries at the end of the 6th century, Cyrene is eighth after Aegina, Athens, Thasos, Chios, Corinth, Naxos and Paros, and precedes several Greek centres of no small prominence, such as Miletus, Samos and Cyprus. Margaret Thompson has examined and discussed the contents of four east Mediterranean hoards and concludes that Cyrenaica had strong commercial connections with Egypt and that the overstriking of Athenian coins is indicative of the connection[27].

By 525 B.C., Cyrene showed signs of economic prosperity. Human figures appear on her coins, showing Athenian influence[28]. In approximately 500 B.C., the first to inscribed coins were struck, in the period of Battus IV. Contemporarily, the façade of the temple of Apollo was adorned with imported Parian marble, to judge from the Gorgon akroterison found[29]. This in turn was probably connected with similar figures to be seen on the city's coins[30].

During the second half of the fifth century, and after the fall of the monarchy, Cyrenaican trade appeared to have gained a consider impetus. The coins of Cyrene, Barka and

16 Diodorus, 17.19.3ff., 19.3.5, 20.6.21.

17 Hopper, *Trade and Industry in Classical Greece,* 71-92.

18 *SEG* IX, 72. See discussion on the section dealing with the exports of Cyrenaica. M. Tod, *A Selection of Greek Historical Inscriptions,* No. 196.

19 C.H. Coster, in *Studies in Roman Economic and Social History*, 1951, 121.

20 Diodorus, 18.19-21. H. Berve, in *R.E.* XVIII, 632F.

21 Le Ridder, *Monnaies Crétoises,* 134ff., 191ff.

22 *BMC* XXViii.

23 Cabinet des Medailles 189. Stibbe, *Cat.* no.194.

24 *BMC* XXViii.

25 *The Inventory of Greek Coin Hoards* inv. 1636. The two coins are illustrated in E. Babelon, *Traite des monnaies Greques et Romaines* II, I 14341-2.

26 Heichelheim, *WGA* (1938), 297-8. Applebaum, *Jews and Greeks in Ancient Cyrene,* 28-29.

27 Thompson, *Expedition* 21.4 (1979), 44.

28 *BMC* XXXIII.

29 Pernier. *Il tempio e altare di Apollo a Cirene,* 55-56.

30 *BMC*, pl.II, 18.

Euhesperides demonstrate technical and artistic progress[31]. In Cyrenaica, the Attic tetradrachm was abandoned in favour of one based on the already existing 'Asiatic' drachm. These coins were copied, down to the smallest detail, by the rulers of Lycia from 450 to 430 B.C.[32], the reason, according to Applebaum, being the Cyrenaican import of silver bullion from Lycia[33]. The transfer to the Asiatic standard must have opened new markets, especially in the eastern Aegean. Indeed the quantity of local coinage of this period struck from imported silver proves that the country's exports were considerable. It may be noted that Cyrene enjoyed an advantage over Attica and many other Greek cities in that she needed no corn from overseas and disposed of sufficient timber. The appearance of the isolated Cyrenean gold issue, minted before 435 B.C., is considered by Robinson as an emergency one[34], as silver was the only metal used in the 6th and 5th centuries[35]. In the fourth century gold issues were plentiful, the Cyreneans appearing to have secured a regular supply of this precious metal. In the period Cyrene's coins depict palm trees, prancing horses, and horses' heads, which appear to reflect a Carthaginian influence[36]. From about 375 B.C. onwards, Carthaginian bronze coins were circulating in Cyrenaica, frequently restruck by Euhesperides[37]. This is explained as an expression of the commercial contact with the Syrtic region, lying between Cyrene and Carthage.

The wealth of the Greek cities of Cyrenaica in this period finds expression in the building activities carried out in Cyrene. The Agora, the Sanctuary of Apollo, and the temple of Zeus were all either replaced or had new architectural elements added[38].

The gold coins of Cyrene continued until about 290 B.C., while silver and bronze issues became abundant in the latter part of the fourth and early third centuries[39].

III. ATTIC POTTERY FROM CYRENAICA AS AN INDICATOR OF TRADE CONNECTIONS

In the study of Attic pottery it is not possible to follow the lead of Boardman and Schaus[40] in their treatment of the material from Tocra and Cyrene. They examined the pottery on both sites and were able to identify with some accuracy the source, and consequently the origin, of the first settlers of Cyrenaica. These sources are Corinth, Sparta, Athens, Rhodes, Chios, Crete, and various other island centers, including Melos and Samos. The significant factors in their study were the quantities found of these non-Attic fabrics at Tocra and Cyrene, and their numbers relative to the amount of other pottery finds.

It has already been stated that since Attic pottery was valued throughout the Greek world and beyond, its trade was not necessarily always in the hands of the Athenians themselves, or transported by their own ships. The Cyrenaican city-states may well have had their own ships. On the well-known Laconian Arkesilaos cup in Paris (pl. 11,1 and already mentioned above)[41], the painting shows Arkesilaos II supervising the weighing of a consignment (silphium or wool) on board a ship that is probably his royal carrier. Thucydides, writing in the second quarter of the fifth century, remarks that Libyan as well as Egyptian ships regularly put in at Cythera[42]. Later in the first century A.D., Flavius Josephus saw a Cyrenean ship in the Adriatic[43].

The presence of Attic pottery on Cyrenaican sites refers more generally to the exchange of goods between the cities of Cyrenaica and Athens, whatever the mechanisms and whoever the actual carriers of the trade were. A pot may well have passed through many hands before it reached its final owners in Cyrenaica.

We do not know under what circumstances the pottery came to Cyrenaica. Was it part of a commercial enterprise, prompted perhaps by Cyrene merchants? Or were the items personal property, gifts and exchanges between officials, or probably portions of commercial consignments that included other luxury goods such as gold and silver objects as much as metal? The other point is the unanswerable issue of whether vases such as the hydria, loutrophoros, oinochoe and olpe (and indeed other closed shapes) were sealed and contained the main item of exchange. Cups, plates, bowls and the like do not present this problem. Regarding Panathenaic amphorae, we do not know whether they were imported empty as well as full. And when full, we can usually only guess at what they contained. (Olive oil was probably the main commodity.) According to Athenaeus, imported smoked fish was among the food served to the guests of the priest of Apollo on the annual festival of the Artemesia[44]. Such items, and other goods, liquid and dry, were probably shipped in transport amphorae. No study has yet dealt with this type of amphorae in the 5th and 4th centuries. So far, very few indications have been found of their presence in the excavated sites of Cyrenaica in this period, but there is some evidence of their use from the 3rd century. The amphorae from Berenice were said to have contained perishable commodities, such as wine, olive oil and fish sauce[45]. These are the same commodities

31 *Ibid,* X/VI, pl.VII, 20.

32 *Ibid,* X/iii

33 Applebaum, *Jews and Greeks in Ancient Cyrene,* 34.

34 *BMC* X/V.

35 Naville, *Les monnaies d'or de la Cyrenaique*, 15.

36 *BMC* 25-37.

37 *BMC* XCVI.

38 Stucchi, *Cyrene,* 41. *Idem, L'Agora di Cirene,* 54-5.

39 Navill, *Les monnaies d'or,* 66f.

40 Boardman and Hays, *Tocra* I 1966, II (1973), *passim*. Schaus, *Archaic Greek Pottery from the Demeter Sanctuary, Cyrene*, 1969-76, Minor Fabric (Ann Arbor 1977) *passim.*

41 Paris (Cab. Med. 189), Bibliotheque Nationale.

42 Thucydides, IV 53.

43 Josephus, *Vita* I, 3 (15).

44 Athen. 549f.

45 Riley, in Lloyd (ed), *Excavation at Sidi Khrebish* II, 113. Fulford, in *Libyan Studies,* 161.

exported to Egypt during the Archaic and Hellenistic periods[46].

The pottery appears to have been a special consignment directed to Cyrenaica, probably as part of a large cargo of luxury goods. Pelike No.42 is the only known pelike by the Jena Painter and hydria No.46 is the only known example by the Painter of the Athens Wedding. The Pasithea painter is known to have painted three pelikai. The name-piece in New York (08.258.20) is without a provenance, but the other two (Nos.39 and 40) are from Cyrenaica. However, from the beginning of the century the picture seems to have changed. It is now possible to compare our finds with those from the Pnyx of Athens, the Greek mainland, and those sites in the eastern Mediterranean, e.g. the Kition in Cyprus. The first decade of the century is best known by the work of the Meleager Painter. A number of fragments painted by him were found in the Pnyx and Kition in Cyprus[47]. Talcott and Philippaki consider the Retorted Painter and the Black Thrysus Painter (No.62) as among those artists whose early work may be associated with the years 380-70 B.C., and who continued to be active well into the second quarter of the century[48]. The two artists appear to have favoured the bell-krater shape. In the early years of the second quarter of the century there was another bell-krater specialist, the Filottrano Painter[49]. Works of these three artists have been found with other material in the Pnyx, Kition, Al-Mina, and, indeed, Cyrenaica[50].

Of the work of the Ochet Group, we have the lekanis Nos.78 and 79. Fragments belonging to the group were found in the Pnyx and Al-Mina[51]. The wide distribution of the work of this group shows its popularity all over the Greek world[52].

Regarding the oinochoi of the F.B. Group, which are found mainly in Spina, fragments of these vessels have been found in Cyrene (No.59), Cyprus, and Naucratis[53].

The picture drawn by these finds confirms the impression that fourth-century Attic pottery finds from Cyrenaica came, in the main part, directly from Athens. Although there are some differences, it is also true that there is common ground between some of the material here and material from Cyprus and Al-Mina, namely those products dated to the second quarter of the fourth century. The number of pelikai of the G. Group from Cyrenaica is not matched anywhere else in the eastern Mediterranean, and among all the overseas cities the number is exceeded only by those from the Crimea region. The Ochet Group pottery is usually not found anywhere in the eastern Mediterranean outside of Cyrenaica: the single fragment from Al-Mina is the only exception[54].

Imports of other contemporary materials from Athens are readily available. Although, since 470 B.C., Cyrenaica had started manufacturing in quantity terracottas and lamps based mainly on Attic models, its imports of these two items from Athens increased in the late fifth and fourth centuries[55]. Such a view of direct trade with Athens is supported by the large number of Panathenaic prize amphorae that reached Cyrenaica in comparison to those found at other sites. Looking at all known Panathenaic amphorae produced in the late fifth and fourth centuries, we find that nearly 50% have come from Cyrenaica. Attica had the largest share of Panathenaics after Cyrenaica. Out of nearly 60 Panathenaics with known provenance, no less than 32 are from Cyrenaica. The Nichomachus series of the second half of the fourth century is nearly exclusively from Cyrenaica. Outside Cyrenaica, in the eastern Mediterranean only one Panathenaic found its way to the area, and this was from Lindos. Can the reason for this large number of Panathenaic vessels be, as Pindar testifies, the active participation of the Cyrenaicans in the Great Panathenaea[56], or were they shipped to Cyrenaica, filled with oil, as commercial consignments? Or perhaps they were acquired as status symbols? These questions cannot be answered while our information is so incomplete. What is most important, however, is that these amphorae are our best evidence for showing the direct line of communication between Cyrenaica and Athens, perhaps independent from other eastern Mediterranean centres.

Another point weighing in favour of direct commercial connections with Athens is the choice of painted subject matter. Further investigation into this interesting field may lead to the conclusion that particular scenes or subjects were in vogue, thus creating a social demand for these items. This issue has been dealt with by Keith De Vries in his publication of Greek pottery from Gordion when examining the distribution of Attic pottery within the Persian Empire[57]. He observed that some vases were decorated with elaborate Persian scenes. Some of these scenes show battles between the Persians and the Greeks, and the Persians were always represented winning. He also observed that some lekythoi had the same elaborate scenes[58]. Numerous vases with scenes of Arimasps and Griffins appear to have been dispatched to the Black Sea region. Indeed, such subjects as fights between Greek and Persians and scenes of Arimasps and Griffins are among the repertoire of fourth-century painting (found on most of the fourth-century forms)

46 Austin, *Greece and Egypt in the Archaic Age,* 37. Frazer, *Ptolemaic Alexandria,* 161.

47 Talcott and Philippaki, 8 Nos. 100 and 128. Robertson, in *Excavation At Kition,* 70, No.50.

48 Talcott and Philippaki, 9-10.

49 Beazley, *BSA* 41 (1945), 19 No.2. *ARV* 1454.

50 Bell-krater, *ARV* 1430, 28 (Retorted Painter). Bell-krater, *ARV* 1453, 5 (the Filottrano Painter).

51 Talcott and Philippaki, Nos.148-175. *ARV* 1499, 17.

52 See the discussion on the distribution of the Ochet Group (Nos 77-79).

53 Beazley, *Some Attic Vases in the Cyprus Museum*, 44. *ARV* 1492, 3.

54 *ARV* 1499, 17.

55 J. Al-Harami J. and D. White, *The Extramural Sanctuary of Demeter,* 21-22. Higgins, *Catalogue of the Terracottas*, see Nos. 681, 701, 709, 711-713, 715, 718, 718-20, 730, 732 and 733. Bailey, *A Catalogue of Lamps in the British Museum*, see Nos. Q36, Q65, Q91.

56 Pindar, *Pyth.* IV, 4-8, 59-63, V 85-95.

57 De Vries, *AJA* 82 (1977), 546 f.

58 The Xenophantos relief lekythos from Kerch showing Persians hunting, *ARV* 1407, 1.

discovered in many areas, including Cyrenaica. De Vries takes this as deliberate orientalizing for the purposes of direct trade with these regions. Boardman seems to doubt this notion and rightly suggests "we should allow ourselves to be impressed only by a mass export of a particular scene which are relatively poorly represented at home, or by single vases which are clearly bespoke for a particular place or occasion"[59].

The fifth-century fragment No.12, showing part of a head of an attendant of Buisiris, is in fact depicting the confrontation between Heracles and Buisiris King of Egypt. This is a very rare representation of the story to be found in North Africa. The only other example is a fragment depicting the same story from the shoulder of an amphora (Oxford) from Naucratis of the Fikellura type (third quarter of the sixth century)[60]. Our piece, however, does not necessarily have any commercial significance. The group of vases Nos.39, 48, 50 are related to a particular place and occasion. The arrival, in the first half of the fourth century, of these vases portraying the story of Heracles in the Garden of the Hesperides is indeed significant. Euhesperides in Cyrenaica is, of course, the location where Heracles was to fulfill his last labour and secure the Golden Apples from the Garden. The three vases from Cyrenaica were very probably intended for Cyrenaica and brought deliberately with the story in mind. This is certainly a valid factor, taken with other evidence, in support of the notion that Cyrenaica had direct commercial trade with Athens.

IV. CYRENAICA AND THE MARITIME TRADE ROUTES

The North-South Axis and Crete

A quick glance at a map of the eastern Mediterranean region is enough to make one aware of the proximity of Cyrenaica to the Greek world and the distance separating it from Egypt: it is only about 300 km from Crete, compared with nearly 900 km from Naucratis. There can be little doubt therefore that a brisk maritime trade was carried on with the Greek mainland, the Aegean islands, and Asian Minor via Crete. We know that it was a Cretan fisher for purple-dye, Korobois, who guided the first Theran settlers to the small islet of Plataea off the Libyan Coast[61]. Crete therefore appears to be the most natural candidate for a transit station on the line of communication between the Aegean and Cyrenaica.

Many scholars have explored the issue of the relationship between Crete and Libya before this actual Greek settlement on the Cyrenaican coast. Sandro Stucchi has argued that a gem and a sherd from Cyrene is late Minoan, but John Boardman shows that they are respectively an island gem and a fragment of an eastern Greek bowl[62]. However, the island's part in the colonization of Cyrenaica has been marked. A sherd was found in Aziris, the first Greek settlement on the Cyrenaican Coast[63].

A further confirmation of the known connection between Crete and Cyrenaica at this time is the influx of people from the island in the second period of colonization under Battus II (580 B.C.)[64]. This was probably the reason for the serious civil strife in the city, followed in mid-sixth-century Cyrene by the invitation for arbitration by the reformer Demonax of Mantina. His solution to the problem was to divide the inhabitants of Cyrene into three new tribes: the Theraeans, the Islanders and, most importantly for our discussion, the group which originated from Crete and the Peloponnese[65].

Cretan pottery from Tocra and Cyrene, dated to 590-565 B.C., has been analyzed to confirm its Cretan origins and consequently the connection between Crete and Cyrene, and influx of people from the island during the reign of Battus II (580 B.C.)[66].

A sixth-century dedication from Cyrenaica on a limestone altar[67] has been published by P.M. Frazer[68]. The dedication is associated with a series of similar fourth-century dedications from Cyrene. These pieces evidently refer to a single deity (one of the *Curetes*) who frequently appears in Crete, the home of the Curetes. The existence of the cult in Cyrenaica is further evidence of the links between the region and Crete.

Classical Crete is little known archaeologically. The Greek pottery on the island takes second place to that of the Minoan. Most of what is exhibited in the museums and storerooms of the island, especially those at the Heraklion Museum, is without provenance. In the case of those with provenances, the publication rights are is restricted to their excavators. On the very few occasions when the writer was allowed to inspect a vase (but not to photograph) the materials were found to be typical of fourth-century Attic vases, and similar to those from Cyrenaica. There are many red-figured pelikai and black-glazed pottery of the middle two quarters of the fourth century.

John Boardman has argued that since the Bronze Age, Cyrenaica was an approach route to Egypt[69]. Although this view cannot be supported by archaeological evidence, it is evident that at this early time the Homeric passage implies

59 Boardman, *Expedition* 21.4 (1979), 35.

60 Oxford G.121.5. Price, *JHS* 44, 1924, 185 fig.5. *CVA* II D, pl.6 (397), 8. Cook, *BSA* 34, (1933-4), 19 No.7, pl.10 d.

61 Herodotus, IV, 151-153.

62 Stucchi, *Cyrene* 143, 149 fig.153. Boardman, *BSA* 43 (1968), 41-42. *Idem, Tocra* I, 15. Vickers, *JHS* 91 (1971), 116.

63 Boardman, *BSA* 63 (1968), 41-42. *Idem*, *Tocra* I, 14, 76, 79 and *Tocra* II, 36-37. Schaus, *op.cit.* 25f.

64 Chamoux, *Cyrene sous la Monarchie Des Battiades,* 136.

65 Herodotus, IV, 161.

66 Boardman, *Tocra* I, 78-80, II 36-38. Schaus, *op.cit.* 25ff.

67 Recovered from the altar on the site of El-Beida. The centre of an important cult of Asklepios, 16 kilometres west of Cyrene. For the excavation of the site see Sichtermann, *AA* (1959), 325-35.

68 Frazer, "Two dedications from Cyrenaica", *BSA* 57 (1962), 24-27.

69 Boardman, *BSA* 63 (1968), 44.

that the trip from Crete to Egypt, via Cyrenaica, was the safest and easiest to make, taking advantage of the winds that blew constantly from the north[70]. From this passage it may be inferred that Crete was a well-known starting point for Greek ships sailing to Egypt, and that of all the Greeks the Cretans were well acquainted with the technique of navigating the eastern Mediterranean. It was Korobios of Itanos who aided the first Greek settlers to reach Plataea (the offshore island close to the coast of Cyrenaica, see above), where the direct crossing from Crete strikes the African shore. We are also familiar with Herodotus' story of Kolaios, who, when bound for Egypt, touched at Plataea[71]. This appears to have been the easiest and shortest open sea route to North Africa and a logical extension of the Aegean world. Strabo (10.4.5) stated that the voyage between Cyrene and the westernmost landfall on Crete takes two days and nights. If Cyrene were then a transit station between the Aegean and Egypt, by the western route, this would have meant first of all a crossing from Crete to Cyrenaica and then eastward along the coast to Egypt. This would have been feasible as there was a natural tendency among early navigators to keep within sight of land as much as possible. A current of moderate strength runs east along this coast, and on this with the aid of westerly winds the early Greek ships sailed to reach the mouth of the Nile[72].

In 404 A.D. Synesius, later to become the well-known Bishop of Ptolemais, described in a letter his voyage by ship to Alexandria along the coast from Cyrene[73]. This must have been a very early route in the eastern Mediterranean and, once established, would have created a regular line of communication between Crete and Egypt during the Archaic and Classical period[74].

The East-West Axis and Egypt

The relationship between Cyrenaica and Egypt stretches back to the days of the New Kingdom (1552-1069 B.C.) when there is increasing reference to Libya, especially in the years between 1552 and 1305 B.C. The relationship, which was in effect an invasion, appears to have been the culmination of sustained long-term Libyan infiltration and settlement in the western Delta resulting in the rise of two dynasties of Libyan origin (22nd and 23rd Dynasties, 845-715 B.C.)[75].

There is, however, a noticeable absence of any Egyptian material in Cyrenaica relating to this early relationship between the two regions. The excavations by McBurney of successive deposits in the Great Cave of Hawa Fteh near Apollonia (occupied continuously from the Paleolithic period until the arrival of the Greeks) failed to produce any Egyptian material[76].

During the Archaic period, Egypt has been proved to have had contact with the western Mediterranean, including Carthage[77], but we do not know the role of Cyrenaica in these commercial ventures. There is evidence of ties between Cyrene and Naucratis since the early years of Greek settlement in Cyrenaica. Vases of the 'wild goat' and Fikellura style, as well as Clazomenia related pottery, were found in both Cyrene and Naucratis, implying a link of some sort between these two Greek centres[78].

We know from Herodotus that later, during the reign of the third Battiad and King Battus II (570-526 B.C.), Amasis, the Egyptian Pharaoh (570-526 B.C.) contracted a friendship and alliance with the Cyrenaicans. He married the Cyrenaican Ladice, who dedicated a statue at Cyrene that could still be seen in Herodotus' time. Amasis also dedicated a gilded statue of Athena and his own portrait at Cyrene[79]. Of this period there is archaeological evidence indicating signs of commerce between Cyrene and Egypt. Objects of gold, alabaster, and faience, as well as scarabs, were found in the Artemision and the Sanctuary of Demeter at Cyrene[80]. Cyrenaican silver coins are the most notable examples of contact with Egypt and they form a high percentage of the contemporary hoards found in Egypt[81].

Archaeological evidence is lacking for the Hellenistic period although there were close political links between Cyrenaica and Egypt (Alexandria)[82]. The only items known to have reached Cyrenaica are the two Pharaohanic statues found at Ptolemais[83], and a single Ptolemaic oinochoe (in Paris) from Benghazi that shows Berenice II 246-222 B.C. as the Tyche of the city of Berenice-Euhesperides[84]. This means that there was no regular flow of material from Alexandria. The reason was probably, as Frazer has suggested, that Cyrenaica was

70 Homer, *Ody.* 14, 264. Herodotus IV, 152. Carpenter, *Beyond the Pillar of Herakles,* 53.

71 Herodotus, IV, 151.

72 Myres, *Who were the Greeks?*, 220f.

73 See discussion in Casson, *Ships and Seamanship*, 289-290. Synesius Epist.4.

74 Pagano, *Quaderni* 8 (1976), 285-352.

75 Desanges J., in *General History of Africa,* 429-433.

76 McBurney, in F. Gadallah (ed.), *Libya in History* 1-7. *Idem*, *The Stone Age of Northern Africa*, 199.

77 J. Vercoutter, *Les Objects Egyptiens et Egyptisants du Mobilier funeraire Carthaginois,* 241.

78 Schaus, *op.cit.* 255.

79 Herodotus, II, 181-2.

80 Pernier, *Il Tempio e altare di Apollo a Cirene*, 96. *Idem*, *Africa Italiana* IV (1931), 195. D. White, *Expedition* 96, 17, 4 (1975), 15.

81 Numismatic Chronicle (NC) 18999, 287. S.P. Noe, *Bibliography of Greek Coin Hoards* (1937) nos.322, 299, 729, 888. M. Thompson, O. Mørkhom, C.M. Kraay, *An inventory of Greek Coin Hoards,* 222, 227-231. Cat. Nos.1626-1637, 1639, 1641-42, 1644, 1647. There are 18 coins from Cyrene and 20 from Barca in the Asyut Hoard. Price-Waggoner, *Archaic Greek Coinage, The Asyut Hoard,* 111-114.

82 Bagnall, *The Administration of the Ptolemaic Possession outside Egypt* 25-37.

83 Frazer, *Ptolemaic Alexandria,* 152, 264 (163). Rowe, *New light on Egypt-Cyrenean relations*, "Two Ptolemaic statues found in Tolmeita", 62-76. Reference obtained from Frazer, *op.cit.* 152, 264 (163). However Frazer disputes Rowe's interpretation of the hieroglyphics and considers the statues as temple or palace ornaments of the Roman period.

84 Paris, Bibliothéque National F.9083. D.B. Thompson, *Ptolemaic Oinochoai,* 134, No.29, pl.C, XI.

self-supporting in agriculture and may have acquired all it needed via the North-South axis to the Aegean world[85].

In our discussion of the east-west trade link we should consider the possibility of a Cyrenaican harbour acting as a transit station for trade between Italy, Sicily and Alexandria. Three main harbours are identified in Cyrenaica: Apollonia, Ptolemais, and Euhesperides (later Berenice)[86]. In the fifth century, Cyrenean pilots were able to direct some Peloponnesian reinforcements to Sicily when their ship had been blown off course[87]. It is also claimed that in the fourth and third centuries large amounts of silphium were already being shipped to Capua[88], although this has not been verified. During the Roman period Apollonia (the port of Cyrene) was considered an important stop on the southerly route during the shipment of 150,000 tons of grain from Alexandria to Rome: a journey that could take one to two months[89].

The appearance of Italianate and Gnathian ware in both Cyrenaica and Egypt in the latter part of the fourth and third centuries is indeed significant. The example catalogued in this work, and those from Donald White's excavation in the sanctuary of Demeter of Cyrene, are probably the start of a flow of pottery of this type to North Africa[90]. Of some 480 fragments of black-glazed ware imported into Berenice in the third century, about 90 percent are composed of Apulian and Gnathian ware. Like those examined in this study, the majority of these seems to represent the product of a single workshop, called the Alexandria Group by J.P. Green as most of the specimens upon which its identification was based had been found in Alexandria[91].

The number of finds from Berenice (and, indeed, those from Cyrene) indicate commercial activity between Cyrenaica and southern Italy from the late fourth century through to the third and second centuries B.C. Dr. P. Kenrick locates workshop somewhere in the vicinity of Taranto, which was exporting selectively along specific long distance trade-route that served the coastal market of Cyrenaica and Egypt[92]. Before the shipment reached the ports of Cyrenaica (Berenice and Apollonia) it probably stopped at Crete. Gnathian ware of a contemporary date has been found there[93]. Despite scepticism over the importance of the port of Apollonia[94], the city's port, together with those of Ptolemais and Euhesperides-Berenice, must have played a prominent role in this trade route. A group of ten ship-sheds of pre-Roman date, similar in nature to those at Piraeus, were recently found on Apollonia[95]. They are now completely submerged to a depth of 2.80 m). After investigation they were shown to have been formed by quarrying the rock and would have contained 0.80 m of water at their footings. It was estimated that they would have had a dry length of 28 m making them capable of hosting all types of shipping, cargo as well as warships.

85 Frazer, *op.cit.* 152.

86 Jones and Little, in *JRS* 61 (1971), 64-79. Kraeling, *Ptolemais,* 48-51. Lloyd, *The Historical Development of Benghazi,* 54-5, 81-85. Casson, *Ships and Seamanship,* 364.

87 Thucyd, 7.50.

88 Plautus, *Rudens,* 631. Friedrich Marx, *Plautus Rudens* 142-3, quoted by Waisglass, *An Historical Study of Cyrene,* 24, and Coster in *Studies in Roman Economic and Social History*, 104-144. It should be noted however that *Rudens*, which was acted in the year 192, was originally a play by Diphilus (360-350 B.C.). Here it is completely remodelled in a Roman setting. So Capua in the original fourth century text was probably Piraeus.

89 See P. Mich., 490 (2nd A.D.), a sailor on his way from Alexandria to Rome. He wrote to his family in Egypt via a traveller he met in Cyrene: "finding someone going your way from Cyrene, I felt I had to let you know I was safe and sound". The reference is taken from Casson, *Ships and Seamanship,* 297, no.4.

90 Reported by F. Kenrick, in C. Barker (ed.), *Cyrenaica in Antiquity*, 251.

91 Green, *Gnathian Pottery,* 12f. *Idem*, "More Gnathian pottery in Bonn", *AA* (1977), 556 f.

92 Kenrick, in Barker (ed.), *Cyrenaica in Antiquity,* 251-2.

93 Green, *Gnathian Pottery,* 28.

94 Chomoux, *op.cit.* 24.

95 Morrison and Williams, *Greek Oared Ships,* 183f., pl.30. Flemming in Du Plat Taylor (ed.), *Marine Archaeology*, 170-8, figs.69-70, pl.30 a and b. *Idem*, "Apollonia Revisited", *Geographical Magazine* 33 (1960-6), 522f.

Chapter Nine

HISTORICAL CONCLUSION

The results reached on all the points of detail have been explicit in the course of this study and there is no need to repeat them here. But it remains to consider what more general Historical Conclusion can be drawn from the study of imported Athenian Pottery to Cyrenaica in the fifth and fourth centuries B.C.

The Cyrenaican cities, namely Cyrene and Euhesperides, were culturally cosmopolitan with connections running across to the rest of the Greek world. They were also multi-racial. Demonax, the sixth-century reformer allowed one tribe for the native "Perioikoi", one for the old Greek settlers and one for the new arrivals to Cyrene[1]. In the Archaic period such a cosmopolitan nature expressed itself clearly in the type of pottery imported, namely the material from Tocra and Cyrene[2]. Then, during the fifth century, the arts appear to have owed a clear debt to Athens. This is indicated by the bronze head of the last King Arkesilaos IV (mid-fifth century) in the style of Pheidias[3].

The commercial activities between Cyrenaica and Athens in this period are difficult to assess since the volume of Attic pottery in Cyrenaica is comparatively small and cannot be taken on its own as sufficient evidence to demonstrate a regular trade link.

One important aspect of the study of pottery in general from Cyrenaica is to assess the contribution of the locally made pottery to the industry of the region and its place within the pottery market as a whole. This task has not yet been undertaken for the fifth- and fourth-century local ware. During the Archaic period the imported ware seems to have impinged more forcefully on the local market[4]. Boardman has remarked that at Tocra the locally produced pottery was restricted to terracottas and votives, where fabric was taken to be visually recognizable[5]. Further investigations have to be carried out in the hope of producing results along the line of the Hellenistic and Roman periods (Berenice). The study of the local ware in these periods showed that there were a variety of shapes and sizes, and some of these were exported. Riley has observed that local amphora production was extensive (over 20 percent of the total amphorae in the Hellenistic and the Augustan periods), which may suggest a measure of self-sufficiency in this shape[6]. By undertaking a similar study we would be in a better position to assess the contribution of imported ware within the economy of the region.

Although small in number, the fifth century Attic pottery finds suggest a peaceful relationship with Athens during, and after, the Peloponnesian war. The aid given to Sparta in 413 B.C. was not then sufficient to involve the Cyreneans in the war on the side of Sparta[7].

In the fifth century there were only two Kings of Cyrene before the monarchy fell, some time between 460-450 B.C., Battus IV and Arkesilaos IV[8]. It was this last king who was mentioned by Pindar as the winner of the chariot race at Olympia, in the Fifth Pythian[9]. This period, however, did not seem to have

1 Herodotus, IV, 161. Applebaum, *Jews and Greeks in Ancient Cyrene*, 18.

2 Boardman and Hayes, *Tocra* I and *Tocra* II, *passim*. Schaus, *Archaic Greek Pottery, passim*.

3 Chamoux, *Cyrene Sous La Monarchie Des Battiades*, 368 f. pl.XX, 3-4. See also G. Richter, *The Portraits of the Greeks*, 104f figs 435-455. B.S. Ridgway, *Fifth Century Styles in Greek Sculpture*, 179f., figs.116-118.

4 Boardman and Hayes, *Tocra* I, 142-148, pl.91-94, *Tocra* II, 65-72, pls. 33-37.

5 *Idem*, in Jones R.E. (ed.), *Greek and Cypriot Pottery*, 707.

6 Riley, in Lloyd (ed.), *Excavation at Sidi Khrebish*, 93-96, 113.

7 Thucydides 8, 19 and 50. See the details in Waisglass, *An Historical Study of Cyrene*, 44 f.

8 For the fall of the monarchy see Michell, in *JHS*, 86 (1966), 99 f.

9 Pindar, *Pyth*. IV, 4-8, 59-63, V 85-95.

been a stable one for Cyrenaica. By the middle of the century Arkesilaos was on the run, fleeing from Cyrene to Euhesperides where he was assassinated. A democracy then replaced the monarchy, lasting for two hundred years. That democracy was probably an oligarchy of a fairly narrow type.

Very few records of this period are available. We know that the cities of ancient Cyrenaica, Cyrene in particular, enjoyed a measure of prosperity great enough to arouse the envy of other Greek states. This was the result of favourable economic circumstances. Aelian reports that the gem-cutters were held in high esteem at Cyrene. Citing a remark made by the comic poet, Eupolis, in his play 'Ο Μαρικάς, which was produced in Athens in 421 B.C. He states that the poorest of the Cyreneans had stones in their rings worth ten minae. This indicates the prosperity of the inhabitants[10]. We also know that a wealthy Cyrenean individual called Epicedes helped Athenian survivors of the Sicilian disaster of 413 B.C.[11]. Instability and disorder arose again as a result of civil strife and this continued for some time after the execution of Socrates. Plato left Athens and visited Cyrene (around 396 B.C.) to attend the lecture of the famous mathematician Theodorus[12]. While there he was invited by the Cyreneans to draw up a constitution and set the government in order, but he refused. There is no space here to go into the controversy over this issue[13], which probably reflected the region's instability. The Oligarchs were then forced to compromise with their opponents by setting up a mixed constitution and share power more widely. A real Kleisthenic democracy on the Athenian model was then established, perhaps about 375 B.C.[14].

There was a peaceful interlude for the next fifty years, just before the campaign of the adventurer Thibron and the subsequent sieges of Apollonia and Cyrene in 322[15]. The Stele of the founders, which commemorates the decision of the Cyrenean demos to grant citizenship to the residents or visiting Therans, is evidence of a fully democratic constitution during this period[16], in which Cyrenaica seems to have enjoyed a prosperity and stability that was expressed in every way. Frazer emphasized that Cyrene and her people made a major contribution to the intellectual life of Greece in the fourth century, above all in mathematics and philosophy[17]. During this period in Cyrene the coinage improved in quality and the minting of gold issues increased. The treasury of Cyrene at Delphi was probably designed by Theodorus, the teacher of the elements of geometry and stereometry to Theaetetus and Plato[18]. During this period the Cyreneans sent a gift of 300 horses and five four-horse chariots to Alexander the Great[19]. Cyrene also donated (or sold on) her corn (806,000 medimni) to the Greek world at a time of shortage. Cyrene's generosity on this occasion was still being cited in Emperor Hadrian's time (second century A.D.[20]). But most important was the fact that the Cyrenaicans were now actively participating in the Panathenaic Games[21]. This probably explains the presence of the large number of Panathenaic vessels found in Cyrenaica.

Egypt does not seem to have made much impact on Cyrenaica, except for a few ritualistic details: the women of Cyrene abstained from veal in deference to Isis worship[22].

It was this period that witnessed the import of the bulk of the Athenian red-figured and Attic black-glazed pottery, as well as the Panathenaic prize vessels.

10 Aelian, *VH,* 12.30.

11 *IG* i. Dem., XX, 41-45 a. Waisglass, *AnHistorical Study of Cyrene,* 47.

12 For the date of Plato's visit to Cyrene see Kurt von Fritz, in *RE* s.v. Theodorus, 1811.

13 Plato, *Lives*, II, 474. Plato, *Ad. Prync.* Inerud.1. Cf. Aelian, *VH.* XII, 30. The reason for Plato's refusal is discussed in Waisglass, *op.cit.* 52 f.

14 Arist. *Pol.,* 1319 b. Applebaum, *Jews and Greeks in Cyrene,* 35.

15 Diodorus, 17.19 3ff.

16 *S.E.G.* 9.3. G. Oliverio, *Riv.Fil.* 56 (1928), 222-232. Discussed in detail by Waisglass, *op.cit.* 56-69.

17 Frazer, *Eratosthenes of Cyrene,* 4f.

18 Herodotus, IV, 186.

19 Diod. Sic, XVII, 49.

20 Diod. Sic, XVIII, 19, 21. Tod, *A Selection of Greek Historical Inscriptions,* 196. Reynolds, in *JRS* 68 (1978), 113, 1.19 and p.117.

21 Abblebaum, *op.cit.* 35.

22 Herodotus, IV, 186.

CATALOGUE

THE BLACK-GLAZED POTTERY

SKYPHOS (1-13, pl.63-66)

Corinthian Type

1) Leiden KVB 109 (miniature type) (pl.63,1)
H. 5.5 cm; D. rim 6.2 cm; D. foot 3.5 cm.

Horseshoe handles, ring foot. Zone above foot reserved, also top and edge of the foot and the underside, with two glazed circles and dot.
Date: Middle of the fifth century B.C.
Cf.: *Ath. Agora* XII, no.1379, pl.45.

Bibl.: Leiden KVB 109. Janssen, *Catalogue* II 1400, 143. Holwerda *Catalogue* XXV 84, 153. Holwerda, no.51, p.12 and pl.1. *CVA* Leiden 3, 64, pl.159,9.

2) Leiden KVB 28 (pl.63,2)
H. 10.4-10.5 cm; D. rim 11.3-11.5 cm: D. foot 6 cm.

Flaring ring foot; horseshoe handles, rim curves inwards. Vase is glazed inside and out. Underside reserved with this circle on as well as on the resting surface.
Date: Third quarter of the fifth century B.C.
Cf.: *Ath. Agora* XII, nos.320-322, Fig.4, pl.15.

Bibl.: Leiden KVB 28. Janssen, *Catalogue* II 1395, 143. Holwerda, *Catalogue* XXV, 81, 135. Holwerda, *Gebruiksaardewerk*, no.6, Fig.1. *CVA* Leiden 3, pl.157,8.

Type A: (3-11) (pl.64,1)

3) Leiden KVB 111
H. 8.6 cm; D. rim; 10.8 cm; D. foot 7.3 cm.

Surface damaged spot as a result of misfiring. Torus ring foot, horseshoe handles. Glazed inside and out. Resting surface and underside reserved with glazed circle and a dot.
Date: Second quarter of the fifth century B.C.
Cf.: *Ath. Agora* X11, pl.16, nos.342-344.

Bibl.: Leiden *CVA* 3, pl.158, 1.

4) Leiden KVB 114
H. 7.5 cm; D. 9.4 cm.

Only one handle remains. Triangular handles. Torus ring foot, glazed all over, including the inside. Underside and resting surface reserved.
Date: Last quarter of the fifth century B.C.
Cf.: *Ath. Agora* XII, pl.16, no.346.

Bibl.: Janssen, *Catalogue* II 1399, p.143. Holwerda, *Gebruiksaardwerk*, no.61, p.13 and p.10, Fig.1. Leiden *CVA* 3, pl.158, 5.

5) Leiden KVB 113 (pl.64,2)
H. 7.7 cm; D. 9.4 cm.

Surface pitted. Triangular handles, torus ring foot. Glazed all over apart from the resting surface and the underside where there is a glazed circle and dot.
Date: Late fifth century B.C. (later than KVB 114).

Bibl.: Janssen, *Cat.* 11, 1398, pl.143. Holwerda, *Gebruiksaardewerk*, no.52, p.12 and pl.1. Leiden *CVA* 3, pl.158, 6.

6) Sèvres 7090, 3
H. 8.5 cm; D. 10 cm.

Torus ring foot, horseshoe handles. Good lustre glaze inside and out. Resting surface and underside reserved.
Date: Last quarter of the fifth century B.C.

Bibl.: *CVA* Sèvres: 1(113), pl.25,15.

7) Louvre (no details available CA 973) (pl.65,1)

Glaze peeled in parts. Torus ring foot, triangular handles. Black glaze all over except resting surface and the underside, which are reserved with a circle and dot.
Date: Last quarter of the fifth century B.C.
Cf.: *Kerameikos* IX: Ker. 8303 p.147, no.265, pl.368; 79,1. *Ath. Agora* XII, P-5145, p.259, no.342, pl.16, Fig.4.

8) Tolmeita 9.2.75(A)

Torus ring foot, horseshoe handles. Glazed all over except for the underside which is reserved. It also bears two glazed circles and a dot.
Date: Last quarter of the fifth century.
Cf.: *Ath. Agora* XII, pl.16, nos.342-344.

9) Manchester M 1272 (pl.65,2)
H. 8 cm; D. 9.2 cm.

Rim chipped, pitted in places. Torus ring foot, triangular handles. Resting surface and underside reserved with glazed circles.

Date: Late fifth to early fourth century B.C.

Bibl.: Rowe, *Cyrenaica Exp.* N.81-AB, pl.35,c.

10) Manchester M 407
H. 8 cm; D. 9.5 cm.

Intact, pitted in places. Torus ring foot, triangular handles. Resting surface and underside reserved with glazed concentric circles.
Date: Late fifth to early fourth century B.C.

Bibl.: Rowe, *Cyrenaica Exp.* N.83-Y, pl.12,b.

11) Apollonia

Torus ring foot, triangular handles. Lustrous glaze.
Date: Late fifth to early fourth century B.C.
Cf.: *Ath. Agora* XII no.345, pl.16.

Bibl.: Ghislanzoni, *Notize: Archelogiche 99*, Fig.49 (below).

Type B: "Glaux" (12-13)

12) Manchester M 1175 (pl.66,1)
H. 5cm: D. 8.5 cm.

Intact. Torus ring foot, round on the outside, convex on the inside with narrow resting surface. Vertical and horizontal handles. Vertical handle reaches the rim. Glazed all over except the resting surface and the underside, which are reserved with glazed concentric circles on the underside.
Date: Third quarter of the fifth century B.C.
Cf.: *CVA* Rennes 1 (30), pl.27,3. *CVA* Tours and Bourges, pl.13,8.

Bibl.: Rowe, *Cyrenaica Exp.* N.81-RR, pl.34,b.

13) Ptolemais 9.2.75(B) (pl.66,2)
H. 9.4 cm; D. 11 cm.

The lustrous black glaze has peeled in places, otherwise in very good condition. The vase has one horizontal and one vertical handle joining directly at the rim. The horizontal handle is a horseshoe shape. Torus ring foot. Glazed all over and inside, apart from the resting surface and the underside.
Date: Second quarter of the fifth century B.C.
Cf.: *Ath. Agora* nos. 360-363, Fig.4, pl.17. *Corinth* XIII, pl.53, deposit 11. *CVA* Oxford 2, pl.66,2. *CVA* Poland 1, pl.46, 11 & 12. *CVA* Norway 1, pl.52, 4. *AM* 81 (1966), pl.25, 6, grave 59.

FEEDER (14, pl.1,1; 67,1-2)

14) Manchester III.L.162 (M 1260) (Cyrene)
H. 5.5 cm; D. 5.6 cm.

Intact and well preserved. Truncated globular form body with small central hole and high moulded foot. A slender tapering spout projecting almost horizontally from belly, just below top at 90° to a vertical ring handle attached to the body. Short broad stemmed and solid foot with heavy disc-base, very slightly concave underneath. Shallow groove at top of foot. On top, surrounding the central opening, a stamp decoration of nine linked palmettes inside this circle, bordering the central opening, is a chain of impressed tongues.
Date: Third quarter of the fifth century B.C.
Cf.: *Hesperia* 32 (1963) 121, D.8, pl.39. *Ath. Agora* XII no. 1197, pl.39. Newcastle 185 (Greek Museum).

Bibl.: Rowe, *Cyrenaica Exp.* 8, N.81-AD, pl.34,a.

CUP (15-25 pls.1-2, 68-71)

i. CUP WITH STEM

Vienna Cup (Vicup) (15-16)

15) Ptolemais Museum (pl.68, 1-2)

The cup has been broken and restored. Parts of the foot and the stem are modern. Shallow bowl with flaring rim. Offset from outside. Handles rather square. Horizontally fixed and rising to the level of the rim. Short stem curving in to bowl and foot without interruption. Black all over except for the inside of the handles, the outside edge and the resting surface of the foot, which are restored.
Date: Second quarter of the fifth century B.C.
Cf.: For Vicup, *CVA* Great Britain 6, 279 (pl.XLI) 32. *CVA* Italy 34, 1528 (pl.2) 3. *CVA* Poland 9, 385 (pl.9) 2,3,5. *CVA* Swiss 1, 26 (pl.26) 2, Fig.B2. *CVA* USA 1, 52 (pl.31) 4. See also *Hesperia* 5 (1936) p.336, and Bloesch, *Foremen Attiche Schalen* p.139, and *Ath. Agora* XII, no.437, and Lezzi-Hafter in *Antika Welt* (1980) no.43.

16) Cyrene Museum (Cyrene) (pl.68,3)

Restored from many pieces. Nearly complete apart from the handles and part of the rim, which are broken. Fine light orange clay, metallic black gloss. Broad shallow curved bowl, straight steep rim, rather heavy stemmed foot with fairly short, thick, concave stem and a thick sloping base with flat beveled edge. Foot only partly hollowed out. Black all over except for bottom of foot.
Date: Second quarter of the fifth century B.C.
Cf.: *Ath.Agora* XII no.434.

ii) STEMLESS CUP

1) Cup with Inset Lip (Castulo Cup) (17-19)

17) Oxford G.P130 (E/AP3/1) (Euhesperides) (pl.1,2)

Rim fragment. Approximately one sixth of diameter remaining.
Date: *c.* 450-425 B.C.
Cf.: For these cups see: *CVA* Tours and Bourges (pl.9) 6-9 Fig.2(4). *CVA* Stuttgart (pl.36) 8. Mainz (pl.41) 9. Geneva I, pl.26,7. Oxford 1 (pl.48). 2 *CVA* Goluchow 1 (pl.46) 6, 9. *CVA* Poland 3 (pl.4) 10. *CVA* Bucarest 2 (pl.32). *Hesperia* 22 (1953), p.73 (1970) Fig.104, 59. Also see *Ath. Agora* XII nos.471-373 Fig.5. Lamboglia *Classificazione* p.188 (form 2). *Quaderni* 9 (1971) Fig.31, pl.xv.

18) Oxford G.P129 (E/AS3/0) (Euhesperides) (pl.1,3)

Foot fragment. Half diameter remaining. Outer edge of foot black and lipped. Reserved resting surface, line at outer edge of underside, central medallion which is painted with a circle, circle and dot.
Date: *c.* 450-425 B.C.

19) Oxford G.P132 (E/AV/1) (Euhesperides) (pl.1,4)

Foot fragment. Approximately one-sixth diameter remaining. Misfired to red at centre of inside. Outer edge of foot black. Reserved resting surface underside.
Date: *c.* 430-400 B.C.

2. Plain Rim

20) Ptolemais Museum (Barka) (pl.69,1)
H. 6.3 cm; D. 20.4, 28.3 cm (including handles).

Spreading ring foot, lipped. Handles come straight and then turn up sharply. Glazed all over except for the underside, where several bands are reserved.
Date: *c.* 425 B.C.
Cf.: *CVA* Gallatin, pl.62,4. *Ath. Agora* XII, 269, no.481, pl.22, Fig.5.

Bibl.: *Liby. Antiqu.* 8 (1971) pl.XX1,b (Vickers).

3. Delicate Class

21) London BM 1866, 4-15.42 (pl.2 69,2-3)

Shallow bowl curves up to a plain rim. Two heavy thick handles, set horizontally halfway down the wall and rising to the rim. Moulded upper foot with raised rings on the underside. Rings on underside and a space within rings are reserved. The rest is black. Floor of the cup is decorated with two zones of tongues (double lines, arcs at outer end).
Date: Last quarter of the fifth century B.C.
Cf.: *Ath. Agora* XII, no.490, pl.50.

22) Manchester M 1098 *bis*, Cyrene (pl.2,2 70,1)

Only the floor of the cup survived. Moulded ring foot raised ring underside. Decoration inside: incised rosettes, surrounded by two grooves, beyond them a zone of linked palmettes, then a zone of ovals. Unpublished.
Date: *c.* 430 B.C.
Cf.: *Ath. Agora* XII, 269, no.483, pls.22,50, Fig.5, 484, pls.23,50 Fig.5. Newcastle 63.

23) Cyrene Museum (Cyrene) (pl.70,2)

The foot and part of the floor preserved. Moulded ring foot, under side reserved with glazed circles and a dot. Decoration inside: a star with a large number of rays closely set, pass beyond their own zone. They are surrounded by two zones of ovals and separated by concentric circles.
Date: *c.* 430 B.C.
Cf.: *Kerameikos* X (1976) 204 K.43 and *Ath. Agora* XII, 269, no.492, pl.51.

24) Cyrene Museum (Cyrene) (pl.70,3)

Only part of the floor has survived. It is flat with moulded ring foot. Glazed zone of inner function of foot and floor rays. The rest is reserved with a glazed circle and dot. Decoration inside: eight-rayed star, placed in the centre and surrounded with a zone of ovals.
Date: Last quarter of the fifth century B.C.
Cf.: *Ath. Agora* XII, 270, no.500, pl.51.

25) London B.M. 1866.4-15.41 (concave lip) (pls.2,3 71,1-2)

Moulded ring foot, lipped. Two raised rings on underside and a raised ring (step?) at the junction of foot and wall. Ribbed wall with arcs above. Reserved line around step above foot, resting surface, underside with glazed circles. Inside on the floor a central rosette, no arcs to indicate leaves, two circles, empty zone, two circles, zone of tongues, no arcs on either end of tongues, two circles.
Date: Last quarter of the fifth century B.C.
Cf.: *Ath. Agora* XII, 270, no.493, pls.22,50, Fig.5. Our vase is listed in *Ath. Agora* XII, 104, no27, no.7.

MUG (26)

Oinoche Shape VIII B (Pheidias shape)

26) Louvre CA 9739 (pl.72,1-2)

Normal ware with lustrous gloss. Rounded (near globular) body with incurved shoulder, short wide neck with flaring rim, wide base with low foot, thin double-strand ring handle from rim to shoulder, with upper ends of strand splayed out and pinched into lip. Foot rounded on outside with small groove on body above; inner face of foot sloping. A string of tiny round impressions surround the base of the neck, regular shallow vertical ribbing around outside of body, probably done with a spatula, no arcs at the top. Orange clay, glazed all over except the base of foot and the underside.
Date: Third quarter of the fifth century B.C.
Cf.: *Ath. Agora* XII, 203, *Kerameikos* IX, pl.112,113 1 (4). *AA* (1972) Fig.23, 1(4); 605 Fig.24 1(4).

BOWL (27-35 pl.3, 73-75)

i) Echinus Wall

27) Oxford G.P118 E/AQ/5/1 (Euhesperides) (pl.3,1)

Approximately half the bowl remaining. Blotchy glaze, perhaps suggesting dipping. Completely painted. No stamped decoration.
Date: 450 B.C. or somewhat earlier.

28) Oxford G.P99 E/A54/2P (Euhesperides) (pl.3,2)

Approximately half the bowl remaining. Thick wax around top rim, moulded disc foot, flat underneath and projected outwards. Glazed all over apart from the underside which is reserved and ruddled. No stamped decoration.
Date: *c.* 450 B.C.
Cf.: *Ath. Agora* XII, no.939, Fig.9. *Kerameikos* IX 151 (2), 228(3), Fig.20.

29) Cyrene Museum (Cyrene) (pl.73,1-2)

Thick walled, round rim sloping inwards, low foot ring with slightly flat resting surface. Decoration inside: zone of ten linked palmettes surrounding a chain of ovules with two circles. Normal ware, fully glazed inside and out, save resting surface and the underside which is reserved apart from glazed bands.
Date: Last quarter of the fifth century B.C.
Cf.: *Ath. Agora* XII, no.859, pl.33. *Tocra* 11, p.93, Fig.42, no.2361.

30) Louvre CA.973 (pl.74,1-2)

Ring foot, concave moulding beneath. Thickened rim sloping slightly inwards. Normal ware black cover except for the resting surface and the underside which is reserved save three glazed circles and a central dot. No floor stamped pattern.
Date: Last quarter of the fifth century B.C.

31) Oxford G.P85 E/AT2 (Euhesperides) (pl.3,3)

Approximately half the bowl remaining. Shallow body with rounded wall and round-topped rim, scraped groove at junction of body and foot. Base-ring with convex exterior, narrow resting surface and wide concave inner face, slightly offset from the flattish bottom of the vessel. Reserved line at outer edge of the top of the foot. Reserved resting surface and underside which is painted with a circle, circle and a dot. Stamped decoration palmettes (four remain) in circle.
Date: Last quarter of the fifth century B.C.
Cf.: *Ath. Agora* XII, no.870, Fig.9. *Kerameikos* X (2), 298(2). Newcastle 170, Hayes. Toronto 66, p.203, K.30, Fig.219.

32) Oxford G.P123 E/AQ511 (Euhesperides) (pl.3,4)

Approximately three quarters of foot and half of the rim remaining. Completely painted black. Inside enclosed small ovules and six palmettes with long stalks.
Date: Last quarter of the fifth century B.C.

33) Oxford G.P117 E/AR3 (Euhesperides) (pl.3,5)

Virtually complete. Largely misfired to green. Resting surface and underside reserved. The latter is painted with two circles and a dot.
Date: 430-410 B.C.

ii) Convex Wall

34) Cyrene Museum (Cyrene) (pl.74,3)

Orange clay, good glaze inside and out, flat underside, reserved.

iii) Out-turned Rim

35) Manchester 111.L.172 (M 694) N.83-B4 (Cyrene) (pl.3,6 75,1-2)
H. 5.4 cm; D. 12.5 cm.

Large bowl with high ring foot and steep wall rim out-turned and projecting. Decoration inside, four linked palmettes surrounded by another row of eleven palmettes, also linked, and these are separated by a chain of ovules. Orange clay. Fully glazed inside and out, save junctions of foot and wall and underside with glazed band and central circle.
Date: From late fifth to first quarter of the fourth century B.C.
Cf.: *Ath. Agora* XII, p.293, no.803, pl.32, Fig.8. Newcastle 188. For decoration *Ath. Agora* no.783, pl.57, Fig.8.

Bibl.: Rowe, *Cyren. Exp.* Pl.10,c.

LEKANIS (36-38)

i) Lidded with Ribbon Handles

36) Ptolemais Museum (Barka) (pl.4,1 76,1-2)

Lid with convex top, broad knob with raised edge and a conic depression at centre reserved resting surface, a zone on top decorated with rays radiating from bases of the handle, edge of knob, edge of the conical depression in the centre.
Body with heavy ring foot, broad resting surface, horizontal ribbon handles which may indicate a metal prototype for the shapes, flange for lid. There is a vertical log on each side of the handle.
Reserved: The handle zone with diagonal zigzag lines and on inside of handles, as well as another reserved zone above foot where rays radiate towards the body from the foot, resting surface and centre of the underside.

Bibl.: Würzburg (163 Langlotz, pl.120, from Arezo). Copenhagen (*CVA* 111, pp.72-78, pl.98-2, Lekanis, no.521, from Nola). There is the example from Canirus, *The Fikelura Cemetery*, *JHS* 60 (1940), p.36-73. *BSA* 47 (1952), p.43. London 64-7 1569. Bern Lezzi Hafter *Antik Welt* (1980), no.36. *Kerameikos* IX, no.263(3), pl.62(6).

37) Ptolemais Museum (from Asleaia) (Barka) (pl.76,3)
H. 9.2 cm; D. 11.7 cm; 17.3 cm (including handles).

Low ring foot with broad resting surface. Horizontal ribbon handles, flanges for lid, slightly convex. The knob sits on a tall stem and has disc top with a raised edge around it and a small depression in the centre. Completely glazed resting surface handle of a lid, resting surface of the foot and the points inside the foot where it joins the body, which are reserved.
Date: 235B.C.
Cf.: Vickers, *Lib. Antiq.* VIII (1971), pl.30. See also similar examples in Sparkes, *Pots and Pans*, Fig.53 (*Ath. Agora* XII, no.1220, pl.40, Fig.11.

ii) Lykinic

38) Manchester 111.L.175 M 1252 (N.81-Ac) (pl.4)

Lid flat-topped slightly convex with vertical side fitting over rim of bowl. Knob high and stemmed with raised band at bottom. The lid is a standard type: flattened sphere surmounted by a disc and divided into two by a horizontal groove.
Rounded bowl with incurving rim, ledged on the outside to receive lid, low spreading ring foot which is lipped, two swung handles attached horizontally to the bowl. They twist upwards and slightly inwards at the top.
Glazed all over except for resting surface of foot and edges of rim.
Date: Late fifth century B.C.
Cf.: Rowe, *Cyren. Exp.* 21, pl.35,b. See similar examples in *Ath. Agora* XII, nos.1242-44, pl.42. Oxford 1885, 498 (*CVA* Oxford, pl.XLVIII, 19. Vickers, *Scythia Treasures* in Oxford (Ashmolean Museum, Oxford, 1979), pp.40-41, Fig.8, pl.IX). Oxford 1966-412 (Beazley, *Gifts*, no.406, pl.LVI, with parallel cited.

PELIKE (39, pl.5,1 77,1)

Lidded Pelike

39) Manchester 111.L.176 (M 681) (M 768 Lid) (Cyrene)
H. 19.5 cm (including lid); D. 13 cm.

Ring foot, rim flanged to receive lid. Strap handles. The black glaze has peeled in some parts. Glaze all over including the inside of the neck.
Lid: Flat top, groove at edge of top, has a flat surface, unglazed underside.
Date: Last quarter of the fifth century B.C.
Cf.: Rowe, *Cyren. Exp.* pl.11. See Athens 18746 (G 894). *ARV* 1460. 72 *Deltion*, 20 (1965), pl.71B. *Ath. Agora* XII, pl.2, no.25. *Clara Rhodes*, 11, 141, Fig.19.

BOLSAL (40-55, pl.6,6 77-82)

40) Ptolemais Museum (from Aslaia near Barka) (pl.77,2)

The bowl has a single curve. Ring foot, U-shaped handles. No decoration inside.

Bibl.: Vickers, *Agora*, P.29725 (Hesperia 42 (1973), no.11 and pl.67,i) and *Agora*, P14133 19:4-U (*Ath. Agora* XII, pl.53, 533) and P.9819 M 18:8 (*Hesperia* XVIII (1949), 319, Fig.1, 156 and pl.94, 156. *Ath. Agora* XII, Fig.6, 534 and pls.24, 534 and 53, 543. Newcastle 572 (Greek Museum).

41) Oxford G.P47 (E/AQ5/1) (Euhesperides) (pl.6,1)

Approximately one third of the foot remains, rest as shown. No concave lower wall, although there are two light grooves present. Black underside. No stamped decoration.
Date: 435 B.C.

42) Oxford G.P45 (E/AS3/2 (a)) (Euhesperides) (pl.6,2)

Half diameter preserved. No concave lower wall or stamped decoration. Underside reserved, ruddled and painted with band

and circle and dot. On outer band of underside the graffito KAT.
Date: 430-420 B.C.

43) Cyrene Museum (Cyrene) (pl.78,1-3)

An open form with shallow floor, curving up to form vertical wall with plain rim, low moulded foot concave on outside, a scraped groove at the lower part of wall before the cavity. Two fairly large loop handles attached horizontally just below rim. Orange clay. Black all over except at a broad band on the underside and four circles. Decoration inside: six linked palmettes around a circle.
Date: Last quarter of the fifth century B.C.
Cf.: *Ath. Agora* XII, no.549.

44) Oxford G.P44 (E/AP3/2 (a)) (Euhesperides) (pl.6,3)

Base complete. Largely misfired to red. Concave lower wall with slight groove above. Underside reserved, ruddled and painted with band and circle, circle and dot. Stamped decoration: circles, five linked palmettes.
Date: Last quarter of the fifth century B.C.

45) Oxford G.P34 (E/AR4/3) (Euhesperides) (pl.6,4)

Approximately one third of foot diameter preserved, rest as shown. Concave lower wall with step above. Underside reserved and ruddled with painted band and circle, central circle. Stamped decoration: palmette cross on small circle (two remain), enclosed ovules set sideways, then palmettes (two remain).
Date: 420-420 B.C.

46) Oxford G.P17 (E/7/1) (Euhesperides) (pl.6,5)

Base complete, although restored. Virtually all walls lost. Reserved line at top of concave lower wall. Underside black with a broad reserved band. Either side of base are pairs of incised circles. At centre of black medallion and incised circle and dot. Stamped decoration: on a circle, ovules then seven linked palmettes, poorly stamped.
Date: End of fifth century B.C. (*c.* 410-400).

47) Manchester III.L.173 (M 752) (Cyrene) (pls.7,1 79,1-3)
H. 6.4 cm.

Flaring ring foot, concave lower part of wall. Black all over except the underside with glazed band and reserved space and two circles and a dot. Decoration inside: five linked palmettes (two are not linked) around a circle. The Cyrene example resembles others from the Athenian Agora that are dated to the last twenty years of the fifth century. The inside palmettes are similar to the previous example from Cyrene and to the Agora P.21359, but the underside differs. This appears to be a later development in the underside decoration closer to a later example from the Agora.
Date: 420-400 B.C.
Cf.: Rowe, *Cyren. Exp.* 16, pl.12, and *Ath. Agora* XII, no.550.

48) Manchester III.183 (M 1225) (B.81-AC) (Cyrene) (pl.7,2)
H. 3.2 cm.

An open form with shallow floor curving up to form vertical wall with plain rim. Low moulded ring foot concave on the outside, loop handles attached horizontally just below rim. Decoration: five palmettes, two are not linked and the other three are linked around circle.
Orange clay. Black all over except the underside with glazed band and reserved space and two circles and a dot.
Cf.: Rowe, *Cyren. Exp.* 18, pl.24,c, pl.35,a. *Ath. Agora* XII, no.550.

49) Oxford G.P125 (E/AP3/P2) (Euhesperides) (pl.7,3)

Complete base and approximately two thirds of wall diameter. Misfired in places. Concave lower wall. Underside reserved, ruddled and painted with ban and circle, circle and dot. Stamped decoration: three palmettes on a circle.
Date: 410 B.C.

50) Oxford G.P12 (Euhesperides) (pl.7,4)

One third of the diameter of the foot remains. Rest as shown. Reserved groove at top of concave lower wall. Black underside with at least two pairs of incised circles. Centre lost and no traces of stamped decoration remain.
Date: 400 B.C.

51) Manchester III.L.177 (M 753) (N.83.BJ) (Cyrene) (pl.7,5 80,1-2)
H. 4.5 cm.

An open form with shallow floor curving up to form vertical wall with plain rim, low moulding ring foot slightly concave on the outside. Loop handles attached horizontally just below rim. Decoration: palmette cross in the floor. Orange clay. Black all over except the underside which is reserved with a glazed band. Inside it a faint small circle and a dot.
Date: Late fifth, to early fourth century B.C.
Cf.: *Ath. Agora* XII, no.558. Rowe, *Cyren. Exp.* 17, pl.12,a.

52) London BM 56.112-9.2 (pl.8,1 80,3)

Flaring ring foot, concave lower part of wall. Black all over except the underside which is partly reserved and partly painted. The centre is glazed with a large circle and another large band around reserved band. Decoration inside: five linked palmettes around a circle, all with rouletting.

53) Oxford G.P64 (E/AR6/1) (Euhesperides) (pl.8,2)

Full height preserved and approximately one third of diameter. Incised line at top of concave lower wall. Reserved and grooved resting surface. Black underside. No stamped decoration.
Date: Second quarter of the fourth century B.C.

54) Louvre (no number) (pls.8,3 81,1-3)

The floor curves up to form vertical wall with thickish rim, moulded ring foot, lower part of wall concave, underside rises to form a nipple in the centre. Handle attached horizontally just below rim, slightly titled upwards. Floor decoration: four stamped palmettes clustered around the centre, surrounded by rouletting. On the underside there is the graffiti: 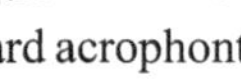
This represents a lot indication of '28' in standard acrophontic numerals.
Date: 350-320 B.C.

55) Cyrene Museum (Cyrene) (pl.82,1-3)

The floor curves up to form the slight rounded wall with thick rim. Moulded ring foot with scraped grooves on resting surface. Slightly concave lower part of the wall underside convex, and rise to form a nipple in the centre. Solid loop handle attached horizontally just below rim, somewhat thickened and joining the wall. Floor decoration: Low stamped palmettes clustered around the centre within rosetting. Orange clay. Black all over including the underside.
Date: 380-350 B.C.

Cf.: *Ath. Agora* XII, no.558. Hayes, *Greek and Italian* BL.Glos., no.61, Clairmont, *Brytus* 12 (1956-57) 19, no.540, pl.V.3.

OINOCHOE (56-67 pls.8/83-86)

i) Shape 5

56) Manchester III.L.171 (M 1248) (Cyrene) (pls.8,4 83,1)
H. 10.8 cm; D. 5.7 cm.

Rounded globular-ovoid body, tapering to a narrow concave neck with flaring rim. Flat base with small moulding at edge. Handle set up on edge of rim. Lip swing slightly concave on outer face to join the body. Orange clay. Glazed all over except the underside.
Date: Last quarter of the fifth century B.C., or slightly later.
Cf.: *Ath. Agora* XII, P.248, no.176, pl.10. *Kerameikos* IX, Fig.41, P.45801.

Bibl.: Rowe, *Cyren. Exp.* pls.246, 38,b.

57) Manchester (M 1247) (Cyrene) (pl.83,2)
H. 10.8 cm; D. 5.7 cm.

See Catalogue entry No.56.

Bibl.: Rowe, *Cyren. Exp.* pls.24,c, 38,b.

58) Manchester (M 658) (N.83.BG) (Cyrene) (pl.8,5)
H. 11 cm; D. 4.3 cm.

Ovoid-cylindrical body, slender in form, curving into flat base with small moulding at edge. The body tapers to a concave neck with flaring rim. The high swung handle is set up on edge of rim, curves in over mouth at top to join the body. Orange clay. Glazed all over save the underside.
Date: Late fifth century B.C.

Bibl.: Rowe, *Cyren. Exp.* 15, pls.9,a.

59) Louvre (no number) (pl.83,4)

Shape is square and round, resting on its flat bottom. The handle rises high, and above, curling over the mouth.
Date: Late fifth, early fourth century B.C.
Cf.: *Ath. Agora* P.4580, P.248, no.176, pl.10.

Bibl.: *CVA* Oxford I, pl.48, 13. *CVA* Copenhagen 7, pl.286, 13.

60) Sèvres Inv. 4156, 4 (Euhesperides)
H. 0.125 m (including handle); D. 0.018 m.

Similar to Catalogue No. 59, but with high handle.

Bibl.: *CVA* Sèvres 13, pl.25,2.

ii) Shoulder Oinoche 'Shape 2'

61) Sèvres Inv. 4166, 3 (Euhesperides) (pl.84,1)
H. 0.13 cm; D. 0.45 m.

Trefoil mouth, low round handle rising slightly above the rim. Disc foot. The outside of the vase and inside of the mouth and neck are glazed. Fine shaped decoration on shoulder angle. Above a row of small linked palmettes, points downwards. Below row of ovules.
Date: Third quarter of the fifth century B.C.

Bibl.: *CVA* Sèvres 13, pl.25 (554) 30.

iii) Kern Class

62) Leiden KVB 62 (Cyrene) (pl.84,2)
H. 0.121 m; D. 0.74 m.

Trefoil mouth, round handle rising slightly above the rim. Disc foot. The body ribbed. The ribs are joined at the top by incised arcs and they end up a little way above foot. The outside of the vase, the inside of mouth and neck are glazed, the underside is reserved.
Date: First half of the fourth century B.C.

Bibl.: Holwerda, *Catalogue* no.59, p.10 and p.13. Beazley, *EVP* (1947), 257. Kern, *Archivo Levant* 5 (1954), 141-5 and pls.1,2. *CVA* Leiden III 55ff., pl.155,6.

63) Manchester M 758 (Cyrene) (pl.85,1)
H. 0.15 m; D. 0.105 m.

Bibl.: Rowe *Cyren. Exp.* 16, pl.12,a.

64) Manchester M 759 (Cyrene)
H. 0.15 m; D. 0.105 m.

Both vases were found in Sarcophagus N.83-Bj from the north cemetery of Cyrene. The material found in this sealed sarcophagus dates from the late fifth century to after the middle of the fourth century.
Cf.: Cyrene (pl.85,2). See Catalogue entry No.64.

Bibl.: Rowe, *Cyren. Exp.* 12, 16ff., 32, pl.12,a.

III. 'Shape 3' (Chous)

65) Leiden KVB 61 (Cyrene) (pl.85,3)
H. 0.148 m; D. 0.125 m.

Squat globular body, flaring ring foot. Trefoil mouth flat on top, low strip handle. The outside of the vase and the inside of the mouth and neck are glazed. Resting surface and the underside reserved.
Date: Last quarter of the fifth century B.C.

Bibl.: *CVA* Leiden, pl.156,8.

66) Leiden KVB 11 (Cyrene) (pl.86,1)
H. 0.105 m; D. 0.66 m.

Trefoil mouth, low round handle. Ring foot, the inside of the mouth and neck and the whole outside are glazed, dipped. The underside is reserved.
Date: Third quarter of the fourth century B.C.

Bibl.: Holwerda, *Catalogue* no.131, p.17 and p.10, Fig.1. *CVA* Leiden III, p.56, pl.155,7.

67) Leiden KVB 12 (Cyrene) (pl.86,2)
H. 0.104 m; D. 0.66 m.

Most of the black glaze has peeled. For description see Catalogue No.66.
Date: Third quarter of the fourth century B.C.

Bibl.: *CVA* Leiden III, p.56, pl.155,8.

OLPE (68-88)

Footed (68-86)

68) H. 8.8 (Cyrene)

Round mouth with thickened rim. Rising strap handle, disc foot, slightly projecting, glazed all over.

Date: 430-400 B.C.

Bibl.: Pernier, *Africa Italinna* IV (1931), 213, Fig.35.

69) H. 8.2 (Cyrene)

Round mouth with thickened rim. Rising strap handle, disc foot, slightly projecting, glazed all over.
Date: 430-400 B.C.

Bibl.: Pernier, *Africa Italinna* IV (1931), 213, Fig.35.

70) Sèvres Inv. 9521, 6 (Euhesperides)
H. 0.105 m, including handle; D. 0.03m.

Round mouth with thickened rim. Rising strap handle, disc foot, slightly projecting, glazed all over.
Date: 430-400 B.C.

Bibl.: Sèvres *CVA* 50, No.3, pl.25,3.

71) Sèvres Inv. 9521, 5 (Euhesperides)
H. 0.110 m, including handle; D. 0.04m.

Round mouth with thickened rim. Rising strap handle, disc foot, slightly projecting, glazed all over.
Date: 430-400 B.C.

Bibl.: Sèvres *CVA* 50, No.5, pl.25.

72) Sèvres Inv. 9521, 7 (Euhesperides)
H. 0.95 m, including handle; D. 0.034m.

Round mouth with thickened rim. Rising strap handle, disc foot, slightly projecting, glazed all over.
Date: 430-400 B.C.

Bibl.: Sèvres *CVA* 51, No.25, pl.25.

73) Leiden KVB 13 (pl.86,3)
H. 8.7 cm (9.4 cm including handle); D. 6cm.

Round mouth with thickened rim. Disc foot, slightly projecting. Rising strap handle. The outside of the vase and the inside of the mouth are glazed. The underside is reserved.
Date: 430-400B.C.

Bibl.: Leiden *CVA* III, p.58, pl.156,12.

74) Leiden KVB 69
H. 8.45 cm, 9.3 cm including handle; D. 5.7 cm.

Round mouth with thickened rim. Disc foot, slightly projecting. Rising strap handle, underside flat. The outside of the vase and the inside of the mouth are glaze dipped. The underside is reserved.
Date: 430-400 B.C.

Bibl.: *CVA* Leiden III, p.58, pl.156,13.

75) Apollonia Inv.66 461 (Apollonia) (pl.87,1)
H. 0.103 m; D. 0.038 m.

The glaze is mottled and peeled on part of the neck and body. Round mouth with thickened rim. Disc foot, slightly protruding from the wall with a torus profile, concave beneath. Raised strap handle. Glazed all over except for the underside, which is reserved.
Date: Middle of the fourth century B.C.

Bibl.: White, in Humphrey (ed.), *Apollonia, The Port of Cyrene*, Tomb 6, 122, pl.XXIf.

76) Apollonia (published in Ghislanzoni, *Notizie Archeologiche Sulla Tripolitania* (1915), 90, Fig.49 *bis*).

The glaze is mottled and peeled on part of the neck and body. Round mouth with thickened rim. Disc foot, slightly protruding from the wall with a torus profile, concave beneath. Raised strap handle. Glazed all over except for the underside, which is reserved.
Date: Middle of the fourth century B.C.

77) Manchester M 685 (Cyrene) (pl.9,2 87,2)
H. 10.5 cm; D. 6.0 cm.

Round mouth with thickened rim. Disc foot protruding from the wall forming a torus profile, concave beneath. Raised strap handle. Glazed all over except for the underside which is reserved.
Date: Middle of the fourth century B.C.

Bibl.: Rowe, *Cyren. Exp.* pl.11,a.

78) Manchester M 683 (Cyrene) (pl.9,3 87,3)
H. 11.4 cm; D. 6.5 cm.

Round mouth with thickened rim. Disc foot protruding from the wall forming a torus profile, concave beneath. Raised strap handle. Glazed all over except for the underside which is reserved.
Date: Middle of the fourth century B.C.

Bibl.: Rowe, *Cyren. Exp.* pl.11,a.

79) Manchester M 761 (Cyrene) (pl.9,4)
H. 10.5 cm; D. 5.2 cm.

Round mouth with thickened rim. Disc foot protruding from the wall forming a torus profile, concave beneath. Raised strap handle. Glazed all over except for the underside, which is reserved.
Date: Middle of the fourth century B.C.

Bibl.: Rowe, *Cyren. Exp.* pl.12,a.

80) Manchester M 760 (Cyrene)
H. 10.0 cm; D. 5.5 cm.

Round mouth with thickened rim. Disc foot protruding from the wall forming a torus profile, concave beneath. Raised strap handle. Glazed all over except for the underside, which is reserved.
Date: Middle of the fourth century B.C.

Bibl.: Rowe, *Cyren. Exp.* pl.12,a.

81) Sèvres Inv. 9521,4 (Euhesperides)
H. 0.12 m; D. 0.032 m.

Round mouth with thickened rim. Raised strap handle. Disc foot, glazed all over.
Date: Middle of the fourth century B.C.

Bibl.: Sèvres *CVA* 50, no.6, pl.25.

82) Sèvres Inv. 9521,3 (Euhesperides)
H. 0.12 m; D. 0.035 m.

Round mouth with thickened rim. Raised strap handle. Disc foot, glazed all over.
Date: Middle of the fourth century B.C.

Bibl.: Sèvres *CVA* 51, no.26, pl.25.

83) Louvre (no number supplied) (pl.83,3)
H. 0.11 m.

Glaze on lip handle and part of the body. Round mouth with slightly thickened rim. Small disc foot, strap handle. Glazed all over, except for the underside which is reserved.
Date: Middle of the fourth century B.C.

84) Leiden KVB 68 (Cyrene)
H. 10.3 cm, including handle; D. 6 cm.

Black glaze has peeled. Round thickened rim. Disc foot, high strap handle. The underside flat, outside of the vase and a small part of the inside of the mouth are glazed, underside reserved.
Date: Middle of the fourth century B.C.

Bibl.: *CVA* Leiden III, p.59, pl.156,14.

85) Leiden KVB 72 (Cyrene)
H. 15.7cm, including handle; D. 6.5 cm.

High slender shape. Round mouth. Low strap handle. Spreading ring foot, underside is slightly concave. The outside of the vase and the inside of the mouth are glaze dipped. The underside is reserved.
Date: Middle of the fourth century B.C.

Bibl.: Holwerda, p.17, 20, no.136, Fig.4. *CVA* Leiden III, p.58, pl.156,10.

86) Sèvres Inv. 9521,1 (Euhesperides)
H. 0.155 m; D. 0.04 m.

High slender shape. Round mouth. Low strap handle. Spreading ring foot. Underside is slightly concave and glazed all over.
Date: Middle of the fourth century B.C.

Bibl.: Sèvres *CVA* 53, no.65, pl.25.

Footless (87-88) (pl.88)

87) Manchester M 759 (Cyrene)
H. 15.6 cm; D. 6.2 cm.

High slender shape. Round mouth. High strap handle, broad shoulder. The wall flares at the bottom. No foot, flat bottom. Neck and all the outside of the vase are glazed.
Date: Middle of the fourth century B.C.

Bibl.: Rowe, *Cyren. Exp.* pl.12,a.

88) Leiden KVB 66 (Cyrene) (pl.88,1)
H. 14.5 cm (including handle); D. 6.9 cm.

High slender shape with round, thickened rim. High concave strap handle. The wall is slightly flared at the bottom. No foot, underside flat. The outside and the upper part of the inside of the neck are glaze dipped. Underside reserved.
Date: Middle of the fourth century B.C.

Bibl.: Holwerda, 14, no.74, and p.10, Fig.1. *CVA* Leiden III, p.57f., pl.156,9.

AMPHORA (89-92, pls.89-91)

89) Amsterdam Inv.934 (Amphora) (pl.89,1)
H. 87 cm.

Black-glazed amphora of a Panathenaic shape with wide spreading lip, raised fillet between neck and body. The body tapers in at the stem. Convex foot, with deep groove on its upper edge, vertical ribbing applied to the surface from the shoulder to the beginning of the stem. Glazed black all over.
Date: Third quarter of the fifth century B.C.

Bibl.: Amsterdam Inv. 934. *CVA* (Scheurleer III, L and N), pl.1,2. Kopeke, *AM* 79 (1964), 40 (119).

90) Fragment (Cyrene Museum) (pl.89,2)

Only the lower part of the body and stem have survived. The body is covered with vertical ribbing. Inside of the hollow stem unglazed. The surface is covered with a metallic black glaze.

91) London BM F 605 1854.2-27.1 (pl.90,1-2)

Black-glazed amphora of a Panathenaic shape. The body tapers sharply into a stem. The mouth has an ogee profile (flaring). There is a raised fillet between the neck and the body at the level of the attachment of the handles. The foot spreads in a convex shape, with a deep groove on its supper edge, which is reserved. Vertical ribbing applied to the surface from shoulder to the beginning of the stem. The underside of the foot and the inside of the hollow stem are unglazed. The outside of the surface and inside of the neck, to the level of the fillet, are entirely covered with a metallic black glaze of high luster. On the shoulder there is the graffito: "Aristarchos, son of Ariston".
Date: 320-310 B.C.

92) London BM 56, 10-1,2 (pl.91,1)
H. 49.6 cm.

Black-glazed amphora of a Panathenaic shape. The body tapers sharply into a stem. The mouth has an ogee profile (flaring). There is a raised fillet between the neck and the body at the level of the attachment of the handles. The foot is spreading in a convex shape, with a deep groove on its supper edge, which is reserved. Vertical ribbing applied to the surface from shoulder to the beginning of the stem. The underside of the foot and the inside of the hollow stem are unglazed. The outside of the surface and inside of the neck, to the level of the fillet, are entirely covered with a metallic black glaze of high luster. On the shoulder there is a graffito.
Date: 320-310 B.C.

Bibl.: Kopcke *AM* 79 (1964). Beil.27, 127.

92 *bis*) BM C 68 (66 4-15, 72)
Description as for Catalogue No.92 above.

Bibl.: Kopcke, *AM* 79 (1964), no.128, Beil. 27, 4.

PELIKE (93-94, pls.91-92)

Ribbed

93) Cyrene Museum (Cyrene) (pl.91,2)

Large pelike with flaring neck, overhanging rim, handles with central ribs, disc foot in two degrees. Underside reserved. The outer edge of the foot is also reserved. On the overhanging rim there is a continuous band of 'egg-and-dot' pattern. Body is ribbed vertically. Gilded wreath around neck of vase.
Date: 360-350 B.C.

94) Apollonia (Cyrene)

Large pelike with flaring neck, overhanging rim, handles with central ribs, disc foot in two degrees. Underside reserved. The outer edge of the foot is also reserved. On the overhanging rim there is a continuous band of 'egg-and-dot' pattern. Body is ribbed vertically. Gilded wreath around neck of vase.
Date: 360-350 B.C.

Bibl.: Ghislanzoni, *Notizie Archeologiche Sulla Tripolitania* (1915), 99, Fig.49 *bis*).

SKYPHOS (95-98 pl.92)

Attic (Type A)

95) Fragment of skyphos Type A (Attic Type), Louvre CA 972 (pl.92,1)
Part of the lip and shoulder missing. Torus ring foot, bulging shoulder tapering below. The rim turns outwards. Glazed reddish in colour (mixture of black and red) cover the whole surface, apart from the resting surface and the underside, which is reserved except for two small, glazed circles.
Date: Second quarter of the fourth century.

Bibl.: *Ath. Agora* XII, P.96019, p.260, no.352, pl.17, Fig.4.

96) Leiden KVB 107 (pl.92,2)
H. 10.9 cm; D. (rim) 11.4 cm.

Out-turned rim. The wall tapers strongly towards the foot. Triangular handles. Torus ring foot. Glaze dipped all over.
Date: Second quarter of the fourth century B.C.

Bibl.: Leiden *CVA* III, pl.159.

97) Sèvres Inv. 4166,11
H. 0.13 m; D. 0.125 m.

Rim turns outwards. Bulging shoulder tapers below. Triangular handles. Torus ring foot.
Date: Second quarter of the fourth century B.C.

Bibl.: Sèvres *CVA* pl.25,4.

98) Sèvres Inv. 4166,12
H. 0.035 m; D. 0.06 m.

Rim turns outwards. Bulging shoulder tapers below. Triangular handles. Torus ring foot.
Date: Second quarter of the fourth century B.C.

Bibl.: Sèvres *CVA* pl.25,7.

HYDRIA (99-111, pls.93-97)

99) Cyrene Museum (pl.93,1)

The two horizontal handles are missing. Part of the surface pitted and the glaze mottled. Ovoid body with wide shoulder, short incurving neck. Overhanging rim developed into two rounded mouldings by groove and prominent ridge at the top. The lower moulding covers part of the vertical handle, but does not cut into it. This handle springs from the shoulder and arches up touching the rim and curves down to join the neck. The side handles are missing. Moulded ring foot, concave with double torus at the edge. Glazed black all over, except for a reserved band setting the opening of the neck and the groove on the rim edge of foot and its functions to the body, the underside including the resting surface. On the rim, the remains of a continuous band of 'egg' pattern. On the neck, the garland of small myrtle leaves in added clay was probably originally gilded.
Date: 370-360 B.C.
Cf.: For comparison, Louvre, Paris, CA 2272. Kopcke, *AM* 79 (1964), pl.23 (1).

100) Cyrene Museum (pl.93,2)

Fragment of neck and rim of an Attic hydria. Overhanging rim partly missing, divided in to two rounded mouldings by a groove and a prominent ridge at the top. Vertical handle springs from shoulder and arch up, curving down to join the neck. Glazed black except a band setting the opening of the neck and the groove on rim. Remains of garland of myrtle leaves in added clay decorate the neck.

101) Sèvres Inv. 4166,1 (Euhesperides)
H. 0.25 m; D. 0.04 m.

Well preserved in good condition. Ovoid body, slightly long neck, overhanging rim marked off by a groove and a ridge at the top. Vertical handle springs from the shoulder and arches up, touching the rim and curves down to join the neck. Side handles are set slightly below the shoulder and re-curve sharply along the body. Moulded ring foot, concave with double torus at the edge. Glazed black all over, except at the edge of the foot and its junction to the body. Garland of small myrtle leaves is added along the neck.
Date: 370-360 B.C.

Bibl.: Sèvres *CVA*, pl.24,7.

102) Apollonia 66-228 (Apollonia) (pl.94,1)

Fragment of neck and rim of Attic hydria. Overhanging rim, moulded and marked off by a groove and a ridge at the top. Incurved neck. Vertical handle area missing. Glazed black except for a reserved band setting off the opening of the neck, with the exception of the handle zone. In glaze and execution the piece is exceptionally fine, and may be dated 375 to 350 B.C.

Bibl.: White, in Humphrey (ed.) *Appolonia, The Port of Cyrene*, pl.XIX, f. For comparison see *Ath. Agora* P-8280, p.239, no.51, p.13.

103) Apollonia 66-45b (Apollonia) (pl.94,2)
H. 0.199 m; D. 0.045 m.

Part of the surface is pitted and glaze mottled. The reserve relief line and dots on the neck have chipped away. Overhanging rim moulded and marked off by a groove and ridge at the top. Vertical handles spring from the shoulder and arch up touching the rim and curve down to join the neck. The side handles spring just above the vessel's greatest diameter and re-curve very sharply along the body. Glazed black except for reserved band around opening to neck, groove on outside of rim, the vertical side of the foot and the underside, including the resting surface. On the neck a reserved line and circle of dot-pattern in added clay
Date: ***375-350 B.C.***

Bibl.: White, in Humphrey (ed.) *Appolonia, The Port of Cyrene*, pl.XXII, f – XXIII, a. For comparison see *Ath. Agora* P-8280, p.239, no.51, p.3. *CVA* Oxford *IBJ*, pl.48, Fig.35.

104) Apollonia 66-228 (Apollonia) (pl.94,1)
H. 0.115 m; D. 0.162 m.

Well preserved and in good condition. Overhanging rim moulded and marked off by a groove and a ridge at the top. Vertical handles spring from the shoulder and arch up, touching the rim, and curve down to join the neck. Side handles spring just above the vessel's greatest diameter and re-curve sharply along the body. Moulded ring foot, concave wall, double torus at the edge. Glazed black except for a band on the opening of the mouth, lower concave moulding of foot and the underside, including the resting surface.
Date: 350 B.C.

Bibl.: White, in Humphrey (ed.) *Appolonia, The Port of Cyrene*, pl.XXII, d-e.

105) Fragment of hydria (Cyrene Museum) (pl.95,1)

Large part of body, foot and neck are missing. Part of the neck and shoulder, and one side of an ovoid body of a hydria ribbed from shoulder to just over the foot. A side handle re-curves along the body.

106) Fragment of hydria (Cyrene Museum) (pl.95,2)

Most part of body missing together with neck, shoulder and foot of the vessel. Vertical ribs applied to the body from shoulder to just over foot.

107) Fragment of hydria (Cyrene Museum) (pl.96,1)

Large fragment of a hydria showing part of the shoulder and the wall. Broad vertical ribbing was applied to the wall.

108) London BM 56, 10-1,4 (British Museum) (pl.96,2)
H. 46 cm.

Ovoid body with wide shoulder sloping down, gradually covered with vertical ribs from shoulder to just above foot. Foot moulded (offset, rests on disc), long incurving (flaring) neck crowned by an overhanging rim with a prominent ridge on the top. Vertical handles at the back and two horizontal ones at either side, re-curving very sharply along the body. The vase is decorated with a continuous band of 'egg' pattern on the rim, and with a wreath of myrtle leaves in relief gilded over white on the neck.
Date: 320-300 B.C.
Cf.: For comparison, British Museum 64, 10-7, 1512. Kopcke, *AM* 7a (1964), no.88, pl.24,1. *Clara Rhodes* VI-VII, p.772, 204. Breccia, *La Necropolis di Sciatbi*, pl.XXXVI (44).

109) Leiden KVB 2 (pl.97,1)
H. 24 cm; D. 15.2 cm.

Surface is pitted and the black glaze has peeled. Overhanging rim moulded and marked off by a growth and a ridge at the top. Round vertical handle springs from the shoulder and arches up touching the rim and curves to join the neck. The two horizontal handles turn upwards and inwards. Ribbed body, the ribs ending a little way above the foot. The ribs are joined at the top by incised arcs. The outside of the vase and the inside of the neck are glazed. Top of the mouth and the groove between the two mouldings of the rim are glazed. Around the neck, in added clay, a tendril with ivy leaves, originally gilded.
Date: 310-300 B.C.

Bibl.: Janssen *Catalogue* 11, 1462, p.146. Holwerda *Catalogue* XXIII, a, 3, p.238. Leiden *CVA* III, pl.154,1, Fig.43.

110) Leiden KVB 49 (pl.97,2)
H. 19.6 – 20.1 cm; D. 11.2 cm.

Foot broken but part of it restored with plaster. The surface is pitted and the black glaze has peeled. Moulded overhanging rim, round vertical handle. The two horizontal handles turn upwards and inwards, touching the wall. Body is covered with vertical ribs from shoulder to just above foot. The inside of the neck and the entire outside are glazed. The top of the mouth and the narrow band between the two mouldings of the rim are reserved. Around the neck, in added clay, a wreath of olive leaves, originally gilded.
Date: 310-300 B.C.

Bibl.: Janssen *Catalogue* 11, 1463, p.146. Holwerda *Catalogue* XXIII, a, e, p.238. Leiden *CVA* III, 53f., pl.154,2, Fig.44.

111) Leiden KVB 50
H. 13.8 cm; D. 7.8 cm.

Moulded overhanging rim, moulded foot. Round vertical handle. The two horizontal handles turn upwards and inwards, touching the raised wall. The body is ribbed, the whole outside of the vase and the inside of the neck are glazed. Top of the mouth and groove between the two mouldings of the rim, the edge of the foot and the underside are reserved. Around the neck, a painted wreath of laurel leaves.
Date: Late fourth century B.C.

Bibl.: Janssen *Catalogue* 11, 1464, p.146. Holwerda *Catalogue* XXIII, a, 4, p.120. Leiden *CVA* III, pl.154,3, Fig.45.

CUP-KANTHAROS (112-115, pls.99-100)

i) Moulded Rim

112) Cyrene (pl.98, 1-2)

Moulded rim foot, concave beneath in several degrees, short stem. Straight ring curved out at the lip in an offset. Long handles, curved and twisted. Four palmettes stamped on floor within a ring of rouletting. All black except for a reserved line at junction of body and stem, and another on the resting surface.
Date: Third quarter of the fourth century B.C.

ii) Squat Rim

113) Manchester (M 656) (Cyrene) (pls.95, 99,1-2)

Concave neck with moulded rim, most of the handles are missing, the part that is left is from the top of the bowl begins to rise upwards. Moulded ring foot, concave beneath, reserved groove separates the two sections of foot. On the floor of cup four linked palmettes enclosing circle within rouletting.
Date: Third quarter of the fourth century B.C.

Bibl.: Rowe, *Cyren. Exp.* pl.8,c (R.1 left).

iii) Bowl-shaped

114) Sèvres Inv. 4166,1 (pl.100,1)

Deep bowl, wall incurving at rim. Handles project from body and re-curve over the rim. The bowl is separated from the foot by a stem. Moulded foot, concave beneath, scraped line at junction of two mouldings on lower part.
Date: 325-310 B.C.

Bibl.: Sèvres *CVA*, pl.25, 22.

115) Cyrene (pl.100,2)

Partly broken section of the upper wall, handles and foot missing, good glaze. Deep bowl, nearly triangular in shape, lip spreads outwards. High stem separates foot and bowl. Two-stepped foot, lower section splayed.
Date: Late fourth or first quarter of the third century B.C.

KANTHAROS (116-121, pls.100-101)

Moulded Rim

116) Sèvres Inv. 9519,14 (Euhesperides)

Moulded rim, thick and projecting. Ring handles. Moulded ring foot, concave beneath in two degrees separated by a reserved groove. Spurs are on same level as the rim. Body covered with vertical ribbing.

Date: Second quarter of the fourth century B.C.

Bibl.: Sèvres *CVA*, pl.25, 37.

117) Leiden KVB 155, (pl.100,3)
H. 0.55 m; D. 0.19 m.

Moulded rim, thick and projecting. Ring handles. Moulded ring foot, concave beneath in two degrees. Separated by a reserved groove. Spurs are on the same level as the rim. Body and foot are separated by high stem.
Date: Third quarter of the fourth century B.C.

Bibl.: Holwerda *Catalogue* p.18, no.146, fig.3.

Plain Rim

118) Sèvres Inv. 9517,6 (Euhesperides)
H. 0.095 m; D. 0.09 m.

Moulded foot, concave beneath. Nearly horizontal tapering spurs. Not leveled with rim, groove between two mouldings on lower part of foot.
Date: Third quarter of the fourth century B.C.

Bibl.: Sèvres *CVA*, pl.25, 45.

119) Sèvres Inv. 7090,3 (Euhesperides)
H. 0.095 m; D. 0.075 m.

Moulded foot, concave beneath, spurs on same level as rim between the mouldings on lower part of foot.
Date: Third quarter of the fourth century B.C.

Bibl.: Sèvres *CVA*, pl.25, 49.

120) Sèvres Inv. 9517,15 (Euhesperides)
H. 0.095 m; D. 0.09 m.

Moulded foot, concave beneath, spurs on same level as rim, between the mouldings on lower part of foot.
Date: Third quarter of the fourth century B.C.

Bibl.: Sèvres *CVA*, pl.25, 51.

121) Cyrene Museum (pl.101,1)

Partly broken, what is left is restored from a number of pieces. Lip and body partly broken. Handle and foot missing. Deep rounded lower body, slightly flaring upper wall with plain rim, slightly tapering handle spurs. Dull black glaze all over. Neck is decorated with olive wreath added in white.
Date: Last quarter of the fourth century B.C.

CALYX CUP (122, pl.101)

122) Manchester M 601 (Cyrene) (pl.101,2)
H. 7.5 cm; D. 8.2 cm.

Intact except for chips on the rim and side. Convex lower body with vertical ribbing (grooving). High upper wall slightly concave, continuous with sharply flaring lip into handle.
Date: After the middle of the fourth century B.C.

Bibl.: Rowe, *Cyren. Exp.* 14, pl.8,b.

ONE-HANDLED (123-125, pl.102)

Conical

123) Louvre CA 973 (pl.102,1)

Deep cup with a small ring foot, concave moulding beneath flaring offset collar (rim) to which the horizontal handle is attached. Black all over except for the resting surface which is reserved apart from glazed circles.
Date: 375-350 B.C.

124) Louvre CA 973 (pl.102,2)

See Catalogue entry No.123 above.

125) Sèvres Inv. 4166,17 (Euhesperides)
H. 0.06 m; D. 0.105 m.

See Catalogue entry No.123 above.
Cf.: Sparkes and Talcott, *Ath. Agor* XII, no.776.

Bibl.: Sèvres *CVA*, 1, pl.25, 12.

SMALL BOWL AND SALT-CELLAR (Fourth-century types) (123-133, pls.10/102-104)

i) Echinus Wall

126) Manchester M 765 (Cyrene) (pls.10,1 102, 3-5)
H. 3.0 cm; D. 8.5cm.

Thick walled, rounded body, with slightly incurving rim, slightly flat resting surface. Inside decoration: stamped palmette-cross. Fully glazed inside and out, except for the resting surface and the underside, which is reserved apart from a glazed broad band and two circles.
Date: Early fourth century B.C.
Cf.: Decoration on bolsal No.40 in this Catalogue and *Ath. Agora* XII, no.556.

127) Tocra Inv. 2362 (Tocra)

Thick walled, small rounded body with slightly incurving rim. Rounded on top, low foot ring with flat resting surface, underside rises to convex shape, scratched groove on resting surface. Normal ware, glazed all over except for resting surface which is reserved.
Date: Early fourth century B.C.
Cf.: *Ath. Agora* XII, nos.948-9, Fig.9. Hayes, *Ontario* no.67.

Bibl.: Boardman and Hayes, *Tocra* II, 94, Fig.42.

128) Tocra Inv. 2360 (Tocra)

The foot and part of the wall preserved. Surface damaged. Sloping sides, short upright rim, rounded on outside. Scraped grooves at junction of body and foot, and on the rest of the surface. The underside rises to a nipple. Glazed all over except for the resting surface which is reserved. On floor four linked shaped palmettes surrounded by rouletting. Graffiti on floor with scratched line below rim.
Date: 350-320 B.C.
Cf.: *Ath. Agora* XII, nos.833-5, Fig.8, pl.33. For graffiti see Boardman and Hayes, Tocra II, 102, where it is suggested that 'Sitrachos' or 'Sitraxos' may be a proper name, abused by references to male and female genitalia.

Bibl.: Boardman and Hayes, *Tocra* II, 94, Fig.42.

129) Oxford G.P104 (Euhesperides) (pl.10,2)

Virtually complete, though part of rim missing. No stamped decoration. Reserved broad resting surface. Black underside with central rising cone.

ii) Echinus Wall (projected rim)

130) Louvre (no number) (pl.104,1-2)

Shallow body, low flaring wall almost vertical on an outward projecting rim, which is also broad. Normal ware, glazed all over.
Date: Middle of the fourth century B.C.

iii) Concave Wall Salt-Cellar

131) Manchester M 767 (N.83-BJ) (Cyrene) (pl.10,3)
H. 2.6 cm; D. 6.4cm.

Concave wall, recesses under rim rounded on top. Normal ware, black all over.
Date: Second quarter of the fourth century B.C.

Bibl.: Rowe, *Cyren. Exped.* 17, pl.12,a. *CVA* Oxford 1 (3), pl.48 (36). *Athen. Agora* XII, no.937. *Hesperia*, Sup. 11, IV (1940), p.133, Fig.98,d.

132) Louvre CA 973 (pl.104,3)

See Catalogue entry No.131 above, and Louvre CA 973 (pl.104,4), also as Catalogue entry No.131 (pl.10,4).

133) Oxford G.P93 (Euhesperides) (pl.10,4)

See Catalogue entries Nos.131-132.

PLATE (134-137) (pls.10/105)

i) Rolled Rim

134) Euhesperides (pl.10,5)

Thick walled plate, wide shallow floor, curving up gently towards the edge. Thick narrow rim, slightly rounded on top, marked off on outside by a groove. Low shallow wall, low foot with wide diameter, concave from inside, convex from outside, with flat resting surface.
Date: Last quarter of the fourth century B.C.

Bibl.: Unpublished.

135) Euhesperides (pl.10,6)

See Catalogue entry No.134 above.
Date: Last quarter of the fourth century B.C.

ii) Fish Plate

136) Leiden KVB 148 (Cyrene) (pl.105,1-2)
H. 3.1 cm; D. 53.7 cm.

Broad floor sloping down to a central depression, ring foot with flat surface.
Date: Third quarter of the fourth century B.C.

Bibl.: Holwerda, *Catalogue* no.75.

137) Euhesperides (pl.10,7)

Broad floor sloping down to a central depression, ring foot with grooved resting surface.
Date: Third quarter of the fourth century B.C.

Bibl.: Unpublished

LEKYTHOS (138, pl.106)

138) Apollonia Inv. 66-182 (Apollonia Museum) (pl.106,1)
H. 0.174 m; D. 0.062 m.

Conical foot with moulded exterior, egg-shaped body. The narrow neck is set off from the body by a flange and from the conical mouth by a groove. The wide rim inclines towards the mouth opening. A wide band of clay applied at the base of neck. Handle projects from shoulder to join the base of conical rim. Body is covered by broad ribbing. Black glaze all over, except for the resting surface and the upper part of moulded foot.
Date: 375 B.C.

Bibl.: White, in Humphrey (ed.) *Apollonia, The Port of Cyrene*, pp.118-19, pl.20,a.

ASKOS (139-146, pl.107-110)

Shallow

139) Leiden KVB 172 (pl.107,1)

Shallow, broad closed body with low wall, sloping into a broad flat base with low moulding at edge. Tubular spout with flaring mouth rising at a right angle. On the shoulder a long arched strap handle (with central ridge on top, and underside flat) applied from the spout to the shoulder of the body at the back on the other side. Slightly high-breasted.
Date: Early fourth century B.C.
Cf.: Massei, *Necropolis di Spina*, Askos no.88 (Inv.6567), pp.145-6, pl/LXXX,1.

Bibl.: Holwerda, *Catalogue* no.90. *Ath. Agora* XII, nos.1176-77, pl.39.

140) London BM 1867, 5-12.45 (pl.107,2)

Broad body with low wall slopes into a broad flat base with low moulding at edge. Trumpet-shaped spout with splayed lip set at a right angle. On shoulder a long arched strap handle, with central ridge on top, connects the spout, the shoulder and the back. Lustrous black glaze was used.
Date: Early fourth century B.C.

Relief Top

141) Leiden KVB 16 (pl.108,2)
H. 4.5 cm.

Deep rounded body with disc foot and convex closed top. Top mould made with relief decoration. Badly worn and therefore difficult to identify what it represents, probably a mask. Trumpet-shaped spout with splayed lip set in an angle near the edge of the top. Double-roll handle overarches across to connect rear of spout to rim-flange on opposite side. Black all over.
Date: First half of the fourth century B.C.

Bibl.: Holwerda, *Catalogue*, P.2.14, no.91, Fig.4.

142) Manchester M 770 (N.83-BJ) (pl.109,1-2)

Deep rounded body with disc foot, convex sloping top with raised medallion at centre. Top mould made with relief decoration. Frontal human mask with puffed cheeks in high relief. Spout and handle are broken and lost, but they must be similar to those on Catalogue entry No.141 above. Lustrous black glaze covers the whole pot.
Date: First half of the fourth century B.C.
Cf.: Alexandrescu, *Histria* IV (1978) 93, no.612, pl.67 (dated to the end of the fifth century B.C).

Bibl.: Rowe, *Cyren. Exp.* 22, pl.40,a-b.

Strainer Top

143) Louvre CA 973 (pl.110,1)

Broad low body with wide round shoulder, raised ring on top. Strap, similar to strap handle, set on shoulder, low flat base. Metallic gloss.
Date: Second quarter of the fourth century B.C.
Cf.: Massei, *Gli Askoi*, body similar to askos no.182 (Inv.9802, pls.LXXI, LXXXII,2). For askos no.108 (Inv.6409, pls.LXIX,3, LXXXII,4).

Guttus Type

144) Louvre CA 973 (pl.110,2)

Deep rounded cushion-like body with vertical offset spout with concave sides ending in flat, projecting lip. Grooved ring handle set on shoulder, low foot with double-base mouldings. Metallic gloss.
Date: Second quarter of the fourth century B.C.
Cf.: *Olynthus* XIII, pl.168. *Ath. Agora* XII, no.1194, pl.39, Fig.11.

145) Leiden KVB 10
H. 8 cm.

Dull black glaze. Cushion-like body, vertical offset spout with concave sides ending in a flat, projecting lip. Grooved ring handle, high moulded foot.
Date: Second quarter of the fourth century B.C.

Bibl.: Holwerda, *Catalogue* no.86.

146) Leiden KVB 93
H. 7.5 cm.

Dull black-glazed body. Similar to Catalogue entry No.144 above; the spout is thinner and shorter, the foot higher.
Date: Second quarter of the fourth century B.C.

Bibl.: Holwerda, *Catalogue* no.87.

LEKANIS, LYKINIC SHAPE (147-152, pls.4/9/111-112)

147) Leiden KVB 7 (Cyrene) (pl.111,1)
H. (inc. lid) 8.1 cm; D. (of body at rim) 6.1 cm.; D. (of body) 7.2 cm (inc. rim 10.5 cm).

Intact, gloss flaked off all over the body and lid except for resting surface of foot. Chipping in places. Thin-walled neck, as with body. Lid: nearly flat top, faintly convex, with vertical sides, fitting over rim of bowl. Flat, disc-like projection on top, profile-moulding at base of dome of 'mushroom'. The knob is high and stemmed, with raised band around bottom. Body: shallow, rounded bowl with slightly incurved rim, ledged on outside to receive lid. Two high swing-handles attached horizontally to belly, twisted sharply upwards and flattened on top with slight inwards twist. Low, heavy flaring foot with moulding at base.
Date: First quarter of the fourth century B.C.

Bibl.: Kern, *Oudheidkundige* pl.5,2.

148) London BM 66. 4-15.30 (pl.4,3 111,2)

See Catalogue entry No.147 above.

149) London BM 68. 0.20-135

See Catalogue entry No.147 above. No lid.

150) Apollonia Inv. 66-459 (Apollonia) (pl.112,1)
H. 0.38 m (to top of bowl); D. 0.078 m (inc. handles).

The knob of the lid is a standard type, flattened sphere surmounted by a disc and divided into two by a horizontal groove. At the base of the stem is a jog. The inset rim inclines inwards to receive the lid. Body with swing handles. High moulded foot. Black-glazed (partly flaking) except for the resting surface of the foot and a band between foot and body, which are reserved.
Date: 375-350 B.C.

Bibl.: White, in Humphrey (ed.) *Apollonia, The Port of Cyrene*, pl.21,e.

151) Apollonia Inv. 65-214 (Apollonia)
H. 0.85 m (inc. handles).

Glaze worn and badly flaking. The knob of the lid is stepped. The inset rim inclines inwards to receive lid. High swing handle, high moulded foot. Black-glazed, apparently by dipping, except for the resting surface and lower edges of the foot.
Date: 375-350 B.C.

Bibl.: White, in Humphrey (ed.) *Apollonia, The Port of Cyrene*, pl.24,d.

Pyre Type

152) London BM 66.4-15.104 (pl.9,1)

Convex lid and wall, decorated with horizontal groove knob in degrees on short stem. Heavy flaring disc foot with broad surface.
Date: 375-350 B.C.

FEEDER (153-155, pls.112-113)

153) Apollonia Inv. 65-162 (Apollonia) (pl.112,2)
H. 0.056 m; D. 0.029 m (of base).

Globular form body, the top of which slants upwards towards the central hole. Short broad stem and solid foot with heavy disc base. Broad vertical ring handle attached to the body. Narrow tapering spout at 90 degrees to the handle. On the top four irregular series of concentric arches (palmette cores), formed by alternating reserved and glazed bands.
Date: Mid-fourth century B.C.
Cf.: For a very similar example from the Black Sea area, see Gaidukjewitsch, *Nekropoli bosporskich gorodow*, 35, Fig.12. *Olynthus* XIII, nos.479-80. Hayes, *Ontario*, no.267, p.165 for palmette core decoration. *ARV* 1522 (1), Vienna 155, *CVA*, pl.32 (2,3) and (2), Vienna 95, *CVA*, pl.33 (5).

Bibl.: White, in Humphrey (ed.) *Apollonia, The Port of Cyrene*, pl.20,f.

154) Leiden KVB 21 (pl.113,1-2)

Gloss flaked off all over the body, buffed clay. Broad rounded body with wide flattened incurved rim. Short broad-stemmed foot, rudely shaped, with heavy disc base, concave underneath. Broad, vertical loop handle on body, narrow tapering tubular spout. Belly, outside of foot and handle glazed. Top reserved, bearing a row of six painted spiral hooks, springing from the lip.
Date: Late fourth century B.C.

Bibl.: Holwerda, *Catalogue*, no.92. Kern, *Mnemosyne*, 4 sev.10 (1957), 17, Figs.1-2.

155) Sèvres Inv. 9519,10 (Euhesperides)
H. 0.055 m; D. 0.025 m.

See Catalogue entry No.154.
Date: Late fourth century B.C.

Bibl.: *CVA* Sèvres, pl.43 (30 and 32).

PANATHENAIC PRIZE AMPHORAE

The Sixth Century Types

1) **A Fragment of a Panathenaic Amphora** (Cyrene Museum) (pl.114,1)

A portion of the picture on the reverse of the vase. The scene represents two wrestlers. Both are of the heavy athletic type, standing foot to foot.

An early amphora, perhaps painted in the early years of the last quarter of the 6th century B.C. The style of drawing is similar to that of the Euphilletos Painter (cf. for the reverse of this vase in Munich, Antikensammlungen 1453 (from Vulci), *ABV* 322 and Boardman, *ABFV*, no.298).

Date: 520 B.C.

Bibl.: White, Libya Antiqua 8 (1971), pl.XIXIV,b.

2) **A Fragment of a Panathenaic Amphora** (Cyrene Museum) (pl.114,2)

A small part of the picture from the reverse of the amphora. What is left of the scene represents a four-horse chariot race. The feet of the hind legs and the wheels remain. It is not easy to recognize the painter from such a small fragment, however this must belong to the later years of the last quarter of the sixth century, or early fourth century B.C. Four-horse chariots are frequently represented in a similar way in this period (cf. *CVA* London 1, pl.3 (27) 29-b).

Date: 520 B.C.

Bibl.: White, *Libya Antiqua* 8 (1971), pl.XIXIV,b.

The Fifth Century Types

3) **Panathenaic Amphora** (Tolmeita Museum) from Aslaia (El-Merj)
H. 68.5 cm (including lid) (pl.115,1-2)

This is a typically late archaic Panathenaic amphora, with long body and short neck. The body of the vase has some flaking as a result of the action of the oil it contained in ancient times. It is, however, possible to detect the thick orange slip added to the body of the pot.

The body is stout and squat with echinus mouth and flat top reserved. Ring at juncture of neck and body. Round small handles, oval in section and torus foot replacing the echinus one. Slight flare in body above foot. Layers above foot. The neck of the vase has a chain of double palmettes on each side, while alternating black and purple tongues appear on the upper part of the shoulder.

Side A) Athena advancing to the left with one heel raised from the ground. She is flanked by two Doric columns topped with cockerels. She wears two garments, the lower of which has many folds. Her Attic helmet consists of a frontlet, neck piece, and is decorated with floral ornaments. The crest overlaps the neck ornaments so that Athena appears taller than on the earliest Panathenaics. Her aegis is covered with scales and framed with snakes. The device on the round shield is Pegasus, the winged horse. In front of Athena, close to the column on the left, is the inscription ΤΩΝΑΘΗΝΗΘΕΝΑΘΛΩΝ ("A prize from the games at Athens"). Added white for Athena's flesh, the details of her dress, the edge of the shield (and the blazon on it), and the plumage of both cockerels. Added purple on the helmet and the edge of the dress, and in dots around the shields' rims. The dress decoration is very carefully done.

Side B) A boy, about to throw a discus, stands between a flute-player on the left and a judge on the right. The flute-player is clad in a foldless chiton, the accepted costume for musicians. There are added white dots around the bottom edge of the flute-player's garment, added purple on both his and the judge's beard, on bands on both their heads, and on the hem of the judge's robe.

This vase has already been attributed by Vickers to the Kleophrades Painter (Vickers, *Lib. Antiq.* (1971), p.94) chiefly by the way the anatomical details (side 2) have been drawn; they compare especially well to other examples of the artist's work (cf. Lo Porto, *Atti e Memorie della Societa Magna Greciae* VIII (1967), 75, and particularly his Panathenaic amphora in Munich, Staatliche Antikensammlungen inv. no.1456, *ABV* 404). It appears that this is probably one of the earliest vases by this artist, whose trade mark on Athena's shield is Pegasus (Beazley, *The Development*, 94).

Date: *c.* 480 B.C.

Bibl.: Vickers and Reynolds, *AR* (1971-72), 38, Fig.14a-b. Vickers, *Lib. Antiq.* 8 (1971), 74, p.15, pl.XXVII a-b, pl.XXVIII a.

4) **Panathenaic Amphora** (Cyrene Museum) (pl.116,2)

This vase was found by a nomad shepherd before 1925 in the surrounding countryside of Barce (El-Merj) and then sold to the Italian authorities for keeping in the town hall at Barce. It disappeared during the last war.

The vessel was attributed to the Berlin Painter (*ABV* 408/11). The subject on side B is a foot race, and we suspect that the device on Athena's shield to be a 'gorgoneion', a favourite device of the artist (Beazley, *The Development*, 95). Comparable to our vase is the artist's further Panathenaic vessel, once in the collection of the Marquess of Northampton at Castle Ashby (*CVA* 9, pls.17,1-2,61,13). Side B on this represents, as with ours, a foot race. Four tall figures compete in a long-distance race. The runners in our vase compete in a short race; this is evident from the way they run, all of them having high leg actions and fast arm movements. On both vases, as in real life, the arm/leg movements are diagonal; the upper parts of the figures are in three-quarter view. Perhaps even closer to our example is the same artist's other vase in Berlin; the poses of the sprinters are identical (Berlin, Staatlich Museum 1832. *ABV* 408 and Boardman, *ABFV* 302).

Date: 480-475 B.C.

Bibl.: Ghislanzoni, *Not. Arch.* 1 (1915), 46-50, Figs.21-22. Beazley *ABV*, 408-11. Luni, *Quaderni* 8 (1976), 262, Fig.31.

5) **Panathenaic Amphora** (Cyrene Museum) (pl.116,3)

Early fifth-century Panathenaic amphora with long body and short neck. It is stout and squat, with an inverted echinus foot but smaller handle. The neck has a chain of double palmettes, while alternating black and purple tongues appear on the upper part of the shoulder.

This vase is also attributed to the Berlin Painter (Beazley, *Paralipomena* 177/12 and p.168). The subject on side B is a foot race. Very similar to this vessel is the Panathenaic by the same artist in Berlin (Berlin, Staatlich Museum 1832 (from Nola). *ABV* 408/4). There are four athletes on each vase, competing over a short distance race. The composition and spacing of the figures are identical on vases, where the two central athletes are close and partly overlapping with one slightly ahead of the other. The placement of the front and rear figures is also the same, but the front racer strides forward, stretching himself to the limit. The upper part of the figure is in three-quarter view.

Date: 480-475 B.C.

Bibl.: Beazley, *ARV* 408. Idem, *Paralip.* 177/12, 618. Luni, *Quaderni* 262, Fig.32.

6) **Panathenaic Amphora** (Berlin, inv. 3979) (pl.117,2)
H. 64 cm.

Echinus mouth, top flat. Ring at junction of neck and body. Round handles, flattish-oval in cross section. Torus foot, palmette-lotus chain on neck. Alternating red and black tongues between neck and panel. The tongues are separated from the fillet at the junction of the neck and body by a black stripe. Red is used for the alternative tongues, white for Athena's flesh, the shield device, and the garments of the charioteers. Relief lines are evident on the horses, chariot, and details of the charioteer.

Side A) Athena advances to left with one heel raised from the ground between two Doric columns, surmounted by cockerels. She wears a chiton and richly decorated ependytes (peplos), with crosses within squares. She also wears the aegis and a high-crested Attic helmet. In her right hand she holds a spear that crosses behind her head at the level of the eyes, pointing in the same direction. The surface of the vase is too pitted and damaged to see the inner details, but one would expect that she might wear a necklace and also a bracelet on her right wrist. In her left ear lobe there might well be a ring-shaped earring. She carries a round shield with a wreath device on her left arm.

Side B) A racing chariot scene. A bearded charioteer wears a long white, belted chiton. He holds the reins in both hands and the whip in his right. The horses are shown at full gallop, with all forefeet off the ground. Both outside horses are ahead of the inner ones. For comparison with our side B, see side B on an amphora in Malibu by the Kleophrades Painter (Frel, *JPG* 4 (1977), 70f., Fig.19).

Date: First quarter of the fifth century B.C.

Bibl.: Neugebauer, 83. Brauchitsch, 46ff., no.87. Schmidt, *Arch. Kunst* 73, pls.2.1 and 3.1. Smets, *L'Antiq. Class.* 5 (1936), 94.

7) **Panathenaic Amphora** London, BM.1903-2-17.1 (Benghazi) (pl.118,1-3)
H. 57 cm.

Echinus mouth, top flat. Ring at junction of neck and body. Round handles, flattish-oval in cross section. Torus foot. On the neck is a double-palmette pattern. On the shoulder, above front panel, a tongue pattern between neck and panel. Above base a ray pattern.

Side A) Figure of Athena strides left, holding a round shield in her left hand, a poised spear in her right. Her face, hands and feet are painted white. Incised vertical lines, rosettes and crosses in purple are used to show the texture and design of her garment. On the shield is a Nike device, with a long sash held in both hands. The crest of Athena's helmet extends up into the tongue pattern. Doric columns with cockerels flank the goddess. The painted inscription ΤΩΝΑΘΗΝΗΘΕΝΑΘΛΩΝ on the column facing the goddess is to be read from top to bottom, with the bases of the inscription towards the column (stoichedon). Purple was used on alternate tongues at the top of the panel and for the bird.

Side B) The scene is a "quintain" game (αφ' ἵππου ἀκοντίξειν). The word in English can refer to the game itself, the "jousting" post used, or the "target" or object attached to the post. This is a form of sport found represented on a number of black- as well as red-figure vases (Gardiner, *JHS* 27 (1907), 270f. Sparkes, *Ant. Kunst* 2 (1977), 8-25. Beck, *Album of Greek Education*, 29.

This vase was attributed, together with another three vases, to the Kuban Group (Beazley, *ABV* 411, 1. *AJA* (1943), 453-54. Peters, *Studien zu den Panathenaisch*, 97-99). The other three have the "tyrant slayers" as shield device. This is not the only Panathenaic with a quintain game as subject. There is another example coming from the fourth century B.C. (entry No.14), and here the shield device is a Nike. It is also smaller than usual and with an earlier date.

Date: 414-403 B.C.

Bibl.: Gardiner, *JHS* 27 (1907), pl.20. Idem, *Greek Athletic Sports and Festivals*, 357, Fig.12,1. London, *CVA* I, pl.1 (31) 1a-b. *ABV* 411, 1. *Addenda*, 53. Boardman, *ABFV*, Fig.304,1. Beck, *Album of Greek Education*, pl.41, 220 (8). Swaddling, *Olympic Games*, 53, above (B). Yalouris, *Athletics*, 301, Fig.105 BJ.

8) **Panathenaic Amphora** London, BM B 606 (Tocra) (pl.118,1-3)
H. 67 cm.

A melon-like form. Echinus mouth, top flat. Ring at junction of neck and body. Round handles, flattish-oval in cross section. Torus foot. On the neck there is a double-palmette pattern. Tongue pattern on shoulder and above base.

Side A) Figure of Athena strides to the left, holding a circular shield in her left hand, and poised spear in her right. Her face, hands and feet are white. She wears a helmet, earrings, necklaces and bracelets. The aegis and her elaborate dress are decorated with star-like flowers. On the lower hem of the dress there is a frieze of dancing girls between a wave pattern. They are painted in white, picked out with yellow on a black ground. Athena's shield device is a mask, probably a 'gorgoneion', surrounded with many rays (or it is a star device in white). The crest of Athena's helmet extends up into the tongue pattern. Doric columns with cockerels flank the goddess. The painted inscription ΤΩΝΑΘΗΝΗΘΕΝΑΘΛΩΝ on the column facing the goddess is to be read from top to bottom, with the bases of the letters inscribed towards the column (stoichedon).

Side B) A charioteer drives a *quadriga* at full speed from left to right; the foremost of the horses has one forefoot advancing just beyond the finish post, which is represented by a white stake; the hair of the charioteer is short, it streaks out behind him, blown by the wind, an attempt to convey the impression of speed. The charioteer wears a white chiton. He holds the reins in both hands, the whip in the right. The horses' collars and elements of their bridles are ornamented with white studs; over their noses they wear metallic nosebands.

This is one of the few vases attributed to the Kuban group, so called after an example found in this district of southern Russia.

Date: 402 B.C.

Bibl.: BM B 606. Brauchitsch, 48, Fig.306. Schmidt 427, *CVA* London 1, pl.1 (31), 292b. Beazley, *Develop.*, 96. *ABV* 411/3. Idem, *Para.* 177. Idem, *Addenda* 52. Shefton, *HGVP* 315, no.8. Swaddling, *Olympic Games*, 67 (B). Simon and Hirmer, pl.234.

9) **Panathenaic Amphora** London, BM B 605 (Tocra) (pl.120,1-2)
H. 72.5 cm.

Melon-like form, with flowing mouth (echinus shape), raised fillet at the junction between neck and body. Round handles, flattish-oval in cross section. Torus foot. Signs of faulty firing on lower part. A double-palmette pattern on the neck, and tongue pattern on the shoulder. Ray pattern above the base.

Side A) Figure of Athena strides to the left, holding a circular shield in her left hand and a poised spear in her right. Her face, hands and feet are white. She wears a helmet, earring, necklace, bracelet, and aegis. Her elaborate dress is decorated with flowers and myrtle branches. Purple has been used for the border of the overfall of her dress and for the tongues on her shoulder. On her shield is a group representing the Tyrannicides, the statues of Harmodios and Aristogeiton by the sculptors Kritios and Nesiotes. The crest of Athena's helmet extends up into the tongue pattern. Doric columns with cockerels flank the goddess. The painted inscription ΤΩΝΑΘΗΝΗΘΕΝΑΘΛΩΝ on the column facing the goddess is to be read from top to bottom, with the bases of the letters inscribed towards the column (stoichedon).

Side B) This is a scene representing a pentathlon competition; an athlete is ready to throw. He is watched by a clothed judge who stands to the left, holding a palm branch in his right hand. Another athlete stands behind, waiting to take his turn.

The choice of Tyrant-slayers as emblem on Athena's shield has been connected with the expulsion of the Tyrants from Athens in 403 B.C. This amphora, therefore, is thought to have been offered in the Panathenaic of 402 B.C.

Bibl.: BM B 605. Brauchitsch, 49-50, Fig.11, p.4a, Fig.11. Schmidt 89, *CVA* London 1, pl.2 (32). Süsserott, 77, pl.1,3 (for dating). Beazley, *Develop.*, 96. *ABV* 411/4. Idem, *Para.* 177. Idem, *Addenda* 52. Part of A. *E.A.A.* 1, 668. Shefton, *HGVP* 315, pl.XXVIII (A). Corbet, *JHS* 85 (1965), 18, pl.Va,b. Simon and Hirmer, pl.1i (A).

10) **Panathenaic Amphora** Tolmeita (Ptolemais) Hildesheim (Pelizaeus Museum) Inv. 1254 from Ptolemais (pls.121,1-2; 122,1-2)
H. 67 cm.

The upper part has been reassembled from several pieces, but apart from very insignificant mends to the foot and neck all remains of the vessel are antique.

Panathenaic amphora with flaring mouth, raised fillet at the junction between neck and body, round handles, convex foot. Double-palmette pattern on neck, tongue pattern on shoulder, ray pattern above base

Side A) Athena strides to the left holding a circular shield in the left hand and a poised spear in her right. Her face, hands and feet are white. She wears a garment with incised vertical lines, zig-zag and star patterns in white. Her aegis is covered with scales and framed with snakes. White paint is also used for the seams and fringe border hanging down from the garment. She also wears a helmet with high crest that extends up into the tongue pattern. The tip of the crest hangs down behind her right arm. The helmet has a neck protector which goes down quite far with an engraved spiral pattern. She carries a large, round shield, the border of which has seven bosses painted in white. The shield device is the Tyrannicides, the statues of Harmodios and Aristogeiton by the sculptors Kritios and Nesiotes (see note to Entry No.2 on BM B 605), painted here in white. Two columns with cockerels flank the goddess. The painted inscription next to the column on the left reads: (ΤΩΝΑΘΗΝΗΘΕΝΑΘΛΩΝ) (painted in stoichedon).

Side B) A victorious charioteer drives a *quadriga* at full speed from left to right, passing the winning post that is painted white. The charioteer's garment is also in white. He is painted stooping forward, holding the reins in both hands as the horses gallop forward, in an attempt to capture the impression of speed. This perhaps explains the fact that the chariot's wheels are not on the same ground level as the legs of the horses. The rims of the eight-spoke wheels are drawn with compasses, as is the shield of Athena on Side A. The inner details of the chariot, and the horses, are all engraved.

Date: 403 B.C.

Bibl.: *AA* (1919), 79, Fig.2 and p.86, b. *JdI* 57 (1949), 145, Fig.1 and pp.150-1, Figs.4-5. *ABV* 412/1.

11) **Panathenaic Amphora** Hildesheim (Pelizaeus Museum) Inv. 1253 from Ptolemais (pls.123,1-3)
H. 68.5 cm.

Panathenaic amphora with flaring mouth, raised fillet at junction between neck and body, round handles, convex foot, with deep groove directly below upper edge. On neck a double-palmette pattern, tongue pattern on shoulder, ray pattern above base.

Side A) Athena strides left holding a circular shield in her left hand and a poised spear in her right. She wears a double wrist-ring on her arm in brown colour. Her face, hand and feet are in white. She (like her counterpart on Entry No.10) wears a garment with vertical lines, and zig-zag and star patterns in white. Her aegis is covered with scales and framed with snakes. She also wears a helmet with a high crest. Both extend up into the tongue pattern. She holds a large, round shield, the border of which has six bosses painted in white. The shield device is the Tyrannicides, the statues of Harmodios and Aristogeiton by the sculptors Kritios and Nesiotes, painted here in white. Two columns with cockerels flank the goddess. The painted inscription next to the column on the left is as Entry No.10 (painted in stoichedon).

Side B) A foot race. Three youths compete in a short distance sprint. They are painted in a rhythmic style with the two athletes on the outside stretching out their arms horizontally while the central figure raises his left arm vertically. They run to the right, their feet not touching the ground. They are depicted here in three-quarter view, in traditional style with left leg and left arm advanced, and showing a diagonal arm/leg movement.

Date: Late fifth century B.C.

Bibl.: *AA* (1919), 79, Fig.1 and p.86, c. *JdI* 57 (1949), 145, Fig.2 and p.153, Figs.7. *ABV* 412/2.

These two vases appear to be by the same hand. This is clear from the treatment of the folds of Athena's garment and the decorative elements of it. The inscription is also written in the same manner.

Both vases have no Archon inscription, but we should find no difficulty in dating them. From the shape and style of the painting (they also share the same shield device) there is a close resemblance to the Kuban Group and so they are likely to have been painted in the same year (402 B.C.), but by a different hand.

12) **Panathenaic Amphora** (Cyrene Museum) (pl.124,1-2)

Panathenaic amphora with flaring mouth, raised fillet at junction between neck and body, round handles, convex foot. On neck a double-palmette pattern, tongue pattern on shoulder, ray pattern above base.

Side A) Athena strides to the left holding a circular shield in her left hand and a poised spear in her right. Her face, hand and feet in white. She wears a helmet, the crest of which extends up into the tongue pattern. She wears a chiton with simple folds and the aegis on it. There is no device on her shield. Doric columns, topped with cockerels, flank the goddess. Next to the left column there is the inscription (in stoichedon): ΤΩΝ[ΑΘΗΝΗΘΕΝΑΘΛΩΝ].

Side B) A foot race. Three youths compete in a short distance sprint. They are painted in a rhythmic style. They run to the right, their feet not touching the ground. They are depicted here in three-quarter view, in traditional style with left leg and left arm advanced, and showing a diagonal arm/leg movement.

The style of painting of the young athletes is very similar to those painted in the Hildesheim Vase (inv. 1253). Only three athletes are shown on each of them. The central figure on both vases shows the upper half of the body drawn in three-quarter view, the arms and legs stretched in a similar fashion.

Bibl.: Luni, *Quaderni* 8 (1976), 26, Fig.27.

The Fourth Century Types

13) **Miniature Panathenaic Amphoriskos** London, BM B 602 (pl.125,1-2)
H. 15cm.

The shape is that of a Panathenaic amphora, but miniature in size, with slightly flaring mouth, hip panels, lower part of the pot and the flaring foot all in black glaze. No palmette design on the neck and no tongues on the shoulder or foot.

Side A) Athena moves to the left, between two Doric columns, holding a spear in her left hand and a shield, shown obliquely, in her right. Her front, head, part of the shield, and the cockerel on the column opposite, are all painted on the amphora shoulder.

Side B) Two athletes are shown exercising (pentathlon?). The figure on the right holds a discus in his right hand, about to throw. The left athlete, shown in profile, is holding a javelin and he, too, is poised ready to throw.

Date: Early fourth century B.C.

Bibl.: London *CVA* 1. *CVA* British Museum 1 (1), pl.5,5. Beazley, *BSA* 40 (1940-45), 10, no.24.

14) **Panathenaic Amphora** Berlin inv. 3980 (pls.126,1 and 127,1-2)
H. 66.5 cm.

The surface damage and the foot are modern. Echinus flaring mouth, raised fillet at junction of neck and body, round handles, flattish-oval in cross section. Torus foot, palmette-lotus chain on neck. Alternating red and black tongues between neck and panel. Red is used for the alternating tongues, white for Athena's flesh.

Side A) Athena strides to the left between two Doric columns, surmounted by a male figure wrapped only to the waist down in a himation and carrying a large cornucopia in the left hand. The goddess wears a richly decorated chiton with incised vertical lines in a zig-zag pattern in white. She holds a circular shield in her left hand and a spear poised in her right. Her face, hands and feet are in white. Her face, hands and feet are in white, she also wears a helmet with a high crest that extends up into the tongue pattern, with its tip suspended from the right arm. Because the surface of the amphora is badly damaged there is no trace of the shield device. Next to the left column there is the inscription (in stoichedon): ΤΩΝΑΘΗΝΗΘΕΝΑΘΛΩΝ. Next to the right column there is a part inscription ending [ ]ΕΡΧΕΝ. Only one name, Philocles, can be made out.

Side B) A quintain scene. Two riders move to the right, each wears a short tunic, Attic helmet, and long boots. Both horses show the same style of movement. Between the riders there is a pole fixed vertically into the ground with a shield attached to it in three-quarter view. The left rider advances towards the pole and readies his javelin to hurl it at the shield. The other rider has past the pole, having already thrown his weapon but missed it. His javelin can be seen in the ground. (Cf. Side B on Entry No.8.)

Date: 392/1 B.C.

Cf.: For inscription, Süsserott, *Griechen Plastik*, p.74, n.157.

Bibl.: Neugebauer, 83. Brauchitsch, *Die Panathenaischen*, p.51f., no.83. Schmidt, *Archaistische Kunst*. Smets, *L'Antique Class.* 5 (1936), 97. Süsserott, *Griechen Plastik*, 72. Beazley, *Develop.*, 97. Sparkes, *Antike Kunst.* 20 (1977), 11, pl.5,3-4. Eschbach, *Statuen auf Panathenaischen* (Kat. 12), pl.5-6 (inscription and report).

15) **Panathenaic (fragment)** Alexandria inv.18239 (Benghazi) (pl.128,1-2)
H. 52 cm.

An amphora with flaring mouth, raised fillet at junction of neck and body, round handles, convex foot. On the neck a double-palmette pattern. Tongue pattern above the fight scene. Mouth, handles, lower part of body, and foot are all glazed black. Top of mouth reserved.

Side A) Athena strides to the left, holding a circular shield in her left hand and a poised spear in her right. Her face, hands and feet are white. She wears a helmet, the crest of which extends up into the tongue pattern. She wears a chiton and aegis. The shield device cannot be made out, nor can we be certain of the symbols on the column. Two figures are holding a Nike. The one on the left is probably Athena. Next to the left column is the inscription: (ΦΡΑΣΙΚΛΕΙΔΗΣ ΑΡΧΩΝ and next to the right one: [ ]ΝΑΘΗΝΗΘΕΝΑΘΛΩΝ.

This is one of the three Panathenaic prize amphorae Beazley assigned to the Astios Group (Beazley, *ABV* 412), the other two being Oxford 572 (CVA Oxford 3, 2 pl.28,4-7. From Athens and inscribed with the Archon's name, Asteios), and the Detroit vase (cf. Entry No.16 below).

The Alexandria vase from Benghazi bears the name of the Archon, Phrasikleides (371-70 B.C.)(Breccia, *Iscrizioni greche e latine*, 233, no.526. Peters, *op.cit.*, p.145), but this may well be by a different hand to the rest of the group.

Cf.: For inscription, Smets, *L'Ant. Class.* 5 (1936), 99.

Bibl.: Schefold, *UKV*, Figs.46-7. *ABV* 412/3. Smets, *L.Ant. Class.* 5 (1936), 97. Schmidt, *Archaistische Kunst.*, 87. Eschbach, *Statuen auf Panathenaischen* (Kat. 15), p.29f.

16) **Panathenaic Amphora** Detroit Institute of Arts 50.193 (Benghazi) (pl.129,1-4)
H. (including lid) 84.6 cm.

Flaring mouth, raised fillet at the junction of neck and body, round handles, convex foot with deep groove directly below the upper edge. The hem of Athena's chiton is retouched, incision of figures of the runners appears to have been emphasized in white paint. The lid does not seem to belong to the vase. Decoration in black glaze on orange ground. Mouth, handles, lower part of body, and foot are all glazed black. Top of mouth reserved, a double lotus and palmette frieze. Long, black, enclosed tongues. Pictures set in panels, framed by dilute glazed lines. The black-glazed lid is surmounted by a knob above a raised fillet; the edge and the interior of the lid are reserved.

Side A) Athena strides to the left holding a circular shield in her left hand and a poised spear in her right. Her face, hands and feet are painted white. She wears a helmet, the crest of which extends up into the tongue position. She wears a chiton and aegis. The device on Athena's shield is a scarcely visible floral wreath surrounding a small quatrefoil. Doric columns with figures of bearded men flank the goddess. Each of these figures is draped from the waist down in a himation. They hold a cornucopia drinking horn in the left hand and a thrysos in the right. The painted inscription is: ΤΟΝΑΘΕΝΕΘΕΝΑΘΛΟΝ, the letters reading from the top down, with the bases of the letters towards the column.

Side B) A foot race scene. Four youths compete in a short-distance sprint. The painting is in a rhythmic style and stereotype poses suggest the act of running: the left arm and left are advanced. A similar representation appears on the Panathenaic amphora in New York by the Kittos Group (*Para.* p.177 below, no.3). On both vases the artists show diagonal arm/leg movements.

The important, fourth-century B.C. innovation of inscribing the Archon's name Panathenaics does not apply to the Detroit vase. This is unusual but there are other examples (cf. the British Museum vessel by the potter, Kittos). They may have been intended as competition samples, or as souvenirs of the Games, rather than as actual prizes.

We also know that the cockerel motifs disappear in the fourth century, or at the time of the introduction of the Archons' inscriptions. They are replaced on column tops by symbols, small designs often representing a statue, which change from year to year and thus serve as clues in the dating process.

The symbols on our Panathenaic do not appear to be gods, but rather magistrates holding the attributes of divinities. If so, then the thrysos of Dionysos and the cornucopia could be a reference to Demeter. If the cornucopia is intended to represent a drinking horn, then Dionysos himself might be invoked. It has been suggested that the figures might be associated with the Eleusinian Mysteries, which were under the control of the Athenians at the time. A Panathenaic amphora in New York by the Kittos Group, referred to above, and dated by its Archon inscription to 367/66 B.C., also has symbols that refer to Eleusis. On the Doric columns are small figures of Triptolemos seated in a winged chariot drawn by snakes. The symbol on the name-piece of the Asteios Group is a Nike holding the stern of a trireme, referring perhaps to Athens.

Bibl.: ABV 412,3. Bell, in Moon, *Greek Vase Painting*, no.125. Eschbach, *Statuen auf Panathenaischen* (Kat. 10), p.18f. puts it with Berlin no.14, the time of Philocles (393/2 B.C.), based on the symbols.

17) Panathenaic Amphora British Museum, BM 604 (Tocra) (pl.130,1-3)
H. 71.3 cm.

Panathenaic amphora with flaring mouth, raised fillet at junction of neck and body, round handles, convex foot with deep groove directly below upper edge. Mouth, handles, lower part of body, and foot are glazed black. A double-lotus and palmette frieze on neck above figure scene, long, black, enclosed tongue.

Side A) Athena strides to the left holding a circular shield in her left hand and a poised spear in her right. Her face, hands and feet are painted white. She wears a necklace, and a more elaborate helmet with crest extends up into the tongue pattern. Her costume is very plain, with simple folds. The device on Athena's shield is a 16-rayed star, between each pair of which is a white spot. Doric columns flank her, each with a seated Triptolemos on top. He sits in his winged chariot with a serpent at his side. He has long hair with a white wreath and a himation over his lower limbs. In one hand he holds two ears of corn. The left column inscription reads:**Τ**ΟΝΑΘΕΝΕΘΕΝΑΘΛΟΝ and the right one: ΚΙΤΤΟΣΕΓΟΙΗΣΕΝ. The writing is now for the first time in 'kionedon', i.e. the letters are to be read horizontally, instead of lengthwise.

Side B) Two athletes engage in a bout of 'pancration' (a combination of boxing and wrestling), watched by two spectators, a nude athlete on the right and a judge on the left. The athlete extends his right hand towards the combatants, as if to encourage one of them. The judge wears a himation wound around the lower half of his body and draped over his left arm. His hair is crowned with an olive wreath painted white. He holds a palm spray in his right hand.

The importance of this vessel rests in that it bears the name of the potter, 'Kittos'. It does not, however, carry the name of the Archon. This may have been a competition sample. The representation of Athena, on the other hand, shows it to be close to the Archonship of Polyzelos (367/6 B.C.), from which date several Panathenaics have been preserved. On these examples several minor changes occur. The form becomes more elegant, especially the mouth and foot, and the traditional rays at the base disappear.

Cf.: For the Polyzelos Group, *AJA* 1943, pp.455-56. A of The Hearst Panathenaic 61 57, p.149.

Bibl.: Brauchitsch, *Die Panath.*, no.86. Peters, *JdI* 57 (1942), 145. Smets, *L'Antique Class.* 5 (1936), 98. Gardner, *Greek Athl. and Sport*, 442. Süsserott, pl.3,3 and pl.12,1. Beazley, *Develop.*, pl.46,4 and pl.47,1. *ABV* 413, (i), 1. *CVA* London 1 (32), pl.2, 1-4. Eschbach, *Statuen auf Panathenaischen* (Kat. 17), p.30ff.

18) **Panathenaic Prize Amphora** Brussels, Musée Roy, A 1703 (Benghazi) (pl.131,1-3)
H. with lid, 93 cm or 85.5 cm, without lid, 73 cm.

A Panathenaic amphora with flaring mouth and top flat. Raised fillet at junction of neck and body, round handles, flattish-oval in cross section. Torus foot with deep groove directly below upper edge. Body restored. Glazed black mouth, handles, broad band between picture panel and tongue panel on Side B, lower part of body, and foot. On the neck a double-lotus and palmette frieze. Below this a black, enclosed tongue panel. The lid is surmounted by a conical knob above a ring.

Side A) Athena strides towards the left. In her right hand she holds a spear that crosses diagonally behind her head. In her left hand she holds a circular shield. Its device, probably a star, has faded and no trace of it remains. Athena wears a chiton and ependytes, the aegis with a scale and snake borders. On her head she has a high, crested, Attic helmet with a plum reaching down to her shoulder. She is presented between two Doric columns surmounted by the figure of Triptolemos, seated in his winged chariot and drawn by snakes. In one hand he holds two ears of corn. Next to the left column is the inscription (kionedon): ΤΟΝΑΘΕΝΕΘΕΝΑΘΛΟΝ, and next to the right hand column: ΓΟΛΥΙΗΛΟΣΑΡΧΩΝ.

Side B) A foot race with three nude athletes running to the right. They have their left hands extended in front and their right hands shown behind them. None of their feet touch the ground.

Attributed by Beazley to the Kittos Group and the Archonship of Polyzelos.

Date: 367/66 B.C.

Bibl.: Brauchitsch, *Die Panath.*, 52f., no.85, Figs.12-13. Peters, *JdI* 57 (1942), 149. Smets, *L'Antique Class.* 5 (1936), 98. Beazley, *Add.*, 52. *ABV* 413, 2. *CVA* Brussels 1, pl.14 (27), 3,a-c. Eschbach, *Statuen auf Panathenaischen* (Kat. 16).

19) **Panathenaic Prize Amphora** Metropolitan Museum, New York, 56.171.6 (probably Benghazi) (pl.132,1-3)
H. with lid, 86.3 cm, without lid, 70.5 cm.

Panathenaic amphora with flaring mouth, top flat, raised fillet at junction of neck and body, round handles, flattish-oval in cross section. Torus foot, with deep groove directly below upper edge. Body restored. Black glaze on mouth, handles, broad band between picture panel and tongue panel of Side B, lower part of body, and foot. Entire neck glazed inside. On the neck a double-lotus and palmette frieze. Above the figure there are black, enclosed tongues, separated and framed by relief lines. The lid is surmounted by a conical knob above a ring. There are broad grooves above and below the ring and a chamfer at the junction of the sloping surface and the flat rim. The edge of the lid, the chamfer, and the grooves are un-glazed.

Side A) Athena strides to the left. In her right hand she holds a spear that crosses diagonally behind her head. In her left hand she holds a circular shield; its device is an incised star with sixteen rays. The goddess wears a chiton and ependytes ornamented with white. Her aegis has scales and borders of snakes. She wears a high-crested, Attic helmet with a plume reaching down to her shoulder. Her long hair is shown as incised lines over the aegis. She is wearing a necklace made up of black-glazed dots. The figure is presented between two Doric columns surmounted by representations of Triptolemos seated in his winged chariot, drawn by snakes. In one hand he holds some ears of corn. By the left column is the inscription (kionedon): ΤΟΝΑΘΕΝΕΘΕΝΑΘΛΟΝ and by the right column: ΠΟΛΥΗΛΟΣ ΑΡΧΩΝ.

Side B) In a foot race, three nude athletes run to the right. Their left hands are extended before them, their right hands behind.

Attributed by Beazley to the Kittos Group and the Archonship of Polyzelos.

Date: 367/66 B.C.

Bibl.: Schmidt, *Archaistisch. Kunst* 82. Peters, *JdI* 57 (1942), 144f.,149, fig.3. Smets, *L'Antique Class.* 5 (1936), 98, no.104. Beazley, *AJA* 47 (1943), 458 II, no.3 and *Para.* 177. *ABV* 413, no.3. *CVA* New York 3, pl.45,1-4. Eschbach, *Statuen auf Panathenaischen* (Kat. 18), p.30ff.

20) **Panathenaic Amphora** British Museum BM B 603 (Tocra)(pl.134,1-2)
H. 64.5 cm.

Panathenaic amphora with flaring mouth, raised fillet at junction of neck and body, round handles, convex foot with deep groove directly below upper edge. Glazed black mouth, handles, lower part of body, and foot. On neck a double-lotus and palmette frieze. Long, black, enclosed tongues above figure scene.

Side A) Athena strides to the left holding a circular shield in her left hand and a poised spear in her right. Her face, hands and feet are painted white. She wears earrings, a necklace, bracelets, and the aegis. On her head is a fanciful helmet and crest that extends up into the tongue pattern. Athena's costume is quite plain with simple folds, the borders of which are painted white. The shield device is a star with sixteen rays and its rim is represented by two concentric, incised circles studded at intervals with white spots. Two Doric columns flank the goddess, surmounted by statues of Triptolemos seated in his winged chariot with a serpent on each side. He has long hair falling to his shoulders; a mantle is wrapped around the lower half of his body. In his right hand he extends an ear of corn.

The painted inscriptions are: ΤΟΝΑΘΕΝΕΘΕΝΑΘΛΟΝ by the left column and ΠΟΛΥΗΛΟΣ ΑΡΧΩΝ by the right, the officiating Archon, Polyzelos (367/66 B.C.). The inscriptions read from top to bottom, with the bases of the letters towards the left column, and the tops of the letters towards the right hand one (stoichedon).

Side B) Two athletes engaged in a bout of pankration, watched by two spectators, another nude athlete on the right and a judge on the left. The athlete holds a palm spray, but he is moving to the right and turns his head towards the wrestlers. The bearded judge also holds a palm in his right hand. He is wrapped in a himation that leaves his right arm and shoulder bare. The design on this side of the vessel is painted entirely black with incised lines.

Date: 367/66 B.C.

Bibl.: Brauchitsch, *Die Panath.*, no.84. Peters, *JdI* 57 (1942), 145. Smets, *L'Antique Class.* 5 (1936), 98. Süsserott, pl.3,4 and pl.12,2. *ABV* 414,3. *CVA* London 1, (32), pl.2.2 and 5. Eschbach, *Statuen auf Panathenaischen* (Kat. 19), p.30ff.

21) **Panathenaic Amphora** British Museum BM B 612 (Tocra)(pl.134,1-2)
H. 53 cm.

Panathenaic amphora with flaring mouth, raised fillet at junction of neck and body. Handle flattish-oval in cross section. Torus foot with deep groove directly below upper edge. Intact and in excellent condition. Glazed black mouth, handles, and broad band between picture panel and tongue panel on Side B. A frieze of lotus and palmettes on the neck, below this an enclosed tongue separated and framed by relief lines.

Side A) Athena strides to the left, holding a spear in her right hand crossed diagonally behind her head. In her left hand she holds a circular shield ornamented with eight white dots on the edge and in the centre an incised, eight-rayed star. Athena wears a chiton and ependytes reaching to the knee with white borders; the aegis has scales and snake border. On her head is a high-crested Attic helmet with plumes of an unusual length. She has long hair rendered in incised lines over the aegis. The goddess is presented between two Doric columns surmounted by rams. There are no inscriptions.

Side B) Two nude boxers with left arms extended and right fists held back at chest level ready to strike. A third youth watches; he is not wearing gloves but perhaps he waits his turn to box.

Attributed by Beazley to the Kittos Group, possibly on stylistic grounds and the design of Athena as the vessel has neither inscriptions nor dating symbols.

Date: 367-66 B.C.

Cf.: For the Kittos Group, *ABV* 413

Bibl.: Gardiner, *Greek Athl. and Sport*, 427. *Idem*, *Athletics of the Ancient World*, 427. Beazley, *AJA* 47 (1943), 456. *ABV* 414, 5.

22) **Fragment of Panathenaic Amphora** (Cyrene 717) (pl.135,1-3)
H. 52 cm.

Approximately half of the vessel only remains, and the handles and foot are missing, but we have sufficient to form a good idea of the Panathenaic and its date. It would have had a flared mouth and a raised fillet at the junction of the neck and body. On the neck there would have been a double-lotus and palmette frieze and black tongues above the figure scene.

Side A) The restored pieces of the obverse show Athena striding to the left holding her shield (shown obliquely) in the left hand and a spear (only a small part remains) in her right.

She wears a helmet and appears to be wearing a long shawl wrapped over her shoulders and then allowed to hang down, ending in a kind of swallowtail. These details are meant, perhaps, to represent an older style of painting. (The same styling appeared on another fragment from Eleusis, dated 363-62 B.C. Cf. Schmidt, *Arch. Plast.*, pl.71 and *AJA* (1943), p.457.) The goddess is flanked by two columns, the shafts of which are apparently decorated with pairs of acanthus leaves and this feature makes Panathenaics of this period unique. The symbol crowning each column is a flying Nike with a lighted torch. (For this type of column and symbols, see the examples from the Kerameikos in Frel, Panathenaic Prize Amphorae, 19-21, Figs.20-21.) Next to the left column is the painted inscription: [ΤΟΝΑΘΕΝΕΘΕΝΑΘ]ΛΟΝ and next to the right hand one: ΧΑΡΙΚΛΕΙΔΗΣ ΑΡΧΩΝ. The inscriptions are in kionedon, that is the letters are inscribed perpendicularly rather than lengthwise.

Side B) A figure is wrapped in a himation, but the right arm and shoulder are uncovered. He is, perhaps, the judge of some sporting event.

We already have a number of examples from the Archonship of Charikleides (363-62 B.C.). As well as the Cyrene fragment, there are the fragment (above) from the Kerameikos (Frel, *ibid*, Figs.20-21), the example from Eleusis (Beazley, *Develop.*, p.98, Schmidt, *ibid*, pl.7, and Peters, *JdI* 57 (1942), p.146), and nine examples from Eschbach's catalogue (27-35, pp.42-45). We associate with the period of this Archon, the innovation of the swallowtail ends to Athena's shawl and the columns, the shafts of which have pairs of acanthus leaves and the flying Nikes as symbols.

This Cyrene Panthenaic is highly significant as it is the only example on which the name of the Archon Charikleides survives complete.

Bibl.: Doubtful, reported in Luni, *Quaderni*, 260, no.3, should rather be *ABV* 715. Beazley, *Addenda*, 414, Charikleides Group No.4.

23) Pananthenaic Amphora Alexandria 18238 (Benghazi) (pl.136,1-2)
H. 60 cm.

Missing some body sections and foot, a Panathenaic amphora with flaring mouth and raised fillet at junction of neck and body. Round handles, mouth and handles glazed black. A double-lotus and palmette frieze on neck and there is an enclosed tongue pattern above figure scene.

Side A) Athena strides to the right (not to the left as with all of the previous vases). Her shield is obliquely shown, but it is the inside that is presented, thus, of course, not allowing us to see any device. In her right hand the goddess holds a poised spear (now faded). Her face and hands are painted white. She wears a shawl over her chiton. This shawl hangs low and ends in a tail of some kind. The aegis is not visible. On her head is a high-crested helmet that extends up into the tongue pattern above. The painted inscriptions on the columns are: Τ[Ο]ΝΑΘΕΝΕΘΕΝ[ΑΘΛΟΝ] and ΝΙΚΟΜΑΧΟΣ ΑΡΧΩΝ.

Nikomachos was Archon in 341-40 B.C. (Breccia, *Iscrizioni greche e latine (Catalogue général des antiquités egyptiennes du Musée d'Alexandria)*, 234, no.527 and AJA 47 (1943), 458.)

Side B) A foot race scene depicts three figures competing in a long distance event. The arms and legs move diagonally. The upper parts of the figures are in three-quarter view. The poses of the sprinters are identical.

We see with this Panathenaic a major change in painting style, especially as regards the figure of Athena, and, indeed, the group name, Nikomachos, (Archon, 341-40 B.C.) derives from this very vessel (*AJA* (1943), 457-8). Vases from this group form a series of dated Panathenaics from one single workshop active during the second half of the fourth century B.C.

The introduction of the rightwards-striding goddess figure appears to have occurred sometime between 359-58 B.C. A good example (although not the earliest one) is represented by a fragment from the Kerameikos of 348-47 B.C, inscribed 'Theophilos Archon' (Frel, *Panathenaic Prize Amphorae*, p.24, Fig.23). The preserved head faces right, according to the new layout. Another example, complete this time but later than the Alexandria find, is in Harvard (Harvard 1925, *ABV* 414, 2 36.124 (from Capua). *AJA* (1906), pl.16. Hoppin, *CVA*, pl.6. Archonship of Theophrastos, 340-339 B.C.).

Bibl.: Schefold, *UKV*, Figs.48, 49. Beazley, *ABV* 414/1. Peters, *JdI* 57 (1942), 146. Smets, *L'Antiq. Class.* 5 (1936), 94.

24) Pananthenaic Amphora Louvre MN 706 (Benghazi) (pl.137,1-3)
H. with cover, 95.5 cm, without cover, 77 cm.

A Panathenaic amphora with flaring mouth, raised fillet at junction of neck and body, round handles, convex foot with deep groove directly below upper edge. The lid is surmounted by a conical knob above a ring (cf. *CVA* Louvre 5, pl.6 (362), 1). The mouth, handles, lower part of body, and foot are glazed black. There is a double-lotus and palmette frieze on the neck, and above the figure scene is a long, black, enclosed tongue pattern.

Side A) Athena strides to the right holding an oblique shield, the inside of which is presented to the viewer. It is secured with a broad, central strap that the goddess' arm passes through, and a narrower strap she grasps with her hand. In her right hand she holds a poised spear. Her face, hands and feet are painted white. She wears a long, plain chiton with simple folds. The aegis is reduced to a mere cross-cord with a small gorgoneion in white. She has a swallowtail shawl over her shoulder. On her head is a fancifully crested helmet that extends up into the tongue pattern above. Two columns flank the goddess. The left column (surmounted by a small figure of Athena, in right profile and holding a sceptre) has the inscription next to it: ΤΩΝΑΘΗΝΗΘΕΝΑΘΛΩΝ. The right-hand column has on the top a small figure of Zeus in a himation. He is shown frontally, with right hand raised and a small Nike flying towards him. To the right of the column, on the outside, runs the inscription: ΘΕΟΦΡΑΣΤΟΣ ΑΡΧΩΝ – 'Theophrastos I, Archon' (340-39 B.C.).

Side B) An athlete appears to have just won a foot race; he is still running and holds a palm branch, the symbol of victory. Another (standing) athlete holds a palm in a relaxed fashion and looks at the judge who is wrapped in a himation; the judge approaches to this athlete's left. Another official (or athlete), wearing a cloak, holds a torch in his right hand. He is walking away to the left, perhaps to announce the victory.

Bibl.: Brauchitsch, *Die Panath. Preis.*, 59f. Smets, *L'Antiq. Class.* 5 (1936), 99. Peters, *JdI 57* (1942), 146. *CVA* Louvre 1, pl.5,8-13 (p.361), pl.6 (p.362). Süsserott, *Greich. Plastik.*, pl.10. Beazley, *AJA* (1943), 462-465. *ABV* 415/3. *CVA* Louvre 5, pl.5,8-4, pl.6,1.

25) Fragments of a Panathenaic Amphora with the same Archon's name were recovered from a tomb in Cyrene in 1911, but never published.

See Hoppin Collection, *CVA*, p.6 and Smets, *L'Antiquité Classique* 5 (1936), p.99, no.119.

26) **Panathenaic Amphora** London BM B 609 (Benghazi) (pl.138,1-3)
H. 60, 63 cm.

A Panathenaic amphora with flaring mouth, raised fillet at junction of neck and body, round handles, convex foot with deep groove directly below upper edge. The mouth, handles, lower part of body, and foot are all glazed black. A double-lotus and palmette frieze on neck and a long, enclosed black tongue pattern above figure scene.

Side A) Athena strides to the right, holding an oblique shield, the inside of which is presented to the viewer. It is secured by a central strap, through which the goddess' left arm passes, and another strap is held in her hand. In her right hand there is a poised spear (now faded). The face, hands and feet are painted white. She is wearing a long chiton with simple folds. Over the chiton, a swallowtail shawl is worn on the shoulder. On her head is the usual helmet with its fanciful crest, both extend up into the tongue pattern. Two Doric columns flank the goddess. Small figures of Athena surmount both columns. They are helmeted and clad in chiton and himation, and hold an aphlaston in their right hands. Next to the left-hand column runs the inscription: ΑΡΧΩΝ ΝΙΚΟΚΡΑΤΗΣ, 'The Archon Nikokrates', who held office in Athens in 333 B.C. On the right is the inscription: ΤΩΝΑΘΗΝΗΘΕΝΑΘΛΩΝ, 'I am one of the prizes from Athena'. Both inscriptions are arranged in kionedon.

Side B) Three tall figures compete in a long-distance foot race. Their poses are identical, with left feet advanced on the ground while the right is behind and higher. Their arms are at right angles. Their torsos are shown in three-quarter view.

Attributed by Beazley to the Nikomachos Series.

Bibl.: Gardiner, *Greek Athl. Sport*, 280. *Idem*, *Athl.*, Fig.93. Süsserot, pl.12,4. Brauchitsch, no.99. Smets, *L'Antiq. Class.* 5 (1936), 100. Peters, *JdI* 57 (1942), 1, 47. *ABV* 415, 5. Beazley, *Addenda*, 52. Boardman, *ABFV*, Fig.305. Swaddling, *Olympic Games*.

27) **Panathenaic Amphora** Sèvres 7230 (pl.139,1-2)
H. without lid, 80 cm.

A Panathenaic amphora with flaring mouth, raised fillet at junction of neck and body. Large handles project from the shoulder and join the neck. A convex foot with deep groove directly below upper edge. On the neck a double-lotus and palmette frieze. Black, enclosed tongue pattern above the figure scene.

Side A) Athena strides to the right, holding an oblique shield, the inside of which is shown to the viewer. Her left arm passes through the shield's central strap and she holds another strap in her hand. A poised spear (now faded) is in her right hand. The face, hands and feet are painted white. She wears a long chiton with simple folds. Over the chiton, a swallowtail shawl is draped across her shoulder. She also wears the usual Attic helmet with a high crest that extends into the tongue pattern above. Two Doric columns flank the goddess and they both have small Nikes on their tops (cf. Smets, *L'Antiq. Class.* 5 (1936), 100). The inscriptions are: [Τ]ΩΝΑΘΗΝΗΘΕΝΑΘΛΩΝ and Α[ΡΧΩΝ ΝΙ]ΚΗΤΗΣ.

Side B) Four athletes compete in a long-distance race.

Attribute by Beazley to the Nikomachos Series.

Date: 332-31 B.C.

Bibl.: Brauchitsch, no.101. Smets, *L'Antiq. Class.* 5 (1936) 100. Peters, *JdI* 57 (1942), 147. *ABV* 415, 6.

28) **Panathenaic Amphora** London BM B 611 (Tocra) (pl.140,1-3)
H. 78.2 cm.

A Panathenaic amphora with flaring mouth, raised fillet at junction of neck and body, round handles, convex foot with deep groove directly below upper edge. Mouth, handles, lower part of body and foot glazed black. On neck a double-lotus and palmette frieze. Long, black, enclosed tongue pattern above figure scene.

Side A) Athena strides to the right, holding an oblique shield, the inside of which is presented to the viewer. It is secured by a central strap, through which the goddess' left arm passes, and another strap is held in her hand. In her right hand there is a poised spear (now faded). The face, hands and feet are painted white. She is wearing a long chiton with simple folds. Over the chiton, a swallowtail shawl is worn on the shoulder. The borders of the shawl and the chiton are ornamented with spots and patches of white. The aegis is reduced to a mere cross-cord (partly faded) with a small gorgoneion in white. She also wears the usual helmet with its elaborate crest; both extend up into the tongue pattern. Two Ionic columns flank the goddess. On each stands a small figure of Athena looking towards the goddess in the centre. These small figures wear high-crested helmets and hold a spear upright in one hand and a figure of Nike in the other. They each wear a peplos with long girt overall and seem to have been inspired by the Athena Parthenos. Next to the left column there is the inscription: ΑΡΧΩΝ ΕΥΘΥΚΡΙΤΟΣ, 'The Archon Euthykriitos', who held office in Athens in 328-27 B.C. Next to the right column is the inscription: ΤΩΝΑΘΗΝΗΘΕΝΑΘΛΩΝ. Both inscriptions are arranged in kionedon.

Side B) A foot race with four competing athletes, shown with none of their feet touching the ground. This is perhaps a long-distance, rather than a sprint race, judging by the easy stride of the runners. They are represented here in the traditional scheme with left legs and arms advanced, showing diagonal limb movements.

For a close parallel see the amphora in the Hermitage, Leningrad (inv. AKB 45), found in a tomb near Kerch (Sokolov, *Antique Art on the Northern Black Sea Coast*, 56, no.41).

Our vase is attributed by Beazley to the Nikomachos Series and dated 328-27 B.C., to the Archonship of Euthykritos.

Bibl.: Brauchitsch, no.102. Smets, *L'Antiq. Class.* 5 (1936), 100. Peters, *JdI* (1942), 147. *ABV* 415, 7.

29) **Panathenaic Amphora** Berlin Inv. 3981 (pl.141)
H. 62.5 cm.

A Panathenaic amphora with flaring mouth, raised fillet at junction of neck and body, long handles that spring from the neck and vertically join the shoulder. The torus foot is relatively small compared with other contemporary vessels and this may indicate that our amphora has been restored. The neck is decorated with olive-branch motifs instead of the lotus and palmette frieze. The usual tongue pattern decorates the area above the figure scene.

Side A) The usual Athena figure. On the columns there are smaller Athenas, each holding a Nike. The inscription next to the left-hand column is: Τ[ΩΝΑΘΗΝΗΘΕΝΑΘΛΩΝ and next to the right-hand one: ΕΥΘΥΚΡΙΤΟΣ ΑΡΧΩΝ.

Side B) Three athletes compete in a short-distance sprint.

Attributed by Beazley to the Nikomachos Series and dated to 328-27 B.C., the Archonship of Euthykritos.

Bibl.: Brauchitsch, no.103. Smets, *L'Antiq. Class.* 5 (1936), 100. Peters, *JdI* 57 (1942), 148. *ABV* 415,8. Eschbach (Kat. 72), pl.36,1-2.

30) **Panathenaic Amphora** Louvre MNB 3223 (Benghazi) (pl.142,1-3)
H. 73 cm.

Panathenaic amphora with flaring mouth, raised broad fillet (band) separates neck from body. Vertical handles, convex foot with deep grooves below upper edge. Mouth, handles, lower part of body and foot are glazed black. The neck has a band of palmettes. Above fight scene a pattern of long, black, enclosed tongues.

Side A) Athena strides to the right, holding an oblique shield in her left arm. It is secured by a central strap, through which the goddess' left arm passes, and another strap is held in her hand. In her right hand there is a poised spear (now faded). The face, hands and feet are painted white. She is wearing a long chiton with simple folds, over which there is a long overfall of ependytes, girt at the waist; its ends fall below her hips. A swallowtail shawl is worn over the shoulder. The border of the shawl and chiton are ornamented with white dots. The goddess has on the usual helmet with a crest that extends up into the tongue pattern. Two columns with Nike figures flank her. Near the left-hand column is the inscription: ΗΓΗΣΙΑΣ ΑΡΧΩΝ 'The Archon Hegesias', who held office in Athens in 324-23 B.C. Near the right column is the inscription: ΤΩΝΑΘΗΝΗΘΕΝΑΘΛΩΝ. Both inscriptions are arranged in kionedon.

Side B) Two athletes are engaged in a boxing match, watched by a judge in a himation. His upper torso and right shoulder are uncovered. He holds a palm frond in his right hand.

Attributed by Beazley to the Nikomachos Series, dating from the Archonship of Hegesias (324-23 B.C.).

Bibl.: *CVA* Louvre 5, pl.6 (362). Brauchitsch, no.10. Smets, *L'Antiq. Class.* 5 (1936), 101, 1-3. Peters, *JdI* 52 (1942), 148. *ABV* 415, 9.

31) **Panathenaic Amphora** (Cyrenaica) (pl.143,1)

Panathenaic amphora with flaring mouth, a raised broad fillet separates neck from body. Vertical handles project from upper part of neck that is decorated with a band of palmettes. Long, enclosed tongues above picture scene.

Side A) Athena strides to the right, holding an oblique shield in her left arm. It is secured by a central strap, through which the goddess' left arm passes, and another strap is held in her hand. In her right hand there is a poised spear (now faded). She is wearing a chiton with simple folds, over which there is a long overfall of ependytes, girt at the waist; its ends fall below her hips. A swallowtail shawl is worn over the shoulder. On her head is the usual helmet with crest, but the modern drawing by Paul Lucas (1710) is inaccurate. Part of the helmet and crest should extend up into the tongue pattern. Two columns flank the goddess; they are surmounted with Nike figures. the tongue pattern. Two columns with Nike figures flank her. Near the right-hand column is the inscription: ΗΓΗΣΙΑΣ ΑΡΧΩΝ, 'The Archon Hegesias', who held office in Athens in 324-23 B.C. Near the left column is the inscription: ΤΩΝΑΘΗΝΗΘΕΝΑΘΛΩΝ. Both inscriptions are arranged in kionedon.

Side B) Two athletes engaged in a wrestling bout, watched by a judge in a himation. The upper torso and right shoulder are uncovered. He holds a palm frond in his right hand. A third athlete watches on.

Attributed by Beazley to the Nikomachos Series, dating from the Archonship of Hegesias (324-23 B.C.).

Bibl.: Lucas, *Voyage*, pl.2. Smets, *L'Antiq. Class.* 5 (1936), 132. Peters, *JdI* 57 (1942), 148. *ABV* 415, 10. Eschbach (Kat.76), p.146.

32) **Panathenaic Amphora** Louvre 3162 MN 704 (Benghazi) (pl.144,1-3)
H. 66.5 cm.

A Panathenaic amphora with flaring mouth, raised fillet between neck and body. Vertical handles, convex foot with deep grooves below upper edge. Mouth, handles, lower part of body and foot are glazed black. A band of palmettes on neck. Long, black, enclosed tongue pattern above fight scene.

Side A) Athena strides to the right holding an oblique shield in her left arm, the inside of which is presented to the viewer. It is secured with a broad, central strap that the goddess' arm passes through, and a narrower strap she grasps with her hand. In her right hand she holds a poised spear (now faded). Her face, hands and feet are painted white. She wears a chiton with simple folds. The aegis is reduced to a mere cross-cord (partly faded) with a small gorgoneion. She has a swallowtail shawl over her shoulder. The border of the shawl and chiton are ornamented with white dots. On her head is the usual crested helmet that extends up into the tongue pattern above. Two columns flank the goddess, surmounted by Nike figures. The left-hand column has the inscription next to it: ΚΗΦΙΣΟΔΩΡΟΣ ΑΡΧΩΝ, 'The Archon Kephisodoros', who held office in Athens in 323-22 B.C. Next to the right-hand column runs the inscription: ΤΩΝΑΘΗΝΗΘΕΝΑΘΛΩΝ. Both inscriptions are in kionedon.

Side B) Three armed runners (hoplites) race to the right. The figures are sturdy and heavy; they are nude apart from Attic helmets. Two shields remain showing star devices. Their poses are identical, with left feet advanced and right feet extending behind them as they run. The right arms are bent at right angles; their torsos presented in three-quarter view.

Attributed by Beazley to the Nikomachos Series, dated to the Archonship of Kephisodoros (323-22 B.C.).

Bibl.: *CVA* Louvre 5, pl.5. Brauchitsch, no.106. Smets, *L'Antiq. Class.* 5 (1936), 101, no.134. Peters, *JdI* 52 (1942), 148. *ABV* 415, 12. Beazley, *Addenda*, 52. Boardman, *ABFV*, Fig.306. Eschbach (Kat.77), p.147ff.

33) **Panathenaic Amphora** Louvre 3164 MN 705 (Benghazi) (pl.145,1-3)
H. 67 cm.

Panathenaic amphora with flaring mouth, raised fillet between neck and body. Vertical handles, convex foot with deep grooves below upper edge. Mouth, handles, lower part of body and foot are glazed black. On neck a band of palmettes above figure scene. Long, black tongue pattern.

Side A) Athena strides to the right holding an oblique shield in her left arm, the inside of which is presented to the viewer. It is secured with a broad, central strap that the goddess' arm passes through, and a narrower strap she grasps with her hand. In her right hand she holds a poised spear (now faded). Her face, hands and feet are painted white. She wears a chiton with simple folds. She has a swallowtail shawl over her shoulder. On her head is the usual crested helmet that extends up into the tongue pattern above. Two columns flank the goddess, surmounted by Nike figures holding an aplustre. The left-hand column has the inscription next to it: ΑΡΧΙΠΠΟΣ ΑΡΧΩΝ, 'The Archon Archippos', who held office in Athens in 321-20 B.C. Next to the right-hand column runs the inscription: ΤΩΝΑΘΗΝΗΘΕΝΑΘΛΩΝ. Both inscriptions are in kionedon.

Side B) A nude athlete prepares to throw a discus. To his left stands a second nude athlete, and on his right is a judge. The judge is partially robed in a himation, leaving right arm and shoulder bare; he holds a palm frond in his right hand.

Attributed by Beazley to the Nikomachos Series, dated to the Archonship of Archippos (321-20 B.C.).

Bibl.: *CVA* Louvre 5, pl.6 (4-7,11). Brauchitsch, no.107. Smets, *L'Antiq. Class.* 5 (1936), 101, no.135. Peters, *JdI* 52 (1942), 148. *ABV* 106, 13.

COLLECTION

THE RED-FIGURE POTTERY

I) The Fifth Century

1	Alabastra, two fragments	Cyrene Museum	pl.11,2
2	Head vase, fragment	Cyrene Museum	pl.12,1
3	Cup, Type C	Cyrene Museum	pl.12,2
4	Cup, fragment	Cyrene Museum	pl.13,1
5	Cup, fragment	Cyrene Museum	pl.13,2
6	Epinetron, fragment	Cyrene Museum	pl.13,3
7	Column-krater, fragment (F11, Tr.2, St.3)	Cyrene Museum	pl.14,2
8	Krater (?), fragment	Cyrene Museum	pl.14,3
9	A fragment	Cyrene Museum	pl.15,1
10	A fragment	Cyrene Museum	pl.15,2
11	A fragment		pl.15,3
12	A fragment	Oxford (from Euhesperides)	pl.16,1
13	Pelike	Cyrene Museum	pl.16,1-3
14	Column-krater, fragment	Cyrene Museum	pl.17,1
15	Column-krater	London, BM 1914-5-20.1	pl.17,2
16	Pelike, fragment	Cyrene Museum	pl.18,1
17	Hydria	Paris, Louvre MN 712	pl.18,1-2
18	Pelike from Asleaia (near El-Merj)	Tolmeita Museum	pl.19,1-2
19	Hydria	Paris, Louvre MN 710	pl.19,3-4
20	Hydria	Paris, Louvre MN 3478 (MN 708)	pl.20,1-2
21	Pelike	Paris, Louvre M 3344	pl.20,3-4
22	Calyx-krater, fragment from Euhesperides	Oxford P513 (E/AR3/2)	pl.21,1
23	Cup with offset lip, fragment (F11/12 Tr. St.2)	Cyrene Museum	pl.21,2
24	Cup, stemless, fragment from Cyrene	Manchester M 1308 (N81-AN)	pl.21,3
25	Cup, stemless, fragment	Manchester	pl.21,4

26	Hydria	Paris, Louvre MN 714	pl.22,1
27	Pelike	Paris, Louvre MN 735	pl.22,2
28	Skyphos, fragments	Cyrene Museum	pl.23,1
29	Loutrophoros	Paris, Louvre MN 558	pl.23,2-3
30	Pelike, fragment	Cyrene Museum	pl.24,1
31	Oinochoe, chous	London, BM 1868.7-5.131	pl.24,2
32	Oinochoe, chous, from Cyrene	Manchester M 1300	pl.22,3
33	Oinochoe, chous	Paris, Louvre N 34V8	pl.25,1-3
34	Oinochoe, Shape II	Paris, Cab. Méd. 471	pl.26,1
35	Askos	London, BM F32 1866.4-15.44	pl.26,2
36	Askos (strainer top)	London, BM F33 1866.4-15.101	pl.27,1
37	Miniature hydria	London, BM 239	pl.27,2
38	Miniature hydria	Leiden KVB 52	pl.27,3

II) The Fourth Century

39	Pelike, from Euhesperides	Paris, Louvre N 3403 (MN 734)	pl.28,1-2
40	Pelike	Paris, Louvre	pl.29,1-4
41	Pelike (Schefold *UKV*, n.483)	Leningrad B4528	pl.30,1-3
42	Pelike	Exeter University	pl.31,1
43	Pelike	Cyrene Museum	pl.31,2
44	Pelike	London, BM G4345	pl.31,3
45	Hydria	Exeter University	pl.32,1-4
46	Hydria	London, BM E226	
47	Cup-skyphos (heavy wall)	London, BM 67.5-12.33	pl.33,1-3
48	Pelike from Derna	Yale University Arts Gallery (Stoddart Collection 1913, 138)	pl.35,1-2
49	Hydria	London, BM G235	pls.35,3-4 and 36,1-3
50	Hydria	London, BM E227	pls.37-40
51	Hydria	London, BM E228	pl.41,1
52	Hydria	London, BM E229	pl.42,1
53	Hydria	London, BM E241	pl.43,1-3
54	Hydria	London, BM E230	pl.44,1-2
55	Hydria	Paris, Louvre N 3371(MN 718)	pl.45,1-2
56	Pelike	Paris, Louvre N 3470 (MN 746)	pl.46,1
57	Pelike	Paris, Cab. Méd. 411	pl.46,2-3
58	Pelike	London, BM F11	
59	Oinochoe, Shape II	Paris, Cab. Méd. 472	pl.47,1-3
60	Pelike (until 1975 in Topsham, Devon, UK (Misses Radford), and now in USA with another branch of the family)		pl.48,1-2
61	Pelike	Manchester M 680 (N83-BH)	pl.49,1
62	Bell-krater, fragment	Cyrene Museum	pl.49,2

63	Pelike	London, BM E434	pl.50,1-3
64	Pelike	Paris, Cab. Méd. 406	pl.51,1
65	Pelike	Paris, Cab. Méd. 408	pl.52,1-2
66	Pelike	Exeter 40 1922.14 (ARV)	pl.53,1-2
67	Pelike	Paris, Louvre MN 752	pl.53,3-4
68	Pelike	Paris, Louvre MN 753, N 3459	pl.54,1-2
69	Pelike	Paris, Louvre MN 756	pl.54,2-3/55
70	Pelike	London, BM F12 (Euhesperides)	
71	Pelike	London, BM F11	pl.55,3
72	Pelike	Paris, Cab. Méd. 407	pl.56,1-2
73	Squat lekythos	Cyrene Museum	pl.57,1
74	Squat lekythos	London, BM E711	pl.57,2-3
75	Oinochoe, Shape III	London, BM E554	pl.58,1-2
76	Lebes gamikos	Cyrene Museum	pl.59,1-2
77	Lebes gamikos	Cyrene Museum	pl.60,1-2
78	Lekanis, lid fragment	Oxford GP509 (E-AQ5-1)	pl.61,1
79	Lekanis, body-wall fragment	Oxford	pl.61,2
80	Lekanis, lid fragment	Paris, Louvre CA963 (CA964)	pl.61,3
81	Lidded lekanis with ribbon-handle	Cyrene Museum	pl.62,1-2
82	Fish plate, fragment		pl.62,3

THE PANATHENAIC AMPHORAE

The Sixth Century

1	Cyrene Museum	Cyrene, last quarter of 6th century BC	pl.114,1
2	Cyrene Museum	Cyrene, last quarter of 6th century BC	pl.114,2

The Fifth Century

3	Tolmeita (Old Ptolemais)	El-Merj, early 5th century BC	pl.115,1-2
4	Lost (Luni Quaderni)	El-Merj, first quarter of 5th century BC	pl.116,2
5	Lost (Luni Quaderni)	El-Merj, first quarter of 5th century BC	pl.116,3
6	Berlin 3979	Cyrenaica, first quarter of 5th century BC	pl.117,1-2
7	London, BM 1903-2-17,1	Benghazi, last quarter of 5th century BC	pl.118,1-2
8	London, BM B 606	Tocra, late 5th century BC (403 BC)	pl.119,1-2
9	London, BM B 605	Tocra, late 5th century BC (403 BC)	pl.120,1-2
10	Hildesheim Inv.1254 (Pelizaeus Museum)	Tolmeita, late 5th century BC	pls.121-122
11	Hildesheim Inv.1253 (Pelizaeus Museum)	Tolmeita, late 5th century BC	pl.123
12	Cyrene Museum	Cyrene, last quarter of 5th century BC	pl.124,1-2

The Fourth Century

13	London, BM B 602	Cyrenaica, late 5th to early 4th century BC	pl.125

14	Berlin 3980	Cyrenaica, 392/1 BC, Archonship of Philokles	pl.126-127
15	Alexandria 182	Benghazi, 371/370 BC, Archonship of Phrasikleides	pl.128
16	Detroit, Inst. of Arts (50.193)	Benghazi, first quarter of 4th century BC	pl.129,1-4
17	London, BM B 604	Tocra, second quarter of 4th century BC	pl.130,1-3
18	Brussels, Mus. Roy. (A 1703)	Benghazi, 367/66 BC, Archonship of Polyzelos	pl.131,1-3
19	New York Met. Mus.(56.171.6)	Benghazi, 367/66 BC, Archonship of Polyzelos	pl.132,1-3
20	London, BM B 603	Tocra, 367/66 BC, Archonship of Polyzelos	pl.133,1-3
21	London, BM B 612	Tocra, 367/66 BC	pl.134,1-2
22	Cyrene Museum 717	Cyrene, 363/62 BC, Archonship of Charikleides	pl.135,1-3
23	Alexandria 18238	Benghazi, 341/40 BC, Archonship of Nikomachos	pl.136,1-2
24	Paris, Louvre MN 706	Benghazi, 340/39 BC, Archonship of Theophrastus	pl.137,1-3
25	Harvard (*CVA* Hoppin 6)	Cyrene, 340/39 BC, Archonship of Theophrastus	
26	London, BM B 609	Benghazi, 333/32 BC, Archonship of Nikokrates	pl.138,1-3
27	Sèvres 7230	Cyrenaica, 332/31 BC, Archonship of Niketes	pl.139,1-3
28	London, BM B 611	Tocra, 328/27 BC, Archonship of Euthykritos	pl.140,1-3
29	Berlin 3981	Cyrenaica, 328/27 BC, Archonship of Euthykritos	pl.141,1
30	Paris, Louvre MNB 3227	Benghazi, 324/23 BC, Archonship of Hegesias	pl.142,1-3
31	Lost (Peters, *JdI* 57 (1942), 148. Pottier, *BCH* 6 (1882), 169)	Cyrenaica, 324/23 BC, Archonship of Hegesias	pl.143
32	Paris, Louvre 3162 MN 704	Benghazi, 323/22 BC, Archonship of Kephisodoros	pl.144,1-3
33	Paris, Louvre 3164 MN 705	Benghazi, 321/20 BC, Archonship of Archippos	pl.145,1-3

THE NON-ATTIC POTTERY

1	Etruscan plate	Cyrene Museum	pl.146,1
2	Campanian hydria	Cyrene Museum	pl.146.2
3	South Italian pelike	London, BM E430	pl.147,1-2
4	Footed Apulian alabastron	London, BM F31	pl.148,1-2

GNATHIA POTTERY

5	Bottle	London, BM 582	pl.149,1
6	Pelike	London, BM C69 (Old Catalogue)	pl.149,2
7	Oinochoe	Cyrene Museum	pl.150,1-2
8	Oinochoe	Sèvres 4166,2	pl.150,3

ABBREVIATIONS

AA	Archäologischer Anzeiger
AAA	Athens Annals of Archaeology
ABV	*Attic Black-Figure Vase-Painters*, J.D. Beazley (Oxford, 1956)
Acta. Arch. Hisp.	Acta Archeologica Hispanica
Addenda	*Beazley Addenda*, L. Burn and R. Glynn
AJA	American Journal of Archaeology
AJP	American Journal of Philology
AKW	BLOESCH, H. (1964), *Antike Kleinkunst in Winterthur* (Winterthur)
Alfieri, Spina	ALFIERI, S. (1979), *Spina, Museo archeologico nazionale di Ferrara*, 1 (Bologna, Calderini)
AM	Athenische Mitteilungen
Annuario	Annuario della R. Scuola Archeologica di Atene
Antiqu. Class.	*L'Antiquité classique*
AR	Archaeological Reports
ARV	*Attic Red-Figure Vase-Painters*, J.D. Beazley (2nd edn., Oxford, 1963)
BCH	Bulletin de correspondance hellénique
Beazley Development	BEAZLEY, J.D. (1951), *Development of Attic Black-Figure*
Beazley Gifts	*Selected Exhibition of Sir John and Lady Beazley's Gifts, 1912-1966*, Ashmolean Museum, Oxford
BICS	Bulletin of the Institute of Classical Studies
BMC	*Catalogue of the Greek Coins in the British Museum: Cyrenaica*, E.S.G. Robinson, 1927
BMFA	Bulletin of the Museum of Fine Arts, Boston
BMMA	*Bulletin of the Metropolitan Museum of Art*, New York
BSA	British School at Athens, Annual of
BSR	British School of Archaeology at Rome, Papers of
Bull. Vereen.	Bulletin van de Vereeniging tot Bevordering der Kennis van de Antike Beschaving
CAH	Cambridge Ancient History
CB	CASKEY & BEAZLEY (1954), *Attic vase painting in the Museum of Fine Arts, Boston*. Vol. 3 (Boston)
Chalk Vases	RUMPF, A. (1927) *Chalkidische Vasen* (Berlin and Leipzig)

Cl. Rh.	Clara Rhodes
Cl. Rev.	Classical Review
CP	Classical Philology
CRAI	Comptes rendus de l'Académie des inscriptions et belles lettres
CVA	Corpus Vasorum Antiquorum
DAI	*Documenti antichi dell'Africa Italiana*, G. Oliverio (Bergamo, 1932-6)
De Ridder Catalogue	DE RIDDER, A. (1901), *Catalogue des vases peints de la Bibliothèque Nationale, Paris* (Paris)
Deltion	Archaiologikon deltion
Development	*The Development of Attic Black-Figure*, J.D. Beazley (Berkeley, 1951)
Duvanlij	FILOW, B.D. (1934), *Die Grabhingelnekropole be Duvanlij in Sudbulgarien* (Sofia)
EAA	Enciclopedia dell' arte antica, classica e orientale
EVB	*Etruscan Vase-Painting*, J.D. Beazley (Oxford, 1947)
FAS	BLOESCH, H. (1940), *Formen Attischen Schalen* (Bern)
FR	*Griechische Vasenmalerei*, Furtwängler and Reichhold
GPP	COOK, R.M. (1960), *Greek Painted Pottery* (London)
GRGSP	STRONG, D.E. (1966), *Greek and Roman Gold and Silver Plate* (London)
HGVP	*A History of Greek Vase-Painting*, P.E. Arias, H. Hirmer and B.B. Shefton (New York, 1969)
Holwerda	HOLWERDA (1936), *Het Laat-Grieksche En Romeinsche Gebruiksaardewerk Uit Het Middellandsche-Zee-Gebied.* (In, Het Rijkmuseum Van Oudheden Te Leiden)
Hundt and Peters	HUNDT, A. & PETERS, K. (1961), *Greifswalder Antiken* (Gedachtnisgab fur Erich Pernice, Berlin)
IG	Inscriptiones Graecae
ILN	Illustrated London News
IJNA	International Journal of Nautical Archaeology
JdI	Jahrbuch des K. Deutschen Archäologischen Institut
JbRGZM	Jahrbuch des Romisch-Germanischen Zentralmuseum, Mainz
JAH	Journal of African History
JEA	Journal of Egyptian Archaeology
JHS	Journal of Hellenic Studies
JRS	Journal of Roman Studies
Lib. Antiqu.	Libya Antiqua
KM	OVERBECK, J. (1871-8), *Atlas der griechischen Kunstmythologie* (Leipzig)
LIMC	*Lexicon Iconographicum Mythologiae Classicae* (Zurich and Munich, 1974)
LM	ROSCHER, W.H. (1965), *Lexikon Der Griechischen und Römischen Mythologie* II.2 (Leipzig 1894-1897, new edition Hildesheim)
MAAR	Memoirs of the American Academy in Rome
MGK	SCHEFOLD, K. (1960), *Meisterwerke griechischer kunst* (Basle)
MM	Mitteilung des Deutschen Archäologischen Instituts, Madrider Abteilung
MemLinc	Memorie della R. Accademia Nazionale dei Lincei
MMS	Metropolitan Museum Studies
Mon. Ant.	Monumenti Antichi

MonPiot	Monuments et memoires publ. par l'Academie des inscriptions et belles letters, Fondation Piot
Not. Arch.	Notiziario archeologica
NSc	Notizie degli Scavi di Antichita
OJh	*Jahreschefte des Osterreichischen Archäologischen Institut*
Paralip	*Paralipomena*, J.D. Beazley (Oxford, 1971)
PEQ	Palestine Exploration Quarterly
phV²	*Phylax Vases*, A.D. Trendall (2nd edn., *BICS*, Suppl. 19, 1967)
Quaderni	Quaderni di Archeoligia della Libia, Rome
RA	Revue archeologique
RAfr	*Revue africaine*
RE	Pauly-Wissowa, *Real-Encyclopadie der klassischen Altertumswissenschaft*
REA	Revue des études anciennes
Rev. Hist.	*Revue Historique*
RIASA	Rivista dell' Istituto Nazionale di Archeologia e Storia dell' Arte, Rome
Riv. Fil.	Rivista di Filologia e d'Istruzione Classica
RM	Mitteilungen des Deutschen Archäologischen Instituts, Römische Abteilung
RStLig	Rivista di Studi Liguri
SEG	Supplementum Epigraphicum Graecum
SEHH	ROSTOVTZEFF, M. (1941), *Social and Economic History of the Hellenistic World* (Oxford University Press)
The Genucilia Group	DEL CHIARO, M.A. (1957), *The Genucilia Group: A Class of Etruscan Red-figured Plates* (University of California Publications in Classical Archaeology, Vol.3, No.4, pp.243-372)
Tocra	*Excavations at Tocra, 1963-1965*, J. Boardman and J.W. Hayes
UKV	SCHEFOLD, K. (1931), *Untersuchungen zu den Kertscher Vasen* (Berlin and Leipzig)
WGA	HEICHELHEIM, F. (1938), *Wirtschaftsgeschichte des Altertum*, 1, 11.

BIBLIOGRAPHY

ACTA of the 1st International Scientific Congress on the Volcano of Thera, Athens (1971)

ALEXANDRESCU P. (1978), "La Céramique d'Époque Archaique et Classique VIIe-IVes" (*Histria* IV)

ALFIERI, S. (1979), *Spina, Museo archeologico nazionale di Ferrara*, 1 (Bologna, Calderini)

AMYX, D.A. (1958), "The Attic Stelai", *Hesperia*, 27, 178-186

APOLLONIA, Les fouilles dans la nécropole d'Apollonia en 1947-1949. I. Venedikov, T. Gerasimov, C. Dremsizova, T. Ivanov, Y. Mladenova, V. Velkov

ANDERSON, J.K. (1961), *Ancient Greek Horsemanship* (Los Angeles)

APPLEBAUM, S.E. (1948), *The Agriculture of Cyrenaica in Classical Antiquity, with special reference to the Jewish revolt leader Trajan* (Oxford, B.Litt. thesis)

APPLEBAUM, S.E. (1979), *Jews and Greeks in Ancient Cyrene* (Leiden, E.J. Brill)

AREA HANDBOOK FOR LIBYA (1969), (Washington D.C., US Government Printing Office)

ARIAS, P.E., HIRMER, M. & SHEFTON, B.B. (1961), *A History of Greek Vase Painting* (New York)

ARNOLD, D. (1969), *Die Polykletnachfolge* (Berlin)

ASHMEAD, A.H. & PHILLIPS K.M. Jr. (1976), *Classical Vases, excluding Attic Black-Figure, Attic Red-Figure and Attic White-Ground*. Catalogue of the Classical Collection Museum of Art (The Rhode Island School of Design, Providence, Rhode Island)

ASHMOLE, B. & YALOURIS, N. (1967), *Olympia: The Sculptures of the Temple of Zeus* (Phaidon Press)

ATALLAH, W. (1956), *Adonis dans la litterature et L'art grecs* (Paris)

ATHANAEUS (1927), *The Deipnosophistai* (translated by C.B. Gulick, Pitman, New York)

ATTIC Red-figured vases in the Hermitage, compiled by Sostavitel' A.A. Peredol'skaia (Artists' Publishing House, Leningrad, 1967) (in Russian)

AURIGEMMA, S. (1965), *Scavi di Spina: La Necropoli di Spina in Valle Trebba* (Rome) Aurigemma, Spina

AUSTIN, M.M. (1970), "Greece and Egypt in the Archaic Age". *Proceedings of the Cambridge Philological Society* (Suppl. No.2), 7-75

BABELON, E. (1901-33), *Traité des monnaies Grecques et Romaines* I-IV (Paris)

BADAWY, A. (1968), *A History of Egyptian Architecture* (Los Angeles)

BAGNALL, S.R. (1976), *The Administration of the Ptolemaic Possessions outside Egypt* (Leiden, E.J. Brill)

BAILEY, D.M. (1975), *A Catalogue of the Lamps in the British Museum* (The Trustees of the British Museum)

BAKALAKIS G. (1967), University of Thessalonike, Annual of the Philosophical School, Supplement No.13

BARKER, G. (ed.) (1985), *Cyrenaica in Antiquity*, Society for Libyan Studies Occasional Paper I, BAR International Series 236 (Oxford)

BARKER, G. "Economic Life at Bernice: the Animal and Fish Bones, Marine Molluscs and Plant Remains" in R. Lloyd (ed.), *Excavation At Sidi Khrebish* Benghazi (Bernice) Vol. II (Suppl. to Lib. Antiqu. V), pp.1-47

BARNETT, R.D. & MENDLESON, C. (eds.) (1987), *Tharros: a catalogue of Material in the British Museum from Phoenician and other Tombs at Tharros, Sardinia*

BARR, F.T. (ed.) (1968), *Geology and Archaeology of Northern Cyrenaica, Libya* (Amsterdam)

BASS, F.G. (ed.) (1972), *A History of Sea-faring, based on underwater archaeology* (Thames and Hudson, London)

BASTET, F.L. (1968), "Die grosse kamee in Den Haag", *Bulletin, Antieke Beschaving*, 43, 2-22

BATES, O. (1914), *The Eastern Libyans: An Essay* (London, Macmillan)

BAUR, P.V.C. (1922), *Catalogue of the Rebecca Darlington Stoddart Collection of Greek and Italian Vases in the Yale University* (New Haven, Connecticut)

BAZANT, J. (1975), "Icongraphy of Choes reconsidered", *Listy filologicke*, 98, 72-76

BEAZLEY, J. D, *Etruscan Vase-Painting* (Oxford) 1947

BEAZLEY, J.D. (1921), "An Askos by Makron", *AJA*, 25, 235ff.

BEAZLEY, J.D. (1929), "Charinos" Attic Vases in the form of Human Heads *JHS*, 49, 38-79

BEAZLEY, J.D. (1943), "Panathenaica", *AJA*, 47, 441-465

BEAZLEY, J.D. (1940-45), "Miniature Panathenaics", *BSA* 41, 10-21

BEAZLEY, J.D. (1951), *Development of Attic Black-Figure*

BEAZLEY, J.D. (1956), *Attic Black-Figure Vase-Painters* (Oxford)

BEAZLEY, J.D. (1963), *Attic Red-Figure Vase-Painters* (2nd edition, Oxford)

BEAZLEY, J.D. & MAGI, F. (1939), *La Raccolta Benedetto Guglielmi nel Museo Gregoriano Etrusco* (Rome, Citta del Vaticano)

BEAZLEY, J.D. (1974 re-issue), *The Berlin Painter and translation of the 1930 Berliner Maler*

BECK, F.A (1975), *Album of Greek Education: The Greeks at School and at Play* (Sydney)

BECKEL, G. (1961), *Götterbeistand in der Bildüberlieferung Griechischer Heldensagen* (Waldsassen/Bayern, Stiftland-Verlang)

BECKER, Reginn-Marie (1977), *Formen attischer Peliken* (Tübingen)

BEHN, F. (1919), "Zwei Panathenaische Preisamphoren des Hildesheimer Pelizaus-Museums", *AA*, 34, 81-98

BELLI, C. (1970), *Il Tresoro Di Taras* (Museo Nazionale di Taranto, Roma)

BERNADBO-BREA, L. & CAVALIER, M. (1955), *Meligunis-Lipara* (II, Palermo: La Necropoli Greca e Romana nella contrada Diana)

BERARD, C. (1974), *Anodoi: essai sur l'imagerie des passage Chthoniens* (Institut Suisse de Rome)

BERARD, J. (1960), *L'expansion et la Colonisation Grecques jusqu'aux Guerres Mediques* (Paris)

BERNARDINI, M. (1963), *Vasi dello Stile di Gnathia* (Vasi Museo Provinciale Castromediano, Lecce, Bari, n.d.c. 1972, and reviewed in *JHS* 83, 208 by A.D. Trendall)

BERNARDINI, M. (1965), *I Vasi attici del Museo Provinciale de Lecce*

BIEBER, M. (1961), *The Sculpture of the Hellenistic Age* (New York)

BIERS, W.R. (1973), "An Attic Head-vase", *Muse*, 7, 17-20

BIERS, W.R. (1983), "Some thoughts on the Origins of the Attic Head-vase", in Moon (ed.), *Ancient Greek Art and Iconography* (University of Wisconsin Press)

BIESANTZ, H. (1965), *Die Thessalischen Grabreliefs* (Studien zur Nordgriechischen Kunst, Mainz am Rhein)

BIMSON, M.J. & FREESTONE I.C. (1982), *Archaeometry* 24.2, 117-126

BLACKMAN, D.J. (ed.) (1973), *Marine Archaeology* (Colston Papers No.23, London)

BLAKEWAY, A. (1933), "Prolegomena to the study of Greek Commerce with Italy, Sicily and France in the Eighth and Seventh Centuries", *BSA* 32, 170-208

BLAVATSKI, V.D. (1953), *History of Ancient Painted Pottery* (Moscow)

BLOESCH, H. (1940), *Formen Attischen Schalen* (Berne)

BLOESCH, H. (1943), *Antike Kunst in der Schweiz* (Zurich)

BLOESCH, H. (1964), *Antike Kleinkunst in Winterthur* (Winterthur)

BOARDMAN, J. (1964), *Greek Art* (Thames & Hudson, London)

BOARDMAN, J. (1970), *Greek Gems and Finger Rings* (Thames & Hudson, London)

BOARDMAN, J. (1973), "Reflection on the Greek Pottery Trade with Tocra", in Gadalla (ed.) *Libya in History* (Benghazi)

BOARDMAN, J. (1974), *Athenian Red-Figure Vases, The Archaic Period: a Handbook* (Thames & Hudson, London)

BOARDMAN, J. (1979), "The Athenian Pottery Trade: The Classical Period", *Expedition*, 21.4, 33-39

BOARDMAN, J. (1986), "Provenance Studies of Greek Pottery of the Historic Period" (R.E. Jones *Greek and Cypriot Pottery*, The British School at Athens, Fitch Laboratory, Occasional Paper I, 627-747)

BOARDMAN, J. & HAYES J. (1973), *Excavation at Tocra: 1963-1965 I, The Archaic Deposit* (British School at Athens, Suppl.Vol.4, London 1966, and *II, The Archaic Deposit II and later deposits*, BAS Suppl.Vol.10, London)

BOARDMAN, J. & LA ROCCA, E. (1978), *Eros in Greece* (John Murray, London)

BOARDMAN J. (1958-59), *Old Smyrna, The Attic Pottery, BSA* 53-54, 152-181

BOARDMAN J. (1973), *The Greeks Overseas* (Harmondsworth)

BOL, P.C. (1972), *Die Skulpturen des Schiffsfundes von Antikythera* (suppl. to *AM* 1972)

BOREAS, *Münstersche Beiträge*, No.16, p.190, pl.33, 1-2

BOTHMER, D. (1957), *Amazons in Greek Art* (Oxford)

BOULTER, C. (1953), "Pottery of the Mid-Fifth Century from a Well in the Athenian Agora", *Hesperia* 22, 59-115

BOVIL, E.W. (1968), *The Golden Trade of the Moors* (Oxford University Press, London)

BRAUCHITSCH, G. (1910), *Die Panathenaischen Preisamphoren* (Berlin)

BRAUN, E. (1962), *Agora VIII*, 'The late Geometric and Proto-Attic Pottery' (Princeton)

BREASTED, J.H. (1906) *Ancient Records of Egypt*, III (Chicago)

BRECCIA, E. (1912), *La necropoli di Sciatbi* (Cairo)

BRIJDER, H.A.G. (ed.) (1984), *Ancient Greek and Related Pottery: Proceedings of the International Vase Symposium, Amsterdam, 12-15 April 1984* (Allard Pierson Series, V, Amsterdam)

BROMMER, F. (1937), *Satyroi* (Wurzburg)

BROMMER, F. (1942), "Heracles and Die Hesperides Auf Vasenbildern", *JdI* 57, 105-123

BROMMER, F. (1973), *Vasenlisten zur griechischen Heldensage*

BROMMER, F. (1977), *Der Parthenonfries* (Mainz)

BROMMER, F. (1979), *Herakles* (Köln)

BROMMER, F. (1979), *The Sculptures of the Parthenon* (Thames & Hudson, London)

BROUSKARI (1974), *The Acropolis Museum* (Athens)

BRUECKNER, A. (1907), "Athenische Hochzeitsgeschenke", *AM* 32, 79-122

BRUNNSAKER, S. (1955), *The Tyrant Slayers of Kritios and Nesiotes* (Lund)

BUCK, D.C. (1948), "The Dialect of Cyrene", *CP* 41, 129-134

BURKE, M.S. & POLLIT, J.J. (1975), *Greek Vases at Yale* (Yale University Art Gallery)

BURKERT, W. (1917), *Griechische Religion der archaischen und Klassischen Epoche* (Stutgart, Berlin, Cologne and Mainz, 251-260)

BURKERT, W. (1985), *Greek Religion* (translated by John Raffan, Harvard University Press, Cambridge, Massachusetts)

BURN, A.R. (1929), "The so-called 'Trade-Leagues' in Early Greek History and the Lelantine War", *JHS*, 49, 30f.

BURN, A.R. (1970), *Greece and Rome 750 BC-AD 565* (Scott, Foresman & Co.)

BURY, J.B. & MEIGGS, R. (1975), *A History of Greece* (Fourth edition, Macmillan and Russell Meiggs)

BUSCHOR, E. (1937), *Feldmäuse* (Sitzungsberichte der Bayerischen Akademie der Wissenschaften, Philhist-Abteilung, Munich)

BUSCHOR, E. (1943), *Satyrtanze und frühes Drama* (München)

BUSCHOR, E. (1969), *Griechische Vasen* (München)

CAMBITOGLOU, A. (1954) (ed.), "Groups of Apulian Red-figured vases decorated with heads of women or of Nike", *JHS* LXXIV

CAMBITOGLOU, A. (1979), *Studies in honour of Arthur Dale Trendall* (Sidney)

CARPENTER, R. (1966), *Beyond the Pillars of Heracles* (Delacorte Press)

CASKEY, L.D. (1922), *Geometry of Greek Vases* (Boston)

CASKEY & BEAZLEY (1954), *Attic vase painting in the Museum of Fine Arts, Boston*. Vol. 3 (Boston)

CASSON, L. (1978), *Ships and Seamanship in the Ancient World* (Princeton, New Jersey)

CHAMOUX, F. (1953), *Cyrene Sous la Monarchie Des Battiades* (Paris)

CHAMOUX, F. *"Sur quelques inscriptions Grecques trouvés à Apollonia de Cyrenaique"*, in Gadalla (ed.) *Libya in History*

CHARBONNEAUX, J., MARTIN, R. & VILLARD, F. (1972), *Classical Greek Art*, 480-330 (Thames & Hudson, London)

CHASE, G.H. & VERMEULE, C.C. (1963), *Greek, Etruscan and Roman Art* (Museum of Fine Arts, Boston)

CLAIRMONT, C. (1954-55), "Greek Pottery from the Near East", *Berytus* 11

CLAIRMONT, C. (1956-58), "Greek Pottery from the Near East: II Black Vases", *Berytus* 12.

COLDSTREAM, J.N. (1968), *Greek Geometric Pottery* (London)

COLDSTREAM, J.N. (1971), *Geometric Greece* (London)

COLDSTREAM, J.N. (1973), "Knossos 1951-61: Orientalizing and Archaic Pottery from the Town", *BSA* 68, 33-63

COLLIGNON, M. & COUVE, L. (1902), *Catalogue des vases peints du Musée National d'Athenes* (Paris)

CONGDON, L.O.K. (1981), *Caryatid Mirrors of Ancient Greece* (Philipp von Zabern, Mainz am Rhein)

COOK, A. (1914-40), *Zeus*, 3 volumes (Cambridge)

COOK, R.M. (1946), "Ionia and Greece, 800-600 BC", *JHS* 66, 67-98

COOK, R.M. (1959), "Bedeutung der bemalten Keramik für den griechischen Handel", *Jdi* 74, 114-123

COOK, R.M. (1960), *Greek Painted Pottery* (London)

CORBETT, P. (1949), "Attic Pottery of the Later Fifth Century from the Athenian Agora", *Hesperia* 18, 298-351

CORBETT, P.C. (1955), "Palmette Stamps from an Attic Black-Glaze Workshop", *Hesperia*, 24, 172-186

CORBETT, P.C. (1960), "The Burgon and the Blacas Tombs", *JHS* 80, 57-58

CARCOPINO, J. (1941), *Daily life in Ancient Rome* (London)

COSTER, C.H. (1951), "The Economic Position of Cyrenaica in Classical Times", in P.R. Coleman-Norton (ed.) *Studies in Roman Economic and Social History*, 104-44 (Princeton University Press)

CROISSANT, F. (1973), Collection Paul Canellopoulos (IV): "Vases Plastiques", *BCH*, 97, 205-25

CUADRADO, E. (1968), "Tombas principescas de El Cigarralejo", *Madrider Mitteilungen* 9, 148 - 186

DALTON, O.M. (1926), *The Treasure of the Oxus and other examples of Early Oriental Metal-work* (London)

DANOV H. & IVANOV T. (1980), *Antique Tombs in Bulgaria* (Sofia Press)

DAREMBERG, C.V. & SAGLIO (ed.) (1877-1904) *Dictionnaires des Antiquités Grecques et Romaines* (Paris)

DAVIDSON, A. (1972), *Mediterranean Sea Food* (Harmondsworth)

DAVIDSON, J.A. (1958), "Notes on the Panathenaea", *JHS*, 78, 23-41

DE JULLIIS, E.M. (1984), *Gli Ori di Taranto in Eta Ellenestica* (Arnoldo Mondadori Editore S.P.A., Milano)

DE MIRO, E. & FIORENTINI, G. (1977), "Leptis Magnia: La Necropoli Greco-Punica Sotto il Teatro", *Quaderni*, 9

DEL CHIARO, M.A. (1957), *The Genucilia Group: A Class of Etruscan Red-figured Plates* (University of California Publications in Classical Archaeology, Vol.3, No.4, pp.243-372)

DEL CHIARO, M.A. (1961), "Caeretan vs. Faliscan: Two Etruscan Red-figured Hydriai", *AJA* 65, 56-57

DEL CHIARO, M.A. (1966), "Distribution of the Caeretan Red-figured Pottery" *Archeologia Classica* XVIII, pp.115-118

DEL CHIARO, M.A. (1974), *Etruscan Red-figured Vase Painting at Caere* (University of California Press)

DELPLACE, C. (1980), *Le griffon de l'archaisme à l'epoque imperiale* (Etudes Iconographique et Essai d'interpretation Symbolique, Bruxelles)

DENNIS, G. (1870), "On recent excavations in the Greek Cemeteries of the Cyrenaica", *Transactions of the Royal Society of Literature*, 2nd Series 9, 135-82

DERBY, W.J. (1977), *Food, The Gift of Osiris* (London)

DE RIDDER, A. (1901), *Catalogue des vases peints de la Bibliothèque Nationale, Paris* (Paris)

DESANGES, J., "The Proto-Berbers", in Mokhtar, G. (ed.), *The General History of Africa II* (Ancient Civilizations of Africa, Heinemann, California, Unesco)

DESANGES, K. (1962), *Catalogue des tribes Africaines de l'Antiquité Classique a l'Ouest du Nil* (Dakar)

DETIENNE, M. (1977), *The Gardens of Adonis* (translated from French by Janet Lloyd, New Jersey)

DEUBNER, L. (1900), ÅÐÁÃËÉÁ, *JdI*, 15, 144-154

DEUBNER, L. (1956), *Attische Feste* (Berlin)

DIEHL, E. (1964), *Die Hydria: Formgeschichte und verwendung im Kult des Altertums* (Munich)

DIERICHS, A. (1981), *Das Bild des Griefen in der frühgriechischen flachenkunst* (Münster)

DE VRIES, K. (1977), "Attic Pottery in the Achaemenid Empire", in *AJA* 82, 544-548

DE VISSCHER, F. (1940), *Les Edits D'Auguste Decouverts à Cyrene* (Paris)

DE VISSCHER, F. (1961), "Heracles Epitrapezios", *L'Antiq. Class.* 30, 67-129

DRACHMANN, A.B. (1910), *Scholia Vetera in Pindari Carmin II* (Scholia in Pythionicas, Leipzig)

DUGAS, C., "Les Vases Attiques à Figures Rouges", *Délos* XXI

DUNBABIN, T.J. (1948), *The Western Greeks* (Oxford)

DUNCAN-JONES, R.P. (1974), *The Economy of the Roman Empire* (Quantitative Studies, Cambridge)

EBERT, M. (1924-32), *Reallexikon der Vorgeschichte* (Berlin)

ECONOMIC DEVELOPMENT OF LIBYA (1960) (John Hopkins Press, International Bank for Reconstruction and Development)

EDRISI (1866), *Déscription de l'Afrique et de l'Espagne*. Trans. R. Dozy, M. J. de Goeje

EDWARDS, G.R. (1957), "Panathenaics of Hellenistic and Roman Times", *Hesperia* 26, 320-349

EDWARDS, G.R. (1975), "Corinthian Helenistic Pottery", *Corinth* VII, Part III (Princeton, New Jersey)

EISMAN, C.J. (1979), *The Porticello Shipwreck, A Mediterranean Merchant Vessel of 415-385 BC* (University of Pennsylvania, Ph.D. thesis)

EL HARAMI, J. (1970), *Greek Terracottas from the Demeter Sanctuary, Cyrene* (University of Pennsylvania, Ph.D. thesis)

ELRASHEDY, F., "Attic imported Pottery in Classical Cyrenaica", in Barker (ed.) *Cyrenaica in Antiquity*

ELRASHEDY, F. (1976), *Garamantian burial customs and their relation to those of other people in North and North-West Africa* (University of Newcastle upon Tyne, M.Litt. thesis)

ESCHBACH, N. (1968), *Statuen auf Panathenaishen Preisamphoren Des 4.JHS. V.chr.* (Verlag Philipp Von Zabern, Mainz am Rhein)

EVANS, A.J., *Scripta Minoa I*, 215f.

EVANS, A.J., *The Palace of Minos I*

EVANS-PRITCHARD, E.E. (1963), *The Sanusi of Cyrenaica* (Oxford, Clarendon Press)

FABRINI, G. (1984), *Numana: Vasi Attici Da Collezioni* (Roma)

F DE VISSCHER (1940), *Les Edits D'Auguste decouverts à Cyrene* (Paris)

FARNELL, L.R. (1909), *The Cult of the Greek States* (Oxford)

FARNSWORTH, M. (1964), "A Mineralogical Study", *AJA* 48, 221-228

FILOW, B.D. (1934), *Die Grabhingelnekropole be Duvanlij in Sudbulgarien* (Sofia)

FINLEY, M. (1973), *Ancient Economy* (London)

FLACELIERE, R. (1965), *Daily Life in Greece at the Time of Pericles* (translated from French by Peter Green, Weidenfeld and Nicolson, London)

FLAGGE, I. (1975), *Untersuchungen zur Bedeutung des Griefen* (Sankt Augustin)

FLEMMING, N., "Apollonia Revisited", *Geographical Magazine* 33 (1960-1), 522-531

FOL, A., NIKOLOV, B. & HODDINOTT R.F. (1986), *The New Thracian Treasure from Rogozen, Bulgaria* (British Museum)

FOLSOM, R.S. (1976), *Attic Red-Figured Pottery* (Noyes Press, New Jersey)

FORTI, L. (1965), *La ceramica di Gnathia* (Napoli)

FÖLZER, E. (1906), *Die Hydria* (Leipzig)

FRANK, T. (ed.) (1938), *An Economic Survey of Ancient Rome IV* (Baltimore, The Johns Hopkins Press)

FRAZER, D. (1935), *The Panoply of the Ethiopian Warrior, AJA* 39, 35-45

FRAZER, P.M. (1970), *Eratosthees of Cyrene: Lecture on a Master Mind* (June, British Academy)

FRAZER, P.M. (1972), *Ptolemaic Alexandria* (Oxford)

FREEMAN, I.L. (1950), *Greek City-States*, London

FREL, J. (1976), "Panathenaische Amphoren", in *Kerameikos* X, 238-245

FREL, J. (1972), "Quelques noms d'archontes sur les amphores panathenaiques", *RA*, 285-290

FREL, J. (1972), "Two Panathenaic Dedications in Eleusis", *AAA* 5, 245ff.

FREL, J. (1973), *Panathenaic Prize Amphoras* (Esperos, Athens)

FREL, J. (1977), "The Kleophrades Painter in Malibu", *The J. Paul Getty Museum Journal* (JPG, Vol.4)

FRICKENHAUS, A. (1911), "Das Herakleion Von Melite", *AM* 36, 113-144

FRONING, H. (1971), *Dithyrambos und Vasenmalerei in Athen* (Konrad Triltsch Verlag, Würzburg)

FROZEN TOMBS, THE CULTURE OF THE ANCIENT TRIBES OF SIBERIA (British Museum Publication, 1975)

FURTWANGLER, A. (1883-7), *La Collection Sabouroff* (Berlin)

FURTWANGLER, A. (1900), *Die Antiken Gemmen* (Berlin)

FURTWANGLER, A. & REICHHOLD, K. (1904-32), *Griechische Vasen Malerei* (Munich)

FURTWANGLER, A. & REICHHOLD, K. (1965), *Antike Gemmen: Geshichte der Steinschneidekunst im Klassischen Altertum* (Amsterdam)

GADALLAH, F. (ed.) (1971), *Libya in History* (Benghazi)

GAIDUKJEWITSCH, V.F. (ed.) (1959), *Necropoli Bosporsckich Gordow* (Moscow)

GARDINER, E.N. (1906), "The Pankration and Wrestling", *JHS* 26, 4-26

GARDINER, E.N. (1907), "Throwing the Javelin", *JHS* 27, 249-273

GARDINER, E.N. (1910), *Greek Athletic sports and festivals* (Macmillan)

GARDINER, E.N. (1930), *Athletics of the Ancient World* (Oxford, The Clarendon Press)

GEMMILL, C.L. (1966), "Silphion", *Bull. Hist. of Medicine* 40, 295-313

GERHARD, E., *Auserlesene Vasenbilder*, 184-85 (Berlin)

GJERSTAD, E. (1948), *The Swedish Cyprus Expedition IV, Pt.2: The Cypro-Geometric Cypro-Archaic and Cypro-Classical Periods* (Stockholm)

GHALI-KAHIL, L.B. (1950), "Vases Attiques De Galaxidi *BCH*, 74, 48-53.

GHALI-KAHIL, L.B. (1955), *Les Enlevements et le retour d'Heléne dans les textes et les documents figures* (Paris)

GHALI-KAHIL, L.B. (1960), *La Céramique grecque* Études thasiennes VII (Paris)

GHALI-KAHIL, L.B. (1972), "Un nouveau vase plastique du potier Sotades au Museé du Louvre", *RA*, 271-84

GHISLANZONI, E. (1915), *Notizie Archeologiche sulla Tripolitania* (Mongrafie e Rapporti Coloniali N.4)

GHIRSHMAN, R. (1964), *Persia from the Origins to Alexander the Great* (translated by Stuart Gilbert and James Edmonds, Thames and Hudson, London)

GHISLANZONI, E (1915), "Notizie archeologiche sulla Cirenaica", 46-50, *Not. Arch.*, 1, 112-113

GILL, D. and TOMLINSON, R. (1985), "Two type B Skyphoi in Birmingham" *BSA* 80, 115-118

GILL, D. (1984), "The workshops of the Attic Bolsal", in Brijder, H.A.G. (ed.) *Ancient Greek and Related Pottery: Proceedings of the International Vase Symposium, Amsterdam* (Allard Pierson Series, Vol.5)

GILL, D., "The date of the Porticello shipwreck: Some observations on the Attic Bolsals", *IJNA*, L6, 1

GILL, D. (1987), "An Attic Lamp in Reggio: The Largest Batch Notation Outside Athens", *Oxford Journal of Archaeology*

GILL, D. (Unpublished), *Attic Black-glazed pottery and related fabrics in the Greek Museum* (The University of Newcastle upon Tyne: a short catalogue)

GILL, D., "Classical Greek Fictile Limitations of Precious Metal Vases", in Vickers, M. (ed.), *Pots and Pans* (unpublished)

GINOUVES, R. (1962), *Balaneutika: Recherches sur le bains de l'antiquité grecque* (Paris)

GOODCHILD, R.G. (1952), "Euhesperides: A Devastated City Site", *Antiquity*, 26, 208-12

GOODCHILD, R.G. (1962), *Benghazi, The story of a City* (Department of Antiquities, Cyrene)

GOODCHILD, R.G. (1963), *Cyrene and Apollonia: An historical record* (guide, Department of Antiquity, Libya)

GOODCHILD, R.G. (1971), *Kyrene und Apollonia* (Zürich)

GOMME, A.W. (1913), "The Legend of Cadmus and the Logographi", *JHS* 33, 53-73; 223-245

GORBUNOVA, K.C. (1973), "Onosy iz Raskopk na Berezani", *Archaelogia Polona*, 14, 79-85

GOTTE, E. (1957), Frauengemachbilder in der Vasenmalerei des 5 Jhn. (München)

GOTZE, H. (1948-1949), "Die Deutung Des Hesperidenrelief", *Jdi* 63-64, 91-99

GRAHAM, A.J. (1964), *Colony and Mother City in Ancient Greece* (Manchester)

GRAHAM, A.J. (1971), "Patterns in Early Greek Colonisation", *JHS* 91, 35-47

GREEK GODS & HEROES (1962), (Fifth edition, Museum of Fine Arts, Boston)

GREEK VASES FROM SOUTHERN COLLECTION (1981) (Introduction and Catalogue by H. Shapiro. New Orleans Museum of Art and Tulane University)

GREEN, J.R. & SINCLAIR R.K., "Athenians In Eretria", *Historia* 19 (1970) 515-527

GREEN, J.R. (1968), "Some Painters of Gnathia Vases", *BICS* 15, 34-49, pls. V-X.

GREEN, J.R. (1971), "Choes of the Later Fifth Century", *BSA* 66, 189-228

GREEN, J.R. (1976), *Gnathia Pottery in the Akademisches Kunstmuseum* (Bonn)

GREEN, J.R. (1977), "More Gnathian Pottery in Bonn", *AA*, 551-63

GREEN, J.R. (1979), "Ears of Corn and Other Offerings", in A. Cambitoglou (ed.), *Studies in Honour of Arthur Dale Trendall*, 81-90 (Sydney)

GREEN, J.R. & SINCLAIR, R.K. (1970), "Athenians in Eretria", *Historia* 19, 515-527

GRIEFENHAGEN, A. (1957) *Griechische Eroten*, Berlin.

GRIEFENHAGEN, A. (ed.) (1960), "Staatliche Museum Berlin", *Antike Kunstwerke* (Berlin)

GRIEFENHAGEN, A. (1979), "Zwei griechische Schmuckstücke", in A. Cambitoglou (ed.), *Studies in Honour of Arthur Dale Trendall*, 91-92 (Sydney)

GSELL, S. (1920), *Histoire ancienne de l'Afrique du nord* (Paris)

GUERRERO, AYUSO, V.M. (1982), *Los Nucleos Arqueologicos de Calvia* (Palma de Mallorca)

GUTHRIE, W.K.C. (1950), *The Greeks and Their Gods* (Boston)

GWYNN, A. (1918), *The Character of Greek Colonization, JHS* 88, 88-123

HAFTER LEZZI, A. (1976), *Der Shuwalow-Maler ein Kannenwerk statt der Parthenonzeit* (Mainz)

HAHLAND, W. (1930), *Vasen um Meidias* (Berlin)

HAMMOND W.M., "What is Trade", in Meyers, E. and West, W. (eds.), *The Archaeology of Trade in the East Mediterranean*

HARRIS, H.A. (1972), *Sport in Greece and Rome* (London)

HARRISON, J.E. (1922), *Prolegomena to the study of Greek Religion* (Cambridge)

HARWOOD, R.M., "Roman Africa", in T. Frank (ed.), *An Economic Survey of Ancient Rome*

HASPELS C.H. (1936), *Attic Black-figured lekythoi*, Paris

HASPELS C.H. (1954), "A fragmentary onos in the Allard Pierson Museum", *Bull. Vereen* 29 (1954), 25-30

HAUSER. F. (1909), "Aristophanes und Vasenbilder", *ÖJh*, 12, 80-100

HAYES, J. (1984), *Greek and Italian Black-Gloss Wares and Related Wares in the Royal Onatrio Museum: A Catalogue* (Toronto)

HAYNES, D.E. (1965), *Antiquities of Tripolitania* (Tripoli)

HAYWOOD, R.M. (1964), *Ancient Greece and the Near East* (London)

HEAD, B.V. (1911), *Historia Numorum: A Manual of Greek Numismatics* (Oxford)

HEICHELHEIM, F. (1938), *Wirtschaftsgeschichte des Altertum*, 1, 11.

HEICHELHEIM, F. (1965), *An Ancient Economic History* (Leiden)

HELBIG, W. (1963), *Führer durch die öffenflichen sammlungen klassischer Altertümer in Rom* (Tübingen)

HERBIG, R. (1929), "Griechische Harfen", *AM* 54 (1929) 164-193

HIGGINS, R.A. (1954), *Catalogue of the Terracottas in the Department of Greek and Roman Antiquities British Museum*, Vol. I (British Museum)

HILL, D.K. (1947), "The technique of Greek metal vases and its bearing on vase forms in Metal Pottery", *AJA* 51, 248-56

HILL, G.F. (1903), *Coins from Sicily*

HILL, G.F. (1951), *Sources of Greek History*, 478-431 (Oxford)

HOFFMANN, H. (1966), *Tarentine Rhyta* (Mainz)

HOFFMANN, H. (1974), "Hahnenkampf in Athen zu Ikonologie einer attischen Bildformen", *RA* 195-220

HOFFMANN, H. (1977), *Sexual and asexual pursuit: a structuralist approach to Greek vase painting* (Occasional Paper No.34. Royal Anthropological Institute of Great Britain and Ireland)

HOLWERDA (1936), *Het Laat-Grieksche En Romeinsche Gebruiksaardewerk Uit Het Middellandsche-Zee-Gebied.* (In, Het Rijkmuseum Van Oudheden Te Leiden)

VAN HOORN, G. (1951), *Choes and Anthesteria* (Leiden)

HOOKER, J.T. (1980), *The Ancient Spartans* (J.M. Dent & Sons, London)

HOPPER, R.J. (1979), *Trade and Industry in Classical Greece* (Thames and Hudson, London)

HOPPIN, J.C. (1973), *A Handbook of Attic Red-Figured Vases* (Washington D.C.)

HUMPHREY, J.H. (ed.) (1976), *Apollonia, the Port of Cyrene* (Excavation by the University of Michigan 1965-1967. A supplement to *Lib. Antique* IV, Department of Antiquities, Tripoli)

HUNDT, A. & PETERS, K. (1961), *Greifswalder Antiken* (Gedachtnisgab fur Erich Pernice, Berlin)

ISSERLIN, B.S.J. (1974), "The Cothon at Motya: Phoenician Harbour Works", *Archaeology* 27, 3

IZ ISTORII SEVERNOGO Prichernomoria V (Antichnuiu epokhu Sbornik Statei. Leningrad, 1979)

JACOBSTHAL, P. (1927), *Ornamente Griechischer Vasen* (Berlin)

JACOBSTHAL, P. (1931), *Die Melischen Reliefs* (Berlin)

JACOBSTHAL, P. (1944), *Early Celtic Art* (Oxford)

JACOBSTHAL, P. & LANGSDORFF, A. (1929). *Die Bronzeschnabelkannen* (Berlin)

JAHN, O. (1870), *Entführung der Europa* (Vienna)

JAMES, T. (1979), *An Introduction to Ancient Egypt* (London)

JENTEL, M.O. (1976), *Les gutti et les Askoi à reliefs etruscques et apuliens* (Leiden)

JEFFREY, L.H. (1976), *Archaic Greece: The City-States c.700-500* (London)

JEHASSE, L. (1978), *Salamine De Chypre* VIII (La Ceramique à Vernis Noir Du Rempart Meridional, Paris)

JEHASSE, L. (1981), "La Ceramique Attique A Vernis Noir De Kition De La Fin Du VI°, A La Fin Du IV° Siecle Avant J.C." *Excavation At Kition*, IV, The Non-Cypriot Pottery (Nicosia)

JETTMAR, K., *Art of the Steppes: The Eurasian Animal Style* (Methuen, London)

JOHNSON, F.P. (1938), "Red-Figured Pottery at Chicago", *AJA* 42

JOHNSON, D.L. (1973), *Jabal al-Akhdar Cyrenaica* (The University of Chicago)

JOHNSTON, A.W. (1978), "Greek vases in Phoenician Clothing", *BICS*, 25

JOHNSTON, A.W. (1979), *Trademarks on Greek vases* (Warminster)

JONES, G.D.B. (1983), "The Excavations at Tocra and Euhesperides", Cyrenaica 1968-1969, *Libyan Studies* 14, 110-111

JONES, R.G. (ed.) (1986), *Greek and Cypriot Pottery* (The British School Athens, Fitch Laboratory Occasional Papers I, 627-747)

JONES, G.D.B. & LITTLE, J.H., "Coastal Settlement in Cyrenaica", *JRS* 64-79

JORY, E.J. (1967), "Some Problems of Festival Competitions", *BICS* 14, 84ff.

JOVINO, M.B. & DONCEEL, R. (1969), *La Necropoli di Nola Pre-Romana* (Napoli)

JUCKER, H. (1961), *Das Bildnis im Blatterkelch, Geschichte und Bedeutung einer Römischen Portraitform* (Lausanne)

JULLY, J.J. (1973), *La céramique attique de la Monédire Bessan, Herault* (Bruxelles)

JULLY, J.J. (1982), Céramiques grecques ou de type grec et autres céramiques en Languedoc mediterraneen, Roussillon et Catalogue I (Annales I, He'raires de l'Universite de Besançon 275, Paris)

KAEMPF-DIMITRIADOU, S. (1979), *Die Liebe der Götter in der Attischen Kunst des 5 Jahrhunderts V Chr.* (A supplement to Antike Kunst)

KANE, S., "Sculpture from the Cyrene Demeter Sanctuary in its Mediterranean Context", in Barker et al., *Cyrenaica in Antiquity*, 237-247

KAROUZOU, S.P. (1945), "Vases from Odos Pandrosou" *JHS* 65, 38-44

KAROUZOU, S.P. (1946), "Choes" *AJA* 50, 245-60

KAROUZOU, S.P. (1970), "Die Schutzflehende Barberini", *Antike Kunst*, 13, 34-47

KELLETT, G. (1963), *Land transport in the Mediterranean in pre-Roman times* (London, M.A. thesis)

KENNER, H. (1935), "Das Luterion im Kult", *ÖJh* 29, 109-154

KENNER, H. (1939), "Flügelfrau und Flügeldämon", *OJh* 31, 81-59

KENRICK, P., "Patterns of Trade in Fine Pottery at Bernice", in Barker (ed.) *Cyrenaica in Antiquity*

KENRICK, P. (ed.) (1986), *Excavations At Sabratha 1948-51* (Society for the promotion of Roman studies. Journal of Roman Studies Monograph No.2)

KERN, J.H.C. (1957), "An Attic Miniature Lekanis-Pyxis from Cyrenaica" *Oudheidkundige Mededeelingen* uit het *Rijksmuseum van Oudheden te* Leiden, 38 53-57

KERN, J. (1954), Notice sur oenochoe attique à glazure noire du Musée de Prehistoire de Valencia (Espagne) *Archivo De Prehistoria Levantina* 5, 141-145

KERN, J. (1957), "An Attic 'feeding bottle' of the 4th Century BC in Leiden" *Mnemosyne*, 4th Series 10, 16-21

KLEBE, H. (1955), Schadewaldt, Gefass zur Kindernahrung im Wandel der Zeit.

KLEINER, F.S. (1972), "The Kalydonian Hunt: A reconstruction of a painting from the circle of Polygnotos", *Antike Kunst* 15, 7-19

KOPCKE, G. (1964), "Golddekorierte Attische Schwarzfirniskermik Des Vierten Jahrhunderts V. Chr", *AM* 79, 22-84

KOSSATZ-DEISSMANN, A. (1978), *Dramen Des Aischylos Auf Westgriechlschen Vasen* (Mainz am Rhein)

KRAELING, C.H. (1962), *Ptolemais, City of the Libyan Pentapolis* (Chicago)

KRAUS, T. (1953-1955), "Antithetisch Bocke", *AM* 68-70

KUNISCH, B.N. (1972), *Antiken der Sammlung Julius C. und Margot Funcke*

KURTZ, D.C. (1975), *Athenian White Lekythoi* (Oxford)

KURTZ, D.C. (ed.) (1985), *Beazley and Oxford* (Lectures delivered in Wolfson College, Oxford, 28 June, Oxford)

KURTZ, D. & BOARDMAN, J. (1971), *Greek Burial Customs* (Ithaca, New York)

LA COSTE-MESSELIERE, P. DE (1950), *Les trésors de Delphes* (Paris)

LACROIX, L. (1934), *La faune marine dans la decoration des plats à poissons* (Verviers)

LAMBOGLIA, N. (1950), "Per una classificazione preliminare della ceramica compana", *Atti del Primo Congresso Internazionale di Studi Liguri*

LAMBOGLIA, N. (1954), "La Ceramica Precampani dell Bastida", *Archivo De Prehistoria Levantina* 5, 105-139

LANE, A. (1948), *Greek Pottery* (London)

LANGDON, M.K. (1978), "Sanctuary of Zeus on Mount Hymettos", *Hesperia* Suppl. XVI

LANGLOTZ, E. (1932), *Griechische Vasen in Würzburg* (Munich)

LAWLER, L.B. (1927), "The Maenads: A contribution to the study of the Dance in Ancient Greece", *Mem. Acad. Rome* VI, 69-112

LAWLER, L.B. (1964), *The Dance in Ancient Greece* (London)

LAZARIDES, D. (1969), *Neapolis Christopolis Kavala* (published in Greek, Athens)

LE RIDER, G. (1966), *Monnaies Cretoises de V au 1er Siecle av. JC* (Paris)

LHOTE, H. (1950), *The Search for the Tassili Frescoes* (Hutchinson, London)

LLOYD, J. (1978), *The Historical Development of Benghazi* (Manchester, Ph.D. thesis)

LLOYD, J. (ed.), *Excavation At Sidi Khrebish Benghazi* (Bernice, Suppl. to Lib. Antiqua V. Published by the Department of Antiquities, Ministry of Teaching and Education, People's Socialist Libyan Arab Jamahiriya)

LO PORTO (1967), *Atti e Memorie della Societa Magna Greciae* 8, 75ff.

LORENTZ, F.V. (1937), "ΒΑΡΒΑΡΩΝ ΥΦΑΣΜΑΤΑ", *RM* 52, 165-222

LUCAS P. (1972), *Voyage du sieur Paul Lucas, fait par ordre du Roy dans la Grece, L'Asie Mineure, La Macedoine et l'Afrique* (Published by Etienne Fourmount, Paris)

LULLIES R. & HIRMER M. (1960), *Greek Sculpture* (Thames and Hudson London)

LULLIES, R. (1968), *Griechische Kunstwerke Sammlung Ludwig Achener* (Düsseldorf)

LUNI, M. (1976), "Storia Della Istituzione Ginnasiale dell Attivita Atletica In Cirenaica", *Quaderni* 8, 259-284

LUSCHEY, VON HEINZ (1954), "Zur Wiederkehr Archaischer Bildzeichen in der Attischen Grabmalkunst des 4 Jahrhunderts V. Chr.", *Beiträge zur Klassischen Altertum Swissenschaft* (Festschrift Bernhard Schweitzer, Reinhard Lullies (ed.), Stuttgart)

McBURNEY, C.B.M. (1960), *The Stone Age of Northern Africa* (Cambridge)

McBURNEY, C.B.M. (1967), *The Haua Fteah, Cyrenaica* (Cambridge)

McBURNEY, C.B.M. (1968), "Libyan Role in Prehistory", *Libya in History* (Historical Conference Benghazi, Fawzi F. Gadallah (ed.) 1-7)

McKCAMP II, J. (1979), "A Drought in the late Eighth Century B.C.", *Hesperia*, Vol. 48, 397-411

MAGGETTI, M. et al. (1981), *Archaeometry* 23.2, 199-207

MAIURI, A. (1940), Monumenti della Pittura Scoperti in Italia 3, I. Pompeii: le case di 'M. Fabius Amandio', del 'Sacerdos Amandus', e di 'P. Cornelius Tegas' (Rome)

MAUNY, R. (1979), Pre-Arab Trans-Saharan Trade-Routes between Libya and the Niger-Chadic Savana", *Trans-Saharan Trade-Route Conference* (Tripoli, unpublished)

MARINATOS, Sp. (1971), "On the Chronological Sequence of Thera's Catastrophes", *Acta of the 1st International Scientific Congress on the Volcano of Thera* (Athens)

MARK, F. (1959), *Plautus Rudens* (Amsterdam)

MASSEI, L. (1978), *Gli Askoi: A Figure Rosse Nei Corredi Funerari della Necropoli di Spina* (Milano)

MATZ, F. (1955), "Belli Facies et Triumphus", *Festschrift für Carl Wiekert*, 41-58 (Berlin)

MAYO, M.E. (ed.) (1982), *The Art of South Italy: Vases from Magna Graeciae* (Virginia Museum, Richmond)

MEIGGS, R. & LEWIS D. (eds.) (1969) *Greek Historical Inscriptions, A Selection* (Oxford)

MEIGGS, R. (1982), *Trees and Timber in the Ancient Mediterranean World* (Oxford)

MERTENS, J.R. (1977), *Attic White-ground: Its development on shapes other than the lekythos*

METZGER, H. (1951), *Les Représentations dans la Céramique attique du IV² Siecle* (Paris)

METZGER, H. (1942-1943), "Lebes gamikos à figures rouges du musée National d'Athenes" *BCH* 66-67, 228-247

MEYERS E. & WEST W. (eds.) (1979), *The Archaeology of Trade in the East Mediterranean* (Symposium papers published in *Archaeological News* 8 No. 2, 3 31-96)

MEZQUIRIZ, M.A. (1954), "La Ceramica de importation en san Miguel de Liria", *Archivo De Prehistoria Levantina* 5, 159-176

MICHELL, B.M. (1956), "Cyrene and Persia", *JHS* 86, 99 f.

MILNE, J.G. (1939), "The trade between Greece and Egypt before Alexander the Great", *JEA* 25, 177-183

MINGAZZINI, P. (1925), *Le rapresentazioni Vascolari del mito dell' apteosi di Heracles*, Memorie della R. Accademia Nazionale dei Lincei 6th Ser., 1, fasc. 6 (Rome)

MINNS, E. (1913), *Scythians and Greeks* (Cambridge)

MOKHTAR, G. (ed.), *The General History of Africa II* (Ancient Civilizations of Africa, Heinemann, California, Unesco)

MOMMSEN, A. (1864), *Feste der Stadt Athen* (Leipzig)

MOMMSEN, H. (1975), *Der Affecter* (Mainz)

MOON, W.G. (1979), *Greek Vase-Painting in Midwestern Collections* (Chicago, The Art Institute)

MOON, W.G. (1983), *Ancient Greek Art and Iconography* (University of Wisconsin Press)

MOREL, J. (1980), '"Les vases à vernis noir et à figures rouges d'Afrique, avant la deuxieme guerre Punique et les problemes des exportations de Grand-Grece", *Antiquites Africaines* 15-16, 29-75

MORRISON, J.S. & WILLIAMS R.T. (1968), *Greek Oared Ships 900-322 BC* (Cambridge University Press, Cambridge)

MOSTRA dell'Etruria Padana e dell cittá di Spina, (1960, Bologna)

MULLER, L. (1874), *Numismatique de l'ancienne Afrique* (Copenhagen 1860-1963, Suppl. Vol.4)

MYRES, J.L. (1930), *Who were the Greeks?* (Berkeley)

NAVILL, L. (1951), *Les monnaies D'or de la Cyrenaique, 450 à 250 avant J.C.* (Geneva)

NEILS, J. (1980), "The group of the Negro Alabastra, A study in motif transferal", *A. Kunst*, 23, 13-23

NEUE DEUTSCHE AUSGRABUNGEN im Mittelmeergebiet und im Vordern Orient (1959, Berlin)

NEUGEBAUER, C. (1932), *Führer durch das Antiquarium*, II, Vasen (Berlin)

NICOLE, G. (1908), *Meidias et le style fleuri* (Geneva)

NIKOLOV, B. (1969), *Musée Archéologique De Vratza* (Sofia)

NOBLE, J.V. (1965), *The Technique of Painted Attic Pottery* (New York)

NOSHY, I. (1968), "Arcesilaos III", in Gadalla (ed.) *Libya in History* 53-78

OAKLEY, J.H., "Double-Register Calyx-krater: A study in workshop tradition", in Brijder (ed.), *Ancient Greek and Related Pottery*, 119-127

OLIVER, A. (1977), *Silver for the Gods, 800 years of Greek and Roman silver* (The Toledo Museum of Art, Toledo, Ohio)

OLIVERIO, G. (1928), "Iscrizioni Di Cirene", *Riv. Fil* 56, 222-232

OLIVERIO, G. (1932-6), *Documenti antichi dell'Africa Italiana* (Bergamo)

ONAIKO, H. (1966), *Antichnyi import v pridneprove* (Moscow)

ONAIKO, H., *Antichnyi import v pridneprove*, 1 probuzhe, Vol.4, pt.2

OOST, S.I. (1963), "Cyrene 96-74 B.C.", *Classical Philology*, 58, 11-25

OTCHET IMPERATORSKOI ARKHEOLOGICHESKOI KOMMISSII (1913-1915, ST. PETERSBURG)

OTTO, W.F. (1965), *Dionysus: Myth and Cult* (an English translation (London 1965) of the 1933 German original)

OVERBECK, J. (1871-8), *Atlas der griechischen Kunstmythologie* (Leipzig)

OXFORD CLASSICAL DICTIONARY (Second edition, 1970)

PAGE, D. (1971), "The Volcano of Santorini and the Devastation of Minoan Crete", *Acta of the 1st International Scientific Congress in the Volcano of Thera* (Athens)

PAGANO, V.P. (1976), "Le Rotte Antiche tra la Grecia e la Cirenaica e gli Itinerari Marittimi e Terrestri Lungo le Coste Cirenaiche e della Grande Sirte", *Quaderni*, 8, 285-352

PAGENSTECHER, R. (1909), *Die Calenische Reliefkeramik*, *JdI*, *Ergnzungsheft* VIII

PARIBENI, E. (1959), *Catalogo Delle Sculture Di Cirene* (Roma)

PARKE, H.W. (1967), *The Oracles of Zeus* (Oxford)

PARKE, H.W. (1967), *Greek Oracles* (London)

PARKE, H.W. & WORMELL, D.E.W. (1958), *The Delphic Oracle*, Vols. I, II (Oxford)

PARKE, H.W. (1977). *Festivals of the Athenians* (Thames and Hudson, London)

PAULY-WISSOWA, *Real-Encyclopädie der Klassischen Alterumswissenschaft*

PAYNE, H. (1932), *Necrocorinthia: A study of Corinthian Art in the Archaic Period* (Oxford)

PEREDOLSKI, A. (1928), "Sotades" *AM* 53, 9-16

PERNIER, L. (1931), "L'Artemision Di Cirene", *Africa Italiana* IV, 173-228

PERNIER, L. (1935), *Il Tempio e altare di Apollo a Cirene*

PETERS, K. (1942), *Studien zu den Panathenaischen Preisamphoren* (Berlin)

PETERS, K. (1942), "Zwei Panathenaische Preisamphoren des Aristophanes" *JdI*, 57

PETROCCHI, C.T. (1941), "Recerche preistoriche in Cirenaica", *Africa Italiana*. Vol. VII

PETRENKO, B. (1967), *Pravoberezhe Spednego Pridneprovyen* (Moscow)

PFUHL, E. (1923), *Malerei und Zeichnung der Griechen* (Munchen)

PHILIPPAKI, B. (1967), *The Attic Stamnos* (Oxford)

PHILLIPS, K. (1976), in Donald White, "Excavation in the Sanctuary of Demeter and Persephone", *AJA* 80, 165-181

PICARD, M. (1955), "Quelques Observations sur le Costume Scythique á propos des Fouilles", in *Studia Antiqua*, in honour of Antonio Salac Septuagenario, 152-159 (Prague)

PICAZO, M. (1979), *La ceramica Atica de Ullastret* (Barcelona)

PICKARD-CAMBRIDGE, A. (1968), *The Dramatic Festivals of Athens* (Second edition, Oxford)

PINNEY, G.F., "Achilles Lord of Scythia", in Moon (ed.), *Ancient Greek Art and Iconography*

POUILLOUX, J. (1973), "Amphore Panathenaique" *Salamine De Chypre IV*, Anthologie Salaminienne, 109-111

POULSEN, F. (1973), *Delphi* (translated by G.C. Richards, Washington, McGrath Publications)

PORADA, E. (1962), *Ancient Iran* (London)

PRAG, A.J.N.W. (1985), *The Oresteia: Iconographic and Narrative Tradition* (Aris and Phillips, Warminster, Wiltshire)

PRICE, E.E. (1983), *The Grand Procession of Ptolemy Philadeplhus* (Oxford)

PRICE, M. & WAGGONER, N. (1975), *Archaic Coinage: The Asyat Hoard* (London)

RAECK, W. (1981), *Zum Barbarenbild in der Kunst, Athens im 6. und 5. Jahrhundert V. Chr.* (Bonn)

REES, D.S. (1979-80), "Industrial exploitation of Murex shells: purple dyes and the line production at Sidi Khrebish Benghazi, Bernice, *Libyan Studies* 11

REINACH, S. (1899), *Repertoire Des Vases Peints Grecs et Etrusques* (Paris)

REINACH, S. (1900), "La Naissance de Ploutos", *Rev. Arch.* 36, 87-98

REYNOLDS, J. (1978), "Hadrian, Antoninus Pius and the Cyrenaican Cities", *JRS* 68, 111-121

RHODES, D.E. (1973), *Dennis of Etruria, The Life of George Dennis* (Cecil and Amelia Woolf, London) (Chapter 6, "Sicily and North Africa", pp.73-99 deals with the period between 1863 and 1887 when George Dennis was in Cyrenaica)

RHOMIOPOLOU, K. (ed.) (1979), *Treasures of Ancient Macedonia* (The Archaeological Museum, Thessaloniki)

RICCIONI, G. (1968), *La Tomba della Panatenaica di Vulci*, Quaderni Di Villa Ginlia No. 3

RICHTER, G.M.A. (1915), *Greek, Etruscan and Roman Bronzes* (New York)

RICHTER, G.M.A. (1904-5), "Distribution of Attic Vases", *BSA* XI

RICHTER, G.M.A. (1965), *The Portraits of the Greeks*

RICHTER, G.M.A. (1967), *Attic Red-Figured Vases: A Survey* (Yale University Press, New Haven and London)

RICHTER, G.M.A. (1984), *The Portraits of the Greeks* (abridged and revised by R.R.R. Smith, Phaidon, Oxford)

RICHTER, G.M.A. & HALL, L. (1936), *Red-Figured Athenian Vases in the Metropolitan Museum of Art* (New Haven)

RICHTER, G.M.A. & MILNE, M.J. (1935), *Shapes and Names of Athenian Vases* (New York)

RILEY, J.A. "The Coarse Pottery from Bernice", in Lloyd (ed.), *Excavation At Sidi Khrebish Benghazi*, 91-449 (Bernice)

ROBERTS, S. (1978), "Evidence for a pattern in Attic pottery production c. 430-350 BC", *AJA* 77, 435-437

ROBERTS, S. (1978), *The Attic Pyxis* (Chicago)

ROBERTSON, M. (1975), *The Parthenon Frieze* (Phaidon)

ROBERTSON, M., "The Attic Black-Figure and Red-Figure Pottery", *Excavation At Kition*, IV, The non-Cypriote Pottery, 51-74

ROBERTSON, M. (1975), *A History of Greek Art* (Cambridge)

ROBERTSON, M., "Beazley and Attic Vase Painting", in D. Kurtz, (ed.), *Beazley and Oxford*

ROBINSON, D.M. (1930), *A Catalogue of the Greek vases in the Royal Ontario Museum of Archaeology* (The University of Toronto Press)

ROBINSON, D.M. (1936), "A new lebes gamikos with a possible representation of Apollo and Daphne", *AJA* 40, 507-510

ROBINSON, D.M. (1945), "A New Onos or Epinetron", *AJA* 49, 488-499

ROBINSON, D.M. (1950), *Excavation at Olynthus* (V: Mosaics, Vases and Lamps of Olynthus (1933); XIII, Vases found in 1934 and 1938 (1955))

ROBINSON, E.S.G. (1927), *Catalogue of Greek Coins in the British Museum* (Cyrenaica)

RODER G. & IPPEL A. (1921), *Die Denkmaler des Pelizäus* (Museum zu Hildesheim)

ROEBUCK, C. (1959), *Ionian trade and colonization* (New York)

ROSE, H.J. (1928), *A Handbook of Greek Mythology* (London)

ROSCHER, W.H. (1965), *Lexikon Der Griechischen und Römischen Mythologie* II.2 (Leipzig 1894-1897, new edition Hildesheim)

ROSENBAUM, E. (1960), *A Catalogue of Cyrenaican Portrait Sculpture* (London)

ROSTOVTZEFF, M. (1941), *Social and Economic History of the Hellenistic World* (Oxford University Press)

ROTROFF, S. (1984), "Spool Saltcellars in the Athenian Agora" *JHS* 53, 343-354

ROWE & HEALY, J. (1959), *Cyrenaica Expedition of the University of Manchester, 1956-57* (Manchester)

ROWE, A. (1948), *New Light on Aegypto-Cyrenean Relations: Two Ptolemaic Statues Found in Cyrenaica*

RUDENKO, C. (1968), *Drevneishie v mire Khudozhestvennye i tkani* (Moscow)

RUDENKO, S.I. (1970), *Frozen Tombs of Siberia* (translated by M.W. Thompson, London)

RÜDIGER, U. (1966-67), "Askoi in Unteritalien", *RM* 73-74, 1-9

RUDOLPH, W. (1971), *Die Bauchlekythos: Ein Beitrag zur Formgeschichichte der attischen keramike des 5 Jahrhunderts v. Chr.* (Bloomington, Indiana, USA)

RUMPF, A. (1927) *Chalkidische Vasen* (Berlin and Leipzig)

RUMPF, A. (1951), "Parrhasios", *AJA* 55. 1-12

RUMPF, A. (1953), *Malerei und Zeichnung, Hd.Arch.*

RUMPF, A. (1976), *Sakonides* (Mainz)

SADAWYA, A., "Greek Settlement in Cyrenaica, with notes on pottery discovered there", in Gadalla (ed.), *Libya in History*, 92-98

SALVADOR, P. (1972), "La primera exploracion sistematica del pecio del Sec, Palma de Mallorca", *R.St.Lig.* 38

SCHLORB-VIERNEISEL (1966), "Eridanos-Nekropol - I. Gräber und Opferstellen hsi-104", *AM* 81, 4-111

SCHAAL, H. (1931), *Vom Tauschhandel zum Welthandel* (Leipzig)

SCHAUENBURG, K. (1962), "Gestirnbilder in Athen und Unteritalien", *Antike Kunst* 5, 51-64

SCHAUENBURG, K. (1974), "Athenabusten des Bowdoin-malers", *AA*, 149-157

SCHAUS, G.P. (1985), *The Extramural Sanctuary of Demeter and Persephone at Cyrene, Libya, Vol. II: The East Greek Island and Laconian Pottery* (University Museum Monograph 56, University of Pennsylvania, Philadelphia)

SCHEFOLD, K. (1930), *Die Kertscher Vasen*

SCHEFOLD, K. (1931), *Untersuchungen zu den Kertscher Vasen* (Berlin and Leipzig)

SCHEFOLD, K. (1960), *Meisterwerke griechischer kunst* (Basle)

SCHEFOLD, K. (1981), *Die Göttersage in der Klassischen und Hellenistischen Kunst* (Hirmer Verlag, Munchen)

SCHEFOLD, K. (1943), *Die Bildnisse Der Antiken Dichter Redner und Denker* (Basel)

SCHMIDT, L. (ed.) (1858-1911), *Die Alterthizmer unserer heidnischenj Vorzeit* (Mainz)

SCHMIDT, E. (1922), *Archaistische kunst in Griechenland und Rom* (Munich)

SCHWARZ, G. (1972-75), "Eine Hydria des Berliner Malers in Graz", *Ojh* 50, 125-133

THE SEARCH FOR ALEXANDER, 1980 exhibition (The Greek Ministry of Culture and Science)

SECHAN, L. (1926), *Etudes sur la Tragedies Grecque* (Paris)

SEGALL, B. (1966), *Tradition und Neuschopfung in der Frühalexandrinischen Kleinkunst* (Berlin)

SEMPLE, E. (1932), *The Geography of the Mediterranean Region: its relation to Ancient History* (London)

SHEAR, T.L. (1970), "The Monument of the Eponymous Heroes in the Athenian Agora", *Hesperia* 39, 145-222

SHEFTON, B.B. (1954), "Three Laconian Vase Painters", *BSA* 49 (1954) 299-310

SHEFTON, B.B. (1958), "Odysseus and Bellerophon Reliefs", *BCH*, 82

SHEFTON, B.B. (1960), "Some Iconographic Remarks on the Tyrannicides", *AJA* 64, 173-179.

SHEFTON, B.B. (1971), "Persian Gold and Attic Black Glaze, Achaemenian Influences on Attic Pottery of the 5th and 4th centuries B.C.", IXth International Congress of Classical Archaeology, in *Annales Archaeologiques arab Syriennes*, 109-110

SHEFTON, B.B. (1982), "Greeks and Greek imports in the south of the Iberian Peninsula". "Phönizier in Western" the proceedings of the International Symposium on the Phoenician expansion in the west, held in Cologne between 24-27 April 1979, *Madrider Beitrage*: BD 8, 337-370 (Deutsches Archalogisches Institut, Madrid)

SHEFTON, B.B. (1982), "The Krater from Baksy", *The Eye of Greece*: Studies in the art of Athens, edited by Donna Kurtz and Brian Sparkes (Cambridge University Press, Studies in Honour of Martin Robertson)

SICHTERMANN, H. (1959), "Archäologische Funde und Forschungen in der Kyrenaiks 1942-1958", *AA* 74, 239-348

SIFAKIS, G.M. (1971), *Parabasis and Animal Choruses*, pls. III-IV (London)

SIMON, E. (1953), *Opfernde Götter* (Berlin)

SIMON, E. (1961), "Zum Fries der Mysterienvilla bei Pompeji", *JdI*, 76, 111-172

SIMON, E. (1966), "Neue Deutung Zweier Eleusinischer Denkmaler des Vierten Jahrhunderts v. Chr.", *Antike Kunst*, 9, 72-92

SIMON, E. (1969), *Die Götter der Griechen* (Hirmer Verlag, Munchen)

SIMON, E. (1976), *Die Griechischen Vasen* (Munich)

SKOMOROSKA, J. & SWIECKI, Z. (1977), "Research in the Construction of Greek Black Vase-Painting" *Archeologia* (Warsaw) 28 37-47

SMITH, C. (1896), *Catalogue of the Greek and Etruscan vases in the British Musuem*, Vol. III

SMITH, H.R.W. (1949), "A goddess from Lebadeia", *Hesperia*, Suppl. VIII

SMETS, A. (1936), "Groupes chronologiques des Amphores Panathenaiques Inscrites", *L'Antiquité Classique* 5, 87-104

SNIJDER, G.A.S. (1934), "Guttus und verwandtes", *Mnemosyne*, 3rd series I, 34-60

SNODGRASS, A.M. (1967), *Arms and Armour of the Greeks* (Thames and Hudson, London)

SNOWDON, F.M. Jr., (1970), *Blacks in Antiquity* (Cambridge, Mass.)

SOKOLOV, G. (1974), *Antique Art on the Northern Black Sea Coast* (translated by S. Chulaki, Aurora Art Publications, Leningrad)

SOURVINOU-INWOOD, C. (1979), *Theseus as a son and a stepson*, Supplement No.40 to *BICS*

SPARKES, B.A. (1968), "Black Perseus", *Antike Kunst* 11, 3-16

SPARKES, B.A. (1977), "Quintain and the Talcott Class", *Antike Kunst* 20, 8-25

SPARKES, B.A. & TALCOTT, L. (1958), *Pots and pans of Classical Athens*

SPARKES, B.A. & TALCOTT, L. (1970), *The Athenian Agora: Vol. XII, "Black and Plain Pottery"* (Princeton, New Jersey)

STAALICHE KUNST SAMMLUNGEN ANITKENABTEILUNG IM ALBERTINUM (Dresden)

STEFFY, J.R. (1985), "The Kyrenia Ship: An Interim Report on its hull construction" *AJA* 89, 83-84, 98-99

STELE: TOMOS EIS MNEMEN NIKOLAOU KONTOLEONTOS (1980), 265-271, Pls. 91-116 (in Greek, Athens)

STENICO, A., "Un Anfora Panatenaica del Pittore di Euphiletos", in Cambitoglou (ed.), *Studies in Honour of Arthur Dale Trendall*, 177-180

STEWART, A. (1977), *Skopas of Paros* (New Jersey)

STEWART, A. (1982), *Scopas in Malibu* (The J. Paul Getty Museum, Malibu, California)

STIBBE, C.M. (1972), *Lakonische Vasenmaler des Sechsten Jahrhunderts v. Chr.* (Studies in Ancient Civilization, New Series I, Amsterdam)

STRONG, D.E. (1966), *Greek and Roman Gold and Silver Plate* (London)

STUCCHI, S. (1965), *L'Agora di Cirene, i, Lati nord ed est della platea inferiore* (Monografie di Archeologia Libica, VII, Roma)

STUCCHI, S. (1967), *Cirene* 1957-1966, un Decennio di Attivita della Missione Archaeologica Italiana a Cirene (Tripoli)

STUCCHI, S. (1976), "Il Giardino delle Esperidi, e le tappe della conoscenza greca della costa Cirenica", *Quaderni* 8, 7-73

STUCCHI, S., "Cyrenaica as head point of two possible caravan routes". *Trans-Saharan Trade-Route Conference*

SÜSSEROTT, H.K. (1938), *Greiechische Plastik des 4. Jahrhunderts vor Christus* (Frankfurt)

SUTHERLAND, C.H.V. (1943), "Corn and Coin", *AJP* 54, 129-147

SWADDLING, J. (1980), *The Ancient Olympic Games* (London)

SWINY, H.W. & LATZEV, M.L., "The Kyrenia Ship Wreck: A fourth century B.C. Greek Merchant Ship", in Blackman D.J. (ed.), *Marine Archaeology*, 349-51

TALCOTT, L. & PHILIPPAKI, B., *Small Objects from the Pnyx: 11*, "Figured Pottery", 1-78, *Hesperia*, Supplement X

TALCOTT, L. (1935), "Attic Black-Glazed Stamped Ware and Other Pottery from a Fifth Century Well", *Hesperia* 4, 477-523

TECHNAU, W. (1929), "Griechische Keramik in Samischen Heraion", *AM* 54, 6-64

TECHNAU, W. (1937), "Die Gottin auf dem Stier", *JdI* 52, 76-103

THEMELIS, P.G. (1969), "Eretria : Procession Way and Panathenaic Amphoras", *AAA* 2, 409-416

THEMELIS, P.A. (1980), "Eretria : Panathenaiko, Amphoreis" *Stele : Tomos eis Mnemen Nikolaou Kontoleontos*, 265-271 Pls. 91-116 (in Greek, Athens)

THIMME, J. (1970), "Griechische Salbgefasse mit Libyschen Motiven", *Jarhrbuch der staatlichen Kunstsammlungen in Baden-Württemberg*, 7ff.

THOMPSON, D.B. (1973), *Ptolemaic Oinochoai and Portraits in Faience* (The Clarendon Press, Oxford)

THOMPSON, H.A. (1934), "Two centuries of Hellenistic Pottery", *Hesperia* 3, 311-480

THOMPSON, H.A. (1949), "The Pedimental Sculpture of the Hephaisteion", *Hesperia* 18, 230-268

THOMPSON, M. (1979), "Hoards and Overstrikes", in *Expedition*, 21.4, 41-47

TITE, M.S., BIMSON, M. & FREESTONE, I.C. (1981), *Archaeometry* 23, 2, 199-207

TOD, M.N. (ed.) (1948), *Greek Historical Inscription: A selection, Vol. II, from 403 to 323 BC* (Oxford)

TOMLINSON, R.A. (1970), "Ancient Macedonian Symposia", *Ancient Macedonia* (Basil Laourdas and C.H. Makaronas (eds.), Thessaloniki)

TONI, Y.T. (1956), *The Social Geography of Cyrenaica* (Durham University, Ph.D. thesis)

TOYNBEE, J.M.C. (1973), *Animals in Roman Life and Art* (Thames and Hudson, London)

TRENDALL, A.D. (1936), *Paestan Pottery* (British School At Rome)

TRENDALL, A.D. (1951), "Attic Vases in Australia and New Zealand", *JHS* 71, 191ff.

TRENDALL, A.D. (1953), "The Choephoroi Painter", in *Studies presented to David Moore Robinson* (Saint Louis, Missouri)

TRENDALL, A.D. (1967), "Phylax Vases", *BICS*, Suppl.19

TRENDALL, A.D. (1983), *The Red-Figured Vases of Lucania Campania and Sicily*, Oxford I, II, and III Supplement, *BISC*, Trendall *LCS*

TRENDALL, A.D. & WEBSTER, T.B.L. (1971), *Illustration of Greek Drama* (Phaidon)

TRENDALL, A.D. & CAMBITOGLOU, A. (1978), *The Red-Figured Vases of Apulia* (Vol. 1, Early and Middle Apulian, Oxford)

TRIAS DE ARRIBAS, G. (1967), *Ceramicas Griegas De La Peninsula Iberica* (Valencia)

TUCKER, T.G. (1901), *The Choephoroi of Aeschylus* (Cambridge)

URE, A.D. (1936), "Red-Figured Cups with Incised and Stamped Decoration", I, *JHS* 56, 205-215

URE, A.D. (1944), "Red-Figured Cups with Incised and Stamped Decoration", II, *JHS* 64, 67-77

URE, P.N. (1927), *Sixth and Fifth Century Pottery from Rhitsona* (Oxford University Press)

URE, P.N. (1913), *Black Glaze Pottery from Rhitsona in Boeotia* (Oxford University Press)

URE, P.N. (1934), *Aryballoi and Figurines from Rhitsona in Boeotia* (Cambridge University Press)

VACANO, VON O. (1973), *Zur Entstehung und Deutung Gemalter Seitenansichtiger Kopfbilder* (Bonn)

VANDERPOOL, E., McCREDIE, J. & STEINBERG, A. (1962), "Koroni: A Ptolemaic Camp on the East Coast of Attica", *Hesperia* 31, 26-61

VATTIER DE BOURVILLE, J. (1849), *Revue Archéologique* 5(1), 15ff., 56f., Rapport au Ministre: *Archives des Mission Scientifique*, 580-86

VENEDIKOVE (ed.) (1963), Apoloniya: razkopkite v. nekropola na Apoloniya 1947-1949 (Sofiyx), B'tgarska Akedemiya na Naukite, Archeologicheski Institute.

VERCOUTTER, J. (1954), *Les objects Egyptiens et Egyptients du Mobilier Funeraire Carthaginois* (Paris)

VERMEULE, E. (1970), "Five vases from the Grave Precinct of Dexileus", *JdI* 85, 103-07

VERMEULE, E. (1979), *Aspects of Death in Early Greek Art and Poetry*

VIAN, F. (1951), *Répertoire Des Gigantomachies; Figures Dans L'Art Grec et Romain* (Paris)

VIAN, F. (1963), *Les Origin de Thebes, Cadmos et Les Spartes* (Paris)

VICKERS, M. ALLAN J. & IMPEY O. (1986), *From Silver to Ceramic* (Oxford)

VICKERS, M. (1970), "A note on a rattling Black-Glaze Cup in Dublin", *JHS* 90, 199-201

VICKERS, M. (1973), "An Ex-Rattling Cup in Oxford", *AJA* 77, 196-7

VICKERS, M. (1974), Two more Rattling Cups? *AJA* 78, 429-30

VICKERS, M. (1979), *Skythian Treasures in Oxford* (Ashmolean Museum, Oxford)

VICKERS, M. (ed.) (1986), *Pots and Pans: Precious Metals and Ceramics in the Muslim, Chinese and Graeco-Roman Worlds* (Oxford Studies in Islamic Art, Oxford)

VICKERS, M. & BAZAMA, A. (1971), "A fifth-century B.C. Tomb in Cyrenaica", *Libya Antiqua*, 8, 69-85

VICKERS, M. & GILL, D.W.J. (1986), "Archaic Greek Pottery from Eusperides, Cyrenaica", *Libyan Studies* 17, 97-108

VICKERS, M. & REYNOLDS, J. (1971-72), "Cyrenaica, 1962-71", *AR*, 27-43

VIERNEISEL, K. (1964), "Die Ausgrabungen im Kerameikos", *AA*, 432ff.

VILLARD, F. (1959), "Vases attiques du ve siècle avant. J.-C. a Gouraya" *Libyca* 7, 7-25

WAISGLASS, A.A. (1955), *An Historical Study of Cyrene from the Fall of the Battiad Monarchy to the Close of the Fourth Century B.C.* (Columbia University, Ph.D. thesis)

WALDA, H. & WALKER, S. (1984) "The Art and Architecture of Lepcis Magna: Marble Origins by Isotopic Analysis", *Libyan Studies* 15, 81-92

WALDHAUER, O. (1929), "Ein Askos aus der Sammlung Chanenko in Kiew und die Altsamische Kunst", *AA*, 235-266

WALTER, O. (1937), "Der Saulenbau Des Herakles", *AM* 62, 41-51

WALTERS, H.B. (1896), *Catalogue of the Greek and Etruscan Vases in the British Museum IV, Vases of the Latest Period* (London)

WALTERS, H.B. (1898), "On Some Black-Figured Vases", *JHS* 18, 282-301

WARD-PERKINS, J.B. (1951), "Tripolitania and the Marble Trade", *JRS* 41, 89-104

WARD, W.A. (1971), *Egypt and the East Mediterranean World* (American University of Beirut)

WARREN, P.M. (1979), "The miniature fresco from the west house of Akrotiri", Thera and its Aegean Setting", *JHS* 99, 128f.

WEBSTER, T.B.L. (1935), *Der Niobiden maler*, Leipsig

WEBSTER, T.B.L. (1951), "Masks on Gnathia Vases", *JHS* 71, 222-32, pl.XLV

WEBSTER, T.B.L. (1956), *Art and Literature in Fourth Century Athens* (London)

WEBSTER, T.B.L. (1967), *Tragedies of Euripides* (Methuen, London)

WEBSTER, T.B.L. (1968), "Towards a Classification of Apulian Gnathia", *BICS* 15, 1-33, pls. I-IV

WEBSTER, T.B.L. (1970), *Greek Theatre Production* (Methuen, London)

WEBSTER, T.B.L. (1972), *Potter and Patron in Classical Athens* (Methuen, London)

WEEGE, F. (1926 & 1976), *Der Tanz in der Antike* (New York)

WEGNER, M. (1949), *Das Musikleben der Griechen* (Berlin)

WEGNER, M. (1963) *Musikgeschichte in Bildern von Griechenland* (Leipzig)

WEILL, N. (1966), "Adoniazousai ou les Femmes sur le Toit", *BCH* 90, 664-698

WEILL, N. (1972), "Un Dionysos Attique á l'Artemision de Thasos", *RA*, 141-50

WEHGARTNER, I. (1983), *Attisch Weissgrundige Keramik* (Verlag Phillipp Von Zobern, Mainz am Rhein)

WHITE, D. (1971), "Excavation of the Demeter Sanctuary at Cyrene 1969", A preliminary report. *Lib. Antiq.* 8, 85-104

WHITE, D. (1975), "Archaic Cyrene and the Cult of Demeter and Persephone", *Expedition* 17.4, 2-16

WHITE, D. (1981), "Cyrene's Sanctuary of Demeter or Persephone: A summary of a decade of excavation", *AJA* 85, 13-30

WIESNER, J. (1963), "Studien zu Dem Arimaspen-motive Auf Tarentiner Sarcophagen, *JdI* 78, 200-217

WILLIAMS, D., "Close Shave", in Brijder (ed.), *Ancient Greek and Related Pottery*, 275-281

WINNEFELD, H. (1889), "Alabastra mit Wegerdarstellungen", Mitteilungen des deutschen Archaologischen Instituts, *AM* 14

WOLTERS, P. (1891), "Rot figurige Loutrophoros", *AM* 16, 371-405

WOLTERS, P. (1913), "Eingeritze inschriften auf Vasen", *AM* 38, 198-199

WOODFORD, S., "Cults of Heracles in Attica", in *Studies presented to George M.A. Hanfmann*, D. Mitten, J. Pedley & J. Scott (eds.), 211-225

WOODWARD, J. (1937), *Perseus* (Cambridge University Press)

WOYSCH-MEAUTIS (1982), *La répresentation des animaux et des êtres fabuleux sur les monuments funeraires grecs de l'Epoque Archaique à la fin du IVe Siecle Av. J.-C.* (Lausanne)

WUILLEUMIER, P. (1939), *Tarente des Origines à la conquête romaine* (Bibliothéque des Ecoles Françaises d'Athenes et de Rome)

YALOURIS, N. (1980), "Astral Representation in the Archaic and Classical Periods and their connection to Literacy Sources", *AJA* 84, 313-318

ZIMMERMANN, K. (1967), "Unteritalische Fischteller. Die Griechische Vase", *Wissenschaftliche Zeitschrift Rostock*, 16

ZUCHNER, W. (1942), *Griechische Klappspiegel* (Berlin)

ZUNTZ, G. (1971), *Persephone: Three essays on Religion and thought in Magna Graecia* (The Clarendon Press, Oxford)

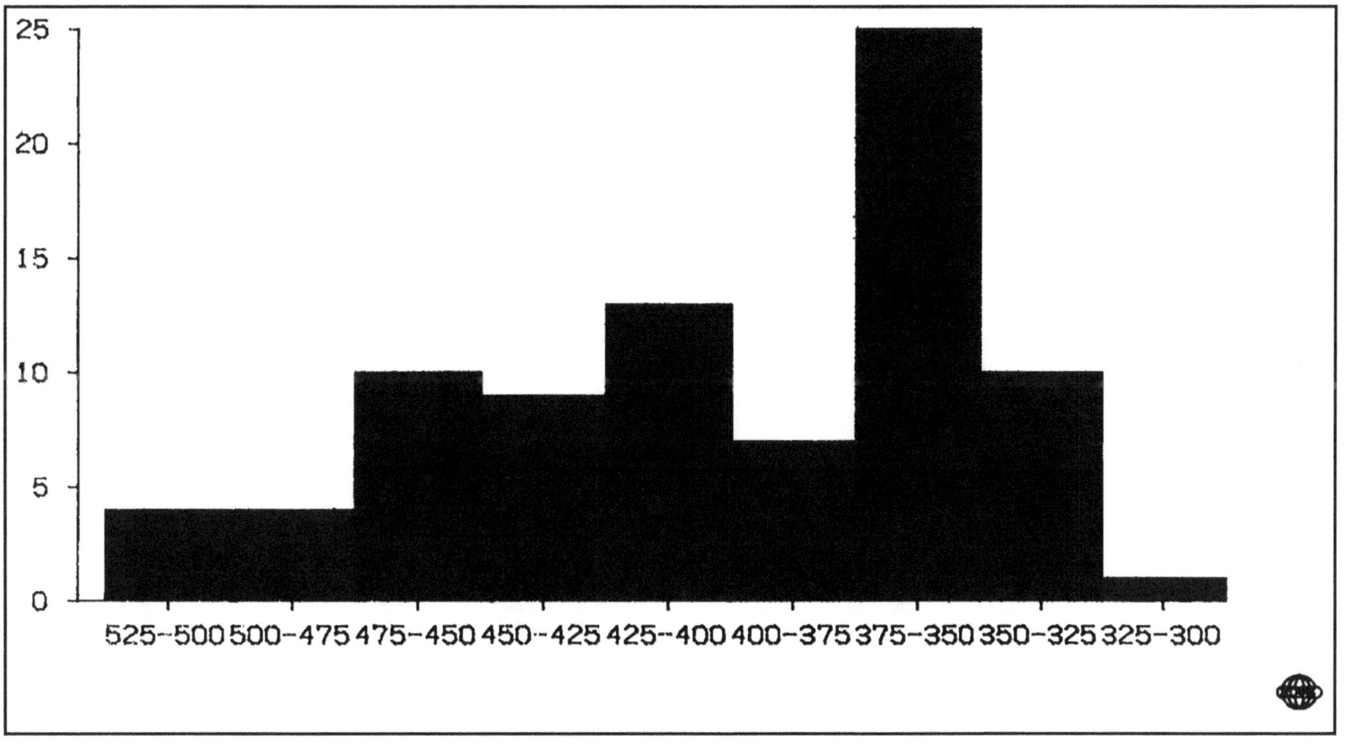

Fig. 1 – Chronological distribution of Attic red-figured ware from Cyrenaica

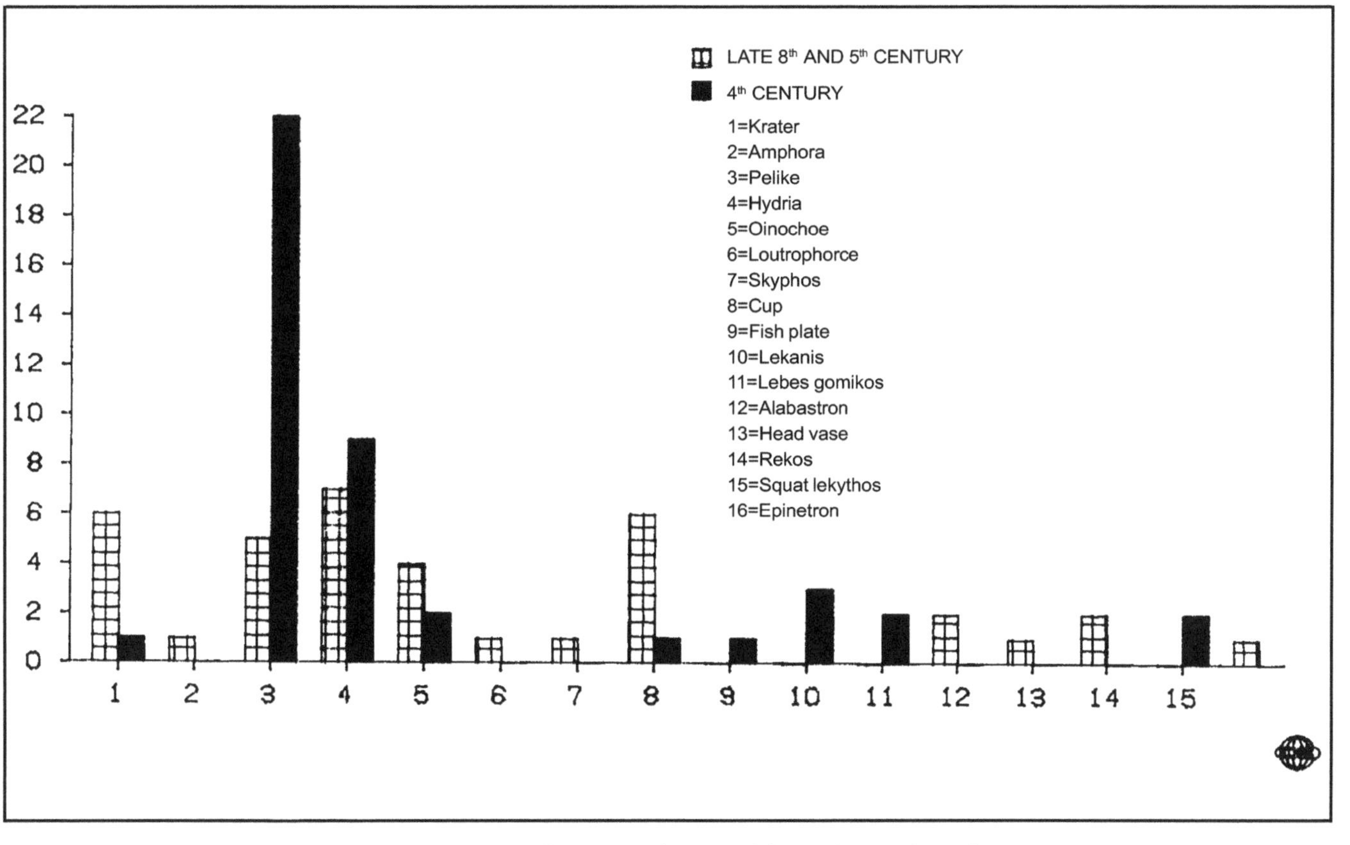

Fig. 2 – Representation of shapes of Attic red-figured ware from Cyreniaca

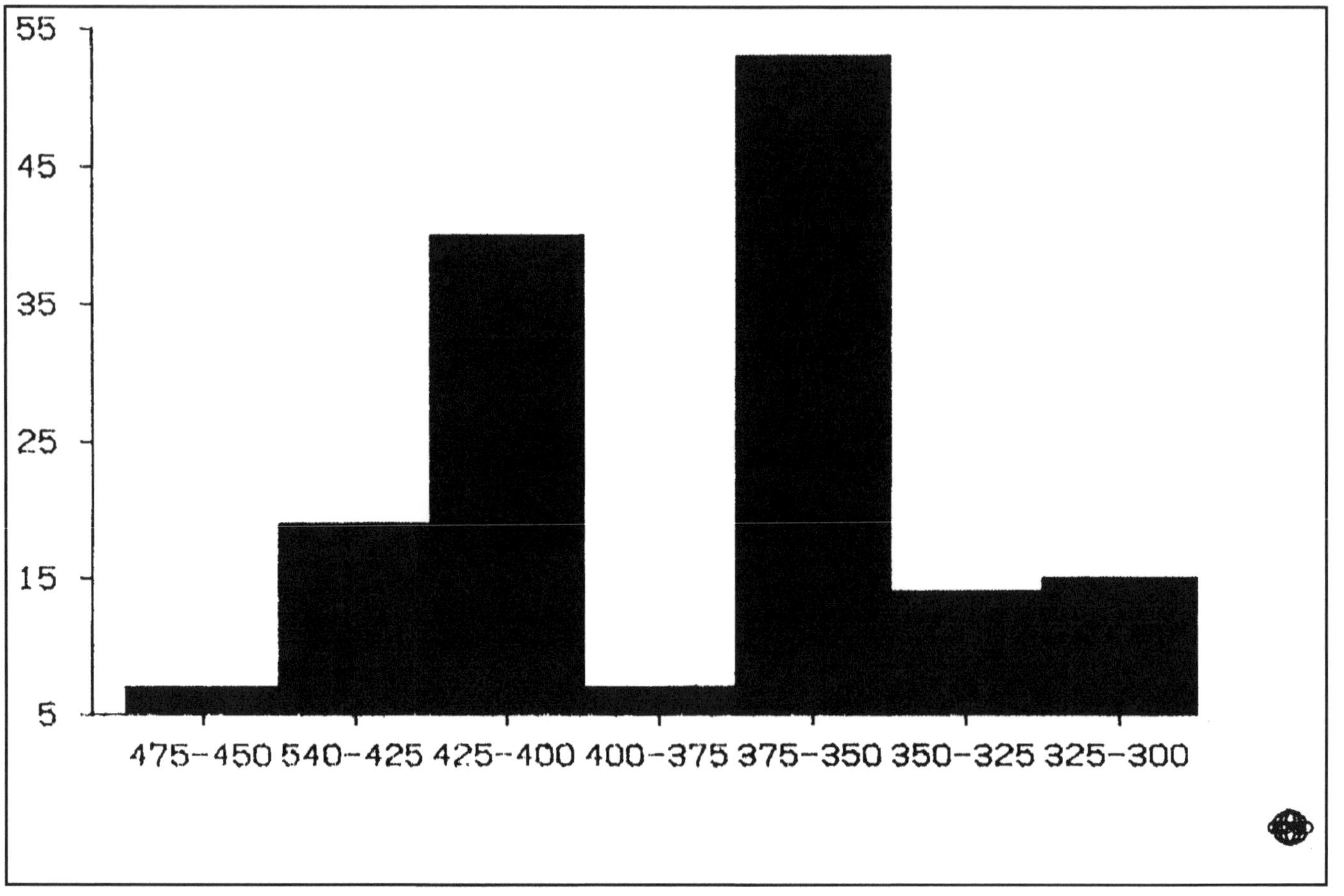

Fig. 3 – Chronological distribution of Attic black-glazed ware from Cyrenaica

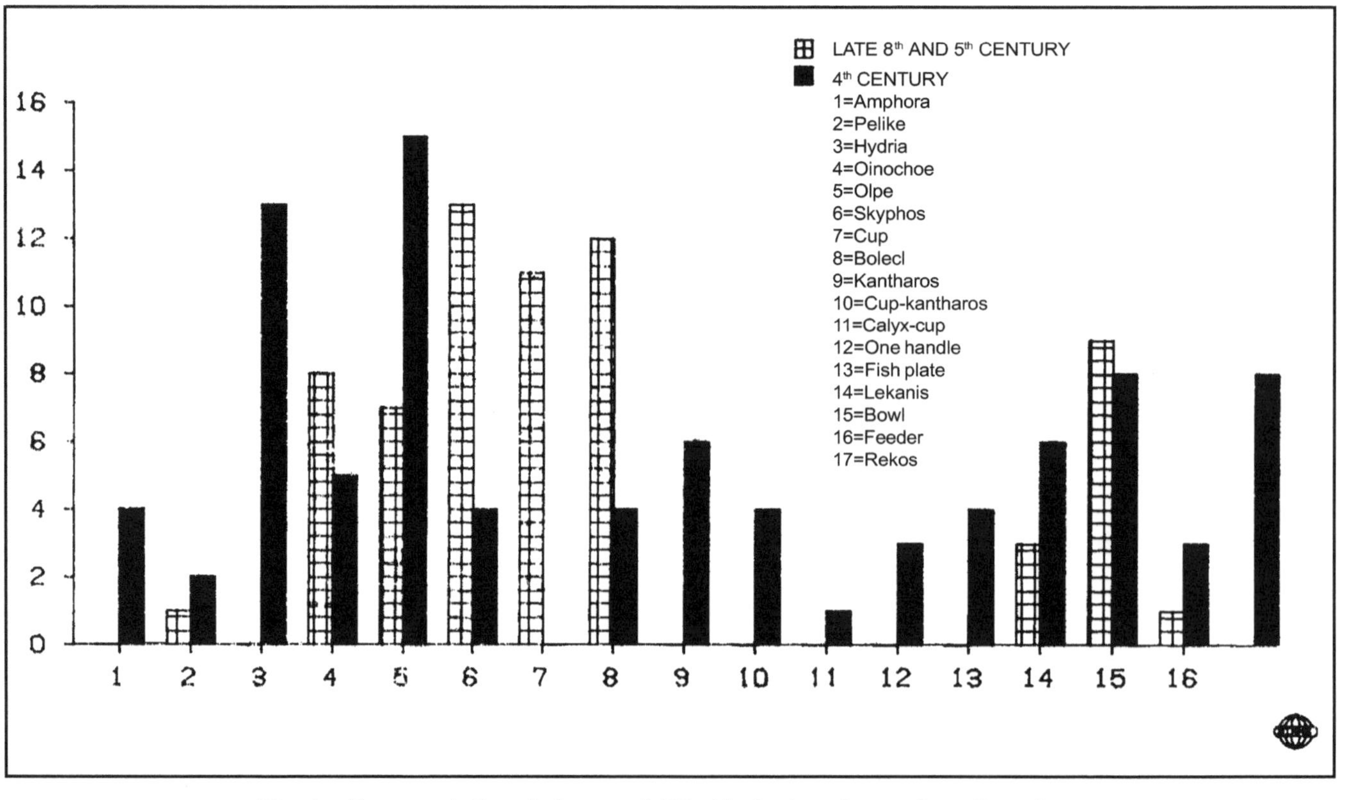

Fig. 4 – Representation of shapes of Attic black-glazed ware from Cyreniaca

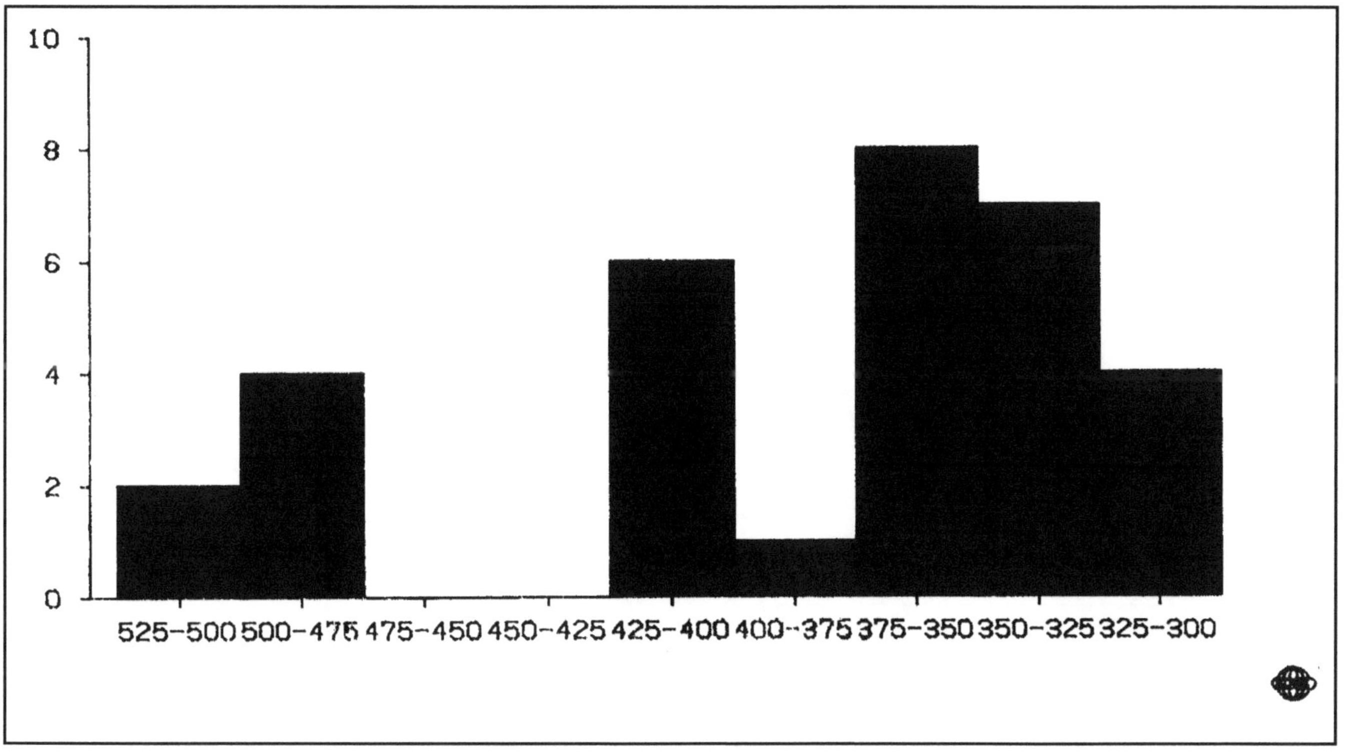

Fig. 5 – Chronological distribution of Panathenaic amphoras from Cyrenaica

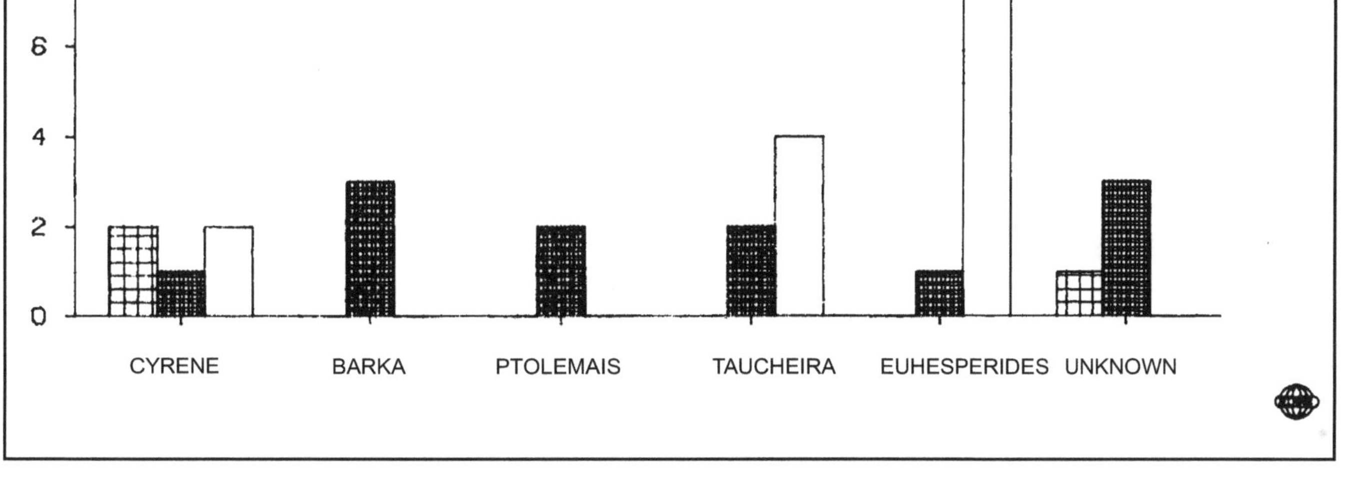

Fig. 6 – Number of Panathenaic amphoras from the Greek cities of Cyrenaica

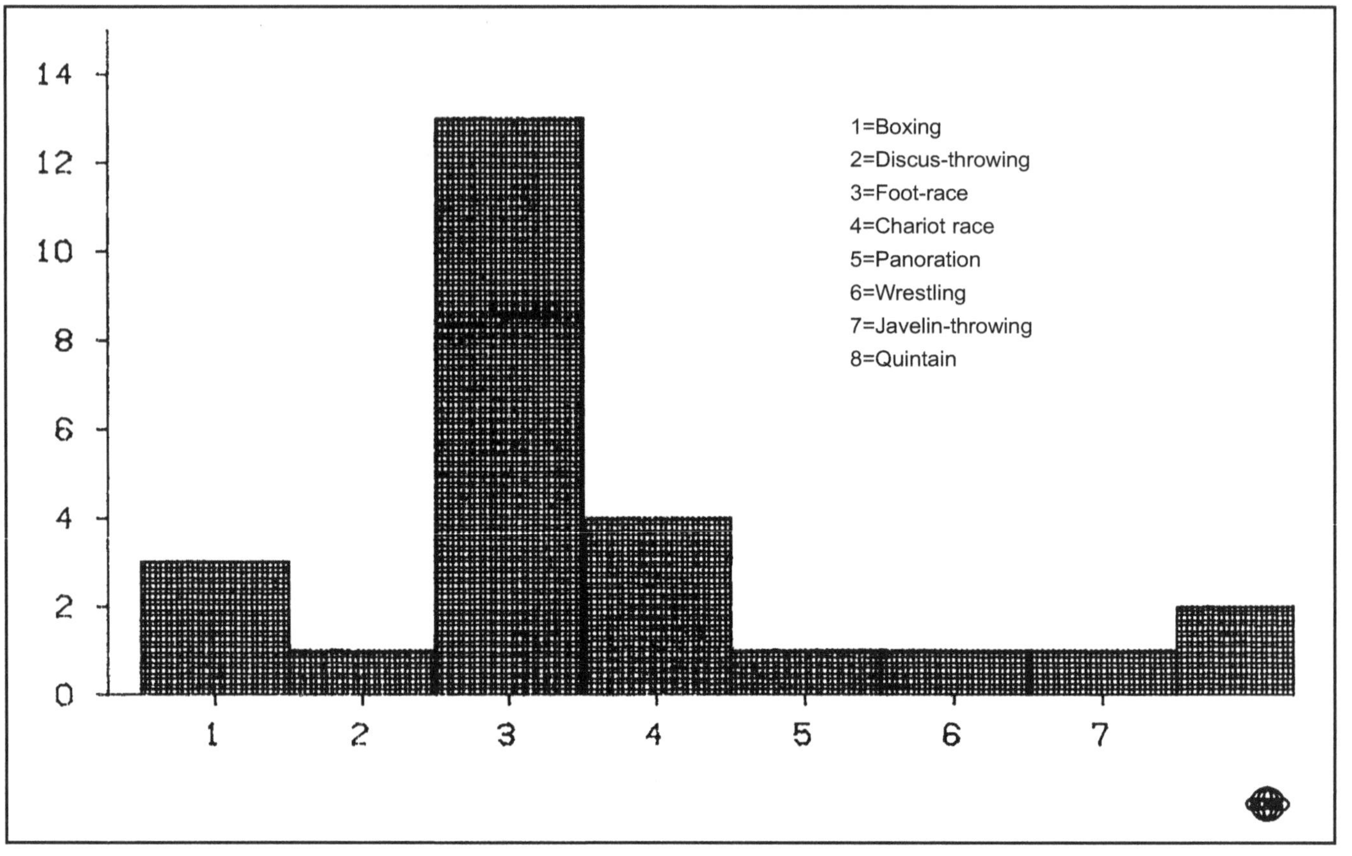

Fig. 7 – Representations of sports on the Panathenaics from Cyrenaica

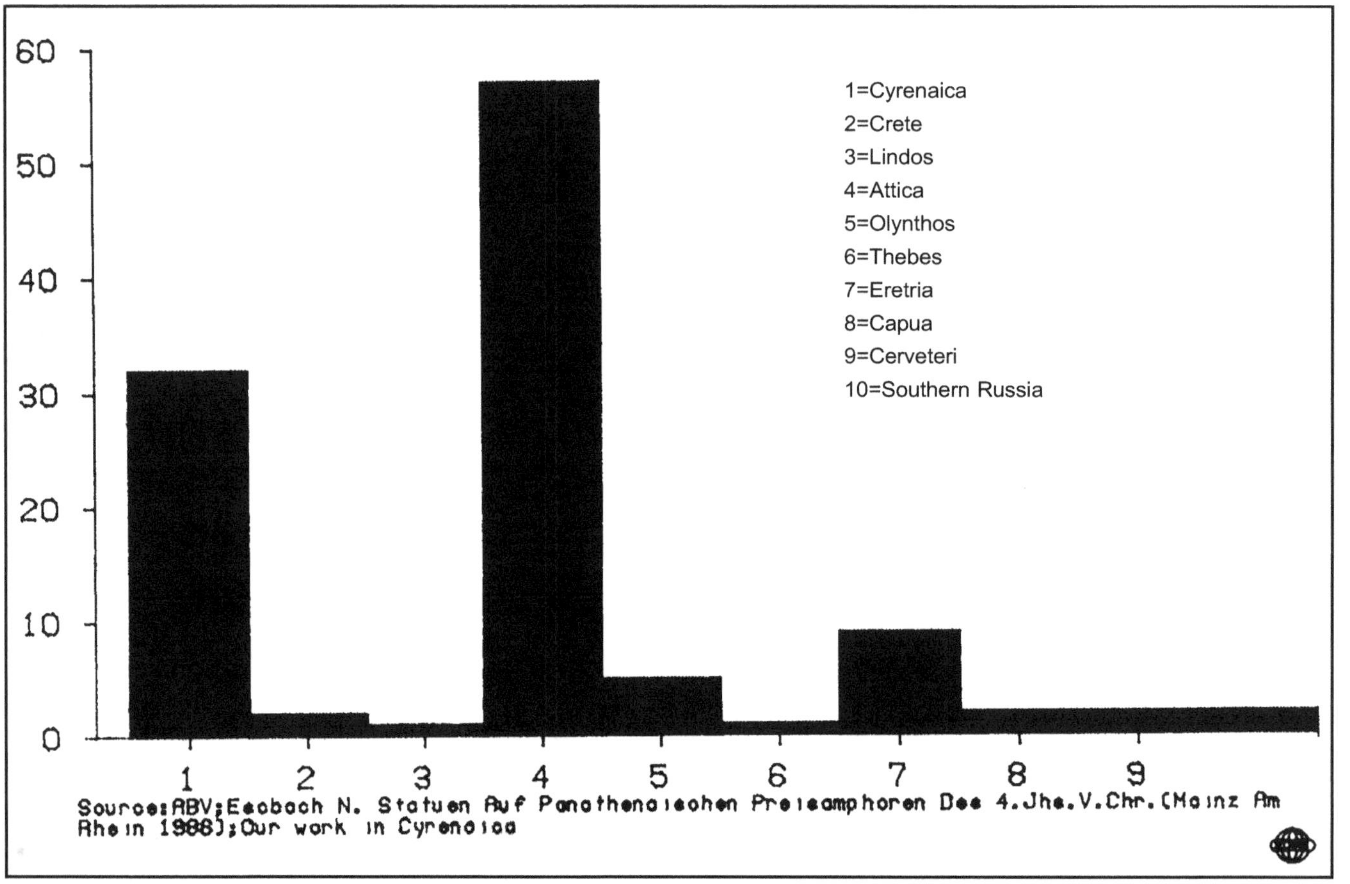

Fig. 8 – All Panathenaics of known provenance from the last quarter of the 5th to the last quarter of the 4th century B.C.

403/2. Eukleides.
402/1. Mikon.
401/0. Xenainetos.
400/399. Laches.
399/98. Aristokrates.
398/97. Euthykles.
397/96. Suniades.
396/95. Phormion.
395/94. Diophantos.
394/93. Eubulides.
393/92. Demostratos.
392/91. Philokles.
391/90. Nikoteles.
390/89. Demostratos.
389/88. Antipatros.
388/87. Pyrgion.
387/86. Theodotos.
386/85. Mystichides.
385/84. Dexitheos.
384/83 Dieitrephes.
383/82. Phanostratos.
382/81. Euandros.
381/80. Demophilos.
380/79. Pytheas.
379/78. Nikon.
378/77. Nausinikos.
377/76. Kalleas.
376/75. Charisandros.
375/74. Hippodamas.
374/73. Sokratides.
373/72. Asteios.
372/71. Alkisthenes.
371/70 Phrasikleides.
370/69. Dysniketos.
369/68. Lysistratos.
368/67. Nausigenes.
367/66. Polyzelos.
366/65. Kephisodoros.
365/64. Chion.
364/63. Timokrates.
363/62. Charikleides.
362/61. Molon.
361/60. Nikophemos.
360/59. Kallimedes (Kallidemos).
359/58. Eucharistos.
358/57. Kephisodotos.
357/56. Agathokles.
356/55. Elpines.
355/54. Kallistratos.
354/53. Diotimos.
353/52. Thudemos.
352/51. Aristodemos.
351/50. Theellos.
350/49. Apollodoros.
349/48. Kallimachos.
348/47. Theophilos.
347/46. Themistokles.
346/45. Archias.
345/44. Eubulos.
344/43. Lykiskos.
343/42. Pythodotos.
342/41. Sosigenes.
341/40. Nikomachos.
340/39. Theophrastos.
339/38. Lysimachides.
338/37. Chairondas.
337/36. Phrynichos.
336/35. Pythodelos.
335/34. Euainetos.
334/33. Ktesikles.
333/32. Nikokrates.
332/31. Niketes.
331/30. Aristophanes.
330/29. Aristophon.
329/28. Kephisophon.
328/27. Euthykritos.
327/26. Hegemon (Dion. Hal. Din. 9).
326/25. Chremes.
325/24. Antikles.
324/23. Hegesias.
323/22. Kephisodoros.
322/21. Philokles.
321/20. Archippos (Dion. Hal. Din. 9).
320/19. Neaichmos (Dion. Hal. Din. 9).
319/18. Apollodoros.
318/17. Archippos.
317/16. Demogenes.
316/15. Demokleides.
315/14. Praxibulos.
314/13. Nikodoros.
313/12. Theophrastos.
312/11. Polemon.
311/10. Simonides.
310/9. Hieromnemon.
309/8. Demetrios.
308/7. Charinos.
307/6. Anaxikrates.
306/5. Koroibos.
305/4. Euxenippos.
304/3. Pherekles.
303/2. Leostratos.
302/1. Nikokles.
301/0. Klearchos (CIA II 611).

Fig. 9 – Athenian Eponymous Archons of the fourth century
(Source, V. von Schoeffer in *RE* II 587; Tod, Greek Historical inscription II, 316).

1 (14)

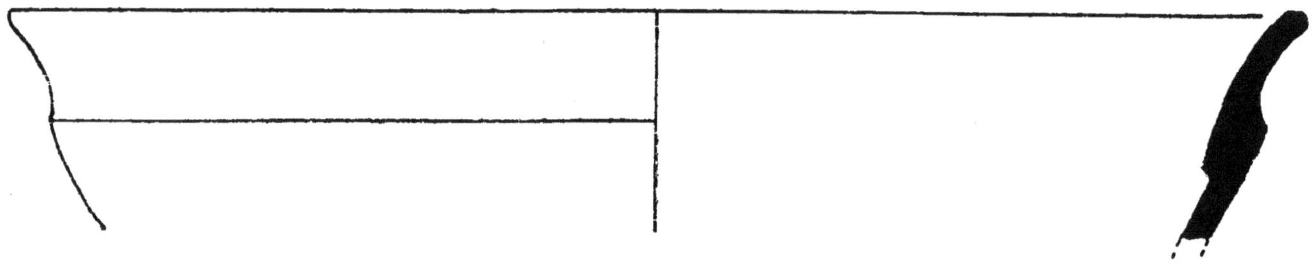

2 (17)

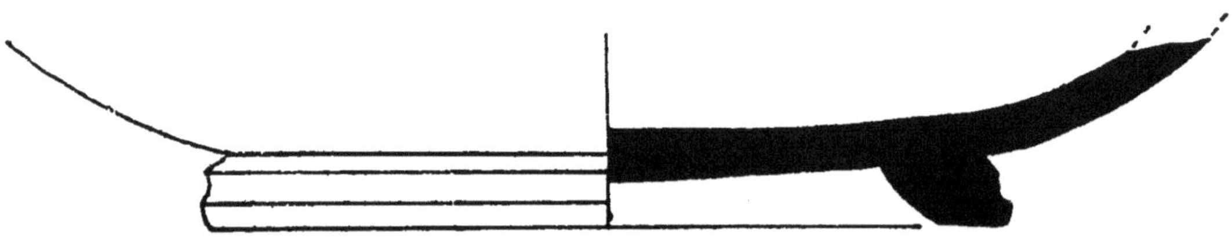

3 (18)

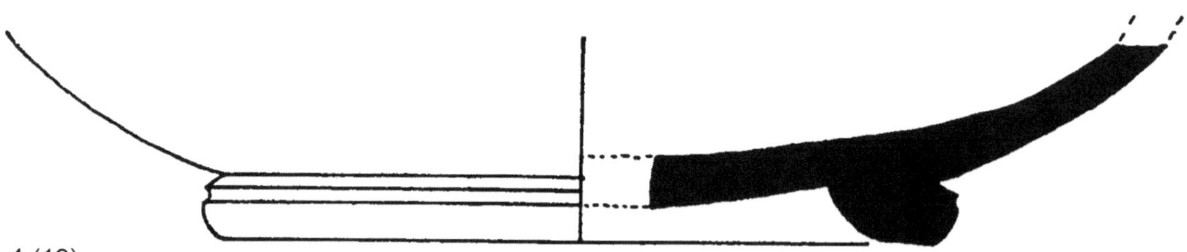

4 (19)

Plate 1

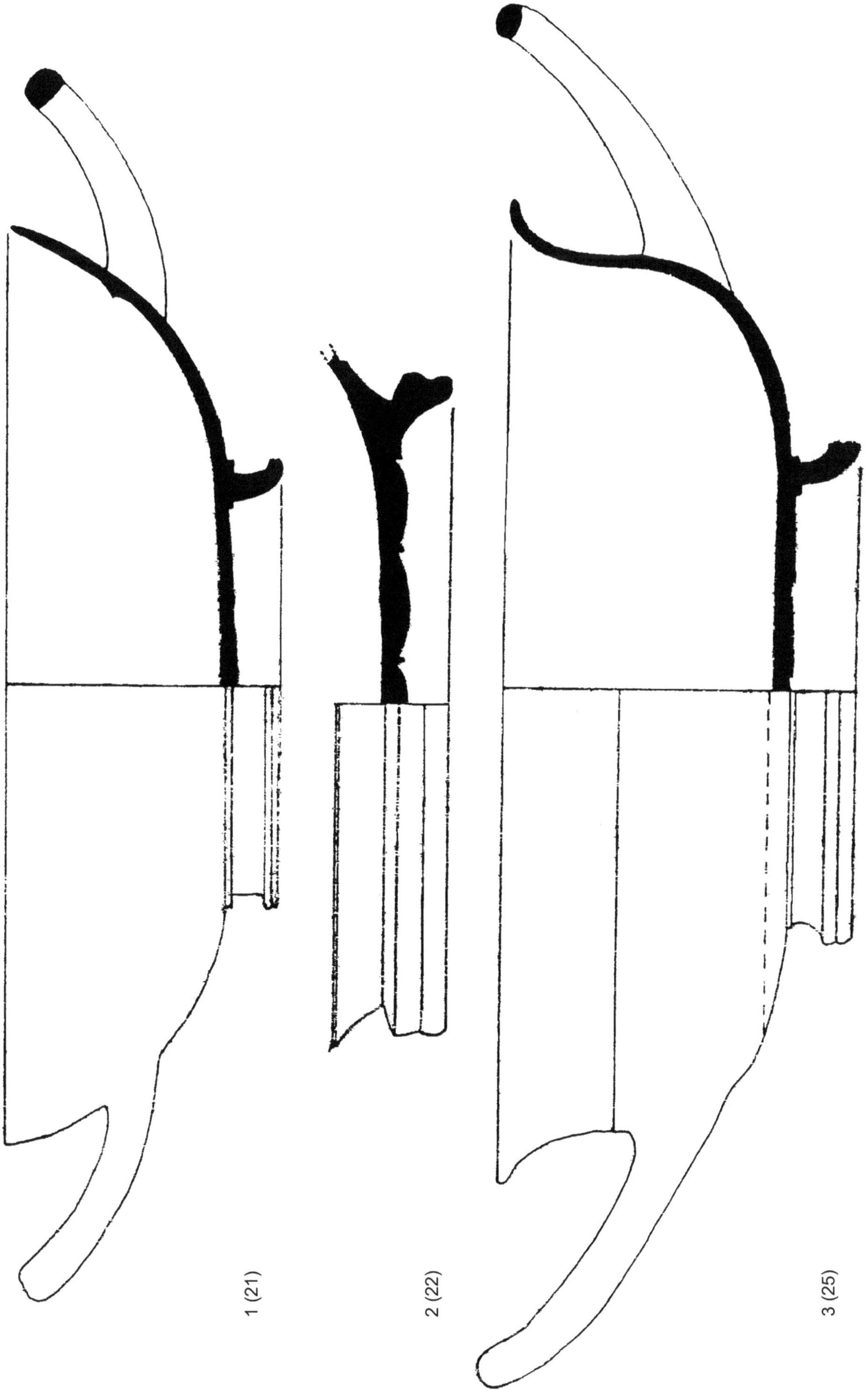

1 (21)

2 (22)

3 (25)

Plate 2

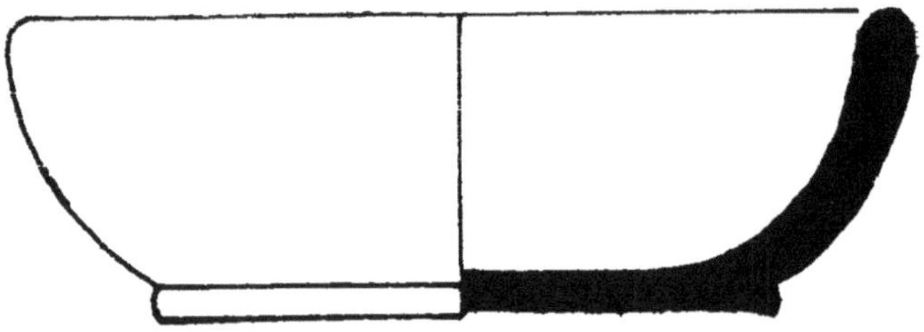

1 (27)

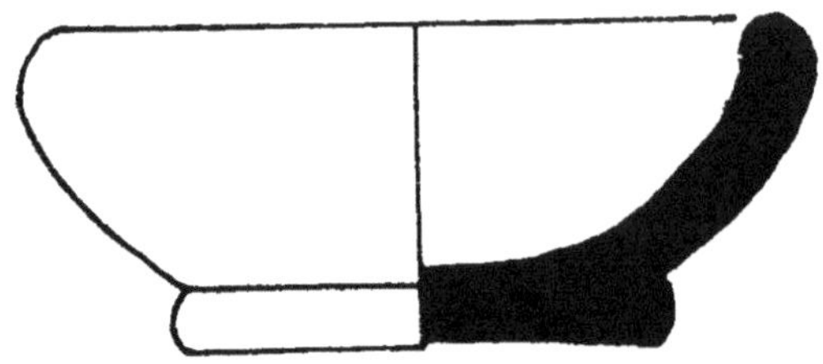

2 (28)

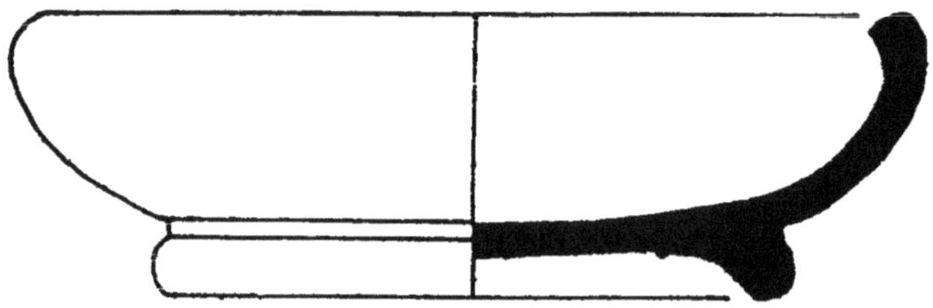

3 (31)

4 (32)

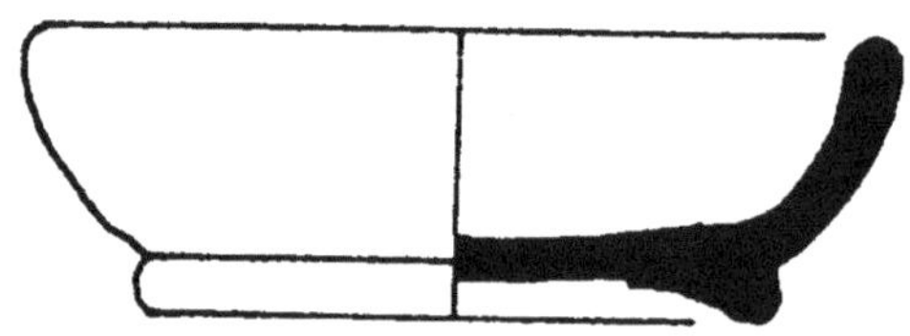

5 (33)

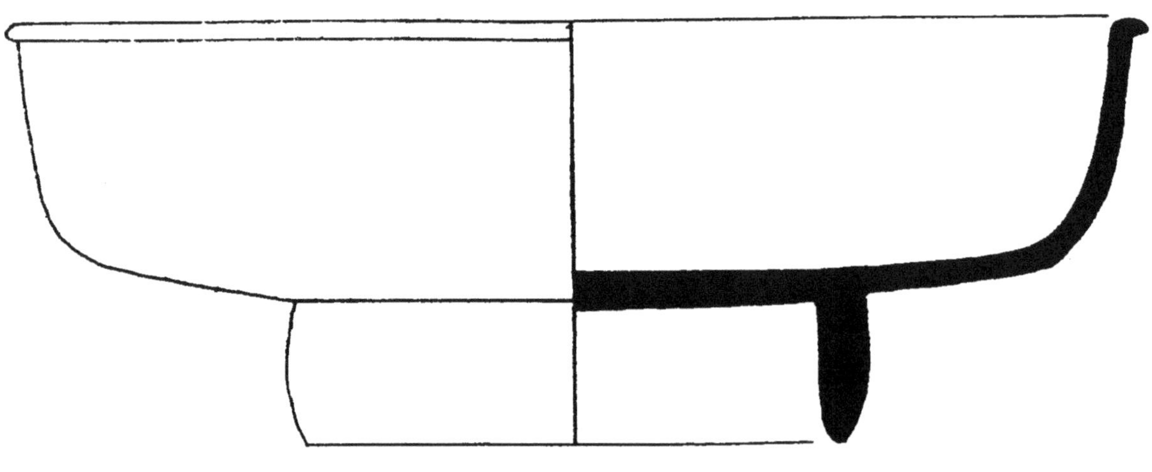

6 (35)

Plate 3

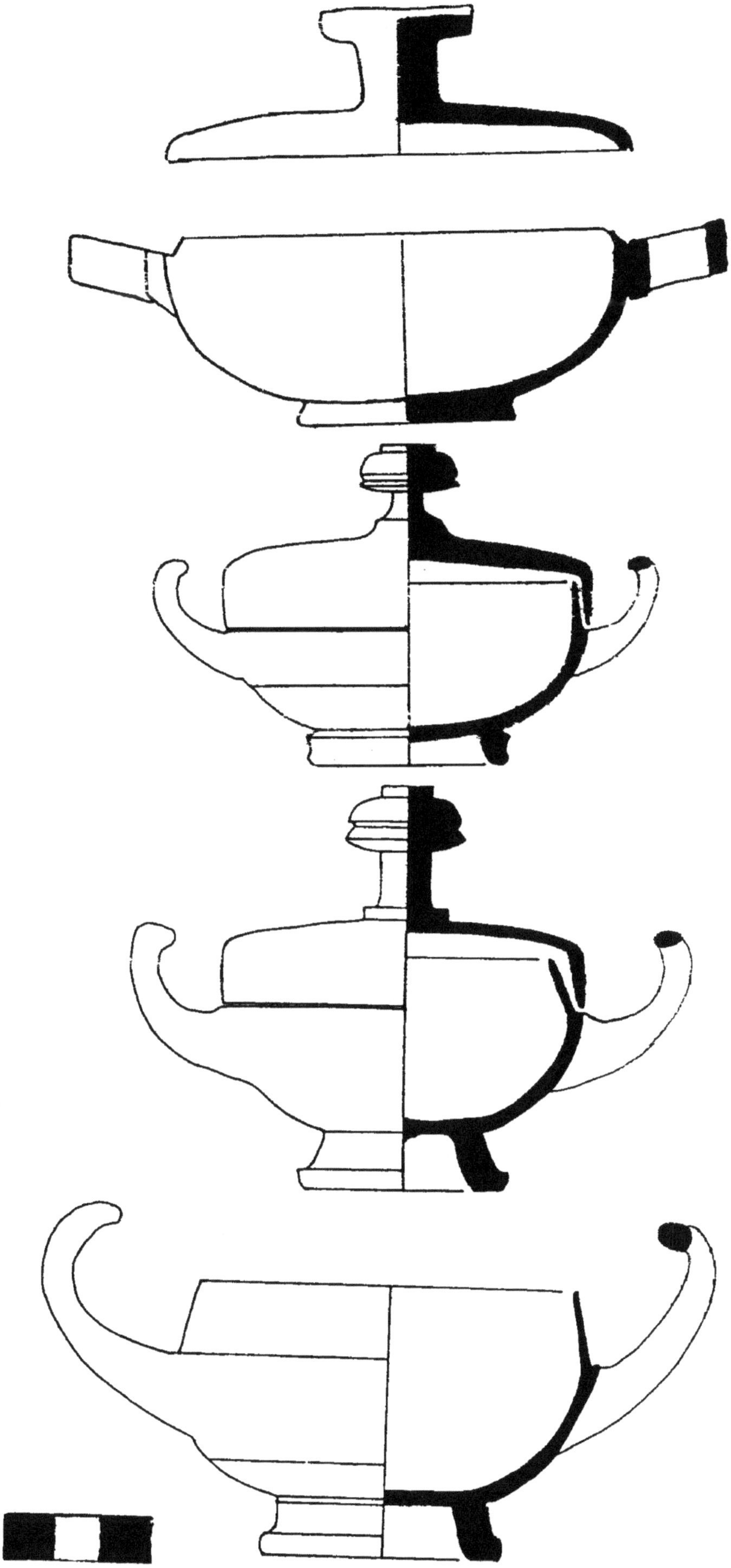

1 (36)

2 (38)

3 (148)

4 (149)

Plate 4

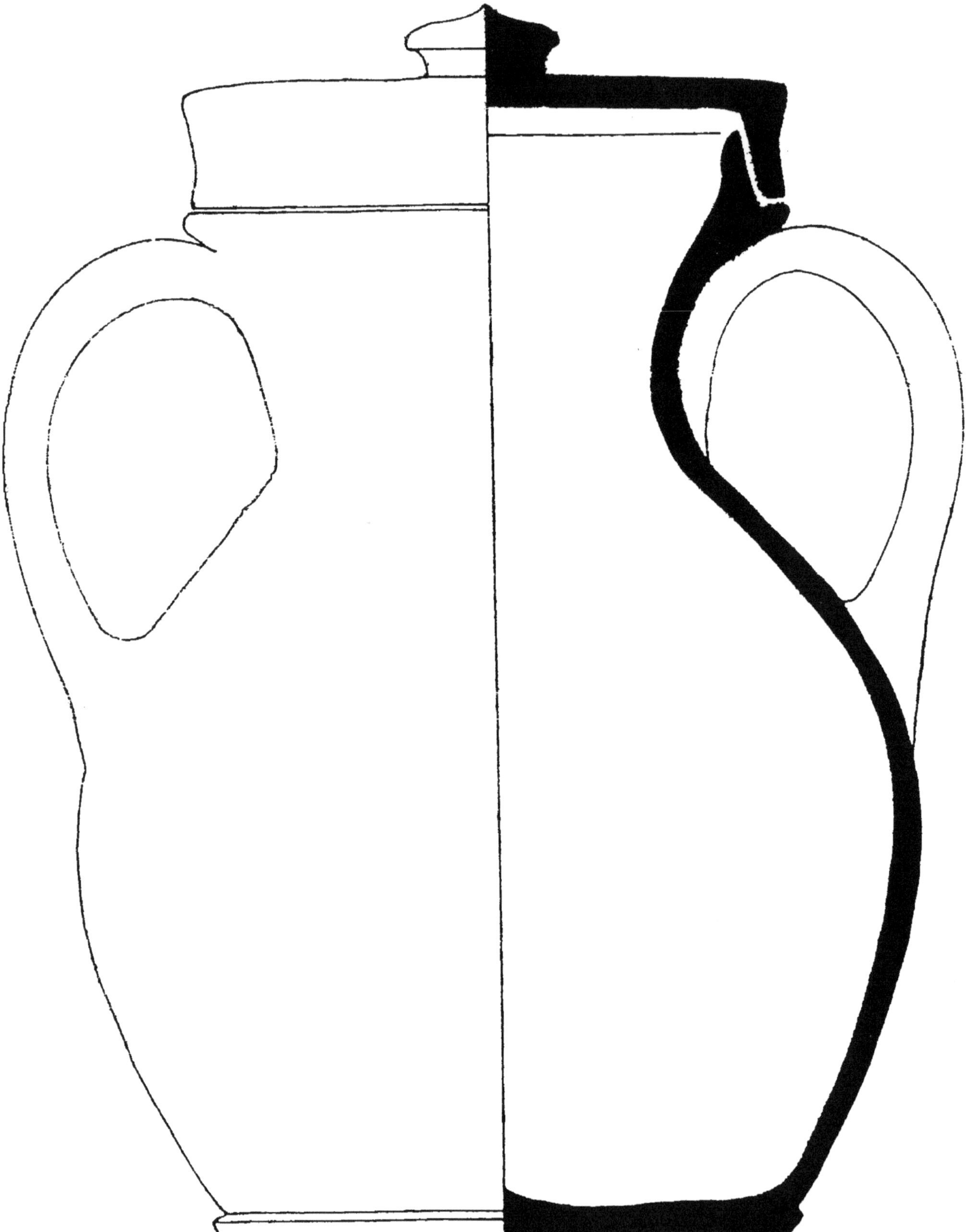

1 (39)

Plate 5

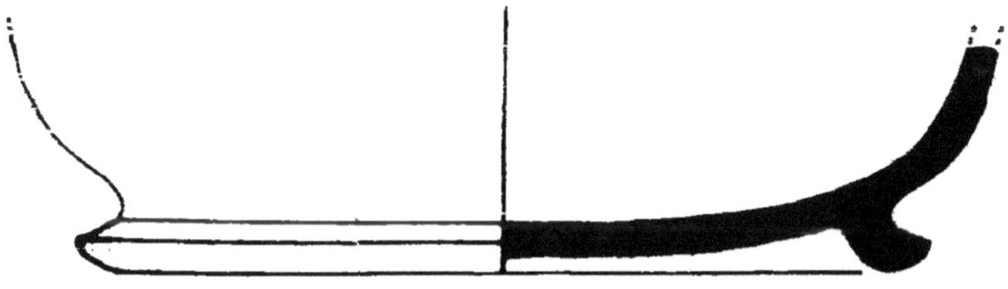

1 (41)

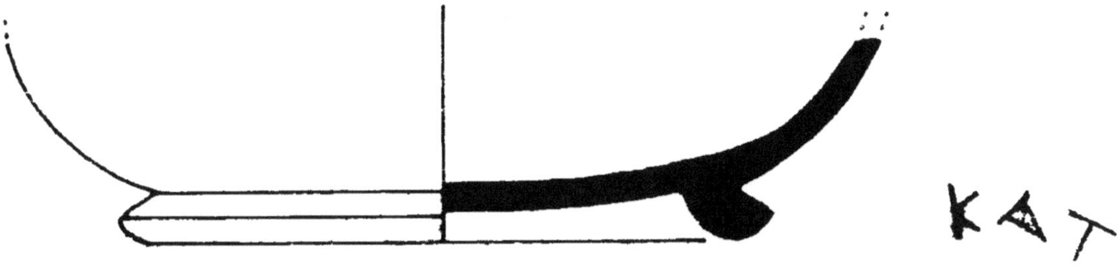

2 (42)

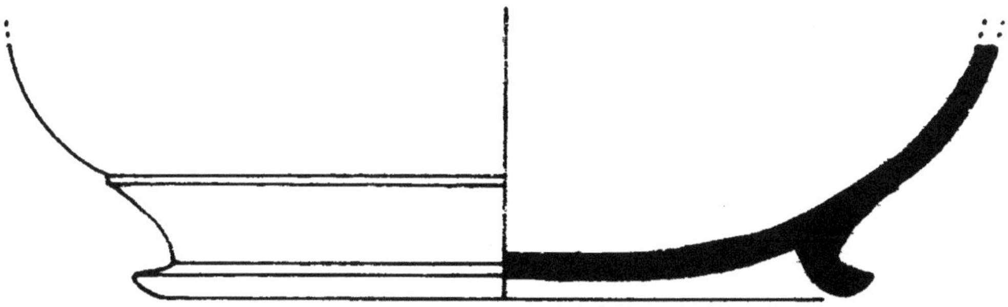

3 (44)

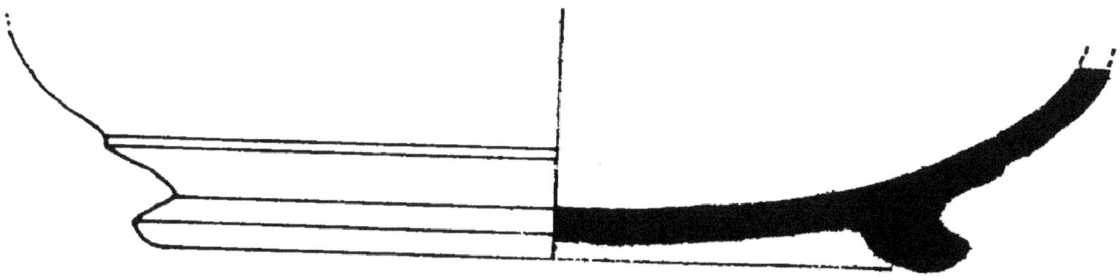

4 (45)

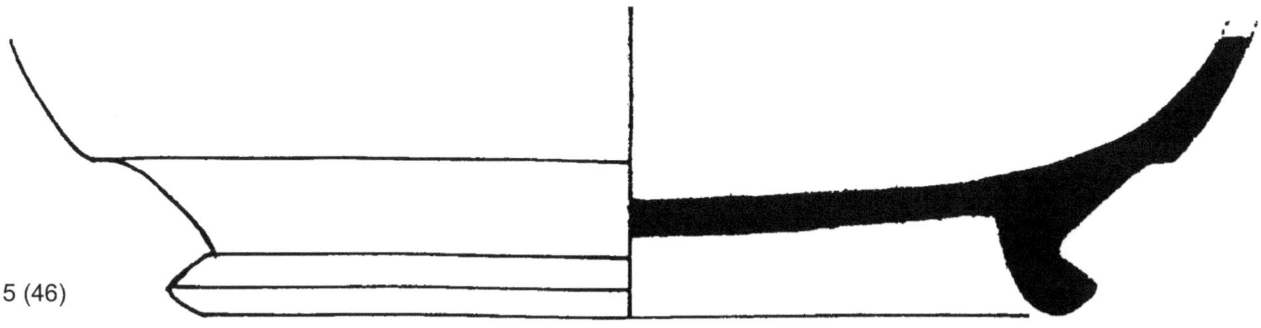

5 (46)

Plate 6

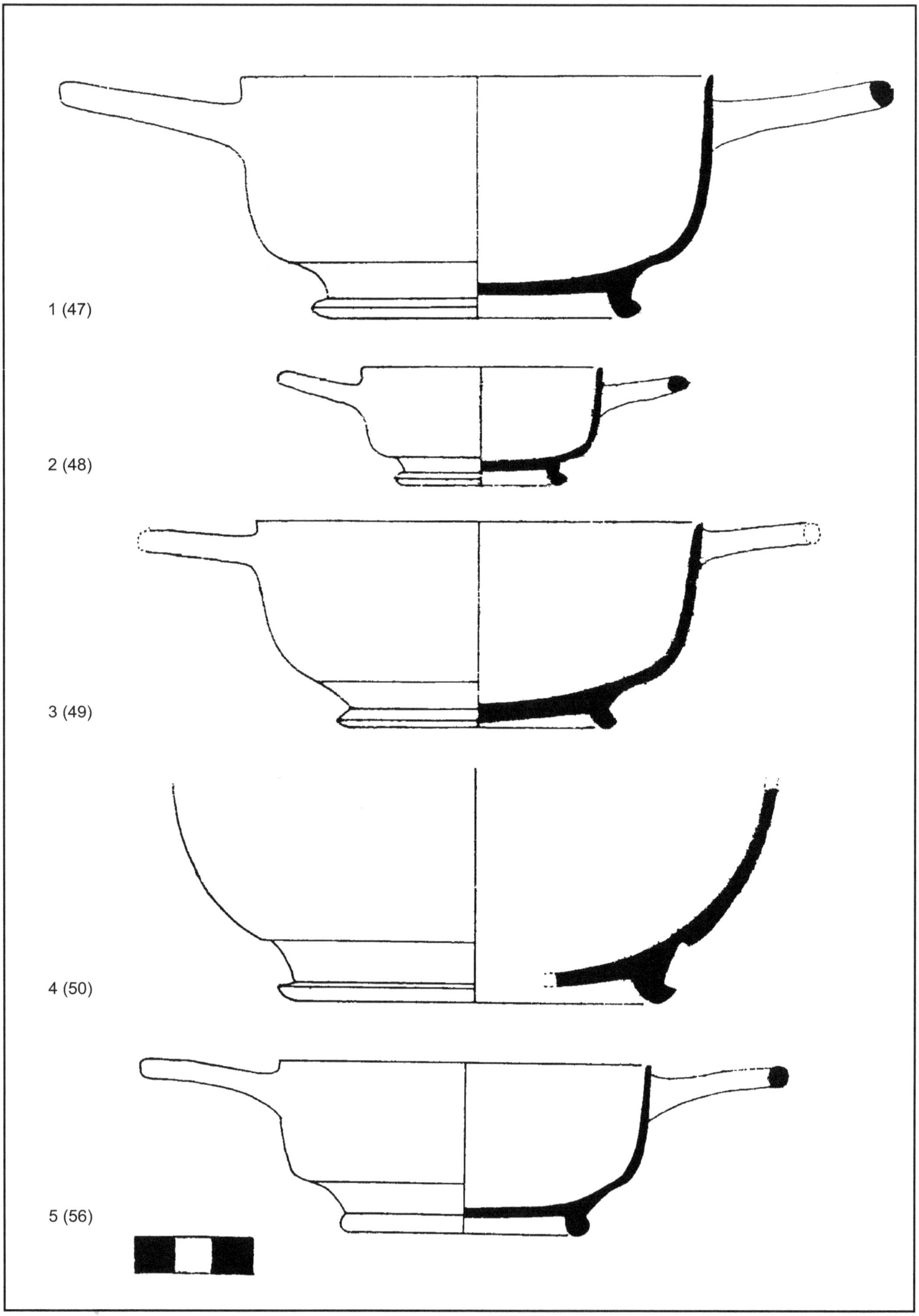

Plate 7

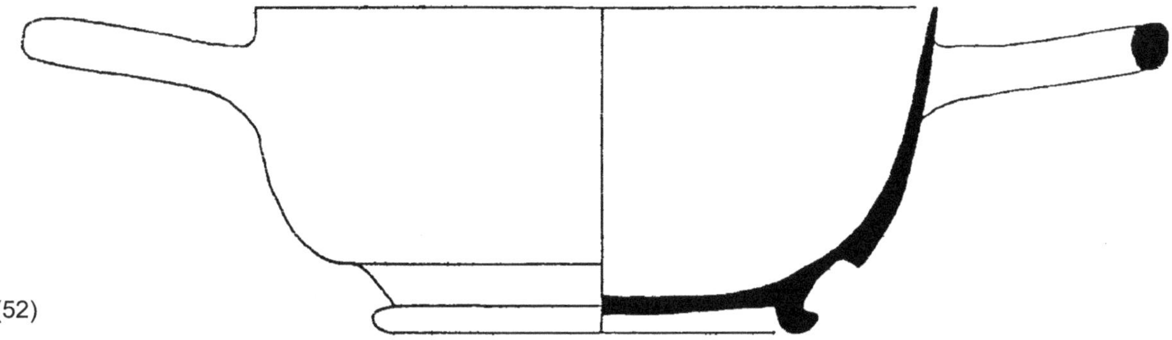

1 (52)

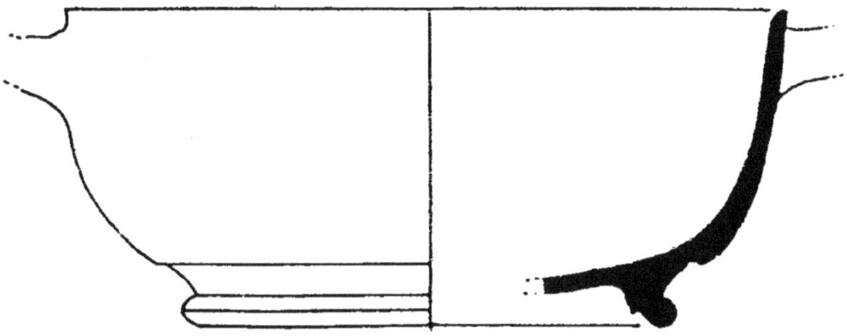

2 (53)

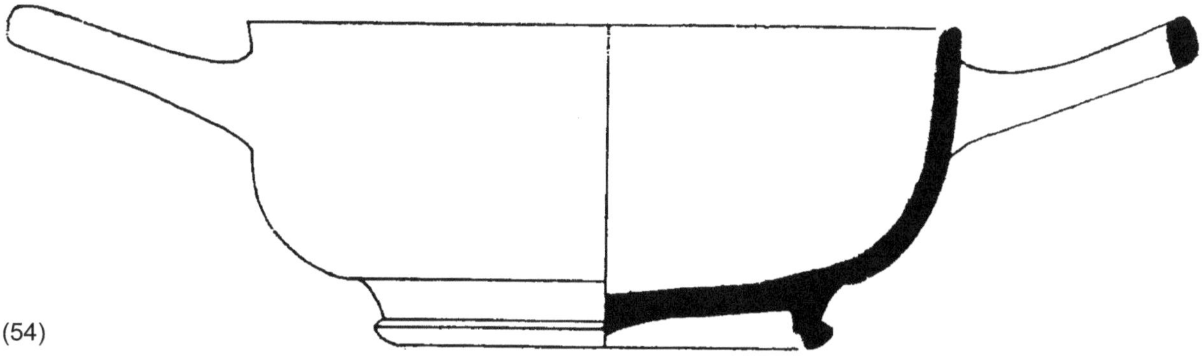

3 (54)

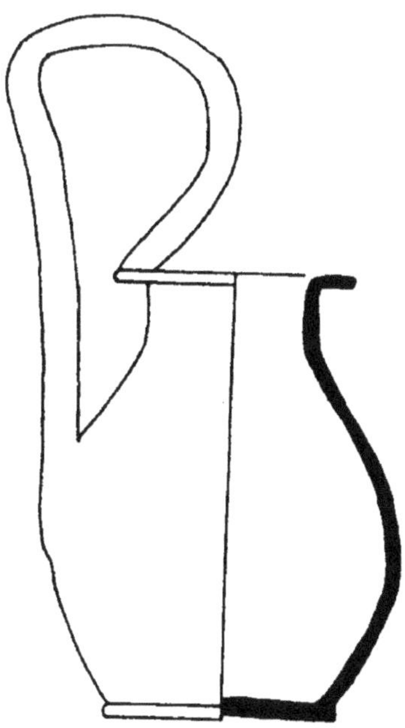

4 (56)

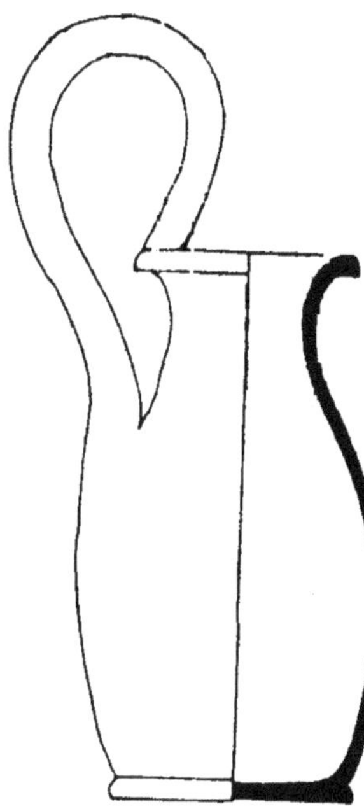

5 (58)

Plate 8

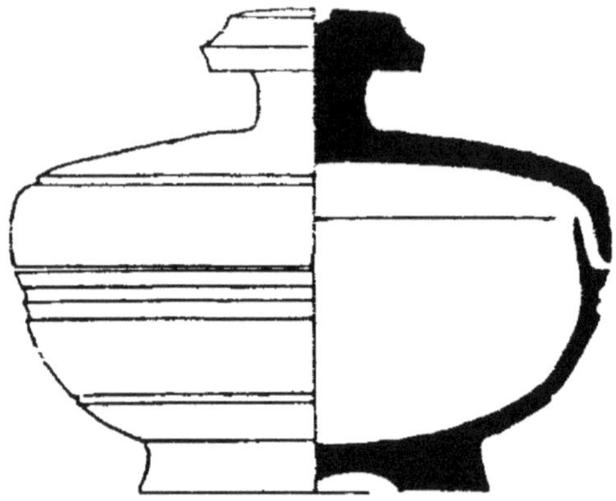

1 (152)

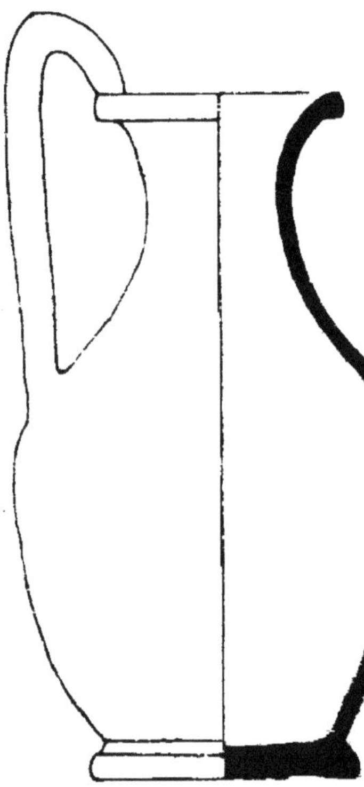

2 (77)

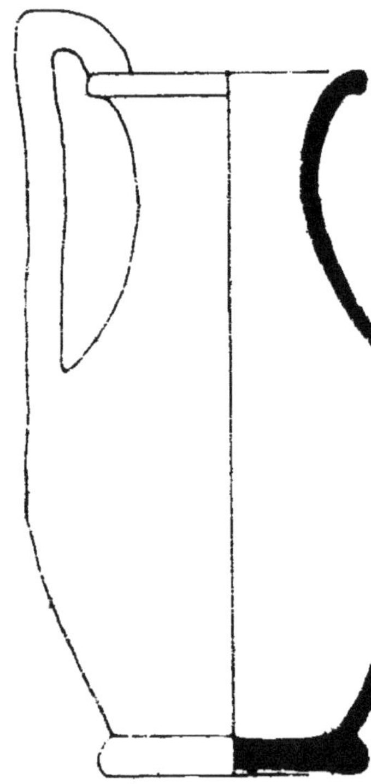

3 (78)

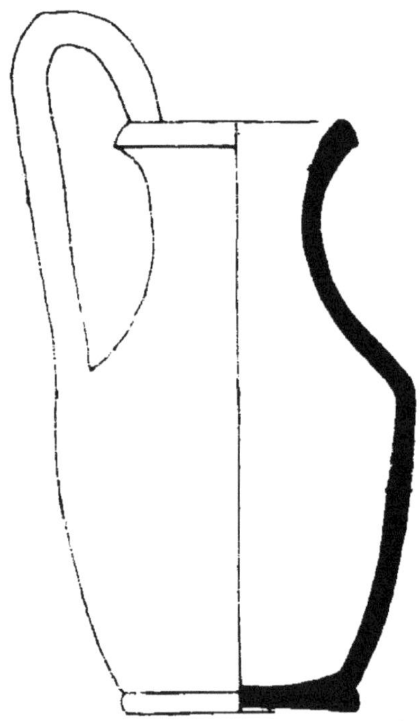

4 (79)

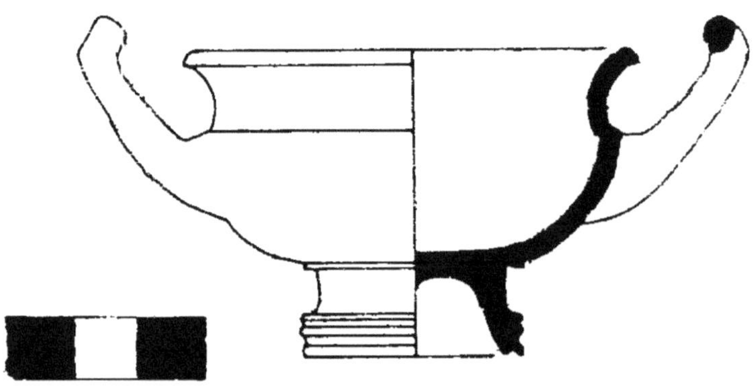

5 (113)

Plate 9

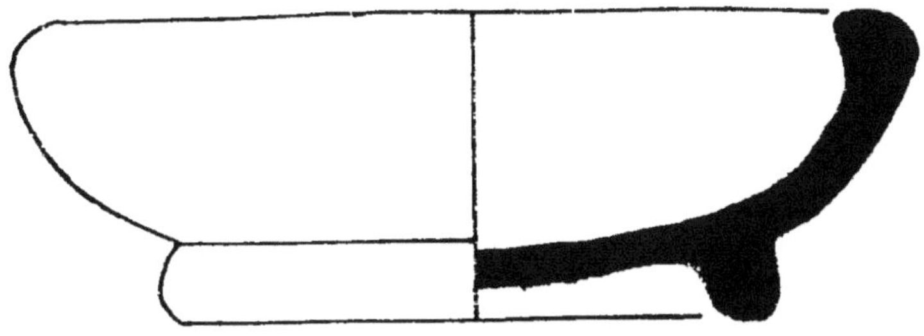

1 (126)

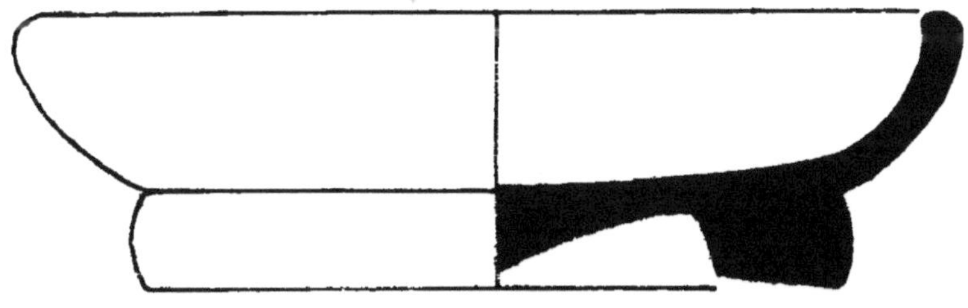

2 (129)

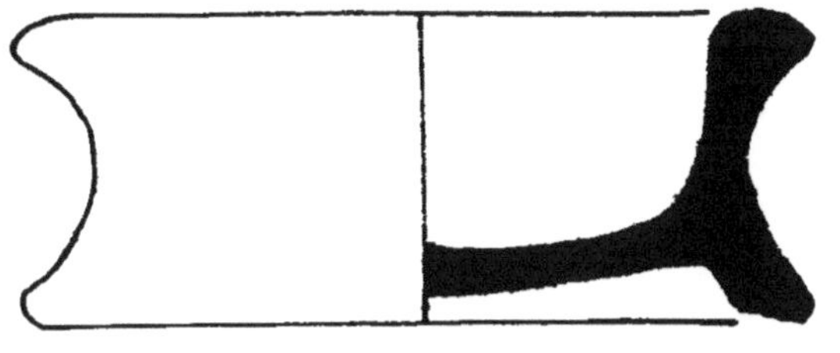

3 (131)

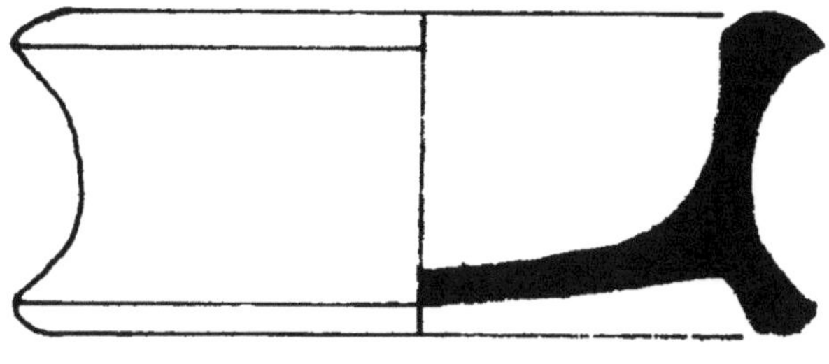

4 (133)

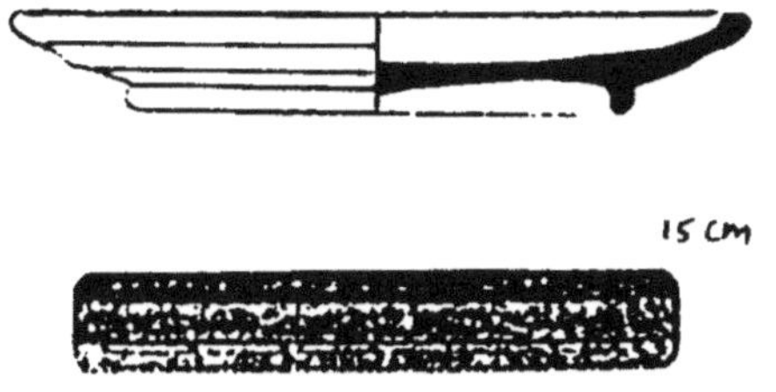

5 (134)

6 (135)

7 (137)

Plate 10

1

2 (1)

Plate 11

1 (2)

2-3 (3)

Plate 12

1 (4)

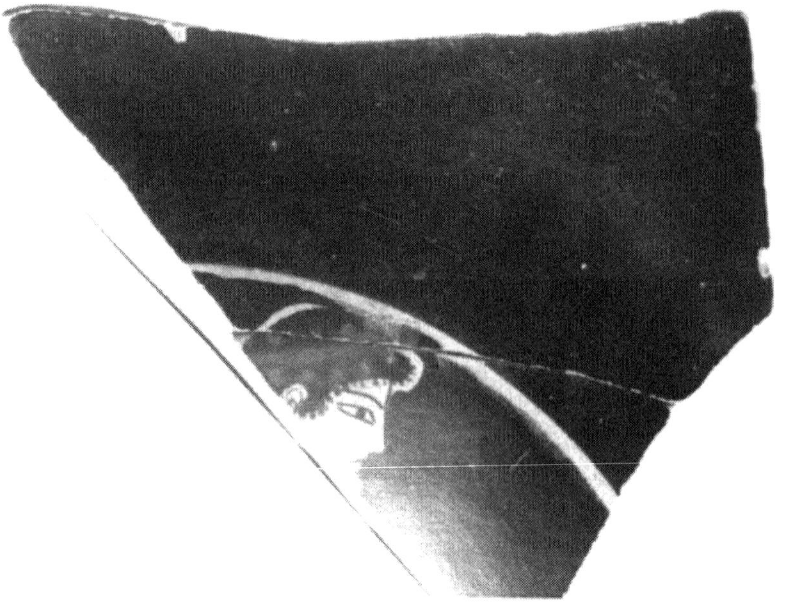

2 (5)

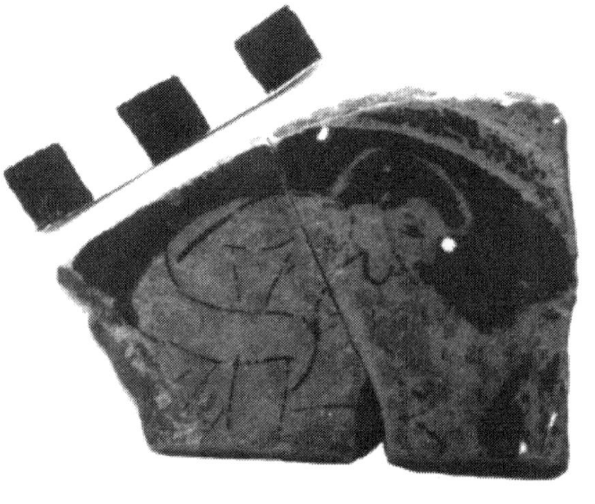

3 (6)

Plate 13

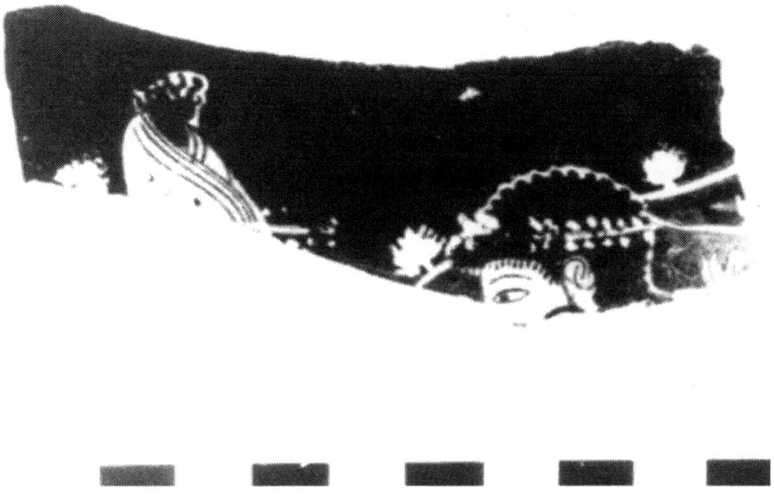

1 (7)

2 (8)

Plate 14

1 (9)

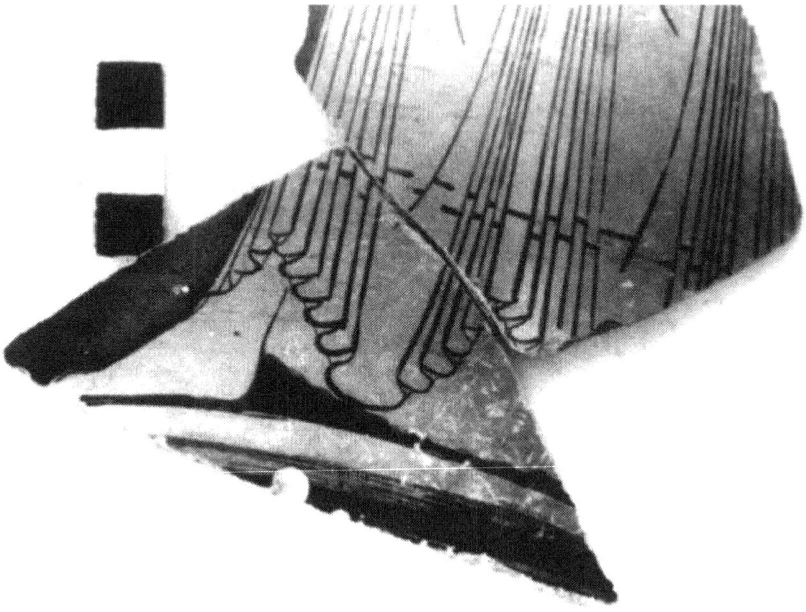

2 (10)

3 (11)

Plate 15

1 (12)

2 (13)

3 (13)

Plate 16

1-2 (14)

2-3 (15)

Plate 17

1 (16)

2 (17)

3 (17)

Plate 18

1-2 (18)

3-4 (19)

Plate 19

1-2 (20)

3-5 (21)

Plate 20

1 (22)

2 (23)

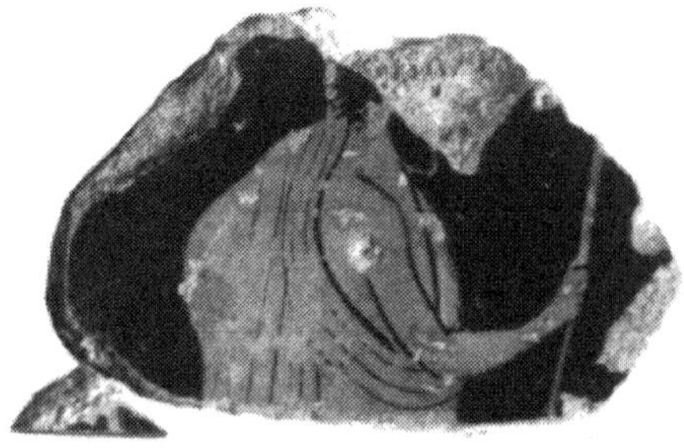

3 (24)

4 (25)

Plate 21

1 (26)

2 (27)

Plate 22

1 (28)

2-3 (29)

Plate 23

1 (30)

2 (31)

3 (32)

Plate 24

1-3 (33)

Plate 25

1 (34)

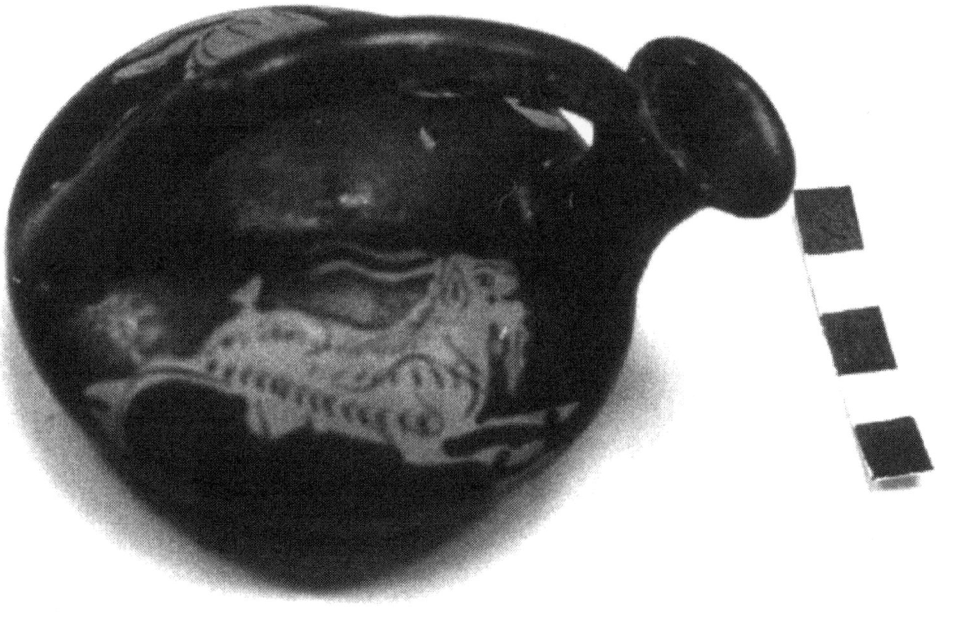

2 (35)

Plate 26

1 (36)

2 (37)

3 (38)

Plate 27

1-2 (39)

Plate 28

1-4 (40)

Plate 29

1-3 (41)

Plate 30

1 (42)

2 (43)

3 (44)

Plate 31

1-4 (45)

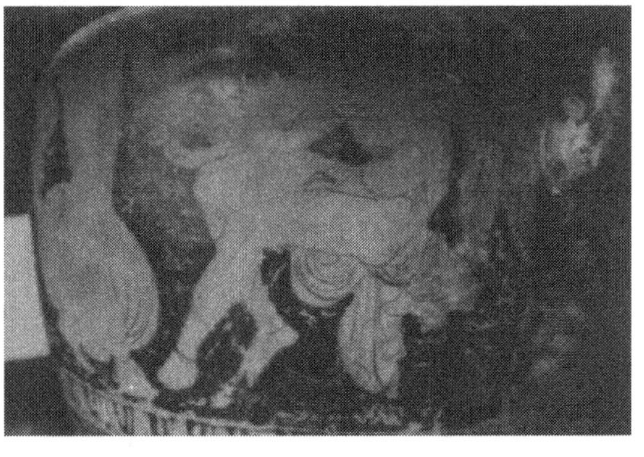

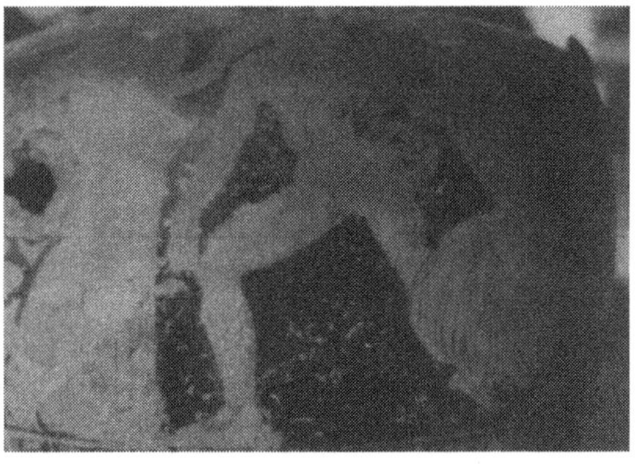

Plate 32

1-2 (46)

Plate 33

1-3 (47)

Plate 34

1-2 (48)

3-4 (49)

Plate 35

1-4 (49)

Plate 36

1-2 (50)

Plate 37

1-2 (50)

Plate 38

1 (50)

Plate 39

1 (50)

2

Plate 40

1 (51)

Plate 41

1 (52)

Plate 42

1-3 (53)

Plate 43

1-2 (54)

Plate 44

1-2 (55)

Plate 45

1 (56)

2 (57)

3

4

Plate 46

1-3 (59)

Plate 47

1-4 (60)

Plate 48

1 (61)

1 (62)

Plate 49

1-3 (63)

Plate 50

1 (64)

Plate 51

1-2 (65)

Plate 52

1-2 (66)

3-4 (67)

Plate 53

1-2 (68)

Plate 54

1-2 (69)

3 (71)

Plate 55

1-2 (72)

Plate 56

1 (73)

2 (74)

3 (74)

4 (74 bis)

Plate 57

1-2 (75)

Plate 58

1-2 (76)

Plate 59

1-2 (77)

Plate 60

1 (78)

2 (79)

3 (80)

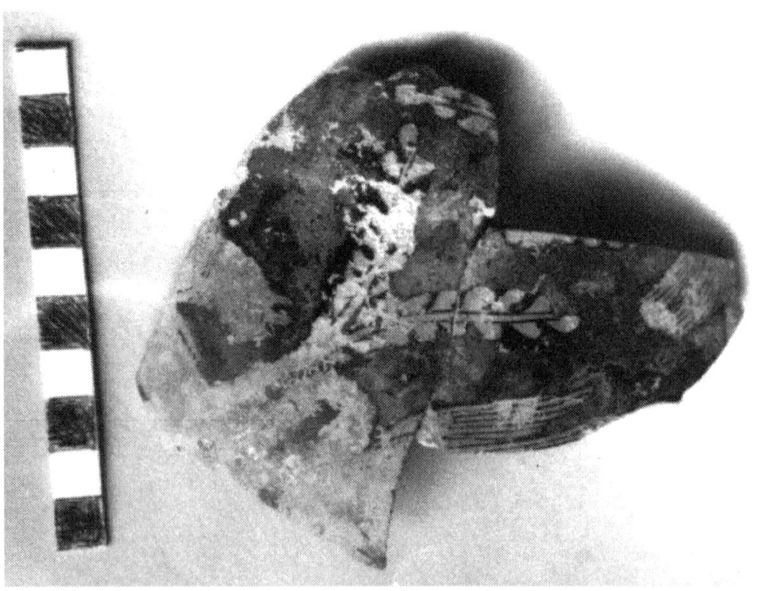

Plate 61

1-2 (81)

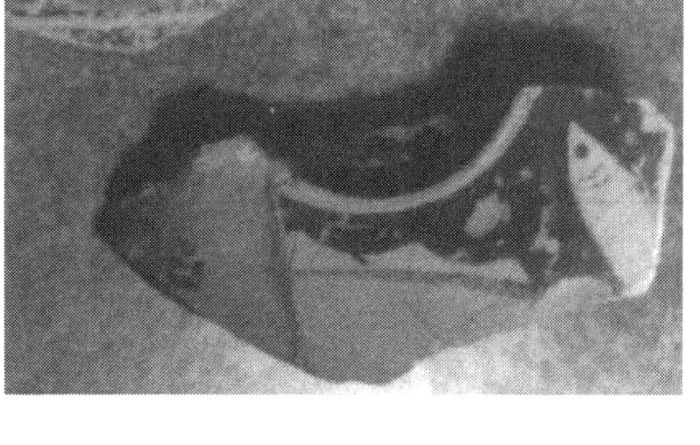

3 (82)

Plate 62

1 (1)

2 (2)

Plate 63

1 (3)

2 (5)

Plate 64

1 (7)

2 (9)

Plate 65

1 (12)

2 (13)

Plate 66

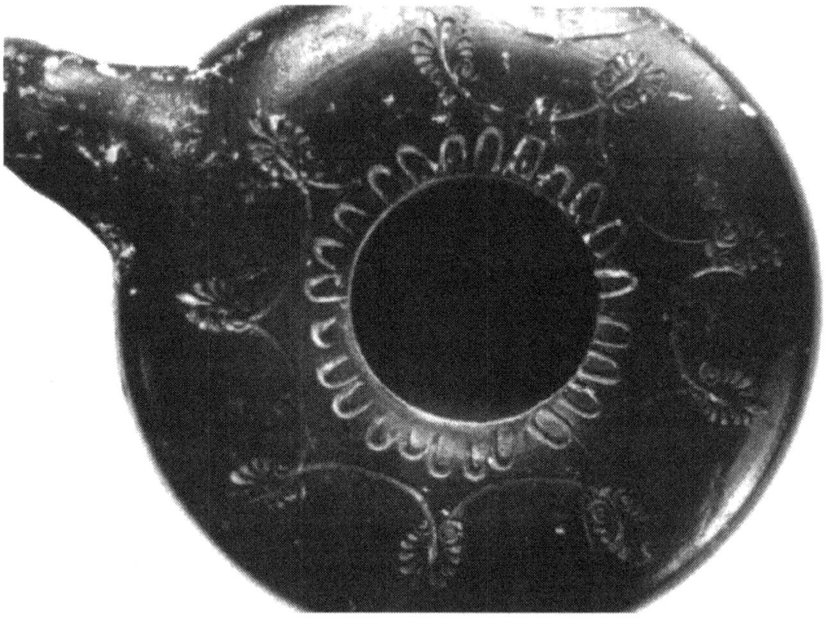

1-2 (14)

Plate 67

1-2 (15)

3 (16)

Plate 68

1 (20)

2-3 (21)

Plate 69

1 (22)

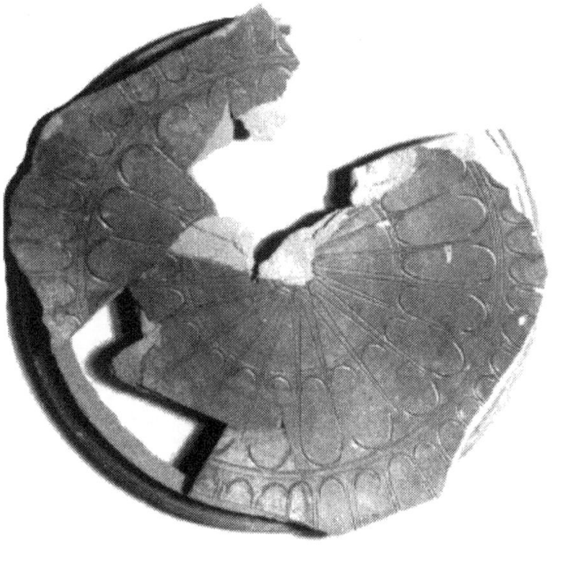

2 (23)

3 (24)

Plate 70

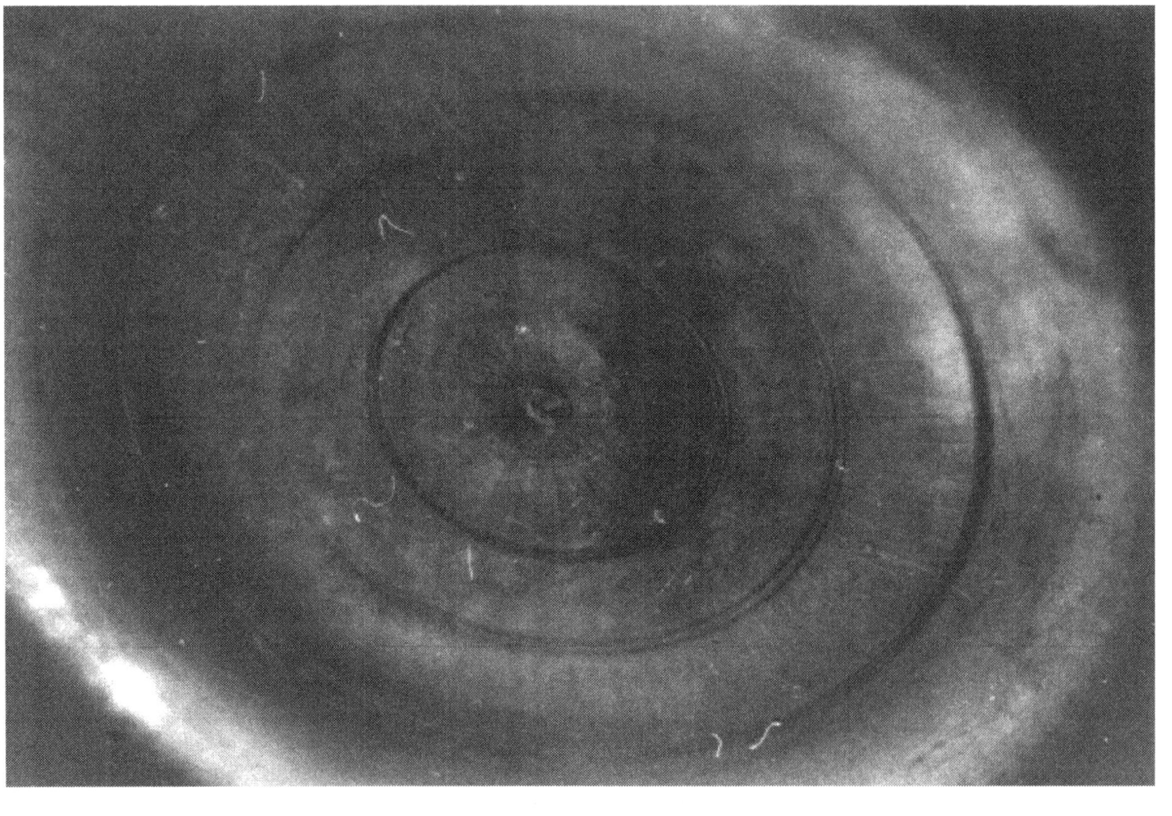

1-2 (25)

Plate 71

1-2 (26)

Plate 72

1-2 (29)

Plate 73

1-2 (30)

Plate 74

1-2 (35)

Plate 75

1-2 (36)

3 (37)

Plate 76

1 (39)

2 (40)

Plate 77

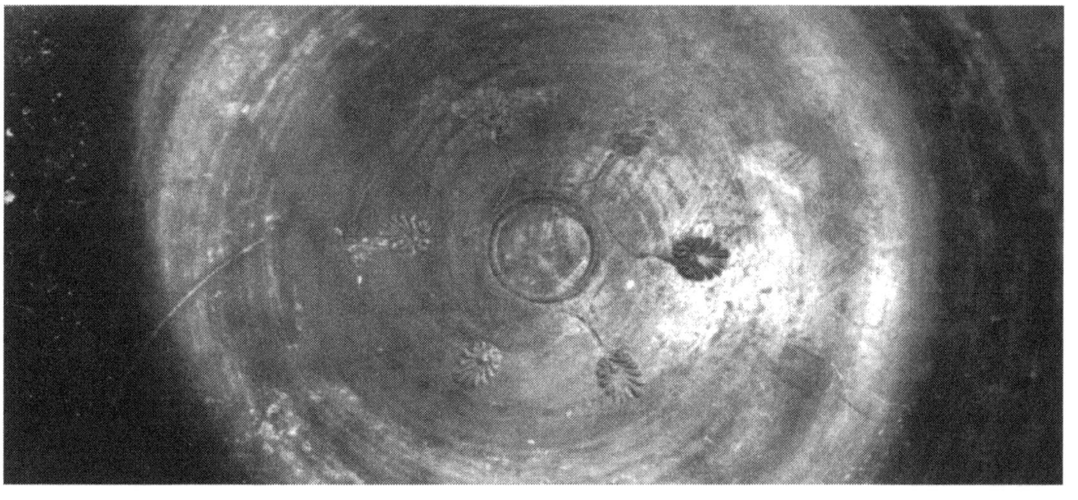

1-3 (43)

Plate 78

1-3 (47)

Plate 79

1-2 (51)

3 (52)

Plate 80

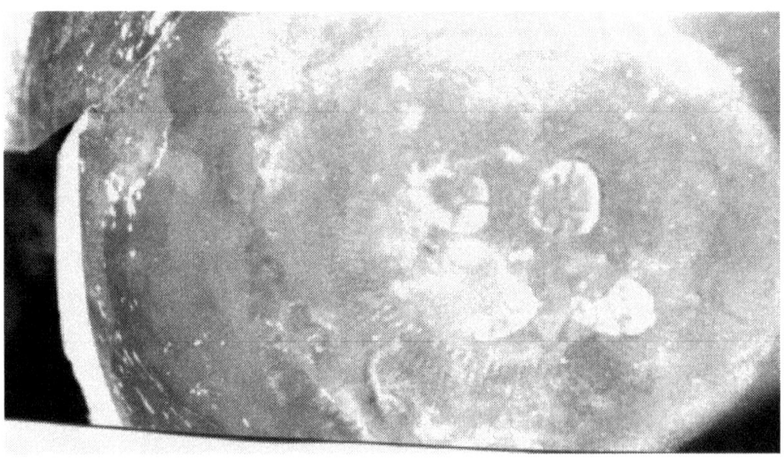

1-2

Plate 81

1-3 (55)

Plate 82

1 (56) 2 (57)

3 (83) 4 (59)

Plate 83

1 (61)

2 (62)

Plate 84

1 (63)

2 (64 bis)

3 (65)

Plate 85

1 (66) 2 (67)

3 (73)

Plate 86

1 (75)

2 (77) 3 (78)

Plate 87

1 (88)

Plate 88

1 (89)

2 (90)

Plate 89

1-2 (91)

Plate 90

1 (92)

2 (93)

Plate 91

1 (95)

2 (96)

Plate 92

1 (99)

2 (100)

Plate 93

1 (102)

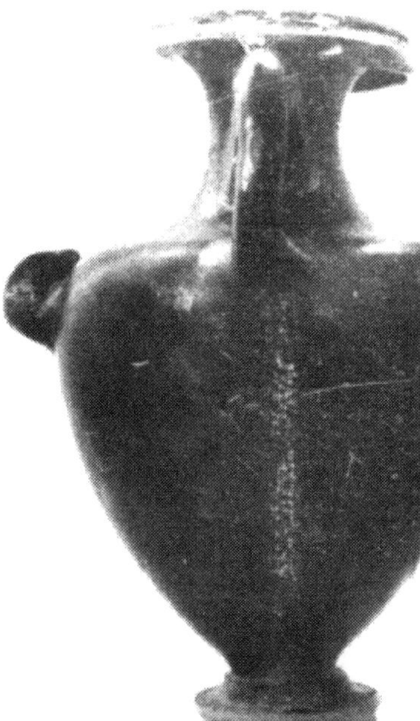

2 (103)

3 (104)

Plate 94

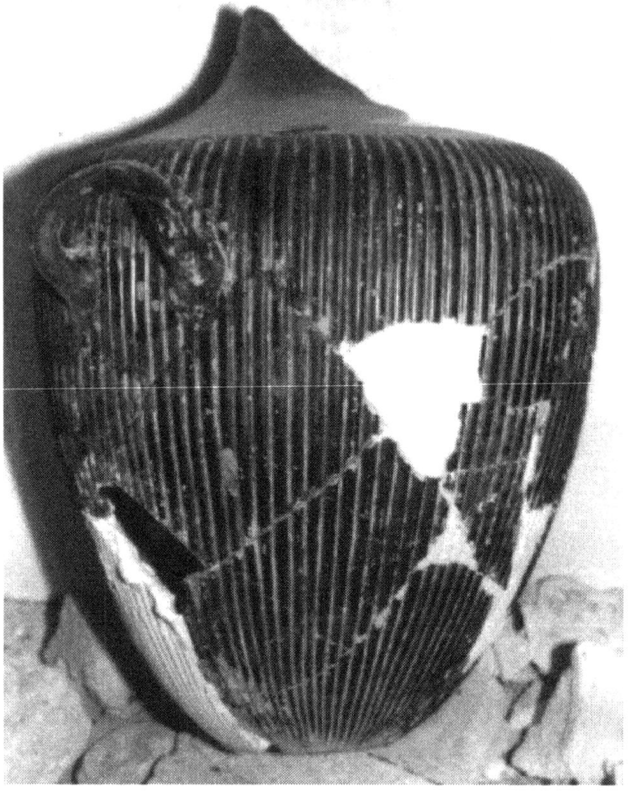

1 (105)

2 (106)

Plate 95

1 (107)

2 (108)

Plate 96

1 (109)

2 (110)

Plate 97

1-2 (112)

Plate 98

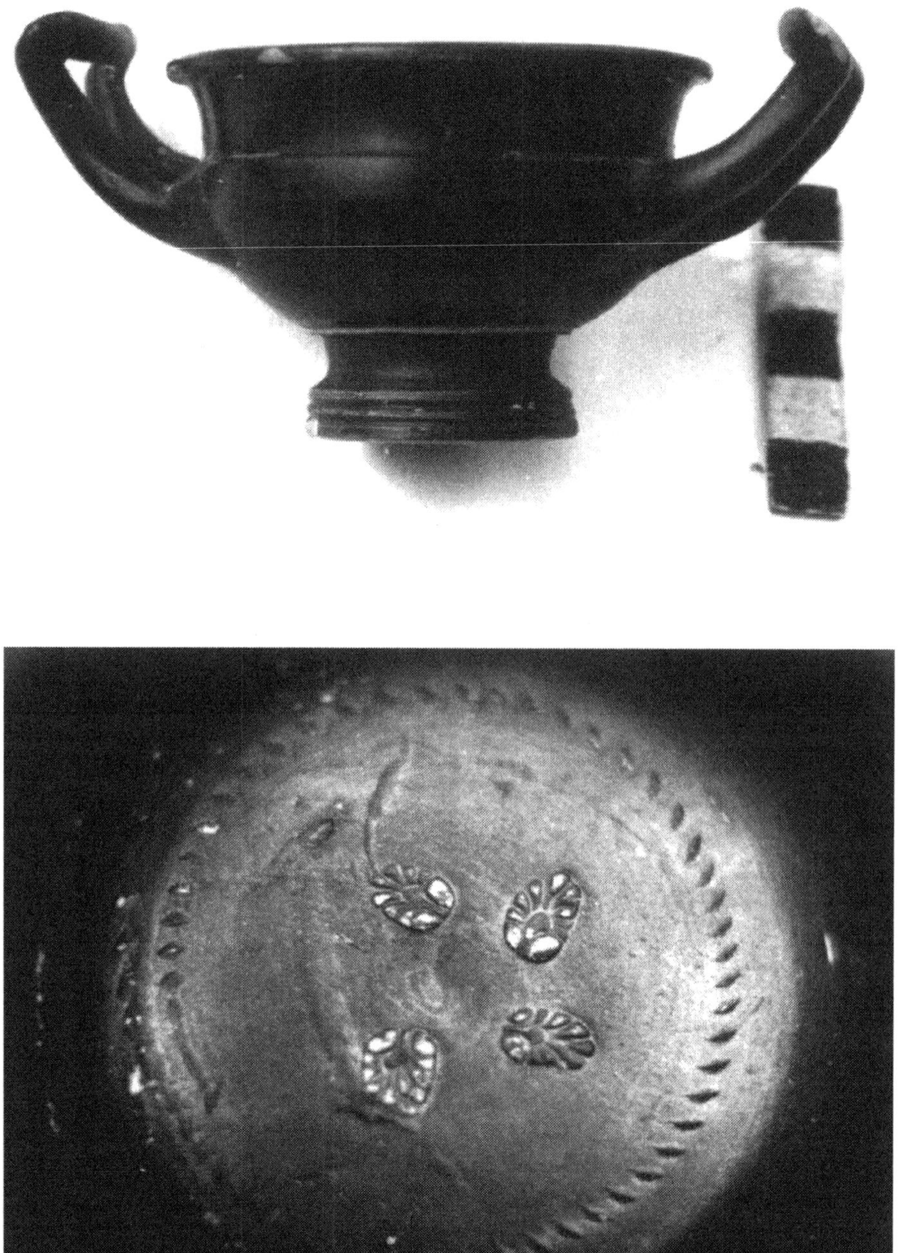

1-2 (113)

Plate 99

1 (114)

2 (115)

3 (117)

Plate 100

1 (121)

2 (122)

Plate 101

1 (123)

2 (124)

3-5 (126)

Plate 102

1-2 (128)

Plate 103

1-2 (130)

3 (132)

4 (132 bis)

Plate 104

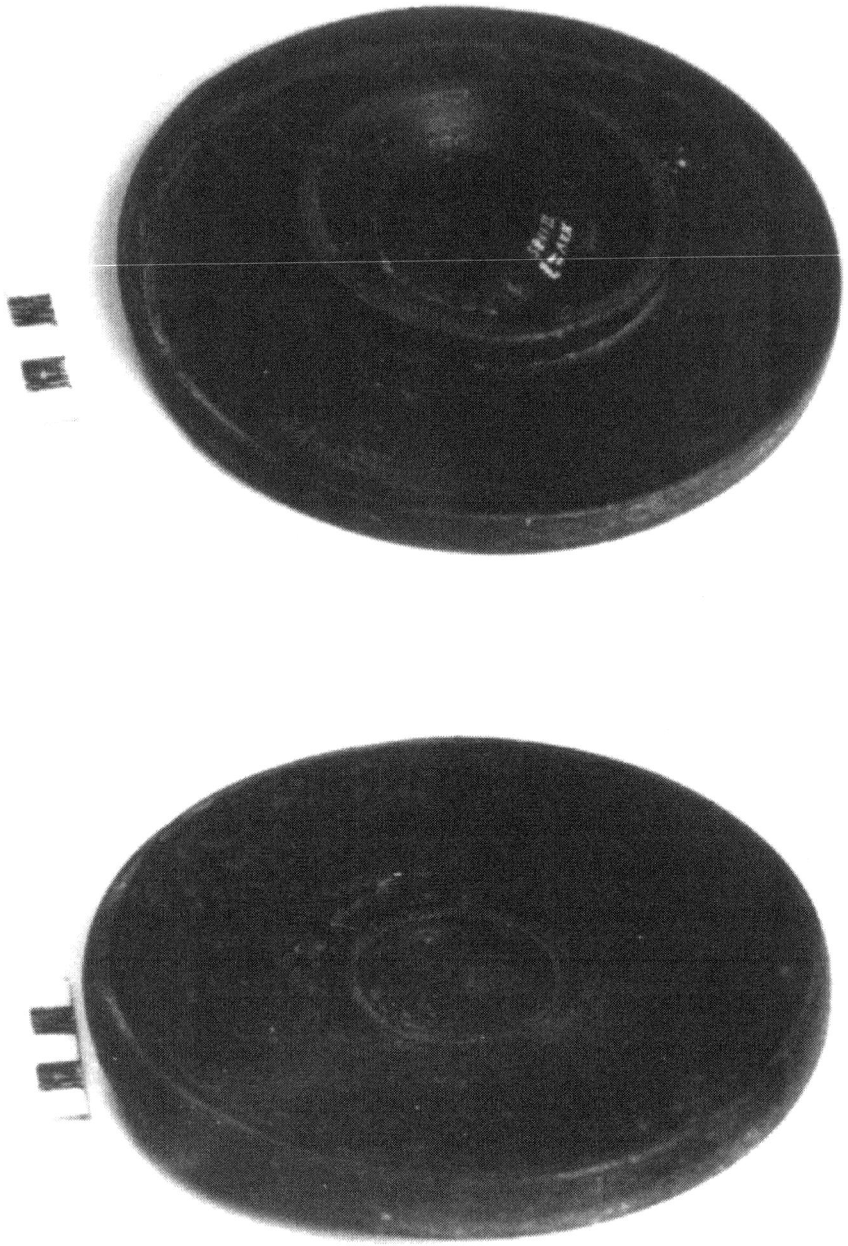

1-2 (136)

Plate 105

1 (138)

Plate 106

1 (139)

2 (140)

Plate 107

1-2 (141)

Plate 108

1-2 (142)

Plate 109

1 (143)

1 (144)

Plate 110

1 (147)

2 (148)

Plate 111

1 (150)

2 (153)

3

Plate 112

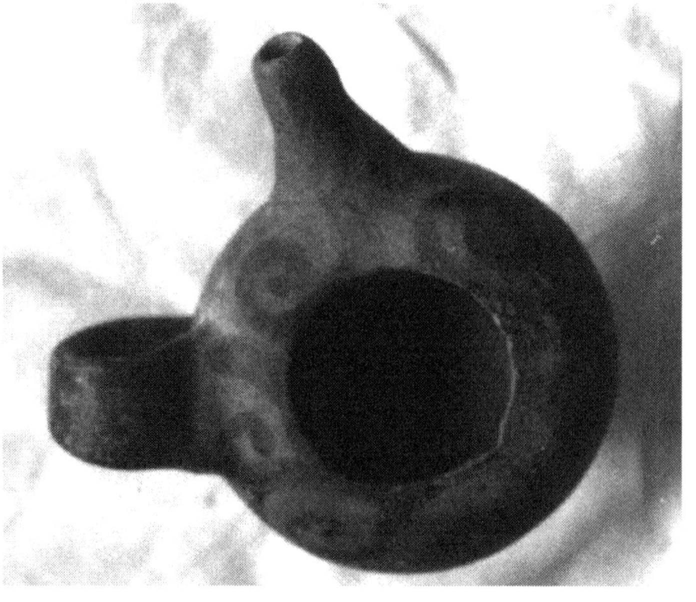

1-2 (154)

Plate 113

1 (1)

2 (2)

Plate 114

1-2 (3)

Plate 115

1

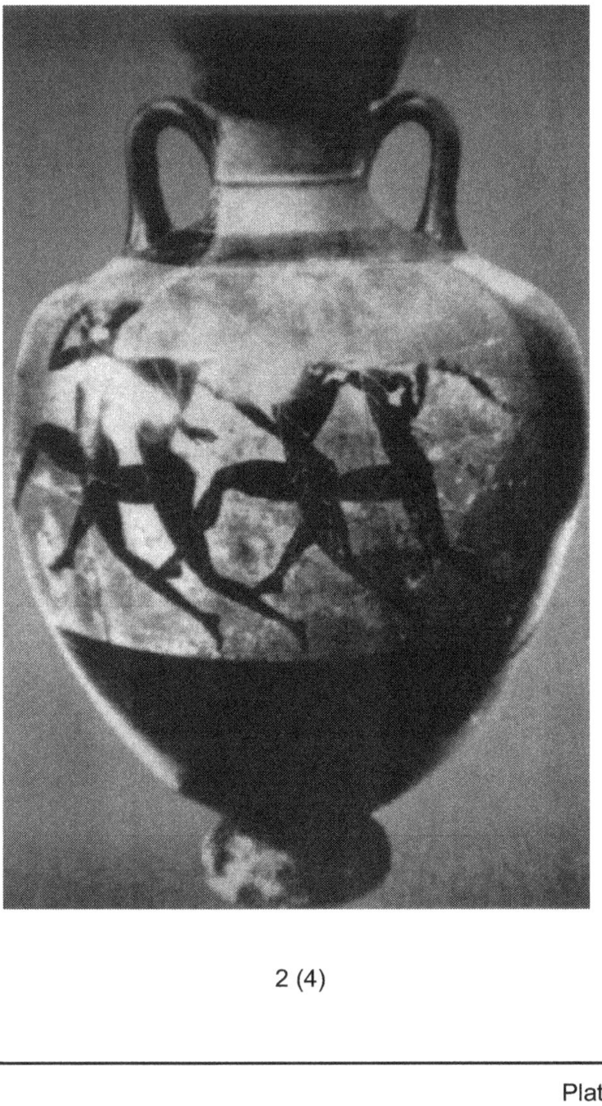

2 (4)

3 (5)

Plate 116

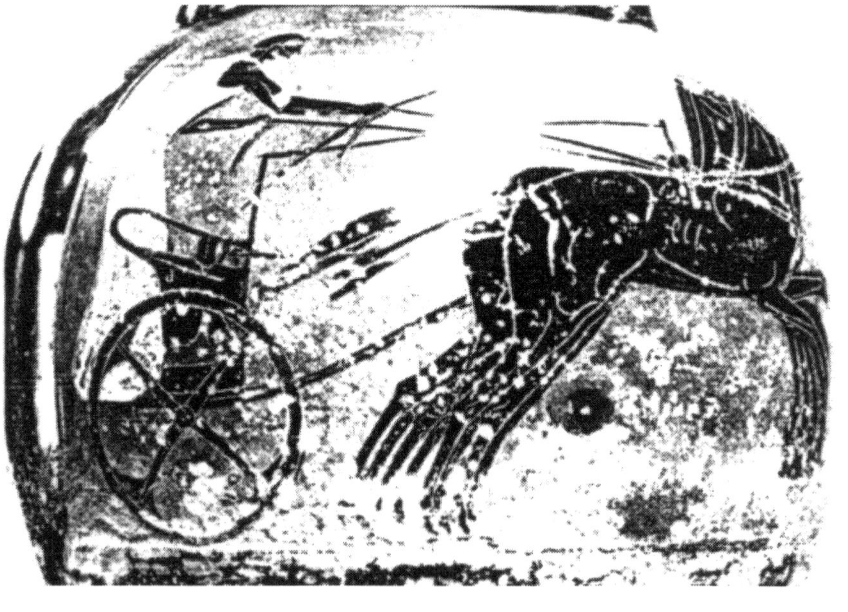

1-2 (6)

Plate 117

1-3 (7)

Plate 118

1-2 (8)

Plate 119

1-2 (9)

Plate 120

1-2 (10)

Plate 121

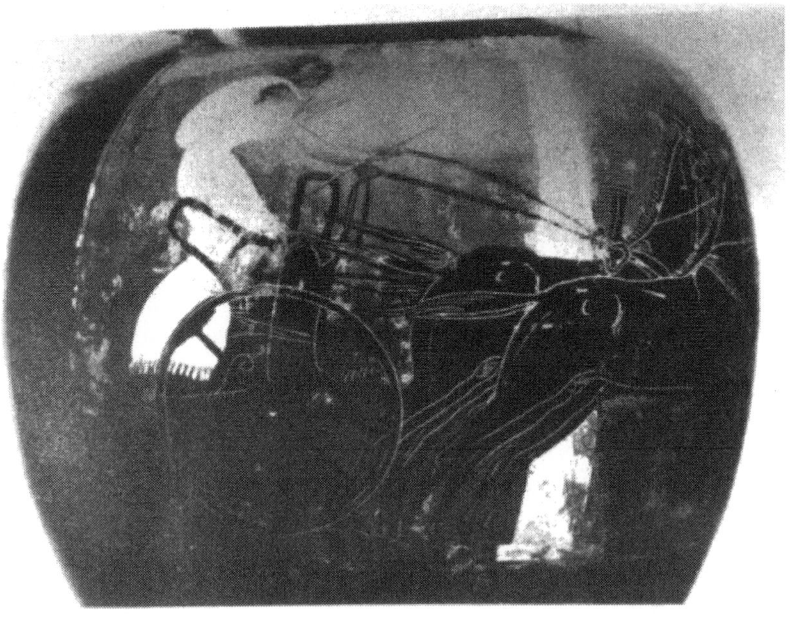

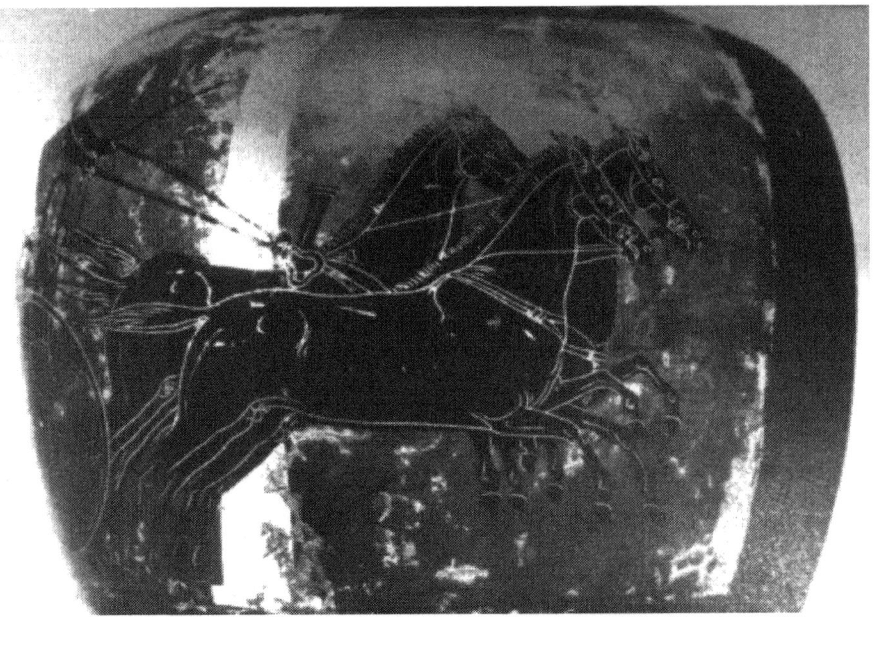

1-2 (10)

Plate 122

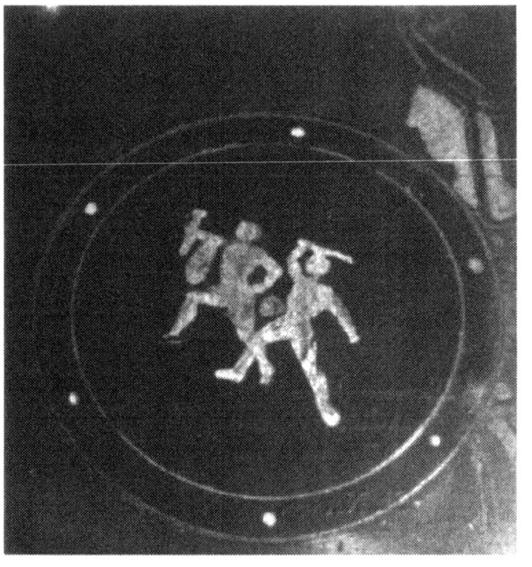

1-3 (11)

Plate 123

1-2 (12)

Plate 124

1-2 (13)

Plate 125

1 (14)

Plate 126

1-2 (14)

Plate 127

1-2 (15)

Plate 128

1-4 (16)

Plate 129

1-3 (17)

Plate 130

1-3 (18)

Plate 131

1-3 (19)

Plate 132

1-3 (20)

Plate 133

1-2 (21)

Plate 134

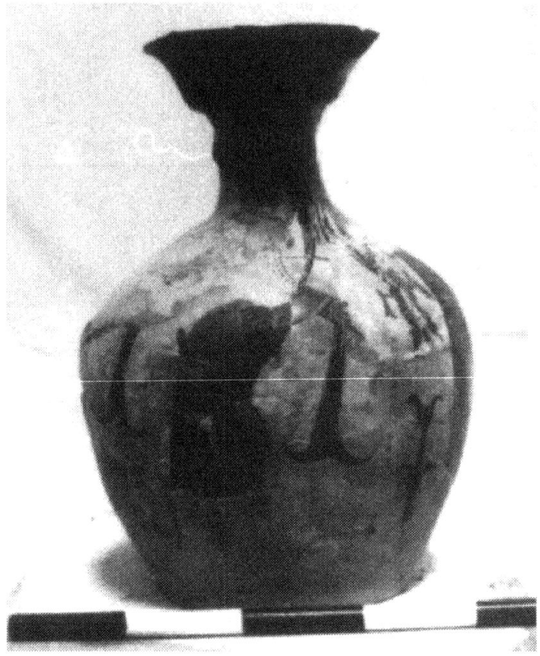

1-3 (22)

4

Plate 135

1-2 (23)

Plate 136

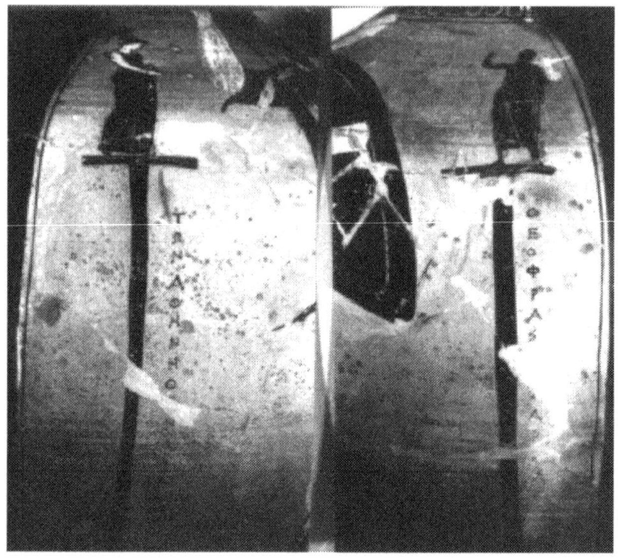

1-3 (24)

Plate 137

1-3 (26)

Plate 138

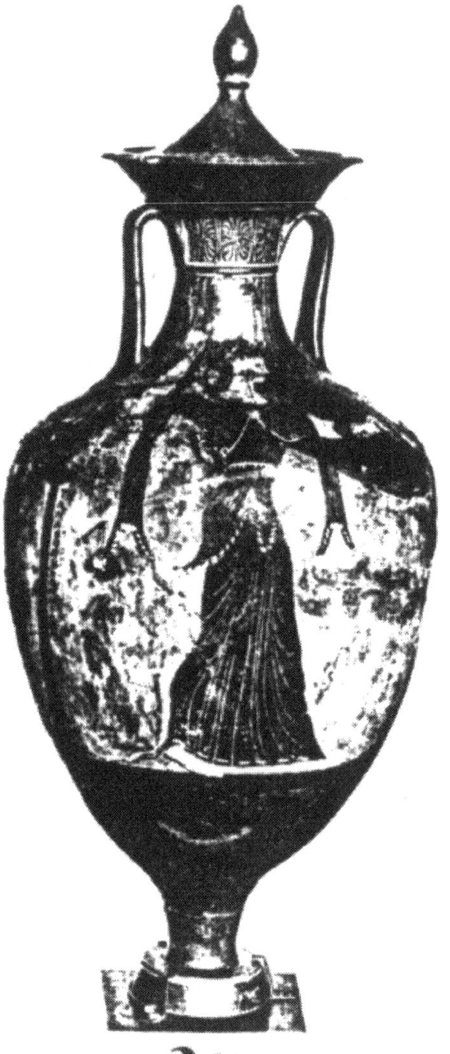

20

1-2 (27)

Plate 139

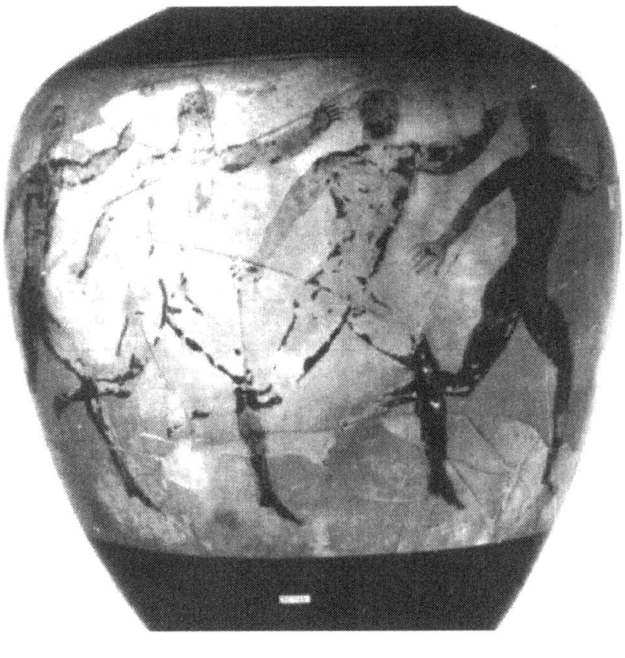

1-3 (28)

Plate 140

29

Plate 141

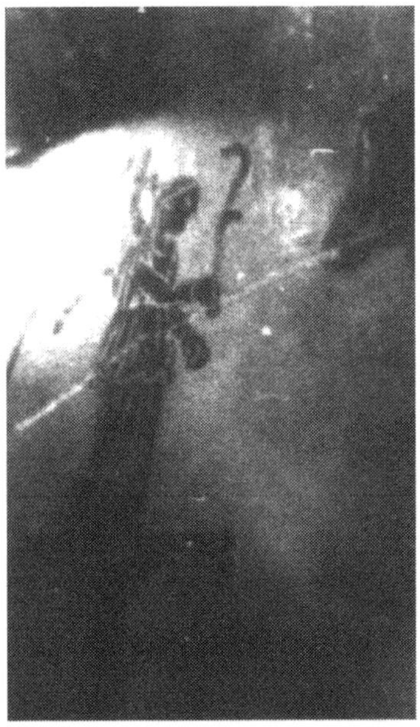

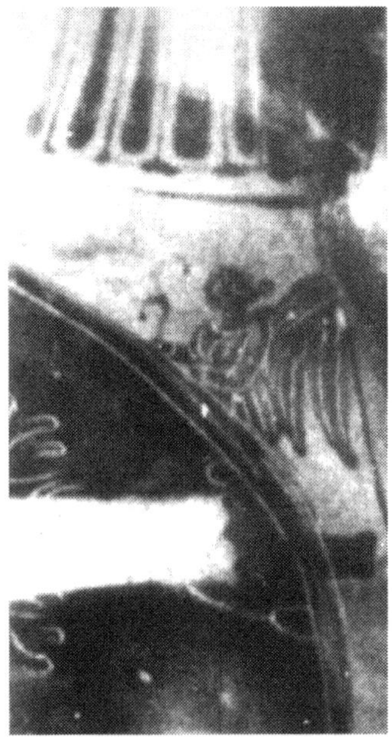

1-3 (30)

Plate 142

1 (31)

Plate 143

1-3 (32)

Plate 144

1-3 (33)

Plate 145

1 (1)

2 (2)

Plate 146

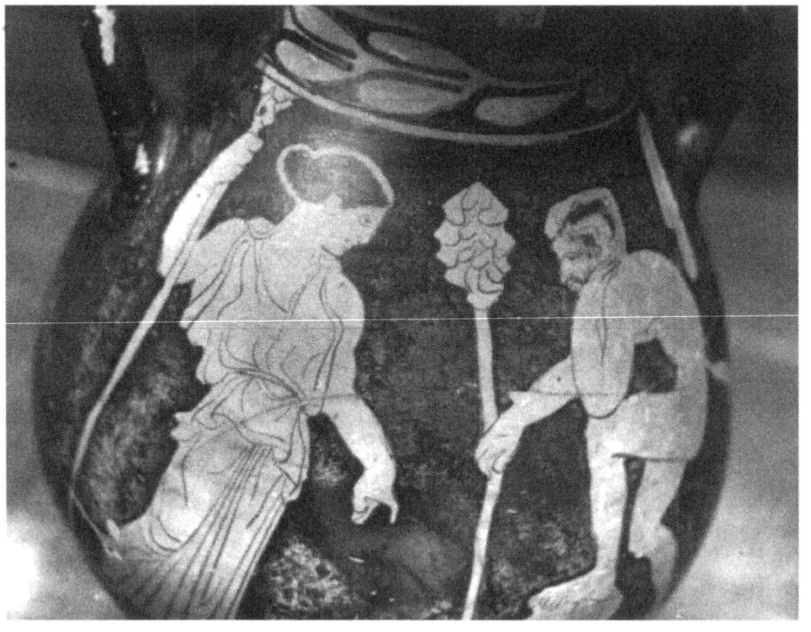

1-2 (3)

Plate 147

1-2 (4)

Plate 148

1 (5)

2 (6)

Plate 149

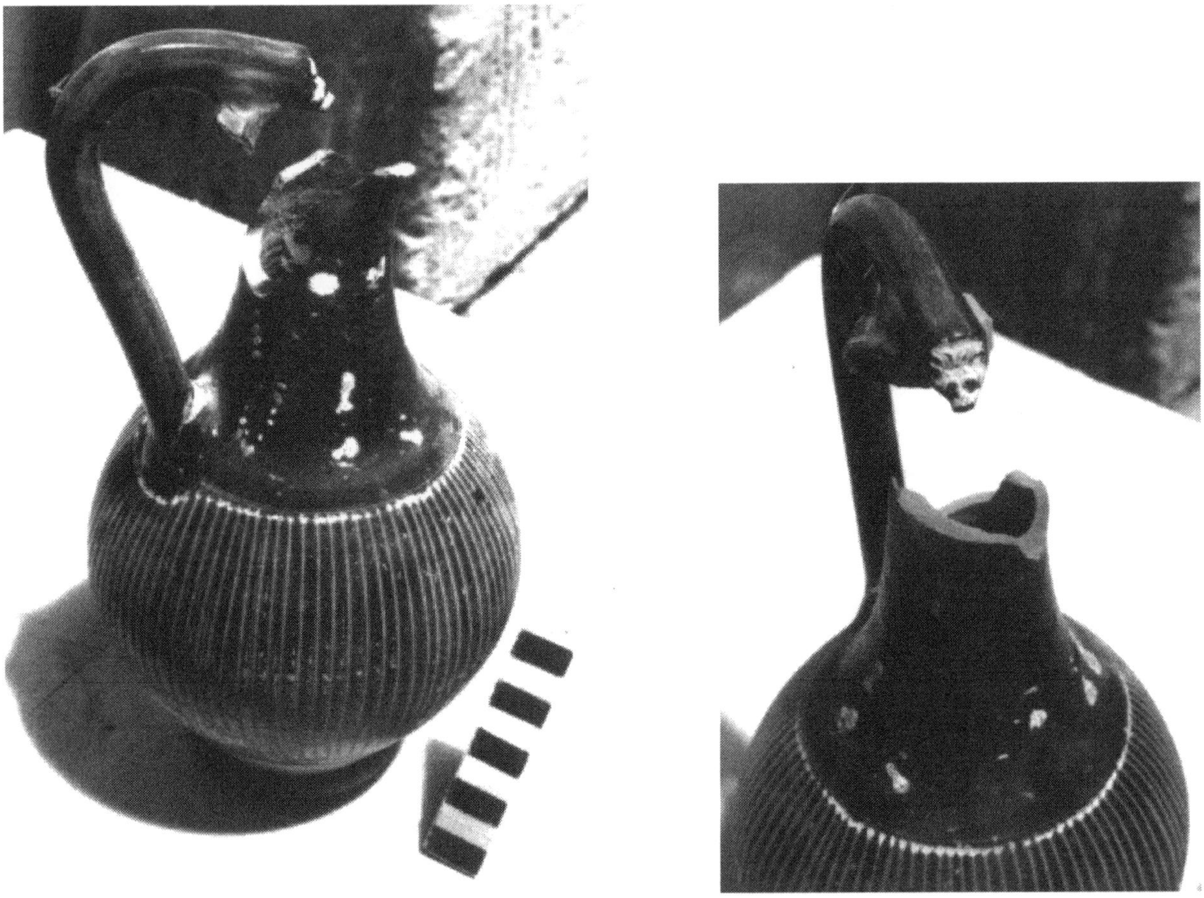

1-2 (7)

3 (8)

Plate 150

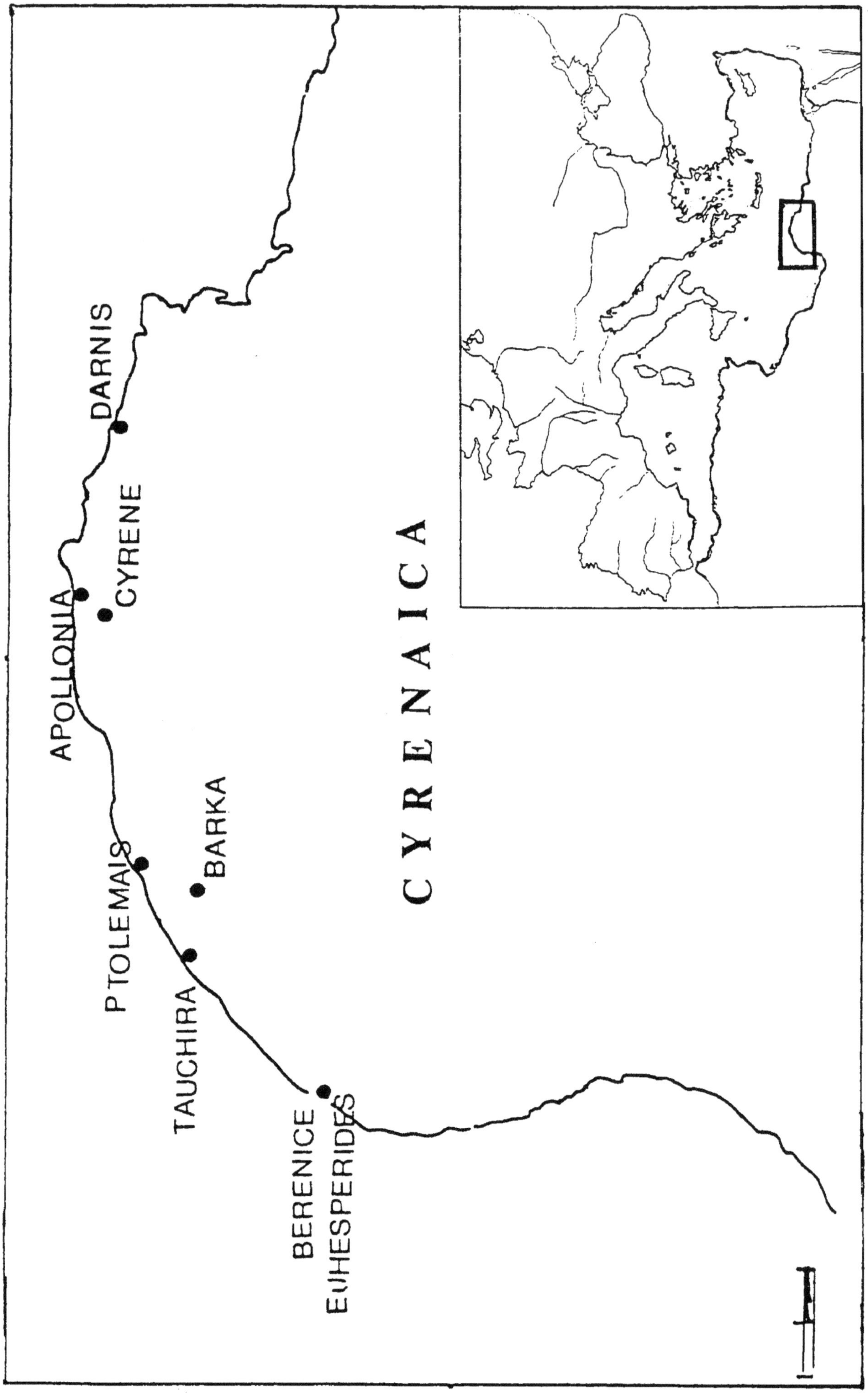

Map 1 – Ancient Cyrenaica with principal cities

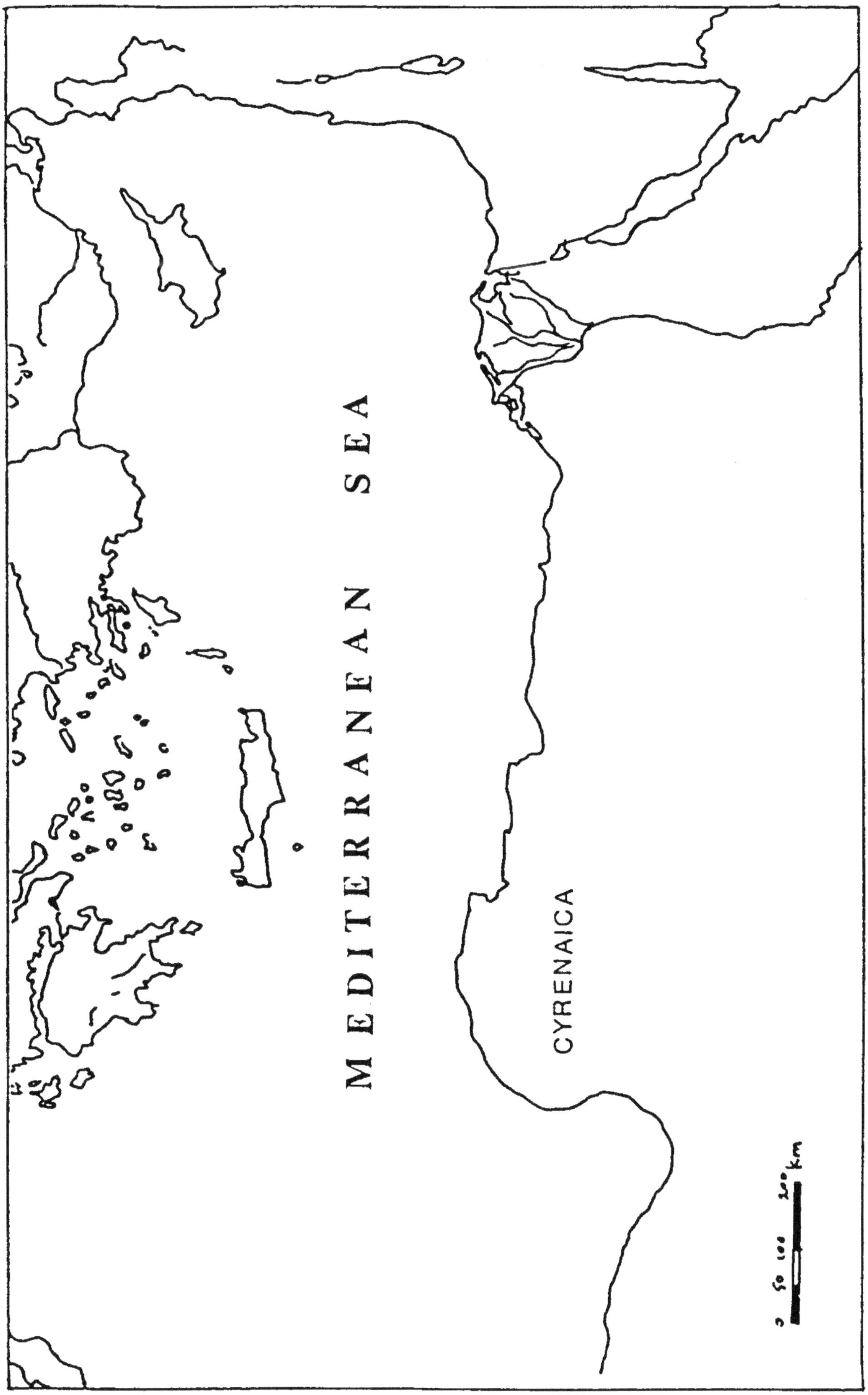

Map 2 – Ancient Cyrenaica and the Eastern Mediterranean

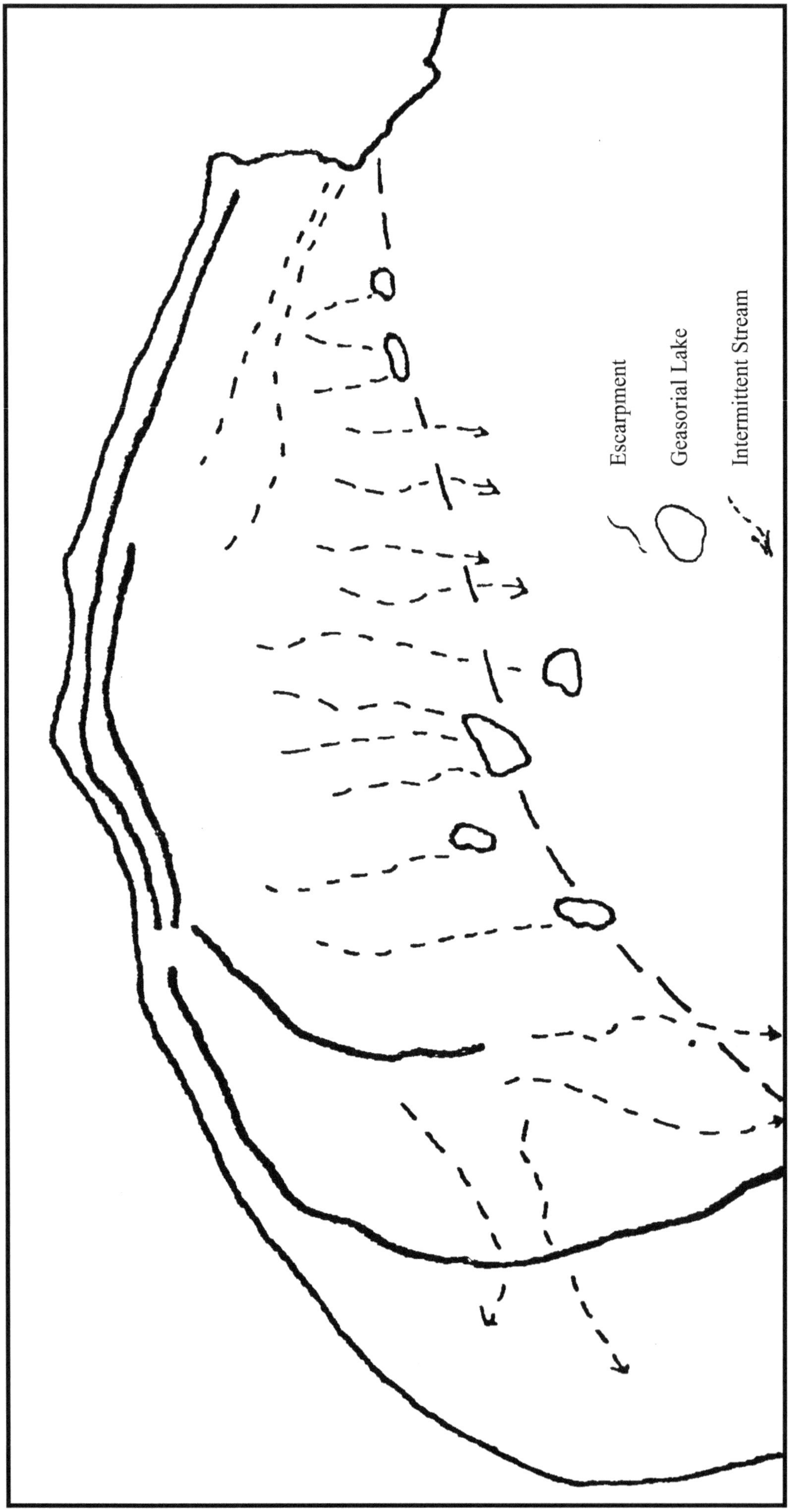

Map 3 – Morphology of Cyrenaica (After D. Johnson and Barker)

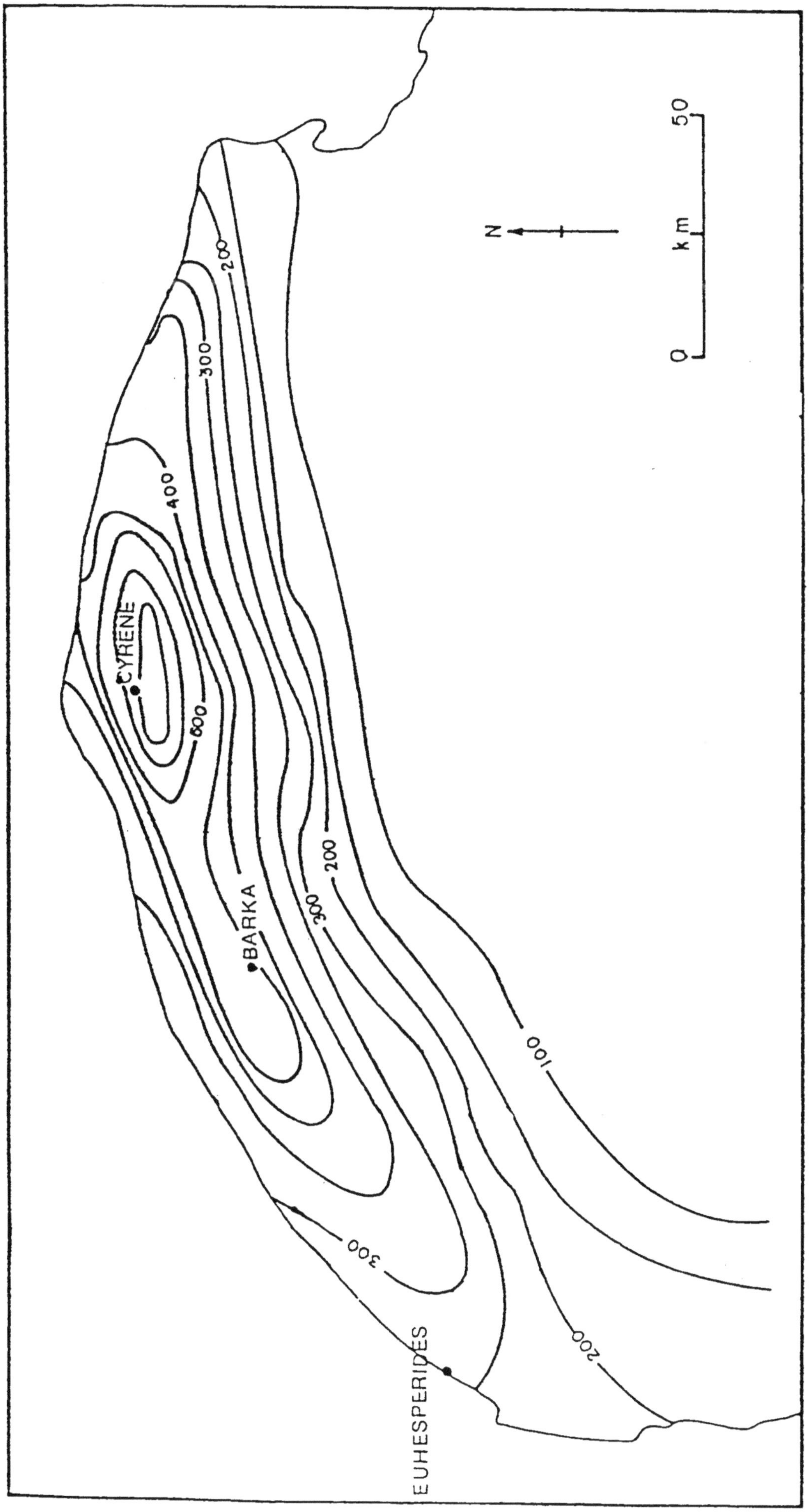

Map 4 – Cyrenaica, annual rainfall, in millimetres (After *Economic Development of Libya*, 1960)

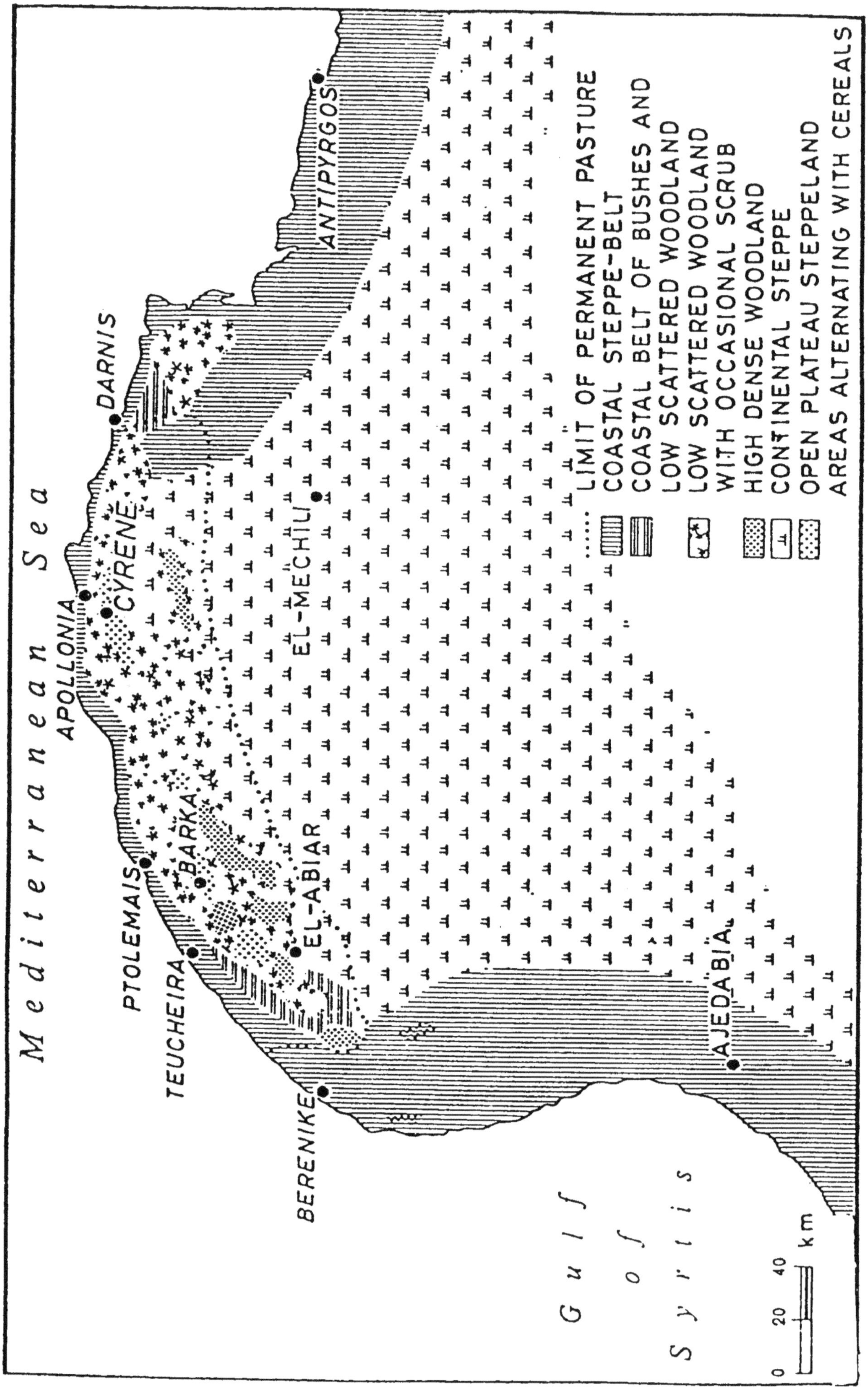

Map 5 – Cyrenaica natural vegetation

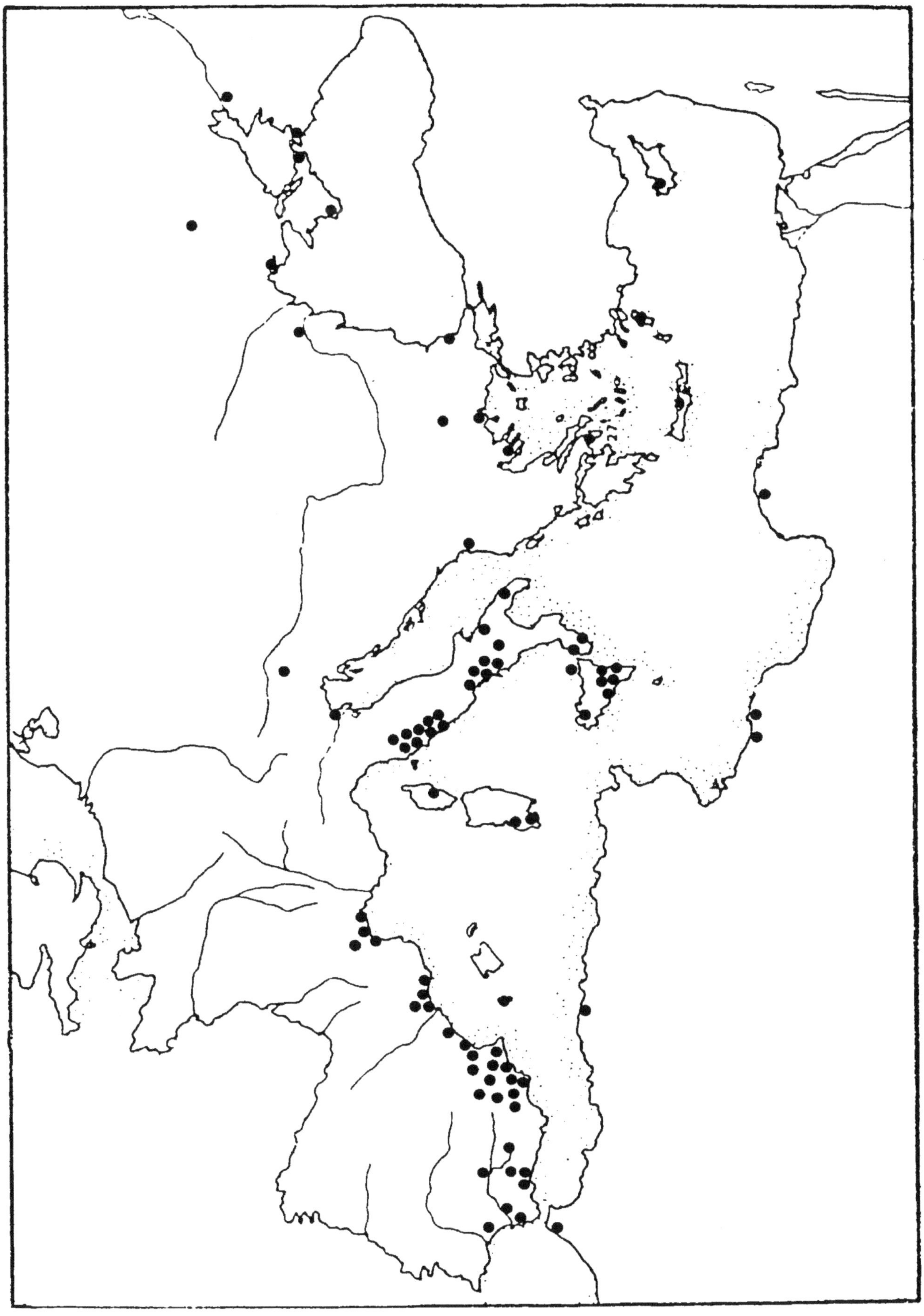

Map 6 – Distribution of Castulo cup (B. B. Shefton and Author)

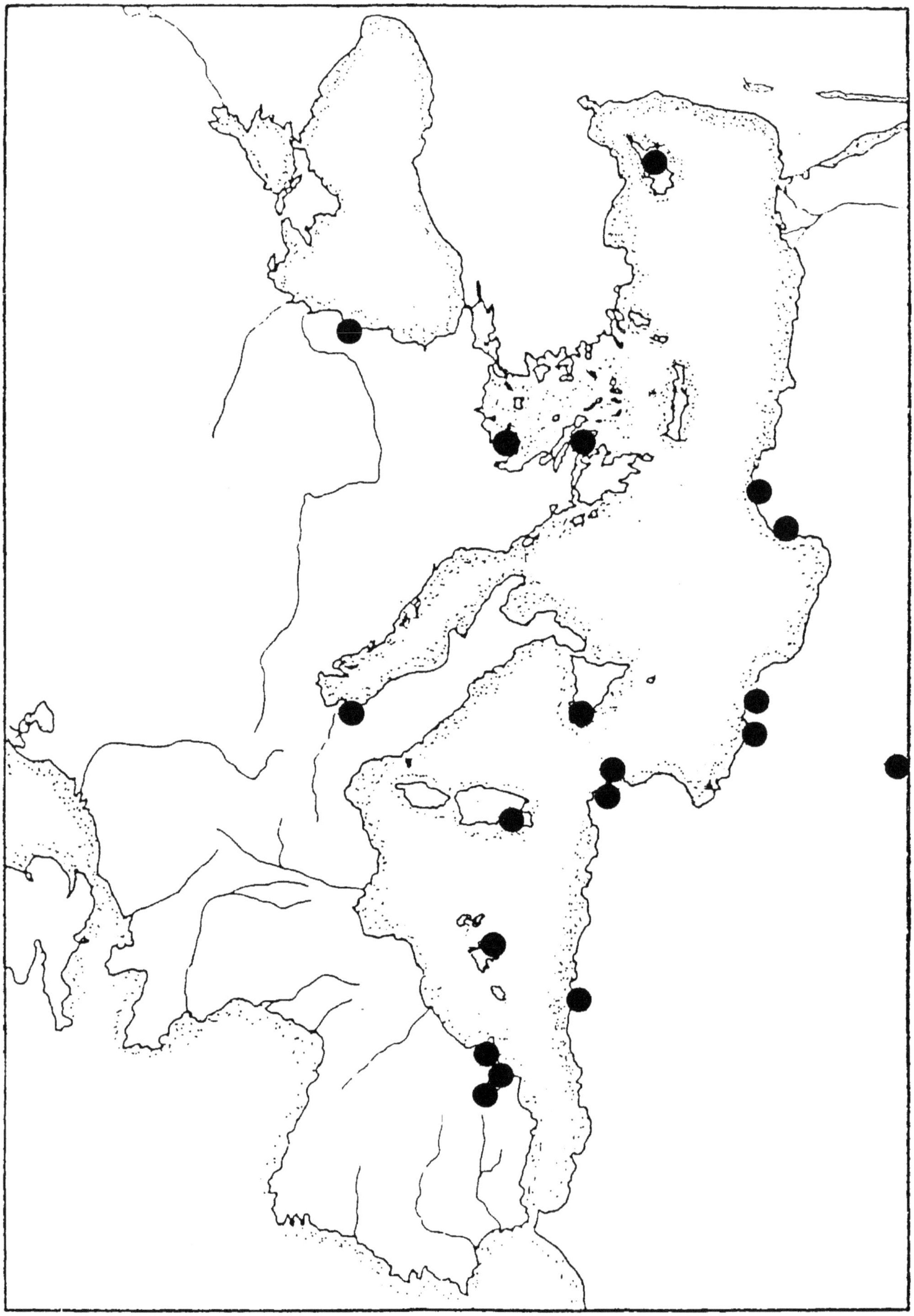

Map 7 – Distribution of fish olates (B. B. Shefton and Author)

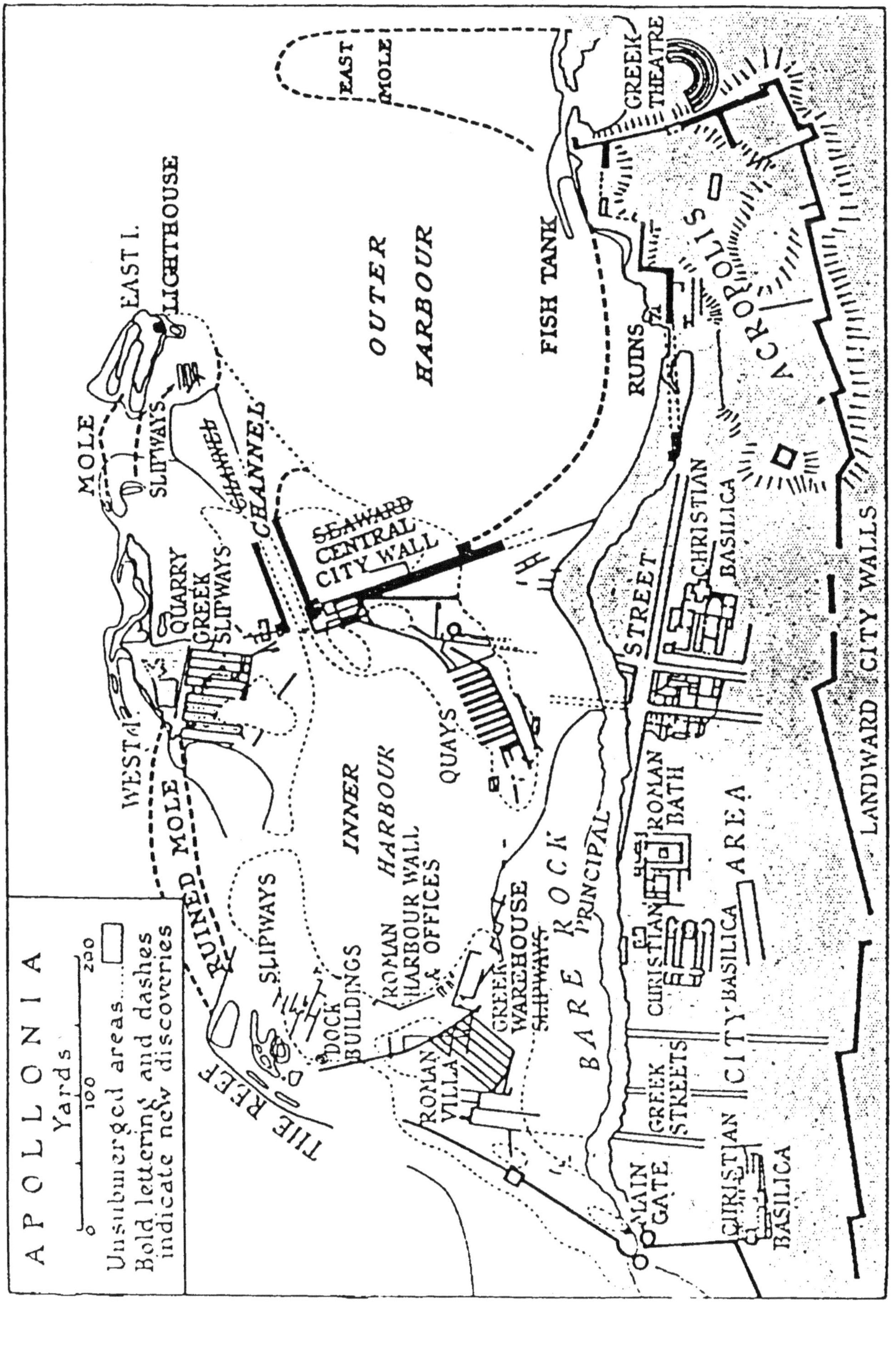

Map 8 – The Ancient Harbour of Apollonia (After Fleming)

www.ingramcontent.com/pod-product-compliance
Lightning Source LLC
LaVergne TN
LVHW071203210926
848482LV00015B/718
* 9 7 8 1 8 4 1 7 1 4 0 3 5 *